Set Lighting Technician's Handbook

Film Lighting Equipment, Practice, and Electrical Distribution

Third Edition

Harry C. Box

Focal Press

An Imprint of Elsevier Science

AMSTERDAM BOSTON LONDON NEW YORK OXFORD PARIS
SAN DIEGO SAN FRANCISCO SINGAPORE SYDNEY TOKYO

Library of Congress Cataloging-in-Publication Data

Box, Harry C.
    Set lighting technician's handbook: film lighting equipment, practice, and electrical distribution / Harry C. Box.—3rd ed.
      p. cm
    Includes bibliographical references and index.
    ISBN 0-240-80495-3 (pbk.: alk. paper)
    1. Cinematography—Lighting—Handbooks, manuals, etc. I. Title.

TR891 .B68 2003
778.5′343—dc21
                                                 2002192744

British Library Cataloguing-in-Publication Data
A catalogue record for this book is available from the British Library.

The publisher offers special discounts on bulk orders of this book.
For information, please contact:

Manager of Special Sales
Elsevier Science
200 Wheeler Road
Burlington, MA 01803
Tel: 781-313-4704
Fax: 781-313-4882

For information on all Focal Press publications available, contact our World Wide Web home page at:
http://www.focalpress.com

10 9 8 7 6 5 4 3 2 1

Printed in the United States of America

Set Lighting
Technician's
Handbook

To my mother and father

Contents

List of Tables

List of Appendices

Preface

Terminology

Imagine that your mother visits you on the set. You introduce her to the gaffer, who she says seems like a nice fellow—that is, until he starts giving orders: "Hang a baby. Kill the midget and have two blondes standing by for the martini."

The set lighting profession uses volumes of peculiar-sounding technical terms. In this book, terms are explained the first time they are used and can also be found in the glossary. You will find, however, that the same equipment has different names from country to country, city to city, and studio lot to studio lot. An *obie* light is called a *basher* in England. In Jamaica, a scrim is known as a *strainer*, while here we often simply call it *wire*. A wall sled is called a *Grumpy* at Paramount Studio (the name people around the lot bestowed on its inventor). There are even a few common terms that are difficult to use in polite conversation.

People who work in rental houses will act as if you are out of your mind if you call something by a name different than that with which they are familiar. This can be frustrating when working out of town with a new rental house.

To make matters even more unpredictable, terms change over time and are constantly being invented and evolving. I adopted the terms that, in my experience, are most universally used, but you will no doubt run across many other names that do not appear here.

The correct terms for the head of the camera and lighting departments are director of photography or cinematographer. To some the abbreviation, DP, is objectionable for various reasons (DP also stands for displaced person, the label given refugees after World War II). Having acknowledged this, I use DP anyway as a matter of convenience in writing and reading. Readers should be aware, however, that for many directors of photography, the use of the abbreviation in conversation does not show proper respect for the title.

Acknowledgments

I am indebted to many individuals for their generous contributions to this book: Darryl Murchison, whose discussions during the early stages of writing helped set the book on course; Michael Skinner, who generously shared his expertise helping me unravel the vagaries of the NEC; Doug Pentek, Earl Gilbert, Larry Parker, Cyrus Yavneh, Russ Brandt, Dean Bray, Frieder Hochheim, Herb Breitling, Michael Kaiping,

xxii SET LIGHTING TECHNICIAN'S HANDBOOK

Scott Toland, and Jon Bart, all of whom read and improved sections of the book; Richard Mula and Pete Romano, who shed much light on the subject of underwater lighting; Frank "the Dinosaur" Valdez and Gary Scalzo, who lent their expertise to the section on rigging; and Vance Trussell, whose suggestions and ongoing interest and encouragement were invaluable to me.

I also gratefully acknowledge the many manufacturers who provided technical information, photographs, and illustrations. The manufacturers are listed in Appendix H. My thanks also to Doug Pentec and Carly Barber of Hollywood Rental and Robert Guzman of Concept Lighting for the use of their rental equipment in creating the artwork.

A special note of thanks to the illustrators, Shawn Murphy and Lisa Cyr, who may well have been inking drawings on their wedding night to make the publication deadline.

My very greatest thanks, love, and appreciation is to Joan Box for her loving attention to my split infinitives and for her unending support.

Acknowledgments for the Second Edition

A great deal of new material appears in this edition, and more people are acknowledged for their contributions to the research. My thanks to Eric King, who shared his expertise on HMIs and electronic ballasts. I owe a debt of gratitude to Chris Barratt, without whose generosity and vast experience I could not have created the new section on generator troubleshooting. My thanks to Bernie Kret at Strand, who helped with the new section on electronic dimmers. Praise, lastly, to the talents of John Huey, who created additional artwork for this edition.

Acknowledgments for the Third Edition

Once again new people have helped shape this ever-evolving work. My thanks first to Mark Crosthwaite, of the Local 728 Safety Training Program and Contract Services. Much of the new material, especially regarding electricity, distribution, and aerial lift safety, was developed in coordination with the training program; and Mark and the other instructors contributed much solid material to this new edition. Thanks to Ron Dahlquist, for his interest in the book and his insight on electricity and distribution. Thanks to Brian Fitt for his work on European electrical distribution systems. Thanks again to the manufacturers who contributed technical data and illustrations to this third edition—especially Lights Up Industries, Dadco, Mole-Richardson Co., and Lightools™. Thanks also to Debra at Cineworks, for use of its equipment in creating some of the artwork.

For the new illustrations in this edition I owe a debt of thanks to a very talented and patient man, Dan Haberkorn. Also thanks to Mark Doering-Powell, for his advice and artwork in the section on blue screen photography. Thanks to Laura Mancini, for modeling for the book, and to Keith Morgan, for lending a hand (and a couple of very nice lights). Thanks to Mike Bauman for bringing me news and pictures from the front lines. My thanks to the many individuals who gave me feedback and suggestions for this edition.

Thanks to my loving wife Stacey, who has endured my bad habit—of continually rewriting this book—with patience, love, and a sense of humor. I love you with all my heart.

Set Lighting Technician's Handbook

CHAPTER 1

Set Basics: Your First Barbecue

All the technical aspects of filmmaking—film stocks, cameras, lighting, sound, effects—involve a myriad of small details that, taken as a whole, seem impossibly complex. As with any craft, to become a master requires years of experience and exposure to many different situations. It has been my experience, however, that no single piece of equipment, procedure, or technique is really complicated; there is no one thing that cannot be explained and understood in less than 10 minutes. Making movies is the artful application of millions of relatively simple details. This book helps with some of those details, describing procedures that save time and promote safety, clarifying aspects of the craft that are confusing and often misunderstood, and supplying a wealth of information about the hundreds of gadgets of which lighting technicians are so fond.

Starting with the basics, we begin with a summary of the role of the lighting crew on a film set.

Job Descriptions of the Lighting Crew

The electric, grip, and camera departments fall under the direction of the director of photography. The gaffer and key grip are the DP's lieutenants. The gaffer is the head of the electric department, in charge of the lighting crew. The gaffer's crew consists of the assistant chief lighting technician, known as the *best boy electric* or *second electrician*. Under the best boy are the set electricians, also called *lamp operators* or *third electricians*.

Director of Photography

Q: How many directors does it take to screw in a light bulb?
A: One. No, two. No, no one.

The director of photography (DP) is the director's right hand; he or she is the one who helps the director make all the hard decisions. It is the DP's responsibility to create on film what the director has envisioned for each scene; to evoke the proper time, place, and atmosphere by means of lighting and to help choose camera angles and camera movement that will be most effective in telling the story. He or she designs the lighting, balancing realism against the dramatic potential of more stylized effects, as called for by the script and the director. The DP has a say in the design and color of the sets and the wardrobe and in the selection of locations. It is often incumbent on the DP to light particular actors with special care (to protect their public image, career, and personal vanity). The DP must maintain proper screen direction (a responsibility shared with the script supervisor) and lighting continuity between setups so the film can be cut seamlessly. The DP usually shoots tests prior to the beginning of photography. He or she may experiment with various lighting effects, with different gel colors, with film stocks and special lab process or different filter combinations, looking for a combination of effects that accomplishes the special requirements of the script. The DP may also conduct his or her own research prior to production to ensure accuracy and authenticity of a period and inspire ideas for the cinematography.

The DP holds a position of immense responsibility, creatively and financially. The producer and director both depend on the DP to achieve photographic excellence within the constraints of the production's budget and schedule. The DP always faces conflicts in fulfilling the needs of the script, director, schedule, and budget and meeting his or her own aspirations for the photography. The lighting crew fights the DP's battles on the front lines. Their ability to light the set quickly and efficiently directly affects the DP's ability to produce great work and do it on a schedule.

Gaffer

Q: How many gaffers does it take to screw in a light bulb?
A: One, no two . . . how many do you have on the truck?

The gaffer is the *chief lighting technician* (CLT). He or she works directly with the DP to implement the lighting plan and help achieve the photographic look of the film. The DP, gaffer, and key grip attend preproduction meetings together and scout the locations where filming is to take place. They discuss the DP's approach to each scene and determine what lighting preparations and equipment are required.

On the set, the gaffer is responsible for the execution of the lighting scheme and the organization and operation of the lighting crew. The DP and the gaffer discuss the lighting. Typically, when talking about the actor's lighting, the DP specifies the placement of each fixture to use to accomplish a particular effect. Sometimes (when lighting backgrounds for instance), the DP may leave it to the gaffer to translate general ideas into specifics. The DP may express the goals in terms of the motivating sources of light for the scene, the mood, and the f-stop at which to shoot. The gaffer then instructs the crew and sees to the exact placement and focus of each light to accomplish the DP's instructions. Typically, once the gaffer has executed the lighting, the DP will "sweeten" to taste, with a few adjustments.

The gaffer must have a very strong eye for lighting and a solid knowledge of which lights to use to create any desired effect. As the lighting starts to come together, the gaffer functions as a second pair of eyes for the director of photography, being always on the lookout for problems—inadequate light, overexposure, hot spots, ugly shadows, and so on. Together the director of photography and gaffer look for opportunities to make the scene look more interesting. A first-rate gaffer has a critical eye for the balance of light and shade, the modeling of facial features, and the separation of foreground from middle ground and background. The gaffer, carrying light meters on a belt, often stands next to the DP at the camera to view and measure the light hitting the subject and to consult with the DP on issues of fill ratio and balance of exposure.

A very important part of the gaffer's job is organizing and running the operation. He or she must constantly be cycling through the many tasks at hand, pushing forward the progress of each project, keeping an eye on the performance of the lighting crew, thinking ahead so that power and lights are readily at hand for each shot, and forestalling delay by maintaining constant vigilance over every possible need.

The gaffer should never have to leave the immediate area in which the action is being filmed. He or she must rely on the crew to be near at hand to make lighting adjustments and fetch equipment when it is needed. If, during filming, it is necessary to clear the set, the grips and electricians remain just outside the set, near the door, during the takes. Because the lighting crew is always under time pressure, an electrician who stays near the action, listens, and thinks ahead can do a lot to help the gaffer and DP win their daily battle against time.

Best Boy Electric

The best boy electric is the gaffer's chief assistant. He or she is in charge of personnel and equipment for the electrical department, a vital role in the smooth running of the lighting crew. The best boy's duties include scouting locations with the gaffer, making scouting notes to help the gaffer compile the list of equipment needed. The best boy supervises the load-in (loading electrical equipment into the truck at the rental house before the first day of production), organizes the equipment and supplies in the truck for easy access, makes sure no equipment gets lost at each location, keeps track of damage, makes repairs, performs maintenance, and supervises the load-out after the last day of production.

In the days when arc lights were in common use, a *running repairman* was used to maintain and repair lights on an ongoing basis during production. This position still exists, mostly on studio lots, and can be a great help to the best boy and electrical crew.

The best boy keeps track of gels and expendables; coordinates equipment orders, returns, subrentals, and special orders; and is in charge of hiring and laying off extra electricians when needed. The best boy supervises the electrical crew's start-up paperwork and time cards. At each location, the best boy plans the routing of the feeder cable and supervises the distribution of electrical power to the lights. If there is a rigging crew, this work will have been done ahead of time by the rigging gaffer.

The best boy is the first person an electrician goes to with a complaint. A chain of command operates on the set; an electrician should not speak directly with the production manager or the director. If necessary, the best boy will take up the issue with the gaffer. It is then the gaffer's responsibility to fight for the needs of the electrical crew. There are always enough opinions on a set. It is preferable that the lighting crew be noticed for its good work, not for its remarks.

Most important, the best boy is the emissary of the electrical department, communicating and negotiating with other departments, with the fire marshal, and with rental houses and other equipment suppliers. A best boy who maintains good relations with each department can get cooperation when it is needed. For example, when the best boy needs to put a light on the roof of a building, the locations team must make the necessary contacts to secure that spot. When the best boy needs some extra equipment delivered quickly, his or her relationships with the transportation department and the contact at the rental house come into play. The best boy's diplomacy is key.

Electricians

Q: How many electricians does it take to screw in a light bulb?
A: It's not a *bulb*, it's a *globe*.

Electricians are affectionately known as *juicers* or *sparks* and are officially titled *set lighting technicians* or *lamp operators*. The electrician's primary responsibility is placing and focusing lights according to the wishes of the gaffer. At each location, the electricians unload and reload the lighting equipment from the trucks, run cabling, and run the distribution of electrical power for the lights. On the set, electricians are responsible for placing and focusing (aiming) the lights; manipulating the intensity, direction, color, and quality of light; wiring practical lamps (such as table lamps and wall sconces), switches, and wall outlets on constructed sets; and anticipating the needs of the gaffer so that equipment is at hand when needed. Electricians usually take responsibility for securing lights and stands for safe use; however, the grip department also plays a role, such as to hang pipe or truss for the lights, secure a stand with straps, or screw it down with grip-chain.

There is a Zen to the job of the lamp operator. An experienced lamp operator handles the equipment with deft speed and smoothness, an economy of movement that comes with familiarity. Through the exchange of a few words or hand signals, or by clairvoyance, the electrician grasps the gaffer's intention and manipulates the lamp to create the desired effect. His or her focused concentration is on two things: the activities of the lighting crew and the behavior of the light. The lamp operator is constantly attentive to the DP and gaffer and to fellow electricians who might need a hand. Simultaneously, the electrician is aware of the light falling, blasting, leaking, and spilling onto the faces and the surfaces around the set.

The set lighting crew may be asked also to provide power for other departments: camera, sound, dolly, and video village. Electricians typically relinquish responsibility for powering vehicles at the base camp to the transportation department. Although powering the base camp is technically within the union jurisdiction of lighting technicians (who are trained to handle electrical distribution), most of the time the gaffer simply does not have the personnel to spare for anything extraneous to the set.

I should add that movie electricians are very rarely licensed journeymen or master electricians. They are not qualified to wire buildings or work on power lines. Their job is lighting movies.

Rigging Crew

A rigging crew is an important part of almost any project, be it a feature, episodic TV series, or even a television commercial. The rigging crew works ahead of the main unit, installing cable and distribution, hanging lights, and taking care of any work that will be time consuming for the main unit to accomplish on the day of filming. This may involve weeks of work to rig a major set or half a day laying in some cable on location. A rigging crew consists of a rigging gaffer, rigging best boy, and rigging electricians. A rigging crew is invaluable to a production, especially to the DP and gaffer. The thought, planning, and careful, unrushed work, testing, and troubleshooting put in ahead of time translates into major time savings for the shooting crew. A properly rigged set means the lighting will look better, the on-set electricians can work with greater efficiency, and the director will be left with more time to get the day's shots. The rigging crew usually also wraps out the set after the first-unit crew has finished with it. The electric rigging crew works in tandem with the grip rigging crew.

The Fixtures Guy

On a production where a lot of practical fixtures and outlets are to be wired, it is valuable to have a fixtures guy (or gal), sometimes also known as a *shop electrician, construction electric,* or *house electrician.* The fixtures guy is responsible for wiring any practical lights and outlets in the set and may also be employed to build and wire special fixtures for the gaffer. A good fixtures guy knows a great deal about dealing with practicals and creating practical lighting effects for production. He will have bookshelves full of light bulb and fixtures catalogues and is an excellent resource for the gaffer when a little R&D is required for a specific problem.

Generator Operator

The generator operator is in charge of the full-time operation and maintenance of the generator. A knowledgeable, experienced generator operator is an extremely valuable person to the set lighting department. This job was traditionally performed by a member of Local 40 (International Brotherhood of Electrical Workers, IBEW), who are trained electricians. However, most genny operators today are teamsters with special 40 cards. The production van driver typically operates the generators on the tractor. To get a 40 card to operate a generator, all a teamster has to do is pay dues to IBEW. There is no training, test, or apprenticeship program. As a result, many generator operators have no special knowledge or training about generators. These individuals are of absolutely no use to you when a generator starts to hick up. Especially when you are on a remote location where a generator cannot be quickly replaced and you encounter a different climate, fuel and other conditions that affect the generators, it is worthwhile for the gaffer and DP to insist on using a qualified generator operator.

Grip Department

Q: How many grips does it take to screw in a light bulb?
A: Grips don't change light bulbs. That's electric.

Alternate:

Q: How many grips does it take to screw in a light bulb?
A: Two. One to hold it and the other to hammer it in.

Nonelectrical lighting equipment is handled by our brothers and sisters in the grip department. (A grip is affectionately called a *hammer*.) Silks, diffusion frames, flags, reflector boards, rigging, dollies and dolly track, cranes, jib arms, and so on are all in the domain of gripology. Lights, dimmers, and generally things with plugs are the domain of the juicers. You could say that the electricians do the lighting and the grips do the shading. Each time an electrician sets up a light, a grip should be right next to him or her with a *grip package*, which includes a C-stand and complement of flags, nets, and diffusion frames that may be needed in front of the light. Electricians graduating from the nonunion world may be used to grips taking charge of placing sandbags on the light stands, providing ladders, and leveling large stands when they are placed on uneven ground. On union jobs in Los Angeles, the electricians generally handle their own ladders, sandbags, and rigging hardware, such as pipe clamps. Grips handle gel and diffusion when it is used on a frame or applied to windows. An electrician applies the gel and diffusion when it goes directly on a light.

Grips are responsible for the safety of the rigging, and they are often called on to rig support for lighting equipment. Truss, speed-rail grids, wall spreaders, and similar rigs are built by the grips. When lights are to be hung from an overhead grid or rigged to the wall of the set, the grips generally rig the support. An electrician then plugs the light in, focuses it, and the like. When lights are mounted on a high platform, on top of parallels, or in the basket of an aerial lift (Condor, Snorkelift, etc.) or on an elevated platform, the grips rig and secure the light and light stand. When an interior night scene needs to be shot during daylight hours, the grips build big black tents around the windows to create darkness outside, while providing space for lights outside the building.

The head of the grip department is the *key grip*. The key grip supervises the grips in the same way that the gaffer supervises the electricians. He or she works for the DP in tandem with the gaffer, supervising the grips in the placement of grip gear in front of each light.

The key grip's chief assistant is the *best boy grip*. The best boy grip coordinates the grip crew in the same way that the best boy electric does the electric crew.

The *dolly grip* is in charge of operating moving-camera platforms, such as dollies and cranes: laying and leveling the dolly track, moving the camera smoothly up and down and to and fro to exact marks with precise timing. Grips also rig support for the camera when it is placed in unusual places, such as on top of a ladder or on the hood of a car.

The Company

Q: How many executive producers does it take to screw in a light bulb?

A: Executive producers don't screw in light bulbs. They screw in hot tubs.

A film crew is composed of freelance artists, technicians, and administrators, who are brought together by the production company when the production is ready to be mounted. The producer and director select the department heads: the DP, production designer, sound mixer, editor, and so on. Each department head usually brings his or her own staff onto the production. The DP recommends a gaffer, key grip, camera operator, and camera assistants with whom he or she prefers to work. The gaffer, in turn, recommends electricians he or she knows and trusts.

Each production brings new faces, new locations, and new circumstances; yet you can count on certain constants in relationships between electricians and the other departments.

Production Staff

Q: How many production managers does it take to screw in a light bulb?

A: None! If you'd just make it a day exterior we wouldn't have to keep screwing around with all these light bulbs!

Officially, the crew is hired by the producer. Although the gaffer usually selects electricians for the crew, once an electrician is offered a job, it is the production manager with whom he signs the deal, memo, or contract. Paychecks are handled by the accounting department through a payroll company.

The duties of the *unit production manager* (UPM) include preparing the script breakdown and production schedule, establishing and controlling the budget, supervising the selection of locations, making deals for locations and services, booking the cast and crew, overseeing daily production decisions (such as authorizing overtime and making schedule changes due to weather), and managing all the off-set logistics, including housing, meals, transportation, permits, security, and insurance. As the UPM is responsible for the budget, he or she must approve all equipment orders and personnel requests.

Some productions have a *production supervisor* instead of, or as well as, a production manager. This title is a technical distinction; a supervisor is a non-DGA production manager (the person does not belong to the Director's Guild of America and therefore can not be called a UPM).

The *production coordinator* assists the production manager. His or her duties include booking the crew, booking and returning equipment, ordering expendables and supplies, monitoring petty cash, distributing production information to the various departments, and coordinating and distributing the shooting schedule and script revisions.

The production manager and production coordinator work out of the production office.

The Director's Team

The "director's team" consists of the assistant directors and the script supervisor.

Assistant Director

The assistant director (1st AD) runs the set. He or she coordinates the actions of every department and the cast, plans the day's schedule, approves the call sheet (which is usually prepared by a second assistant director), keeps everyone informed about the shots, and plans ahead to minimize the amount of time used for each setup. The AD must stay informed of any potential delays or problems and facilitate, coordinate, and motivate the actions of the crew, solving problems before they occur. He or she is responsible for keeping the production moving and on schedule on an hour-to-hour basis.

ADs are responsible for coordinating the actions of all the departments. For example, if an electrician needed some furniture moved to place a light and the set decorator is nowhere in sight, the 1st or 2nd AD would take the matter in hand.

The AD staff take care of the actors: coordinating their schedules, ushering them through makeup and wardrobe and to and from the set. The AD also directs the background action, supervises crowd control, and determines safety precautions during stunts or complicated setups. The AD calls out, "Rolling" just before the cameras roll and "Cut" after the director calls "Cut." It is the nature of the job that the AD has to tell everybody what to do all the time. One shouldn't hold it against him or her, though; a good AD can make the difference between a 12-hour day and a 16-hour day.

The AD is aided by a 2nd AD. They in turn are helped by second 2nd ADs and a squad of production assistants (PAs). You can usually enlist the help of a PA for any odd job that presents itself; just ask first to be sure that the 2nd ADs can spare the PA.

Script Supervisor

Details such as the hand in which an actor holds his beer, at what point in the scene he puts out his cigarette, whether his shirt sleeves are rolled up or not are observed and noted by the script supervisor. All these details are noted in a log for future reference for the editor and the director. For this reason, it is vital for her to be able to see the action on every take; if you stand in her way, you risk being jabbed by her sharp little pencil. The script supervisor also keeps track of the scene and take numbers, lenses used, shot scale, movement, eye-line direction, good takes, flawed takes (and reason), line changes (including ad libs and mistakes), and so forth. The gaffer sometimes has the best boy take detailed notes on the placement of the lights, especially if the scene may be replicated at another time. The script supervisor can provide the best boy with the applicable scene numbers for these notes.

Camera Department

Q: How many ACs does it take to screw in a light bulb?

A: Five. One to screw it in and four to tell you how they did it on the last show.

The camera department is made up of the DP, camera operator, 1st Assistant, 2nd Assistant, and a loader. When shooting in High Definition, the camera crew may include a Digital Image Technician (known as a DIT) and a camera utility person in place of the loader. The first camera assistant (1st AC) is responsible for the camera, including building it, configuring it for each shot, making lens changes, threading the film, running tests, and performing regular maintenance as needed. During the take the 1st AC keeps the camera in focus and may perform any of a multitude of other tasks—zooming, making an aperture change, or ramping the shutter speed or angle. The 1st AC never leaves the camera's side.

From time to time, the 1st AC calls on the lighting crew to help get rid of stray light hitting the lens. (When a light shines directly into the lens, it causes a flare on the image.) The AC and the grips watch for "hits" during setup and rehearsal.

The 2nd AC and loader aid the 1st AC with lens changes and magazine changes, mark the actors' positions, slate each shot, and keep the camera reports and film inventory. Almost all camera equipment runs on batteries, but a 2nd AC needs power to run a video monitor. When a director uses a video monitor, it quickly becomes habit to supply power to the monitor as soon as the camera is placed. Similarly a stinger should be supplied for the dolly at all times.

Sound Department

The sound mixer oversees the recording of audio, monitors the sound levels, and is generally responsible for the quality of the sound recording. The sound mixer is the one person on the set lucky enough to perform his or her job from a sitting position. He or she can usually be found reading the paper at the sound cart.

The boom operator is the person who actually positions the microphone within range of the actors, by holding it on a pole over their heads, wiring them with radio mikes, or planting hidden microphones on the set. When a power cable must cross the microphone cable, the electrician should run it under the microphone cable so it doesn't restrict the boom's movement.

The boom operator has to contend with shadows cast onto the actors and backgrounds by the microphone and boom pole. Boom operators are very good at analyzing the lighting and use great ingenuity to avoid casting shadows. The gaffer and DP can usually help the boom operator by setting toppers on one or two lights to eliminate shadows cast onto the back wall. Particularly difficult for the boom is flat-on hard light from the direction of the camera, because it tends to throw mike shadows onto the back wall. Shooting the light so that it lights only the face or raising it higher, so the light is angled downward, then topping the light, can eliminate the problem. Steep, top-down lighting tends to throw microphone shadows across the actor's clothes or table surfaces. Sometimes, the lighting is such that a boom microphone simply cannot be used, and the sound department must accommodate by using other methods.

The sound department has a vested interest in the good placement of the generator. Even with baffles to deaden it, engine noise can be a nuisance.

Ballasts and dimmers usually hum and can become a concern for sound. Place them as far from the microphones as possible (preferably in another room or outside). (If you wear a pager, don't forget to put it on silent (vibrate) mode.)

Dimming, light cues, and effects create electrical "noise" in the power supply. The sound cart should be powered off separate utility power. All crew members must check with an electrician before plugging in their own electrical equipment; plugging a monitor mistakenly into a dimmer channel, for example, would provide an unexpected fireworks display.

Locations

Q: How many fire safety officers does it take to screw in a light bulb?
A: One, but it's an 8-hour minimum.

A script might call for a city street, department store, hospital, church, factory, private residence, prison, airport terminal, office building, hotel lobby, or post-apocalyptic tundra. Many settings can be more easily (and cheaply) filmed at an existing real site than re-created on the studio stage or lot. Whatever the case, the locations department finds, secures, and coordinates the film's locations.

When on location, any questions or problems pertaining to the building or grounds (such as rigging lights to the structure or access to locked rooms or circuit breaker panels) are handled by the building engineer through the locations manager or their assistants. The locations manager obtains permission to place lights in unorthodox places, such as on a roof. Care must be taken not to damage the floors, walls, or garden. When a house has hardwood floors, for example, the grips and electricians can put rubber crutch tips on the legs of the stands and ask that layout board be put on the floors to protect them. Some locations make restrictions on the use of their property. Working on a period movie, for example, you may well find yourself shooting in a historical building with irreplaceable architectural detail. It is often the locations manager's task to enforce whatever rules have been established at the location—rules that may conflict with the needs of the lighting department. In these situations, keep in mind that it is the director's desire to film the location and our job to make it work. It will usually involve extra time and trouble, but it is more important to keep the locations manger an ally and help preserve good relations with every location the company uses. In the greater scheme of things, it is better for our whole industry if the public views film production as a positive experience.

Transportation

Q: How many teamsters does it take to screw in a light bulb?
A: Four. You got a problem with that?

The drivers are responsible for operating and maintaining all the production vehicles. In addition to the "production van" (usually a 40-ft truck that carries all the lights), transportation usually provides vehicles with hydraulic lift gates to the electric department. These are particularly useful on location when equipment needs to be shuttled to several sites in one day or must be dispersed over a large area. Drivers may also be dispatched to make runs, return equipment to, or pick it up from suppliers. It is a good idea for the best boy to give the transportation coordinator as much advance warning as possible, as needs arise.

Art Department

Q: How many art directors does it take to screw in a light bulb?

A: Does it have to be a light bulb? I've got a really nice candelabra we could use.

Construction builds the sets, *set dressing* decorates the set with items not handled by an actor, while the *props department* is responsible for anything that is handled by an actor. Wall lamps, practicals, "oil" lanterns, and the like are provided and placed by the set decorators. Wiring them is taken care of by an electrician. Employees of the set decorator move furniture.

Hair, makeup, wardrobe, stunts, special effects, first aid, craft service, and catering are the remaining departments on the set with which electricians need to consult from time to time. It pays to stay on good terms with every department.

Civilians

One more group you are going to come into contact with, especially when working on location, is the general public. Everyone on a film crew knows how important it is to establish and maintain good relations with the public. No one knows this more than the locations manager. On location, more often than not, a film crew is a guest in someone else's house. We constantly hold up traffic and ask people to be quiet during takes. By our very presence, we often put someone out. Although, typically, the location is being paid well for the trouble, every flower that gets trampled in the garden, every unthinking curse uttered within earshot of sensitive ears, every piece of equipment left in someone's way makes the public less inclined to cooperate and let us do our work. A disgruntled neighbor may confront the first person he or she sees, sometimes quite rudely. The locations manager and production manager's job is to deal with complaints. As lighting technicians, our role in all this is minimal but important. Treat any comment or question from the public with politeness and professionalism. Help the locations manager stop trouble before it starts by pointing any complaints or problems his or her way. Get approval before placing a light somewhere it is going to annoy civilians; that way the locations manager has a fighting chance at preemptive diplomacy. Any kind of rigging that might do harm to a location or otherwise alarm the owner must be preapproved through the locations manager. When locations or production make specific rules or requests with regard to working in a location, know that they are doing so because the issue is *already* sensitive. If they tell you to wrap out quietly, they are doing so because there have already been complaints about the noise. In cities like Los Angeles, New York, and more recently Toronto and Vancouver, a large segment of the population have had bad experiences with film productions and make it very difficult for production to work on location. There are also those who have learned they can extort money from a desperate production manager and make noise and get in the way until they are paid. As much as possible, these are behaviors we'd like to change.

Okay, let me just finish off the list . . .

Q: How many stunt men does it take to screw in a light bulb?
A: Five. One to screw it in and four to tell him how bitchin' he looked doing it.

Q: How many studio execs does it take to screw in a light bulb?
A: No one knows. Light bulbs last much longer than studio execs.

Q: How many actors does it take to screw in a light bulb?
A: 100. One to screw it in and 99 to say they could have done it better.

Q: How many screen writers does it take to change a light bulb?
A: The light bulb is IN and it is staying IN!

Q: How many editors does it take to change a light bulb?
A: If we change the light bulb we'll have to change everything.

Block, Light, Rehearse, Tweak, Shoot

Progress on the set is measured in *setups*. A feature film crew may shoot 20–30 setups per day. The assistant director tries to schedule the shots so that all the shots in a scene in which the camera is looking in one direction, requiring one particular lighting setup, are shot together at one time. When possible, wider master shots are photographed first, establishing the lighting for the scene. Closer coverage, which usually requires refinements to the master setup, follows. Once coverage from one direction is complete, the AD calls, "Turning around," "Moving on," or "Next setup," and the camera is moved around to shoot the other way. The crew then relights the scene for the new camera angle. Once a scene is completed, the AD calls, "New deal," the company clears out the set, and the director and actors block out the next scene on the schedule.

Although it is convenient when the shots can be scheduled in an order that is efficient for lighting, the AD may have other priorities. Shot order may be arranged to give precedence, for example, to a particularly difficult performance or a stunt that destroys part of the set.

The only sensible way to proceed in filming each new scene is to follow the following five steps in order:

1. Block.
2. Light.
3. Rehearse.
4. Tweak.
5. Shoot.

Lighting without blocking first always causes delays when the actors arrive and do things differently. Trying to shoot without rehearsing and tweaking almost always results in an imperfect take. As fundamental as this rule sounds, it is often the first thing forgotten on set. A well-run set works as follows.

First the director, DP, and actors block the entire scene (plan the staging). During blocking rehearsal, the set is usually cleared so that the actors and director can work without distraction. The director and principal actors are called the *first team*. The DP, gaffer, and key grip watch the rehearsal to determine lighting needs and constraints. The 2nd AC marks the actors' positions with tape at their feet.

Once the scene has been blocked, the actors are sent to makeup and the DP begins lighting. Often, the lighting crew has already roughed in some of the lights during a prelight. The actors are replaced by costumed stand-ins, who act as models for the gaffer and DP while the lights are placed. The *stand-ins* are known as the *second team*. The camera crew sometimes rehearses complicated camera moves using the stand-ins to save the principal actors from technical rehearsals that might dull their performance.

Once the lighting is in place, the AD calls the first team back to the set for final rehearsal. He calls, "Quiet please. Rehearsal's up." The actors run through the scene with the camera and sound crew to iron out any remaining problems. The AC gets final focus marks. The timing of the actions and camera movement may be adjusted. After one or two rehearsals, the scene is ready to shoot.

As a courtesy to the actors and director, everyone must hold their work while the actors are on the set. However, final rehearsals may take place while the lighting crew still has final touches to add. Also, during the rehearsal the DP may see a problem that needs to be addressed before shooting. It is therefore essential that the lighting crew be allowed a moment to tweak after the rehearsals, before the first take.

To save time between setups, electricians may begin lighting a new part of the set while the rest of the crew is filming, but before the camera rolls. When the AD calls, "Hold the work," the work stops immediately.

When it is time for cameras to roll, the AD calls, "Picture's up," followed by, "Roll sound." Second ADs and set PAs, who are equipped with walkie-talkies, echo "Rolling" in every part of the set. Everyone remains absolutely silent once "Roll sound" is called. Be careful not to stand in an actor's eye line. It distracts an actor to see a technician standing directly in his or her line of sight (staring blankly) while trying to perform. When the take is finished, the AD broadcasts, "That's a cut" on the walkie-talkie, at which time work can resume.

The AD makes other announcements, such as these:

"Going again right away." The electrical crew may not have time to resume work because a second take will be rolling immediately.

"Hold the roll." There has been a momentary delay. It cues the sound mixer to stop rolling tape while the problem is fixed.

"That's lunch, one half-hour."

"Abby Singer is up." The Abby Singer is the second to last shot of the day. It was named for (former) assistant director Abbey Singer, who always had "just one more shot" after the last shot of the day.

"Martini is up." The martini is the last shot of the day. (Your next shot will be out of a glass.)

"That's a wrap." This announcement is made after the last shot of the day has been successfully completed. Electricians then begin wrapping: taking down the lights, coiling the cable, and loading the truck. When filming will resume in the same place on the following day and the equipment can simply be left where it is, it is a "walk away."

"MOS." This phrase means that sound will not be recorded for the shot. The term comes from the early days of sound. It is an acronym for minus optical stripe.

"Fire in the hole!" This is announced before a shot in which there will be gunfire or explosions. Be prepared for a loud noise to follow.

CHAPTER 2

Preproduction Planning: Lighting Package, Expendables, and Personal Tools

Preproduction Planning

One of the first responsibilities of the DP and gaffer during preproduction is to prepare an equipment list (lists of equipment and expendables are given in Appendix J and K). To come up with a complete equipment list, the gaffer needs pretty clear ideas about how each scene will be lit. In scouting the locations and looking at the sets, the DP, gaffer, key grip, and rigging keys are confronted with the particular challenges they'll need to address. The gaffer reads the script carefully, making notations and raising questions for the DP. He discusses scenes with the DP. The input of the director, production designer, and costume designer often steer important lighting decisions.

While absorbing the aesthetic choices of the director and DP, at every stage, the gaffer must consider three things: equipment, personnel, and time.

Equipment   What basic equipment is needed to light the scenes? Which scenes require special equipment (condors, xenon spotlights, or what have you)? Will the transportation department need to furnish extra vehicles on particular days to move equipment from place to place?

Personnel   How many extra electricians are needed to operate this special equipment or to prerig or wrap out cabling and equipment? Are certain days on the schedule particularly difficult, or will large locations require extra hands?

Time   What prerigging is required to achieve efficiency during shooting? How much time does it take to get into and wrap out of each set? What might cause lighting delays the DP and production department should take into account? What workable solutions can the gaffer suggest to the assistant director and UPM?

Additionally, the gaffer and DP, in coordination with the production designer, determine what special considerations should be given to the lighting in designing the sets. Designers are generally very conscious of lighting and design the sets with windows in places that will make for good lighting; however, looking over the designer's plans forestalls impediments to the lighting and may inspire ways to incorporate the DP's lighting ideas into the design.

During preproduction, the gaffer and DP also discuss how to approach the material. What is the mood and style of the film? When will the shots be fairly conventional, and when will steadicam shots reveal every corner of a room, requiring that all lights be hung above or outside the set? What gel colors are needed? What film stocks are used? Will the lighting be at a low level or a high level? Each of these questions affects the equipment the gaffer needs.

Scouting Locations

The director, assistant director, and department heads scout each location in a group; the director and first AD present an overview of how the scenes are played out. This is the crew's opportunity to ask questions and coordinate crew members' actions. The DP and gaffer formulate a rough idea of how they light each space. If the lighting is complex, they may also draw light plots and make notes on the placement of windows and doors in each room as well as wall sconces or chandeliers that may be seen on camera. These notes are invaluable during future discussions. The gaffer, best boy, and rigging gaffer consider the special rigging required, special equipment required, cable routing, generator placement, location of the staging area, and placement of the production van. During the scout, the DP, gaffer, and key grip constantly work out plans to adapt the space for lighting. Aerial lifts or parallels may need to be employed outside the windows to support large lights. Wall spreaders or other lighting support may need to be rigged near the ceiling. Windows may need to be gelled or tinted.

In addition to absorbing this information, the best boy and rigging gaffer need to determine routes of access to each set for cabling. They must coordinate with the transportation and locations departments to ascertain where the generator can be placed so as to be as close to the set as possible without causing sound problems. They must learn from the DP, AD, and director how the feeder cables can be run to the set without entering into the shots. If a tie-in may be necessary, the best boy inspects the power boxes to determine their suitability. If house circuits may be used, he locates and examines the breaker box to determine its capacity and the layout of circuits. He locates the light switches for sconces and house lights. He works with the locations manager and the contact at the location to gain access to locked rooms or arrange for lights to be placed on a neighboring property or the roof. He must find the service entrance through which to bring in carts and equipment without encountering stairs. He must locate the elevators. If large numbers of fluorescent lights are needed, he must get a count of the number of tubes to be ordered. In short, he must fully think through the lighting needs at each location.

Once the locations have been scouted, the gaffer and best boy look over the production schedule; evaluate personnel, equipment, and time requirements; and apprise the production department of their needs. It is helpful to create a calendar that outlines when extra workers and equipment are required.

Production Meetings

At least one major production meeting is held before production begins. This is scheduled after all the tech scouts have been completed and is attended by (at least) all the department heads. The meeting is led by the first assistant director. Typically either the shooting script or the production schedule is used as an itinerary. Taking the shoot scene by scene, the AD lists all the major elements of each scene. Questions and concerns from any department are raised and discussed. Issues that involve a great deal of interdepartmental cooperation are the most important to flush out in detail. Decisions involving only two parties can be identified and deferred to separate meetings. The gaffer and key grip are required to attend, listen, and contribute when it is helpful. This is usually a long and painful meeting, but it may often be the only opportunity for everyone to learn about the plans and needs of other departments that might affect them.

Equipment Package

The load-in is the first day of work for an electrician on a feature film. It is the first day the electrician puts his or her hands on the lights.

The best boy supervises the checkout and load-in, making sure the lighting order is correctly filled and all the equipment is in full working order. The checkout must be extremely thorough. Even at the best rental houses, you cannot assume that all the equipment is in perfect working order or leave the counting to someone else. At the completion of filming, any broken or missing items are charged to the production as "lost and damaged." An infinite number of circumstances can conspire to foul things up: Orders are often changed at the last minute, special equipment may come from more than one rental house. Almost always, a few items require maintenance or are miscounted by the rental house, so count and check the equipment carefully. To prep and load the equipment package for a medium-size feature film into a 40-ft. truck takes two days for three electricians.

Lights

In film, we call them *lights, lamps, fixtures,* or *heads*. Each light should be tested at checkout. Take the time; you do not want to discover problems on the set when production is in full swing. Once you establish a routine for checking lights, it takes very little time to check all the items listed in Checklists 2.1 and 2.2.

Stands

There are many different kinds of light stands, from short to very tall, from lightweight to heavy steel. All types of stands are covered in detail in Chapter 6. Checklist 2.3 enumerates the checkout procedure for stands.

Figure 2.1 Complete scrim set with box. The set includes (from left to right) a half double, half single, two doubles, a single, and a set of gel frames.

Checklist 2.1 Fresnel and Open-Face Tungsten Lamps Checkout

☐ Check that each light is complete. Each must have a full set of scrims, a scrim box or bag, and barn doors. Count the scrims. A complete five-piece set includes two doubles, one single, one half double, one half single, and one gel frame (Figure 2.1).

☐ Check the fit of barn doors. Check for floppy doors. Most gaffers prefer four-leaf to two-leaf doors. Doors should be fitted with safety chain.

☐ Plug in each fixture and turn it on to check the bulb and the switch. Make sure you have any needed connector adapters. Wiggle the cord at the switch and lamp housing to ferret out any intermittent discontinuity (problem with power cord or lamp base contacts).

☐ Check flood spot mechanism for smooth, full travel. Observe the beam as it changes. An uneven or odd-shaped beam is evidence of an improperly aligned bulb or a bent or damaged reflector.

☐ Especially with hot-burning lights such as baby-babies or baby-juniors, the reflector can get cooked by prolonged use tilted steeply downward. The reflector must be properly aligned, unbent, clean, and in good condition. With the power off, open the fixture and *check the condition of the reflector.*

☐ Inspect the *bulb* for blisters and bulges, evidence the bulb has been mishandled and burnout is imminent.

☐ Check that the *lens* is clean and free of cracks. A little dust buildup on the lens cuts the light output in half.

☐ Check that the T-handle threads properly. The threads sometimes get stripped.

☐ Check that the tilt lock knuckle holds the light firmly. The cork disks at the swivel point wear out and occasionally need to be replaced.

Checklist 2.2   HMI Lamps Checkout

- ☐ Each unit should be complete with scrim set, barn doors, lens set (PARs only), two-head feeder cables, ballast, and power feeder cable. With units using large size Socapex connectors, a J-box is needed to connect the head feeders to one another.
- ☐ Check for floppy barn doors, bad fit, or a missing barn door safety chain.
- ☐ Hook-up and *turn on* each light, using both head feeders. Inspect the head cables for bent pins or misthreaded connectors, cuts in insulation, and a loose strain relief collar at connector. Check READY and ON indicator lights on the head and ballast.
- ☐ Allow several minutes to reach full output. Using a three-color color temperature meter, *measure the color temperature* and green/magenta shift of each unit. Mark these measurements on a piece of white camera tape and tape it to the bail of the light. Also include the date and the unit number.
- ☐ *Number* each head, ballast, and globe box, so that the same head, globe, and ballast are always used together.
- ☐ Check the flood spot mechanism for smooth, full travel. An uneven or odd-shaped beam is evidence of an improperly aligned bulb or a bent or damaged reflector.
- ☐ Watch for unstable arcs. If in question, use a welder's glass to observe the bulb.
- ☐ You may want to check for ground faults and leakage current from the head and the ballast. Current leaking to the lamp housing or ballast casing give you a nasty shock if you become well grounded (as when standing in wet grass). This is rarely a problem with new equipment but often occurs with older, poorly maintained equipment. You can run into this problem if the wires in the head feeder cables are crossed, or if there is a short in the cable, the head, or the ballast. With the lamp on, use a voltage tester to check for current between the lamp housing and ground and the ballast casing and ground. Use a GFI-protected duplex outlet box to test the smaller HMI units. This special circuit breaker trips if it detects leakage current.
- ☐ You may also want to test the restrike capability of the light by turning it off and attempting a restrike after 15 seconds. If the light will not restrike, try again once every 60 seconds to see how long you have to wait. Note: Repeated unsuccessful ignition attempts discolor the inside of the bulb; don't overdo it.
- ☐ Inspect the bulb for blisters and bulges, evidence that burnout is imminent.
- ☐ If the ballast uses a fuse, get a couple spares (Lightmaker 575/1200 ballasts).
- ☐ Check that the lens is clean and uncracked. Dust on the lens cuts light output in half.
- ☐ Check that the T-handle threads properly. The threads sometimes get stripped.
- ☐ Check that the tilt lock knuckle holds the light firmly. The cork disks at the swivel point wear out and occasionally need to be replaced.

Checklist 2.3   Stands Checkout

☐   Raise each stand to full extension. Check for binding and corrosion. Test the lock of each T-handle.

☐   Inspect for bent or broken braces and loose or missing brace bolts.

☐   Crank stands and motorized stands should be tested by raising and lowering the stand with a sandbag on the top. The weight is necessary to prevent the stand's inner mechanism from binding when lowered.

☐   Pneumatic tires should be fully inflated and roll smoothly.

☐   Check that the wheel swivel locks, brace hinges, collars, and so on operate properly.

Checklist 2.4   Cable and Distribution Checkout

☐   The main disconnect or bull switch is a high-amperage (200 or 400 amps), fused, switch box used as a main on/off switch for power to the set. Be sure that at least one spare fuse is included.

☐   Heavy-gauge (4/0 or 2/0), single-conductor feeder cable is used to run power from the power source to the set. Check the lug and pin connectors for bent or broken ends. Inspect cable for cuts in the insulation, showing exposed copper.

☐   Deuce boards are fused remote switches, usually used with DC systems, that subdivide current into 200A subcircuits. *Stock spare fuses.* (The AC version uses 100A breakers.)

☐   Banded cable, stage extensions, Bates cable, and plugging boxes are types of heavy extension cable that carry power to various areas of the set and to high-amperage lights. Check for melted, overheated plastic on connectors. Check for bent or broken pins. Check for gashes in cable insulation.

☐   Edison boxes, or gang boxes, plug into the larger feeder cable to provide a number of Edison outlets. Stock replacement fuses.

☐   Stingers are Edison extension cords used to carry power to medium and small lights (2000 W and less). Inspect each stinger. Check the connectors for melted or blackened plastic. Test any suspicious-looking ones.

Electrical Distribution System

Lighting a set can require heavy loads of electricity. When shooting on location, where necessary electrical service is unavailable, the production is powered by one or more generators, which are designed to run quietly and produce the quantities of power needed. Electricity is fed to the lights through the distribution system. Electricity and distribution are covered in detail in Chapters 11–13. Checklist 2.4 gives a brief description of the components of the distribution system, with some notes on things to watch for during the checkout.

Loading the Production Van

When shooting on location, the lighting crew works out of its truck. Depending on the size of the production, the vehicle may be anything from a cube van, to a 10-ton truck, to a fully customized, 40-ft, 18-wheel production van. A fully equipped production van like the one shown in Figure 2.2 is complete with dual generators mounted on the tractor. The truck comes equipped with shelving for the lights, brackets on the doors to hold stands, a large hydraulic lift gate, one or more side doors with stairs, interior lighting, and a well-organized design. Smaller 5- and 10-ton trucks have jockey boxes underneath both sides of the truck that carry cable and sandbags. Larger trucks have doors along the length of the belly that can hold a substantial quantity of cable and distribution equipment.

A head cart (Figure 2.3) is a customized cart with large pneumatic tires and sturdy shelves onto which a variety of the most commonly used lights are packed. The cart shown also carries a variety of stands (or gel rolls).

Head carts provide convenience and mobility during shooting and expedite loading and unloading. You typically have several carts, some for tungsten units, for example, others for HMIs. When the truck travels, the carts are simply secured in the aisle. Lights are packed tightly and neatly onto the shelves of the carts and the truck, grouped according to size. Once the lights are packed, the best boy labels the shelves of the carts and the truck to show where each type of light is kept. It is helpful to include the number of lights on each shelf. This makes it easy to conduct a fast inventory at the end of a day's shooting. Before the truck travels, the lights

Figure 2.2 A 40-ft production van with two tractor-mounted generators. Note that stands are mounted to the rear doors. The small door on the side provides access to 12ks. (Courtesy of Hollywood Rental, Sun Valley, CA.)

Figure 2.3 Pictured here are a "tungsten cart" holding a crate of Peppers and shelving for a variety of tungsten lamps, a "distro cart" containing crates of splitters and adaptors, and a cable cart (far right).

are secured with rubber bungee cords. Large lights (5k and 10k fixtures and large HMIs) are kept on the floor of the truck along with HMI ballasts.

The electric crew typically also has a milk crate cart for stinger crates, practical bulbs and wiring devices, dimmers, a gel crate, expendables, and rolls of gel (Figure 2.4).

Cable dollies (Figure 2.5) also are typically part of the equipment package. Cable dollies can be stowed in the aisle of the truck during travel, convenient for keeping cable ready to be wheeled out.

When packing the truck, be sure you provide immediate access to equipment that is routinely needed. Don't bury your distribution boxes under cable or behind big lights. Put spare items (fluorescent tubes, spare globes) on the top shelves, along with fixtures that are seldom called for. During night shooting, reserve a special spot for the items that will be packed away last—the work lights and associated cable and distribution.

The workbox (a wooden chest of drawers) is usually secured inside the truck. It is used to store spare bulbs, electrical expendables, tools, paperwork, and supplies.

Expendable Supplies

Expendables (see also the Appendix K checklist) are supplies purchased and used up in the course of production. In addition to equipment inventory and checkout, the best boy and electricians use prep days for organizing and prepping expendables,

Figure 2.4 The electrical cart carries various types of stands. Milk crates contain hand dimmers, variacs, stingers, adaptors, three-fers, cube taps, zip cord, practical bulbs, and other electrical expendables. An electric cart may also hold rolls of gel and a milk crate of cut gel. (Courtesy of Backstage Studio Equipment, Sun Valley, CA.)

cutting gels for the lights, and completing any similar tasks to get everything ready for the first day of shooting.

Gels and Diffusion

Gels are used for three purposes:

1. To correct the color of one light source to match that of another (tungsten correction, daylight correction, carbon arc correction, and fluorescent correction gels).
2. To alter the color of a source to create an effect (theatrical or effects gels).
3. To reduce the intensity of a source without altering its color (neutral-density gels).

Diffusion media soften light. Gels come in wide rolls and in sheets. They can be applied to lights or windows or put in frames that are placed in front of the light source.

Cuts of gel are kept in a crate or box, sectioned according to size and color (Figure 2.6). This practice makes gel use fast and easy on the set and ultimately saves gel because less is wasted. Precut color correction gel and diffusion into squares of 6 in., 8 in., 10 in., and 12 in., and a couple cuts of 20 in. and 24 in. (A 6-in. square fits inside the barn doors of units 1k or smaller. An 8-in. square fits

Figure 2.5 A cable dolly for moving cable from place to place. (Courtesy of Backstage Studio Equipment, Sun Valley, CA.)

studio babies and baby juniors. The 10-in. and 12-in. sizes fit inside the doors of regular juniors and outside the doors of lamps 650 W and smaller. The larger cuts of gel fit on the outside of the doors of 2ks, 1200 HMIs, and PAR lights.) Anything larger than 24 in. can be gelled using a frame supplied by the grips.

The best way to cut gel from the roll is to use a template. Cut a 24 × 48 in. piece of ½-in. plywood and mark out a grid pattern of 6-, 8-, 10-, and 12-in. squares. Use a skill saw to score along the marks, making grooves ⅛ in. deep. The matte knife blade slices down the grooves and makes cutting gel very fast and easy. The smaller cuts can be made from the scraps left over from the larger cuts. Once the gel is cut and organized, the gel crate finds a home on the cart, where it will remain close at hand during shooting. Assorted rolls of gel may be kept on the head cart; the remaining rolls are stored in boxes on the truck.

Electrical Expendables

A production may or may not require all of the items described here. During prep these items are organized in the drawers of a work box, crates on the milk crate cart, and boxes on the shelves of the truck. Label each drawer, crate, and box with its contents. A large capacity toolbox with drawers makes an excellent storage place for all the small expendable items. You can also keep gel swatch books, special tools, and meters in the toolbox. The tool box fits right on the milk crate cart (see Figure 2.6).

Figure 2.6 Cut gel and diffusion are marked with permanent marker and stored according to size and type in a sectioned milk crate.

Black wrap Black wrap is a durable black foil used on hot lights to control spill and shape the beam. It is available in rolls of 12 in. (50 ft), 24 in., and 36 in. (25 ft). White wrap is also available.

Clothespins (nicknamed C-47s or bullets) These are used to attach gels and diffusion to the lights.

Rubber matting Matting is used to cover power cables where they cross doorways and other traffic areas. It comes in rolls 24 in. wide, up to 100 ft long.

Sash cord Sash cord is made of white cotton rope. It is used for tying cable to pipe, among other things. Commonly used weights are #6, #8, and #10.

Trick line and mason line These are #4 weight nonstretch rope. Trick line is black. Mason line is white. It comes in handy for odd jobs, such as making stinger tie strings and power cord hangers.

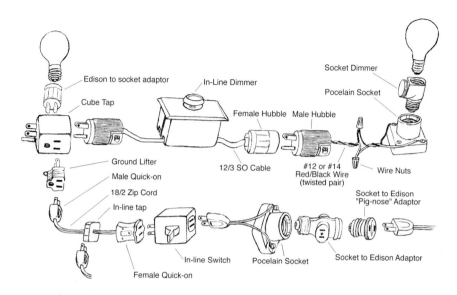

Figure 2.7 Electrical supplies.

Bungee cords and S-hooks Black rubber bungee cords come in various sizes and should be ordered to fit the shelves of the truck and carts.

Cube taps Cube taps are used for plugging several low-amperage lights into one outlet. General Electric makes a cube-shaped tap from which the device gets its name, but any connector that serves the same function may be called a *cube tap* (15 A max). See Figure 2.7.

Ground plug adapter A ground plug adapter is used to adapt grounded plugs to the ungrounded outlets found in older houses. It is also called a *cheater, ground lifter,* or *two-to-three adapter.* See Figure 2.7.

Quick-on plugs These are small, low-amperage Edison sockets and plugs that can be connected to #18 zip cord quickly with no tools. Quick-on plugs provide a speedy way to rig small lamps. See Figure 2.7.

Add-a-taps or in-line taps These are female Edisons that can be spliced onto a piece of #18 zip cord without cutting the cord. See Figure 2.7.

Zip cord Light 18-gauge household lamp cord is used for rigging practicals and other small lights. See Figure 2.7.

Wire nuts A wire nut is a an insulated cap used to splice two bare wires together. See Figure 2.7.

Dimmers Household dimmers of 600 and 1000 W are commonly used to dim small lights and practicals. See Figure 2.7.

Porcelain sockets Lamp sockets (medium screw base, E26) are used to mount light bulbs in set pieces and soft boxes. Use porcelain sockets, as photo bulbs will melt plastic sockets. See Figure 2.7.

Socket dimmers A socket dimmer (150 W max) screws in between the lamp socket and the light bulb, allowing the bulb to be dimmed. See Figure 2.7.

In-line switches   When rigging practical lights in sets, it is sometimes handy to have a plug-in, 15A switch on the line. See Figure 2.7.

Hubble Edison   The best boy stocks male and female Hubble Edison plugs to replace the plugs on stingers and power cords when they burn out. See Figure 2.7.

#12 copper wire   The best boy may want to have rolls of black, white, and green #12 wire, which is handy for wiring special lights and devices. A twisted pair of red/black wire is commonly used, too. See Figure 2.7.

Bus fuses   Spare bus fuses for deuce boards and bull switches are usually provided by the rental company.

Gang box fuses   These are 20-A BAF bus fuses, the essential replacement fuses for gang boxes. Gang box fuses blow quite frequently, so be sure to have plenty on hand.

Splitter fuses   These 60-A fuses are used in in-line fuses on 100-A to two 60-A Bates splitters.

Electrical tape   Electrical tape is used for color-coding cables and spider boxes. It comes in a variety of colors (red, white, blue, black, and green) and is handy for insulating wire splices.

Gaffer's tape   Gaffer's tape is a heavy 2-in. fabric-based tape that rips cleanly in the direction of the weave. It is used to tape just about everything.

Paper tape   Paper tape has less adhesion than gaffer's tape. Black 2-in. paper tape is handy for masking light. It has less of a tendency to pull the paint off walls than gaffer's tape.

White and colored cloth tape   This 1-in. and 2-in. cloth tape is used for labeling and color coding equipment.

Snot tape   This is a sticky film that is handy for mounting gels in gel frames (3M transfer tape).

Best boy paint   Best boy paint is white, heat-resistant paint used to repaint the reflective surfaces of soft lights without altering the color of the light emitted.

Dulling spray   This is a spray applied to shiny surfaces to tone down reflective glints.

Streaks and tips   Colored hair spray is used to tone down or black out surfaces that are too bright. It is water soluble, washes off easily after filming, and comes in shades of auburn, beige, black, blond, brown, gray, pink, silver, white, etc.

Practical bulbs   These are bulbs used in practical lamps, usually household (medium screw base) bulbs. Various types are used, among them photoflood bulbs, household bulbs, floodlights, spotlights, and small fluorescents. Specifics appear in Chapter 9 and Appendix Table E.1.

Fluorescent bulbs   High color rendering index (CRI) tubes replace fluorescent tubes in offices and commercial buildings where the existing fluorescents are not correct for photography.

Flashlight bulbs   These are replacement bulbs for electricians' flashlights.

Batteries   Use AA for flashlights and pagers; AAA for light meters; disk batteries for DM73 voltage/continuity meter; 9V for amp probe and light meters.

Cotter pins   Cotter pins are used when hanging lights to prevent the receptacle from slipping off the pin.

Visqueen heavy plastic sheet   A Visqueen heavy plastic sheet is used to protect equipment and electrical connections from rain, precipitation, dew, dust, and sand. It comes in 100-ft rolls, 20 ft wide (folded to 5 ft).

Crutch tips   Crutch tips are put on the legs of stands to protect floors, in sizes $^3/_4$ in. for small stands and $1^1/_4$ in. for large stands.

Refracil   Refracil is a heat-resistant cloth that will not burn when a hot light is placed on it. It protects ceiling and wall surfaces from heat damage.

Bailing wire   Bailing wire is a stiff wire, also called *stovepipe wire*, that can be used as a barn-door safety, although a grip chain is preferable.

Preparations may include the following:

Set box   The best boy often prepares a set box, which is kept close to the action at all times and contains all the commonly needed items—tape rolls, zip cord and quick-ons, cube taps, dimmers, and a supply of clothespins.

Tape rolls   Put together a selection of tape rolls on a loop of sash cord: one roll each of 2-in. gaffer's tape, 2-in. black paper tape, and 1-in. white cloth tape. Snot tape should also be readily available. The electrical tape rolls (all colors) go together on a separate rope.

Practical bulbs   Mark and organize practical bulbs so their wattages and types are easily readable. Label the boxes. Insert (foamcore) dividers in a couple of milk crates. Stock compartments with various types and wattages to keep near the set. PH-bulbs (211, 212, and 213) do not have their rating printed on the top of the bulb. It is helpful to mark the top of these bulbs with a permanent marker: one dot for 211, two dots for 212, and three dots for 213.

Zip cord stingers, porcelain sockets   Put together a number of zip cord stingers (zip cord fitted with quick-on plugs). They will come in handy when wiring practical lamps.

Homemade boxes   Homemade lighting fixtures, such as soft boxes, are wired by an electrician. Soft box construction is discussed in Chapter 8.

Tools and Personal Gear

Tool Belt

When working on set, a lamp operator carries the needed tools and supplies on a tool belt (Figure 2.8). The best arrangement for our work is to carry most of the tools (shown in Figure 2.9) in a compartmentalized pouch. A flap folds over the tools to prevent them from falling out. Sharp tools (a knife) and delicate instruments (a voltmeter) are best stowed out of harm's way in their own protective leather pouches. Spread the weight around the belt to avoid putting stress on your back. Some electricians try to carry everything but the kitchen sink on their belts. They have tools hanging, clanking, and jangling from every part of their outfits. Carrying humping heaps of tools around all day wears you out and slows you down. It is better to keep yourself lean, streamlined, and unencumbered. Keep additional tools in a toolbox. Every electrician should own the following tools. What you carry on

Figure 2.8 Tool pouch.

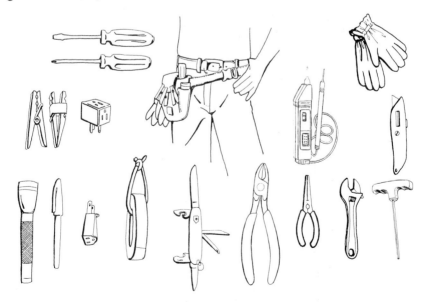

Figure 2.9 Tools and supplies carried on an electrician's tool belt.

your belt varies, depending on the circumstances. (Keep in mind, all the gear you buy for work is tax deductible. Keep your receipts.)

Leather work gloves Made of cowhide or some equivalent, these are used for handling hot lights or dirty cable and hardware. Clip them onto your belt when not wearing them. Leather gloves protect your hands from heat, abrasion, and grime. They cannot necessarily be counted on to protect you from electrical shock. While they may provide electrical insulation when clean and dry, typically they are moist with sweat, making them a conductor. For work requiring better finger dexterity (though less protection), goatskin gloves are about one third as thick.

Glove clip A glove clip loops over a belt and provides a small spring clamp to hold gloves.

Screwdriver Carry a flathead screwdriver and a Phillips screwdriver, or better, a single screwdriver with a reversible tip, flathead on one side, Phillips on the other.

Utility knife with retractable blade Knives are used for cutting gels, foamcore, rope, and so on.

Scissors Small, sharp scissors are often handy for making more careful cuts of gels and the like.

Wire snips These are used primarily for cutting wire for practical lamps and making wire splices but have other important uses discussed later in this book.

Crescent wrench An adjustable wrench is used to adjust the friction of a bail, tighten a pipe clamp, and perform countless other jobs. The standard 6-in. crescent wrench has a $^{1}/_{2}$-in. maximum jaw opening that is too small to fit the $^{5}/_{8}$-in. bolt used on many pipe hangers. You can find 6-in. crescent wrenches with an extra wide jaw, which are ideal, or carry an 8-in. wrench, which is bulky.

Speed wrench A ratcheted $^{3}/_{8}$-in. square wrench is used for securing sister-lugs (square-headed setscrews) onto bus bars.

Needle-nose pliers A needle-nose pliers is used for pulling hot scrims out of a light, small repairs, and so forth.

Bates cable tool This tool performs three functions necessary for maintaining Bates connectors. It has a pin-cleaner, pin-straightener, and pin-splitter. It comes in its own pouch.

T-handle Allen wrench A $^{3}/_{16}$-in. Allen wrench with a long insulated T-handle is used for tightening the setscrews on sister-lugs inside a spider box. You can insulate several inches below the handle by applying heavy shrink-wrap insulation or wrapping the tool with electrical tape.

Voltmeter/continuity tester A voltmeter/continuity tester is used to check line voltage (120 V, 208 V, or 240 V), check for voltage drop, and locate broken connections in power cords. A continuity tester tests for burnt-out bulbs and fuses and continuity in wires. Some models have a pushbutton on/off switch, which helps prevent inadvertently running down the batteries.

Circuit tester Plugs into an Edison outlet and tells you if the line is hot. Also indicates if the polarity and grounding are correct.

Line sensor (voltage tick) This device indicates if a wire has current flowing through it by sensing the magnetic field.

Flashlight   Electricians frequently find themselves working in the dark. When dealing with electricity, you always need to see what you are doing. Small, rugged, focusable flashlights are very popular and easy to carry on your belt.

Clothespins   Keep a dozen or so on your belt. Figure 2.8 shows an inverted C-47 (a C-74), which is handy to pull hot scrims out of lights.

Permanent marker   This is used for labeling gels, fixtures, connectors, cables, and so forth.

Ballpoint pen   A pen is used for taking notes, filling out paperwork, taking down phone numbers, and so on.

Ground plug adapter   When on location it is good to keep a couple cheaters in your pouch.

Cube taps   Keep a supply of two or three on you.

Gaffer's tape   Loop sash cord through the tape and attach it to your belt with a carabiner. If the roll is too bulky, you can make a "tape cube." Fold about 9 in. of tape onto itself, then continue to wind tape around until about 5 or 6 ft of it is wound onto the strip. The tape cube can go in your back pocket.

Meters

More sophisticated electrical measuring equipment may be useful to a best boy, generator operator, rigging gaffer, or dimmer board operator. These meters are used for troubleshooting and close monitoring of the power supply and electrical system. (Meters are covered in detail in Chapter 11.)

Amp probe   The amp probe clamps around a single conductor and measures current (in amps) running through it. It is used to check that the load does not exceed the capacity of the system and is balanced between phases.

RMS multimeter   This is a high-end, precision electrical meter used to measure AC or DC voltage, check line loss, find continuity, read amperage, read resistance, check line Hz rate, and detect rapid voltage fluctuations, among other things. Meters having a memory function can give peak and average values over an extended period of monitoring.

Circuit finder   This device shows which circuits share a given circuit breaker and which circuit breaker is connected to each outlet. It has two parts: one connects into an outlet, the other is used at the breaker panel. A circuit finder can be very useful when house multiple circuits are used to power movie lights.

Other Hand Tools

Some supplemental tools can make life easier. These are usually part of the gaffer's kit, kept in a workbox in the truck.

Automatic wire stripper   This tool provides a fast, precise way to strip insulation off the ends of wires. It is handy when wiring a lot of fixtures.

Rope wrench   This heavy-duty snip can cut cable or rope cleanly, like butter. It saves a lot of time and aggravation when making up stingers, wiring fixtures, or rigging with rope.

Crimper   These are used for crimping connectors onto wires, useful when wiring some types of fixtures.

Spider wrench   A special T-handle wrench for use on sister lugs, the wrench fits over the outside of the sister lug bolt. It can be very handy when an Allen slot gets stripped.

Electrician's scissors   These extra-tough scissors (they can cut through a penny) are especially useful for cutting metal gobo patterns but also great for cutting gels, rope, and the like.

Thumbscrew-type $^5/_8$-in. wrench   A small, convenient alternative to carrying a big crescent wrench, it does not provide as much leverage as a wrench but is great for $^5/_8$-in. bolts on stirrup hangers.

Hand rasp (also called a rat-tail rasp)   This rasp can pierce and saw through luan. It is useful for cutting a quick rat hole in a set wall.

Allen wrench sets or hex set (English and metric)   These wrenches are used for fixing stands, among other things.

Full set of screwdrivers   The set should include a large and small Phillips, a very small flat-head screwdriver, a large flathead screwdriver, and a right-angle screwdriver for lamp head repairs.

Vice grips   These include small, needle-nose grips for clamping onto small parts while making repairs and large, crescent vice grips for getting a tight grip in a jammed pin connector.

Soldering iron and solder

Cordless electric drill/screw gun   Especially useful when rigging, this tool is used to affix devices to a wooden structure to keep them neat and organized.

Hammer

Steel tape measure

Glue   Super-glue has a multitude of uses.

Large flashlights   It is handy to have some big flashlights when shooting at night. They can be passed out to electricians at the end of the night to perform a walk-around "idiot check."

Can handle   This is a handle that fits over the bull switch to provide comfort and leverage when throwing large, spring-loaded switches. If you throw a lot of switches, a handle can save you a lot of strain.

Personal Gear

Electricians get dirty: jeans, a T-shirt, and work boots or sneakers are normal apparel. Weather permitting, it is advisable to protect your legs and arms with long pants and a shirt. Be prepared for the weather. In southern California you might need only sunscreen, a baseball hat, sunglasses, and a jacket and jeans for after sunset, but be prepared for all weather conditions. When shooting on location you might want to keep the following personal gear in your duffel bag:

- A full rain suit.
- Boots.

- Cold-weather jacket.
- Hat and gloves.
- A change of clothes in case you get wet.
- Consider the terrain. Hiking boots or work boots are often desirable.
- Sunscreen.
- Lip ointment.
- Mosquito repellent.
- Ear protection (disposable earplugs or head gear for when firearms are used).
- Eye protection (goggles or safety glasses). The special effects department usually supplies eye protection to everyone who is needed near the action during explosions and stunts.
- Goggles and a bandana are needed when working in the desert. Blowing sand gets in your eyes, nose, and mouth and can practically blind you.
- Map book. In any metropolitan area, carry a map book with detailed illustrations of the streets. This will save you from getting lost and being late for work when the location map and directions aren't so good.

Grip Equipment

Grips and electricians work together closely, and it is important to have a working knowledge of grip equipment. A brief description of common pieces of equipment follows.

Shiny Boards

Reflector boards (shiny boards)   This is a 42 × 42 in. silver-covered board that mounts on a junior stand. Reflectors are used to bounce light, usually sunlight. They can be panned, tilted, and locked into position. They normally have a hard side that reflects a hard squarish patch of light and a soft side that reflects a slightly broader, less intense, area with soft edges. These are also called *shiny boards*.

2 × 2 ft. shiny board   Similar to the larger ones, this uses a baby stand.

Mirror boards   A mirror board is a shiny board with a mirror surface. Quite a bit heavier than shiny boards, it gives off a very bright, sharply delineated square of light.

Combo stand   This stand with a junior receptacle (1 1/8 in. female) is used for shiny boards or lights.

Low combo stand   A short combo stand (36 in. instead of the standard 48 in.) is also called a *low boy junior*.

Overhead Sets

Overhead set   A large frame with one of several types of material stretched across it. Overhead sets are used on exteriors to shade the action (Figure 2.10). Standard sizes are 20 × 20 ft, 12 × 12 ft, 8 × 8 ft, and 6 × 6 ft. An overhead set

Figure 2.10 A 20 × 20-ft. overhead silk reduces and softens direct sunlight.

includes a single net (which cuts light by a half stop), a double net (cuts a full stop), a silk (diffuses light, softens shadows), and a solid made of black duvetyn (shades action completely). A set may also include a griffolyn, a silver, a gold, grid cloth, or diffusion.

Griffolyn (griff)   A nylon/plastic sheet that is white on one side and black on the other. When stretched in an overhead frame, the white side provides a big bounce source for exterior fill; the black side absorbs light for negative fill (Figure 2.11).

Silver and gold lamé   A *silver lamé* is a reflective silver fabric used as a large, strong exterior bounce source. A *gold* has a reflective gold side to create a golden bounce light. They are stretched on an overhead-type frame.

Stands: medium roller, high roller, hi-hi roller   A stand has a 4 1/2-in. gobo head suitable for holding an overhead frame and usually a receptacle for a junior stud. It comes in various sizes, medium, high, and hi-hi. A hi-hi makes it possible to get lights and grip equipment as high as 20 ft in the air.

Carts

Grips typically have a grip cart (called a *taco cart*). The cart holds C-stands, apple boxes, wedges, cup blocks, and cribbing as well as provides drawers for hardware and expendables and space for milk crates (which hold mounting hardware). A flag box attaches to the front and holds 2 × 3 ft and 18 × 24-in. flags, nets, and silks. Grip clips are also found on the taco cart.

A 4-by cart holds 4 × 4-ft flags, nets, silks, and bounce boards. Grips may have an additional large-wheeled flag box to hold large cutters and additional flags, nets, and silks.

Figure 2.11 A white griffolyn can be used as a giant soft bounce source. Gold and silver lamé give even stronger light.

Items Kept on the Carts

C-stands (century stands) This stand is used to hold just about everything, from flags, nets, and silks to tree branches, bead board, and lights that have a ⅝-in. baby receptacle. The standard height is 53 in. A hi-boy is 73 in. high, and a lowboy is 26 in. high.

Flags Black duvetyn fabric is stretched over a metal frame and used to cut a selected portion of a light beam. Common sizes include 18 × 24 in., 24 × 36 in., and 4 × 4 ft.

Nets Bobbinet is stretched over a metal frame and used to reduce the strength of a selected portion of a beam of light. Common sizes include 18 × 24 in., 24 × 36 in., and 4 × 4 ft.

Silks White silk is stretched over a metal frame and used to reduce and soften a beam or light. Common sizes include 18 × 24 in., 24 × 36 in., and 4 × 4 ft. Thinner silks, called *half silk* and *quarter silk*, are also available.

Frames Diffusion gel is mounted (using snot tape) into an empty metal frame to diffuse or color a beam of light. Common sizes include 18 × 24 in., 24 × 36 in., 3 × 3 ft, and 4 × 4 ft.

Cukes and celo cukes A cuke is a piece of ¼-in. plywood with holes cut in it in random shapes. It is used to break up a beam of light into a pattern. A celo cuke uses painted wire mesh instead of plywood to give a more subtle effect. Common sizes include 18 × 24 in., 24 × 36 in., and 4 × 4 ft.

Cutters   Long narrow flags are used to create shadows or cut the light. Common sizes include 10 × 42 in., 18 × 42 in., and 24 × 72 in.

Dots and fingers   Very small flags and nets are used to make very small cuts.

Flex arm   A jointed, lightweight arm is used to support small flags (postage stamps, fingers, and dots).

Apple boxes   Solidly constructed, internally reinforced plywood boxes are used for everything imaginable. They come in a variety of sizes: full, half, quarter, and a pancake. A wall plate mounted on a pancake is useful to position a light on the floor. Apple boxes are also used to raise cable connections off the ground when water or moisture is present.

Cup blocks   Wooden (cup) blocks are placed under the wheels of light stands for leveling on uneven ground and to prevent stands from rolling.

Foamcore holder   This is a device used to mount foamcore and bead board on a C-stand. A vice grip clamps two 6 × 6 in. plates around the bead board. The baby stud provides a means of attaching it to the C-stand. It is also known as a *duckbill* or *platypus*.

Grip clips   These are metal spring clamps, usually kept on a loop of rope hung on the taco cart. They are sometimes referred to by their size number. A #1 grip clip clamps onto objects up to 1 in. thick, a #2 up to 2 in., and a #3 up to 3 in.

Mounting Hardware

Mounting hardware provides either a baby stud or a junior receptacle for mounting a light in just about any position imaginable: mounted to a pipe, ceiling, wall, floor, pillar, or false ceiling or outstretched on an arm, camera, or dolly. The typical grip package has a good selection of hardware available to accommodate any situation. Mounting equipment includes C-clamps, furniture clamps, chain vice grips, mafer clamps, gator clamps, junior and baby offsets, junior drop downs, stud adapters, nail-on plates, and putty knives with baby studs. The use of stands and mounting equipment is covered in detail in Chapter 6.

Dollies

Doorway dolly   Although designed as a simple camera platform, this small, steerable dolly is great for moving sandbags. Electricians use them for cable and large lights.

Western dolly   This is similar to a doorway dolly but bigger.

Camera dollies   The camera is mounted on a dolly for moves during takes and for general ease in moving between shots. Dollies feature a hydraulic boom arm and a heavy, smoothly controllable chassis. Dollies generally run on a track, although a smooth floor will do.

Wedges   Triangular wooden blocks are used to level the dolly track, keep doors open, and so on. They are kept in a milk crate.

Cribbing   Blocks of 2 × 4 in. are used to level the dolly track. They are kept in a milk crate.

Other Grip Equipment

Ladders   A-frame ladders are available in heights of 4, 6, 8, 10, and 12 ft; extension ladders are 24 ft tall. They are also referred to by the number of steps (four-step, eight-step, and so on). Use only wooden or fiberglass ladders when handling electrical equipment. Aluminum ladders conduct electricity and are unsafe.

Parallel set   Similar to scaffolding, but simpler and quicker to assemble, a parallel set provides a high platform for lights or the camera. It comes in 6-ft sections, with 18 ft the maximum.

Ratchet straps   Nylon straps with a ratchet tightening device are commonly used to secure camera- and light-mounting equipment to automobiles, to secure a stand on scaffolding, or to secure similar rigging.

Sandbags   Sandbags are used as deadweight to stabilize stands. Shot bags are filled with lead shot and therefore are smaller per pound. Bags come in various sizes, from 5 lb up to 50 lb; 15- and 35-lb bags are normally used to secure light stands.

Stair blocks   Blocks of 2 × 4 in., assembled in a stair shape, provide increments of adjustment for raising furniture by a small amount.

Furniture pad   A packing blanket has a multitude of uses. Furniture pads are used to protect floors from being scratched by stands. Also called *sound blankets*, they are used to deaden live rooms.

Other equipment carried on the grip truck may include a water cooler, sun/rain umbrella, ice chest, shovels, rakes, brooms, trash can, traffic cones, pickax, sledgehammer, and fire extinguishers.

Grip Expendables

Safety chain   Also called grip chain or sash chain. In addition to barn door safety, safety chain is used for such tasks as chaining the legs of a stand to a high platform.

Automatic tape gun (ATG)   An ATG is a dispenser for snot tape used to attach gels to windows and gel frames.

Bead board   Styrofoam $3/8$, $1/2$, or 1 in. thickness comes in 4 × 8-ft sheets. It is used to bounce light and gives off a softer and weaker light than foamcore.

J-lar tape   Clear 2-in. tape is used to repair ripping gel and to stop gel from rattling in frames or on windows.

Chalk   Chalk is used to mark dolly positions on the floor.

Duvetyn   This thick, black canvaslike cloth is used to obstruct light in a multitude of situations, such as blacking and tenting windows and covering distracting objects. It comes in 50-yd rolls.

Foamcore   This extremely lightweight bounce board is made from $1/4$-in. foam reinforcement glued between two sheets of white, glossy card stock. Foamcore also comes with flat black on one side and is available in 4 × 8-ft sheets.

Hardware Hardware includes drywall screws for mounting wall plates, staples, pushpins, nails, bolts, nuts, and so on for general construction.

Lumber It is useful to stock lumber in a variety of sizes and forms. For example, 1 × 3-in. (batten) board is used to build soft boxes; 2 × 4-in. and 2 × 6-in. boards are used for wall spreaders. Plywood may be laid on the floor to make a dance floor for smooth dolly moves.

Rope Manila hemp (rough brown rope) comes in $\frac{1}{4}$ in., $\frac{3}{8}$ in., and $\frac{1}{2}$ in. thicknesses. Among the many uses, $\frac{1}{2}$-in. rope is used for tag lines and guy wires.

Show card Thick card stock, usually white on one side and black on the other, is used to bounce light or absorb it. Show cards come in a range of colors, including silver.

Silicone spray This is a dry lubricant used on the dolly track.

Tracing paper Vellum 1000H translucent paper is used to white out windows. It is available in rolls.

CHAPTER 3

Light Fixtures—The Basic Tungsten Arsenal

Light fixtures come in all shapes and sizes. An electrician should learn the name, weight, power, bulb, and accessories for each. The design of the fixture, bulb, lens, reflector, and accessories determines the nature of the beam and provides some methods of controlling it. A fixture's beam characteristics (such as brightness, focusability, evenness, punch, softness, size, shape, and color) dictate its function in our lighting arsenal. Each type of fixture has specific advantages in certain applications, and there are tricks to using each. In this chapter, we concentrate on the most common types of tungsten fixtures: Fresnels, soft lights, open face, PARs, and ellipsoidal spotlights (Lekos), area lights, and cyclorama lighting. Other commonly used lights such as HMIs, fluorescents, xenons, and specialty lights are covered in subsequent chapters. A great deal of specific, up-to-date information about equipment is available from lighting manufacturers' catalogues and websites (manufacturers and their websites are listed in Appendix H). Lamp catalogues available from GE or Sylvania list specifications for every bulb and socket manufactured.

Tungsten Light

Tungsten Color Balance

Color motion picture films are designed to reproduce colors accurately when lit with light having a particular color makeup. The color makeup of a light source is quantified by its *color temperature*. Since tungsten filaments burn most efficiently at a color temperature of 3200 K (degrees Kelvin), *tungsten-balanced* film stock is designed to reproduce colors accurately when the subject is lit with tungsten (3200 K) light. Note that color temperature, expressed in degrees Kelvin, is a measure of the color output, not operating temperature. *Daylight-balanced* films are designed to reproduce colors accurately when lit with light having a color temperature of 5600 K, or daylight.

Tungsten light and daylight include every color across the visible spectrum and are therefore said to have a *continuous spectrum*. The graph of spectral power distribution (Figure 3.1) compares the distribution of energy across the spectrum of a tungsten source to that of daylight. Daylight is much stronger in the blue end of the spectrum, and tungsten light is much stronger in the red end. (Color balance and color correction are explained in more detail in Chapter 8.)

The Tungsten Bulb

In a *tungsten bulb*, light is created by running current through a tungsten filament (held in a near-vacuum or inert gas in the glass bulb) until it glows; that is, until it is heated to incandescence. Tungsten lights can be powered by either AC or DC.

Tungsten Halogen versus Standard Tungsten Bulbs

A *tungsten halogen bulb* is a type of incandescent bulb that contains special regenerative elements to prevent deposits of tungsten from blackening the sides of the globe. The regenerative elements carry the evaporated tungsten back to the filament, where it is reused, thereby increasing the life of the bulb. For the regenerative process, called the *halogen cycle*, to occur, a high temperature (at least 250°C) must be maintained inside the globe; and for this reason, tungsten halogen globes tend to be compact and made of quartz, which can withstand the high temperature. In the old days, large 10k lamps contained a cleaning agent that had to be manually swished around the inside of the globe between uses to clean off the tungsten blackening.

The standard type of globe used in each fixture is listed in Appendix A. There are often alternatives to the standard type: a bulb with a different wattage or color temperature, or one that uses frosted instead of clear glass (see Table E.3).

Fresnels

The Fresnel (pronounced *fre nel'*) is one of the most flexible fixtures to work with, being designed to create a relatively even field of light with adjustable intensity and field size. The light from a Fresnel makes clean, hard shadows. Its clean beam makes it a good choice for lighting actors' faces, either directly or through diffusion. For these reasons, it is the most commonly used fixture in film and television (Figure 3.2). Figure 3.3 illustrates some Fresnel fixtures that every electrician must be able to identify.

The light is named for its Fresnel lens, which bends the diverging rays of light emitted by the bulb into a controlled beam of light. The Fresnel lens has the same light-bending characteristics as a standard plano-convex lens, but the Fresnel's design compresses the convex curve into jagged steps (Figure 3.4), making it lighter and thinner so that it retains less heat.

Equally important, the fixture uses a *spherical* reflector. Because the bulb is at the focal point of the spherical reflector, light rays coming from the back of the bulb are reflected straight back through the bulb (not directly out the front of the

Figure 3.1 Spectral power distribution graphs (SPD) illustrate the distribution of energy over color spectrum for four primary light sources. Incandescent lamps are strong in the yellow-orange and red and weak in blue and violet. As color temperature increases, the curve shifts toward the blue spectral band. In contrast, daylight is stronger on the blue end of the spectrum. Shown here are spectral distributions for (A) clear noon sky (10,000 K); (B) clear north sky (7000 K); (C) sun plus sky (6500 K); (D) overcast sky (6800 K); and (E) direct sun (5600 K). Incandescent and daylight sources have a continuous spectrum, as shown by their smooth spectral distribution curves. HMI and fluorescent sources have no continuous spectrum. An HMI has a multiline spectrum (correlating to 5500 K), which appears to the eye much the same as daylight. Note that generally the HMI graph has a similar distribution as line C or E on the daylight graph.

The fluorescent graph shows a standard cool white bulb (correlating to 4500 K). Note that most of its energy comes from narrow peaks. The color rendition of this bulb is poor.

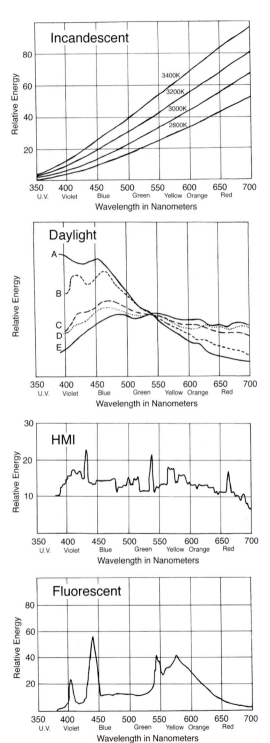

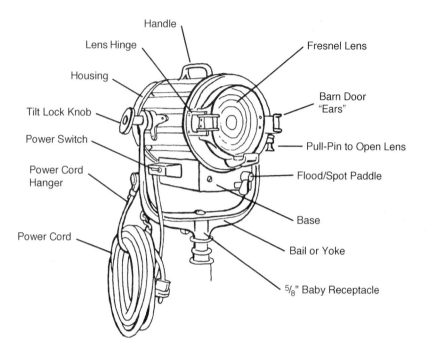

Figure 3.2 Anatomy of a Fresnel fixture.

fixture, as in a parabolic reflector). All light therefore emanates from a single point within the fixture (the bulb), which is what allows the Fresnel lens to control the beam so cleanly.

Inside the housing, the globe and spherical reflector are mounted together and can be moved toward or away from the lens by an exterior adjustment knob. Moving the globe and reflector toward the lens *floods* the beam, increasing its spread and decreasing its intensity (Figure 3.5A). Moving the globe and reflector away from the lens *spots* the beam, making it narrower and more intense (Figure 3.5B). The adjustable focus makes it quick and easy to obtain the desired intensity or beam width.

Fresnel Beam

To anticipate how the light will behave when an actor walks through it, it is helpful to have a three-dimensional mental picture of the beam's shape and intensity, the manner in which intensity falls off toward the edges, and how varying the amount of spot or flood changes these characteristics. Figure 3.6 illustrates the terms *field* and *beam*, terms used in describing the photometric[1] qualities of a fixture. A polar

---

[1] Photometric data provided by manufacturers denote the range of spot and flood achieved by each light by giving the beam angle at the two ends of the range. A typical Fresnel has a range from about 10° to 45° or 50°. (Such data may also be expressed by giving the beam diameter and peak intensity, in foot-candles, at various distances from the fixture.) Table B.2 gives the beam diameter at various distances for given beam angle.

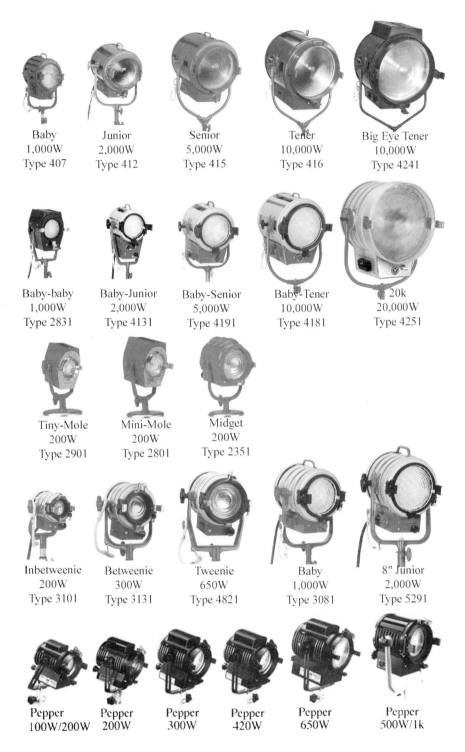

Baby	Junior	Senior	Tener	Big Eye Tener
1,000W	2,000W	5,000W	10,000W	10,000W
Type 407	Type 412	Type 415	Type 416	Type 4241

Baby-baby	Baby-Junior	Baby-Senior	Baby-Tener	20k
1,000W	2,000W	5,000W	10,000W	20,000W
Type 2831	Type 4131	Type 4191	Type 4181	Type 4251

Tiny-Mole	Mini-Mole	Midget
200W	200W	200W
Type 2901	Type 2801	Type 2351

Inbetweenie	Betweenie	Tweenie	Baby	8" Junior
200W	300W	650W	1,000W	2,000W
Type 3101	Type 3131	Type 4821	Type 3081	Type 5291

Pepper	Pepper	Pepper	Pepper	Pepper	Pepper
100W/200W	200W	300W	420W	650W	500W/1k

Figure 3.3 Fresnel fixtures. (Courtesy of Mole-Richardson Company and LTM Corporation, Los Angeles, CA.)

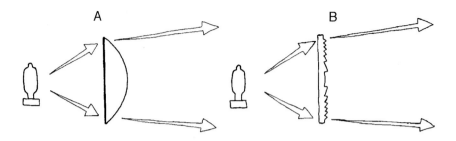

Figure 3.4 Fresnel and plano convex. (A) A plano-convex lens pulls together the divergent rays of light. (B) A Fresnel lens has the same optical effect as the plano-convex lens, but it is cut away to reduce weight and heat retention.

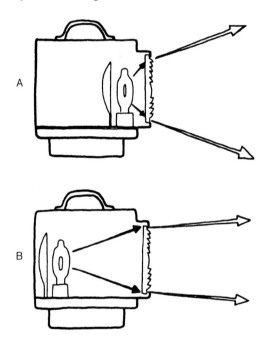

Figure 3.5 (A) A Fresnel lamp and reflector in flood position: Rays are refracted into a wide beam. (B) A Fresnel in spot position: The lamp and reflector are positioned so that the rays are concentrated into a tighter, more intense beam.

distribution graph (Figure 3.7) gives a clear picture of the "shape" of the beam intensity and how it changes from flood to spot.

At full flood, the beam is relatively even across a 40° sweep, then falls off quickly toward the edges. Note that, in full flood, the beam has no central hot spot; the field is very even. As the lamp is spotted in, the rays become less divergent, more nearly parallel. The beam narrows and gets brighter in the center, falling off rapidly on either side. At full spot, the usable portion of the beam is narrow, about a 10° angle. The term *throw* refers to the distance from the lamp to the subject.

Figure 3.6 The *field* defines the "usable" light—the area of light that has an intensity of at least 10% of the peak value. *Beam* is defined as the area of light that has an intensity of at least 50% of the peak value. The *hot spot* is the brightest spot within the beam. The terms *beam angle* and *field angle* refer to the angle, from the fixture, of the beam and field, respectively.

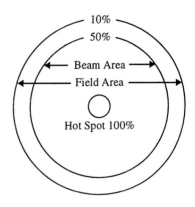

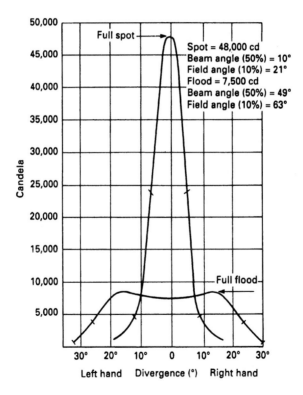

Figure 3.7 A polar distribution graph depicts light intensity across the diameter of the field of light. The upper tick marks denote the beam angle (the "working" light); the lower tick marks denote the field angle (the "usable" light). In the flood position, the light offers virtually even intensity across the wide spread of the beam; in the spot position, beam intensity falls off rapidly outward from the central hot spot. Note: cd is an abbreviation for candela or candle power. It is a measure of brightness: cd = foot-candles $\times$ (distance)^2.

A lamp in spot position has a greater throw; it illuminates the subject to the same brightness at a much greater distance. Table B.3 gives the intensity at any distance for a variety of fixtures.

Photometrics, beam angle, and *field angle* are terms used in light manufacturers' sales literature; they are rarely mentioned on set; but in practice, electricians use these concepts all the time. For example, say, a large room is to be lit using several lights spaced evenly along one wall of the room. To make the light intensity even across the whole room, the lamps are set at full flood, and the edge of the *beam* of each light is feathered into that of the next. The beams overlap slightly at the 50% point, creating an even 100% intensity across the entire space.

Creative Uses of Flood and Spot

A Fresnel creates its hardest, most delineated shadows at full flood. The more spotted-in the fixture, the *less* sharp the shadow lines appear. In full spot position, rays from the Fresnel travel more nearly parallel, and some converge slightly and cross one another. This creates a fuzziness to any shadow cast from an object. If one wants to project a sharp shadow or make a silhouette (for example, the silhouette of a person cast on a closed curtain as seen from outside a house at night), one would want to use a light at full flood.

Usually a Fresnel is employed when even light is desired, so Fresnels end up used in flood position a lot. The brightness is even across the beam, and brightness falls off evenly as objects are farther from the light source. This gives a nice natural appearance, for example, to light coming through a window. The flood/spot mechanism might be used only to fine-tune the intensity very slightly.

A beam spotted in farther can be used to advantage if you do not want the light level to fall off so much at a distance from the light. If you spot in the light, the center of the beam reaches deeper into the set, while the edge of the beam lights objects closer to the light source to a more equal intensity. Conrad Hall ASC (two-time Academy Award winner) is a DP who uses this technique in situations such as a long hallway where there is no place to put a frontal fill light because it would be seen in the shot. A Fresnel set at full spot is aimed over everyone's head deep into the hallway; the edge of the beam skims the faces all the way down the hallway, giving a nearly even light level from foreground to background.

The Globe and Its Installation

Bulbs are referred to by a three-letter code assigned by the American National Standards Institute (ANSI). For example, a typical 1k Fresnel uses an EGT bulb. ANSI codes are listed with other specifications in Appendixes A and E.

Most larger Fresnels used in motion picture work have a bipostal lamp base. Smaller lamps, such as the 200W FEV, have a bayonet base. Bulbs are listed by base type in Table E.3. Figure 3.8 shows how to open up various models of lights to get at the globe.

On small units, the bulb simply plugs straight into the lamp base and is held in place by friction. When removing the bulb from this type of base, be careful not

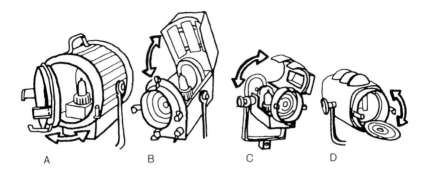

A B C D

Figure 3.8 Four common ways to access the inside of a Fresnel fixture. (A) With most lights 1000 W and larger, the lens door swings open on a hinge. (B) On a baby-baby, the top of the housing swings back on a hinge at the back of the fixture. (C) The top of a Pepper's housing swings open to one side. (D) The lens of a midget is held in place by a spring.

to break the glass off its porcelain base. Firmly grasp the porcelain base and wiggle the globe out. Do not handle the glass. On lights 2000 W and larger, a screw in the fixture's lamp base tightens the base around the pins of the bulb. With this type of base, the globe comes out freely when the thumbscrew is loosened.

The position of the bulb relative to the reflector is critical to the proper operation of the light. The filament of the bulb sits precisely at the focal point of the reflector. Therefore, if the bulb is not seated properly or the reflector is bent, the lamp's performance is drastically reduced.

Tilt Angle

To ensure proper heat dissipation, manufacturers recommend that Fresnels be hung with the base down. Each type of globe has a limit to the amount it can be tilted on its side without shortening the life of the globe. For example, a senior (a 5k Fresnel fixture) should burn with the bulb oriented within 45° of vertical. In addition to damaging the bulb, a 2000-W baby junior light hung at an extreme downward tilt will melt the reflector. In practice, the tilt angle is a concern only with lights that have large, expensive globes. Small lights are hung in whatever manner is required.

Fresnel Accessories

Each Fresnel should always be accompanied by the barn doors and a set of scrims in a scrim box or scrim bag. A typical equipment package also includes snoots and at least one focal spot in various sizes to fit the various lights.

Scrims

A scrim is a stainless steel wire screen used to reduce the intensity of the light. A single scrim has a loose wire weave, is identified by its green ring frame, and cuts the intensity of the light by approximately a half stop. A double scrim has a tighter weave, is identified by its red ring frame, and cuts the light by approximately

Figure 3.9 A bottom-half scrim is used to even out intensity as the subject moves closer to the light fixture.

one full stop. A standard set of scrims includes a single, two doubles, a half-single, a half-double, and a gel frame. Quarter scrims and graduated scrims are also available for some fixtures.

Half scrims affect just one half of the beam. A bottom-half double can be used to even out the intensity of the light as the subject moves closer to the fixture (Figure 3.9). It reduces the light falling on objects close to the light, bringing the light level down to that of objects farther from the light.

A gel frame can be used to hold light gels or diffusion for short spans of time; however, because of the heat close to the lens, many lights melt gels mounted in the gel frame. Similarly, hot scrims melt the gel in a gel frame (and make a big gooey mess on the scrim). Therefore, gels and diffusion materials are often attached to the barn doors, where the heat is less intense.

Appendix A lists the appropriate scrim sizes for various lighting fixtures.

Barn Doors

Barn doors provide the most basic control over the placement of the edges of the beam of a Fresnel or open-face fixture. Because the doors are so close to the fixture, the cut is fairly soft (Figure 3.10).

Barn doors typically have two large leaves and two smaller triangular ones. When the bigger doors are horizontal, they are said to be "Chinese"; when vertical, we call them "American." By closing the two large leaves into a narrow slit and folding the small leaves out of the way, you can make a narrow slash. The slash can be horizontal—for an eye light, for example—or turned diagonally to make a slash across a background.

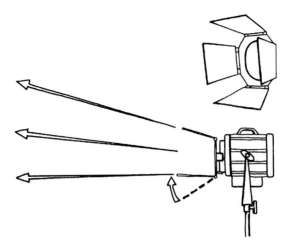

Figure 3.10 Barn doors contain the light, putting a straight edge on the beam.

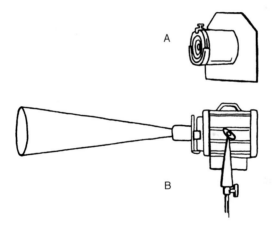

Figure 3.11 (A) A snoot with multiple aperture rings allows some flexibility in beam width. (B) A snoot confines the beam to a narrow circle.

Snoot

When a very confined, narrow, circular beam is desired, replace the barn doors with a snoot. Snoots come in various sizes, from wide (called a *top hat*) to very narrow (*stovepipe*). Some snoots are fitted with four rings with different aperture sizes so that you can adjust the beam width (Figure 3.11).

Focal Spot

A focal spot essentially changes a Fresnel into a spotlight. The focal spot lens assembly creates a narrow, bright, even circle. Like an ellipsoidal reflector spotlight,

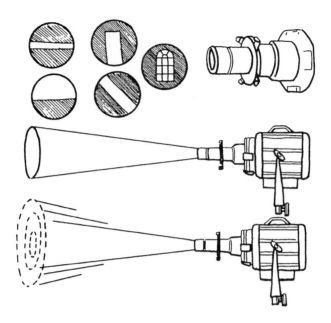

Figure 3.12 A focal spot. The four framing shutters can be pushed into the beam to form hard cuts in any shape: a narrow slit for an eye light, a rectangle to frame a doorway, a straight line cut, or a diagonal slash, for example. It can also project gobo patterns. The gobo fits into a slot on the barrel. The beam can be focused to create hard edges or defocused to soften them.

a focal spot has framing shutters. It accepts design patterns called *gobos* and *mattes*, which can be projected and focused onto the scene. It has interchangeable lens tubes—wide beam and narrow beam. It also comes with a gel ring to add color gels (Figure 3.12).

Shutters

Shutters are like heavy-duty venetian blinds; they have rows of parallel slats that open and close. The shutter is mounted on the front of the light (Figure 3.13). The shutter can be controlled to smoothly reduce the amount of light getting to the subject. Shutters are handy when the light level needs to change during a shot. Care must be taken to avoid projecting a venetian-blind pattern on the subject. Keep the light some distance from the subject and use diffusion material between the two. Be watchful also for a vertical shift in the position of the beam as the shutters are closed. Shutters are frequently used to create a lightning effect; a sudden flash can be produced by opening and quickly closing the shutter. Use appropriate caution; the shutters will warp from the heat buildup if kept closed for too long.

Figure 3.13 Shutters can be manually activated or motorized as shown here. These DMX-controlled shutters are activated from a dimmer board or DMX remote slider. (Courtesy of Mole-Richardson Company, Los Angeles, CA.)

Soft Lights

Soft lights (Figures 3.14 and 3.15) are designed to produce soft light with less-defined shadows. Light from the long tubular globes is directed into a white concave reflector. Because it is indirect, bounced off a diffuse white surface, and exits through a relatively large aperture, the resulting light is soft and has a wide, even, uncontrolled spread. Soft lights are commonly used for fill and general room ambiance. Table A.2 (Appendix A) provides soft light specifications.

Because soft lights use indirect light, they produce far less light per watt than Fresnels. Most soft lights have multiple globes, each switched individually, making it easy to increase or reduce the light's intensity. Figure 3.15 shows the egg crate and snoot, which can also be used to contain and control soft light. Soft lights do not generally have scrims, but you can improvise by inserting a baby scrim between the base and the white reflector surface, sandwiched with the egg crate and held in place with a grip clip.

To maintain maximum intensity and proper color temperature, the white reflector must periodically be cleaned or repainted. When repainting the interior surface, use "best boy white" paint. Best boy white reflects light without changing the color of the light and withstands high temperatures. If regular white paint is used, it will appear off-color.

To gain access to the globes, loosen the finger screws that lock the basket to the reflector and hinge the base open. The globes are double-ended and held in place

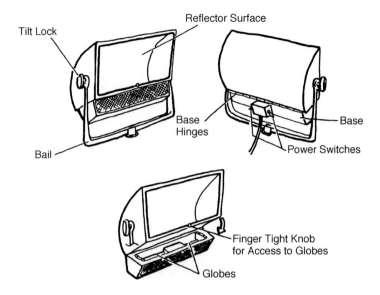

Figure 3.14 Anatomy of a 2k zip soft light.

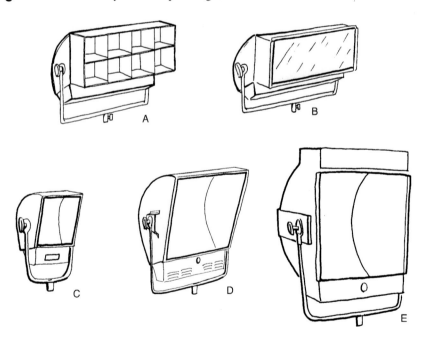

Figure 3.15 Soft lights and their accessories. (A) Egg crate: This black, metal grid helps control spill and also reduces the overall intensity of the light. It is a good idea to keep an egg crate with each soft light because they are used frequently. (B) Diffuser frame (shown here placed on the front of the egg crate): This square gel frame fits in the front of the unit to hold colored gel or diffusion. (C) 750-W zip. (D) 4k soft. (E) 8k Softlite with eight 1k globes.

in a spring-loaded porcelain base. To install the globe, insert one end and push back the spring until the other end can slide in.

Open-Face Lights

As the name implies, open-face lights have no lens and are therefore slightly brighter per watt than a Fresnel. However, the beam is not focused, so it is less even and less controllable. Open-face lights make good bounce lights (directed into a white bounce surface) or can be handy for lighting elements of the background set. To be used for lighting actors, a medium to heavy diffusion is needed to take the garish curse off the light.

Open-face fixtures can be divided into three categories: prime fixtures, broads and nook lights, and portable kit lights. Figure 3.16 illustrates open-face lights with which an electrician must be familiar. Table A.3 (Appendix A) lists their specifications.

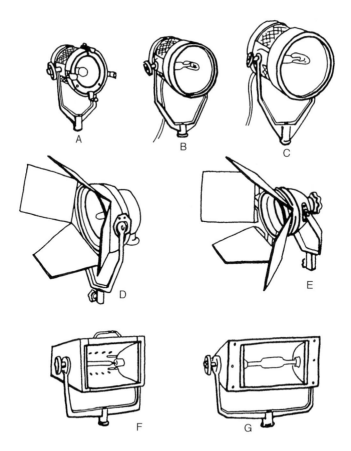

Figure 3.16 Open-face fixtures: (A) 650-W teenie-weenie, (B) 1k Mickey, (C) 2k mighty, (D) 2k blonde, (E) 1k redhead, (F) 1k broad, (G) 1k or 2k nook light.

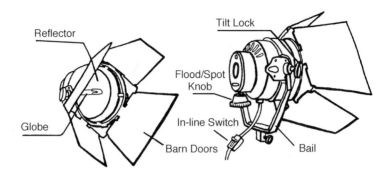

Figure 3.17 Anatomy of a blonde 2k open-face fixture.

Prime Fixtures

Prime open-face fixtures (Figure 3.17) use a double-ended lamp. They have a round face and an adjustable reflector for flood/spot control and come with barn doors and a scrim set. They are lightweight, durable lights with a relatively high intensity per watt and are more controllable than broads and nook lights. All sizes mount on a baby stud.

Compared to a Fresnel, the flood/spot mechanism is very unrefined. The mechanism alters the globe's position relative to the reflector. When the globe is close to the reflector, the reflector sends out a wide beam; when the globe is pulled away from the reflector, it reflects more of the rays in a narrower beam. Because light emanates from both the bulb and the surface of the silver reflector, open face lights tend to spill light everywhere. To compensate they need large barn doors.

Open-face prime fixtures are often bounced into a white surface such as foamcore to create soft light. Note that open-face lights tend to burn very hot and can melt a foamcore bounce board or destroy a flag if it is placed too close to the light. Think twice before rigging a light close to set pieces, and allow ventilation above the fixture.

Broads and Nook Lights

Broads and nook lights (Figure 3.16F and G) consist of little more than a long, double-ended bulb and a curved or V-shaped silver reflector. Nook lights are small and light and can be easily hidden in the set. Because broads and nook lights create raw, hard light, they tend to be used for jobs such as throwing light on a background or illuminating a soft box. They are also handy as work lights.

Light Kits

Portable open-face lights are normally used by small, mobile camera crews for documentary, industrial, and promotional video and film work. The lights come in kits with a full complement of accessories, including adaptive, lightweight mounting hardware and lightweight stands. The units are small and usually draw 1000 W or less (Figure 3.18).

Figure 3.18 Lowel open-face lighting kit with accessories. The DP kit shown includes 4 1k DP lights, stands, scrims, special barn doors, diffusion frames, mixed gels, color correction blue gels, super spot reflector, a space clamp (special furniture clamp), a spare globe case, power cords, and extensions. (Courtesy of Lowel-Light Manufacturing, Inc., Brooklyn, NY.)

Lightweight, portable soft lights are also available. Compact fixtures can illuminate only a limited area, but they can be useful to supplement heavier lighting equipment.

The quality of the light can be manipulated using gel frames to alter color or diffuse the light. Because the raw light from an open-face fixture is often hard and unattractive, cinematographers seek to soften the source, bouncing the light into silver umbrellas, or attaching a chimera light box to the fixture (see Chapter 8).

PAR Lights

A large range of light fixtures use parabolic aluminized reflector (PAR) lamps. We get to the fixtures in a moment, but the most important part of a PAR fixture is the lamp.

PAR Lamps

The PAR lamp itself includes all the most important parts of a light: the globe, lens, and reflector are one permanently sealed unit, like a car headlight (Figure 3.19). PARs are popular because they put out a lot of light per watt, more than any other incandescent fixture.

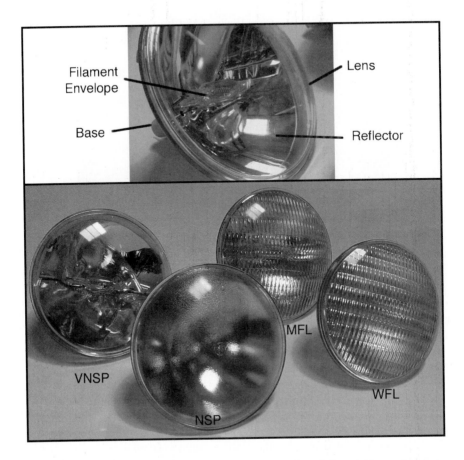

Figure 3.19 Anatomy of a PAR lamp. The lens types from left to right are very narrow spot (VNSP), narrow spot (NSP), medium flood (MFL), and wide flood (WFL). (Extrawide flood (XWFL) is not shown.)

The most common size is the PAR-64 (which has an 8-in. diameter). PAR-64s are available in various wattages (1000 W is most common, but wattages from 100 to 1200 are available) and with various spreads as shown in Figure 3.19. (See also Tables E.4, E.5, and E.6.) PAR lamps tend to have an elliptical beam rather than a circular one. The lamp can be turned in its fixture to orient the beam as required.

For an even narrower, very intense beam, an aircraft landing (ACL) light can be fitted into standard PAR-64 housings. ACL lamps operate on 28 V but can be run in series in gangs of four and connected to a 110-V circuit. (The Italian company IRIDE S.R.L. makes a variety of fixtures designed to use 28-V, 600-W ACL lamps, including a monster "Concorde Senior," which houses 31 ACL lamps in a circular array, making it an 18,600-W fixture. The fixture runs on 220 V.)

There are smaller PAR lamps with lower wattages: PAR-56 (7-in. diameter, up to 500 W), PAR-46 (5¾-in. diameter, up to 250 W), and the PAR-36 (4½-in.

diameter, up to 650 W). (The nomenclature for PAR lamps is simply the globe's diameter in eighths of an inch. A PAR-64 diameter is therefore: $64 \div 8 = 8$ in.)

Dichroic PAR Lamps

PAR-64 and PAR-36 lamps are also available with a dichroic reflector, which absorbs much of the yellow light and reflects a color temperature closer to daylight (about 5000 K). "FAY" lamps are daylight-balanced PAR-36 lamps (5000 K, 650 W per bulb, $4\frac{1}{2}$ in. diameter) (see Figure 3.21D, E). Dichroic lamps are used for daylight fill. Although HMIs can also fulfill this objective, dichroic lamps can offer an inexpensive alternative, which may suffice for some situations. Bulb designations are listed in Appendix E.

PAR Fixtures

PAR Cans

PAR cans are simple, lightweight, inexpensive, maintenance free, and made for the heavy-duty life of the concert tour (Figure 3.20). Their design is as simple as they come—a PAR lamp mounted inside a can that provides a gel frame slot at the front of the barrel. PAR cans generally do not come with scrims. The gel frame of a PAR-64 is typically 10 in. in diameter and any 10 in. scrim (Mighty-Mole) fits the slot. PAR cans come in many sizes. The 1k PAR-64 is the most useful for lighting; the smaller PAR-56, PAR-46, and PAR-36 sizes are sometimes used as on-camera set decoration.

PAR cans are the workhorse of rock-and-roll lighting because they can drive light through even the most saturated gel colors. Narrow-beam PARs can pound light onto a performer or produce strong shafts of light in the atmosphere. The wider PARs fill the stage with a wash of color. In motion picture and television work, narrow PARs are often used to splash a bright streak of sunlight across a part of the set or to bounce light off the floor. Because the narrow spot globes are so punchy, PARs are ideal for creating a strong water reflection effect (the moving light off a swimming pool, for instance). They can also throw light long distances, which is handy, for example, for lighting foliage or buildings at night. The light they produce

Figure 3.20 PAR cans come in either a chrome or black finish. (Courtesy of Mole-Richardson Company, Los Angeles, CA.)

is hard and unpleasant when used directly on faces; but a beautiful glowing light can be created by bouncing a PAR into a light-colored surface near an actor. Stunning examples of this effect can be found in the work of Robert Richardson, ASC (in *Casino, JFK, Natural Born Killers*, and others). Richardson creates beautifully dramatic scenes by bouncing a very narrow PAR (VNSP) off the tabletop in front of an actor, then obscures the table top from the camera with set dressing. Another great example is Conrad Hall's beautifully naturalistic work in *Searching for Bobby Fisher*, in which he used PARs to create beautiful bright sun splashes that glow on actors' faces and in their eyes.

MolePARs, Master Lite, Cine-Queen

The MolePAR (Figure 3.21A), Master Lite, and Cine-Queen are essentially the same simple fixture by different manufacturers. They comprise a PAR-64 lamp housing with a power cord, yoke, and ears to hold barn doors and scrims. The main difference, in practice, between a PAR can and a fixture like a MolePAR is spill. An open fixture like a MolePAR tends to spill light in all directions and is more useful for lighting trees at night, for example, where spill is not undesirable. Spill can be managed with blackwrap and barn doors, of course, but a PAR can is often cleaner to use when you want to contain spill.

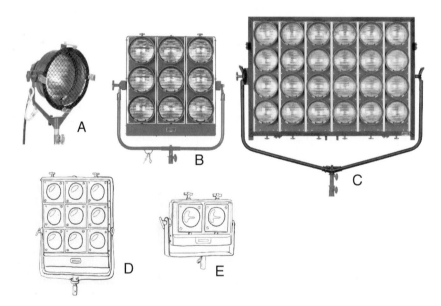

Figure 3.21 In the MolePAR fixture (A), the lamp rotates to allow adjustment of the elliptical beam. The Maxibrute (B) offers three pods of three lamps each. The two outside pods can be panned individually. The Moleeno (C) and similar Deeno light arrays have 24 or 36 lamps. Because they can be lamped with any of the lenses shown in Figure 3.19, PARs offer a lot of flexibility and punch. The most commonly used FAY lamps (smaller 650 W lamps) are the nine-light FAY (D) and two-light FAY (E). (Courtesy of Mole-Richardson Company, Los Angeles, CA.)

PAR Arrays

Many fixtures simply house clusters of PAR lamps on a single base. The lamps are individually switched, with 1, 2, 4, 6, 9 (Maxibrute), 12, 24 (Dino or Moleeno), or even 36 (Super Dino) lights to a cluster (Figure 3.21B and C). They are referred to by the number of lights in the cluster; for example, a four-light, six-light, or the most common, a nine-light. *Maxi-brute* is a common name for a nine-light using PAR-64 lamps (Figure 3.21B). *Mini-brute* or *nine-light* refers to the smaller PAR-36 nine-light (Figure 3.21D). (Table A.4 in Appendix A lists the common types.)

Large PAR arrays can put out a lot of light. They are often used to light large spaces at night or bounced into a 12 × 12 white griff for soft fill. A nine-light works well as a bounce light because you can adjust the intensity quickly by snapping lamps on or off. On stage in large exterior sets, multiple PAR arrays can create a dominant direction of light to simulate sunlight.

PAR arrays are designed in rows, or *pods*, of three to six lights. The pods are mounted into a metal frame held in place at the ends. Usually, the pod can be swiveled and tightened with a knuckle at one end. This affords the some versatility. The pods can be individually focused—splayed out to cover a large area or focused to concentrate light in a smaller area. Additionally, the gaffer can have the fixture fitted with any kind of PAR lamps, from wide flood to very narrow, or can use a combination, as desired. One may even choose to mix color temperatures by including dichroic lamps. However, relamping a large PAR array is time consuming, something you want to take care of well ahead of time.

The Arri Ruby 7 is a unique arrangement of seven PAR-64 globes mounted in a circle that hinges from the outside ring, so the beams can be made to converge at a selected distance, diverge into a wide flood, or unite into one powerful parallel beam (Figure 3.22).

Ellipsoidal Reflector Spotlights (Lekos)

Each lighting venue has its own set of demands. The ellipsoidal reflector spotlight (known as an *ERS, ellipsoidal,* or *Leko*[2] in the United States and as a *profile spotlight* in England) gives the stage lighting designer the strong throw, versatility, and control needed to light a stage from some distance (Figure 3.23). Ellipsoidal spotlights are listed in Table A.12. Naturally, these fixtures are often employed when filming stage performances, but their special qualities are also very handy in other situations. A Leko can make a hard cut where there is no room to make a hard cut with a flag. For example, a woman answers her front door; she is lit by light bounced off a piece of show card taped to the inside wall beside the door. An ellipsoidal can make the hard cut necessary to prevent direct light from hitting anything but the card.

The fixture is designed to give a long controllable throw to light a stage from fairly distant positions. The fixture is able to project a beam that can be shaped by shutters, an iris, or a gobo pattern. The shape of the beam is determined by the shape

---

[2]Leko is the trademark of Strand Lighting but is widely used to refer generally to ellipsoidal spotlights.

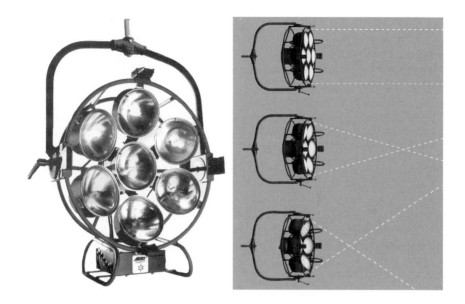

Figure 3.22 The Ruby 7 is a unique seven-light PAR array with flood spot control (the knob is located on the back of the fixture). The seven on/off switches are on the base. (Courtesy of Arri Lighting, New York.)

or pattern in the gate aperture. Light collected from a highly efficient ellipsoidal reflector passes through the gate; the shape or pattern in the gate is then brought into focus by a lens assembly in the barrel. The gate can be brought into sharp or soft focus by sliding the barrel forward or backward. The narrower the beam angle of the lens, the greater are the throw and intensity.

The four cutting *shutters* (top, bottom, left, and right) can be pushed into the path of the beam to shape it into a square, rectangle, triangle, or whatever is needed. Immediately in front of the shutters is the *gobo* slot, into which a metal cutout pattern can be inserted. Hundreds of gobo patterns are available—a wide variety of window and venetian blind patterns, foliage patterns, clouds, cityscapes, stars, flames, practically anything you can name. Motorized rotating gobo devices are available that create theatrical moving flame and water patterns by projecting two counter-rotating gobo patterns. Many fixtures also have a rotatable front barrel, which provides flexibility in the positioning of shutter cuts and gobo patterns. An *iris* can be placed in the beam near the gobo slot to adjust the aperture of the circular beam or to use the lamp as a follow spot. Colored gel is placed in a gel frame holder at the front of the light. A *donut* is a metal mask that slides into the gel frame slot. It is used to sharpen gobo patterns and clean up color fringes at the beam edge (at the expense of some light output).

Bulb Adjustment and Installations

The field of an ellipsoidal is normally very even. If the bulb gets out of alignment in relation to the reflector, the lamp shows a noticeable hot spot. On a Source Four (a popular fixture manufactured by ETC), the rear lamp housing has

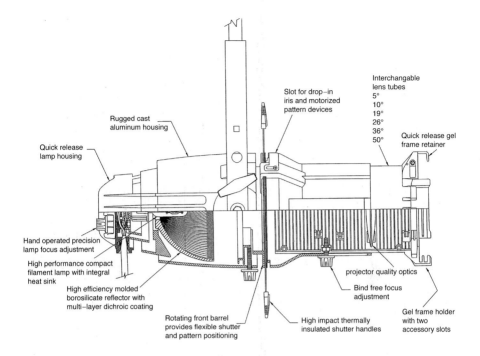

Interchangable
lens tubes
5°
10°
19°
26°
36°
50°

Slot for drop–in
iris and motorized
pattern devices

Rugged cast
aluminum housing

Quick release
lamp housing

Quick release gel
frame retainer

Hand operated precision
lamp focus adjustment

High performance compact
filament lamp with integral
heat sink

High efficiency molded
borosilicate reflector with
multi–layer dichroic coating

projector quality optics

Bind free focus
adjustment

Gel frame holder
with two
accessory slots

Rotating front barrel
provides flexible shutter
and pattern positioning

High impact thermally
insulated shutter handles

Figure 3.23 The Source Four. Innovative advances in the design of the bulb, reflector, and lens assembly allow this 575-W light to outperform standard 1k ellipsoidals while providing exceptionally sharp shutter cuts without halation, even distribution of light through the field, extended pattern life, and eliminating shutter jams due to heat warping. You can put two Source Fours on a 1.2-kW dimmer circuit, doubling the dimmer capacity. (Courtesy of ETC—Electronic Theatre Controls, Inc., Middleton, WI.)

two concentric adjustment knobs: The outer one centers the lamp; the inner knob adjusts the flatness of the field (Figure 3.24A). A "flat field" is as even as possible, all the way to the edges. A "peak" field is as bright as possible and less flat.

To center and adjust the lamp,

1. Aim the light at a flat surface, so you can clearly see the field.
2. Loosen the outer knob on the rear of the lamp housing.
3. Gently move the outer knob left, right, up, and down until the lamp is centered in the reflector.
4. Tighten the outer knob (clockwise) to lock it in position.
5. Turn the inner knob either clockwise or counterclockwise until you find the optimum flat field.

To change a burnt-out bulb,

1. Remove the back of the lamp housing by loosening the knurled bolt on the back of the housing and lifting out.
2. Hold the lamp by the base. (Do not touch the glass. If you accidentally smudge the glass clean it with rubbing alcohol and a lint-free cloth.) Note: Lamps come in 115 V and 120 V in the United States. They are also available in

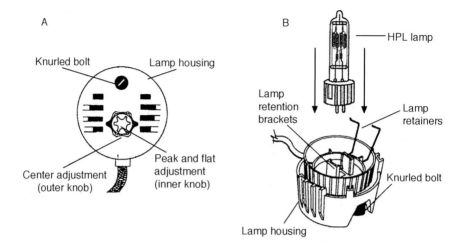

Figure 3.24 (A) The outer knob centers the lamp; the inner knob adjusts the flatness of the field. (B) The lamp base, lamp, and retention bracket. (Courtesy of ETC—Electronic Theatre Controls, Inc., Middleton, WI.)

different color temperatures (the 3050 K bulbs last quite a bit longer that the 3200 K bulbs).

3. Line up the flat sides of the lamp base with the retention brackets on either side of the socket.
4. Push the lamp into the base until it seats firmly. The top of the lamp base should be even with the top of the retention bracket (Figure 3.24B).
5. Press the lamp retaining clip across the lamp base to secure the lamp in place.
6. Reinstall the lamp housing by aligning the bolt hole and tightening the knurled bolt.
7. Center the bulb and adjust the field flatness, as described previously.

Detailed information about how to clean the lenses and reflectors, as well as the many adjustments that can be made to these fixtures, is available on the manufacturer's website.

Ellipsoidal fixtures are designed with either a fixed beam width or a "zoom" barrel. Some manufacturers refer to individual fixtures by lens diameter and focal length (6 × 9 in. has a 6-in. lens and a 9-in. focal length). Others refer to lamps by field angle (such as 40°, 26°, 20°, 10°, and 5°). They correlate roughly as follows:

By field angle (degrees of spread)	By lens diameter and focal length
19°	6 × 16
26°	6 × 12
36°	6 × 9
50°	4½ × 6

Gaffers often scratch their heads when they see these figures, not knowing which type works for a given application, but you can easily calculate the beam diameter and light intensity of any fixture using data given in Appendix B (the explanation at the beginning of Appendix B tells you how to use the tables). Generally speaking, wide-beam Lekos of 250 and 500 W are used above stage in small theaters, 750 and 1000 W 6 × 9 and 6 × 12 fixtures are used above stage and in the front of the house in medium-sized theaters, and 6 × 16 or 8 × 16 1k and 2k fixtures are used for long throws from the house.

Theater and concert lights usually come ready to be hung in a theater, with a pipe clamp bolted to the bail and a short-tail power cord with 20 A Bates connector. When ordering theatrical lights be sure to order *bail blocks* and Bates to Edison *pigtail adapters* to adapt the fixtures for your use (on stands with an Edison outlet box). A bail block bolts to the bail in place of the pipe clamp and typically fits both baby and junior stands.

Area Lights and Backing Lights
Chicken Coops and Space Lights

Chicken coops and space lights are commonly hung throughout a very large set to fill the space with a general soft overhead illumination. The chicken coop (Figure 3.25A) hangs on a chain and uses six 1000-W silver bowl globes. The globes are silvered on the bottom to prevent direct hard light from shining downward. A space light (Figure 3.25B) consists of six 1k nook lights configured like spokes of a wagon wheel, pointing down into a silk cylinder. At the bottom is a round diffusion ring to which a diffusion material or gel can be clipped. The Mole versions of this design (6k and 12k) incorporate a Socapex input. Thus, the lights are individually

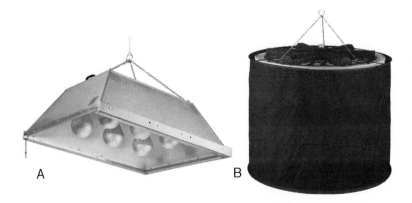

A   B

Figure 3.25 Coops and space lights are available with either a single 60-A connector or Socapex input, which allows individual control of all six lamps. Space lights are made in a 2k version (two 1k lamps), a 6k version (six 1k lamps), and a 12k version (six 2k lamps). (Courtesy of Mole-Richardson Company, Los Angeles, CA.)

Figure 3.26 A 5k Skypan hung on a trapeze. A gaffer can choose from 2k, 5k, 10k, or 20k versions of this light. (Courtesy of Mole-Richardson Company, Los Angeles, CA.)

controlled either on a dimmer or by individual on/off switches at the distribution point (Chapters 12 explains more about Socapex and switch boxes).

Scoop Lights and Sky Pans

Scoops and sky pans (Figure 3.26) are very simple lights that have been around since incandescent lights were first used in motion pictures. They consist of an exposed bulb mounted in a large white reflector. Scoops are 1k or 2k; sky pans can be 2k, 5k, 10k, or 20k.

Sky pans are used for lighting scenic paintings, backdrops, or backings evenly from side to side and top to bottom. The light can be made softer and more even by employing a frame of spun glass diffusion. The gel frame fits into a metal skirt that one attaches to the face of the light.

Cyc Strips, Ground Rows, and Borders

A cyc strip is a row of open-face lights having a specially shaped reflector used to illuminate a cyclorama, or *cyc*, evenly from top to bottom and side to side. Cyc strips come in either short strips of 1, 2, 3, or 4 lights or longer strips of 6, 8, 9, or 12. The larger strips are wired in groups to provide three or four separate circuits for different colored gels, with one circuit of several lights per color (Figure 3.27).

A four-circuit cyc strip might have the three primary colors of light—red, green, and blue—plus either a white circuit or a second blue circuit. (Blue gel absorbs more light than the other colors and is therefore weaker.) By mixing the primary (or other)

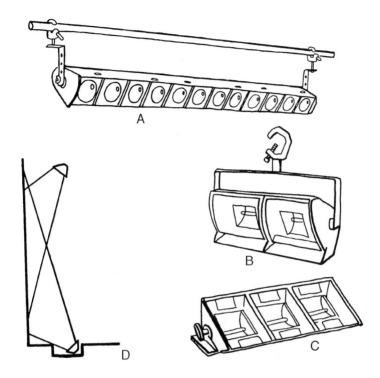

Figure 3.27 Cyc lighting: (A) a border light, (B) a two-light far cyc (also made in strips of many lights and in groups of four), (C) a ground row cyc strip (comes in strips of 1, 2, 3, 4, 6, 8, 9, and 12 or more lights). (D) The typical cyc lighting method lights the cyc evenly from top to bottom.

colors using dimmers on each circuit, the cyc can be made any color or can take on a gradation of colors from top to bottom, simulating a sunrise, for example.

Cyc strips may be positioned on the floor, called a *ground row*, or in a trench below floor level, pointing up at the cyc; and they may be hung from pipes or battens in front of or behind the cyc, pointing down at it. The angle of the strip and its distance from the cyc are critical for achieving even lighting from top to bottom.

Strips of PAR lights, called *border lights*, are also used to light cycs and curtains. PARs have a better throw and a tighter, more intense beam, which is sometimes needed on a very tall cyc to carry light into the center of the cloth.

Small Fixtures

Screw-Base Fixtures

The Lowel K5, Desisti Pinza, and similar fixtures provide a regular screw socket that can be fitted with a photoflood (or any other type of medium screw-base bulb) of up to 500 W. Because K5 kits are lightweight and can be easily hung, clamped, dangled, or taped to walls and ceilings, they are easy to rig. Fitted with

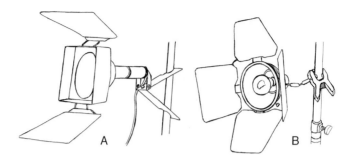

Figure 3.28 Molite (A), an R-40 bulb with attachable barn doors: Pinza (B), a reflector lamp that takes photoflood bulbs.

Figure 3.29 The stick-up illustrated is 3 in. tall, and weighs 9 oz with its 9-ft power cord. It takes either 100-W, 120-V or 125-W, 12-V bulbs. It comes with a wire frame for securing gel and diffusion. (Courtesy of Great American Market, Hollywood, CA.)

R-40 mushroom floods and hoods (Figure 3.28), they can create nice pools of light from above. (Photoflood and mushroom flood bulbs are discussed in detail in Chapter 9.)

Stick-up Kits

A stick-up is a very small open-face light that can be taped or clipped into the smallest of places. It can be fitted with a 100-W or 200-W, 120-V bayonet-base bulb or with a 100-W, 12-V bulb. The latter is ideal as a dome light in an automobile because it can run off the car battery (Figure 3.29).

Because a stick-up is so small and light, it can be taped in place or hung on pushpins. When the light is placed against a surface, insulate the surface with a double or triple layer of refracil heat-resistant cloth. You can wrap a piece of black wrap around the back of the fixture to act as barn doors.

Figure 3.30 The refined beam of a 100-W Dedolight. (Courtesy of Dedotec USA, Inc., Lodi, NJ.)

Dedolights

Dedolights (manufactured by Dedotec) are small, compact fixtures that use two specially designed lenses in an assembly that is more efficient than a Fresnel and provides a hard, adjustable beam with exceptionally even light across the field (Figure 3.30). In set lighting, the DLH2 kit has become an important part of the equipment package. This kit includes three 100- or 150-W fixtures, a power supply, cables, and accessories.

The special lens assembly gives the fixtures punch for the long throw and an unusually wide range of adjustment (model DLH2 ranges from 40° in full flood to $2^1/_2$° in full spot). A 100-W Dedolight has roughly the same light output as a 300-W Fresnel. The lights are so small, lightweight, and unobtrusive that they can easily be hidden in the set.

The lights have various accessories, including barn doors, gel frames, lightweight mounting hardware, suction mounts, camera clamps, and a focal-spotlike projection attachment. The projection attachment allows extremely precise control of the beam. It can be shuttered in on a beer label, for instance, providing a hard edge cut with no color fringing or softness around the edges. For this reason, the lights are useful in tabletop setups and miniature work.

The 100-W Dedolights run on 12 V. The 150-W version runs on 24 V. The power supplies power three, four, or five lights at a time. Three power settings are on the power supply for each light: high (3300 K, maximum light output), medium (3200 K, medium light output), and low (about 3000 K, lower light output). The lights can also be powered directly off a 12-V battery belt.

Dedo's 400 Series lights are larger versions with the same optical technology. The DLH436 (400 W) runs off a power supply at 36 V. The low voltage allows the fixture to use a small lamp, which can be precisely collimated by the lens assembly. The power supply can be switched to different color temperatures (3200, 3400, or 3600 K). The DLH 650 (650 W) runs off the main power with no separate power supply. The DLH400D is a 400-W daylight fixture described in detail in Chapter 4.

The Dedocool is a 250-W tungsten-balanced light designed for lighting small areas when a great deal of light is needed (e.g. for an extremely high shutter speed). Used at close range, the light can provide 220,000 FC at 8–12 in., while giving off very little heat. Insects, plants, food, plastics, paper, and other such items that would be adversely affected by the heat of any other source of this intensity can be filmed using this light. A cooling fan at the back of the fixture is necessary to cool the bulb. The special power supply keeps the fan running for a short time after the light is turned off to cool the light. If the light is unplugged hot, damage to the fan can result.

CHAPTER 4

Light Fixtures—The Basic HMI Arsenal

HMI Fixtures

HMI lights[1] are a highly efficient source of daylight-balanced light (5600 or 6000 K, depending on the globe manufacturer). Having daylight-balanced lights is essential in a number of scenarios:

1. When artificial light needs to mix with natural daylight, as when shooting day exterior scenes or inside a building with lots of windows.
2. When shooting tungsten-balanced scenes that require blue "moonlight" (e.g., *Terminator II*, or any other James Cameron movie for that matter).
3. When shooting a tungsten-balanced scene, if you have no other big lights. In this case, a full correction (CTO) gel would be used in front of the light.

An HMI puts out about four times as much light as a tungsten light of the same wattage, 85–108 lumens per watt of electricity, compared to 26 lumens per watt for tungsten halogen bulbs. This is partly because an incandescent bulb expends 80% of its energy creating heat (infrared wavelengths), whereas HMIs convert that same percentage of its energy into usable illumination. As a result, HMIs operate somewhat cooler than their tungsten equivalents.

An HMI light uses a ballast connected between the AC power source and the lamp head. The component parts of an HMI are the head, the head cable, the ballast, and in most cases a separate ballast cable (Figure 4.1). Standard HMIs run on AC power only (Lightmaker AC/DC models have gone into retirement).

---

[1]HMI is the registered trade name of Osram for its discharge lamps; however, HMI has become the common name referring to all lamps of its class, regardless of manufacturer. The many other manufacturers and trade names are covered later in this chapter.

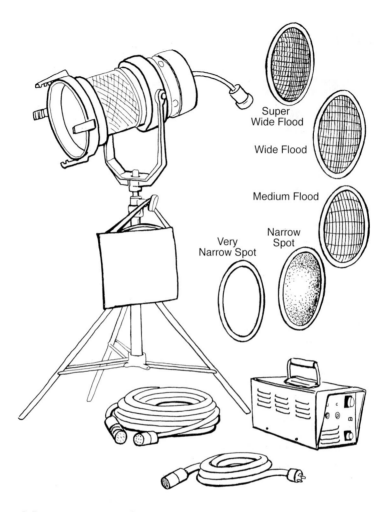

Super
Wide Flood

Wide Flood

Medium Flood

Narrow
Spot

Very
Narrow Spot

Figure 4.1 LTM 1200 HMI PAR head, head cable, ballast cable, ballast, scrims, lens case, and set of spreader lenses.

There are two types of ballasts: *magnetic*, the original type of power supply, and *electronic* (also called *square wave* or *flicker free*), which are becoming more and more common. More about this shortly.

There are several types of HMI fixtures: Fresnels, PARs, open face, soft lights, and battery-powered sun guns. Specifications for HMI fixtures appear in Appendix A.

HMI Fresnels

Small Fresnels of 200, 575, and 1200 W are commonly used as interior direct light or bounce light when daylight color balance is needed. They are equivalent in function to a tweenie, a baby, and a junior, respectively. These sizes have the advantage of plugging into a standard household outlet when necessary. Medium-size

HMI Fresnels of 2500, 4000, and 6000 W are used in much the same manner as 5k and 10k tungsten units—to light large interiors, to double as sunlight, to provide fill on exteriors, or to provide key light and backlight on night exteriors.

Large HMI Fresnels—12k and 18k—have replaced the carbon arc as the workhorse large light. A necessary part of almost any equipment package, 12ks are used for fill on day exterior shots or to cover wide exterior night shots. One or two are very often mounted to an aerial lift (Condor) to light up a city block from 80 ft in the air. Another common application is making sunlight effects through windows, both on location and inside the studio. They may be put through diffusion or bounced to create a large, bright soft source.

HMI PARs

PAR lights are more efficient than Fresnels, and they deliver a strong punch of light with a longer throw. They come with a case of three or four spreader lenses (Figure 4.2 and Table A.6). They come in sizes 200 W, 400 W, 800 W, 575 W, 1200 W, 2.5k, 4k, 6k, and 12k.

The term *PAR* is actually somewhat outdated for HMIs. When HMI PARs were first designed, they were built like a PAR-64, with bulb, reflector, and UV lens all in one sealed unit. Today's HMI PAR lights use a single-ended HMI globe. It is axially mounted in the fixture in front of a highly efficient parabolic reflector.

Figure 4.2 A workhorse of film production: the LTM 2500W Cinepar. (Courtesy of LTM Corp., Los Angeles, CA.)

UV-protective glass covers the front of the unit, and the spreader lens slides into slots in the ears (see Table A.6).

The spreader lenses affect both the shape and angle of the beam. For example, for a typical 1200-W PAR, the very narrow and narrow spot lenses give a circular beam of 6° and 8°, respectively. The medium and wide flood lenses give a wide elliptical beam of 27° × 11°, and 60° × 25°, respectively. The superwide flood gives a circular beam of about 54°. To turn an oblong beam, the operator rotates the lens.

Some PAR fixtures also have spot/flood adjustment. When used with spreader lenses, the spot/flood functions best as a focusing adjustment, to smooth out the field. The adjustment for a smooth field differs depending on the lens in use.

Accessories for HMI Fresnel and PAR Lights

HMI Fresnels and PARs use the standard accessories as their tungsten counterparts: barn doors, scrims, gel frames. Chimera lightbanks are often used to turn direct light into soft light. When HMIs are used for theatrical (stage) and event lighting, DMX-controlled shutters enable the light to be controlled from the dimmer board. DMX-controlled shutters and color scrollers are valuable accessories when this kind of control is required. (DMX-controlled ballasts are covered under Square-Wave Electronic Ballasts, later in this chapter.)

HMI "Open-Face" Lights

The Arri X series and Desisti Goya lights are open-face lights in the sense that they have only clear UV protective glass in front of the bulb and reflector, no lens (Figure 4.3). Specifications are given in Table A.8. While their beam is broad

Figure 4.3 Arri X Light. (Courtesy of Arri Lighting, New York.)

and unfocused, these fixtures have the unique ability to be oriented in any direction. They can be used pointing straight down as an overhead soft light (through heavy diffusion) or straight up for architectural lighting. They cast a hard shadow and would be a good choice if a hard silhouette were needed. They come sizes 200 W, 575 W, 1200 W, 2.5k, 4k, and 6k.

HMI Soft Lights

As with incandescent soft lights, the lamp of an HMI soft light is aimed into a white concave reflector. The bounced light and large aperture create a soft, even field of daylight-balanced light. The HMI soft light, of course, produces much greater quantities of light than an incandescent (see Table A.8). Although they are more popular in Europe, you see few HMI soft lights on set; they are expensive and softening accessories like chimeras make them somewhat redundant.

The Aurasoft light is a large round soft-light fixture that can be fitted with either an HMI lamp or tungsten lamp. It is popular among some DPs mainly because the round shape makes a pleasing eye light.

Small HMI Fixtures—Sun Guns and Modular Multiuse Fixtures

Sun Guns

A sun gun is a small (125, 200, 250, or 400 W) light powered by a 30-V nickel-cadmium (nicad) battery, usually in the form of a battery belt (Figure 4.4, Table A.7).

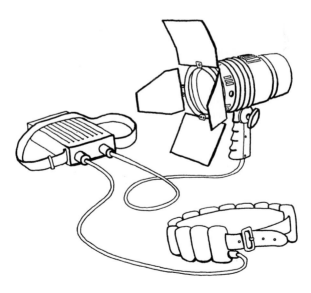

Figure 4.4 This HMI sun gun takes a 250-W SE HMI globe and has a color temperature of 5600 K. It operates on a 30-V battery belt and is adaptable to a 24-V car-type battery.

The light has a handgrip as well as a mounting stud. Sun guns are sometimes employed in remote locations where power is not available (e.g., a cave in the mountains of Mexico) and in situations where the expediency of a battery-powered light takes priority (e.g., a moving vehicle or on a moving elevator).

Although the 30-V nicad belt batteries are supposed to last as long as an hour, rented batteries rarely keep the light going for more than 20–25 minutes. Lithium batteries have greater amp-hour capacity and are preferable. When battery-powered lights are to be relied on over the course of a whole scene or a whole day, it is necessary to have many batteries on hand. They must be fully charged overnight (8 hours), and it helps to have them "topped-off" again within an hour prior to use.

Joker-Bug

A number of manufacturers have adaptations for small daylight-balanced fixtures worthy of special note. K-5600 Lighting manufactures the Joker-Bug lights (200, 400, and 800 W), which are small fixtures designed with a unique range of applications: a highly directional PAR light, a soft light or lantern, a linear tube light, or an ellipsoidal spotlight (Figure 4.5). In the Joker mode, the light is a small PAR fixture using an axially mounted single-ended MSR bulb in a parabolic, highly efficient reflector. The lights are very bright for their size. The spreader lenses allow wide control (the 400 ranges from a punchy 5° beam to a generous 55° spread). In the Bug mode, the "beamer" (the front housing containing the reflector) is removed, leaving only a bare omnidirectional bulb held in a UV protective beaker. The Bug is used to illuminate a Chimera light bank or china lantern. The bulb can be oriented in any position. For this application, the clear beaker is exchanged for a frosted one, which helps diffuse the source. Both the 200 and 400 Joker-Bug can run on battery packs using the Slimverter power supply, making the 400 one of the brightest sun guns available. They can also be run on any type of AC power.

The Softtube is a 45 in. long by 6 in. wide white transluscent tube that attaches to the front of the Joker-Bug light. It radiates soft light and inhabits a very small space, making it ideal for small spaces where daylight fill is needed (e.g., lighting a bus interior).

The Bug can be adapted to the Source Four ellipsoidal spot by removing the Source Four lamp housing and inserting the "bug-a-beam" adapter with the Bug 400. The result is a daylight-balanced ellipsoidal spot with four times more brightness than normal. The short-arc MSR bulb is well suited to the task; the Source Four's beam is clean, sharp, and free of color fringing.

Cinespace

LTM has a similar light design, the Cinespace 125 W/200 W and Cinespace 575 W. These lights have a set of lenses that includes a frosted Fresnel as well as an assortment of spreader lenses. The front reflector housing twists off to adapt the light to a lantern or chimera lightbank. Again, you have the option of a frosted or clear globe cover.

Pocket PAR

Arri's variation on the theme is the 125-W Pocket PAR, which is a miniature light with its own unique set of accessories. These include a Light Pipe (same idea

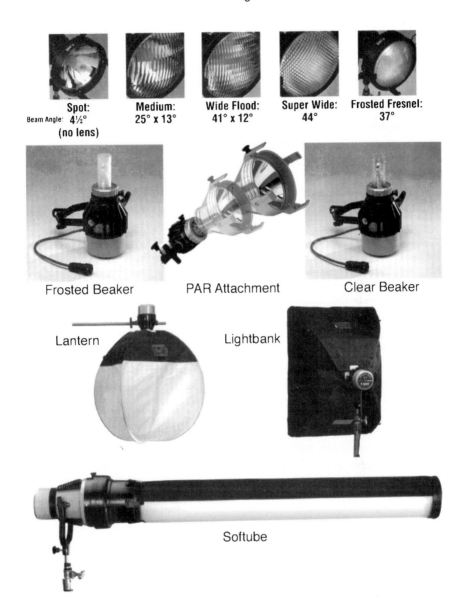

Figure 4.5 The Joker 800 in its many forms. (Courtesy of K5600, Los Angeles, CA.)

as the Joker Softtube), a set of four pattern projection lenses (like a focal spot), and a Flex Light system. The Flex Light is like a fiber optic system but uses a liquid optic tube that increases light transmission and does not suffer from the green tendency of fiber optic glass (and it cannot break). The system consists of a flexible liquid optic tube (in $1^1/_2$-m and 3-m lengths) that attaches to the face of the Pocket PAR via a light collector attachment. On the other end, a front lens slides into small flashlightlike holder. The Flex Light kit comes with three lens choices as well as color correction filters, a mounting adapter ($^5/_8$-in. female) for the flashlight end. The Pocket PAR has no omnidirectional Bug mode but can be fitted with an XXS chimera lightbank to be used as an obie, eye light, or lantern. It can be powered from any type of AC service or from a 30-V battery pack with a DC power supply.

Dedo 400D

The Dedo 400D is another small daylight fixture with unique characteristics and accessories. Dedo lights are known for their extraordinarily sophisticated optical control. They offer superior light output per watt, a totally clean beam that has a wide focusing range (from 5° at spot to 50° at full flood). In the flood position, they project a completely even field distribution. The ballast is dimmable, plus it has a boost position for additional light output. It has automatic input voltage selection (90 to 255 V AC). The projection attachment for the 400 series Dedo lights has the sharpest, cleanest beam I have seen on any light. The projection attachment accessories include framing shutters, iris, and gobo holder.

HMI Operation

Setting Up

The ballast circuit breakers should be off or the ballast unplugged while connecting or disconnecting head cables. The breakers should remain off while plugging in the power (Figure 4.6).

Head cable connectors (Socapex or VEAM) have multiple pins and a threaded collar that screws onto their receptacle. Use the keyway to orient the plug into the socket. VEAM connectors for 575-, 1200-, 2500-, and 4000-W fixtures are identical, except that the keyway is oriented differently. To tell the cables apart many manufacturers and rental houses color code the connectors or cables as follows:

Green	575
Yellow	1200
Red	2500
Blue	4k

Be sure to tie a tension relief so that the weight of the head cable does not pull on the connector, especially with larger lights that have heavy head cables.

Many electronic power supplies provide dual outputs so they can be used with more than one wattage light (1.2k/2.4k, 2.4k/4k, 4k/6k, 6k/12k, etc.). Note that both sockets are continually hot when the ballast is powered and on. Use a cover or tape over the unused socket.

Junction Boxes

The large Socapex connectors used on some head feeders can be connected only to a panel-mounted receptacle and not to another head cable. A junction box (J-box) provides the means of connecting one head cable to another.

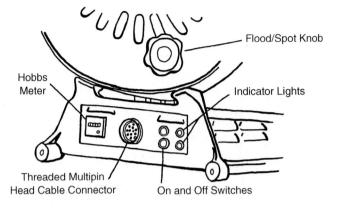

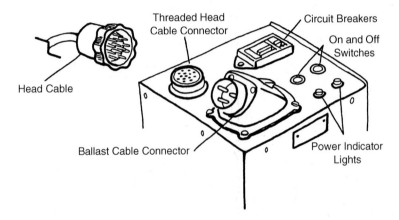

Figure 4.6 Anatomy of an HMI head and ballast.

Striking

Once the head cable is connected to the head and ballast, plug in the ballast and switch on the circuit breakers. With 12k and 18k lamps, place the bulb in the full spot position before pushing the on switch. This backs the bulb away from the lens, so that the lens does not crack from thermal shock. Also, in the (rare) event that the globe explodes during warm-up, the chance of shattering the lens is minimized. When 12k bulbs do explode, they often go within the first 5 or 10 minutes of ignition or reignition.

Before pushing the on switch, call out "Striking" to warn people that the light is about to be ignited. HMIs have on/off switches on both the head and the ballast, and most models can be turned on and off from either place. When you press the on switch, the ballast briefly sends a high-voltage ignition charge to the head, and this makes a sparking sound. On many electronic ballasts, there is a pause before the ballast sends the ignition charge, which can be as long as 10 seconds.

The igniter circuit provides an ignition charge of 5,000–17,000 V, depending on the size of the globe. The ignition charge creates a brief arc between the electrodes in the globe. Once the flow of electrons is initiated, the ballast brings the voltage down to the operating level and regulates the current.

Once sparked, the HMI begins to emit light. From a cold state, it takes 1–3 minutes for the substances in the globe to vaporize. At the same time, lamp voltage, lamp current, luminous flux, and color temperature all reach their nominal values.

Reigniting a globe that is hot from recent use may present difficulty. Hot gasses inside the globe are under great pressure, creating very high resistance. To overcome this resistance and ionize the gas between the electrodes, a much higher ignition voltage is necessary. The electronics of most newer ballasts take this into account and have better hot restrike performance; often, however, an older magnetic ballast cannot produce sufficient voltage and you have to wait until the lamp has cooled (2 or 3 minutes) before you can restrike.

Troubleshooting

When an HMI goes down—won't strike or starts to flicker—you need to quickly identify the source of the problem and give the gaffer the information right away. If the problem is immediately fixable, you can give the gaffer a time estimate. If it is more complicated, you need to explain the situation so the gaffer can decide what to do, usually based on the time available.

If an HMI will not work, first double-check all the obvious possibilities. Are the ballast breakers turned on? Are the cables connected properly? Is a bulb installed? Is the HMI plugged into the proper voltage? (Some are 120 V, others are 208, 220, or 240 V.) If the HMI still doesn't work, isolate the problem: Is it the head cable, the head, the globe, the ballast, or the power? Isolating the problem requires a logical, methodical approach. You can eliminate possibilities by temporarily borrowing a ballast and head cable known to work; this will usually get you to the heart of the problem quickly. If the problem is hidden, you may have to change each component before you find its cause. In the worst case, more than one faulty part conspires to confuse things.

Problems with the Head Cable

The cables, specifically the connectors, are the most common source of the problem. If the indicator lights are on at the ballast and off at the head and you get absolutely no response from the head when you try to strike it, the problem is most likely in the cable or the ballast. Swap the head feeder for a new one to see if it is malfunctioning. (Note: The neon indicator lights in the head sometimes burn out. The light is often integral to the switch, and it is an expensive part for the rental house to replace, so you cannot always count on them being in working order.)

Very often, the pins of the connectors get pulled back into the connector because the strain relief is loose, or the wires get twisted inside the connector because the keyway that locks the inside of the connector to the outside sleeve has broken off.

Check that all the pins on the connector are flush (same for the receptacles on the female connectors).

When the head cables are checked out at the rental house—and periodically during shooting—check for missing screws on the strain-relief part of the connectors. If the strain-relief clamp comes loose, the connections inside can get pulled out and twisted. Dirty connector pins may also be at fault, in which case the pins should be blown out with compressed air and cleaned with contact cleaner. Also look for damaged insulation along the length of the cable. Treat head cables with care; avoid dragging them across pavement or throwing them on the ground because this can bend the connectors, making them impossible to connect. Never run head cables where heavy equipment and vehicles will run over them; this damages the wires inside, causing endless headaches later on.

For long head feeder runs, it is advisable to go with longer cables rather than string together several shorter ones. Using 100-ft cables (available for the larger units from Arri) cuts down the number of connection points, which are always the weakest link.

The pins and keyway are oriented differently for different sizes of HMIs and the products of different manufacturers. Check that you are using the right head cable. The keyway orientation normally prevents you from using the wrong kind of connector, but if the connector is forced into place, it may appear to be connected. Again, color-coding by wattage of similar-looking head cables helps.

Problems with the Head

If the indicator light shows that there is power at the head but nothing happens when you press the button or if the HMI shuts itself off when tilted down, it is likely that the lens door is slightly loose, allowing the UV protection microswitch to shut off the unit. Check that the door is tightly closed, even when the light is tilted forward. You may need to adjust the rod on the microswitch so that the switch engages. Once in a great while, the microswitch becomes overheated, breaks, and must be replaced. On newer fixtures, the lamp base tightening knob is also part of the safety loop circuit. Be sure the lamp base knob is tight or the lamp may not strike.

If the light makes a striking sound but does not take, the problem is most likely with the globe, igniter circuit, or internal cables. If the globe is hot from prior use, it is very likely that the globe simply needs a minute to cool before it will restrike.

As globes get older, they have more difficulty striking. As the electrodes wear away and the gap between them becomes wider, the igniter has to generate more voltage to bridge the gap. You may have to try several times before the globe takes. Wait 20 seconds between strikes. It is time to replace the globe when its electrodes have worn down so far that the igniter can no longer induce an arc.

With 12k lamps, if the light makes a loud buzz and arcing sound when you attempt to strike but does not take, check the high-voltage (HV) cables and lamp cables. The lamp cables connect the lamp to terminals at the base of the lamp holders. The high-voltage igniter cables run from the base of the lamp holders to the igniter circuit in the base of the head (Figure 4.7).

If the lamp cables hang close to a metal part (such as the reflector), the start-up charge may arc. This deprives the bulb of the necessary start voltage and, over

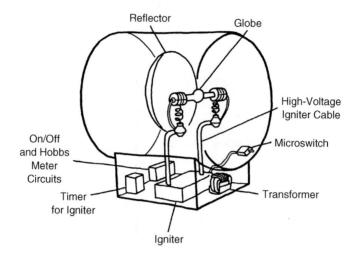

Figure 4.7 Interior anatomy of an HMI head.

time, burns away the lamp cables. When installing the globe, position lamp cables so they have plenty of clearance and do not arc to the reflector or lamp housing. If you find a lamp cable partially burnt (blackened, fraying strands of cable), do not use that globe until the lamp cables have been replaced.

Another cause of HV cable burnout is overheating. The cables get jostled around and the terminal screws loosened, causing overheated contacts, which eventually burn right through the igniter cables or lamp cables. Check and tighten the terminals each day when the lights are moved around a lot.

Problems with the Ballast

Some magnetic 12k ballasts have a selector switch that must be set at the appropriate input voltage (208 or 240 V). Improper input voltage selection can cause trouble in striking and operating the light. The Cinemills ballast has an internal patch panel instead of a selector switch: To check or change the input voltage selection, remove the front panel of the ballast and repatch the plugs inside. Some ballasts are self-regulating and require no adjustment to be used with 208- or 240-V power.

Ballast hum is normal; nonetheless, it is the electrician's duty to remedy any annoyance to the sound mixer. It is best, from the start, to place HMI ballasts in a separate room. When one ballast is particularly noisy, exchange it for a new one. In the meantime, placing sandbags above and below the ballast helps dampen vibration. Building a tent with furniture pads also helps, but do not block ventilation.

If a magnetic ballast starts to buzz, it can be a symptom of low input voltage. When operating on a low input voltage, the ballast has to draw more current to provide the needed voltage to the head. This can cause overheating and nuisance circuit breaker trips. Check the line voltage.

Problems with Flicker

Flicker is one of the most aggravating problems you can have because it can occur from a number of different causes. Most commonly, it is due to a bad connection in the distribution system but may result from a wandering arc in the globe, improper voltage, bad power cable connection, or faulty head cable. An intrepid and dauntless electrician is needed to track down the actual cause of the flicker.

First, let me stress that we are now talking about *visible* flicker. It is a common misconception that a visible "flicker" in the light is cause for concern about the generator's Hertz regulator. Electricians are generally aware that, to avoid flicker, HMIs require a precisely regulated Hertz rate; however, one must realize that this type of "flicker" is a pulsation recorded *on film only*—it is not visible to the eye on set. (More about this horror later under HMI "Flicker" and Flicker-Free Ballasts.)

Visible, random, intermittent flicker is almost always caused by a bad connection in the distribution system, head feeder, or ballast feeder cable. In the worst case, a bad contact in the power feeder or distribution cable can cause the light to stop working altogether. Try to determine if more than one light is being affected; if so, what part of the distribution do they share? Are they on the same 100-A whip (maybe a bad Bates plug)? Are they on the same leg (maybe a loose connection on that phase)? If a neutral connector is loose in the distribution, all phases flicker.

When using Bates cable, check for loose-fitting pins and hot connectors and black pitting on the hot pin of the power feeder. Use your dikes or a pin-splitter to spread the pins if the pin is squished together. Contact cleaner also works miracles to restore dirty pins. When working in dirt, dust, or sand over an extended time, it is a good idea to give the HMI connectors a cleaning every week or so. Blow out dirt with compressed air, and clean the pins and receptacles with contact cleaner.

A visible ongoing pulsation or a flutter in the light is evidence of a wandering or unstable arc in the globe. Arc instability may be due to a nonhorizontal orientation of the globe or a defective globe. Double-ended lamps may develop a wandering arc when the inner globe is positioned on a tilt. Arc instability may also be due to excess current on the electrodes, which points to faulty voltage regulation by the ballast or improper input line voltage. Excess current wears down electrodes at an accelerated pace, aging the globe before its time. Before discarding a globe as unstable, check it by using a different ballast.

The condition of the arc can be checked by viewing the globe through a welding glass. Because of the other lights in use, a wandering or fluttering arc may not be apparent to the eye when looking at the subject onto which the light is falling, but it will register on film. The problem becomes clearly apparent when you observe the arc in the globe. This is harder to do with Fresnels because you cannot see through the lens very clearly. Do not attempt to view the bulb directly.

Momentary spikes or flashes in an HMI, other than during the warm-up period, may be an indication that the Hertz rate of the generator is jumping (magnetic ballasts only). The generator's frequency meter may not detect very short, erratic frequency pulses. Measure the current with a frequency meter that has a high sampling rate to determine if the governor in the generator is faulty.

HMI "Flicker" and Flicker-Free Ballasts

Standard Magnetic Ballasts

The light intensity of an HMI increases and decreases 120 times a second, twice every AC cycle. This fluctuation is not visible to the eye but is captured on film as a steady pulsation if the camera is not in precise synchronization with the lights. To avoid capturing light pulsation on the filmed image, you must (1) use a crystal-controlled camera, (2) run the camera at one of a number of specific frame rates, and (3) use a line current maintained at exactly 60 Hz.

The safe frame rates are those that divide evenly into 120 (120, 60, 40, 30, 24, 20, 15, 12, 10, 8, 6, 5, 4, 3, 2, 1). Additional HMI-safe frame rates at any shutter angle are listed in the tables in Appendix D. At any of these frame rates, the camera motor must be crystal controlled. A wild or non-crystal-controlled camera cannot be used with magnetic HMI ballasts.

Standard ballasts also create light pulsation on film if the AC Hertz rate is not precisely controlled (if, for example, the generator's governor is out of adjustment). The Hertz rate for any power line can be checked using an in-line frequency meter or by measuring the light's flicker rate with a photosensitive Cinecheck frequency meter pointed at the HMI head itself (magnetic ballast only). Rental companies can supply a frequency meter with their equipment. Additionally, most generators have built-in frequency meters.

Square-Wave Electronic Ballasts

Square-wave ballasts eliminate the flicker problem. They allow you to film at any frame rate, at changing frame rates, and with a wild camera (Figure 4.8).

When filming an action sequence—an explosion or a car crash, for example— some of the cameras shoot at a high frame rate (slow motion). To give the DP the flexibility to choose any speed, the light output from the HMIs must be flicker free.

A square-wave ballast maintains a virtually constant output of light over the whole AC cycle by squaring off the curves of the AC sine wave. The changeover period is so brief that the light is virtually continuous (Figure 4.9C and D).

Unfortunately, the square wave causes the globe, igniter, and other parts of the head to make a high-pitched whistle. The head becomes a resonating chamber, amplifying the noise and projecting it toward the set and the microphones. To make the ballasts quiet when recording dialogue, electronic ballasts are fitted with a switch to change between *flicker-free* operation and *silent operation*. In the silent mode, a special circuit electronically rounds off the sharp corners of the square wave, which eliminates the noise (Figure 4.9E).

In the silent mode, a square-wave ballast provides flicker-free light at frame rates up to about 34 frames per second (fps), and in flicker-free mode, up to 10,000 fps. Make sure that all ballasts are set to the same setting.

Figure 4.8 Electronic flicker-free ballasts. Power Gems and Arri ballasts are *constant power* ballasts. Most models are dual wattage with autosensing. Note: When ballast is operating *both* outputs are hot. Cover the unused outlet. On Power Gems (A) 18k/12k, (B) 12k/6k, (C) 6k/4k, (D) 4k/2.5k, and (E) 2500/1200W controls include start and stop momentary switches, breakers, dimmer pot, silent/flicker-free selection switch, and liquid crystal operation/diagnostic display. The 1200/575W model (F) has a wattage selection switch and separate output connectors. Arri ballasts shown are (H) 12k/6k, (I) 4k/2.5k, and (J) 1200/575W. Arri also makes DMX-controlled ballasts in all sizes. (Courtesy of Power Gems, Van Nuys, CA, and Arri Lighting, New York.)

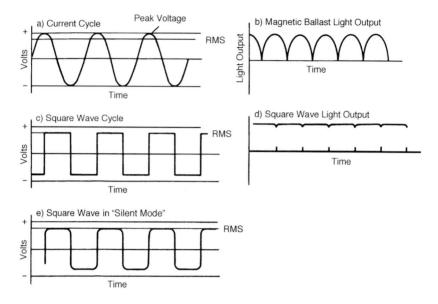

Figure 4.9 The normal sinusoidal 60-Hz current cycle of a magnetic ballast (A) creates a fluctuating light output (B), requiring that the camera frame rate be synchronized with the light fluctuations to obtain even exposure from frame to frame. The refined square-wave signal of an electronic ballast (C) creates virtually even light output (D), rendering the fixture flicker free. The sharp corners of the normal square-wave signal create noise in the head. When operated in the silent mode, the ballast electronically rounds off the corners of the square wave (E).

Square-wave ballasts completely process and regulate the input power, and as a result, they offer additional advantages and features, including

- Light weight: A lot less backache than their ship-anchor magnetic counterparts.
- Wide tolerance for voltage and Hertz rate discrepancies: Variation of up to 10% in voltage or line frequency has no adverse effect on operation.
- "Dimming" capability: By controlling current, the ballast can dim the lamp 50%, or about one stop of light. At 50% power, a globe's color temperature is 75K–200K higher (bluer) than normal.
- Increased light output (5%).
- Increased globe life (as much as 20%).

In addition, modern *constant-power* electronic ballasts are able to regulate not just lamp current but lamp power, enabling the ballast to compensate for changing lamp voltage as a lamp ages. *Constant power* means the lamp has a stable, optimal color temperature that remains uniform regardless of lamp age or line voltage. Constant-power designs are also less prone to overheating than constant-current ballasts (in situations where line voltage is low, current can become excessive).

The more-sophisticated electronic ballasts (like those shown in Figure 4.8) incorporate warning lights or self-diagnostic messages on an LED display. After shutdown, the display identifies the problem: an overheated power module, improper input voltage, a short in the output circuits, current on the ground wire, a misconnected cable—everything but a readout of the gaffer's blood pressure. If the ballast shuts off, be sure to check the display before rebooting the ballast.

Most electronic ballasts we use are of European origin and have a 50-Hz/60-Hz output selection switch. This switch controls the timing of the output waveform from the ballast. With these ballasts, the output waveform has no reference to the input voltage Hertz rate, so it will work with any supply Hertz rate. Normally, this switch would be set to 60 Hz in the United States (because we normally shoot at 24 fps); however, you can use this switch to gain alternative flicker-free speeds when operating in silent mode. On the 50-Hz setting, safe frame rates include 100, 50, 33.33, 25, 20, 10, and 5 fps. Of course all the HMIs on the set have to be on the same setting. (Additional safe frame rates with 50-Hz output appear in Appendix D.)

Power Factor Correction Circuits

Power factor is explained in greater detail in Chapter 11, but for now I'll offer a simplified explanation. A purely resistive load (e.g., an incandescent light) has a power factor of 1.0. Voltage and current increase and decrease *simultaneously* in a sinusoidal waveform, 120 times a second. Volts × amps always equals watts. The circuitry in magnetic and electronic ballasts is not purely resistive; it has other properties that knock voltage and current slightly out of phase with one another. This lowers the power factor. Electronic ballasts with no power factor correction circuit have a power factor of around 0.7, which means the ballast can use only 70% of the power it draws, or to put it another way, it has to draw 30% more power than it uses: (Volts × amps × pf = watts). This has several consequences, none of them good. It means the generator has to work 30% harder, use 30% more fuel, and have 30% less capacity available for lighting. It also means the ballasts have to work harder, generate more heat, and age sooner.

A power factor less than 1.0 also means a high *return current* on the neutral wire in the distribution cable, and the neutral wire needs to be doubled or even tripled to handle the excess current. With a power factor of 1.0, when the phase wires (red, blue, and black) are evenly loaded, the current cancels out between the phases, and the neutral wire carries only the difference between phases. With a power factor of less than 1.0, the load on each of the phase wires does not cancel out even when they are evenly loaded. With a power factor of 0.7, for example, 30% of the current does not cancel between phase wires but instead it adds up on the neutral. So you would have to carry 90% of the load on the neutral even though all phase wires are evenly loaded (assuming you have three-phase service).

Additionally, some types of ballast electronics also create *spike currents* that can reach $2\frac{1}{2}$ times those of the equivalent sinusoidal waveform. This happens because the capacitors are charging only at the peak of the sine wave. Generator suppliers complain that this creates extremely high loads on the service or generator and can interfere with the generator's voltage regulator and even burn out the alternator. To contend with spike currents, some suppliers recommend the generator

Table 4.1 Electronic Ballast Power Consumption

	Lightmaker AC/DC	Lightmaker AC/DC	B & S (Arri, Sachtler)	Power Gems (LTM, Strand, Leonetti)	
	DC Amps	AC Amps	AC Amps	AC Amps	
				240-V Input	120-V Input
200	3 A, 120 V	5.1 A, 120 V		1.5 A @ 240 V	3 A @ 120 V
575	8 A, 120 V	10 A, 120 V	9 A, 120 V	5 A @ 240 V 3 A @ 240 V w/pfc	10 A @ 120 V
1200	17 A, 120 V	20 A, 120 V	18 A, 120 V	8.3 A @ 240 V 5.6 A @ 240 V w/pfc	17 A @ 120 V
2500	27 A, 120 V	39 A, 120 V	32 A, 120 V	16 A @ 240 V 11.5 A @ 240 V w/pfc	32 A @ 120 V
4000	42 A, 120 V	56 A, 120 V	52 A, 120 V	25.7 A @ 230 V 18 A @ 240 V w/pfc	51 A @ 120 V
6000	65 A, 120 V	75 A, 120 V	41 A, 120 V	41 A @ 240 V 27 A @ 240 V w/pfc	
12,000	120 A, 120 V	145 A, 120 V	81 A, 120 V	80 A @ 240 V 52 A @ 240 V w/pfc	
12/18k			61 A/91 A, 240 V	53 A/79 A, 240 V w/pfc	

w/pfc = unit with power factor correction.

be oversized to at least twice the size of the load, when the load has a low power factor. And they warn spikes may also affect other units running on the same service.

A *power factor correction circuit* realigns the waveform and induces a smoother waveform. Power factor correction circuits successfully increase the power factor to as much as 0.98. The ballast uses power more efficiently with minimized return current and line noise and also reduces heat, thereby increasing reliability. Table 4.1 lists power consumption for three prominent makes.

European electrical codes require the use of power factor correction with main power, but it is not required in the United States. Almost all manufacturers now include power factor correction on 12k/18k ballasts (for these high-current units, power factor correction becomes not just desirable but necessary to protect the electronics from extremely high currents and overheating). All major manufacturers offer power factor correction as an option on medium-sized ballasts. However, because of the added cost, weight, and complexity of power factor correction, rental houses may or may not stock them. The gaffer or best boy must specify that power factor corrected ballasts are required when ordering the equipment. For smaller lighting setups, power factor correction is usually of no consequence; however, when large numbers of ballasts (4k and up) are to be used, power factor correction is advisable. Arri calls their optional power factor correction feature an *active line filter* (ALF).

DMX-Controlled Ballasts

Both major ballast manufacturers now offer DMX-controllable versions of their ballasts. By linking multiple ballasts with a DMX-control cable and setting an address on each ballast, you can turn units on and off and dim (electronic ballasts) to 50% from a central dimmer console. This is a great convenience with large location rigs and in the studio, where dozens of lights are spread out all over the perms and throughout the set. Manufacturers offer DMX-controllable ballasts in all sizes 575 W and up and DMX control as a retrofit to electronic and magnetic ballasts. These power supplies tend to be sensitive to crosstalk on the DMX cable. Keep the DMX runs away from the power cables and use an Opti-splitter if control problems occur.

Troubleshooting

The development of electronic ballasts with features such as constant power output, sophisticated diagnostic and protection circuits, and power factor correction is the result of years of struggle by ballast manufacturers to master reliability. Electronic parts in the older, simpler electronic ballasts were susceptible to trouble. For example, repeated hot stabs could burn out the inrush resistor that protects the front-end rectifier bridge diodes and capacitors during start-up. The most common repairs to older electronic ballasts revolved around damage to input rectifiers, vented (blown) capacitors, open inrush resistors, or blown power module fuses—all caused by high inrush current. To protect the inrush resistor, be sure to turn off the main on/off switch or breaker after use and make sure it is off before plugging in the power cord.

Another common repair on older ballasts is damage to the output transistors (IGBTs and FETs) caused by a short or arc path in the head or head cable. A shorted igniter circuit can burn out ballast after ballast. In some cases, the ballast continues to work even though internal parts are damaged. The result is that other parts overheat and short out, and the repair bill and turnaround time keep going up.

Newer ballasts include back-end protection circuits, so that a sensor shuts off power if it senses a short. This protects the ballast but it doesn't lower the blood pressure of the gaffer, who is waiting for that light to come on. As a precondition to operation, sophisticated ballasts demand that the head and cables be in good condition, with no shorts in the power line or ground, and a continuous ground.

Once an electronic ballast craps out, there is seldom anything you can do but replace it. Nothing inside an electronic ballast is user-serviceable; you have to leave it to a qualified electronics technician. For this reason, preventative steps become all the more important. There are many things electricians can do to prevent a failure. The main one is to *treat the equipment as you would any electronic device*. Electronic ballasts must be handled gently and thoroughly protected from heat, moisture, condensation, precipitation, dirt, sawdust, and so on. They cannot be left baking on a hot beach or outside overnight in the dew. Magnetic ballasts are just about bulletproof, being made mostly of copper and iron. They can take all kinds of abuse, both physical and electrical, without failing. Electronic ballasts are made of circuit boards, relays, capacitors, and transistors, like your home stereo, and although they have rugged casings and use heavy, commercial-grade components, electronic ballasts cannot be treated like magnetic ballasts. The electrician must enter a solid-state frame of mind when handling this equipment.

Ballast Electronics

A magnetic ballast is a very simple device. Input power is routed through the main breakers to a choke coil connected between the main input and the lamp. The coil may be tapped in several places to provide for various input voltages and a high start-up voltage. Capacitors are also included to compensate for the inductance of the coil and restore a unity power factor. The coil provides the start-up charge for the igniter circuit, then acts as a choke, regulating current to the lamp once the light is burning. Power from the coil is routed to the main contactors (which are controlled by a low-voltage control circuit) and the igniter circuit wire.

An electronic ballast is quite a bit more complicated (Figure 4.10). There are three primary stages to a square-wave ballast. The first stage, the DC intermediate circuit, converts power to DC. As a preliminary, power flows from the mains supply through the circuit breakers and earth leakage detection circuit to the RF mains filter. This filter restricts the flow of noise back onto the supply service. Contactors K1 and K2 and the start-up resistor form a circuit that charges the

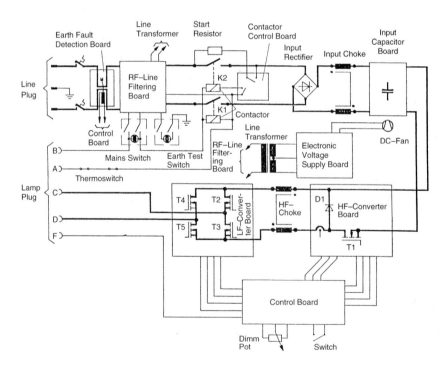

Figure 4.10 Block diagram of a 2500-W electronic ballast. (Courtesy of Arri Lighting, New York, and B & S Elektronishe Gerate GmbH, Germany.)

capacitors before the power electronics are activated at start-up. The input rectifier and capacitors then convert the current to DC: The input rectifier inverts the negative half of the AC cycle, and the capacitors level it out to one continuous positive DC voltage.

The second and third stages are referred to as the *power electronics* or *power modules*. The second stage is a step-down or buck converter (HF-converter board and HF-choke) that draws a constant current from the DC intermediate stage, then precisely regulates current flow to the final power electronics. Actual current flow is constantly monitored by the control board and adjusted by controlling the high-frequency (20 kHz) duty cycle of transistor T1. This circuit (T1, D1, and HF-choke) allows a constant power ballast to maintain a lamp at optimum color and output performance as lamp voltage increases with age.

The final stage (LF-converter board) serves as an inverter, turning the DC current into an AC square wave using four specialized transistors (insulated gate bipolar transistors, or IGBTs). The IGBTs switch back and forth in pairs (T4 and T3, then T2 and T5), reversing the polarity at a frequency controlled by the control board. (Frequency is not referenced to the line Hertz rate. Thus, an electronic ballast is not affected by a generator that is slightly off speed.) A transformer and voltage supply board circuit provides power for the control boards.

Whether the ballast is electronic or magnetic, seven wires run through the head feeder to the head (except in some Arri ballasts, which get away with six): two (thicker) power wires, *VOH* (voltage out hot), and *VOR* (voltage out return); a *ground wire*; the *igniter's power* line; and three 15-V logic signal wires: *switch common* (15 V from ballast), *on momentary* (a remote on switch at the head), and *safe on* (which is wired to the microswitch in the lens door and to the off switch on the head. Both switches must be closed for the main contactors in a magnetic ballast to close; in the case of an electronic ballast, the power modules act as an electronic circuit breaker).

In the head, VOH and VOR run directly to the terminals of the globe. The ground wire is connected to the lamp housing. The igniter's power line and VOR are connected to the primary step-up transformer of the igniter circuit. This transformer steps voltage up to about 5000 V. From there, current runs through a spark gap to a secondary transformer, which boosts voltage up to the starting voltage of the lamp, on the order of 17 kV. When the operator pushes the strike button two things happen: The contactors in the (magnetic) ballast are closed (in an electronic ballast, the control board turns on the power control circuits, FETs, and IGBTs), which apply voltage to VOR and VOH, and a 200–350-V strike voltage is sent to the head on the igniter power line.

Taking it in extreme slow motion, the strike sequence happens as follows: The ignition voltage climbs from zero, increasing until the voltage potential is sufficient to bridge the spark gap. When a spark bridges the gap, a very high-voltage start charge is delivered to the electrodes of the lamp from the secondary transformer. After $1-1\frac{1}{2}$ seconds, a timer circuit removes igniter power from the circuit. Once the flow of electrons is initiated in the bulb, the ballast starts to hold back current. The lamp arc stabilizes and voltage rises to the normal operating value.

The spark gap is set to deliver the proper strike voltage for the bulb. To some extent, increasing the spark gap can improve hot restrike characteristics because it increases strike voltage; however, adjusting the spark gap involves special tools and an experienced technician—the parts are fragile and extremely small. Too narrow a gap produces insufficient voltage to arc the bulb; with too wide a gap, the voltage does not bridge the spark gap.

The lamp is turned off when the "safe on" line is interrupted, by either the lens door microswitch or the off button on the head or ballast. This opens the main contactors in a magnetic ballast or shuts off the power control circuits in an electronic ballast.

DCI Lamps and Ballasts

Direct current iodide (DCI) lamps were introduced in 1993 by L.P. Associates. Like a xenon bulb, a DCI lamp uses DC current. It creates a constant, flickerless light and therefore has no light pulsation problem. DCI lamps have many of the same characteristics as HMIs: 5600-K color temperature, cool operating temperature, high luminous efficiency, bright light output, and hot restrike capability. DCIs have a dimming capability, like HMI electronic ballasts, but unlike them, DCIs operate silently and are flicker free at any frame rate. DCI lamps are made in sizes from 500–10,000 W that match the dimensions of corresponding HMI lamps: 750 or 1,000 DCI (575 HMI), 1,500 DCI (1,200 HMI), 3,000 DCI (2,500 HMI), 5,000 DCI (6,000 HMI), and 10,000 DCI (12,000 HMI). With a simple modification to the lamp holder, standard HMI fixtures can use DCI lamps by operating on a special DCI power supply. The small, lightweight power supplies take AC input power and deliver DC power to the lamp. On L.P. Associates' 750- and 1500-W fixtures there is no separate ballast and feeder cable; the power supply and igniter are built into the housing on the base of the light.

Operating characteristics, such as lamp warm-up time, the need for care in handling and cleaning the lamp, lamp installation with nipple pointed forward, the use of UV emission safeguards, and lamp life (200–300 hours), are the same as for standard HMI lamps. Unlike HMIs, DCI lamps have a positive electrode (anode) and a negative electrode (cathode). Installing the lamp with correct polarity is critical to proper operation; therefore, the diameter of the positive end is slightly larger, requiring that one lamp holder on a standard HMI fixture be enlarged for use with a DCI lamp. To prevent an AC ballast from being connected to a DCI lamp, the feeder cable connectors are also different.

Like other electronic power supplies, DCI ballasts have a fairly low power factor, and with 120-V ballasts there is return current on the neutral.

Three-Head, Three-Phase Solution

One way to get around the HMI pulsation problem when operating at off speeds or with a wild camera and magnetic ballasts is to use three standard HMI ballasts connected to three heads, each powered from a different leg of a three-phase source. Because the three phases peak a third of a cycle apart, when taken together,

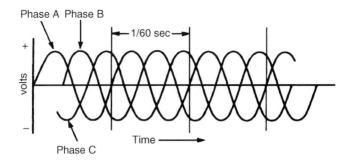

Figure 4.11 With three-phase power, the peak of each leg is a third of a cycle out of sync with the last, creating six peaks in each cycle. At 60 Hz, that amounts to 360 peaks per second, which is a high enough frequency to be flicker free at any frame rate.

the three lights have an actual frequency of 360 peaks per second (3 × 120 = 360). At this frequency, the camera does not detect the pulsation (Figure 4.11).

The lights must be bounced or mounted close together and placed far enough from the subject not to create separate shadows. The light created is flicker free at any frame rate.

HMI-Type Lamps

HMI (Hg [mercury] medium-arc iodide; Osram), HMI/SE (single ended; Osram), MSR (medium source rare earth, single ended; Philips), GEMI (General Electric metal iodide), CID (compact indium discharge; Thorne, UK), CSI (compact source iodine; Thorne, UK),[2] DAYMAX (made by ICL), and BRITE ARC (Sylvania) are trade names of lamps in the HMI family registered by the various manufacturers. All these consist of two tungsten-coated electrodes surrounded by mercury vapor and other metal halides held in a quartz envelope. The flow of electrons switches electrons in the gas from one highly excited state to another, releasing energy in the form of visible and UV light. While the mercury is responsible for most of the light output, an optimal mix of halides of rare earth metals in the mercury vapor brings a balance of color output. The result is a quasi-continuous *multiline spectrum*, meaning that the color is made up of narrow peaks of various wavelengths rather than a continuous spectrum, which closely resembles the makeup of daylight and renders colors faithfully on film. There are two kinds of HMI globes: single ended and double ended (Figure 4.12).

Single-Ended Globes

The design of single-ended (SE) globes allows for greatly improved efficiency when mounted axially and used with a bright reflector, as in SE PAR fixtures. They are also used mounted vertically in some models of Fresnel fixtures.

---

[2]CID and CSI are used in stadium lighting. CID is also used in small sun-gun fixtures and has the same color characteristics as HMI globes.

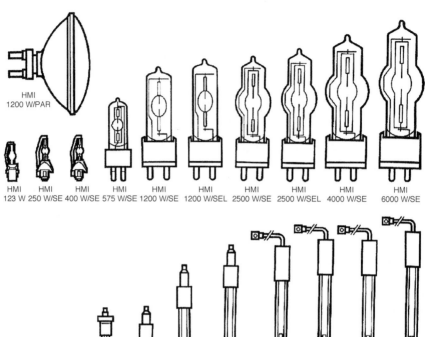

Figure 4.12 HMI globes. (Courtesy of Osram Corp., Van Nuys, CA.)

Single-ended globes of 575 W and larger can generally be burned in any orientation. The design and short overall length of SE globes make it easy for them to restrike while hot.

Double-Ended Globes

HMI Fresnels and soft lights use double-ended globes. The range of sizes is shown in Figure 4.12. Double-ended globes of 4k and larger must be burned with their arc within 15° of horizontal; never tip these larger HMIs on their side.

Relamping HMI Heads

Before relamping a light, be sure that the breakers are off, the fixture is unplugged, and the lamp is completely cooled. HMI bulbs build up internal pressure when in use. It is dangerous to handle them when hot; if broken, they will explode, sending shards of hot quartz in all directions.

The golden rule when relamping any fixture is never to touch the quartz envelope with your fingers and never to allow moisture or grease to come into contact with the bulb. Even a light smudge of finger grease causes a hot spot on the quartz envelope, which weakens the quartz and causes the envelope to bubble. When the globe loses its shape, the globe's photometric and structural properties are compromised and the globe could explode. HMI globes are too expensive to handle carelessly. At this writing, a single-ended 12k HMI globe is priced at around $2299. When an HMI globe explodes, it shatters the lens and destroys the lamp holder and reflector, bringing the total loss to a staggering sum. Always handle globes with a clean and dry rag, with clean cotton gloves (editor's gloves), or with the padding in which the globe is packed. Make it a practice to clean the globe once it is mounted in the fixture. Use a presaturated alcohol wipe or isopropyl alcohol and a clean lint-free tissue.

Double-ended HMI globes have metal ends that are laid into the lamp holder. HMIs of 2500 W and larger have clamps that close around the globe ends and are tightened with a screw. Finger screws, Allen screws, nuts, or standard screws are used. HMI globes of 6k, 12k, and 18k have connection wires that have to be attached to terminal screws on the base of the lamp receiver. Globes of 575 and 1200 W are held in a U-shaped receiver. Their ends are threaded and are tightened in place with knurled nuts. The 200-W globe has a knife plug, a flat tab that slides into the connectors on the base, and is locked in place with tightening screws.

Insert double-ended globes into the fixture with the molybdenum ribbon horizontal so that it does not block light returning from the reflector (Figure 4.13).

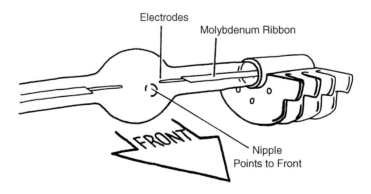

Electrodes

Molybdenum Ribbon

FRONT

Nipple
Points to Front

Figure 4.13 Proper installation of an HMI globe. Note that the ribbon is horizontal and the nipple is oriented outward (it may also be oriented upward). Connections are tight. HMI globes should be cleaned with an alcohol-impregnated cloth as a part of daily maintenance.

Orient the nipple on the bulb upward or outward toward the lens, not downward or toward the reflector. The nipple should always be above the arc to prevent a cold spot from forming where chemicals in the globe enclosure may condense and interfere with the burning cycle.

Be sure the globe's contact pins are tightly secured in place. Contamination in the contacts or a loose contact will impair proper cooling. A bad contact, evidenced by pitting and discoloration on the contact pins, causes premature lamp failure. A loose HMI globe may also vibrate.

With some SE PAR fixtures, it is impossible to install or remove the globe without handling it by the glass. Great care must be taken to avoid breaking the glass where it attaches to its ceramic base. Hold the glass with a clean rag, and wiggle the globe gently along, not across, the axis of the pins; any stress across the axis can very easily snap the quartz. The better single-ended PAR fixtures provide a globe release. When the knob is loosened, the globe can be inserted and removed with ease.

HMI Lamp Characteristics and Hazards

Color Temperature

Factors that affect the color output of HMIs are the type of globe (5600 K or 6000 K), the number of hours the globe has been used, lamp cooling, and the regulation of the power by the ballast. It is good practice, especially with HMIs larger than 2500 W, to match heads to ballasts and number and label both the head and the ballast with the color temperature and the amount of green that the light emits. For example, a head and ballast would be labeled "#1, 5500 K, +2, 5/13/96." This indicates ballast 1, which is matched to head 1, 5500 K color temperature, has a +2 CC of green on the date shown.

Globe Life

When an HMI globe is brand new it often shows a very high color temperature (10,000–20,000 K). This is sometimes accompanied by some arc instability, causing flicker. You may want to "burn in" the globe before filming starts, or color correct the lamp. During the first couple hours of use, the color temperature comes down quite quickly to the nominal value (5600 K or 6000 K) and the arc stabilizes. Thereafter, the color temperature changes over the life of the globe at the rate of 0.5–1 K per hour, depending on conditions. The color temperature decreases because as the gap between electrodes increases, more voltage is required to maintain the arc, and as the voltage increases, the color temperature decreases. For safety reasons, manufacturers recommend that globes not be used for more than 125% of their rated service life. As the bulb ages, changes in the quartz glass envelope make the globe increasingly fragile.

Lamp Cooling

You can overheat a lamp and cause damage to the reflector or lens by pointing the lights at an extreme up or down tilt. Also, if the light receives inadequate ventilation, the color temperature shifts toward green and blue.

Ultraviolet Emissions

All HMI globes produce light that has harmful amounts of UV radiation. Skin and retinal burns can result from direct exposure to the light. For this reason, a special housing and protective lens must be used. UV rays are reduced to a safe level when the light passes through the glass lens or when the light is indirect, bouncing off the inside walls of the fixture, for example. HMIs always have a safety switch that shuts off the globe if the lens door is opened or if the lens breaks. You can get a nasty burn very quickly by tampering with these safety features or by using broken or homemade equipment that doesn't have them.

A damaged or poorly made fixture that leaks direct UV radiation can, and has, caused skin burns, retinal burns, and even skin cancer. If prolonged proximity is unavoidable, as when operating a 12k in a condor, and you start to feel some burning on your skin, place a flag to block radiation from the fixture and have the fixture replaced ASAP.

Mercury

HMI globes contain very small amounts of mercury, which is poisonous. If a globe breaks, take sensible precautions to prevent ingestion of toxic chemicals. Keep chemicals off your hands. Wash your hands. Dispose of broken and burnt-out bulbs in an appropriate place. Normally, burnt-out globes must be returned to the rental house for inventory.

CHAPTER 5

Fluorescent Lights

History of Fluorescent Lights

Until relatively recently, cinematographers regarded fluorescent lighting as a minefield of photographic headaches, virtually incompatible with motion picture photography. Fluorescents were associated with ghoulish green skin tones, poor color rendering, anemic light output, noisy humming ballasts, and the same shutter speed restrictions that existed with HMIs (with magnetic ballasts).

In the 1980s, confronted with the inevitable need to shoot in fluorescent environments, many gaffers started putting together their own fluorescent systems. They wired newly available solid-state ballasts to kluged lamp harnesses, and sought out new commercially available tube designs that provided a better color spectrum. A range of fluorescent color correction gels were developed for fluorescent lights. The results rendered fluorescent environments filmable, but color balance and light output were still far from ideal.

It took the innovations of a determined gaffer and his best boy to overcome these obstacles. Freider Hochheim and Gary Swink designed fixtures, ballasts, and lamps tailored to the needs of film production. Their company, Kino Flo, Inc., continues to make groundbreaking advances in the photographic applications of fluorescent technology. Various manufacturers now offer stand-mounted fluorescent fixtures with high-frequency, flicker-free ballasts (Table A.10), which operate with commercially available lamps. Kino Flo makes its own lights, which are high output and color corrected (Table A.11). Cinematographers discovered the positive qualities of fluorescent lights: lightweight fixtures that put out soft, controllable light that wraps around the features and creates a pleasing eye light. They can easily be built into sets when a fluorescent environment is called for and can be used purely as a low profile, soft lighting instrument.

Kino Flo

Kino Flo makes fluorescent lighting systems specifically for film production work (see Table A.11, Appendix A). Kino Flo tubes are specially designed to be used with Kino Flo high-output ballasts. The Kino Flo KF55 (5500 K), KF32 (3200 K), and KF29 (2900 K) broad-spectrum fluorescent lamps are engineered to correspond to the spectral sensitivity curves of color film emulsions. Kino Flo tubes mix wideband and narrowband phosphor crystals with rare earth elements. The phosphor blend displays a complete spectrum of light (Color Rendering Index of 95) and no green spike when operated with Kino Flo high-output ballasts. In Appendix E, Table E.2 lists all Kino Flo tubes and Figure E.1 illustrates the different tube types. Kino Flo also makes green and blue tubes specifically suited for green-screen and blue-screen work. Matte photography is discussed in detail in Chapter 10. Red, pink, yellow, and UV (black light) tubes are also available, which are great for decorating a set with neonlike lines of light. All Kino Flo tubes are safety coated to make the lamps more durable and ensure that no glass fragments, mercury, or harmful phosphors are released if the lamp breaks (Parts are shown in Figure 5.10D).

Kino Flo ballasts run at high frequency (most at 25 kHz, the Diva-Lite at >30 kHz), resulting in flicker-free operation at any frame rate or shutter setting. The lights turn on instantly, even when cold, requiring no warm-up time. Kino Flo ballasts provide switches for individual lamps or pairs of lamps, so controlling brightness is a simple matter of adding or subtracting lamps. They can also be dimmed about one stop on a variac dimmer, or better still, using a Kino Flo dimming ballast you can reduce output to 3% without flicker. (You cannot use an electronic SCR dimmer or household resistance-type dimmer with a fluorescent light.) Kino Flo ballasts are lightweight and run silently.

Kino Flo 120-V Systems

Detailed, up-to-date information can be found on Kino Flo's website. See Appendix H for web addresses.

Portable Fixtures

Kino Flo fixtures come in various configurations and sizes. The four-bank systems, double-bank systems, and single-bank systems each have their own corresponding ballast and head cable (Figure 5.1). Each fixture is equipped with a lightweight egg-crate louver that controls the spread (and slightly reduces the intensity) of light. The fixture has a snap-on mounting plate for attachment to a C-stand (Figure 5.2), but because the fixtures are lightweight, they can also be taped or stapled into place.

The most commonly used Kino Flo fixtures for lighting on sets are the versatile 4-ft and 2-ft units. The four-bank, 4-ft units provide sufficient output to serve as key light at moderate light levels, or as a soft fill at higher light levels. The double-bank and single-bank fixtures are handy for hiding in sets, to glow a background wall or set dressing. The small fixtures are perfect to light actors close to the fixture; the fixture might be attached to a nearby wall, propped hidden behind a TV, or built into the set.

Diva-Lite

The Diva-Lite 400 (four-bank) and Diva-Lite 200 (double-bank) fixtures (Figure 5.3) are designed with compactness and portability in mind. The ballast is in the head and can be dimmed its full range using a knob on the back. The fixtures

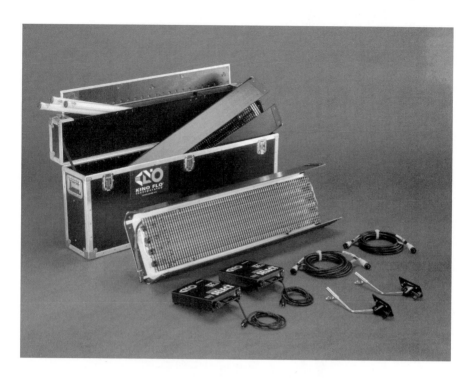

Figure 5.1 The Kino Flo four-bank, 4-ft fixture, here as part of a kit with two fixtures, Select ballasts, head cables, baby stand mounting plates, and traveling case. (Courtesy of Kino Flo, Inc., Sun Valley, CA.)

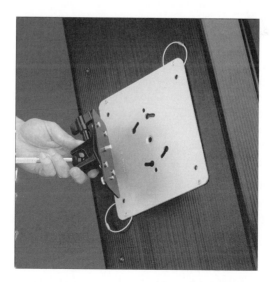

Figure 5.2 The removable mounting plate. (Courtesy of Kino Flo, Inc., Sun Valley, CA.)

Figure 5.3 Diva-Lite four-bank and two-bank fixtures use integral dimming ballasts and high-output lamps. (Courtesy of Kino Flo, Inc., Sun Valley, CA.)

use a lollipop attachment that adapts directly to a standard baby stand. Diva-Lites utilize the U-shaped compact fluorescent lamp (CFL). The Diva-Lite 400 is as bright as a 4-ft, four-bank fixture. Because of its brightness and handy dimming feature, it is a good head for use as an obie light over or under the camera lens or as a soft key. The Diva-Lite 400 is available with an optional universal ballast, which can be used around the world on any current source (100-V AC–265-V AC, 50/60 Hz).

Flathead 80

The Flathead 80 is a 4-ft, eight-bank fixture capable of putting out quite a bit of light (60 foot-candles at 10 ft) while remaining lightweight (26 lb) and less than 5-in. deep (Figure 5.4). It is a good light when you must tuck one against a wall and light a relatively large area. The Flathead 80 employs a pair of Select four-bank ballasts, so it can be controlled two tubes at a time (in a center out pattern). It comes with a parabolic silver louver that controls the spread and direction without cutting too much light output. Cardholders at the corners allow the electrician to fabricate

Figure 5.4 (A) The Flathead 80 fixture is lightweight and has high output (eight lamps). The head is connected to two Select ballasts. Card-holders at the corners (B) enable the easy use of extension doors. The detachable mounting plate (C) swivels in all directions and locks with a knob. The mounting plate pictured fits $1\frac{1}{8}$-in. junior receiver. (Courtesy of Kino Flo, Inc., Sun Valley, CA.)

Figure 5.5 Wall-o-Lite's ballast is on board and can be DMX controlled. (Courtesy of Kino Flo, Inc., Sun Valley, CA.)

foamcore barn doors in custom shapes and dimensions and attach them with grip clips. This is an especially useful feature when trying to control spill or get a very even light level (e.g., when lighting a green screen).

Wall-O-Lite

The Wall-O-Lite is a bright, DMX-controllable fixture with integral ballast. It houses 10 4-ft lamps, giving it an output of as much as 75 foot-candles at 10 ft (about as much light as a 2.5 HMI Fresnel bounced) and a weight of 48 lb (Figure 5.5). Because it creates a broad, even light and is DMX controllable (on/off control from 1 to 10 tubes) (Figure 5.10C), this fixture has proved especially useful for lighting matte screens (green screens or blue screens). Up to 512 Wall-O-Lite fixtures can be daisy-chained together. Stacked or positioned side by side, they have been enlisted to create a seamless wall of light for special set pieces or special effects. The fixture is also useful as an area light or Northlight. It mounts on a junior stand.

Blanket-Lite 6 × 6

The Blanket-Lite is composed of 16 6-ft lamps hung in a 6-ft square arrangement on a fabric base. A silver fabric reflector is mounted behind the tubes (Figure 5.6). The light can be hung in a frame or mounted to a wall. The frame, which is 80-in. square, provides for the attachment of diffusion. The whole thing is only 10 in. deep.

Figure 5.6 The 6-ft × 6-ft Blanket-Lite suspended in a frame with diffusion and a soft crate to control spill. (Courtesy of Kino Flo, Inc., Sun Valley, CA.)

It can be used as an overhead soft light or mounted on stands as a large soft key. It puts out 137 foot-candles at 10 ft. The Blanket-Lite weighs only 30 lb. The frame weighs an additional 60 lb.

Studio Fixtures

The Kino Flo studio fixtures (Image 80, 40, and 20) are designed for studio applications and green- and blue-screen work. They are DMX controllable, yoke mounted with metal housings, metal barn doors, and built-in ballasts. The Image 80 (4-ft) has eight tubes, the Image 40 (4-ft) has four tubes, and the Image 20 (2-ft) also has four tubes.

12-V DC Kits: 12-V Single, Mini Flo, and Micro Flo

Kino Flo makes a variety of 12-V DC fixtures that can run on battery power or a 12-V transformer power supply (120-V AC or 220-V AC).

12-Volt Single

In a car, helicopter, or elevator, where AC power is unavailable, you can run any of the standard Kino Flo fixtures from a 12-V DC battery. The 12-V single ballast can power T-12, T-10, or T-8 lamps, ranging in size from 15 in. to 4 ft. Four 12-V ballasts can power a four-bank 4-ft fixture—all that is required is a single to four-bank combiner (see Figure 5.10F). For greater power requirements in remote situations, you can also use an inverter system, described in Chapter 13.

With the proper adapter cables, you can power a standard four-bank fixture from four 12-V ballasts. The 9-in. or 15-in. lamps are ideal in a nighttime car scene to give the appearance of dashboard light. Kino Flo makes 12-V "car kits" with either 15-in. or 9-in. single-tube fixtures, dimmable ballasts, all the usual accessories, cigarette lighter connector, and spring clamps to connect to a car battery.

Figure 5.7 12-V DC Mini-Flo kit: Two 9-in. fixtures, mounting plates, and armature wire to mount the light in any position, 12-V DC ballasts, cigarette lighter adaptor, and clip-on car battery cables. (Courtesy of Kino Flo, Inc., Sun Valley, CA.)

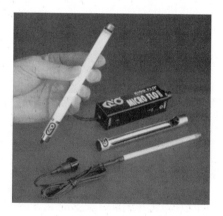

Figure 5.8 A 9-in. Mini-Flo (reflector and doors removed) and 4-in. Micro-Flo tube Kino Flo lights. (Courtesy of Kino Flo, Inc., Sun Valley, CA.)

Mini-Flo and Micro-Flo

The 12-V Mini-Flo kit has a 9-in. lamp with a corresponding fixture, ballast, and head cable (Figure 5.7). The Micro-Flo kit consists of tiny 6-in. and 4-in. tubes, thinner than a pencil (either tungsten or daylight) (Figure 5.8). Their size makes them uniquely suited for many special applications, such as to light a face inside a space suit helmet. They are commonly used for tabletop and miniature photography.

Using Kino Flo Fixtures

The components of each fixture (fixture with barn doors, reflector, egg-crate louver, lamp harness, and tubes) can be disassembled and employed in any number of configurations as needed (Figure 5.9). The fixture can be used with or without the egg-crate louver. For greater control of the spread of light, *combiner clips* can be used to stack several louvers on the same fixture. The spread is reduced to 67° with one louver, 37° with two, and 25° with three. On the other hand, if a softer, less-controlled light is wanted, the reflector can be removed, leaving the white backing as a soft bounce.

The fixture is designed so that, if the whole fixture is too bulky for a particular application, the tubes, wiring harness, and reflector can be quickly stripped out of the fixture. Bare tubes might be taped under a bar counter, for example. You can increase the brightness of bare tubes by taping the reflector to them. Bare tubes can be neatly mounted to a surface using plastic cable ties and adhesive cable tie mounts (and staples if necessary, Figure 5.10G) or by applying double-stick tape to the tube.

You can order a special Y-splitter (Figure 5.10E, F), which splits a four-bank (or two-bank) cable into single harnesses, so you can mount tubes end to end, for example. Be sure to order additional single harnesses and cables with the splitter.

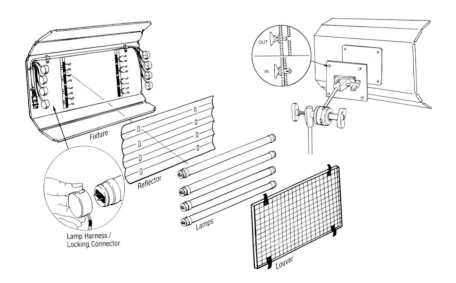

Figure 5.9 The components of the portable Kino Flo fixtures. The tubes can be used with or without the fixture, the reflector, and louver. The lamp harness uses a simple spring-loaded locking connector. The mounting plate pops on and off quickly using plastic locking pins. No tools required. (Courtesy of Kino Flo, Inc., Sun Valley, CA.)

Ballasts

With all fluorescent ballasts it is important to connect the fixture to the ballast *before* the ballast is turned on, or the electronics will suffer. Newer Kino Flo ballasts have circuits to protect the electronics from this problem, but many ballasts do not. Kino Flo standard ballasts (four-bank, double, and single) provide either a three-position toggle selection switch (all lamps/off/half the lamps) or individual switches for each tube. Kino Flo *Select* ballasts (four-bank, double-bank, and single) feature an additional high-output/standard-output toggle switch. Use the high-output setting for 4-ft lamps and the standard setting for 2-ft and 15-in. lamps. Operating 2-ft and 15-in. lamps in the HO setting raises the color temperature and green output. The Select ballast also features more advanced electronics than the standard ballast, which makes its performance more reliable and consistent.

Kino Flo *dimming ballasts* (double-bank and single) feature a slider to adjust light output in a full range with no change in color temperature. A trim adjustment allows you to set and return to a particular setting easily and to turn the lamp on at a preset level. Dimming ballasts provide a jack for attachment of a remote cable. Multiple dimming ballasts can be wired to and controlled by a standard dimmer board.

Mega-Flo Fixtures

Kino Flo makes 8- and 6-ft Mega-Flo systems that run on high-output *mega-ballasts*. Double- and single-bank fixtures are available. The megaballasts also power the Blanket-Lite.

Troubleshooting

From time to time, one or more tubes in a fixture will not light. The problem could be in the ballast, the lamp harness, or the lamps. The best way to proceed is as follows:

1. Double check that the ballast is plugged into live 120-V AC service.
2. Check that the extension is properly connected at the ballast and harness.
3. Check that the harnesses are properly secured to the tubes and the head cables are fully connected at both ends. Harness connectors are color coded; the same color must be on both ends of the lamp.
4. Switch the ballast to full on position. Note which lamps do not work, and try another ballast. If the same lamps still do not fire, change those lamps. If the lamps still do not fire, change the harness.

When renting four-bank Kino Flos in large numbers, it is prudent to include a few extra backup four-bank ballasts (1 for every 12 systems). The Kino Flo Select ballasts have a latch-up feature to protect the solid-state circuitry from abuse during operation. However, many older ballasts are still in circulation. Single and double systems generally do not require backup ballasts.

Kino Flo portable fixtures are made with wire barn door "hinges" (the flexible metal rods at the corners of the doors), which are made to be disposable. If one breaks, it can be easily replaced by removing the end screw, pulling out the broken wire, and replacing it with a length of good wire (Figure 5.10I).

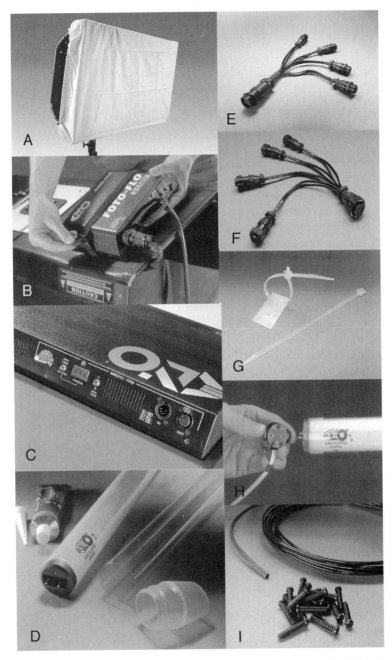

Figure 5.10 (A) "Flosier" diffusion on a Diva Lite. (B) Velco straps hold the Foto-Flo ballast to a four-bank fixture. (C) Dimmable DMX-controlled ballast. (D) Kino tubes are sealed in plastic tubes for safety. These parts can also be purchased. (E) Four-bank to single splitter—it allows four tubes with single harnesses to be connected to a four-bank ballast. (F) Single to four-bank combiner—it allows four 12-V single ballasts to power a four-bank fixture. (G) Adhesive mounts and releasable ties, handy for mounting bare tubes (you can also staple the plastic mount if the adhesive doesn't hold). (H) Harness connector. (I) Barn door wire repair kit. (Courtesy of Kino Flo, Inc., Sun Valley, CA.)

Building a Film-Friendly Fluorescent System from Commercially Available Parts

High-Frequency Ballasts

High-frequency ballasts bypass the problem of intensity fluctuation by converting a 60-Hz input frequency to between 20,000 and 40,000 Hz. The period of time between the off and on pulse of each cycle is so short that the illuminating phosphors do not decay in light output. The phosphors are essentially flicker free.

Some off-the-shelf fluorescent electronic ballasts have another flicker problem, called an *ersatz ripple*. Even though the ballast puts out a high-frequency cycle, that cycle can start to have a waveform itself. In a number of incidents, 24p video cameras and film cameras operating within a flicker-free window have picked up flicker from architectural lights operating near the filming area. Some ballasts simply are not designed to remove this ripple. In some instances, the ballast was found to be faulty. When shooting on constructed sets, using solid-state high-frequency ballasts for built-in fluorescent light fixtures, it is worthwhile to shoot a test with the ballasts you will be using. On location, solid-state ballasts are the norm in any modern installation. Older installations may not have high-frequency ballasts and therefore are limited to fewer shutter speeds and shutter angles.

Color-Correct Fluorescent Tubes

Until recently Duro-Test manufactured standard tubes suitable for color photography, Optima 32 (3200 K) and Vita-Lite (5500 K). Unlike those of other commercial manufacturers, these tubes incorporated wideband phosphor crystals and produced close to correct color rendering. When filming in a location with ceiling fluorescents, the lighting crew would typically replace all the existing fluorescent tubes with color-correct tubes. Duro-Test is now out of business; at this writing, it is not known if another manufacturer will offer the Optima phosphors under a new name.

Note: Tubes like Optima 32s, which have very little green when powered by a conventional ballast, require magenta correction when powered with a Kino Flo high-output ballast. High-output ballasts overdrive the fluorescent tube, which raises the color temperature and green output.

Some Additional Notes about Fluorescent Lights

Effect of Temperature

Fluorescent lamps are sensitive to extremes of temperature. Standard fluorescents are designed for operation above 50°F. Fluorescents operating on high-frequency ballasts operate in temperatures below freezing. With all fluorescents, even those operating on high-output ballasts, the operating temperature affects both the color and the intensity of the light. Under freezing conditions, the high-intensity ballast can get the tube started, but it takes a few minutes for the tube to reach the proper color and output. In hot temperatures or if the tubes are enclosed in an unventilated space, the color may wander toward the blue-green end of the spectrum, and additional color correction may be needed.

Effect of Voltage Shifts

Voltage shifts do not appreciably affect the color temperature of fluorescents. If the voltage is *too* low, however, the light will go out completely or will not start. A 10% decrease in power will yield a 10% decrease in light output.

Calculating Power Needs

Fluorescent lights are generally of nominal wattage and therefore pose no special power demand concerns. However, when a large number (hundreds) of fluorescent lights are to be powered, one must keep in mind some additional factors. The wattage rating on a fluorescent tube is the power consumed by the tube alone. The ballast typically consumes an additional 10–20%. Therefore, a 40-W tube actually consumes as much as 48 W of power (20% of 40 = 8, 40 + 8 = 48). In addition, the power factor must be taken into account (reactive current and the power factor are explained in Chapter 11).

CHAPTER 6

Stands and Rigging

We constantly need to hang lights in awkward places, so naturally, over the years, ways have been devised to secure a light almost anywhere. People are constantly inventing and reinventing these devices. The basics are described in this chapter but check manufacturers' websites for up-to-date information (Arri, Matthews, Norms, American, Modern Studio Equipment, Versales).

Stands

Stands come in two basic types: babies and juniors. *Baby* stands (sometimes called *750 stands*) have a $\frac{5}{8}$-in. pin that fits into the baby receiver found on the smaller lights, baby-2k or smaller (Figure 6.1A).

Junior stands (sometimes called *2k stands*) have a $1\frac{1}{8}$-in. receiver that takes the junior pin found on larger lights. Stands of both types come in short, "low-boy" versions as well as the standard height with two or three risers. Stands may be made of aluminum, which is lightweight, or steel, which is stronger.

Baby Stands

The most versatile baby stand for location work is a steel three-riser stand with a mountain leg (Figure 6.2). The legs can be quickly retracted by loosening the T-handle on the top collar and pulling up. The legs have a wide base for stability, and the mountain leg makes it easy to level the stand when it is placed on uneven ground, on a stair, over the edge of a curb, or leaning against a set wall (Figure 6.2).

Rolling Stand

Baby rolling stands are convenient when working in the studio on a level surface. Many rolling stands have brakes that snap into a locked position.

Blade Stand

Blade stands are extremely lightweight, which is their one advantage. They are also somewhat flimsy and unstable. They are best used with small lights. Stabilize a lightweight stand by hanging a small shotbag on the lower T-handle.

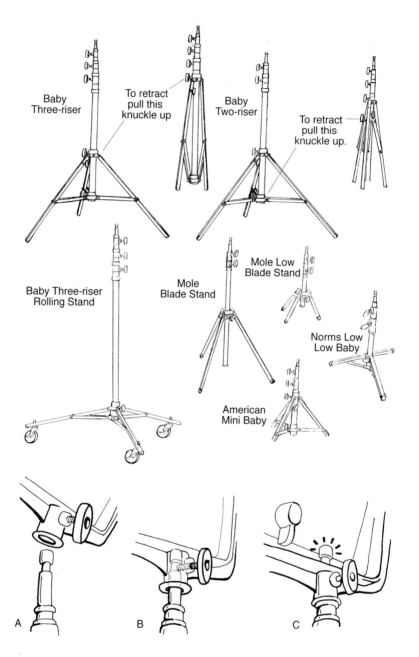

Figure 6.1 To retract the legs of most stands, loosen the upper tie-down knob and pull the legs up and in. With some stands, the legs retract by loosening the bottom tie-down knob and sliding that collar upward. A $5/8$-in. baby pin inserts into the receptacle on a fixture (A). When mounting the light, the pin should be flush with the receptacle and not stick through. This assures that the T-handle engages the indent of the pin (B). Also some lights (notably the baby junior) do not tilt properly if the pin sticks (C).

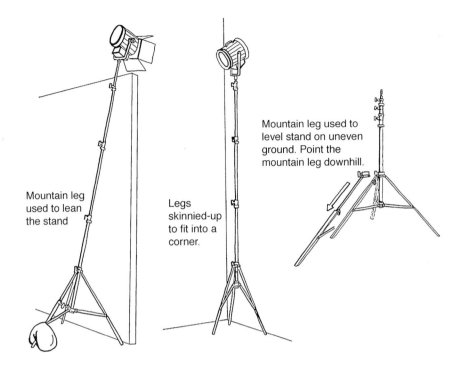

Figure 6.2 Alternative stand configurations.

Low Stands
When you need a light placed low, a mini-baby (22–50 in.) or preemie (31–70 in.) stand comes in handy. Table 6.1 lists the basement and top floor for many common stands.

Junior Stands
Combo
The junior combo stand is so named because it was designed to handle both lighting units and reflector boards. Larger fixtures, Studio 2k and larger, have a $1\frac{1}{8}$-in. junior pin. A typical two-riser combo has a maximum height of 11 ft. A three-riser combo has a maximum height of 14 ft. Figure 6.3 illustrates the junior stand and some common stand accessories: the baby pop-up pin, the angled drop-down offset, and the baby pin adapter.

Low Boy
The minimum height of a typical combo stand is 48 in. If the light must be lower than that, you need a low-boy junior stand, which has a minimum height of around 33 in. If you need to mount a light lower than 33 in., you have to under-hang the light from an offset or use a turtle stand or T-bone.

Table 6.1   Stands

Name	Type	Risers	Minimum Height	Maximum Height	RM Leg	Brand
Low Baby Stands						
Low blade stand	Al	2	15¼"	38⅞"		Mole
Mini preemie	St	2	20"	39"		Matthews
Preemie baby	Al	2	31"	5' 10"		Matthews
Mini baby	St/Al	2	22"	50"	X	American
Low low baby	Al	2	20"	3' 3"		Norms
Low hefty baby	Al	2	33"	5' 7"		Norms
Baby Stands						
Steel maxi	St	3	34"	10'		Matthews
Beefy baby standard	Al	2	37"	8' 3"		Matthews
Beefy baby, 3-riser	Al	3	45"	12'	X	Matthews
Baby, 2-riser	St/Al	2	40"	9' 4"	X	American
Baby, 3-riser	St/Al	3	44"	12' 5"	X	American
Baby light, 2-riser	Al	2	44"	9' 4"		Norms
Baby light, 2-riser	St	2	52"	10' 6"		Norms
Hefty baby, 2-riser	Al	2	47"	9' 10"	X	Norms
Hefty baby, 3-riser	Al	3	50"	12' 10"	X	Norms
Low Junior Stands						
Runway base only		0	11"	11"		Matthews
Low boy	St	2	33"	6' 9"	X	Matthews
Low boy	Al	2	37"	6' 9"	X	Matthews
Low combo, 1-riser	St	1	29"	4' 0"	X	American
Low combo, 2-riser	St	2	32"	5' 6"	X	American
Low combo, 2-riser	St	2	33"	5' 7"	X	American
Low boy		2	36"	5' 8"	X	Norms
Rolling folding stand	St	1	22¼"	32"		Mole
Junior Stands						
Combo	St	2	48"	11"	X	Matthews
Sky high	St	3	52"	14'	X	Matthews
Mombo combo	St	4	76"	27'	X	Matthews
Light duty combo	St	2	48"	10' 5"	X	American
Heavy duty, 2-riser	St	2	50"	11' 3"	X	American
Heavy duty, 3-riser	St	3	51"	14' 3"	X	American
Alum combo, 2-riser	St/Al	2	48"	10' 3"	X	American
Alum combo, 3-riser	St/Al	3	51"	13' 9"	X	American
Mombo combo	St	4	5' 8"	23' 5"	X	American

Table 6.1 Stands (continued)

Name	Type	Risers	Minimum Height	Maximum Height	RM Leg	Brand
Standard		2	54"	11' 2"	X	Norms
Sky high		3	58"	13'	X	Norms
Sky high	Al	3	61"	13'	X	Norms

Notes: RM leg stands for Rocky Mountain leg.
St/Al means the stand has steel legs and aluminum risers.

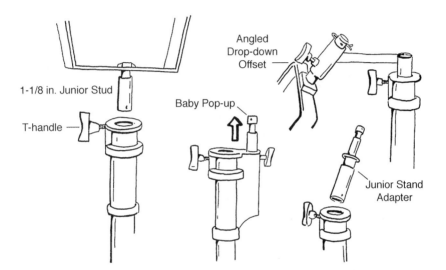

Figure 6.3 The 1⅛-in. junior pin fits into the receptacle on the stand. The T-handle should engage the indented part of the pin. Some stands have a baby pop-up, which allows the junior stand to support either a baby or a junior fixture. An angled drop-down offset allows a light or reflector to hang lower than the lowest height of the stand. The 45° angle holds the light away from the stand. In the absence of a baby pop-up, a junior stand adapter can be used.

T-Bones and Turtle Stands

A T-bone is simply a metal T fitted with a junior receiver (Figure 6.4). A T-bone can be nailed or screwed into place (typically in green beds or on parallels). It sits flat on the floor, providing a low position for larger lights. A turtle stand is nothing more than three legs joined in the center to a junior receiver. Matthews's C+ stand has removable legs, which serve as a turtle stand. The riser section of the C+ stand can be used as a stand extension. Matthews and other manufacturers also make wheeled turtle stands. Matthews calls theirs a *runway stand*.

Mombo Combo

A mombo combo is a very substantial, four-riser, steel stand with a very wide base (no wheels), which allows a maximum height of more than 26 ft.

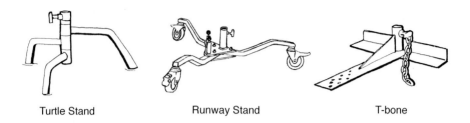

Turtle Stand   Runway Stand   T-bone

Figure 6.4 Three ways to place a light near the ground. A T-bone can be nailed or screwed into place in green beds or on parallels.

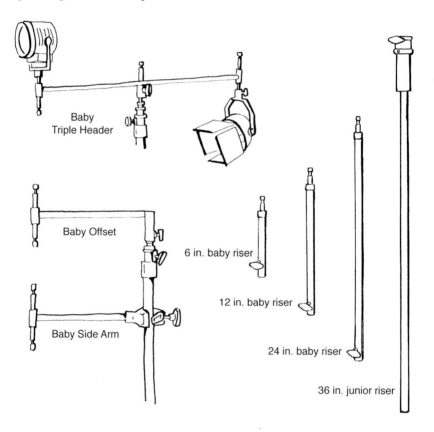

Baby
Triple Header

Baby Offset

6 in. baby riser

12 in. baby riser

Baby Side Arm

24 in. baby riser

36 in. junior riser

Figure 6.5 Offsets, side arms, double headers, and triple headers are available in baby and junior sizes (babies are shown here).

Offsets, Side Arms, Extensions, and Right Angles

Offsets

Figure 6.5 shows various types of baby offsets that can be used to locate the head out from the stand. They are useful when some obstruction, such as furniture or a set piece, prevents the stand from being placed under the light. Note that an offset or side arm puts the stand off its center of balance. Use sandbags on the legs as counterweights.

Risers

Risers come in many sizes; typical sizes would be 6, 12, 18, and 24 in. A riser is a handy piece of hardware when a light mounted to a plate or clamp is not quite high enough. A 36-in. junior stand extension essentially adds an additional riser to a stand. It can also be inserted into the receiver on the dolly or the crane when a light is to ride with the camera.

Using Stands

- See Chapter 2, Checklist 2.3, for check-out procedure for stands.
- Remember, "Righty tighty, lefty loosey." Lock-off knobs (T-handles) tighten when turned to the right (clockwise) and loosen when turned to the left.
- Extend the top riser first. If you extend the second riser first, you will raise the first riser out of your reach and look like a bonehead. However, if the light is heavy for the stand, you can add strength to the stand by not using the first riser or using only part of it.
- Bag any raised stand. A good rule of thumb is one sandbag per riser. If the light is extended all the way up on a three-riser stand, you would use three bags. Place the sandbags on the legs so that the weight rests on the stand, not on the floor.
- Get help when needed. As a rule, use two people to head up any light 5k or larger. Depending on the height of the stand and the awkwardness of its position, heading-up a 12k or Dino can require three or four people. Don't hesitate to round up the other electricians and grips when you need them. It is poor judgment to underestimate your needs. A heavy light can get away from you and cause injury and damage. Moreover, handling large lights alone tires you out before the day is over and, in a short time, is likely to lead to back and knee problems. I know too many people in their middle and late thirties who have done permanent damage by abusing themselves when they were younger. Lifting equipment is not a contest; the lighting crew works as a team.

Crank-up and Motorized Stands

Crank-up stands provide a mechanical advantage needed for raising heavy lights. Table 6.2 gives the weights and weight capacities of crank-up and motorized stands. They have a chain-, cable-, or screw-driven telescoping extension system with a crank and clutch, so that the crank does not reverse and spin out of control under weight. Do not crank up a stand without some kind of weight on it, as this can cause problems in the inner mechanisms.

The Cine-Vator, Molevator, and similar motorized stands power the telescoping mechanism with an electrical motor that is operated by a single up/down toggle

Table 6.2   Weight Capacities of Crank-up and Motorized Stands

	Floor	Ceiling	Capacity	Type
American				
Roadrunner 220	4' 2"	11' 3"	220 lb (100 kg)	Crank
Big Fresnel lamp stand (BFL)	4' 2"	12' 6"	300 lb (136 kg)	Motor
Arri				
Baby 2-section Supercrank	3' 2" (97 cm)	5' 5" (165 cm)	220 lbs (100 kg)	Crank
Short-base 3-section Supercrank	4' 8" (153 cm)	11' 3" (345 cm)	154 lbs (70 kg)	Crank
2-section Supercrank	4' 10" (147 cm)	7' 7" (232 cm)	198 lbs (90 kg)	Crank
3-section Supercrank	5' 5" (165 cm)	11' 5" (348 cm)	176 lbs (80 kg)	Crank
4-section Supercrank	5' 11" (182 cm)	15' 7" (477 cm)	154 lbs (70 kg)	Crank
5-section Supercrank	7' 9" (237 cm)	20' 4" (620 cm)	154 lb (70 kg)	Crank
Matthews				
Lite Lift	4' 1"	8' 6"	85 lb (38 kg)	Crank
Crank-O-Vator	4' 11"	12'	150 lb (68 kg)	Crank
Low Boy Crank-O-Vator	3' 2"	5' 5"	150 lb (68 kg)	Crank
Super Crank	5' 9"	12' 6"	200 lb (90 kg)	Crank
Cine-Vator	4' 6"	12'	300 lb (136 kg)	Motor
Mole-Richardson				
Folding Crank-up Litewate Stand	4' 5"	10'	—	Crank
Molevator	5' 1"	11' 1"	250 lb (113 kg)	Motor

switch (Figure 6.6). These stands can handle the heaviest lights made (up to 300 lb). The motor is usually 115-V AC (at about 6 A) but can be 115-V DC, 220-V AC, or 220-V DC.

- When rolling a large light on a crank stand or motorized stand, push the stand from the back with the swivel locks *unlocked* on the two rear tires and the front tire *locked*. Steer by pushing the back wheels left or right. This way you are less likely to catch in a rut and tip over the whole stand.
- When the stand is in place, prevent the stand from rolling by swiveling each wheel straight out from the stand and locking each swivel. Additionally, wedges in the tires and cup blocks under the tires prevent them from turning (grip department).
- Before raising the stand, make sure it is totally leveled with cup blocks, wedges, and apple boxes, if necessary (grip department).
- Use your strong arm to turn the crank to raise and lower the light. Never release the clutch without having a good grip on the crank. A properly adjusted crank should not spin when the clutch is released. However, they often do. If the crank gets away from you, there is a good chance you will not be able to

Figure 6.6 A Cine-Vator stand. (Photo courtesy Matthews Studio Equipment, Burbank, CA.)

get hold of it again before the lamp hits you in the head. There is also a good chance you'll hurt yourself trying to grab hold of the spinning crank. If you lose control, let go of the clutch and get out of the way of the light.

Grip Stands

For the most part, the grip stands are used for flying overhead sets and setting flags, nets, diffusion frames, and so on. However, in special situations, they are needed as light stands.

C-Stands

Q: How do you drive an electrician crazy?
A: Lock him in a small room with a C-stand.

The Century stand is a versatile, all-purpose, rigging gadget that is the centerpiece of the grip's equipment. Its components are like the parts of an erector set, and setting C-stands is a little-appreciated art form. Given enough time and enough C-stands, a grip could build a scale model of the Eiffel Tower. When a C-stand is used as a light stand, however, it becomes the electrician's responsibility (Figures 6.7 and 6.8).

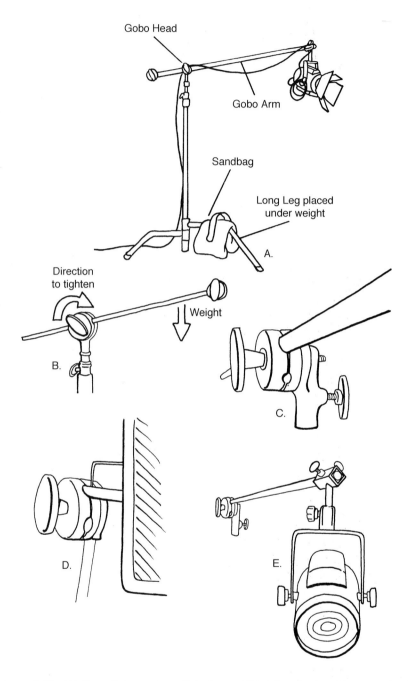

Figure 6.7 (A) C-stand supporting a light fixture. (B) Orient the knuckle so that gravity tightens it ("righty tighty"). (C, D) The grip head accepts various sizes: a ⅝-in. hole for the gobo arm or a baby pin; a ⅜-, ½-, or ¼-in. hole for nets and flags. (E) The light fixture shown uses a bar clamp adaptor (used on furniture clamps) to attach to the gobo arm.

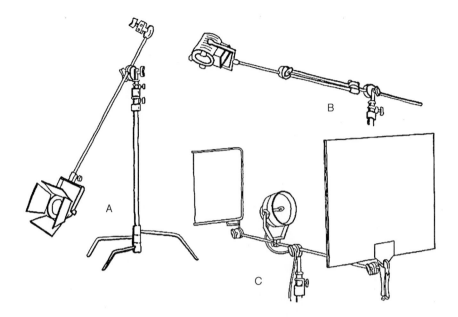

Figure 6.8 Some special uses for C-stands: (A) to place the light in a low position; (B) to arm the light out over the action (here, two gobo arms a coupled together); (C) a bounce card rig like this uses a single stand to support the light, bounce card, and a net.

Knowing the proper technique will save you much embarrassment; grips like nothing better than to heckle an electrician who is making a mess of a job with a C-stand.

- Place the longest leg under the extended arm. This helps stabilize the stand. Always sandbag the legs when putting weight on an extended arm (Figure 6.7).
- Work with gravity, not against it. When you are standing behind the stand with the arm pointing away from you, the knuckles should be on your right. In this way, when weight is put on the arm, gravity pulls the grip head clockwise, which tightens it. If the knuckle is on the left, the weight will eventually loosen the knuckle, and the whole rig will collapse (very bad form).
- Avoid configurations in which the back end of the arm sticks out, especially at eye level; it could hurt someone. There is almost always an alternative configuration that eliminates the hazard. If it's unavoidable, place a tennis ball or styrofoam cup on the end of the arm so people will see it.
- Place the sandbag on the top leg so that the weight is on the leg and not resting on the ground.
- Always place the C-stand on the "off-camera side" of the light—the outside, as viewed from the camera. This helps keep grip equipment out of the movie.
- When a lot of torque is placed in the gobo head, configure the stand so that the flag rests on the T-handle (Figure 6.9). Do not rely on the strength of the grip head alone. I've strayed into the domain of gripology here, but what the heck, I'm on a roll.

Figure 6.9 Large cutters can be supported by the knuckle on the C-stand.

- Take wind into account. When setting 4-by frames or flags in a wind, use a larger stand with a wide base, such as a combo stand. A C-stand does not handle big flags or frames well in any kind of wind.

Medium, Hi, and Hi-Hi Rollers

A medium roller stand is slightly taller than a junior combo, about 14 ft maximum, and has wheels, which makes it easy to move around. The wheels have brakes that should be locked once the stand is placed. In addition to a junior receiver, roller stands typically provide a 4-in. grip head for mounting overhead frames, large flags, and other grip gear. A hi-hi roller is especially useful when height is required; it has a maximum height of 20 ft.

Booms

Boom poles allow a fixture to be cantilevered over or behind the actors in places where it could not be mounted by other means. Booms vary in size and strength. The small ones mount on a baby stand and provide about a 4-ft arm with almost as much counterweight length. The larger ones mount on a junior stand, have more length and more counterweight, and provide either a junior or a baby mount for the light. Sandbags can be added for additional counterweight.

Stand Maintenance

Modern stands are made of stainless steel and aluminum. Stainless steel stands are extremely weather resistant. A well-made stand will not rust or corrode. When stands get muddy, they should be cleaned so that dirt does not get inside, between the risers. Wipe each riser down with a rag or towel. If a riser starts to bind, lubricate it with silicone spray.

Occasionally the Allen screws that secure the bonnet castings and the riser castings to the tube parts of a stand get loose and the castings come off. It is a simple matter to push the castings back into place and tighten down the Allen screws. Be sure to keep the castings tight. If the casting comes off while you are raising a light, the riser will separate from the stand and you'll wind up balancing the light on a pole like an acrobat with tea cups.

Rigging Hardware

Baby and Junior Nail-on Plates

A nail-on plate, also called a *wall plate* or *pigeon plate* (Figure 6.10), mounts to a surface with screws. Use a cordless electric drill with a Phillips bit and wood or drywall screws. The plate can be mounted to a horizontal surface, a wall, or a

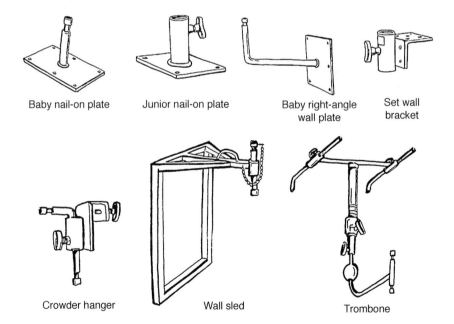

Baby nail-on plate   Junior nail-on plate   Baby right-angle wall plate   Set wall bracket

Crowder hanger   Wall sled   Trombone

Figure 6.10   Plates and hangers for set walls.

ceiling, but be sure you are screwing into something solid. If you are screwing into a set wall (usually $\frac{1}{4}$-in. plywood), place a piece of cribbing on the other side of the wall to give the screws something to hold to.

The grips usually prepare several apple boxes with nail-on plates. When mounted on an apple box, a nail-on plate provides a stable lighting position that is handy for setting a light on the floor or on a counter top.

Set Wall Mounts

Figure 6.10 shows a variety of set wall mounts.

Set Wall Bracket

A set wall bracket is a right-angle plate that mounts to any right-angle corner, such as the top of a flat.

Crowder Hanger

A crowder hanger fits over the top of a door or on a 2 × 4-in. beam. It can be used with a baby adapter that provides two mounting positions, one above and one below the hanger.

Edge Plate Bracket

An edge plate bracket is similar to a crowder hanger. It is used to mount lights to the side edge of a green bed.

Wall Sled

A wall sled is suspended on rope from the top of a set wall. The weight of the light holds the sled in position against the wall without screws or tape. Wall sleds are made with either a junior or a baby mount.

Trombone

Like the crowder hanger, a trombone also fits over the top of the set, but it is adjustable to any width of wall. It provides an adjustable drop-down position for the light. Use a rubber ball on the telescoping arm to prevent it from scraping the wall. A trombone can have either a junior or a baby mount.

Clamps

C-Clamp

C-clamps (Figure 6.11) come in various sizes: 4, 6, 8, and 12 in. Each one has two baby pins or a $1\frac{1}{8}$-in. junior receiver welded to it. The feet are either round and flat or squared off. The squared metal clamps are designed for mounting to pipes.

With any of the clamps shown, to prevent puncturing or marring the beam and to increase the surface area of the clamp, insert two pieces of 1 × 3 in. cribbing between the clamp and the surface. Wrap the cribbing in duvetyn when it is important not to scratch the finish.

A common problem when mounting lights to a C-clamp on top of the set wall is that the light cannot be tilted down far enough. Use the angled pin on a C-clamp to get around this problem.

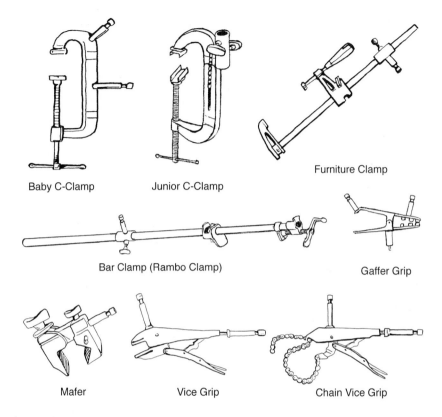

Baby C-Clamp   Junior C-Clamp   Furniture Clamp

Bar Clamp (Rambo Clamp)   Gaffer Grip

Mafer   Vice Grip   Chain Vice Grip

Figure 6.11 Clamps.

Furniture Clamp and Bar Clamp

Furniture clamps and bar clamps are normally used by woodworkers to clamp workpieces together during glue-up. Furniture clamps come in various sizes (6, 12, 18, 24, and 36 in.); standard bar clamps are 48 in. (but can be any length), all of which are adjustable. Furniture clamps are typically used to undersling lights from ceiling beams or square pillars that are too wide for a C-clamp. As with C-clamps, use cribbing to increase the surface area of the clamp and to protect the surface to which you attach the clamp.

Gaffer Grip

A gaffer, or gator, grip is a spring clamp with rubber teeth. It is used to mount smaller lights to doors, pipes, and furniture.

Mafer

A mafer (pronounced *may fer*) is a very strong, versatile mount, a favorite clamp-type mount. A cammed screw mechanism closes and opens the rubber-lined jaws. It can attach to any round surface from $\frac{5}{8}$–2 in. in diameter and any flat surface from $\frac{1}{16}$–1 in. thick. The baby pin snaps into place with a spring-loaded lock.

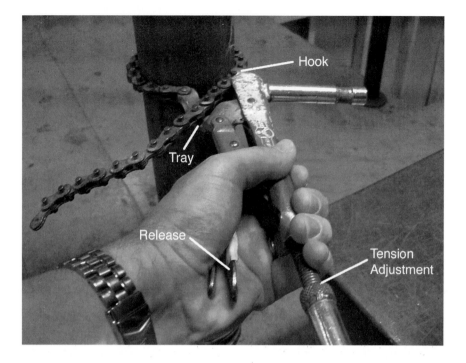

Figure 6.12 Face the tray up, toward you. Wrap the chain around the post and into the tray. Engage the chain's pins into hooks and squeeze the vice handles until they snap closed. To loosen or tighten the tension, turn the knurled knob before closing. Wrap tape around the handles to ensure the vice does not open if it gets accidentally bumped. To release, remove the tape and pull the release lever.

The removable pin can be exchanged for accessories, such as a flex arm, a double-header offset arm, or a right-angle baby pin.

Vice Grip

The adjustable width of a vice grip provides a strong grip. As with any vice grip, the clamp is released by pressing the unlocking handle.

Chain Vice Grips and "Candlesticks"

Figure 6.12 shows a correctly threaded chain vice grip. A chain vice grip provides a very solid mount to any pipe up to 6 in. in diameter. It is used to mount a light to a standing pipe or pillar. Using a chain vice grip is preferable to using a clamp in this application because a clamp can crush a pipe, while a chain vice grip applies force more evenly around the diameter of the pipe. Chain vice grips are often used to secure a "candlestick" to a standing post. A candlestick is nothing more than a heavy metal tube, one end of which is sized to receive a junior pin. It is like a junior riser but is stronger because it does not have a cast aluminum receiver. (When heavy lights are rigged to an aerial lift, for example, a great deal of sideways force may be exerted on the receiver when the aerial lift stops and starts. A normal

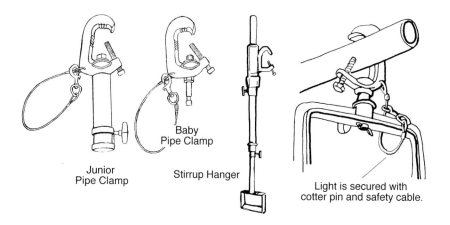

Junior Pipe Clamp

Baby Pipe Clamp

Stirrup Hanger

Light is secured with cotter pin and safety cable.

Figure 6.13 Pipe clamps.

junior receiver casting can crack open under such stresses.) To make sure that the vice grip does not open, always wrap tape around the handle after the chain vice grip is in place.

Be very careful if you are considering mounting small lights to plumbing pipe on location. Although it may look sturdy, old cast iron pipes can be paper thin, corroded on the inside after years of use. In any case, do *not* use a pipe clamp or C-clamp, use a chain vice grip, as you stand a better chance of not rupturing the pipe. *Never* mount lights to fire sprinkler system pipes. It is against fire codes and a bad idea. If you rupture the pipe, it can flood the set.

Grids and Green Beds

Pipe Clamp

Pipe clamps (Figure 6.13) are used when hanging lights from an overhead pipe or grid. Pipe clamps come with a safety pin attached to the clamp with a safety chain. The cotter pin prevents the receiver from slipping off the pin. Always use the safety pins when hanging lights.

Telescoping Stirrup Hanger

To get a light lower than the height of the grid, use a telescoping hanger to lower it to the desired height. Hangers have a stirrup to which you attach a pipe clamp. They are also made with a baby pin or junior receiver instead of a stirrup.

Greens and Bazookas

In most studio sound stages, wooden catwalks called *greens* or *decks* are suspended above the set to provide lighting positions. Along the edge of the greens, at 18-in. intervals, are holes onto which a junior pin fits. A light may be inserted directly into this receiver or a *bazooka* can be inserted into the hole. A bazooka is like a one-riser stand with no legs. An L-shaped bracket fits over the catwalk's hand rail to support it.

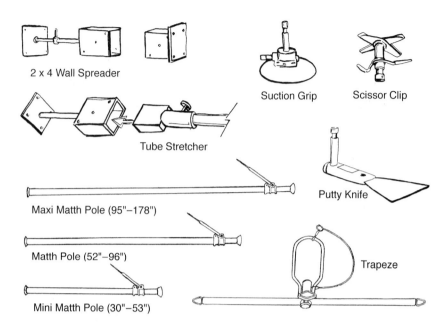

Figure 6.14 Location (and stage) rigging equipment.

Location Rigging Hardware

Wall Spreader and Tube Stretcher

Wall spreaders (Figure 6.14) support lights by exerting pressure against two opposite walls or the floor and ceiling. A 2 × 4-in. or 2 × 6-in. piece of lumber creates the span. The hardware mounts to either end of the lumber and uses a threaded post to apply pressure against the walls. Lumber must be cut to fit the particular span needed.

A wall spreader can create a secure overhead beam of up to about 16 ft from which lighting fixtures can be hung. With a long span, be sure the hardware is aligned with wall studs and screw the wall spreaders to the wall. A *tube stretcher* essentially adapts a wall spreader for use with speed-rail pipe instead of lumber.

Matth Pole

A matth pole, or pole cat, is a smaller, lighter-duty version of a wall spreader, especially useful in doorways or narrow halls or used vertically between floor and ceiling. A Matth pole can support lightweight fixtures and grip equipment.

Suction Grip

Suction grips of 4 or 6 in. can be used to affix small lighting units to nonporous surfaces, such as a window or car hood. These grips generally use a cam to create the suction; they are not as strong as the larger, pump-type grips. Suction grips come with baby pins only and should be limited to use with smaller lights.

Scissor Clip

A scissor clip is used to mount a light to the metal supports of a dropped ceiling. The scissor closes over the metal strips that support the ceiling tile. It is tightened in place by turning the $\frac{5}{8}$-in. pin. Cables can be dressed above the ceiling or clipped to the metal strips with small grip clips.

Putty Knife

A putty knife can be wedged in a windowsill or door frame. It provides a baby pin for a small light fixture.

Trapeze

A trapeze is used to dead hang a light of any size from a rope. It provides a junior receiver. Eyelets at each end of the trapeze are provided for guy wires, which aim the light and hold it in place once in position.

CHAPTER 7

Lighting Objectives and Methods

We've talked a lot about equipment. Let's put hardware aside for the moment and discuss the bigger question of what we want to accomplish with lighting and how we go about it. What considerations do the director of photography and gaffer keep in mind when making lighting decisions? To begin, we look at the objectives in lighting a scene. Next, we make a foray into some of the technical considerations the DP and gaffer are concerned with, including taking and interpreting light meter readings, using and controlling contrast. We discuss the zone system and how it helps to understand the placement of light and dark values. We also consider what factors affect the working lighting levels for a given scene.

With these questions out of the way, we examine the conceptual basis the DP and gaffer use to generate ideas and devise schemes for lighting each scene. Finally, we look at lighting method: the critical matter of light placement, lighting actors' faces, and lighting a scene.

Lighting Objectives

What do we think about as we face an unlit set, before we can name and place the particular lights we will use? Take a moment to consider the overall objectives of lighting.

Visibility (or Selective Visibility)

A film without sound is a silent movie. A film without light is radio. Obviously, you must have light to expose the film. Exposure and contrast are two essential elements of selective visibility in cinematography. Much of the artistry of cinematography is in the control of lightness and darkness throughout the film's latitude, selectively exposing objects and characters to appear bright and glowing, slightly shaded, darkly shaded, barely visible, or completely lost in darkness, as desired.

Equally important is the direction of light. One of our first concerns is how to light the actor's face. What angle of light shall we use to reveal the face? How much of the face do we wish to reveal? Where will the actor stand? Which way will he or she face?

Naturalism

Lighting helps set the scene: It locates the scene in time and space. The quality and direction of the light and the sources it implies are part of what makes a scene convincing. Often unconsciously, we recognize lighting that portrays time, season, place, and weather conditions. The lighting is evocative of the way the air feels and smells, whether it is musty or clear, cool or hot, humid or dry.

In lighting a scene, the DP strives to evoke as much about the place and time as he or she can imagine. The crew won't necessarily shoot a given scene at the time specified in the script. In fact, day scenes are often shot at night and night scenes during the day. To create natural-looking lighting and keep things consistent, one must control the existing light sources and utilize or invent techniques to re-create realistic, natural lighting using artificial sources.

The opposite of natural lighting is lighting that *gives away* the artificial setting to the audience: when multiple shadows are cast on the walls and floor by an actor, when a lamp or wall sconce casts its own shadow, when you can trace the diverging rays of light back to a lamp outside a window, when "direct sunlight" comes into a room at different angles at each window.

Composition

Lighting is used as a means of emphasis and delineation. It helps separate the layers of the three-dimensional world on a flat, two-dimensional screen. It can also create purely graphic effects that contribute to the design of the composition.

Emphasis

In some situations, the DP needs to selectively emphasize characters or elements, letting the lighting direct the eye within the frame. For example, imagine a wide shot looking down over the congregation in a large church. The shot immediately conveys the grandeur of the ceremony, but without further help, our eye wanders without a focus. An increased light level surrounding the figures at the front of the church draws the eye to our hero and heroine making their vows at the altar. The light falls off a little on peripheral figures.

Separation

When the three-dimensional world is telescoped onto a piece of celluloid and projected onto a flat screen, our natural stereoscopic ability to detect depth is lost. The cinematographer can reemphasize depth in the image by accentuating the outlines of characters and objects, contrasting the brightness and color of the different layers, and moving the camera, which reveals depth with the relative motion of different planes.

A common problem is that, when foreground and background share the same value, they blend together. Suppose we are shooting a courtroom drama. The district attorney (DA) has dark hair and is wearing a dark blue suit. The courtroom is paneled in dark wood, and the reporters and onlookers in the audience are wearing dark gray and black suits. The DA's dark hair will blend into her dark surroundings, making it hard to say just where her head stops and everything else starts.

The cinematographer may choose to remedy this with a strong backlight that creates a rim around her hair and shoulders, to separate her from the background. The amount of backlight needed depends on the reflectance of the subject and how pronounced an effect is desired. Suppose the public defender is dapper, blond, and sporting a cream linen jacket. He will require little or no backlight to separate him from the dark background, but a small amount of backlight might be used if the DP wants to glamorize the character with highlights in his hair. If we were to measure the intensity of the backlight, the light might be one stop under the key light. The dark hair of the DA will absorb light like a sponge, so her backlight would be set one or two stops over the key light.

There was a time in movie history when a bright glamorous backlight was an accepted convention. Today, audiences tend to recognize it as artificial. Strong backlight can still look natural if it is well motivated; otherwise, it has to be subtle. Perhaps the DA's kicker could be motivated by a shaft of sunlight. A bright window in the background of the shot often helps in this type of situation; it provides a sense of source.

Backlight is not the only way to create separation. The cinematographer might choose to separate the foreground, middle ground, and background simply by lighting them to contrasting levels of brightness. The dark-haired DA could be separated by lightening the background behind her. A DP who does not want to lose the sense of solemn darkness in the audience might choose to throw a shaft of sunlight across just one or two rows of the dark suits. The gaffer places the shaft so that it lines up behind the DA in a pleasing composition. A light dose of smoke in the air gives substance to the translucent shaft of light, leaving the audience in atmospheric dimness behind it. The DA's dark hair stands against lighter values, nicely separated and defined.

Depth

Another important compositional element is depth. A composition that includes surfaces at various distances receding into the distance increases the shot's sense of perspective and scale. If the shot includes some sense of space beyond the plane of the facing wall, outside a window or through an open doorway into other rooms, the gaffer can create planes of light and dark that recede deep into the picture. Depth offers nice opportunities for interesting lighting and composition.

Graphic Effect

A DP often wants light that simply creates graphic shapes or lines that enhance or distort shapes in the scenery. This could be done by throwing a diagonal slash across the background, a pattern of moving foliage, a window frame, a venetian blind, or using objects in the set dressing to create irregular shadows.

Lighting a textured surface at an oblique angle emphasizes the texture of the surface. The wall of a corrugated metal building appears as a pattern of vertical lines, a brick wall becomes a pattern of regular rectangles. Breaking up the background with textured light goes a long way toward creating an exciting image from one that would otherwise be dull.

Time Constraints

One final objective that has been conveniently ignored up until now is working within the time frame permitted by the production schedule. In an ideal world, the DP can devote planning and attention to all the objectives previously discussed. In real life, however, speed often becomes the top priority, and the lighting has to be designed accordingly. There is little time to contemplate stylistic concerns; it is simply a matter of getting the scene lit fast and making it look as good as possible. The lighting crew spends all its energy trying to get out of the fire and back into the frying pan.

The speed of the lighting depends a great deal on the complexity of the DP's approach. One cinematographer might light a scene beautifully with a single soft source. Another might have a very detailed, painstaking approach, using dozens of fixtures and lighting practically every person and every object on the set individually, which takes much more preparation time.

Speed also depends on the gaffer's and best boy's planning and the flexibility of the rigging. With thoughtful planning and some prerigging time, the time spent on lighting during shooting can be quite minimal and yet the lighting complex. Without proper planning and a flexible rigging design, much time is wasted (rerouting cable, rigging and hanging new lights, and so on), stress is higher, more effort is expended, and the lighting can become rushed and sloppy.

Light Level, Exposure, Contrast, and Metering

An incident light reading can be expressed one of two ways, in foot-candles (FC) or f-stops. Thinking in foot-candles has advantages when working with the lights, but ultimately, the f-stop is set on the camera, and most DPs think of their exposure range in terms of f-stops.

Foot-Candles

A light reading expressed in foot-candles is an absolute measurement of light level. A light reading expressed in f-stops depends on additional variables (the film speed, shutter angle, frame rate, filtration, etc.). A light meter, such as the digital Spectra Professional IV (Figure 7.1), can tell you the intensity of light in foot-candles (Figure 7.2 shows the foot-candle scale). This meter also gives the reading as a working f-stop, taking into account the film ISO and shutter speed.

The advantage of working in foot-candles rather than f-stops is that a gaffer very quickly learns how many foot-candles to expect from a given light at a given

Figure 7.1 Spectra Professional IV digital/analog light meter. This meter reads incident light directly in f-stops and photographic illuminance in foot-candles or lux, with a range from 0.1 to 70,000 FC. (Courtesy of Spectra Cine, Inc., Burbank, CA.)

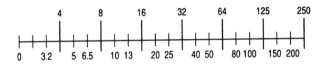

Figure 7.2 Actual numerical increments between standard foot-candle readings.

distance (Table 7.1 lists some approximate data. Table B.3 [Appendix B] is a more comprehensive list). If lighting to a given FC level, the gaffer will always call for the right light for the job. F-stops, on the other hand, do not correspond directly with light level. It is not as straightforward to know what light fixture will give a particular f-stop.

F-Stops

F-stop settings are inscribed on the aperture ring of the lens of the camera by the manufacturer in standard increments: 1, 1.4, 2, 2.8, 4, 5.6, 8, 11, 16, and 22. Figure 7.3 shows the entire range of f-stops and the increments between f-stops. The lower the f-stop, the larger the aperture and the more light passes through the lens. The range of f-stop on a given lens depends on its design. A lens designed for speed might open up to f-1. An extreme telephoto lens might only open up to f-5.6.

A light meter gives the f-stop by taking into account the film speed and exposure time. (For normal filming at a crystal sync speed of 24 fps and with a standard 180° shutter, the exposure time is $^1/_{48}$th of a second.) Many meters (e.g., Minolta) read out only in f-stops.

Table 7.1 Relative Strengths of Various Sources

Source	FC Spot	FC Flood
Direct sunlight		6400–8000
Skylight on an overcast day		450–1800
Brute arc at 30'	9000	1190
12k HMI at 30'	8250	500
9-lite PAR 64 at 30'	NS lens 3600	WF lens 450
2500 HMI PAR at 30'	NS lens 2880	WF lens 247
4000 HMI Fresnel at 30'	2305	247
10k at 30'	2465	460
5k baby senior at 30'	655	110
PAR 64 at 30'	VNS lens 560	MF lens 150
2k junior at 20'	1000	130
1k baby at 20'	440	45
2k zip soft light at 10'		100
650 pepper at 10'	528	110
750 soft at 10'		30
200 mini at 10'	195	25
100 pepper at 10'	55	23

Figure 7.3 The actual numerical increments between f-stops.

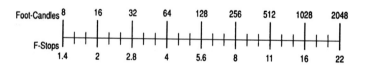

Figure 7.4 Comparison of foot-candles to f-stops with 320 ASA film.

The f-stop scale in Figure 7.4 shows how foot-candles compare with f-stops for 320 ISO film. As you can see, the foot-candles double with each f-stop.

Each incremental f-stop cuts the light by a half: f/4 lets half as much light through as f/2.8, so it takes twice as many foot-candles at f/4 (64 FC) to get the same exposure as at f/2.8 (32 FC). Table 7.2 correlates f-stop to foot-candle level for all film speeds.

Table 7.2 F-Stop vs. Foot-Candles for Various Film Speeds

ASA	f/1.4	f/2	f/2.8	f/4	f/5.6	f/8	f/11
25	100	200	400	800	1600	3200	6400
50	50	100	200	400	800	1600	3200
64	40	80	160	320	640	1250	2500
100	25	50	100	200	400	800	1600
125	20	40	80	160	320	640	1250
160	16	32	64	125	250	500	1000
200	13	25	50	100	200	400	800
320	8	16	32	64	125	250	500
400	6.4	13	25	50	100	200	400
500	5	10	20	40	80	160	320

Notes:

Incident light in foot-candles.

Frame Rate: 24 fps.

Exposure time: $^1/_{50}$ second (180° shutter opening).

Taking Readings with an Incident Light Meter

Incident light meters measure the amount of light falling on the face of the light meter. A *hemispherical light collector*, or *photosphere* (commonly known as the *ball*), collects light from the sides, top, and bottom as well as the front. The reading is taken by holding the meter up in the position of the subject. When the ball faces the camera, the meter gives an average reading of the total amount of light falling on the subject as viewed from the camera.

Alternatively, by pointing the ball at the light source, you can read the amount of light from that source. However, keep in mind that, when light hits the subject from the side or back, relative to the camera, less light is reflected toward the camera than when that light hits the subject from the front. Making allowance for this, the reading of a side-light can be accurately taken by turning the meter, splitting the angle toward camera.

When reading the output of individual lights, some cinematographers replace the hemispherical collector with a flat disk collector. The flat disk reads only light coming from the front. The disk is also used when photographing flat artwork, such as a painting or front-lit titles.

When taking a reading, use your free hand to shade unwanted light off the photosphere. If you were reading the intensity of frontal lights, you would shade off any light coming from high backlights. The facial tones are not affected by the light hitting the back of the hair and shoulders, and if you do not shade the meter from the backlights, the reading will be incorrect. Back light would be measured separately.

You can get an impression of the relative strengths of various lights, key and fill, for example, by shading the photosphere from one source, usually the key, and noting the change in the reading. You would use this technique to determine the *contrast ratio*.

A reading halfway between two numbers is called a *split*. For example, a 2.8/4 split would be halfway between f/2.8 and f/4. Increments between stops are also commonly expressed in thirds of a stop, so you might say "one third stop closed from a 4" to indicate that the aperture is one third of the way toward 5.6.

For even smaller increments, a DP might specify "4 and a quarter" (which means a quarter stop closed down from f/4). Going the other way, the DP would say "a quarter stop open from 4." An even smaller increment would be a "heavy 4" or a "light 4." A heavy 4 would be just over a 4, a light 4 would be just under a 4 (opened up from a 4). Establish common terminology with the people you work with and use clear language. Double-check if you are not sure what someone means.

Reading the light meter is only part of the determining the aperture that will be set on the lens. The DP can use underexposure and overexposure selectively to affect the amount of apparent grain in the image as well as the contrast and the amount of detail the film will retain at the extremes of the film's latitude. The DP gives the lab specific instructions on how to handle these manipulations of the negative so that exposure on the final print or transfer is correct.

F-Stops for the Electrician

When setting a light, an increase of one stop means doubling the light level. The gaffer might tell the electrician to "remove a double," "spot it in a double's worth," or "move the light in one stop closer." An experienced electrician can approximate this by eye.

Contrast, Latitude, and the Zone System

Contrast Ratios

The key light is angled so that the actor's face takes on a light side (the key side) and a shadow side (the fill side). The *contrast ratio* is the ratio of brightness of one side to the other. As a rule, the exposure is set for the key side (this is a rule a good DP almost always breaks; we get to that in a minute). The darkness of the fill side greatly influences the emotional tone of the image. The *fill light* typically comes from the direction of the camera and fills in the whole face. The *key light* hits selected parts of the face, favoring one side. Therefore, to determine the contrast ratio you compare the light on the key side, which is key plus fill, to the shadow side, which is fill alone:

key + fill : fill alone

If key plus fill reads 120 FC and fill alone reads 60 FC, the contrast ratio is 120:60, or 2:1. A 2:1 ratio has a one-stop difference between key plus fill and fill alone. A 2:1 ratio is relatively flat, a typical ratio for ordinary television productions. It provides modeling while remaining bright and void of noticeably strong shadows. With a two-stop difference, or 4:1 ratio, the fill side is distinctly darker and paints a more dramatic, chiaroscuro style. For most normal situations, the contrast ratio is kept somewhere between 2:1 and 4:1. A three-stop difference, or 9:1 ratio, puts the fill side in near darkness, just barely leaving detail in the shadow areas. A bright, sunny day typically has about a 9:1 ratio, requiring the addition of fill light to lower the contrast ratio.

Contrast Viewing Glasses

A contrast viewing glass is a dark-tinted (ND) glass that typically hangs around the gaffer's or DP's neck like a monocle. By viewing the scene through the glass, the gaffer can evaluate the relative values—highlights and shadow areas. The glass darkens the scene so that the highlights stand out clearly and shadow areas sink into exaggerated darkness. The glass helps evaluate if a particular highlight is too bright or a shadow too dark. On the other hand, if nothing stands out when viewed through the contrast glass, the scene has gotten too flat and monotonic; you might want to reduce the fill level, flag or net light off the backgrounds, and find places to add highlights. Contrast glasses are available in various strengths, which are meant to approximate the contrast characteristics of different film stocks. The glass becomes ineffective when it is held to the eye long enough for the eye to adjust to it. Encircle the glass with your hand so that your hand forms a lighttight seal around your eye. Use the rest of your hand to shade the contrast glass from flare. You can also evaluate contrast without the aid of a contrast glass in the old-fashioned way, by squinting.

Gaffers also frequently use a contrast glass to check the aim of the lights. By positioning herself on the actors' marks, a gaffer can center the aim of the light fixtures (without blinding herself) by viewing each light through the dark glass. Similarly, a contrast glass can be used to view the movement of clouds in front of the sun on days with intermittent cloud cover. A "gaffer's glass" or "welding glass" is an even thicker glass, which should be used if you are looking directly at the sun. Another way to check if clouds are about to move in front of the sun is to take off your sunglasses and view the sun's reflection in them.

The Zone System

The human eye can see detail in a much wider range of contrast than film emulsion. Although a person looking at a scene may see detail in every shadow and every highlight, on film, anything too dark or too bright relative to the chosen exposure starts to lose definition as it approaches the extremes of the film's latitude. Details disappear into obscurity, and objects become either more and more bleached out or increasingly lost in blackness.

It is helpful to think of the tones in a black-and-white picture. Between pure black and pure white lies a range of *values*, shades of gray that define the picture. The goal in choosing the exposure and illuminating the scene is to place those values so that they will be rendered on film as the cinematographer envisions them.

Ansel Adams, the American still photographer, invented the zone system as a tool for understanding how the values in a scene will be rendered on film. With the still film and printing process he was using, he could create 11 zones, as shown in Figure 7.5. Zone 0 is pure black and zone X is pure white. Each zone is one stop lighter than the last.

The range of brightness and darkness in which film emulsion can capture an image is known as its *latitude*. Each film emulsion has its own latitude characteristics

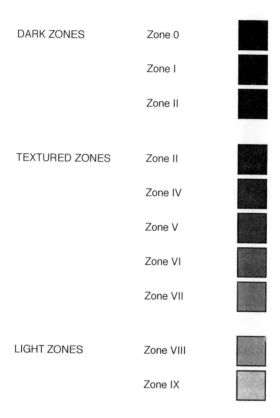

DARK ZONES	Zone 0	
	Zone I	
	Zone II	
TEXTURED ZONES	Zone II	
	Zone IV	
	Zone V	
	Zone VI	
	Zone VII	
LIGHT ZONES	Zone VIII	
	Zone IX	

Figure 7.5 The 11 values of the zone system. Zone X is pure white. It is not shown here. (From Chris Johnson, *The Practical Zone System: A Simple Guide to Photographic Control*, p. 31. Boston: Focal Press, 1986. Reproduced with permission of Focal Press.)

within this 10-stop range. Cinematographers must therefore be familiar with the response of different film stocks.

Zone V, middle gray, is a very important value for determining exposure. Middle gray is 18% reflective and commonly called *18% gray*. An incident light meter works by defining this midpoint in the latitude of the film. It gives an exposure reading that will make a middle-gray object appear middle gray on screen. When you define the exposure of middle gray, all the other values fall into place (to the extent of the film's latitude). On the outer edges of the exposure latitude, the image begins to lose detail and textured areas become less defined until, at the extremes of the scale, in zones I and IX, no detail is visible and, in zones 0 and X, only pure black and pure white are seen. Ansel Adams described the appearance of each zone on film something like this:

0: Total black. With a film stock that holds blacks well, the blacks on the edge of the frame merge with the black curtains surrounding the screen.

I: Threshold of tonality but with no texture.

II: First suggestion of texture. Deep shadows represent the darkest part of the frame that still shows some slight detail.

III: Average dark materials and low values, showing adequate texture.

IV: Average dark foliage, dark stone, or sun shadow. Normal shadow value for white skin in sunlight.

V: Middle gray (18% reflectance). Clear northern sky near sea level, dark skin, gray stone, average weathered wood.

VI: Average white skin value in sunlight or artificial light. Light stone, shadows on snow, and sunlit landscapes.

VII: Very light skin, light gray objects, average snow with acute side lighting.

VIII: Whites with texture and delicate values. Textured snow, highlights on white skin.

IX: White without texture, approaching pure white. Snow in flat sunlight.

X: Pure white. Spectral reflections, such as sun glints or a bare light bulb.

The way the cinematographer lights the set and sets the exposure determines the various values of the scene. Suppose that the exposure outside a room with windows is five stops brighter than inside the room. If the aperture is set for the interior exposure, all details in the exterior portion of the image will fall into zone X and be completely bleached out; the edges of the windows will likely get "blown out," with soft fringes around them. A compromise somewhere between the exterior and the interior exposures is not much better; the interior will still be very dark and muddy (zone III) and the exterior will be hot (zone VIII). The lighting must bring the outside and the inside exposures closer together.

To look natural, the exterior should be brighter than the interior, but by two or three stops, not by five. To close the gap, you could reduce the exterior exposure two stops by gelling the windows with 0.6 neutral-density gel; you could light the inside, bringing it up to a level that is two stops less than the outside exposure; or you could combine these techniques.

Previously, I said that, as a rule, the key side of the actor's face is set *at exposure*; in other words, you would take a light reading of the key side (key plus fill) and set that exposure on the lens. In reality, a much more expressive image is created by carefully placing the values of the face in response to the natural sources within the scene and the dramatic feeling of the scene. In fact, a creative cinematographer will tell you, as a rule, *never* place the key side at exposure. For example, overexposing the key side by one stop while underexposing the fill side by one and a half stops gives a greater sense of light entering a space (through a window for example). In another shot, the DP might underexpose the key side of the face by one stop and let the fill side fall into near darkness, three stops underexposed. The exposures on the actors faces are balanced to some extent by other values in the image. If the scene is largely underexposed but some bright sources are within the frame, there is a reference point for the viewer's eye. The values of backgrounds, practical lights, windows, and so on can be manipulated to place their relative intensity in the zone desired. A spot meter can be used to measure and compare reflective values, but with practice, one mostly balances levels by eye.

Negative film stocks tend to have greater latitude in overexposure than they do in underexposure. As a general rule, a neutral-gray object can be overexposed by as much as four stops and underexposed by up to about three stops before it becomes lost, either washed out or lost in dark shadow.

Reversal film stocks have the opposite response: They have greater latitude in underexposure and lose definition faster in overexposure. Reversal stocks tend to be more contrasty and have less latitude in general than negative stocks. Similarly, video cameras have narrow latitude: Typically, detail is well rendered only within a four- or five-stop range.

Spot Meters

A spot meter (Figure 7.6) is a reflected light meter with a very narrow field of acceptance (less than 2°). An incident meter reads the amount of light hitting the light meter, and a reflected meter reads the amount of light reflected back from the subject.

The reading depends on the reflectance of the object as well as the amount of light. From behind the camera, the DP or gaffer can sight through the meter and pick out any spot in the scene to measure, taking readings of various areas of the scene, to compare the exact values of face tones, highlights, and shadows.

Digital spot meters typically display readings in either f-stops or EV (exposure value) units. Some meters display readings only in EV units; the corresponding f-stop is found using the conversion dial on the meter. Table 7.3 shows how spot meter readings correspond to reflectance. The f-stops listed down the left side of the table

Figure 7.6 Sekonic L-608 Cine Super Zoom Master digital spot meter. A parallax-free zoom spotmeter (1°–4°) with a retractable incident lumisphere for incident light readings. Frame rates from 1 to 1000 fps can be set on the meter. Shutter angles from 5° to 270° and filter compensation can also be set on the meter. Reads in f-stops (f/0.5–f/45), foot-candles (0.12–180,000 FC), lux, Cd/m^2, foot-lamberts, and EV (incident and reflected). The meter notes and remembers readings using nine memory banks, handy for evaluating contrast. (Courtesy of Seconic Professional Division, Mamiya America Corporation, Elmsford, NY.)

Table 7.3 Spot Meter Readings, Reflectance, and F-Stops

Aperture Setting: f-stop	0	I	II	III	IV	V	VI	VII	VIII	IX	X
1.0	—	—	—	0.5	0.7	1.0	1.4	2.0	2.8	4	>5.6
1.4	—	—	0.5	0.7	1.0	1.4	2.0	2.8	4	5.6	>8
2.0	—	0.5	0.7	1.0	1.4	2.0	2.8	4	5.6	8	>11
2.8	<0.5	0.7	1.0	1.4	2.0	2.8	4	5.6	8	11	>16
4	<0.7	1.0	1.4	2.0	2.8	4	5.6	8	11	16	>22
5.6	<1.0	1.4	2.0	2.8	4	5.6	8	11	16	22	>32
8	<1.4	2.0	2.8	4	5.6	8	11	16	22	32	>44
11	<2.0	2.8	4	5.6	8	11	16	22	32	44	>64
16	<2.8	4	5.6	8	11	16	22	32	44	64	>88
22	<4.0	5.6	8	11	16	22	32	44	64	88	>128

represent the aperture setting on the camera lens. The zones across the top of the table indicate the actual reflectance, which corresponds to spot meter readings taken off various areas of the composition.

EV units are handy because they put reflectance value on a linear scale in one-stop increments. Each EV number represents a one-stop difference in value from the last. It eliminates the mental gymnastics involved in counting on the f-stop scale. For example, if a skin tone reads f/8, and a highlight reads f/45, how many stops brighter is the highlight? Before you start counting on your fingers, let's ask the same question in EV: The skin tone reads EV 10, the highlight EV 15; it's easy, the difference is five stops. You can even set the ASA on the spot meter so that EV 5 represents the f-stop on the lens. By so doing, you calibrate the meter to read out in zones: EV 0–10 equal zones 0–X. EV readings are not affected by the shutter speed setting of the meter, only the ASA.

A great many DPs rely almost exclusively on a spot meter for light readings. Knowing that the reflectance of average white skin is about zone VI and one stop lighter than 18% gray (zone V), the DP can base the f-stop on a spot reading taken off an actor's face or a fist held out. The DP makes the necessary one-stop compensation mentally.

When reading the reflectance of white skin, the reading will be a half to one and a half stops brighter than the setting on the lens. Brown and olive skin falls around zone V, and dark brown and black skin values fall between zones II and IV. When lighting and exposing black skin, the shininess of the skin plays a larger role in determining the light value than with lighter skin. Reflective glints off black skin may range up into zone VI or higher. There is a tremendous range of tonal values in human skin that the cinematographer observes and takes into account. You can find out the exact reflectance of a particular actor by comparing the reading of the face to that of a gray card or one's own hand.

A spot meter is particularly handy for measuring naturally luminescent sources, such as television screens, table lamps, illuminated signs, stained glass windows, neon lights, or the sky during sunrise and sunset. It is also handy for getting readings on objects that are inaccessible or far away.

Light Level

A single parameter that greatly affects all a gaffer's major decisions is the amount of light the DP wants to film a scene. One DP I worked with always shoots ASA 50 film at a f/4 or f/5.6, indoors or out, requiring a light level of 400–600 foot-candles. To do this requires many large HMI units, heavy 4/0 cable, many large power plants, and lots of hard-working hands. Another DP shoots ASA 500 film with a very low f-stop, requiring only about 32 foot-candles of illumination. Sometimes the biggest light needed might be a 2k or baby and the biggest cable is banded #2 cable. The choice of light level affects everything: what lights to order, the power requirements, and the time and personnel needed.

Film Speed

A DP's choice of film stock depends on many factors, including the subject matter of the film, the director's ideas about how it should look, the types of locations, the need for matching with other stocks (matte work and opticals), and personal style of lighting and preferences about grain and color.

As illustrated in the preceding examples, the *speed* of the film, or ISO (also termed ASA or EI), is the primary determinant of light level. A high-speed film emulsion is very light sensitive and requires little light to gain an exposure. Slower film stocks require more light but have less apparent grain, finer resolution, and more deeply saturated colors.

The choice of film stock also affects the look of the lighting. If a slow film stock is used in an interior scene, a fairly drastic increase in light level is required, virtually replacing all natural light with brighter artificial sources. The large lights must very often be hung above the set, giving limited realistic lighting angles. Faster film stocks and lenses enable a more subdued lighting approach, with fewer and smaller artificial lights brought to bear. The small lights are easier to hide, allowing more realistic angles for the light. The cinematographer can use existing light to a greater extent.

Optimizing Lens Characteristics

Lenses tend to have the greatest clarity and definition in the middle of the f-stop scale, between f/4 and f/8. Some loss of quality occurs at the ends of the scale. For this reason, many cinematographers ask for sufficient foot-candles to work in the center of the scale. Also, because lens characteristics change very slightly at different f-stops and for simplicity of lighting, DPs often prefer to shoot all the shots for a particular sequence at the same f-stop.

Depth of Field

Depth of field is the amount of depth that appears in focus. As the iris is opened up to lower f-stops, the depth of field decreases. (Depth of field also decreases with an increase in the focal length and a decrease in the subject's distance to the lens.)

Depth of field is directly proportional to the f-stop. The DP who wants shallow focus with a given lens needs to use a low f-stop (f/2 or f/2.8) and, therefore, low light levels or filters must be used. Lots of depth requires a higher f-stop, necessitating higher light levels. Thus, the depth of field also affects the size and type of lighting fixtures used to light the scene.

Varying Exposure Time

When the camera is operated at high speed for slow-motion photography, the exposure time is decreased and the aperture must be opened up to compensate. For example, when filming a car stunt at night with multiple cameras, the working light level must be high enough to accommodate a lower f-stop setting on high-speed cameras. An f/4 (uncompensated) would force a camera running at 120 fps to expose at under an f/2. This could be accomplished with the use of super-speed lenses, which open up to about f/1.4, but could not be accomplished with many standard lenses, which typically open up to between f/2 and f/2.8, or zoom and telephoto lenses, which are slower still. Similarly, if the shutter angle is reduced, the exposure time is reduced.

When shutter speed or shutter angle is not standard, everyone must be very clear when giving f-stops as to whether the f-stop compensation has been taken into account. When giving the f-stop, you would say it is an "f/4 on the lens," meaning that the compensation has been taken into account. If not, you should say you are giving an uncompensated reading.

The Genesis of Lighting Ideas

If ten world-class DPs each planned the lighting for a particular room, each lighting scheme would be different from the rest, as different as the mind and imagination of its creator. There can be no set prescription for "good lighting"; it is not the object here to present formulas. In fact, a gaffer or DP who always lights by formula or habit undervalues the potential impact of the lighting. The psychological effect of the script is played out not only through the dialogue and acting but also in the lighting and camera work. Good lighting comes from the ability to visualize how light can underscore the drama and mood of a written scene. Mood is perhaps the most powerful contribution of lighting to a motion picture. It starts in the DP's imagination. The DP looks at the room he or she is going to light and mentally returns to the script: the events, the emotions, the personalities that inhabit the space in the story. In collaboration with the director and production designer, the DP arrives at a sense of what each scene should feel like. The lighting may be gritty and hyperrealistic, slick and clean, high-tech and stylish, or lush and glamorous.

It may be naturalistic or it may be stylized and theatrical. The DP seeks conceptual ideas that inspire the approach to the lighting:

- What kind of world does the story exist in? What kind of images convey the basic tone of the film?
- What color and quality of light support the character's inner emotional state, and what light sources could be introduced in the scene to motivate that light on the actor or in the room?
- How should the audience experience this character—radiant with charisma, frazzled and imperfect, strong and determined, or what?
- What are the conditions, the weather, the time of day? Are they dictated by the script? If not, does the tone of the scene suggest an approach to take?
- How is light treated by the character in the story? Would she invite sunlight to pour into the room like butterscotch or close it out, leaving us in a musty dark room, the sunlight seeping around the edges of thick curtains?
- Does light connect the central character to his surroundings or does it isolate him? Is he surrounded with glowing human faces with whom he might interact or anonymous figures who leave him alone and alienated?
- Where does the arc of the story take us? How does the space change in appearance and feel from one part of the film to the next? Is it a long day's journey into night, an emergence from darkness into light, or what? How will each scene in this progression be augmented?

The lighting does not necessarily follow a literal interpretation of the script's mood. It can be ironic—a miserable lonely person faced with a beautiful sunny day. This might be more compelling than giving the character a dull rainy afternoon to mope about, especially if the writer uses irony as a device elsewhere.

Infinite creative possibilities wed the lighting to the story. New ideas constantly suggest themselves from the dialogue, the setting, the actual location. Even the props, the set dressing, and the characteristics of the actors themselves can contribute to lighting ideas. Very often on location scouts, the natural fall of the light lends itself to a particular scene, stimulating ideas for how that feeling can be recreated. A set painter's work light might do something interesting quite by accident.

Imaginative previsualization of each scene, based on story-driven concepts, stimulates an inexhaustible supply of lighting ideas. It brings variety to the cinematography and avoids a monotonous, formulaic approach. It offers the DP and gaffer a cohesive vision, which will result in creative, effective, and appropriate lighting design.

The Process of Creating Natural Lighting

Many DPs have said that the best lighting is usually the simplest; with each additional light, you add at least one new problem. Two carefully placed lights usually give far better results than lighting a subject with five or six lights. DPs strive to find lighting that is deliberate, clean, and simple.

This is not to say that a DP will never use dozens, or even hundreds, of lights to illuminate a scene. A scene may call for many small pools of light. Each light is controlled and serves a distinct purpose. As an actor walks through the room, he may pass through 20 lights, but at any one moment no more than two or three sources illuminate him.

Motivating Light Sources

It is sometimes helpful for the DP and gaffer to designate the motivating sources of light for a scene. These sources may be real or imagined; identifying them gives the DP and gaffer a starting point, a quality of light to emulate. Ostensibly, a scene could be lit by direct sunlight pouring through the windows, by soft light filtering through a skylight, by candles on a dining room table, by a table lamp and wall sconces, by moonlight, by torchlight, by the light of an instrument panel (in an airplane, a car, a spaceship, a submarine), by a flashing neon sign outside the window of an urban apartment, by the flashing lights of an ambulance, by the headlights of a passing car, or by the flickering glow of a bonfire on a beach. The DP who has previsualized the scene already knows what type of light source is appropriate. Now, taking into account the specific blocking, architecture of the set, and placement of practical lights in the set, the DP determines which source will act as key light on the actor's face, which source might motivate lighting on the background, and which source to use to motivate backlights.

Reinforcing the Motivating Source

A source may be shown on screen (a table lamp, for example) or may simply be suggested. In either case, the actors are illuminated either by the source itself or by lighting fixtures that strengthen the effect of the motivating source.

In most cases, if the source is bright enough to provide illumination for the actors, it will appear too bright itself. Suppose an actor is sitting on a couch beside a table lamp. If we rely solely on the lamp to provide the exposure on the actor's face, the lamp will be greatly overexposed. Conversely, if we dim down the lamp to look natural (zone VIII), the actor's face will be too dark. The actor's face therefore needs to be illuminated separately by a source that mimics the soft, golden quality of the table lamp. This also affords us the opportunity to "cheat" the key light where it will look best on the actor's face. What matters is that the quality of the light—of the key source in particular—be that of a realistic and plausible lighting source and that the general direction of the light have continuity and not shift between camera angles. A diffused Fresnel aimed around the front of the lamp would serve this purpose. Care must be taken not to let light spill onto the lamp itself or to let the lamp cast a shadow from the Fresnel, as this would destroy the illusion of light originating from the lamp.

Consider the movement of the actors in relation to the placement of lighting sources. Light naturally influences behavior. For instance, a patch of sun moves across my living room floor during the afternoon, and my cat moves every 15 minutes to keep up with it. People also gravitate to light to read, work, and talk to one another. It is therefore natural that the lighting fall into place with the blocking, and to some extent the director and production designer will want to place windows and light sources to facilitate the lighting.

When no plausible sources exist to light the actors, as in a dark bedroom at night, a little dramatic license must be taken. The idea is to create a look that is psychologically palatable to the audience, if not wholly realistic. One approach to lighting a supposedly unilluminated night scene is to create a low base level of nondirectional blue light and underexpose it. Then, very selectively, add chips and slivers of light, and perhaps use subtle backlight to define the contour of the actor where he disappears into dark shadow. The success of such an effect is a delicate matter requiring an experienced eye and judgment.

Establishing the Key Light

The first light to establish is the key light. The key light typically establishes the exposure for the scene. All the other lights—fill light, backlight, practicals, scenery lighting, and so on—are set relative to the key light. The key is the strongest light on an actor's face. It may cover a large area (the sun, for example, is one of the larger key lights) or it may cover only the immediate area around the motivating source. If the set is large, a number of different sources will be key lights in different areas of the set. For example, as an actress moves from a window to a sofa in front of a fireplace, she walks out of the soft, blue, window light and into the warm, flickering firelight.

The shape of a face is revealed to the eye by the way light falls on the curves and planes of features. Tonal variations, the shading and shadows, are what tell our brain the shape of an object. Certain features can be emphasized or deemphasized by the placement of the lights. Often a DP's efforts are focused on deemphasizing trouble spots, such as wrinkles, a double chin, or sunken eyes. We may hide a double chin by keeping the light high and the chin in shadow.

The placement of the key light and the angles at which light strikes the subject greatly affect the associations evoked in the audience. Yet no particular meaning is necessarily associated with a given angle of light. You don't want to be limited by pedantic assumptions—a low light always denotes something sinister or that the classic key position bestows glamour. Lighting is a subjective matter. The art of the gaffer and DP is to respond to the context of the moment being photographed.

Rembrandt Cheek-Patch Lighting

The conventional, textbook key light position is at 45° above and 45° to one side of the actor (Figure 7.7). This position throws the shadow of the nose across the opposite side of the face, leaving a patch of light on the cheek. This patch is known as the *Rembrandt cheek patch*, after portraits by the 17th-century Dutch painter. This lighting angle puts light in both eyes and models the nose, lips, chin, and cheeks nicely. It is considered the most natural key light position. It is very important to realize, however, that every actor has a different face: One has a large nose; another has a broad face or a chin that sticks out or droops. Some have deeply

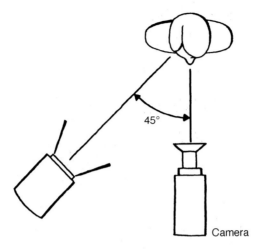

Figure 7.7 Conventional key position, 45° above and 45° to one side of the actor.

set eyes that are difficult to get light into, or hair that interferes with the light, or wrinkles they wish their public not to see. The DP responds to these differences in the treatment given to each face; the 45° rule quickly becomes academic.

Most often the key is somewhere between 0° and 90° from a frontal position to the subject and between 0° and 45° above the subject's head; however, it can come from any direction that reveals at least some of the features of the face: from below, from high overhead or high to the side, and even from a three-quarter back or side position.

Far-Side Key

This is an important concept in selecting the key light position. Once the DP and gaffer have seen the blocking and know where the actors will move, which way they will face, and from where the camera will view them, the next decision is where to place the key light (or lights). The DP will juggle a number of considerations, but all things being equal, it is photographically more pleasing to light with a *far-side key* than a *near-side key*. When the camera faces an actor, her face is lit either from camera left or camera right. If the actor faces toward camera left she presents more of the right side of her face to camera than the left side. The left side is therefore the *far side* and the right side is the *near side*. A far side key light makes the near side of the actor's face the fill side (Figure 7.8A). This arrangement models the facial feature by presenting contrast (created by the shadow line of the nose, lips, eyes, jaw, chin, etc.) toward the camera.

If we do the opposite, placing key light on the near side (camera right in this example), we light the side of the actor's head rather than her eyes and face; the nose shadow falls across the far side of the face where the camera won't see it as well and the predominant side presented to camera is in front light, generally flatter and less appealing (Figure 7.8B). Placing the key light on the side opposite from

Figure 7.8 (A) Far-side key (key light is on the other side of the line of action), (B) near-side key (key is on the same side of the line as the camera).

the direction the actor is looking is called placing a *near-side key*, which some people like to call the *dumb-side key*.

Figure 7.9 shows an actor facing three-quarters to camera. From the camera's perspective, the key light, which is lighting one whole side of the actor's face, is a deeply set side light. The effect is to give the far side of the actor's face an illuminated edge and to place a patch of light on the near-side cheek, while leaving the rest of the near-side portion of the face in shadow. By adding a limited amount of fill light, the far-side key conveys darkness in the room. If we want to lighten the face without filling more from the front we can "wrap the key"; that is, wrap the key light around the face more by adding a soft light on the same side as the key light but in a slightly more frontal position.

Side Light

A direct side light at eye level puts one whole side of the face in shadow. When this half-light effect is desired, the best position for the key light is not at 90° to the face but slightly less than 90°. At 90°, the cheek on the key side of the face tends to make an unattractive shadow (Figure 7.10A). By bringing the light slightly

Figure 7.9 Deep set, far-side key with soft wrap.

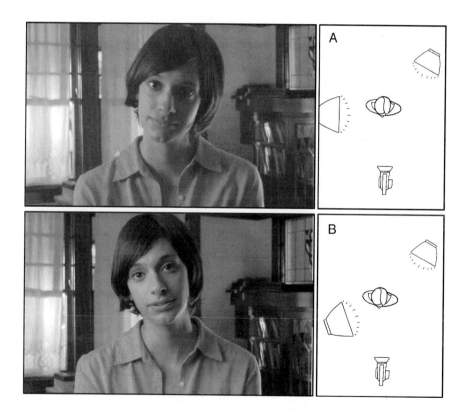

Figure 7.10 (A) Side light with opposite side kicker. (B) Same setup with soft wrapping key.

forward of 90°, the shadow disappears, and the result is a pleasing half-light effect. It models the face nicely and gives a pronounced sense of contrast and direction (Figure 7.10B). Light does not fall on the far eye. If desired, fill light or eye light may be added to put a glint in both eyes. Young children's faces tend to have less predominant features and a soft side light wraps around their faces even without further help.

Again, a nice addition to a side light key is to use a second light to *wrap* the light around onto the far cheek with a very subtle soft source in a three-quarters frontal position on the same side as the key with little or no additional fill. The result, a very soft, high-contrast side light, gives an appealing gradation of tones across the face. This look came into vogue in the 1980s in testimonial commercials, a yuppie talking candidly and presumably impromptu about his stockbroker or the merits of his long-distance service. The technique is useful in all sorts of situations.

One pitfall of a side light position is that, if the actor turns his head away from the source, the face goes completely into shadow. The addition of a back or side kicker on the nonkey side can help define the features in such a case (as was done in Figure 7.10). Alternatively, you could let the face go dark and define the profile by silhouetting it against a lighter background.

When two actors are side by side, an eye-level side light tends to cast the shadow of one actor onto another. This problem can be remedied by raising the light higher, throwing the shadow downward.

In dance performances, floor-level side lights are used because they accentuate the form and musculature of the dancers. The low position allows the light to be cut off the stage surface, which increases the apparent height and duration of dancers' leaps and enhances the illusion of effortless flight.

Front Light

When a key light is brought to the front, the scene becomes flatter. Using a direct frontal soft light as the key light is a technique of glamour photography, where the goal is to reveal less of the form (make the nose look smaller) and to fill in the blemishes. Actors who have undesirable wrinkles are often given stronger doses of super-soft front light.

Front light was a convention of glamour cinematography of the black-and-white era. By placing the light so that it shoots dead onto the face, the nose and chin shadows are minimized to a small underline. The eyes appear very bright, and the sides of the face, the temples, and jaw fall off in brightness.

To prevent the front light from flattening out the entire scene, it is often desirable to angle the light down such that it can be cut off the background with toppers and siders (Figure 7.11). It is also helpful to have some distance between the actor and the background; otherwise, a hard shadow becomes unavoidable.

Bottom Light

The thought of frontal bottom light conjures up images of eerie, unnatural visage with lighting under the eyebrows, nose, and chin casting shadows upward from the eyebrows. However, a low light source does not necessarily have that effect.

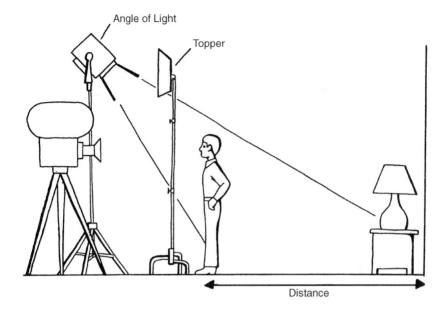

Figure 7.11 An on-the-nose key usually requires a topper to prevent the front light from flattening out the background.

Light that is bounced up from a light-colored floor or table surface can lend the face a soft radiance. Again, lighting angles do not necessarily have any particular meaning.

Naturally, a low position may be used when a light source is at ground level (a camp fire, for example) or the actor is elevated. Any time you place a light in a low position, you have to be prepared to deal with, or learn to love, the shadows cast upward on the background and ceiling.

Placing soft or bounced light on the ground from the side and three-quarter back position highlights the line of the neck and jaw and the edges of arms. This is a fast way to get some nice definition without having to worry about the lights getting into the shot. If the lens has a narrow angle of view (doesn't see below the waist) or the set dressing can provide hiding places for low lights, this can be a great, fast option. Kino Flos placed on the floor, small tungsten soft lights on beaver boards, or PAR cans bounced onto a show card laying on the ground—all these techniques achieve similar results. A floor-bounce also works well for a touch of frontal fill.

High in Front or High to the Side

A high position can give a dramatic effect by putting the eye sockets in deep shadow and underlining the nose, lips, and chin in shadow. In *The Godfather*, Gordon Willis used soft, high frontal sources to give Marlon Brando a low-key, intimidating presence.

Eye Light

An eye light makes the eyes twinkle by creating a reflection in the eyeball. The light is usually placed as close to the camera lens as possible. The bigger the dimensions of the source, the bigger the reflected dots. Eye light does not have to be very intense, however, because the eyeball is very reflective. An eye light need not flatten out the overall composition.

An *obie light* is a light positioned directly over the camera lens, mounted to the matte box. It has the advantage of panning, tilting, and dollying with the camera. The obie light maintains a minimal level of frontal fill on actors as they pass in and out of other lights while the camera moves with them through a set. An obie light typically has some sort of dimming device. It is convenient to use dimming shutters or a dimmable fluorescent (e.g., Diva-Lite 400) so brightness can be adjusted without affecting color temperature.

I find camera-mounted lights most helpful when tracking actors through caves, corridors, air ducts, or tunnels when the overall feel needs to remain dark but a minimum amount of fill light needs to be maintained on the faces.

Backlights, Kickers, and Hair Lights

Backlight highlights the edges of the face, hair, and shoulders of an actor. It strengthens the lines that delineate the figure from the background. The various backlight positions can also emphasize features of the face and hair. Scenes that occur in relative darkness are often backlit to give delineation to the figures and set dressing without lighting them. Backlight is also the best angle to make rain and smoke visible to the camera.

Three-Quarter Backlight Kicker

A kicker is normally relatively low, from a three-quarter backlight position. A light glancing off the side of the face and hair gives form to the jaw, cheek, and hair and separates that side of the figure from the background. Because of its low, back position, it does not cause problems by spilling onto walls and can easily be kept off the ground. As with all backlights, the problem is always keeping it out of frame and preventing flare on the lens. It is nice to be able to hide the light behind a set piece or furniture.

High Side Backlight

High side backlights, one on either side of the subject, soak the performer in backlight; the effect is powerful and dramatic. You see this technique used in rock concerts and dance performances. It works equally well in motion pictures. When blended with the frontal lights and applied with more subtlety, a pair of high side backlights rims the head and shoulders evenly and highlights the hair. News reporters and talk show hosts seem to have one or two backlights with them wherever they go. High backlights tend to light up the ground, table tops, and other horizontals.

Rim

A rim light is a high direct backlight that rims the head and shoulders, pulling the actor out from the background. A rim light is a thin highlight. Again, the light spills onto the floor and must be shaded off the lens.

Hair Light

Positioned somewhere between a rim and a top light, a hair light creates a flattering halo effect. Applied with subtlety, it brings out the color and texture of the hair.

Top Light

A top light (directly overhead) primarily lights the actor's hair and shoulders. It does not light the face at all, other than the forehead and the bridge of the nose. Although it can be used for dramatic effect, this is not a great position from which to light a person, unless the person is reclining. It can be effective to create a sense of faceless anonymous figures in a room, lighting table tops and horizontal surfaces, without illuminating faces. Sometimes a DP bounces a top light off of a table to illuminate an actor's face.

Fill

The next important consideration is fill. The object of fill light is to bring up the light level in the dark shadow areas of the face created by the key light. To do this soft light must come from a more frontal position than the key light, usually from near the camera. When low light levels are used, the ambient light level may be sufficient to fill the shadows; often the fill can be accomplished with a white board placed to bounce light into the shadow areas of the face. When a fixture is used, it must be a large, soft source that will not create additional shadows—a light bounced into a 4 × 4 piece of foam core or put through heavy diffusion such as 216 or a large source such as a soft light, chimera, or other soft box.

The amount of fill light determines the contrast ratio and has a great deal to do with the apparent lightness or darkness and, to some extent, the mood of the scene. If the fill light is strong, bringing the contrast ratio up to 2:1, the scene appears very bright and flat, a look termed *high key*. Reducing the amount of fill light brings out the directionality of the key lights, separates the elements of the frame, and makes the colors appear more saturated. Reducing the fill even more allows deep shadows to appear. A high key/fill ratio gives the sense of night or darkness in the room, especially if the scene is lit with edge and side light. This kind of look is termed *low key*.

Most DPs fill by eye rather than by using a meter. Judging fill light takes some experience and familiarity with the characteristics of the film stock. It may be helpful to turn the fill light off and on to judge its effect.

Ambience

A close cousin of fill light, ambience is general fill throughout the set (as opposed to the fill on the actors' faces). All the lights used to light the set bounce around to some extent to create ambience. Sometimes DPs need more ambient light; other times they seek ways to reduce the ambient light. Typically 6k coops or space lights are hung above sets to provide ambience. On location, large bounces are often used to create ambient light. On smaller sets, very often the bulbs in the coops are exchanged for a smaller wattage so the ambience doesn't take over. It is helpful to have these lights on a dimmer as well, as a quick way to set the ambience once the other lighting is in place.

If ambience is too high, limit the amount of light spilling and bouncing around the set. Flags and 4 × 4 floppies are used to cut light. Blacks can be erected to create "negative fill," reducing the area of ambience around the subject by sucking it up with black duvetyn.

Set Light

Sometimes the key lights illuminate the set and very little further treatment is needed. It may be lit with practicals, which give it pools of light and dark, or the gaffer may place bulbs behind items of set dressing to add interest. When light needs to be added to bring out the background, it is best to be selective. Light tends to build up on backgrounds and can start to flatten everything out. Look for ways to break it up or create variation, gradation, or specific highlights.

Backdrops

On a sound stage, the exterior scene outside the windows of the set is very often created using a translight or scenic backing. A translight is a gigantic photograph that is back lit (usually with sky pans). Day and night translights are created depicting a backyard, the view from a high-rise office building, and so forth.

Specials

If some object in the set requires a separate treatment, for example, a crystal ball, that object is given a special. In the case of the crystal ball, a special might shoot up into the ball through a hole in the table.

Lighting the Scene

The discussion thus far has dealt with lighting a single, stationary actor. Very few movies, however, are about a single individual who never moves. The following light plots show how two different sets might be lit for a scene.

Living Room Scene

Figure 7.12 shows a living room set built on a sound stage. The scene at hand is set on a cold, overcast winter day. A fire is burning in the fireplace. The actor starts the scene at the window, looking out at the falling snow, then he moves to the armchair and sits down in front of the fire.

The motivating sources for the scene are the lights from the window, the table lamp next to the armchair, the fire, and the chandelier in the front hall. Before we can plan how these sources will function, we first need to know where the camera will be placed. For the shot at hand, the camera will be placed on the right side of the fireplace, taking a profile angle of the actor at the window, panning with him as he moves to the chair, and taking a three-quarter frontal angle of him as he sits down.

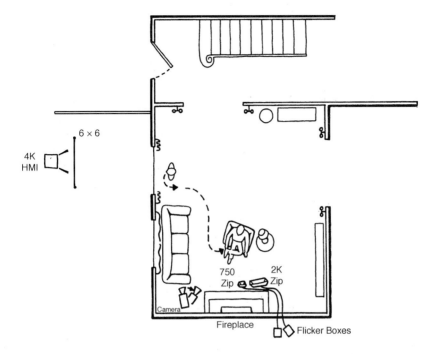

Figure 7.12 Living room scene and key light positions. The 4k HMI through silk gives a soft cool light through the window while the two small soft lights on the flicker boxes create the illusion of firelight.

The key light at the window naturally comes from outside. The light should be soft, diffuse, and slightly blue in contrast to the warm interior. We use a 4k HMI Fresnel shining into a 6 × 6-ft frame of light grid cloth. A half CTO orange gel is applied to the light to correct the blue HMI source halfway to tungsten. We adjust the light's intensity so that we read the target f-stop on the subject's face when he stands by the window. The intensity falls off as he moves away from the window. The window frame cuts the light, reducing the spill on the back wall and preventing it from spilling onto the armchair.

As the actor approaches the chair, the key shifts from the window to the fireplace. A firelight rig is placed on the floor just out of the frame. The firelight is exposed a half-stop under the target f-stop, colored slightly orange, and made to flicker randomly. (Some techniques for creating this effect are explained in Chapter 8.) The shadows in the room should shift slightly with the dancing movement of the make-believe flames. Because the light from the fire is close to the subject, intensity rapidly falls off behind him. Shadows are cast on the chair but do not reach the back wall.

Backlights and Kickers   Now that the two key lights are set, we can consider what other lights we would like (Figure 7.13). The position of the table lamp motivates a nice kicker for the seated position. A 650-W Fresnel is placed on a stand just out of the frame to the right, aimed around the back of the table lamp.

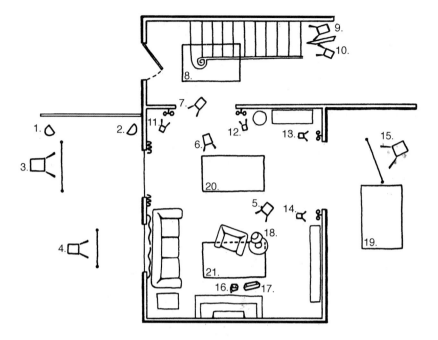

Figure 7.13 Living room scene with back and fill lights added: (1, 2) sky pans lighting the painted flat, (3) key at the window, (4) light giving glow around the edges of the closed curtains, (5) rim light motivated by the table lamp, (6) backlight at the chair motivated by the hallway light, (7) backlight at the window, (8) soft box to fill the hallway with top light, (9) light on the stairs and banister poles, (10) slash on the back wall, (11–14) small Fresnels producing light around the wall sconces, (15) light spilling into the living room from the dining room, (16) 750-W soft firelight, (17) 2k zip firelight, (18) table lamp, (19) dining room soft box to light the visible walls of the next room, and (20, 21) soft top fill, put low on dimmers for ambient warm fill.

The combined light reading of the practical and the kicker is to be one stop over the target f-stop.

We could also introduce two backlights coming in from the hallway: one to rim the actor's back at the window and one for his shoulders when in the chair. The backlight at the window should be cut so that it does not throw light on the wall and curtains next to him.

Fill Finally, we will need some fill light. We want to keep contrast in the scene, so we need only enough fill to give a little detail on the shadowy part of his clothes at the window and as he moves to the chair. A soft source next to the camera would have to be carefully positioned so as not to light up the camera-left wall and to avoid causing a glare in the paneling on the far wall. The scene might also be filled by hanging soft boxes overhead.

Background Additionally, we must consider treatment of the back walls, hallway, stairs, dining room, and scenery outside the windows, all of which are in the background of the various shots filmed in this room. As the scene continues, we are likely to have actors coming into the hallway, the dining room, the stairway, and so on. We must consider each area that may be used or seen.

In the firelight scene described earlier, it may be enough to bring out the back walls with the glow from the sconces on either side of the hallway entrance. We may want to reinforce the sconces with small Fresnels or Source fours positioned overhead, throwing soft blobs of light on the walls around the sconces. A light shining down from the top of the stairway would provide an edge light to an actor standing in the hall or on the stairs and create a diagonal slash on the far back wall. The hallway might also be lit with a skirted overhead soft box. The scenery flat outside is lit with several blue-gelled sky pans.

Exterior Night Scene

Typically, when shooting moody, dark scenes or night scenes, the key lights move around to side and back positions. "Back cross-light" is a common technique used to light two or more people from the back.

Figure 7.14 shows a setup for a face-to-face conversation at night. The camera position for the master shot has both actors in profile. Actor A is keyed from the back right, actor B from the back left. From the camera's point of view, these two lights are far-side keys; they put very little light on the visible side of either actor's face, giving a sense of overall darkness. Note that actor B's key light acts as a kicker, or backlight, for actor A, and actor A's key light does the same for actor B.

A small amount of fill light is required to keep the side of the faces visible to the camera from going totally black; however, the fill light's intensity must be

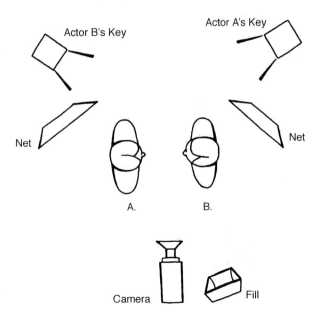

Figure 7.14 Back cross master shot.

very carefully controlled to get detail in the faces without overfilling. I drew the fill light here as a soft zip light; however, the fill light for a large night exterior is often made by bouncing larger lights into a 12 × 12 white griffs or provided by ambient light from an overhead light such as a balloon light. Similarly the key lights I drew might actually be large lights placed far from the action, often mounted in an aerial lift platform to light a larger area. In any case, the back cross-light is created with the angle of light drawn here.

Once the master shot is completed, individual, over-the-shoulder (OTS) close-ups will be shot. Figure 7.15 shows the camera placements.

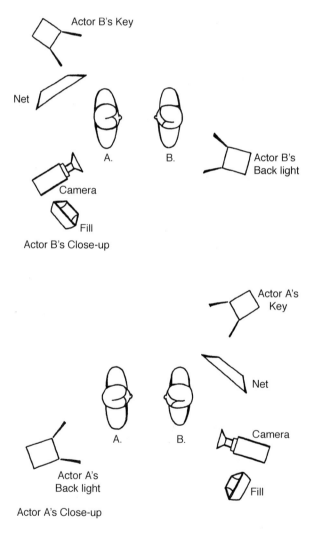

Figure 7.15 Back cross setup for OTS reverse close-ups.

Note that our key lights are already in good positions to light the faces. We now bring in backlights to keep a rim on the nonkey sides of the faces. The fill light moves with the camera, placed on the nonkey side, and is cheated back and forth for each close-up.

Moving into position for the first close-up, we want to check the intensity at which actor B's key hits actor A's back. Because A is closer to the light, it may be too bright. Placing a net to bring down the level of B's key solves this problem. Similarly, when we move the camera for the second close-up, we reduce the level of A's key hitting B. When shooting the first close-up, we turn off actor A's backlight.

The background consists of storefronts across the street. The DP wants the background shadowy and underexposed two to three stops. Starting with total darkness, we need to bring the light level on the street and storefronts up to a low base level. Our aim is to create an ambient light: moonlight or streetlight. The whole background must be covered completely. If the camera sees the edge of a light's field, where true darkness begins, the ambient effect will be destroyed. To accomplish a widespread, even field, we need to put a fairly big fixture high up and a long way off, typically a 12k HMI on a condor crane 50–80 ft in the air and perhaps 150 ft away. The size of the light, its height, and its distance depend on the size of the area to be lit. Note in Figure 7.14 that, for each shot, a new background is seen and quite a bit of real estate may have to be covered.

To accentuate the darkness of the background, it would be nice in this situation to have a few self-luminous sources in the picture: practical lights, illuminated windows, neon signs, car headlights, or perhaps some steam (backlit) rising out of a manhole. Cinematographers often like to wet down the pavement during night scenes so they can pick up reflections from the shiny surface.

CHAPTER 8

Manipulating Light: Tools, Techniques, and the Behavior of Light

I can't stand a naked light bulb any more than I can a rude remark or vulgar action.
—Tennessee Williams, *A Streetcar Named Desire*

Light has five properties: color, brightness, form, shape or pattern, and movement. The set electrician uses the techniques discussed in this chapter to manipulate and control these five properties.

Color

The lighting crew has two goals when it comes to color. The first is the technical process of matching the *color temperature* of the light sources to each other and to the rated color balance of the film stock. The second is aesthetic: introducing color into the light to simulate realistic sources, such as late afternoon sun, firelight, neon light, or blue moonlight. The DP may use tints to enhance the colors of the actors' faces, their clothes, and their surroundings, and give the scene mood—warmth, eeriness, bleakness.

Color Correction

Light is a narrow band of the electromagnetic spectrum, as shown in Figure 8.1. Wavelengths from 380 to 760 nanometers (nm) are detectable to the human eye as visible light.

The color of a light source is determined by the intensity of the various wavelengths that make up the light. When the full range of wavelengths is combined,

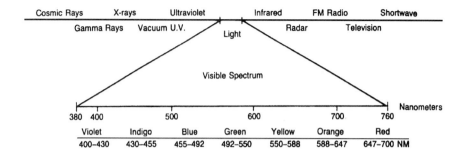

Figure 8.1 The color spectrum is a narrow band within the electromagnetic spectrum. Individual colors of light within the visible spectrum combine to make "white light."

the result is said to be "white" light. Nonetheless, all "white" light has colored tint to it depending on its particular balance of wavelengths. Because the human eye adapts to its surroundings, shifts in balance are not always apparent to the human eye unless one light source is next to another in direct contrast. An incandescent light produces light that is orange compared to an HMI, which is stronger on the blue end. Standard fluorescent tubes produce light that has strong spikes at several places in the spectrum, which give it a strong green hue.

Unlike the human eye, film stock cannot adjust to these variations. Color rendition is always relative to the color balance of the film stock, either tungsten (3200 K) or daylight (5600 K). To appear white on film, the color balance of the light must match that of the film. This is accomplished by applying color correction gels to unmatched sources. The gels redistribute the spectrum by reducing the intensity of selected wavelengths in a given source. CTO (color temperature orange) must be applied to daylight sources to match with tungsten film. CTB (color temperature blue) must be applied to incandescent sources to match to daylight film. A magenta gel must be applied to fluorescent lights to remove the green appearance.

A gel having a secondary color diminishes the amount of the opposite primary color in the light (see Figure 8.4 later in this chapter). Conversely, a gel having a primary color diminishes the strength of the opposite secondary color in the light. For example, amber gel diminishes blue light, and blue gel diminishes amber light. Magenta gel diminishes green light, and green gel diminishes magenta light.

Kelvin Color-Temperature Scale

The color makeup of any source that has a continuous spectrum, such as an incandescent light, can be measured on the color-temperature scale and quantified in degrees Kelvin. Figure 8.2 shows how the distributions of wavelengths differ for sources of different color temperatures.

You may be wondering why the Kelvin scale (a temperature scale) is used to quantify color balance. In order to give us a fixed reference point, scientists decided to compare the color make up of any source to that of a theoretical "perfect black body radiator" when it is heated. The idea is that light is emitted when a substance

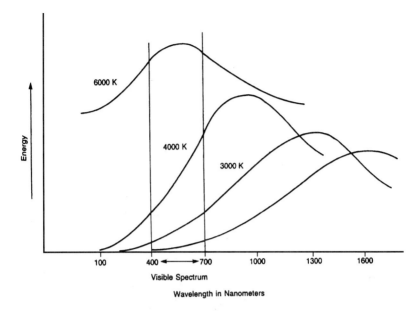

Figure 8.2 Distribution of energy for various color temperatures across the visible spectrum. Note the distribution of energy in a tungsten source (3200 K) favors the red end of the spectrum, while in a daylight source (5600 K), the curve slopes downward at the red end and the distribution of energy is more even over the visible spectrum.

is heated. How much it is heated determines the color makeup of the light. When heated a little, it glows red. Heated more, it becomes yellow, then white, then pale blue, and finally brilliant blue. So the color makeup of a tungsten light is the same as that emitted by a "perfect black body radiator" heated to 3200 K. The higher the Kelvin reading, the bluer the light.

The color makeup of sources that do not have a continuous spectrum (HMIs and fluorescents) can also be given a Kelvin rating, termed the *correlated color temperature* (CCT).

Using MIRED Units to Calculate Color Shifts

If you want to change a source to a particular color temperature, you have to make calculations using values called *MIREDs*. These calculations have been made for you in Table 8.2 and in Appendix F. Table 8.2 shows the color temperature resulting from applying common color correction gels to different light sources. Tables F.1–F.3 (Appendix F) tell you what gel to use to get from any color temperature to any other color temperature.

Although the Kelvin scale is useful for defining the color temperature of a source, it is an awkward scale to use when quantifying the effect of a color correction gel or filter. You cannot simply state that a particular gel creates a 200 K shift.

Table 8.1 Color Temperature of Various Sources

Source	Kelvins	MIREDs
Match or candle flame	1900	526
Dawn or dusk	2000–2500	500
Household bulb	2800–2900	357–345
Tungsten halogen bulbs	3200	312
Photo flood bulbs	3400	294
1 hour after sunrise	3500	286
Late afternoon sunlight	4500	233
Blue glass photoflood bulb	4800	208
3200-K lamps with dichroic filter	4800–5000	208–200
FAY lamps	5000	200
Summer sunlight	5500–5700	182
White flame carbon arc light with Y-1 filter	5700	175
HMI light	5600 or 6000	179 or 167
Sunlight with blue/white sky	6500	154
Summer shade	7000	141
Overcast sky	7000	141
Color television	9300	108
Skylight	10,000–20,000	100

Table 8.2 Color Temperature Resulting from Applying Common Color-Correction Gels

Gel Applied	Daylight Source, 5600 K	Tungsten Source, 2900 K	Tungsten Source, 3200 K
⅛ CTO	4900 K	2700 K	2950 K
¼ CTO	4100 K	2450 K	2650 K
½ CTO	3450 K	2200 K	2350 K
Full CTO	2950 K	2000 K	2100 K
⅛ CTB	6200 K	3050 K	3400 K
¼ CTB	7000 K	3250 K	3600 K
½ CTB	9900 K	3750 K	4250 K
Full CTB	23,800 K	4800 K	5700 K

Note: Results are rounded to the nearest 50°. Exact results vary depending on the brand of gel and exact color temperature of source.

Table 8.3 Color Temperature and Output at Various Voltages

Voltage	Color Temperature		Light Output
	Kelvins	*MIREDs*	
120 V	3200 K	313	100%
110 V	3100 K	322	75%
100 V	3000 K	333	55%
90 V	2900 K	345	38%

The Kelvin shift of a given correction filter depends on the color temperature of the *light source*. A blue gel that alters a tungsten source 200 K (from 3200 K to 3400 K) alters a daylight source 650 K (from 5600 K to 6250 K).

When gel manufacturers quantify the effect of color correction gel, they use micro reciprocal degrees (MIRED units) rather than degrees Kelvin. MIREDs provide a linear scale on which to calculate the shift of a given gel on any source.

The MIRED value is equal to 1 million divided by the Kelvin color temperature:

$$\frac{1 \text{ million}}{K} = \text{MIRED value}$$

Table F.4 lists the MIRED value for any Kelvin number from 2000–9900 K. Tables F.5–F.7 list the color shift in MIREDs of color correction gels of various manufacturers.

The MIRED shift of a particular gel needed to get from any Kelvin temperature (K_1) to any other Kelvin temperature (K_2) is as follows:

$$\text{MIRED shift} = \frac{1 \text{ million}}{K_1} - \frac{1 \text{ million}}{K_2}$$

Note that tungsten color temperature is 312 MIREDs, and daylight is about 179 MIREDs. To correct a daylight source to tungsten, a shift of +133 MIREDs is required. To correct a tungsten source to daylight, a shift of −133 MIREDs is required.

Color-Temperature Meter

A color-temperature meter gives a Kelvin reading of the light hitting the cell of the meter. It is important to realize that, although a cinematographer's color meter, such as the Minolta Color Meter II (Figure 8.3), is calibrated at the factory, the readings of two identical meters will often differ.

This type of color meter is accurate for comparing the color temperatures of several light sources, but no Kelvin reading should be taken as an absolute value. When more than one meter is being used to take readings on the set, the meters should be checked side by side under the same light to determine the variation between them.

Figure 8.3 Minolta Color Meter II. (Courtesy of Minolta Corp., Cypress, CA.)

Light-Balancing Scale—Orange/Blue Shifts

The Minolta color meter automatically calculates the MIRED shift from the Kelvin reading. Minolta calls this shift the *light-balancing* (LB) index number. This number indicates the amount of amber or blue correction gel needed to match the source to the color temperature of the film stock (refer to Tables F.1–F.3 to determine the closest correction gel to use). To use the LB scale, the color balance of the film stock must be preset on the meter. A three-position selection switch offers the standard film color temperatures: film type B, 3200 K; film type A, 3400 K (which is used for some still film stocks); or film type D (daylight), 5500 K. The meter also has a manual mode that allows you to enter any target Kelvin temperature. The manual mode comes in handy when the cinematographer needs to have all the lights balanced to a nonstandard Kelvin rating. A chart on the back of the color meter also gives the Kodak filter number and the amount of exposure change corresponding to the LB reading (Table F.8). Kodak filters are used in the camera in situations where an overall color correction is needed. For example, when filming a scene in which the practical lamps are unavoidably yellow, the DP can add $\frac{1}{4}$ CTO to the lights to match them to the practicals, then, if desired, cancel out the yellow cast in the lab (or telecine) or even with a blue filter on the lens.

Color-Compensation Scale—Green/Magenta Shifts

The color temperature meter also gives a *color-compensation* (CC) reading that indicates the amount of green or magenta gel needed to correct a source to appear white on film. Such a correction is typically required by fluorescent lights and sometimes on HMIs. A CC reading of 30M (+13 on Color Meter II) is typical for a cool white bulb, for example. This excess green can be filtered out with a full minus-green (magenta) gel. Table F.9 lists green/magenta correction gels and the corresponding color meter readings.

Color-Correction Gels

All correction gels come in densities of full, half, quarter, and eighth correction. Correction gel typically comes in rolls 48 or 54 in. wide and 22 or 25 ft long. When gel is cut from the roll, the cut pieces should be labeled (F, H, Q, or E) and organized by size and color.

Converting Daylight Sources to Tungsten

CTO gels are orange, and they "warm up" a light source. The 85 gel corrects sunlight and HMI sources to 3200 K. Full CTO or extra CTO correct skylight to tungsten, or 5500 K sources to a warm yellow 2800 K.

Gelling Windows

When the outside of the window is accessible, gel can be stapled or taped over the outside window frame, which hides the gel more easily. When stapling gel, apply a square of gaffer's tape to the gel and staple through the tape to prevent the gel from ripping. The key to gelling windows is to keep the gel tight and free of wrinkles.

CTO correction is also available in 4 × 8-ft acrylic sheets. Using acrylic sheets avoids the problems of wrinkles, movement, and noise that gel makes.

With a very light dusting of spray adhesive (Spray 77), you can stick gel directly onto a window or acrylic sheet. Press bubbles and wrinkles out to the edges with a duvetyn-covered block of wood. If gelling windows promises to become an everyday process on a particular location, an elegant system is to cut acrylic inserts to fit the windows, then add ND and CTO gel (using the spray adhesive technique) as needed to suit the light conditions and time of day. Move the inserts around from shot to shot depending on the camera angle.

You can also use snot tape (3M transfer tape) or secure it by carefully taping around the edge of the gel with tape that matches the color of the window frame. Another fast method is to spray water on the windows and apply the gel with a squeegee. This method will not last all day, but it saves so much time that it doesn't matter if it must be redone.

Neutral-Density and Combination Neutral-Density/CTO Correction Gels

Neutral-density (ND) gel is gray; it decreases the intensity of a light source without altering color:

Type	Light Reduction
ND 0.3	1 stop
ND 0.6	2 stops
ND 0.9	3 stops
ND 1.2	4 stops

Combination CTO/ND gel and acrylic sheets are commonly used to reduce the brightness of windows.

Converting Tungsten to Daylight

CTB correction gels change the color temperature of a tungsten source toward that of daylight. Typically, a quarter or half CTB is used when the DP desires a cool blue look to a particular light source.

When the DP uses a daylight-balanced film, tungsten sources are typically avoided. HMI fixtures provide daylight-balanced light that is cleaner, brighter, cooler, and a more efficient use of power. Tungsten lights are very weak on the blue end of the spectrum. Full CTB reduces light transmission by 85%, or about two stops. (The gel has to absorb 85% of the energy from the light; consequently the hot-burning lights also burn out blue gel very quickly.)

Dichroic Filters and Reflectors

The most common type of dichroic filter (dike) is a coated silver reflector or glass filter that fits onto some open-face lights to make a tungsten-to-daylight conversion (3200 K to 5600 K). The filter or reflector reduces light output by two stops. The filter or reflector is easily identified by its strange red/blue reflective appearance, like gasoline in a water puddle.

A dichroic filter works by optically canceling out certain wavelengths of light. It does not involve dyes or pigment but rather reflects selected wavelengths of light by the thickness of a chemical coating on the glass. The thickness of the coating is one-quarter of the wavelength of the selected color's chromatic opposite. Manufacturers can custom make dichroic glass filters in practically any color. Their advantage over gel is that they never fade. They are ideal for long-term installations, where the cost and trouble of replacing faded gel every week outweighs the initial expense of buying glass filters. The trick to them is that light has to pass through the filter exactly perpendicular to the plane of the glass or the color will start to vary. For some lights, a curved glass filter is necessary. Manufacturers include Rosco (Permacolor Glass Filters) and Automated Entertainment Manufacturing (HD Dichroic).

Before the dichroic filter came along, the *MacBeth* filter was used. It is simply a blue glass filter.

Green/Magenta Color Correction

Green and magenta color correction gels were developed primarily to allow color matching between fluorescent lights and other sources. A comprehensive table of fluorescent lamp types and the correction they require is given in the *American Cinematographer Manual—Color Balancing for Existing Fluorescent Lighting*. This table represents the result of comprehensive testing and is by far the best reference. For copyright reasons, it cannot be reproduced here.

However, many variables remain that no table can account for, so testing with a color meter remains the best approach. Table F.9 lists green and magenta correction gels and Kodak filter numbers and corresponding color meter readings that may be useful in this process.

There are three general approaches to matching the color temperatures of fluorescent lights, tungsten lights, HMIs, and daylight: (1) Match all the sources to daylight (5600 K), (2) match all the sources to tungsten (3200 K), or (3) match all the sources to fluorescent daylight (5600 K plus green). Table 8.4 details each approach.

Gelling Fluoros

When gelling fixtures that have frosted plastic panels, you can cut sheets to lay inside each fixture. If you have to gel tubes individually, place tabs of snot tape along the tube and roll the tube up in gel. Carefully cut away excess gel.

Rosco makes tubular sleeves of color correction gel that can make gelling tubes easier. You can also get clear plastic sleeves that are meant for protection in case of lamp breakage; cut and roll the gel inside them.

Fluorescent Tubes, Color Rendering

Manufacturers provide two ratings to indicate the type and quality of the color rendered by their fluorescent tubes: the correlated color temperature (CCT) and the color rendering index (CRI). The CCT and CRI are printed on the packaging of the tubes and sometimes also on the tubes themselves. While CCT and CRI ratings give the gaffer valuable information about the general performance characteristics of a given tube, they can be misleading in terms of the color rendering of fluorescent light *on film*. CCT and CRI are based on the color perception of the human eye, not the peculiarities of film emulsions. Specific color information must be gathered with color-temperature meter.

Correlated Color Temperature

The CCT gives the effective color temperature of the tube to the human eye when the spikes in the color curve are combined together. Fluorescent lights come in various color temperatures. Daylight tubes are designed to light spaces that have supplementary daylight, such as offices with large windows. The light is color balanced toward the blue end of the spectrum (5000–6500 K) to blend with the window light. Warm lights, which have a color temperature closer to that of household bulbs (3000 K), are for use in enclosed spaces where supplementary light comes from table lamps and wall sconces.

Color Rendering Index

The CRI is a rating, from 1 to 100, of the accuracy of a light's rendering of color when compared with a perfect reference source (daylight is a perfect 100). A rating above 90 is considered accurate color rendition for photography. With a CRI above 80, the eye can still make accurate color judgments and the color rendering is termed *acceptable*. Between 60 and 80 color rendering is *moderate*. Below 60 color rendering is *poor* or *distorted*.

On location, you will run into *standard* fluorescents and *full-spectrum (high-CRI)* fluorescents. Table E.2 (Appendix E) lists specifications for various types of fluorescent tubes. A high CRI tells you that the tube has a nearly complete spectrum of light frequencies and is therefore capable of rendering colors well; however, they often have a strong green spike and require color correction, which typically involves

Table 8.4 Strategies for Matching Mixed Color Sources

Strategy	Ceiling Fluorescents	Tungsten Fixtures	HMI Fixtures	Windows	Fluorescent Floor Fixtures	Film Stock and Camera Filters
Match to Tungsten Used when the daylight sources are small and manageable (e.g., sound stage, a night scene, or a location with small windows).	Replace with high CRI, lamps with good tungsten-balanced color rendering. Add ¼ or ⅛ minus green as necessary. Gel warm whites with full minus green. Gel cool whites with fluoro filter.	**Use Tungsten lights to light the scene.** Use it as is.	Apply full CTO gel.	Apply Sun 85 or full CTO gel.	Kino Flo (with KF-32 tubes).	Tungsten balanced film, no filter.
Match to Daylight Good approach in room with many large windows.	Replace with high CRI, lamps with good daylight-balanced color rendering. Add ¼ or ⅛ minus green as necessary. Gel cool whites with full minus green.	Apply full CTB gel (very inefficient).	**Use HMI's to light the scene.** Use it as is.	Use it as is or with ND as needed.	Kino Flo (with KF-55 tubes).	Tungsten balanced film with 85 filter. Daylight balanced film, no filter.
Match to Fluorescent Daylight Resort to this if the ceiling lights must remain on and (1) there are too many fluorescent lights to gel or replace them all, (2) the lights are not accessible, or (3) there is no other alternative.	Cool whites. Use it as is.	Apply plus green 50 or full CTB and full plus green gel.	Apply full plus green gel.	Gel with window green.	Kino Flo with KF-55 tubes and full plus green. Other types use same type of bulb as in ceiling fixtures.	Tungsten balanced film with 85 and FLB filter, or correct green in lab printing. Daylight-balanced film with FLB or take out green in lab printing.

a combination of magenta and CTO gels. The amount of magenta filtering varies and does not necessarily correspond to CRI rating. For example, the Optima 32 (CRI 82) has excellent color rendering on film and requires little or no color correction. A Chroma 50 (CRI 92) shows a strong green spike on film that must be removed with half minus-green gel. (Both Chroma 50s and Optima 32s were manufactured by Durotest, which is now out of business.)

A low CRI rating indicates the tube emits a very limited spectrum of light and is incapable of rendering all colors. These fluorescents are designed to maximize lumen output and raise energy efficiency. They produce 2–4 times the light output per watt of an incandescent bulb, and they last 5–15 times longer. So, for economic reasons, standard fluorescent tubes are widely used in office buildings, warehouses, factories, and commercial buildings. However, they generally have low CRI ratings, 50–70, and should be replaced with better tubes.

Coloring Light

Color Chips and Gray Scale

When the film laboratory makes a print or video transfer from a developed negative, the timer or colorist adjusts the exposure and colors of the print to make them look natural. A DP who introduces colors into the lighting must take steps to prevent the timer from removing the color in the lab. To give the lab a reference at the beginning of each film roll, the camera assistant films about 10 seconds of color chips or gray scale under white, properly color-balanced light. The *chip chart*, or color chart, has a set of standard colors or a scale of gray tones from white to black from which the timer can work. The chip chart must be filmed under light that is exactly the proper color temperature. A light that has been checked beforehand with a color temperature meter should be standing by for chip chart shots. When filming the chip chart, no other light should fall on the chart. You may need to turn off or block lights momentarily to prevent extraneous light from discoloring the chip chart. It is also helpful to the colorist to see skin tone with the chip chart, and even to see the scene in the background with all its "nonstandard" color.

A DP who wants the lab (or telecine house) to give the film print (or video transfer) an overall color cast might modify the color of the light hitting the gray scale. For example, for the lab to warm up the dailies (make them more golden and yellow), the DP might film the gray scale with ¼ or ½ CTB on the chart light. When the lab puts in the color settings to compensate for the blue gray scale, it will add yellow, which will show in the footage.

When working with television cameras, the engineer puts up a chip chart in front of each camera before beginning shooting and electronically adjusts the signal from each camera for proper color rendition.

Color Correction Gels for Tints

Color correction gels are used for tints largely because they are readily available and warm or cool the light in a way that occurs naturally in real life and is familiar, in the Kelvin scale. They shift the color along a single dimension between orange and blue.

Eighth, quarter, and half CTO and CTB gels are often used to warm up or cool down a source or even an entire scene. A fire light might use half, full, or even double CTO. A sunset or dawn scene might be filmed with a full CTO on the lights to simulate the golden light of the low sun. An exterior winter scene shot on a sound stage might use soft overhead lights gelled with a half CTB to cool the scene to 4200 K. "Clean" ungelled directional sources would be added to make sunlight.

When using HMI lights in a tungsten-balanced scene, the amount of blue tint in the light is controlled by the amount of CTO correction applied to the light. When a slightly cool light is desired, a half CTO is applied, bringing the 5600 K source down to about 3800 K. This accomplishes the same thing as applying a half CTB to a tungsten source.

Theatrical Gels for Tints

For a more complete palette of tints, theatrical gels offer a vast array of alternative possibilities (Table F.10). Theatrical gels, also called *effects gels* or *party gels*, come in more than 400 shades (in sheets 21 × 24 in. or 20 × 24 in. or in 4 × 25-ft rolls). Instead of using a quarter CTO, the DP can choose from dozens of warming shades, such as gold, amber, straw, fire, salmon, pink, rose, apricot, and so on. For bringing color to face tones, there are various *cosmetic gels*: cosmetic peach, burgundy, rose, rouge, and so forth (also listed in Table F.10). Colors such as salmon, pink, and even chocolate are also used to enhance skin tones. Straw and bastard amber often simulate a low afternoon sun or a flame.

Film emulsions vary in their sensitivity to different colors. A tint may not look quite the same on film as it does to the eye. It must also be remembered that tints must be compatible with the pigments of the wardrobe and set. The color of the light mixes subtractively with these colors. The cinematographer may even conduct screen tests to see on film exactly what effect a given tint will have on a particular face or costume. A test is also the best way to compare the effects of several possible tints side by side.

Saturated Colors

A deeply colored gel effectively narrows the range of wavelengths to those of a specific color. For example, a red gel transmits only the wavelengths around 650 nm. All other wavelengths are absorbed by the gel. The more deeply saturated the gel, the more heat it retains and the more susceptible it is to losing its color and melting. Pairing tungsten lights with red, orange, and yellow gels and HMI or arc lights with blue and purple gels uses the fixture's light spectrum more efficiently and puts less stress on the gels. Protect saturated gels by affixing them away from the heat of the lens, on the barn doors or a grip frame. Narrow-beam punchy sources, such as PARs, play havoc on saturated gels. *Heat-shield* is a clear, heat-resistance film used to protect colored gels from fading or melting under heat stress. Leave a couple inches of space between the Heat-shield and the gel. Rosco's *Therma-shield* is a beefier (and more expensive) version that will hold up better than standard heat shield films. PAR lights and 2k open-face units often require Heat-shield, especially with dense colors.

Heat-shield retards the fading of a gel but is ineffective when a light is simply burning through a gel. In that case, the gel must be placed further from the source,

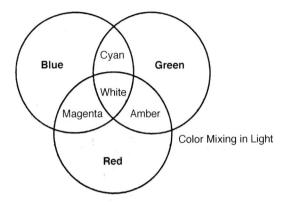

Figure 8.4 Additive mixing of colored light. The overlapping of all three primary colors creates white light. The combination of two primary colors creates the secondary colors (amber, cyan, and magenta). (Reprinted with permission from *Backstage Handbook* by Paul Carter. New York: Broadway Press, 1988.)

spreading the light over a greater area of gel. Sheets of gel may have to be seamed together with clear J-lar tape to cover the larger beam.

Additive Mixing of Colors

When differently colored lights overlap, they mix to make new colors. This is sometimes desirable, sometimes undesirable. Either way, it is important to know how colored lights mix.

The primary colors of light are red, blue, and green. By mixing these three colors of light, all other colors can be made. Theoretically, if three lights gelled primary red, blue, and green are aimed at a white surface with their beams overlapping, as in Figure 8.4, the area of intersection of all three lights is white. The intersection of two primaries makes the secondary colors (cyan, magenta, and amber).

Subtractive Mixing of Colors

When two gels are combined in one light or when colored light is directed at a colored surface, the colors combine subtractively: Only the colors common to both are seen. Having a feeling for subtractive mixing is important for anticipating how the set, wardrobe, and actor's skin tone appear in tinted or colored light. A red light directed at a blue-green dress, for example, will turn the dress black.

Brightness

Methods of Control

There are many ways to adjust a lamp's intensity. On the set, you quickly learn to consider not only which method is the quickest and easiest but which method best accomplishes the effect needed.

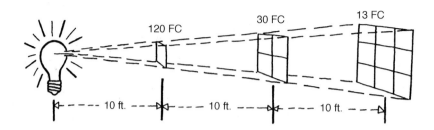

Figure 8.5 Inverse square law (law of squares). If a square surface of 1 ft × 1 ft is illuminated to 120 FC 10 ft from the light source, at 20 ft the same amount of light is now spread over a 4 ft × 4 ft area. The amount of light on a 1 ft × 1 ft area is a quarter of what it was at 10 ft (120 ÷ 4 = 30 FC). At 30 ft, the intensity is one-ninth of what it was at 10 ft (13FC).

Scrims   Dropping a scrim in the light is the fastest and easiest way to reduce intensity without affecting anything else.

Distance   It is often surprising how little you need to move a light to make a big difference in the brightness. This is because the intensity of a light decreases in proportion to the *square* of its distance from the subject. This is known as the *law of squares* or *inverse square law*. Figure 8.5 shows that, if a fixture produces 120 FC at 10 ft, at twice the distance (20 ft) the intensity is *one-quarter*, or 30 FC. At three times the distance (30 ft), the intensity is *one-ninth*, or about 13 FC. (See Falloff—Your Friend, the Inverse Square Law section.)

Flood or spot   Flooding dims the light and increases its coverage; spotting brightens the light and narrows its coverage. With PAR lights, you can change to a wider or narrower lens.

Dimmers   Dimmers provide a variable control of intensity but also affect color temperature. See the section on Dimmers.

Nets   Nets are especially useful to control a selected portion of the beam. They are framed on three sides and open on one side. The open side makes it possible to hide the shadow line of the net, also called the *grip single* or *grip double*.

Fingers and dots   Fingers are used to reduce the intensity of a sliver of the beam. Dots are used to reduce the intensity of a very small circular area and can be used to even out hot spots in the center of beam field. Both come as single nets, double nets, silks, and solids.

Bobinette   Black net fabric that comes in bolts. It is handy because it can be cut to any shape and size and draped or taped in place. It would be a quick way to dim down a too-bright neon or fluorescent practical, for example.

Neutral-density gel   Neutral-density gel is useful for controlling the brightness of an otherwise unmodifiable fixture such as a ellipsoidal spot.

Diffusion   Diffusion media dim and soften the light. The many kinds of diffusion media affect brightness and softness to varying degrees.

Wattage   You can replace the fixture with a bigger or smaller unit or, in some instances, replace the globe with a higher or lower wattage (bulb substitutions are listed in Table E.3).

Shutters   Shutters can smoothly reduce the amount of light getting to the subject. They are handy when the light level needs to change during a shot.

Falloff—Your Friend, the Inverse Square Law

A tiny Kino Flo placed 2 ft from a face gives the same light level as a 2k at 15 ft, or a 20k at 45 ft, so which one would you use? The gaffer tries to use the inverse square law to his advantage, rather than fighting it, forcing him to employ an arsenal of gadgets and grip equipment. If you use a *big* light and place it *far* from the action the light level will be relatively *even* from one side of the acting space to the other. If you use a *small* light source and place it *close* to the actor the light level will *falloff quickly* on the objects surrounding the actor. In Figure 8.6, for the subject lit with the 20k at 45 ft, the change in brightness within 10 ft of the subject is only about $2/3$ of a stop. For the subject lit with the 200W softlight at 2 ft, the light level 10 ft behind the actor is more than 5 stops less—total darkness on film. For the subject lit with the 2k at 15 ft, the background is a pleasing $1\,1/3$ stops down from the subject's brightness. Note, however, any subject that passes through the foreground position will be blown out by three stops. All three of these scenarios offer definite advantages in the right situation. A small light source close up will put less light on the backgrounds, allowing the DP to build more mood, and making practical lights and other highlights pop. A large light far away allows the actors to move through a large space without drastic changes in level or having to light many areas separately. The size of the space, the motivating light source, the mood of the scene, the color and distance of the backgrounds, the details of a particular actor's face—these are all considerations that inform the decision of how to best take advantage of the inverse square properties of light.

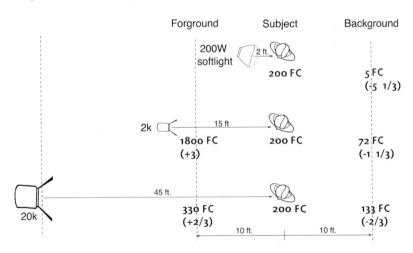

Figure 8.6   The inverse square law in practice. All three subjects are lit to 200 FC, but the light level in the foreground and background positions varies a great deal depending on where the light is placed. The numbers in parentheses give the difference in f-stops from the subject's position.

Dimmers

Dimmers allow the DP to set light outputs to precise levels and to plan controlled changes in light levels during the scene. Very often these changes are designed to be invisible—hidden by the movement in the shot. Commonly a DP will put back lights on a dimmer if the camera moves around the subject in such a way that back lights turn into front lights. Of course dimmer cues are also handy for creating effects where some sort of light appears or disappears in the scene. A dimmer reduces light intensity by reducing the voltage to the light. Unfortunately, this in turn reduces the color temperature of the light, turning it gradually more yellow and orange as it is dimmed, as shown in Table 8.3. As a rule of thumb, the light changes 10 K per volt. Ten volts over or under line voltage increases or decreases the Kelvin temperature by 100 K. Dimmers are useful, therefore, only to the extent that the color change is not noticeable or when it is acceptable to the DP.

Several kinds of dimmers are used in film production: household dimmers and socket dimmers are commonly used to set the intensity of practicals. Variac dimmers are on hand to dim tungsten lamps: 1k, 2k, and 5k on AC power. A similar array of plate dimmers are available for DC power. Electronic dimmers are commonly used when large numbers of dimmer circuits are prerigged throughout the set. A control console (dimmer board) is used to control all the dimmers. Hundreds or even thousands of dimmer circuits may be in such a setup. Specifications for many commonly used types of dimmers are listed in Table G.3. Electronic dimmers also come in a stand-alone, single-dimmer type. More specific information about dimmers is found in Chapter 12, "Distribution, Equipment, Rigging, and Dimmers."

Household dimmers   Small 600-W and 1000-W household AC resistance dimmers (*squeezers*) are often used to control practical lamps and small fixtures. Prepare each dimmer with a plug and socket so that it can be plugged into the line when needed. (Use grounded connectors and at least 14/3 wire for 1000-W dimmers.)

Socket dimmers   A 150-W socket dimmer screws into the bulb socket. They are handy for controlling low-wattage practical lamps.

Variac dimmers   The variac dimmer, an AC dimmer, is a type of variable transformer called an *autotransformer*. It can boost the power up to 140 V or decrease it to zero. These dimmers come in 1k, 2k, and 5k sizes (Figure 8.7). Typically, they are fitted with an on/off switch as well as a large rotary knob. Some have a three-way 120-V/off/140-V switch.

There is an important difference between a household resistance dimmer and a variac dimmer. A variable resistor, or rheostat, works by interposing a resistance on one wire of the circuit, in series with the light. The resistance opposes the flow of current to the light, which causes the light to dim. A variac does not use resistance; instead, it uses coils to induce a current (like a transformer), the voltage of which can be varied. For dimming filament lamps, the effect of either dimmer is the same; however, for controlling fluorescent ballasts or fan motors (inductive loads), a rheostat will not work. A variac must be used.

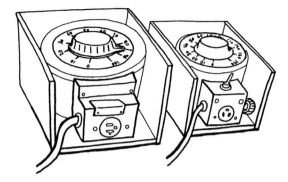

Figure 8.7 Variac dimmers in 2k and 1k sizes. The 1k dimmer knob is marked in volts, from 0 to 140 V. The scale on the larger variacs runs from 0 to 100 percent, which does not refer to volts. When set at 85%, the dimmer delivers line voltage (120 V). At 100%, the variac boosts voltage to 140 V.

Figure 8.8 Mole-Richardson 2k plate dimmer. (Courtesy of Mole-Richardson Co., Los Angeles, CA.)

Plate dimmers Plate dimmers are large variable-resistance dimmers that can be used with either AC or DC circuits running incandescent lights (Figure 8.8).

Electronic dimmers The 2.4-kW, 6-kW, 12-kW, and 20-kW stand-alone electronic dimmers are single electronic dimmers with a slider fader on the dimmer unit as well as a DMX port to control the dimmer from a console.

Figure 8.9 Strand CD80 dimmer pack. The 12-channel pack shown here has 12 dimmer circuits each protected by a 20-A circuit breaker. The dimmer pack's brain (the controller card) is attached to the face plate (below the breakers), which contains the control cable inputs/outputs, diagnostic indicators, and set-up switches. (Courtesy of Strand Lighting, Inc., Rancho Dominguez, CA.)

When a large number of incandescent lights are to be controlled, dimmer packs, or modular dimmer racks, are commonly used. Multiple dimmer circuits are controlled remotely from a control console (a dimmer board). A simple console provides sliding faders to set output levels for each channel. Two or more packs may be daisy-chained and controlled by a single control console when larger numbers of channels are needed. Electronic dimmer packs come in standard sizes: 1.2 kW (10 A per dimmer), 2.4 kW (20 A per dimmer), 6.0 kW (50 A per dimmer), and 12.0 kW (100 A per dimmer). Electronic dimmers are also available for use in DC-powered installations. A complete list is given in Table G.3. A portable unit like the 12-channel pack shown in Figure 8.9 is compact and relatively lightweight, ideal for location work. Electronic dimmers are covered in more detail in Chapter 12.

Shape, Pattern, and Form

In the following sections, we look at how light can be manipulated as it travels from the light source to the subject. We begin by discussing the manipulation of hard light, then move on to ways of creating and manipulating soft light. This discussion encompasses the properties of form, shape, and pattern.

Once a light is placed and turned on, the gaffer cuts it off areas where it is not wanted (be it with barn doors or flags). Often a key light must be cut off a background wall or an actor who stands closer to the light source must be net off. The gaffer might break up the background with a pattern, a streak, or a line of shadow. Side-spill leaks should automatically be cleaned up with a flag or black wrap. To accomplish any of these important goals requires awareness of a few basic laws of physics as well as a number of tricks.

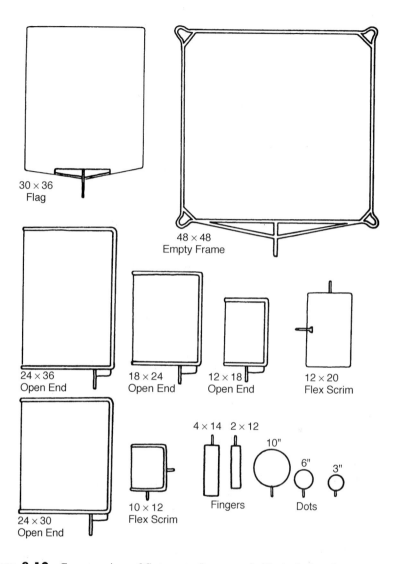

Figure 8.10 Common sizes of flags, nets, frames, and silks including fingers, dots, and 10 × 12-in. postage stamps.

Making Cuts and Patterns

A *topper* is a flag or net used to cut the top of a light. Toppers are often used to keep light off background scenery, which also helps the boom operator avoid casting shadows on the walls. Similarly, *siders* and *bottomers* trim light from the side or bottom. A *lenser* cuts light off the camera lens to prevent flair in the filters and lens. A *courtesy flag* is set up to shade glaring light off the director, DP, camerapersons, or others.

Flags and nets come in various standard sizes, as shown in Figure 8.10.

A few simple, but very important, rules apply when using any flag, net, pattern, or set piece (such as a window) in front of a light.

To make a soft cut (fuzzy shadow line), place the flag closer to the light. To make a hard cut (cleanly defined shadow line), place the flag closer to the surface onto which the shadow falls. For example, if you put a slash of light on a background wall and want the light to gradually taper off toward the top, use a soft-cut topper (a barn door works fine). If you want a hard, defined shadow line, on the other hand, place the flag well out in front of the light. For the sharpest definition, back the light up and place the flag as close to the wall as possible (without it encroaching into the frame). A larger flag may be necessary to cover the whole beam.

When setting a *lenser*, a hard cut is preferable. Halfway between the camera and the light is usually an effective placement when practicable. If the camera is on a long lens, the flag can be placed close to the camera. However, when a wide lens is used, you will run into trouble with the flag encroaching into the frame and it must be worked closer to the light.

To avoid the encroachment problem, always place the stand on the off-camera side of the flag. First prepare the flag on the stand, then slide it in from the offstage side until the shadow covers the lens and filters. A lenser must block light from the entire inner face of the matte box. If light hits the filters in the matte box, the image may flare. Try to overhear or observe what lens is being used and learn to guesstimate the frame line accurately.

With Fresnel lights in flood position, the beam width is roughly equal to the distance from the light. If the flag is placed 3 ft in front of the light, a 2 × 3-ft flag is sufficient. If a harder shadow is needed, use a longer cutter (24 × 72 in.) placed further from the light.

Use of the Net

A net can reduce the intensity in a specific area with much greater accuracy than a half-scrim in the light. You can help hide the shadow line of a net by making a soft cut. If a double net makes an obvious shadow line, you can use two single nets clipped together and staggered, so the thickness builds up gradually. You can fine-tune intensity with a net by angling the net slightly. The more oblique is the angle, the thicker it gets.

Break-Up Patterns

A break-up pattern is very often used to give texture to the background of a shot. Breaking up the light with a tree branch, gobo pattern, venetian blind, window pattern, or just random streaks of shadow gives the image greater contrast and tonal variation and helps set off the foreground subject. The gaffer may want to exploit whatever shadow-projection possibilities are offered by the set and set dressing: foliage moving in the wind, a slow-turning fan, water running down glass, lace curtains, a banister.

Again, for the pattern to be cleanly defined, the pattern maker must be as close to the surface as possible.

You get a cleaner shadow

- From a point source than from a larger one.
- From a stronger light placed further away.
- From a Fresnel fixture than from an open-face reflector fixture.
- At full flood than when spotted in.
- From the edge of the beam than from its center.
- By removing the lens from the fixture altogether (though you also lose intensity and flood/spot control).
- By using a donut to remove the edges of the beam with ellipsoidal and xenon lights.
- Of venetian blinds from a Fresnel if you place a C-stand arm through the center of the beam a foot or so in front of the fixture. (No one ever believes me on this one. Just try it.)

The distance also affects the size of the projected shadows. When close to the subject and far from the light, the pattern is of only slightly larger dimensions than the pattern maker itself. When the pattern maker is very close to the light, however, the pattern is projected over a large area, extremely enlarged and distorted in shape, more expressionistic. Therefore, the size of lamp used, the size of the pattern maker needed to cover the beam, and the distance of the light and the pattern from the subject must all be taken into account before placing the light. In fact, these considerations may have to be taken into account when designing and placing the sets. For example, if a light is to shine through a window and needs to be placed a considerable distance from the window, ample space must be provided for lights around the set.

Cucaloris

A *cucaloris*, also called a *cookie* or *cuke*, is a plywood flag with odd-shaped holes cut in it. It is used to break up the light into random foliagelike splotches. A *celo cuke* is made with painted wire mesh and creates a more subtle effect because the mesh reduces the light rather than blocks it completely. A cookie does not look convincing if it moves during a take. For realistic moving foliage, use a branchaloris.

Branchaloris

A *branchaloris* is nothing more than a leafy branch found on the ground or broken off a bush and placed in front of a light on a C-stand. It breaks up the light, projects the shadows of branch and leaves onto the scene, and can be made to move naturally, as if in the wind.

Tape on an Empty Frame

To make lines through the light (to simulate the frame of a window, for example), take an empty frame (18 × 24 in., 2 × 3 ft, or 4 × 4 ft, depending on the size of the source and the frame's distance from it) and run strips of black tape across it. It is easiest to build the pattern with the fixture in place and turned on, so you can see the effect it creates.

Soft Light

Soft light results when light is bounced or diffused over a relatively large surface by one of several means: light shining through a large frame of diffusion; light bouncing off of a large white surface.

With soft light, we are no longer dealing with parallel (slightly diverging) rays of light from a single point source but with rays bounced or diffused so they are diffracted at all angles, moving away from the diffusion surface in all directions. Light from a soft source comes to the subject from all points of a diffuse luminous surface, resulting in three qualities that are often very desirable:

1. *Soft shadows.* No clean, sharply discernible line is projected. The shadow lines are broad and fuzzy. Shadows appear as gradations of tone, so that the entire image is imbued with a softness that is natural and also very beautiful. The fuzzy quality of soft shadows also makes them easier to hide in situations where multiple shadows would be distracting.
2. *Soft light around the features of the subject.* Whereas a face lit from one side by hard light is like a half moon (bright on one side and black on the other), lit by a large soft source, it shows a gradual drop off of light from one side to the other. Soft light tends to fill in blemishes in the skin. The overall picture has a full tonal range, light to dark, with no harsh shadow lines and lower overall contrast than when lit with harder light.
3. *Interesting reflections.* When lighting shiny or glossy subjects or surfaces with glossy finish, a soft source is reflected as an amorphous highlight. Hard light, on the other hand, is reflected as a bright, glaring hot spot.

A soft source can be used to create a soft highlight in dark wood, bringing out dark furniture or paneling by catching a reflection of the light source. The gaffer places the light where it is seen by the camera as a reflection in the surface. Especially in cases where you don't want to throw a lot of light onto the walls, this approach yields a subtle, more natural effect.

Along the same lines, a soft source makes a nice eye light. It reflects in the shiny part of the eye, giving the eyes a special brightness. A large, soft source reflected in this way need not actually shine a lot of light onto the subject; it need only be bright enough to create a visible highlight reflection.

Softness of Light

Three factors affect the softness of light: the size of the face of the source, its distance from the subject, and the amount direct rays are diffused by the bounce surface or diffusion material. The larger the source, the softer the shadows and the greater the wrapping effect, because the larger source yields more light rays, which can come from angles that encircle the features of the subject. This is why it is important when focusing a light fixture onto a diffusion frame or bounce board to completely fill it with light. The surface of the diffusion frame or bounce board becomes the source of light for the scene; the larger the source, the softer the effect.

The smaller the subject, in relation to the face of the source, the more the light engulfs it. If the subject is too small, it becomes overwhelmed and the image starts to appear flat.

Obviously, the size of the source in relation to the subject also depends on the distance between them. The further away the source, the smaller its effective size. (The sun, for example, is a very large source but, as it is 93 million miles away, its rays are completely parallel, so direct sunlight is about as sharp a light as you'll find.)

Bringing a soft light in as close to a subject as possible maximizes its softening effect. This also localizes the light, creating a soft pool around the actor, which falls off very quickly into darkness. This happens because the light level falls off with distance at a geometric rate, so the closer the source is to the actor, the more dramatic the fall off. Conversely, if you want the light to carry across more space you would want to move the source further away. The further the light is from the action area, the less light intensity falls off across the space.

Controlling Soft Light

A DP wants to control the foreground lighting and background lighting separately and light the actors without also flattening out the background. One can do this by cutting and containing the lighting with flags, black wrap, and the like. Soft light is more difficult than hard light to cut and control, and the softer the light (the larger the source and the heavier the diffusion), the more difficult it becomes. The larger the source, the larger the flags required to block the light. Boxing in a 4 × 4 frame of heavy diffusion typically requires 4 × 8 flags. Large cutters, 2 × 6 ft, are necessary as toppers, placed well out in front of the source. Boxing in larger frames (8 × 8 or 12 × 12) can require a lot of grip work. Flags and nets used close to a large source are ineffectual: The light engulfs the flag. To be useful, the flag must be far enough from the source that it blocks a direction the light is traveling, rather than merely blocking a portion of the face of the source. Grips often need to fabricate a *teaser* 12- or 14-ft long by stapling a length of duvetyn to a 1 × 3 batten.

Nets are often ineffective with a large soft source. You can, however, use a solid where normally you would use a net. Because the shadow is so nebulous, the flag serves to create an area of lesser brightness, rather than a cut. The flag can be angled to increase or decrease its effective size.

Controlling Soft Light Using Egg Crates

The best way to easily contain soft light is using an egg crate or louver directly in front of the diffusion surface. Lighttools™ makes fabric egg crates (Soft Crates™) for all types of chimera-type light banks as well as for larger diffusion frames, butterfly sets, and overhead frames from 4 × 4 ft up to 20 × 20 ft (Figure 8.11). A Soft Crate is a collapsible fabric grid that controls the light by dividing the source into bite-size portions, or cells. The Soft Crate reduces neither the softness nor the brightness of the light source appreciably but does control how much the light spreads to the sides. This approach has the advantage of being extremely space efficient. It avoids cluttering the set with a forest of flags and C-stands, which can be a real problem especially in smaller sets. Soft Crates used on large frames come in four cell sizes, referred to by their maximum beam spread: 20°, 30°, 40°, or 50°.

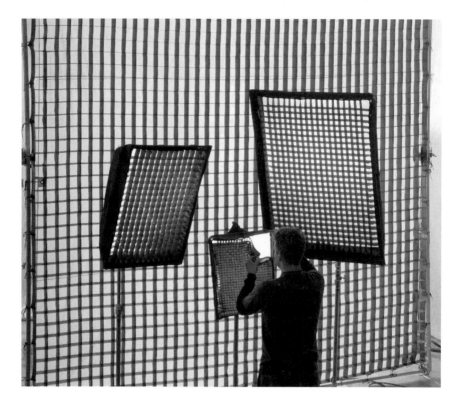

Figure 8.11 Lighttools Soft Crates being made ready for use on three lightbanks and a 12 × 12-ft frame. (Courtesy of Lighttools™, Edmonton, Alberta, Canada.)

Soft Crates for Chimera-type light banks are offered in 20°, 30°, 40°, 50°, and 60° cell sizes.

While the main purpose of an egg crate is to contain the light, on larger frames it also tends to even out the brightness of the light as you move toward the light source. This happens because, as you move closer to the light source, the fabric cells occlude progressively more of the diffusion surface. The egg crate effectively reduces the exposure range in the acting space by reducing the rapid increase of brightness, what DPs like to call *sourcyness*, showing the audience the light source. The egg crate effectively circumvents the inverse square law.

Diffusion

Diffusion Materials

There are five basic types of diffusion material, each with its own character: spun, frost, white diffusion, silks (and other fabrics), and silent diffusion. Each type is manufactured in several densities (Table F.11). Spun, or spun glass, is used mainly on very hot little light fixtures, because it is very heat resistant. Spun gives the beam a mild soft edge but with minimal spread, so that the shape of the beam and the effectiveness of barn doors are maintained. Frost, such as opal or Hampshire frost, yields slightly more beam spread and softening but still maintains a discernible beam center. The original direction of the beam is still dominant.

A medium-weight diffusion material, such as 250, diffracts much more of the light. As a result, the beam spreads as it passes through the material. As the diffusion surface itself becomes the source of rays of light equally with the light fixture, the effective size of the source is enlarged to the size of the diffusion frame. Shadows are softened. The light starts to wrap around the edges of objects.

A dense diffusion, such as a heavy frost, 216, or grid cloth, causes a wide beam spread. The original direction of the beam becomes secondary to the diffuse multidirectional rays emitted from the diffusion material. The light rays are deflected in all directions over the entire area of the diffusion frame. This creates the ideal source for shadowless, wrapping light because the greatest number of light rays are diverted at angles that can accomplish these ends and the dominant direction of the light from the fixture is completely removed. It creates an even field of light with no discernible beam center or edge.

Fabrics such as silk, muslin, and grid cloth with their dense diffusions often are used on large frames. Many gaffers like the diffusing effect of muslin. You can bounce light off it or use it as a diffuser, directing light through it. The fabric is inexpensive and durable and can be made in any size, even huge 40-ft squares and larger. Unbleached muslin has a yellow tint, which warms the light without the need for gels. Bleached muslin has less of a tint but retains some warming effect.

Silk is commonly used on a 12 × 12 or 20 × 20 overhead frame. Full silk has a relatively low transmission; it reduces light intensity by about $2^2/_3$ stops, but despite its density, silk has only a moderate diffusing effect. A light passing through silk still casts a hard shadow, but the silk helps to fill. China silk or $^1/_4$ silk is much lighter, reducing transmission by only a half stop.

Silent diffusions, such as soft frost and Hilite, are made of a rubbery material that does not rattle and crinkle when caught by wind, as other diffusions do. These materials are not as heat resistant as normal diffusion material, however, and should not be used directly on a light fixture.

Diffusion on the Fixture

As with colored gel, label each piece of diffusion material when it is cut from the roll. Mark the type on the corner of the piece with an indelible marker.

Attaching diffusion material to the barn doors of a Fresnel or open-face light takes the hard edge off the beam. It diffuses the light, evens out the intensity across the field, and reduces or removes the central hot spot.

To create as large a source as possible, open the barn doors wide and attach the diffusion material to the outside. When using dense diffusion medium, the flood/spot mechanism works in reverse. To maximize the light output, flood the light to fill the diffusion with light. Maximum output is often found just shy of full flood.

Diffusion attached inside the barn doors allows them still to have some effect and creates fewer problems with spill and reflections off the back of the diffusion;

Figure 8.12 A Croney cone. (Equipment courtesy of Hollywood Rental, Sun Valley, CA.)

however, it does not increase the size of the source and therefore does little more than take the curse off the hard light.

Other Ways of Making Soft Light

Croney cone   The Croney cone, named for its inventor, Jorden Crownenweth, ASC (*Blade Runner*), is a cone that fits in place of the barn doors on the front of the light. A frame fitted with grid cloth or some other diffusion slides into slots on the front of the cone, turning the Fresnel into a soft source with a larger face (Figure 8.12). The diffusion frame can be exchanged easily when a different type of diffusion is desired.

Chimera   Chimera Photographic Lighting makes a variety of collapsible, heat-resistant, fabric soft boxes (Figure 8.13) that incorporate a great many refinements on the basic Croney cone design.

Chimeras are made of heat-resistant fabric stretched and held in shape by flexible, interior, stainless-steel poles. The interior fabric is soft silver reflective material, which increases light output and further diffuses the light. The design includes two effective ways to reduce side spill, 60° and 90° honeycomb grids, and louvers. A second interior diffusion baffle can be added to double-diffuse the light. This ensures that even an intense and punchy light source will be fully diffused.

Chimeras can be fitted to almost any Fresnel, PAR, and open-face fixture in place of barn doors. A "speed ring" is needed to adapt the chimera to each light (see tables in Appendix G). Figure 8.14 shows one gaffer's own handmade adaptation, which incorporates control of color temperature and intensity by use of individually switchable globes and an on-board dimmer control. The chimera

Figure 8.13 Chimera lightbanks in use on a variety of heads: (from small to large) a Video Pro bank on a 150-W Dedo fixture, a small Quartz bank on a 1k baby (fitted with a fabric louver), and large one, a 2k junior and a Daylight bank on a 2.5k HMI. (Courtesy of Chimera Photographic Lighting, Boulder, CO.)

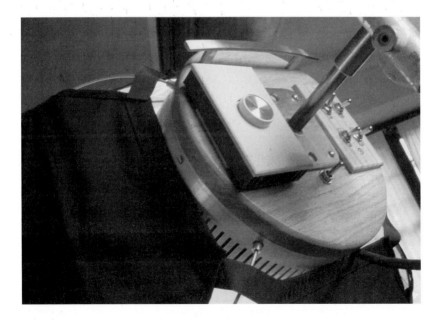

Figure 8.14 Gaffer Keith Morgan designed the "Woody Light" (the back plate is oak). Designed for speed and flexibility, the base houses a 1k EGT and four photoflood globes wired to individual switches and a master dimmer. See Appendix H.

light banks are available in four models. Video Pro and Quartz banks are standard depth and are best used with open-face fixtures. Daylite and Daylite Junior banks are deeper; they are useful for narrower-beam fixtures, such as Fresnels.

The flaps that close the chimera around the face of the light get burned by most lights. The flaps are fitted with Velcro, so they can be folded back away from the face of the light. *Always* fold the flaps and open the ventilation holes.

Homemade diffusion box   You can build an inexpensive soft box with many of the same advantages as the chimera. This type of soft box diffuses light from a fixture while containing the light (Figure 8.15A). It has two separated layers

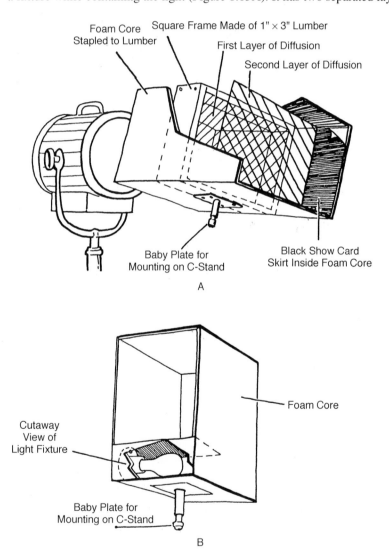

Figure 8.15   (A) A portable diffusion box, (B) the "garbage box," so named because it was improvised in a hurry on set from materials found in the garbage.

of diffusion material. Light becomes diffused as it passes through the layers, and it bounces between the layers, further scattering the rays and softening the light. The hood, made of black show card, adjusts the spread of light. A nail-on plate is screwed on for mounting the unit on a C-stand.

A box like this can be made any size or shape, but if you make it just slightly larger than the size of standard frames (24 × 36 in. or 18 × 24 in.), you can make a slot in the side of the box so that diffusion and color can be easily changed by sliding in a new frame.

Homemade soft box   Another approach to take is to construct a soft box with light bulbs installed inside the soft box itself. The advantage is that it is self-contained and very lightweight. You can position such a box without having to contend with a heavy light fixture (a short C-stand easily supports it).

Soft boxes can be made quite simply out of light lumber, foamcore, staples, screws, and diffusion material. Remember that these materials are flammable and light bulbs get very hot. Be sure to cut ventilation flaps or holes in the bottom and the top of the box to create a ventilation flow. Leave plenty of space on all sides around the bulbs. Do not put power cords or tape on the inside of the box, where they could come loose, fall near a bulb, and catch on fire. Use #14 or #12 red/black wire, not zip cord. Build these home-made devices with large doses of common sense and caution.

Construct the box with black foamcore on the outside, white inside. Use porcelain medium screw base sockets for regular bulbs, photofloods, and mushroom floods; or bayonet mount FEV sockets for small tungsten bulbs. Use several bulbs, and wire each socket separately so that you can vary the brightness by switching bulbs on or off. Cut flaps so that you can reach inside to change bulbs when needed. Place the mounting plate at the center of gravity so that the box balances on the plate and does not create excessive torque on the C-stand. (If you build a snoot for the box, you may need to determine a second center of gravity with the snoot in place and add a second nail-on plate.)

Garbage box   This type of soft box got its name when an inventive gaffer (now DP, Greg Gardener) hurriedly pulled a cardboard box from the garbage and transformed it into a soft light (Figure 8.15B). The box is lined with foamcore. A ledge shields direct light from the bulb. A white wrap foil lining around the bulb should be used to protect the foamcore from heat. This type of light is used close in to a subject.

Chicken coop   A chicken coop hangs overhead on rope. This kind of light might be used, for example, over a large dinner table. It is usually rigged so that it can be raised and lowered to increase or decrease the intensity of the light. The one shown in Figure 8.16A is fitted with six photoflood bulbs. A small, single-bulb version is shown in Figure 8.16B. The coop has a duvetyn skirt that can be lowered or raised independently on all four sides to control the amount of light falling on the walls of the room.

Nook light coop   Figure 8.17 shows nook lights mounted in a chicken coop frame and pointing upward into the foamcore to create an even, less direct soft light.

China lanterns   Paper Chinese lanterns are an inexpensive, lightweight soft light or ambient light source. They come in various sizes (12-, 24-, and 30-in.

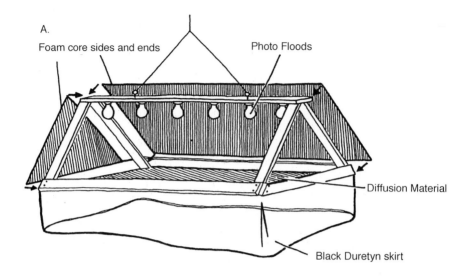

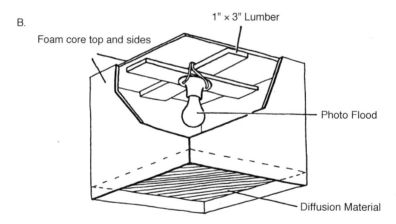

Figure 8.16 (A) A homemade skirted six-light chicken coop, (B) a single photoflood soft box.

spheres) as well as rectangular boxes. Rig the lantern to a C-stand, with a photoflood bulb in a porcelain socket (do not use the 60-W plastic sockets sometimes sold with the lanterns; the photoflood bulbs will melt them). I always use them on a variac. Hidden in the set, or positioned just off screen and used in close, the lanterns are nice soft "glow lights" and give a localized warm glow. A large ball hung above the set achieves a nice low ambient light level. The ball can be skirted, if desired, to keep spill off walls. The popularity of lanterns inspired manufacturers to come up with more durable fixtures of this type. K 5600 Lighting makes a 200-W HMI lantern in 20- or 30-in.

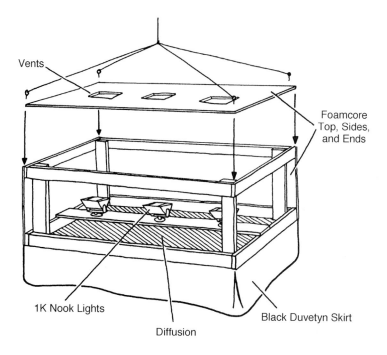

Vents

Foamcore
Top, Sides,
and Ends

1K Nook Lights

Black Duvetyn Skirt

Diffusion

Figure 8.17 A homemade skirted nook light bounce box.

diameter. Chimera has 22- and 30-in. lanterns that fit video pro ring sizes or can be fitted with a tungsten halogen socket.

Bounce Light

Soft light can be created by simply bouncing a specular source off a white surface. The following are some examples.

Bead board and foamcore   In many situations, a piece of white board can be used to bounce existing light onto the shadow areas of the face to reduce contrast. This is especially common when shooting outside in direct sunlight, where the contrast is very high. A 2- or 4-ft square of foamcore, taped to and reinforced by a piece of bead board, is standard equipment for fill light. Similarly, a piece of show card placed in the lap of the driver of a car helps fill in shadows.

To fill a fairly large room with soft light, a strong light, such as a 2500 HMI PAR, can be aimed at a 4 × 4-ft or 4 × 8-ft piece of bead board or foamcore (Figure 8.18).

Remember that the angle of incidence equals the angle of reflection. If you put the bounce board up high and angle it downward, you can place the lights below and in front of the board, pointing up into it.

Show card, cove light   In a small room where it is difficult to hide lamps, you can tape a piece of white show card into an off-screen corner (Figure 8.19).

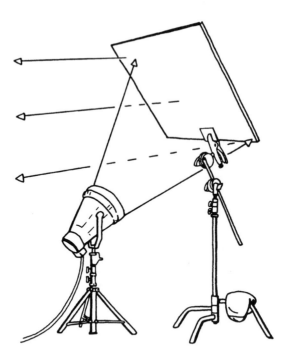

Figure 8.18 A strong, large, soft source produced by bouncing a 2500-W HMI PAR off a 4 × 4 bead board.

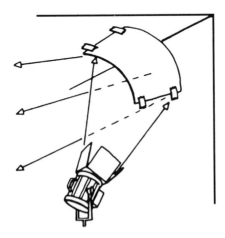

Figure 8.19 A show card taped into a corner creates a soft source without rigging a fixture into the corner.

The reflected light can be better controlled if the show card is curved into a parabola. The fixture is hidden under or above, pointing at the show card, creating a soft light from that direction. You can also use a silver or gold show card.

Ceiling   A fast and easy way to fill a room with soft, even illumination is simply to bounce a strong light off a white ceiling. If the ceiling is not white, you can rig a sheet of foamcore to the ceiling.

Griff   To create a very big, soft source that might simulate skylight when shooting inside a studio or when a large area needs to be covered with soft light, the gaffer may bounce light into a 12- or 20-ft square of griffolyn. A couple of large HMIs, one on each side, do the trick. For exterior scenes, a griff works the same way, bouncing sunlight.

Negative fill   To some extent the shine in people's faces reflect the color and lightness of surfaces around them. Placing a 4 × 4 floppy near an actor removes these reflections, as well as shading off any wayward light.

Movement

The final property of light that can be manipulated is motion: the jumping glow of a television screen, the dancing flames of a fire, the passing of car headlights at night, disco and concert lights, the movement of a handheld lantern or flashlight, a swinging bulb hanging from the ceiling, the projection of rain running down a windshield, the slow, smooth motion of sunlight through an airplane's windows as it banks and turns. Movement contributes to a scene's naturalism, mood, and visual interest.

Flicker Effects: Television Screen, Flame, and Fire

Sit in a dark room with only the television on but don't look at it. Watch the way the light shifts on the walls and faces in the room. You will notice that the blue television light quickly changes in intensity and color when there is a cut on screen and gradually shifts in intensity as the camera pans or as characters move around.

The pace of the shifts depends on what you are watching. A music video creates a constantly changing image. Old movies, on the other hand, tend to play scenes in wide master shots or intercut reverse close-ups, leaving at least several seconds and even 20 or 30 seconds between cuts. When you create an off-screen television effect, you must find a way to mimic the pace of the shifts with the intensity of the light.

There are many different ways to do this, and any method that works is as good as another. A common way is to make a soft box out of foam core and light lumber, then place several small lights inside it. Use blue gel and diffusion material on the front of some or all the lights, as desired. To make the lights flicker, some sort of controller must be used.

Figure 8.20 Magic gadgets flicker box supplies three 20-A circuits, each of which can be set to flicker up to a set peak and down to a set base level. The three circuits can be programmed to create a variety of chase effects, fire effects, and television effects. The box can also serve as three 2k dimmers. (Courtesy of Magic Gadgets Inc., Seattle, WA.)

Flicker Boxes

Television screen and flame effects are often created using a flicker box such as that shown in Figure 8.20. A variety of such boxes are on the market. Specifications are listed in Table G.4 (Appendix G). A flicker box typically creates increase and decrease in intensity at random intervals. The rate of flicker as well as the brightness of the light at its peak and lowest intensities can be set with controls. Some flicker boxes also make blinking light effects and lightning flashes. Flicker boxes having three circuits can produce coordinated flicker effects and chase effects.

Some gaffers use a circular disk of mercury switches to flicker the lights. The switches contain liquid mercury, which completes the circuit when tilted such that the mercury sloshes over the contacts. By artfully tipping and rotating the disk, different lights turn on and off in a controllable yet unregimented way that is very convincing. Operating this type of controller requires a practiced hand.

Another gaffer uses two short fluorescent tubes and has an electrician move his arms in front of the light—simple but effective.

Fire Effect

Flicker boxes are also commonly used to create a fire effect. When a flame moves, the shadows from the firelight move up and down and from side to side. To get a convincing effect, it is necessary to use at least two lights to simulate a flame.

The best way to get a fire effect is to use fire. If practical considerations (such as the location, the need for fire marshals, and so on) allow it, a fire bar (a gas-fueled pipe with holes along it) can be supplied by the effects department and used as a portable lighting source. If the intensity of the flame is insufficient, supplemental light can be imbued with the look of flame by shining a fixture through the flame of the fire bar.

Moving Lights

Lights are often mounted to a crane or dolly or handheld by an electrician to make the light move. Reflecting a PAR 64 into a shiny silver tray of water creates lively water striations. Sequences of dimmer cues can be set up to create breathtaking shifts in angle and color. Various special effects lights can be used to create moving projections (*scene machine*) or dynamic concert lighting effects (automated fixtures). There are many exiciting ways to move light. The possibilities are limited only by your imagination.

CHAPTER 9

Electrician's Set Protocol and Aerial Lifts

Set Protocol

Staging Area

On arrival at each new shooting location, one of the first jobs is to establish a staging area where electrical equipment is kept, ready to go onto the set when needed. The best boy will have scoped out a spot that is convenient to the set but not so close as to block access. Stake out the good spot early before another department claims it. The entrance to the staging area must be clear of obstructions. You don't want a line of director's chairs sitting in front of the area. You need to be able to carry equipment in and out fast.

While the director and DP decide on their shots, the electricians can "head-up" a selection of lights on stands in the staging area, ready to be brought into the set when called for. Line up the lights on stands. Organize them in rows—row of midgets, row of tweenies, row of babies, row of juniors, and so on—so that each type of light is readily accessible. Skinny up the legs of the stands so they can be packed together closely. To be totally proper about it, the lights should be arranged with the stand fully lowered, T-handles lined up in a straight line down the back of the stand, power cord hanging on hanger, gels and scrims hanging on the stand (not in the light), and doors closed.

The staging area should be arranged in an orderly fashion for easy access to all the equipment, which includes crates of 25- and 50-ft stingers, gel crate, gel rolls, boxes of practical bulbs and associated electrical parts (zip cord, quick-ons, plugs, porcelain sockets, etc.), variac dimmers, black wrap, tape rolls, clothespins, and similar electrical expendables. It is often convenient to keep a selection of essentials (tape, black wrap, clothespins, and gel) even closer at hand, in a set box, a crate kept on or immediately outside the set.

When a light, stinger, or cable is no longer needed on the set, it goes back to the staging area where it will not create clutter. The light should be "head wrapped": the stand fully lowered, the cord coiled, the barn doors closed, and the scrims removed and hung on the stand. If a particular gel or diffusion is being used on all the lights, store it in the scrim box. Some gaffers like to have specific precut gels kept with each light.

Lighting the Set

Electricians have to be alert and always have one eye on the gaffer. You tune into the sound of his voice and learn to pick it out from the general rumble of noise. An experienced electrician has a sense of the ebb and flow of activity on the set and knows when he needs to work fast and when there is time to spare. When lighting begins on each new setup, all the electricians should automatically come to the set. There is a great deal of activity as the broad strokes of the lighting are put in. The director's monitor and the camera dolly should be provided power immediately if need be. The director often needs the monitor to set up the new shot.

A period of tweaking and adjusting follows the broad strokes; a few small lights may be added. Finally, the DP declares that the lighting is ready, and the AD calls the actors into the set. Each time the first AD announces a new shot, the electricians working the set should quietly get close to the lights that they may need to move and watch the gaffer and DP for orders. Even when lighting activity is at a minimum, one electrician should always be on the set (unless the AD clears the set for a particular reason). Before you leave the set to grab a soda, conduct business, or go to the restroom, be sure another electrician is on the set and knows that you are stepping out. If the gaffer needs to step out, he will assign a set electrician to cover him, and that person must remain next to the DP until the gaffer returns.

Setting Lights

The gaffer gives an instruction: "Put a baby over in that corner to key these two actors. Give it opal and quarter CTO." You need a baby stand, a baby with scrim set and barn doors, and precut gels and diffusion. You probably also need a 25-ft stinger to run power to the light. A grip will usually be right behind you with a C-stand and flags, and he should provide a sandbag.

A complete set of appropriate-size scrims and a set of barn doors should be brought to the set with every light. Hang the scrim box on the stand. When the gaffer wants a little less from a light, you should be able to drop in the scrim in seconds. It is very bad form to have to search for scrims. They should always be with the light.

It is also worth repeating that each raised stand should be bagged. The more time you spend on sets, the more you see just how easily stands are toppled. It becomes second nature to check that stands are properly bagged. Similarly, when working in a wind, around Ritter fans, or around helicopters, the grips may need to tie guy lines (no less than three) to the top of the light stand and secure them to bull stakes driven well into the ground. Prop-wash from a helicopter will blow over a Dino on a supercrank like it was a piece of paper, even with 130 lb of sand on it.

Focusing Lights

Ideally, an electrician has some idea what the light is to be used for. Either the gaffer explains it briefly when calling for the light or the electrician already knows because the gaffer and DP use particular lights for the same general purpose on each setup and the electricians have set similar lights numerous times before. The electrician comes in with the light, sets it up, powers it, aims it to light the prescribed area at approximately the desired angle, adjusts the barn doors, and has the diffusion ready, all this without turning the light on. The electrician then notifies the gaffer he or she is ready. When the gaffer gives the go ahead, the electrician turns the light on and makes any small adjustments called for by the gaffer.

Don't make the mistake of turning on the light as soon as you arrive with it, especially if you're not clear on exactly what the gaffer has in mind. This can be annoying to the gaffer and DP because it disrupts the process; the gaffer and DP may be in the middle of focusing other lights or taking light readings. If a light suddenly comes on, blasting everywhere, it can mess up what they're working on and give false meter readings. Usually background lights can be turned on and focused by the electrician without the gaffer. The gaffer is notified for final approval after the light is totally set, before the electrician walks away. This saves the gaffer time. But, if in doubt, check before you hit the ON switch.

When you turn the light on, the grunt work stops and the real craft begins—manipulating the light so that it accomplishes the desired effect. While the electrician handles the light, the gaffer either stands on the set with the light meter or views the scene from the appropriate camera angle. Very often the gaffer starts with the light at full spot to aim the beam. A gaffer will hold out a fist where the beam should be spotted. The electrician spots the light onto the gaffer's hand, then returns the light to full flood. Another way gaffers sometimes focus the light is to view the light fixture through a contrast glass. The gaffer then directs the lamp operator with hand signals (Figure 9.1) or verbal instructions. The following are common instructions:

Pan lamp-left or lamp-right   Lamp-left is your left when you face the direction the light is facing. Lamp-right is your right.

Camera-left or camera-right   Camera-left is your left when you face the direction the camera is facing. Camera-right is your right.

Upstage   A term that originates in the Shakespearian Theater where the stage is sloped toward the audience. Upstage is away from the audience. In film and television it is taken to mean the direction away from the camera (e.g., the upstage lights are backlights).

Downstage   The direction toward the audience, in our case, the camera (e.g., move the junior downstage 3 ft).

Offstage   As above, as if the camera is the audience. Offstage is the direction away from the center of the shot laterally (e.g., always place the C-stand on the offstage side of the light).

Onstage   The direction toward the center of the shot laterally (e.g., "You can move your light 2 ft onstage before you get in the shot").

Tilt up   Tilt the light up.

Tilt down   Tilt the light down.

Flood it out   Turn the flood/spot knob slowly toward flood until told to stop. Reply, "Flooding."

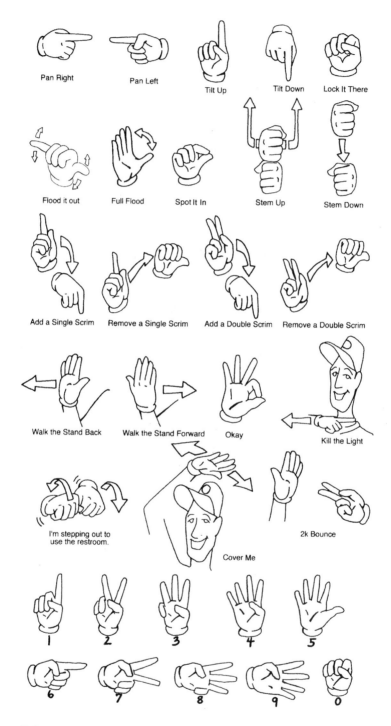

Figure 9.1 Hand signals.

Full flood   Go directly to full flood.

Spot it in   Turn the flood/spot knob slowly toward spot until told to stop. Reply, "Spotting."

Full spot   Go directly to full spot.

Stem up   Raise the stand.

Stem down   Lower the stand.

Walk it back   Move the stand and light back.

Walk it in   Move the stand and light closer to the action.

Lock it down   The light is aimed correctly; tighten the T-handles to lock that position.

Walk away   It's perfect. Make sure that everything is secure. You're done with that one. "That's a purchase" is a similar phrase.

A scosh   Technical term for an increment slightly less than a smidge or a tad, as in "Flood it out a scosh."

Door it off the back wall   Lower the top barn door.

Drop in a double   Put in a double scrim. Reply, "Double in" when finished. You also hear expressions like, "Slow it down" or "Bring it down to a dull roar."

Home run   Two doubles in a light.

Grand slam   Two doubles and a single in a light.

Pull the wire   Pull out all scrims. Reply, "It's clean" when no scrims remain.

Bottom half-double   Put in a half-double scrim oriented to cut the bottom. Reply, "Bottom half-double in."

Waste some of that   Pan or tilt the light so the hot spot isn't directly on the action.

Do off/on or A-B   Switch the light off and on so that the gaffer can observe what the light accomplishes. Announce "On" as you turn it on and "Off" as you turn it off.

Shake up that shiny board   As the sun moves, shiny boards have to be readjusted. Move the board to check that it is properly aimed. The phrase can refer to lights in the same way.

Flag the light   Pass your hand back and forth in front of the lens to show where the beam is hitting.

Give me a slash here   Bring the barn doors together to create a line where indicated.

Rotate the beam   PAR lights have an elliptical beam, rather than a round one. You can turn the lamp housing to orient the beam horizontal, vertical, or at any angle.

Dress the cable   Neaten up the cable or run it out of sight or out of the way.

Dress the light   Something is hanging off the light (that is, a safety chain or diffusion is hanging into the shot). Clean it up.

Change that out for a deuce   Replace the light with a 2k fixture.

Count to 10   Hold off on what you are doing; things are changing and it may not be needed after all.

Cancel the baby   Yup, sure enough, we don't need that light.

Fire it up   Turn it on.

Cool the light   Turn it off. You also often hear, "Save the lights."

Strike the light   When referring to an HMI, strike means turn it on, as in "Strike it up."

Strike the set   Take down all the lights and return them to the staging area.

It is customary for the electrician to respond to the gaffer's directions by repeating each direction back as he performs it. This assures the gaffer that she has been heard and someone is following her instructions. When she says, "Flood it out," the electrician responds, "Flooding" as he does so. When a delay is involved, he lets the gaffer know he has heard her before proceeding; if she asks for a light, the electrician responds, "Flying in" as he goes to fetch it.

Sometimes a gaffer and DP will try to sneak in some final accent lights while the director and actors are already rehearsing on set. The gaffer needs this to be done without drawing attention to what is being done. The electrician should be especially careful to focus and contain the light before turning it on and to work quietly.

Applying Gel to the Fixture

The most common way of attaching gel or diffusion to a Fresnel or open-face light is to clip it on with clothespins (Figure 9.2B). Look out for light reflecting off the back of the gel and bouncing onto the walls of the set. Encircle the gaps in the barn doors with black wrap to block gel-reflection spill.

Don't be stingy with gel; cut a square of gel big enough that light does not leak around the side of the gel, causing white spill. Placing the gel on the inside of the barn doors (Figure 9.2A) also prevents spill but puts more heat stress on the gel. Generally this works well with Fresnel fixtures when they are flooded out. When using a dense gel, a particularly hot fixture (PAR or open face), or when the lamp is spotted, the gel is liable to lose color.

Gel frames can be used in some circumstances with some types of fixtures but generally the scrim slot is too hot a place for gel. Never put a scrim next to a gel frame. The hot scrim will melt the gel.

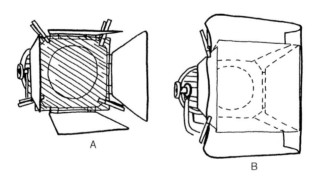

A

B

Figure 9.2   Gel and diffusion can be attached either inside (A) or outside (B) the barn doors.

Communications: Walkie-Talkies and Hand Signals

The clamor of the crew calling out these sorts of instructions to one another can be a distraction for the director, actors, and DP when they are trying to communicate on set. Walkie-talkies with earpieces or radio headsets are an invaluable tool for the grip and electric crew. They cut down the noise on the set and save the electricians a lot of running. If you need something from the staging area and someone has just gone over there, for example, you can quietly ask that person to bring you what you need on the way back without yelling or running.

When using headsets or walkie-talkies, be sure to use proper mike technique: Press the button fully, allow a second for the transmitter to engage *before* you start speaking and don't let up on it until *after* you have finished your last word. Otherwise, your first and last words will be cut short. When speaking, keep the mike about an inch from your mouth for a clear, strong signal.

Typically a walkie-talkie has many channels, which may be assigned to various departments. Usually, the assistant directors are on channel 1, while the electric, grip, and transportation departments claim their own channels.

The gaffer initiates a conversation by asking for someone by name, "Dave, come back," or simply a general call for aid, "Electric." Respond with your name: "Go for Dave." Always acknowledge a transmission by saying "copy" or some similar response. If the transmission is interrupted by another transmission say, "You were stepped on, say again." If the signal breaks up during transmission say, "You broke up, come again" or repeat what you think the other person said and ask for confirmation. A broken signal is often an indication that the battery on the transmitting walkie-talkie is low and should be exchanged for a fresh one. Common usage has evolved to include various CB radio codes, such as

Q: "What's your 20?" Where are you?
A: "I'm ten one-hundred." I'm in the john.

Use concise phrases. Brevity is the soul of wit, as Shakespeare said; try not to clutter up the frequency with rambling. If a lengthy explanation is unavoidable, you may want to change to an unused channel so as not to monopolize the frequency. Say, "Go to 3" (or whatever channel is free). Then change to channel 3 and wait for a response. When the conversation is finished, say "Back to 5" or whatever the original channel was.

Last but not least, if you do not have an earpiece or headset and are operating with an open speaker, turn the volume on your walkie-talkie to 0 during takes, and remember to turn it back up again when the take is finished. Few blunders are more embarrassing and unforgivable than ruining a take by allowing your radio to blurt out, "Hey Dave, what's for lunch?" in the middle of a tense performance.

Teamwork

It is important for each electrician to watch for a chance to back up another electrician and jump into the game. When a light is called for, one electrician sets the light, while another runs the power. When an HMI is called for, one person connects the head, the other connects the ballast. If a light is called for at the last minute, all the electricians work in a team: One person carries the head, another grabs a stand, and two more carry the ballast together, throwing the head cables over their shoulders. By the time the head is on the stand, the ballast cable is attached to the ballast and someone has run power to the ballast. The whole drill takes only a minute.

The trick to teamwork is communication and jumping in to help without getting in another person's way. Communicate. If you're running someone's power or fetching a gel for the person's light, be sure to tell that person so. Some things are better accomplished by one person alone. If three or four people all jump to set one light, the set becomes like a grade-school soccer game, with everybody playing out of position, chasing after the ball in one roving mass. When things gel between crew members, setups come together like a well-practiced play on the sports field, allowing the director of photography time for finesse. In this way, a sharp crew can vastly improve the look of the photography, not to mention keeping the days a reasonable length.

Warnings

When carrying large, heavy, or hot equipment through the set, call out warnings such as, "Coming through—watch your back" or "Hot points—coming through." You don't want to singe the director's arm with a hot light. I once heard a grip carrying dolly track use the warning, "Duck or bleed!" This cleared the way quite effectively.

When turning a light on, call out, "Light coming on" before you hit the switch. This is a courtesy to the actors, stand-ins, and crew who are in front of your light. It is meant to warn them not to look at the light. (Unfortunately, when novices hear the warning, they often do just the opposite and momentarily blind themselves but learn quickly after that.) It is a good idea to tilt the light up, away from the set, or put a gloved hand in front of the light as you turn it on. That way the light doesn't come on suddenly, and you give the actors or stand-ins a second to adjust to it before you pull away your hand. This kind of courtesy is not just a matter of politeness but also one of professionalism.

Similarly, avoid blinding people in general. If a working light needs to be moved, don't let it swing around and blast into people's faces.

If you are about to plug in a light and you can't tell if the switch is on or off, you can give the warning, "Possible hot stab." This is especially important if the light is aimed at someone or if the light coming on is likely to be an annoyance to the DP or gaffer. An accidental hot stab can be forgiven if you give a warning. It is important to make a habit of turning lights off at the switch before unplugging them to avoid hot stabs.

Whenever a flash camera is used on the set, the photographer should call out, "Flashing" before snapping the shot. This is mainly a courtesy to people in front of the camera, but it also alerts the electricians that a camera is about to flash. This way, the flash is not mistaken for a bulb burning out or an electrical arc.

Safeties

When a light is hung above the set (suspended from the ceiling, set walls, or overhead pipes), a safety line should be tied around the yoke and around a permanent structural support capable of holding the weight of the light if it should come off its stud. The best type of safety line is aircraft cable, sometimes called a *dog collar* because it has a loop in one end and a carabiner or dog leash clip at the other. In the absence of aircraft cable, sash cord or safety chain can be used. Be sure to leave enough slack in the safety line for the light to be panned and tilted.

Barn doors should also come with safety chain connecting them to the light to prevent them from falling. If a light does not have a barn door safety chain, use bailing wire or safety chain to attach the doors before hanging the light.

Stingers and Cabling

A set can quickly become a rat's nest of tangled cables if care is not taken when running cables and stingers. Here are some guidelines.

Circuit Balance and Capacity

The best boy electric is responsible for distributing the loads on the cables and the power source so that circuit loads are balanced and cables are operating within their capacities. Each electrician must know the cable layout, know where you can find outlets, and keep tabs on the amperage on circuits that are operating near capacity. When balance (between phases) or circuit capacity is critical, keep the best boy abreast of new lights being added. With large lights (5k or larger), consult with him as to which circuit should be used before plugging in.

It is normal for cables to run warm, but if they become hot to the touch replace cables as necessary and notify the best boy electric.

If a fuse blows repeatedly, something is wrong: The circuit is overloaded or there is a short in the light, the plug, or the outlet. Redistribute the plugs, add more circuits, repair the short. Do not replace the fuse with an oversized fuse or copper slug—it'll eventually cause a meltdown.

2k Plugging Policy

To help other electricians know which duplex outlets are maxed out and which still have amperage to spare, make it a policy within the department to always *plug a 2k into the top duplex outlet.* If you are plugging a *1k or smaller use the bottom outlet first.* This way any electrician knows at a glance which duplex outlets have capacity to spare and which are already maxed out. It is also helpful to label the plug of 2k lights so that you can identify them among the many cords at the outlet box, and keep them on separate 20-A circuits.

Figure 9.3 Cable crossover. (Courtesy of Peterson Systems International, Duarte, CA.)

Cables Crossing the Set

Keep cables out of the shot and out from underfoot. An electrician rarely runs a cable in a direct line from power to light. Before running the cable, consider the best way to run it. Avoid crossing doorways, especially if there is a chance that the door will work in the scene. Run stingers around the edge of the set. Gaffers often say you can tell a good electrician by the cable you *can't* see. The most convenient setup is to have the distribution cables run above the set with power drops in strategic locations. This eliminates a lot of cable running around the set.

Cables Crossing Work Areas

When cable has to cross an area where there is foot traffic (a hallway or doorway) use cable crossovers (Figure 9.3) or put a rubber mat over the cable and tape it securely to the floor with wide gaffer's tape.

If there is a danger of people tripping on the bulge of the mat, put diagonal stripes of yellow tape across it so that it will be noticed. When cables cross an area where vehicles or carts will be moving, protect the cables with cable crossovers. HMI cables especially should never be left vulnerable. Another way to protect cable from damage from wheels and foot traffic is to lay 2 × 4 lumber on either side of the cable and tape it down to the floor.

Appropriate Length

Use an appropriate length stinger to reach the light. A *clothesline cable*, one that is taut and off the floor, is an accident waiting to happen—someone is sure to trip on it. Stingers normally come in lengths of 25 and 50 ft. Use the appropriate length. A rule of thumb for fast identification is as follows: A 25-ft stinger has about 7 coils and a 50-ft stinger has roughly 14. When a light is on a stand, the power cord should fall straight to the ground at the base and have some slack coiled or in a figure-eight at the base. Keep excess cable coiled neatly. Place the coil such that, if the stand is moved, the cable will play out from the top of the coil, not from the bottom.

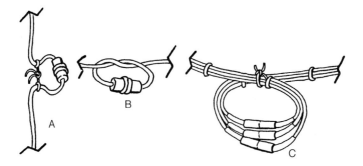

Figure 9.4   When there is danger of an accidental kick-out, use a strain relief. (A) A dangling connection held with the tie ropes, (B) a simple strain relief for a stinger running along the ground, (C) banded cable connection point.

When lights are hung from pipe, be sure to leave two loops of slack cable hanging at the light. If the light later needs to slide down or pan around 180°, you need slack to play with. Run the power cable down the pipe to the service or to the end of the pipe. Tie it to the pipe at intervals with mason line or sash cord. Never wind a cable around a pipe; this makes it impossible to move later.

Preventing "Kick-Outs"
When connecting two cables, use a stress knot or the cables' tie-rope to hold the connection together (Figure 9.4). This helps prevent a "kick-out" (accidental unplugging). In the event of a kick-out or "gap in the line," the electrician must quickly track down the culprit connection. As with everything else on the set, remaining aware of what is happening around you will help you spot kick-outs immediately.

Repatching
You will sometimes need to unplug a light that is in use to replace a cable, run power from a different direction, or readjust the loads of various circuits. Before you unplug the light, inform the gaffer of the need for a repatch, and as you disconnect it, call out, "Repatch." This assures everyone that the light has not gone out accidentally. Frequent repatches can be irritating for the gaffer and DP. In many situations it may be best to find another way to solve the problem.

The Gak Package
Accessorize each distro location. Next to each distro box (600A, 900A, 1200A, or what have you) the following package of cables and adapters should be neatly stowed.

- 2   50-ft 100A Bates
- 2   100A lunch boxes

- 2 milk crates containing:
  - 4 25-ft stingers
  - 4 50-ft stingers
  - 2 100A to 60A splitters
  - 1 100A to 100A splitter
  - 1 100A gang box

Standby Stingers at Outlet Boxes

To streamline the process of powering lights as they are added, have at least two stingers standing by at each power drop or gang box, coiled and ready for use.

Labeling Stingers and Power Cords

Labeling cables helps immensely in identifying problems and recabling lights when needed. When a cable runs out of the set through a rat hole, over the top of the set, or up into the pipes or greens above the set, both ends of the cable or stinger should be labeled with tape. Indicate the lights it is powering; for example, "2k window light" or "stair sconces." Similarly, when using a dimmer board, the gang box or female receptacle of the power cord is marked with the channel number. See the discussion of Rules for Cabling in the subsection on Rigging the Set in Chapter 12 for notes on labeling and laying out distribution equipment.

When lights are hung from a grid it is helpful to be able to identify each light by number. Label each light so the number is visible to the gaffer on the ground below. Write the numbers large and legible on 2-in. tape on the underside of each unit. Mark the tails (the plugs) with the same numbers. With the lamps numbered, it is easy for the gaffer to communicate what she wants: "Plug lamps 10, 14, and 18 into the same dimmer and work them on a cue."

Labeling Dimmer Settings

When setting a dimmer level, start with the dimmer at line voltage. Say, "Line voltage." The gaffer may then specify a setting to try, "Set it at 90%" or just say, "lower, . . . lower, . . . lower, good." Keep replying with the level, "that's 80, . . . 70, . . . 60." Once it is set, make a mark on tape to indicate the setting. If several settings are used, number them. After the shot is completed, leave these markings on the dimmer until you're sure they won't be needed again.

Dimmers hum. At close range they will create problems for the sound recordist. The electrician can anticipate this and position dimmers accordingly.

Coiling Stingers and Cable

All cables and stingers are coiled clockwise. Each loop puts a twist in the cable. When uncoiled it must be allowed to untwist, or it will start to twist onto itself.

The stranded copper wire inside a cable has a natural twist; coiling counter-clockwise works against the grain. When a cable is consistently coiled in the same

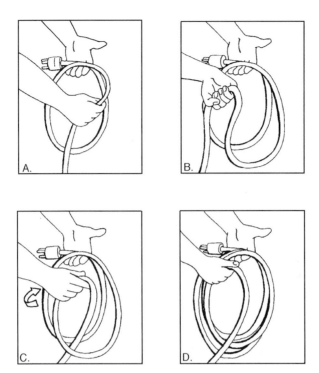

Figure 9.5 When you coil a stinger, use your wrist to put a slight twist on each loop; the stinger will coil easily. When a cable wants to twist too much, you can use the over–under method of coiling. Always use this method with control cables: (A) Start with a normal loop, (B, C) give the second loop a twist to the inside, (D) make the next loop normal. Alternate back and forth between a normal loop and a twisted loop.

manner each time it is used, the cable becomes "trained" to coil that way. A trained cable coils easily. If a cable is coiled different ways with each use, it becomes confused and unmanageable.

The over–under method shown in Figure 9.5 is used for coaxial cable, dimmer control cables, and audio cable. Every other loop counteracts the twist so the cable can be unraveled without twists. Using the occasional underhand loop sometimes makes a cord more cooperative.

Small Bulbs, Practicals, Wiring, and Switches

Types of Bulbs

Photoflood bulbs and PH bulbs   Photoflood bulbs are color-balanced for use in photography (3200 K, 3400 K, and 4800 K) and come in various wattages, as shown in Appendix E. The 211 (75 W) and 212 (150 W) are often used in table lamps and suspended China-hat practicals. Higher-wattage photofloods are often used in soft boxes, Japanese lanterns, and scoop lights such as Smith Victor lights. Most photoflood bulbs burn very hot and have a short life, in order to provide the high color temperature.

Household bulbs A selection of low-wattage household bulbs (15 W, 25 W, 40 W, 60 W) is handy for making practicals glow without being overly bright. A household bulb's color temperature falls between 2600 and 2900 K, which appears yellow on film. In most instances, a warm color shift is appropriate for the scene (for example, lamps naturally appear slightly warm), and the DP leaves it. If the color shift is objectionable, it can be removed with CTB gel. Alternatively, the DP may add $\frac{1}{4}$ CTO to the artificial lights to match the warmth of the practicals. The color shift can be removed in the lab or with the use of a blue filter on the lens (Kodak 82 series, see Table F.8).

Candella base bulbs Some candelabra wall sconces and chandeliers take candela-base bulbs; this is something to check during location scouts. The bulbs, usually of low wattage, are very warm. Round makeup table bulbs (40 W and 60 W) are small, soft, very warm (2600–2700-K) bulbs that can be grouped to make an inexpensive, soft glow light.

Mushroom floods—R-40 and others Flood- and spotlights of the mushroom-shaped variety incorporate a silver reflector inside the bulb for better output and throw. Common wattages are 75 W, 150 W, 300 W, and 500 W (EAL). 3200-K R-40 bulbs are available in 200 W, 300 W, 375 W, and 500 W wattage (see Table E.1). The rest fall between 2800 and 2900 K. The R-40 size is the most commonly used. A Lowel K-5 kit includes sockets, mounting bracket, and barn doors that fit snug onto the front of an R-40 bulb. There are a wide variety of other reflector bulbs. The size is indicated by the number; for example, in R-40/FL, R stands for reflector and 40 is the size (in eighths of an inch: 40/8 = 5 in.). FL indicates flood. Smaller R-30 and R-20 bulbs are great for track lighting or lighting wall art at close range.

MR-16 MR-16 bulbs are tungsten halogen projector bulbs with a 2-in. parabolic reflector. They are 3200 K and very bright. Now commonly used in track-lighting fixtures, they come in a variety of wattages, voltages, and reflector types. The track-lighting type is 12 V, uses a transformer, and has a GX-5.3 base, shown in Figure E.1, Appendix E. Fortunately, 120-V versions of MR-16s are also available with a standard medium screw base in 75 and 150 W. The VNSP MR-16, which has a mirrorlike parabolic reflector, makes an amazingly bright narrow column of light. The tiny size, brightness, and color temperature of MR-16s make them a very useful bulb for making small pools of light.

Linestra tubes These are incandescent, tube-shaped bulbs 12, 20, or 40 in. long and $\frac{3}{4}$ in. in diameter. Their color temperature is 2800 K. They are very lightweight and can be attached with tape or bailing wire. They are used in sets, lighting shelving, for example.

Fluorescent bulbs The most common type of practical fluorescent bulb you will encounter is T-12 base (bi-pin) in 4-, 3-, and 2-ft sizes. In industrial spaces, you often run into 8-ft slimline-base tubes (Appendix E). These bulbs can be easily replaced with high CRI bulbs. Older desk lamps sometimes take small T-5 tubes.

Controlling Practicals

It is standard practice to put practical lamps on dimmers so that their intensity can be easily adjusted. However, there are other ways to dim a bulb that do not alter the color temperature. Spraying the bulb with a light speckle of black streaks and tips is a fast way to reduce the bulb's intensity. (Don't spray a hot bulb; it will burst.) Sometimes you want to reduce brightness in only one direction. This can be done by spraying one side and not the other. Holding a lighter close to the bulb and letting the carbon build up on the bulb is another good way to dim it. The carbon wipes off more easily than streaks and tips. Placing diffusion on the inside of the lamp shade and installing ND gel around the bulb are also ways to dim a practical.

Light Cues

Hand Cue

If an actor turns a wall switch on or off during a scene, the wall switch can be wired to a deuce board switch that controls the lights. Usually, however, an electrician performs the lighting cue with a dimmer or switch when the actor reaches for the light switch. The electrician must be positioned somewhere out of the way and out of the shot but able to see the action to hit the cue. Experienced actors help sell the cue by covering the switch with their hand so that the camera does not see the exact moment that the switch flips.

Switchover

In a night scene, when an actor turns off a bedroom light and the room goes dark, the lighting must switch from practical sources to moonlight or exterior sources. Darkness is commonly simulated by underexposed, blue, directionless lighting. The transition may require a switchover in which some lights are turned off and others are turned on in the instant that the actor turns off the lights. The problem is that the time required for one group of filaments to dim and the other group to heat up prevents the switchover from being instantaneous, and the audience can see the new lights coming on. Some special techniques can be helpful to sell the switchover.

One solution is to have the night group ON the whole time. Unfortunately, this can look phony because the moonlight appears to be as bright as the light in the room, and the blue color of the night group discolors the lamplight. However, if the change happens before any of that becomes too noticeable, this can be a workable solution. If the scene ends with the lights turning off, the blue group can be kept very low so as not to distract for the bulk of the scene.

If the scene carries on in darkness after the lights go off and the actors must be visible in the dark, then a special transition is needed. Here is a clever way to handle this transition: Keep the night group on throughout the scene, but at levels that are one and a half to two stops below the lamplight. This will look natural. When the interior light is turned off, begin to open the camera aperture on a slow 5-second change. The effect is similar to that of the human eye adjusting to the dark. Additionally, the audience's eyes will be adjusting to the new light level, which hides the aperture change.

Wiring Small Fixtures

Practical Lamps

On any interior set, the art department will provide *practical fixtures*: table lamps, wall sconces, floor lamps, desk lamps, china hats, chandeliers, and so forth. Each time you begin working on a new set, one of the first things to take care of is the wiring and testing the practicals and changing the bulbs as desired by the gaffer.

Lamps and sconces often come from the prop house with bare wires and need to be fitted with plugs. If a lamp or sconce is metal and not UL listed, a grounding wire is required and zip cord (18/2) may not be used. UL-listed lamps do not require a ground wire and 18/2 wire can be used up to 6 ft. When necessary, use wire nuts to insulate wire splices, as shown in Figure 9.6.

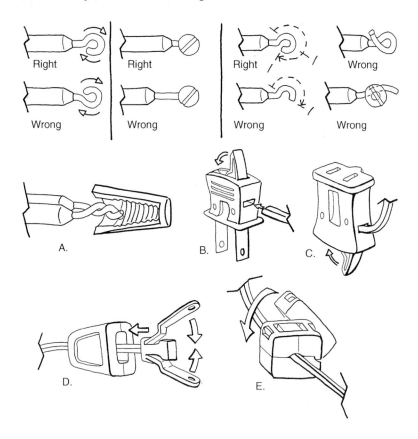

Figure 9.6 (Top) Tips on connecting wires to terminals. (A) Wire nuts on wire splices. Note: The wires need not be twisted as shown here; in fact, wire nuts are designed with a threaded metal insert that crimps the wires together when the nut is screwed on. Nonetheless, it is often necessary to twist the wires to hold them securely together. (B) Male quick-on, (C) female quick-on, (D) male quick-on, (E) in-line tap.

Quick-on plugs stab the zip cord with copper spikes, eliminating the need for screw terminals. Quick-on plugs and sockets are designed to be used with 18/2 zip cord only. Note that in-line taps don't have polarized sockets, so a polarized plug won't fit. You may have to clip the flare off the male plug with wire snips, or use a cube tap as an adapter. It is best to use a female quick-on for the terminal end of zip cord; if an in-line tap is used, fold the wire back once it is through the tap and *wrap it with electrical tape.* Do not leave an exposed end—someone is bound to get bit.

Some notes about zip cord: 18 AWG (American wire gauge) zip cord is often used to wire practicals. It may not extend more than 6 ft from the fixture. It may not be used with any fixture having a ground wire. It is rated for 10 A maximum and will not withstand overamping. It can be dangerous to make long zip cord runs, because the resistance in the cord is so high that a dead short at the end of a long run of cord will not trip the circuit breaker. The cord will burn up before it will trip the circuit protection.

Practical Outlets

A well-made set has *practical wall outlets.* These are very convenient for plugging in practical, set dressing appliances (a toaster, for example) and small lights. On the outside wall, the outlet box usually has a short tale with an Edison plug, which should be connected to a dedicated 20-A circuit.

Wiring Plugs, Sockets, Switches, and Connectors

When wiring or repairing electrical devices, be sure to *make as solid a connection as possible*, bringing together as much surface area of copper at each terminal and making each terminal tight and secure. *Plugs, sockets, connectors, and switches* are the weak spots in a circuit. They create resistance that can eventually heat up the wires, which further degrades the conductors and their insulation, further increases resistance and heat, and eventually poses a shock or fire hazard (or simply causes a nuisance by burning out).

Also for safety reasons, any time you install or replace a switch or connector, *pay attention to the proper polarity.* On plugs and sockets, the gold terminal is for the hot (black) wire, and the silver terminal is for the neutral (white) wire. The green terminal is for the green grounding wire. (On zip cord the hot wire has a rib on the insulating jacket, while the neutral wire does not.)

If an electrical device is connected with reverse polarity (i.e., the neutral and hot wires are reversed), a potential safety hazard exists. The switch controlling the fixture, which normally interrupts the hot wire, now interrupts the circuit on the *return* wire (neutral). Although the fixture still functions, it has a hot lead running to the lamp when turned off—a hot lead looking for a place to ground. So, even though the fixture is off, it is still *hot.* For example, someone attempting to change the bulb, thinking that because the switch is off the light is safe, could be in for a jolting surprise. This is precisely why one should always unplug a fixture before putting a hand inside it, even if the switch is off.

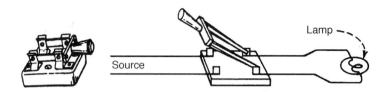

Figure 9.7 Both wires are disconnected when the fixture is turned off with a double-pole switch. Most fixtures 2k and larger use a double-pole switch. (From H. Richter and W. Schwan, *Practical Electrical Wiring*, 15th ed. New York: McGraw-Hill, 1990. Reproduced with permission of McGraw-Hill.)

Figure 9.8 (A) A *double-throw*, or *three-way*, switch has three terminals. It switches current flow from A-C to A-B.
(B) When connected as shown, three-way switches allow the circuit to be switched from two places. The circuit can be made live or dead at either switch, regardless of the position of the other switch. (From H. Richter and W. Schwan, *Practical Electrical Wiring*, 15th ed. New York: McGraw-Hill, 1990. Reproduced with permission of McGraw-Hill.)

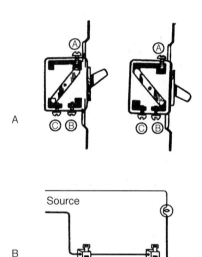

For the same reason, when installing a switch, *a single-pole switch must be connected on the black wire*, not the white.

Double-Pole Switches

For 240-V circuits and lights 2k or more, it is necessary to have a switch that interrupts both wires at once. This is known as a *double-pole* switch (Figure 9.7).

Three-Way and Four-Way Switches

It is sometimes handy to have two or more switches in different locations to control a circuit. To do this, wire two *three-way* switches as shown in Figure 9.8. When more than two switches are needed, a three-way switch is connected at the beginning and end of the chain of switches, and any number of *four-way* switches can be connected between them (Figure 9.9). In either case, any of the switches will close and open the circuit, regardless of the position of the other switches.

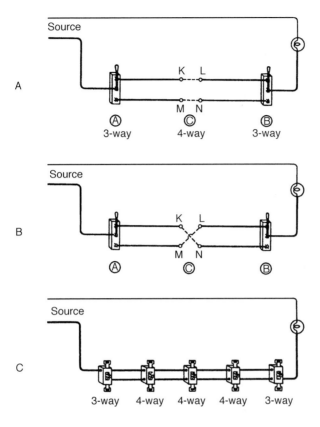

Figure 9.9 A *four-way* switch is used when controlling lights from three or more places. (A) and (B) show the way a four-way switch works. (C) Any number of four-way switches can be connected between two three-way switches. (From H. Richter and W. Schwan, *Practical Electrical Wiring*, 15th ed. New York: McGraw-Hill, 1990. Reproduced with permission of McGraw-Hill.)

Safety

You don't have to work on sets long before you see that, in a rush, people can forget their common sense. This is how people get hurt and equipment gets broken. Make safe work practices habitual and you will avoid needless injuries, especially when working under pressure. Work swiftly but never run.

Ladders

When working with suspended lights, you must often work from a ladder. If the ladder seems at all shaky, have someone hold it and spot you at the bottom of the ladder. Use the appropriate size ladder. Don't use the top step. Don't stretch to reach a light that is too far from the ladder; instead, get a taller ladder, or climb down and move the ladder.

Two people often need to work from two sides of the same ladder when rigging two lights very close together. When you step onto someone's ladder, say, "On your ladder," and when you step off again, say, "Off your ladder."

Parallels

Parallels are quite frequently used as a lighting platform. They are quick and easy to assemble and, if used with proper caution, can be safe. However, *caution* is the watchword. Almost any veteran electrician can tell you a story about an accident involving parallels.

Parallels must be set on level ground or be leveled with leveling jacks. On uneven ground it can be hard to tell what is level; a plumb line or bubble level should be used. A leaning parallel is an accident waiting to happen. Be sure that weight is distributed evenly on the platform, especially when people are climbing or lifting equipment up to the platform. Use bodies as counterweights when necessary. Never mount lights outside the perimeter of the railing.

Large light stands should be strapped down to the platform. Ratchet straps and nylon webbing are ideal, although chain or rope can do the trick if properly used. Remember to take into account the force of the wind blowing on 4-by frames. Tie guy lines to the bail or stand when needed. Tie the power cable to a vertical post on the platform, leaving plenty of slack to maneuver the light.

Working Aloft

Anytime you work at a height—on a ladder, greens, catwalk, parallels, or truss—remove your tool belt. Tie any tools you need to your belt. If you do drop something, yell a warning, such as, "Heads up," "Headache," or just "Look out below!" Dropping a tool from the catwalks can get you kicked off a studio lot.

Remember to bring a tag line so you can hoist equipment as you need it. The tag line should be tied off at the top end so that it cannot fall. Call, "Line out" before you toss down the line. When you toss an item up to a worker, call, "Airmail" to alert the people around you; then, if the catcher misses, no one gets cracked on the head.

Protecting Floors

Protecting the floor becomes a concern when shooting in a private home or on a set where the floors might be scratched by metal stands. A number of precautions can be taken. One is to put crutch tips on the feet of each stand. Tape the rubber tips in place with gaffer's tape. A stock of crutch tips should be ordered in advance after the location is initially scouted.

Layout board ($\frac{1}{4}$ in. hard cardboard that comes in 4×8-ft sheets) can provide a protective covering over the floor. It is usually laid out over the entire area and taken up wherever it will be seen in the camera's frame. A more temporary substitute is a furniture pad placed under the stand.

Sprinkler Systems

With the fire marshal's permission, make a practice of putting Styrofoam cups over sprinkler heads to insulate them from the heat of the lights. In the category of big blunders, few are more conspicuous than activating the emergency sprinkler system and dousing the actors and sets in water. Placing a hot light too close to a sprinkler head can easily melt the soft alloy valve that normally holds back the flood. There is no way to stop an activated head from flowing once it has started, and the water in the pipes will continue to drain for hours, even if the sprinkler system is immediately turned off at the source.

Smoke, Fire, and Other Bad Smells

Lights get very hot and can easily start a fire. Common sense and proper care are essential to the prevention of accidents. In the event of a small fire, a quick electrician may be able to smother the flames with gloved hands or with a furniture pad. Know where the fire extinguishers are.

An electrician with a good nose and good eyes can detect a potential fire before it becomes serious. If you smell smoke, don't cause a panic, but let the other electricians and grips know so they can help look for the source. The smell of burning wood may be caused by a toasting clothespin or a light placed too close to a wooden set piece. The smell of burning plastic or rubber may be traced to smoldering insulation on a cable connection or in-line switch. An overheated stinger is a common offender. Check the lights for burning gel or diffusion and smoking flags or nets. Check the set walls and ceiling for bubbling or smoldering paint. On DC stages, keep your nose open for the sharp, metallic-burning smell of an arcing paddle connector. When a paddle comes partially unplugged it will arc, which eventually burns up the contacts on the plugging box. Keep looking until you find the source of the smell. The problem may be something obscure, such as burning bakelite plastic in a defective deuce board.

A smoking light is usually the result of some foreign matter getting into the light and burning up. Dusty lights often smoke for a short time when they are first turned on. Moths are relentless kamikazes. They will keep an open-face fixture smoking all night as they bake themselves one after another. Outside in a ventilated area this does not pose a danger to anyone but the moths. Inside, though, it may be necessary to turn off a smoking light and clean it out. Sometimes the only way to clean the light is just to let the substance burn off. For example, after a light is repainted, it should be taken outside and turned on for 10 or 15 minutes until it stops smoking.

Lamp Repair

When a lamp fails, be sure to label the light so that it isn't brought back onto the set by mistake. Put an X across the lens with 1-in. tape, and write *NG* (no good) or *BO* (burnt out) on it. If you know what is wrong with the light, write that on it also (for example, blown bulb, bad switch, bad plug).

Common repairs include changing the globe, replacing the power switch or plug, reconnecting the power cord to the head, repairing the flood-spot mechanism, and cleaning corroded contacts with contact cleaner. Most lights are not too complicated and can easily be repaired if replacement parts can be obtained. Before starting any type of repair, double-check that the fixture is disconnected from the power. If time allows, the best boy simply has new equipment delivered in exchange for the broken equipment.

The Wrap

When filming is completed at a given location, all the equipment has to be packed back into the truck. This may take 2 or 3 hours when a lot of equipment is in use. Especially after a long day, it is everyone's dearest wish to get the truck packed as quickly as possible and get home. One of the best boy's responsibilities is to begin the wrap early and have as much of it done as possible before the actual wrap is called. Early in the day, the best boy organizes the removal of superfluous equipment from the set and the coiling of cable no longer needed. Once the last setup is lit, any equipment not in use should be stowed and ready to drive away.

When wrap is called, lights are switched off and the equipment starts coming back to the truck. I find it works best if the best boy remains at the truck and packs the equipment as it is brought to the lift gate by the electricians. This avoids equipment piled up at the gate. Wrapped lights should look like the one shown in Figure 9.10.

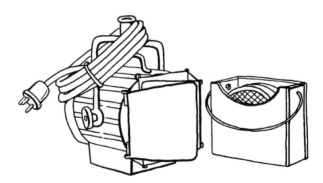

Figure 9.10 A properly wrapped light. Some electricians prefer to tuck the cable inside the bail to prevent it from getting caught on other equipment.

The bail is swiveled up over the top of the light. The power cord is coiled, tied, and hung over the bail or tucked under the bail. The barn doors are shut. Scrims, diffusion, and gel have been removed and returned to the scrim and gel boxes. Spreader lenses are removed from PAR lights. The globes should be removed from larger lights (12k and 18k HMIs) before travel.

Coiling Feeder Cable

The fastest way to coil feeder cable (banded, 2/0, or 4/0) is to stand with your legs apart and coil in a clockwise circle on the ground. With a little practice you can get into a rhythm, pulling the cable toward you with one hand, then the other, guiding it into a coil. If you are fighting the natural twist of the cable, the coil will not want to lie flat, and the unnatural twist will age the cable. The ideal size for a coil is tight enough not to be floppy and unmanageable, but not so tight and tall that it becomes impossible to stack. Use the tie strings to secure both ends firmly. Loose ends tend to swing around, hit people, and generally get in the way. Lift with your knees, not with your back. Never jump down (off the gate, for example) with heavy cable on your shoulder. You will know as soon as you do it that it was a mistake. Your knees and ankles may never forgive you.

Inventory

The best boy conducts an equipment inventory during loading. If each shelf has been labeled with the type and quantity of lights it holds, this process is quite straightforward. Bungee off each shelf as soon as it is complete; this helps keep track of what is still missing; and once all the shelves are filled, the truck is ready to go without further delay. Putting each light in its proper place is not just a matter of organization, it can be crucial to fitting everything on the truck. Before leaving any location, someone should run an idiot check of the set, looking in each area where lights were placed during filming.

Aerial Lifts and High Platforms for Lighting

Figure 9.11 shows various types of aerial lifts commonly used as platforms for lights and lamp operators: a straight mast boom (Condor), articulated boom (knuckle boom), scissor lift, and man lift. Aerial lifts are invaluable tools, both on the sound stage and on location. With the right lift, riggers and lamp operators can move easily into hard-to-reach places to hang and adjust lights and cable.

The standard moonlight rig for night time street exteriors consists of one or two large lights mounted to the basket of a telescoping straight mast boom, raised over one end of the street. Condor, Snorkelift, JLG, Genie, and Simon are the dominant makes, but *Condor* is the common name for a straight mast boom. An electrician is designated to operate the platform and the lights mounted on it. Productions often need to bring on an extra hand for "Condor duty," so knowing how to operate an aerial lift is an important skill for getting your foot in the door with different crews.

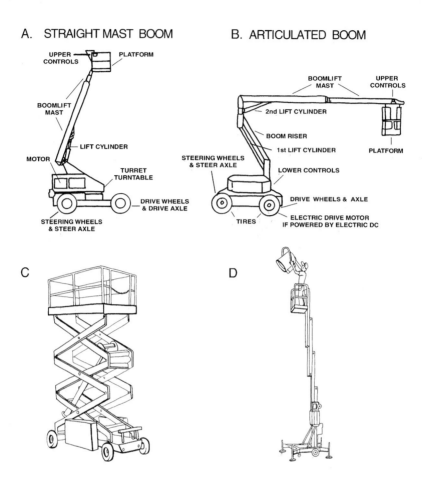

Figure 9.11 (A) Straight mast boom, (B) articulated boom, (C) scissor lift, (D) man lift.

Aerial lifts are engineered to be stable and safe within the parameters for which they are designed; nevertheless, the operation of aerial lifts presents a host of potential hazards, for which the operator of the lift must assume responsibility. Tragic accidents do occur. Potential hazards include tipping over, falling into a pit, being electrocuted by power lines, falling or being flung from the basket, running over equipment or people, mechanical or hydraulic failure, and dropping tools or equipment on others, to name some of the big ones. These kinds of accidents are avoided by consistently adhering to safe work practices. Such practices include allowing only trained personnel to operate the equipment, making a thorough preuse inspection of the equipment, never disabling safety features, selecting the proper equipment for the job at hand, making a thorough inspection of the workplace, locking in with a lanyard and four-point fall protection harness, carefully and fully preparing any rigging attached to the lift to prevent cables being snagged or stretched, making all necessary weight and balance calculations, taking into account the center of gravity when operating the boom arm, never operating on a slope or grade, assuring the platform is on a completely stable footing, knowing and maintaining minimum safe distances from power lines and electrical buses, maintaining downward lines of sight, and tying off equipment with a safety chain or lanyard including hand tools. These procedures are not just good practices, they are required by law. Your employer has legal responsibility to provide appropriate, properly maintained equipment, and never has the right to ask you to operate the equipment in a manner inconsistent with safety. As the operator, you must say when something is not safe. If you are asked to do something that could be hazardous, explain the problem and do not put yourself in harms way. Rest assured, they can always find another way to get the shot they are after.

In the sections that follow, we discuss these safety procedures in greater depth. The discussion here, however, is a starting point. Nothing can replace taking a training class given by qualified safety personnel, operating the equipment yourself, and working with and learning from experienced, veteran riggers who can show you better and safer ways to rig and operate lifts.

Getting the Right Machine for the Job

The main considerations when selecting lift equipment are working height, platform weight capacity, platform size, lift type (ability to reach to the necessary position), fuel type (indoor or outdoor use), terrain (two-wheel or four-wheel drive, ground clearance), and cost. Table 9.1 lists data for some common models.

Straight mast boom lifts give the most height (Figure 9.11A). Common sizes are 30-, 40-, 60-, 80-, and 110-ft platform heights. A straight boom lift uses hydraulic cylinders to lift the boom from horizontal to vertical. The boom also turns on a turret. The telescoping mast extends and retracts. Most straight mast booms are diesel powered. The smallest sizes may be propane or electric powered or both. Propane fuel can be used inside buildings when there is ample ventilation to the outside. The electric motor must be used inside when there is little ventilation. The electric motor is less powerful and tends to be slower, usually allowing only one primary function to operate at a time.

Weight capacity also varies with size and model. The largest machines can handle a 1000-lb basket capacity, which is usually sufficient to carry multiple lights plus one operator. The smaller ones have a 500-lb maximum that limits you to fewer or smaller units. The larger-capacity machines have more ample basket size. This is a clear advantage when working with multiple lights. The smallest units have quite cramped basket dimensions, but their smaller overall size makes them better for working in narrow spaces. Typically the best boy and gaffer know well ahead of time what locations require aerial lifts and what lights will be rigged. Weight capacity calculations and size requirements should be ironed out during prep. You want to avoid a situation where the Condor is suddenly being rigged with more equipment than expected. (We get to weight calculations shortly.)

An articulated boom lift or "knuckle boom" has two lifting cylinders (Figure 9.11B). The primary cylinder lifts the boom riser, the secondary cylinder lifts the mast. This allows the articulating boom to get up and over obstacles. Articulated models

Table 9.1 Specifications for Genie Aerial Lifts and Work Platforms

Model	S-40	S-45	S-60	S-65	S-80	S-85	S-100	S-105	S-120	S-125
Telescope Booms										
Working Height (ft)	46	51	66	71	86	91	106	111	126	131
Platform Height (ft)	40	45	60	65	80	85	100	105	120	125
Horizontal Reach (ft)	31	36	51	56	71	76	75	80	75	80
Lift Capacity (lbs) 6-ft platform	500	500	600	500	600	500	—	—	—	—
Lift Capacity (lbs) 8-ft platform	500	500	500	500	500	500	750	500	750	500
Platform Size	6' × 30" 8' × 36"	6' × 30" 8' × 36"	6' × 30" 8' × 36"	6' × 30" 8' × 36"	6' × 30" 8' × 36"	6' × 30" 8' × 36"	8' × 36"	8' × 36"	8' × 36"	8' × 36"
Power Source G = gas D = diesel	82 HP g 56 HP d 36 HP d	82 HP g 56 HP d 36 HP d	82 HP g 56 HP d 60 HP d	82 HP g 56 HP d 60 HP d	82 HP g 56 HP d 60 HP d	82 HP g 56 HP d 60 HP d	75 HP d 77 HP d 81 HP d	75 HP d 77 HP d 81 HP d	75 HP d 77 HP d 81 HP d	75 HP d 77 HP d 81 HP d
Drive	4 × 2	4 × 4	4 × 2	4 × 4	4 × 2	4 × 4	4 × 2	4 × 4	4 × 2	4 × 4
Fuel Capacity (gal)	33	33	33	33	33	33	40	40	40	40
Weight (lbs)	11,650	14,790	26,060	28,400	33,380	35,860	39,700	40,000	44,340	44,640
Drive Speed Stowed Gas (mph)	4.0	3.5	4.4	3	3.8	3.1	—	—	—	—
Drive Speed Stowed Diesel (mph)	3.8	2.8	4	2.8	3.3	3	3	3	3	3
Drive Speed Raised (mph)	0.68	0.68	0.6	0.6	0.68	0.68	—	—	—	—
Gradeability	30%	40%	30%	40%	30%	38%	42%	42%	40%	40%

Table 9.1 Specifications for Genie Aerial Lifts and Work Platforms (continued)

Model*	Z-20/8	Z-30/20N	Z-34/22	Z-45/25	Z-60/34
Articulating Booms					
Working Height (ft)	26	36	40	51	66
Platform Height (ft)	20	30	34	45	60
Horizontal Reach (ft)	7	21	22	24	34
Up and Over Clearance (ft)	16	12	15	22	28
Lift Capacity (lbs)	500	500	500	500	500
Platform Size	46" × 30"	46" × 30"	56" × 30"	72" × 30"	6' × 30" 8' × 36"
Power Source E = electric G = gas D = diesel	E	E	E, E & D, G or D	E, E & D, G or D	G or D
Drive	—	4 × 2	4 × 4	4 × 2	4 × 4
Fuel Capacity (gal)	—	33	33	33	33
Weight (lbs)	7000	14,500	11,200	17,100	21,890
Drive Speed Stowed (mph)	0–2.7	0–3.3	0–3.7	4.8	3.5
Gradeability	20%	30%	37%	30%	30%

Table 9.1 Specifications for Genie Aerial Lifts and Work Platforms (continued)

Model	GS-1530	GS-1930	GS-2032	GS-2668	GS-3268	GS-2046	GS-2646	GS-3246	GS-4390	GS-5390	GS-2668	GS-3268
Scissor Lifts												
Working Height (ft)	21	25	26	32	38	26	32	38	49	59	32	38
Platform Height (ft)	15	19	20	26	32	20	26	32	43	53	26	32
Lift Capacity (lbs)	600	500	800	1250	1000	1200	1000	700	1500	1500	1250	1000
Platform Length	64"	64"	89"	99"	99"	89"	89"	89	212"	212"	99"	99"
Platform Length Extended	103"	103"	128"	159"	159"	128"	128"	128"	258"	258"	156"	156"
Platform Width	29"	29"	31"	61"	61"	46"	46"	46"	72"	72"	61"	61"
Power Source E = Electric G = gas D = diesel	E	E	E	E	E	E	E	E	G or D	G or D	G or D	G or D
Drive	Front wheel	Front wheel	Front wheel	Front wheel	Front wheel	Front wheel	Front wheel	Front wheel	4 wheel	4 wheel	4 wheel	4 wheel
Weight (lbs)	2658	2858	3503	6583	7550	4324	4646	6172	13,780	18,425	6550	7520

*Notes: Several models also come in a narrow version (denoted by N after the model number). These are good when space is a particular problem. Models with an internal combustion engine (gas or diesel) are denoted with IC after the model number. Electric are denoted DC, or bi-energy (DC and gas).

are smaller and have less capacity than the straight booms. Most are propane/electric powered. They are particularly valuable for getting over sets for rigging and adjusting lights.

Scissor lifts and vertical lifts are self-propelled elevated work platforms (Figure 9.11C). The larger models have large solid platforms onto which light stands can be placed. Small and medium-sized scissor lifts are electric powered and have very little ground clearance, so they are best used on a flat surface where there is no terrain. The platform usually is made to extend out on one end so you can reach over the obstacles a limited amount. A typical scissor lift has a 500- to 1500-lb capacity and a maximum height of 20 to 40 ft (see Table 9.1). The large platform size of some scissor lifts has a tendency to invite lots of people and equipment onto the platform. Know the maximum weight capacity and stay within its limits. A large platform with a 500-lb capacity can fit many more people than it is rated to lift.

When fully charged, the batteries should last for many hours of intermittent operation; however, scissor lifts should always be plugged in and charged overnight. If the lift will not operate, check the DC voltage across the batteries (usually 24 V powered from four 6-V batteries arranged in series). If the batteries are drained, the lift needs to be charged for several minutes before it can be operated, and it should remain on charge until fully charged.

Straight Mast Boom Lifts (Condors)

Walk-Around Inspection

Before taking the controls of an aerial lift, personally make an inspection of the equipment. Like the pilot of a plane, you entrust your life to a machine, and like every pilot, you need to make a walk-around inspection of the equipment before *every* "flight." During this inspection, if you find any problems with the equipment, be they serious or superficial, make a note of them on a piece of paper along with the equipment ID number, date, time, and your name; and turn a copy in to the best boy. This is required legal protection for you and it helps the best boy and the equipment rental company track and fix problems. Try to arrange to inspect the equipment in daylight. If this is impossible, set up a work light or use a powerful flashlight to get a good look. The inspection only takes a few minutes.

Basket

Control console Be sure you can read the labels on the console. Take a moment to identify each switch, control lever, and indicator light (including the horn and the shut-off switch). If the unit has been used previously by painters, you may have to do some deciphering (or a little scraping).

Symbols/colors Because forward/reverse and left/right controls are relative (depending which way the turret is facing), the control levers are color coded. Make a note of the color of the arrow painted on the front of the chassis (the steering end). Remember this color always drives you in the direction of the steering wheels.

Rails   The guard rails are rated to withstand 500 lb of force. If they have been bent, crushed, or drilled through, their strength is greatly reduced. Note that specific places are provided to clip on your lanyard (fall-protection harness). These supports are beefed up and rated to support 5000 lb of force. That is why you should not just hook to the guardrail at any convenient place. If you were to fall, the load on the rail when it arrests your fall would almost certainly be in excess of 500 lb.

Toe board   A toe board is required by law to assure that the operator does not accidentally kick something out of the basket. If for some reason you lack a toe board, a legal toe board can be made of standard 1 × 3 lumber.

Basket floor   Be sure you have full visibility through the floor of the basket. Clear out any garbage.

Arm

Track cover   Electrical and hydraulic lines running up the arm to the basket are housed in a track that pays out as the boom is extended. The track protects these vital lines. Be sure the track and the pins that hold the track together are in good condition.

Welds and pins   The basket is held to the arm by a single steel pin and a hydraulic cylinder. Check for rust around the welds (rust indicates the welds are corroded and weakened). This point will be under great stress if the basket is overloaded. It must be in good condition.

Hydraulic lines   Check the condition of the hydraulic lines. When rigging grip and electric equipment to the basket and arm pay special attention to stay clear of hydraulic lines where they are unprotected, such as where they enter and exit the track at either end of the arm. If a cable should get wrapped around a hydraulic line or a line get pinched between the grip rigging when the basket is swung around, the line could be stretched or cut and the basket would flop, dumping its operator.

Safety switches   Boom arms are equipped with safety switches on the arm, which tells the machine if the boom is raised or extended. The machine limits speed and functions when the boom is up or extended. These safety switches should be clean and in working order.

Wheels

Matched set   The condition of the wheels is perhaps the single most important factor in the stability of the lift. All the tires must be the same size, brand, and tread. They must all be filled with the same material. They must be in good condition. It is a relatively simple matter to have tires replaced if necessary, but be sure they are replaced with exactly the same size, brand, tread, and fill.

Engine Compartment

Oil   You are looking primarily for oil leaks and the condition of the hoses.

Bubble level   The electronic bubble level is a required safety switch mounted somewhere on the chassis or inside the turret, sometimes in the engine compartment, sometimes on the front left side inside the turret. The bubble level is meant to prevent boom arm functions when the chassis is not on a level surface. If someone has disabled the level, the vehicle is not safe to operate. This level can be disabled a number of ways, by disconnecting it or by screwing or taping it down.

Fuel

Propane   If the propane tank is not full, be sure transportation has spares readily available.

Diesel   Normally, the vehicles are delivered with a full tank. If you have been operating the equipment a lot, you may want to have the tank topped off. Most vehicles do not have a fuel gauge. You can check the level with a dip stick.

Hydraulics

Main valves   The main hydraulic valves are located in the chassis. Manual valves are provided near the ground control console. There are two hand levers or valves that can be opened in an emergency, if the main valves fail or the engine quits and won't restart. Opening both valves releases pressure in the hydraulic lines and causes the main hydraulic cylinder to lower the boom. You may find it reassuring to locate these valves so you can instruct ground crew how to operate them should the engine fail.

Control Panel (Ground)

Start up   Start the engine from the ground control console. Check that the oil pressure, engine temp, and ammeter gauges are in the green.

Controls   Operate each ground control switch. You want these switches to work in case you get hurt and the ground crew has to bring you down.

ID plate   The ID plate is located near the ground control console. This plate displays the ID number of the vehicle as well as its weight limit and other specifications, such as two-wheel or four-wheel drive. If your walk-around inspection has found any faults, note the ID number and file a report with the best boy.

That's it for the walk around. Chances are you will start by positioning the condor for rigging. This gives you an opportunity to check each of the controls from the basket as well.

Driving the Aerial Lift

Before starting up the lift, take a walk along your route of travel. Keep an eye out for low overhead, cables, curbs, ramps, steep grades, potholes, and traffic. Get ITC police to help lock up traffic if you have to go on a busy street.

The first thing to do when you climb into the basket is put on the fall-protection harness and clip it to the designated attachment point. When operating an aerial lift,

OSHA requires the use of a safety-body harness attached to a lanyard (not more than 4 ft of free fall) and a snap hook that hooks to specified places on the guardrail.

This type of lift is self-propelled at speeds of 0.7–3 miles per hour (mph). When the boom is raised and extended, the platform automatically drives at a slower speed. The boom and turret can be controlled from either the basket or a side panel on the chassis. The drive train can be controlled only from the basket. The operation of different makes varies slightly. The Snorkelift TB-A80, which has an 80-ft boom, is shown in Figure 9.12. The controls are similar for most other types and sizes. Rental companies are required (by OSHA) to provide an operator's manual, usually in a weatherproof canister on the equipment, so if you are unfamiliar with a particular model, consult the manual. Most operations are self-evident, however, once you understand the basics.

Very often the hardest part of operating an unfamiliar lift is learning its safety devices. All machines require that you step on the dead-man's pedal for the functions to operate. Because people try to defeat this (by sticking a weight on the pedal), some machines now require you to put your foot on the pedal within 3 seconds of applying the controls. If the controls stop working, you waited too long; you have to take your foot off the pedal and put it back to regain control. Some lifts require you to hold a switch to operate the vehicle when the turret is reversed (pointing backward). This is meant to make you think twice before engaging the control levers, as the controls are reversed left/right and forward/reverse from the driver's reversed perspective.

Make it a practice to beep the horn to alert those nearby of your intentions before you begin to move. The better machines have electronics to provide ramping in all the controls, including boom operations, which helps smooth out the natural jerkiness of the machinery. You will run into older or less-sophisticated models for which the controls act very abruptly. All models, especially these, require considerable care in operation, especially when lights are rigged in the basket.

When driving the platform from place to place, drive with the boom fully retracted and parallel to the ground. This position gives the operator the best field of view over the top of the chassis. The most natural (and therefore the simplest and safest) configuration for driving is with the steering tires toward the front and the boom slung off the back (see Figure 9.12D). This also puts the weight over the drive wheel, which improves traction. Never drive the platform down an incline boom first. Avoid making turns on an incline. On an incline, the vehicle often does not stop on a dime, it drifts to a stop. Keep people well clear when you are driving on an incline. Do not use reverse or forward as a brake when moving in the opposite direction.

Operating the Boom Arm

Aerial platforms are normally very stable, even when the arm is fully extended. However, physics being what it is, stability is severely compromised if the chassis is not level. Do not operate the machinery on more than a 5° gradient (6-in. rise in 10 ft). Most lifts have an automatic safety device that precludes operation on uneven ground. The transportation or grip department can help level the vehicle. Make sure leveling boards are secure and completely stable. Keep in mind the chassis bounces when the boom arm stops suddenly, which can (and has) caused the chassis to roll

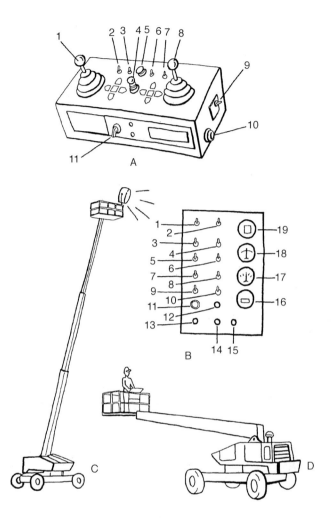

Figure 9.12 Snorkelift operation. (A) Platform basket control panel: (1) boom control lever (up/down, rotate left/right), (2) engine throttle (low/high), (3) drive range (low gear or high gear), (4) boom arm (retract/extend), (5) shut-off button (this button must be pulled out before the lift can be started), (6) platform level (tilts the basket), (7) emergency power on/off switch (battery power), (8) drive lever (forward/reverse, steering left/right), (9) platform rotate, (10) horn, (11) ignition switch and circuit breaker. (B) Ground control panel on side of chassis: (1) platform/ground control selector switch, (2) boom/axles selector switch, (3) engine throttle (high/low), (4) emergency power on/off switch, (5) boom arm (extend/retract), (6) boom control lever (up/down), (7) boom control lever (rotate left/right), (8) platform level, (9) platform rotate, (10) ground controls (on/off)—works like dead-man pedal that must be held on to operate boom functions, (11) start button, (12) choke, (13) system circuit breaker, (14) throttle circuit breaker, (15) choke run circuit breaker, (16) Hobbs meter, (17) amp meter, (18) oil pressure, (19) engine temperature. (C) Boom arm extended. (D) Boom arm retracted in position to drive chassis. Note that the boom is raised so that the driver can see over the top of the chassis. The steering wheels are at the front. (Equipment courtesy of ADCO Equipment Rental, City of Industry, CA, and Snorkelift, St. Joseph, MO.)

or slide off leveling boards. Never perch the wheels on the top end of the leveling boards. On an incline, this can be very dangerous. If leveling boards are used, they should be as wide as the tires.

When a slight gradient is unavoidable, orient the chassis pointing up and down the hill, and rotate the boom with the weight on the uphill side or, if necessary, the downhill side, but not out to one side. Be sure the chassis is completely level side to side. Chock the wheels. The chassis can creep if left on an incline.

On the larger aerial lifts, the wheel base must be expanded before boom operations can be used. With early models this was accomplished by lifting the wheels off the ground with the boom arm. Later models incorporate a hydraulic jack that lifts the chassis and hydraulic cylinders that extend and retract the wheels (controlled from levers on the chassis). On more recent models, the entire process is controlled with a single switch by the operator in the basket. The wheels extend out several feet on either side. When working over pedestrian or automobile traffic, use cones, signs, or flags to mark the area and control traffic around the base of the boom.

For best stability,

- Raise the arm up to above 45° before you start to extend.
- The steeper the boom angle, the more centered the center of gravity.
- Retract the boom before starting to bring the arm back down.
- The arm is more stable over the front or back of the chassis than over the side of the chassis.
- On an articulated boom lift, lift with the primary (lower) cylinder first, raise the arm upward second, and extend the boom last.

A chassis can be driven when the arm is raised; however, this is not recommended when the chassis is not on perfectly level ground or when the weight is off-center. Driving the chassis with the boom extended, called *towering*, should be avoided. Jerky starts and stops make the boom sway violently, which throws the operator around in the basket and can even catapult him or her out of the basket entirely.

Some additional do nots:

- Do not use the boom arm as a crane.
- Do not sling objects below the basket.
- Do not step out of the lift onto another surface; the arm can move unexpectedly with the change of weight and leave you stranded or hanging.
- Do not stand or sit on the guardrails.
- Do not attempt to climb down the arm, rappel out of the basket, or use a rope ladder.
- Do not extend the boom if the wind is greater than 25 mph. If you have frames 12 × 12 or larger rigged to the lift, it is not safe to go up in even a moderate wind.
- Do not go up if lightning is reported in the area. Come down immediately if lightning is sighted or thunder is heard.

Weight, Center of Gravity, and Range of Motion

The stability of an aerial lift is maintained as long as the combined center of gravity of the boom and the chassis stays inside the perimeter of the tire base. If it does not, the lift tips over. Three factors affect the center of gravity: the weight of the load (in the basket and on the boom arm), the distance of that load laterally from the center of the chassis, and other forces on the arm (such as wind or an unlevel wheel base). Figures 9.13 and 9.14 show two examples of manufacturers' range of motion diagrams. (Look in the operator's manual for specific data for the lift you are using.) Note that, in both illustrations, the weight rating is reduced when the mast angle is less than about 45° from horizontal and extended. Whatever our weight, these diagrams point out the range of motion that is most stable and the areas that are less so.

In film work, we typically operate *at* maximum weight capacity. In addition, we mount our lights at the outside edge of the basket. This puts the center of gravity even closer to the edge of instability. To stay within the center-of-gravity limits of the machine, we must do four things:

1. Calculate the reduction in capacity caused by the placement of the load at or outside the guard rail.
2. Limit our range of motion so we always remain within the envelope for our load rating.
3. Take wind and exposure (surface area) into account.
4. Place the chassis on a firm and level surface.

Special Training for Reduction of Capacity Calculations

The only formal data available at this writing has been put together by Genie Industries in conjunction with special aerial lift training provided by Local #728 Set Lighting Technicians and Local #80 Studio Grips. Genie Industries prepared a supplemental manual giving guidelines for use of approved models of Genie lifts to allow trained technicians in our industry to make specific exceptions to the standard operator's manual, to allow their lifts to be safely used as lighting platforms. This includes computation methods and tables used to recalculate the maximum weight capacity of the basket, based on the actual position of the lighting and grip equipment. It also includes specific guidelines with regard to wind speed and surface area of diffusion frames. It outlines many important additional requirements.

Anyone using aerial lifts as lighting platforms should take the special training course. The training is first rate, and regardless of one's experience level going in, graduates come away with new and valuable knowledge. The efforts of the union locals and manufacturers such as Genie Industries are to be applauded. In a very real way, their efforts make our workplaces safer and allow technicians to gain the technical knowledge necessary to make confident, informed decisions and recommendations. It also makes trained technicians ever more-valuable members of the crew.

Example of Weight Calculations

The maximum weight limit is printed in various places, including the ID plate and placards on the basket and next to the panel door on the chassis. As already

Maximum Load Rating Chart for Material Lifting Applications Only

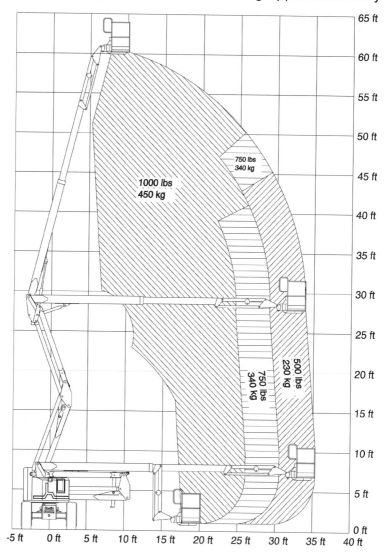

Z-60/34

Figures 9.13 and 9.14 These diagrams illustrate critical areas in the range of motion in terms of stability. When the lift is used *strictly to lift equipment* (without personnel in the lift), a multiple load rating range of motion diagram such as this can be used (by trained personnel, in accordance with a number of important rules and restrictions set forth by the manufacturer). Figure 9.13 depicts the load rating for various areas in the range of motion for a particular make and model of articulating boom. Figure 9.14 is for a particular make and model of telescoping boom. Notice the load rating decreases when the boom angle is less than about 45 degrees when the jib starts to get near full extension. The load rating decreases even more as you extend the boom horizontally. These are the critical areas in the range of motion for any lift in terms of stability.

234

Maximum Load Rating Chart for Material Lifting Applications Only

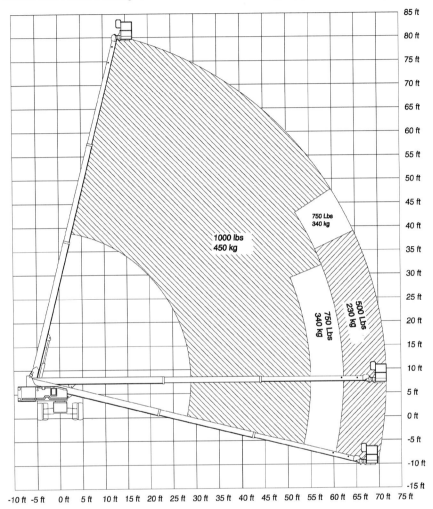

S-80

These figures are excerpts from the Special Supplement to Genie Industries Operator's Manual for Authorized and Trained Members of IATSE Local #728 Set Lighting Technician's Union and Local #80 Studio Grips Union. They are reprinted here by permission of Genie Industries. They are included here only to illustrate how the position of the boom affects stability generally. The load ratings shown here are for use by trained personnel only, and for unmanned material lifting applications only. When manned, most lifts have a 500-lb maximum capacity (see Table 9.1). Be sure to refer to the operator's manual for the particular make and model lift you are using. You can receive a copy of the supplement in full and learn how to use special tables like this by taking the Union training courses.

mentioned, calculations about the type and number of lighting units are made during prep, so that the lift equipment ordered is of sufficient capacity for the job at hand. In addition, as the operator, you want to make your own weight calculations, because it may affect your range of movement and the order in which you angle, extend, and rotate the boom arm.

Table 9.2 analyzes the weight limits for a typical lighting situation: a basket loaded with two 20k Fresnels and six PAR 64 lamps. Although the actual weight in the equipment in the basket is 823 lb, the position of the lights and grip equipment makes that load equivalent to 1111 lb. Assuming a 1000-lb limit, the lift is overloaded.

Table 9.2 Example Weight Calculations

Quantity	Item	Actual Weight	Reduction in Capacity
Cables on Boom Arm			
2	100-A Bates 240-V, 100-ft extensions (60 lbs)	120 lb	
1	100-A Bates 240-V, 100-ft extension	60 lb	
	Total load on arm	180 lb	180 lb
Lighting Equipment (at guardrail)			
2	20k Fresnel (100 lb)	200 lb	
2	Scrim bags and scrim sets (12 lb)	24 lb	
1	Condor bracket—T-bar	60 lb	
6	Chain vice grips (2.5 lb)	15 lb	
6	MolePAR (5 lb)	30 lb	
6	8-in. baby C-clamps (6 lb)	36 lb	
1	Lunchbox	16 lb	
2	Apple boxes (10 lb)	20 lb	
1	Lamp operator	180 lb	
1	Tools, personal gear, food, and drinks	18 lb	
	Total load at guardrail	599 lb	825 lb
Grip Equipment (3 ft out from guardrail)			
2	4 × 4 frames (4 lb)	4 lb	
2	Sets of ears (5 lb)	10 lb	
2	24 × 72-in. cutter (7 lb)	14 lb	
4	C-arms (4 lb)	16 lb	
	Total load 3 ft out from guardrail	44 lb	106 lb
Total Load		823 lb	1111 lb

Note: Weights listed in this example are taken from manufacturers' published specifications. "Reduction in load" calculations are taught in union-organized training courses. I encourage all readers to take this training.

Power Lines

At high voltages, current can arc 10 ft or more if given the chance to ground, especially in moist salt sea air. Assume any power line is energized. It is possible in some circumstances to have them deenergized but this must be carefully coordinated so there are no misunderstandings. Minimum safe distances from power lines depend on the voltage of the service. Figure 9.15 and Table 9.3 gives minimum safe distances for various voltages. City power lines are typically 135 kV or less. Residential power lines are typically 480 V. The transformers on residential streets drop this down to 120/240-V service. The wires running to the houses and apartments are typically 120/240 V. In most urban situations the minimum safe distance from power lines is 15 ft and, if the wires are residential, 10 ft. Never operate a boom closer than 10 ft to power lines.

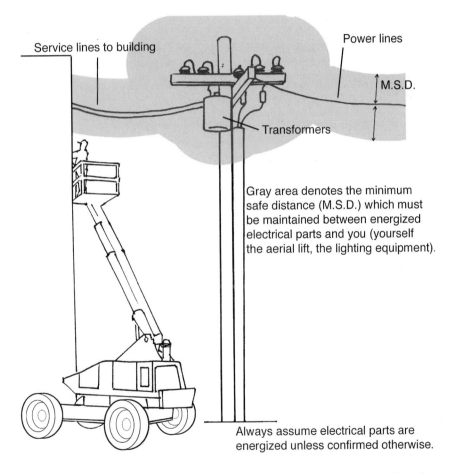

Figure 9.15 For typical residential wiring, the power lines are 480 V and the lines from the transformers to buildings are 240/120 V. The minimum safe distance (M.S.D.) is 10 ft (the area shown in gray). Keep all parts of the aerial lift and lighting equipment at least this distance from live power lines and poles.

Table 9.3 Minimum Safe Approach Distance to Energized (Exposed or Uninsulated) Power Lines

Voltage Range	Minimum Safe Approach Distance	
	Feet	Meters
0–300V	Avoid Contact	
300–50kV	10	3.05
50kV–200kV	15	4.60
200kV–350kV	20	6.10
350kV–500kV	25	7.62
500kV–750kV	35	10.67
750kV–100kV	45	13.72

Do not allow machine personnel or conductive materials inside the prohibited zone.

Maintain MSAD (minimum safe approach distance) from all energized lines and parts as well as those shown.

Assume all electrical parts and wires are energized unless known otherwise.

Do not operate *over* live power lines; the boom is powered by hydraulics, and occasionally they have been known to spring a leak, causing the boom to slowly drop. In this scenario, being over power lines would be deadly.

Hanging out over a lake (with hot power running up the arm) presents a similar hazard if the arm loses hydraulic pressure. In such cases, provide the aerial lift operator with a remote switch in the basket (such as a deuce board remote) so that, in an emergency, the operator can turn off the main power running to the basket. Do not rely on someone on the ground to get to the switches in time.

Rigging Lights and Cable

Mounts

Various manufacturers make hardware for securely mounting large lights to the basket of an aerial lift. The grips who rig the mount need an idea of which way the light will face to position the mount conveniently. There are two basic types of mounts: candlesticks and T-bar Condor brackets.

A candlestick is a solid iron pipe with a junior-size receiver in one end. The pipe is mounted inside the basket to the vertical posts of the guardrail using chain vice grips with the T-handle facing the operator (Figure 9.16). (Bazookas, junior risers, and lights stands should not be used for big lights. The castings are not strong enough and will split. Only solid metal candlesticks should be used.)

A T-bar consists of two vertical posts that hold a horizontal mounting bar just above the top guardrail. Junior mounts can be slid around the horizontal mount to support lights. The vertical posts are attached to the guardrail posts using chain vice grips or U-brackets and bolts. Some people prefer to use chain vice grips because they wrap around the tubular guardrails (distributing the pressure more

Figure 9.16 A candlestick is rigged to the basket post with chain vice grips. Note the chain vice grips are oriented so they do not stick out and become a hazard. A light can also be underslung below the basket by rigging a candlestick upside down outside the basket.

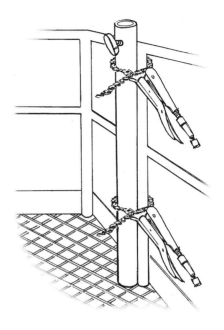

evenly) and have less of a tendency to crush them. Always orient the chain vice grip so it is flush with the basket (it should not stick into or out of the basket) as someone is liable to run into it. If you use U-brackets, don't overdo it; tightening the brackets until they crush the tubular posts does nothing to increase the strength of the rig.

When an 80-ft arm is resting on the ground, the light mounts are still 6 ft above ground level. This makes mounting big heavy lights from ground level a challenge. The best way to mount lights onto a Condor mount is to work from the lift gate of a stake bed or other truck. Two electricians can lift a light into place from a lift gate. If no lift gate is available, you can mount the light by tilting the basket forward so that it is easy to reach from the ground. Lift the light onto the mount. Then, while two people hold the weight of the light, hook a safety line from the back of the light to the inside guard rail and tighten it until it takes up the weight of the light. This keeps torque off the junior pin, which is not strong enough to withstand the weight at right angles. With someone stabilizing the light, tilt the basket back to level.

Always tie a safety around the bail to the basket. The safety should be $1/2$-in. hemp, aircraft cable, or, best of all, 1-in. tubular webbing. A 10-ft length is sufficient to run a loop through the knee rail and over the yoke with plenty of slack for maneuvering the light. Loop the safety around the knee rail so that, if the light falls, it will swing *under* the basket and not smash into it.

Once the lights are rigged on the basket, the operator must use a light touch on the controls and operate the chassis and boom as smoothly as possible. Jerking the lights around with abrupt movements puts a great deal of stress on the mounts.

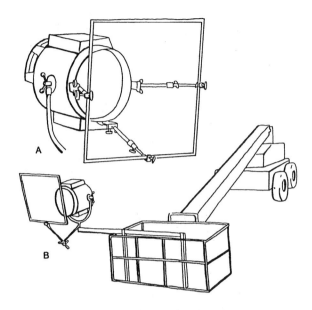

Figure 9.17 Mounting 4-by frames. (A) Ear extensions made by American Studio Equipment. (Equipment courtesy of American Studio Equipment, Sun Valley, CA, and Concept Lighting, Sun Valley, CA). (B) Grip helper and Condor bracket manufactured by Matthews Studio Equipment, Inc., Burbank, CA.

Grip equipment, such as a 4-by gel frame, can be secured out in front of the light using ear extensions (Figure 9.17A) or a grip helper (Figure 9.17B).

A meat ax is commonly secured to the rail of the basket to provide a means of manipulating nets and flags out in front of the light. A cut is often needed.

The grips supply additional flags and nets tied to the basket in case they are needed once you are aloft.

Underslinging from the Basket

In some circumstances the shot requires that the lights undersling below the basket. This does not present any real problems in terms of rigging; however, it does make it impossible to operate the lights from the basket. A second lift must be used to focus and adjust the lights.

Cabling

Figure 9.18 illustrates how to support and control cables. The head cable must be long enough to reach the ground when the boom is at its full height. A head cable extension is usually required to make the run. As always, the head cable should have a strain relief at the head. Leave enough slack head cable so that the fixture can be maneuvered. Tie off the cable to the middle rail, running it around the basket to the center of the basket next to the control console. When there is more than one cable, run all cables together in a single bundle. Tie the cables off before they exit the basket. Run the cables down to the top of the arm and, leaving

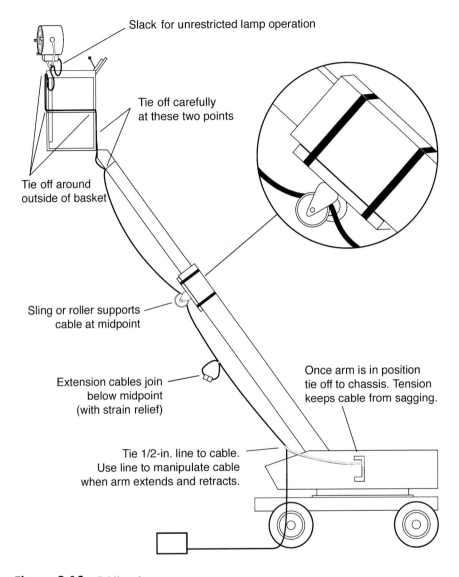

Slack for unrestricted lamp operation

Tie off carefully
at these two points

Tie off around
outside of basket

Sling or roller supports
cable at midpoint

Extension cables join
below midpoint
(with strain relief)

Once arm is in position
tie off to chassis. Tension
keeps cable from sagging.

Tie 1/2-in. line to cable.
Use line to manipulate cable
when arm extends and retracts.

Figure 9.18 Cabling the arm.

enough slack so the basket can be fully rotated left and right, tie off the cables to the top of the arm.

Extend the arm out fully at ground level. At the end of the second telescoping section, loop a line loosely around the cables and tie the line around the arm (be sure to position the line so it stays clear of the moving parts). As the arm extends and retracts, you want the cables to pull freely through this loop. The junction between head feeder cables should be tied securely with a strain relief and always remain below the loop. Better yet mount a boat roller to the arm instead of using a loop. This is an innovative improvement used by many of the best rigging gaffers. The roller supports the cable but allows it to freely pay out as necessary.

Usually, only one loop or roller is required. The remainder of the cable can be controlled from the ground by tying a $1/2$-in. line to the cable about one-third of the way up. The spotter on the ground uses this line to help control the cables when the arm is moving. Once the arm is set, the line is tied off to the chassis, holding the cables taught along the arm. Always have a ground spotter present when a rigged condor arm is in motion.

Never place the ballast behind or in front of the chassis. If you need to move the chassis, this causes delay. In the worst case, you could run it over.

Condor Duty

An evening of "Condor duty" is made up of a period of rigging (preferably in daylight), a period of positioning the arm and focusing the lights (usually as night falls), occasional radio calls to refocus, and long hours of sitting at the top of the lift doing nothing. Make yourself comfortable and stay warm. Square away the following items in the basket well before it is time to take the condor up:

- Walkie-talkie.
- Tools (secured so they cannot fall).
- 100-ft tag line (to pull things up to the basket).
- Furniture blankets (to sit on).
- Apple boxes (to sit on).
- A reading and work light.
- Layers of additional clothing.
- Gloves and hat.
- Snacks and drinks.
- A good book (this book, for example).

Once in position some people like to drape furniture pads or duvetyn around the sides of the basket and put rubber matting on the floor of the basket as protection from the wind. You can construct a very comfortable chair with one furniture blanket and seven to nine large grip clips. Use three grip clips to clamp one edge of the blanket to the top rail on the narrow side of the basket. This will be the back of the chair. Now clamp the sides of the blanket to the knee rail on either side (next to the control console and next to the gate). The sides of the chair provide a wind block. Before lowering the basket, be sure to remove the blanket so that you have an unobstructed view below you.

Very often, as the machinery and hydraulic lines cool, the arm settles. It can suddenly droop a few inches. This happens on all machines and need not be a cause for panic.

Marking Placement

If you need to mark the placement of the basket so you can return to that position (to take a meal break for example), make a plum bob by attaching a weight (a crescent wrench works well) to the tag line. Lower the line until the crescent wrench just barely touches the ground below. Tie off the tag line at that length and have your spotter mark the position of the plum bob on the ground. If you have to mark several positions, you can tab the line with tape instead of tying it off; and label the tabs.

Shooting in the Rain

The primary concerns when shooting in the rain, real or artificial, are that all the electrical circuits are safe and the lights are covered and stay dry.

Cabling and Distribution

Electrical safety hazards posed by water are discussed in Chapter 10. Similar hazards exist any time the ground is thoroughly wet. In fact, water is a better conductor when it is mixed with the minerals of soil. A muddy field is more conductive than a freshwater pool. Guard against bare contacts coming into contact with water and ground by elevating all connection points on milk crates or apple boxes. Wrap all electrical connections in Visqueen or heavy-duty plastic garbage bags to prevent water falling onto connection points. When cable is to be run in wet areas, it should be inspected prior to use. Look for deep nicks in the outer sheath.

Rain poses an additional hazard: Everything and everyone tends to get wet, and wet hands and feet pose little resistance should you come into contact with a fault. Light fixtures must be grounded. It is a wise precaution to test lighting fixtures for ground fault leaks prior to use in a wet environment. GFI protection should be used on circuits that are in close proximity to water (see Chapter 10, section Shock Block).

Rain Tents

Lights must be protected from falling and blowing moisture. If water falls or blows onto the hot lens, the thermal shock can crack or shatter the lens, especially when the bulb is in flood position, where it makes the lens hottest. If water leaks into the housing and touches the globe, the globe will burn out or explode. With HMIs, water causes serious problems with the electronics. Water can also cause corrosion to the metal parts of the fixtures.

Protect the lens with a gel frame of heat-shield gel or a thin color ($1/8$ CTO or $1/8$ CTB). Place rain hats over the lights. Celo screen (a tough, plastic-covered, wire screen) works well to cover fixtures. Bend it over the light and grip clip it to the bail on either side. Alternately, a flag covered with a garbage bag works for small lights. Larger lights require a 4-by flag wrapped in Visqueen. A 12-by or 20-by griff is handy to cover a number of units at once. (Check for holes in the griff first.) Rain hats should be positioned so that rain runs off away from the fixture; don't let rain collect and form a pool in the flag.

Lighting Rain

Falling water is most visible to the camera when lit from the back. Rain shots are typically done by placing rain between the lens and the actors and the general area before the camera and supplementing it with rain falling in puddles, on the tops

(A)

(B)

Figure 9.19 Rigging lights to a moving vehicle. (A) Shotmaker truck towing a car. (B) A car on a process trailer. (Photos courtesy of Shotmaker Co., Valencia, CA.)

of cars, and in places where it would be noticeably lacking were it not there. A gentle trickle of rain might also be used over the actors to keep them dripping.

Shooting on Moving Vehicles

The standard method of shooting a scene in a moving car is to tow the car and mount the camera to the side door or the hood of the car. The tow vehicle is equipped with a sound-baffled generator and various rails and platforms to which lights can be mounted. Some very specialized vehicles, such as Shotmaker trucks, support the camera on a crane arm, which makes placing the camera a relatively easy task and provides an opportunity to approach a driving scene with some dynamic camera moves (Figure 9.19A).

Another approach is to put the car on a low-riding flatbed trailer, a *process trailer*, and tow the trailer (Figure 9.19B). The trailer rides low to the ground so that the height of the car above the pavement looks normal to the camera. Taking the air out of the car's tires once it is on the trailer also helps. The largest trailer for this purpose is two lanes wide, allowing room for the camera, lights, and crew. It usually works out well to tie HMI ballasts to the speed-rail frame around the roof of the cab. Run cables along the speed rail, keeping them neatly tied and out of the way. Be sure nothing will slip loose, rattle, drag, or get under the tires when the car gets on the road.

Many techniques are used for lighting the interior of a car. The basic problem with daytime car interiors is the contrast between interior and exterior. The light level on the faces has to be brought up so that the exterior scenery is not overexposed. When lighting a car on a sunny day, one approach is to use large HMI sources on the tow vehicle to simulate sunshine on the actors' faces. On an overcast day, the supplemental lights may be shone through diffusion material attached to the windshield (assuming that the camera does not see the windshield).

Shooting at night poses a different set of problems. For a city street scene, an open aperture is needed to make naturally lit storefronts visible. You would therefore shoot at relatively low light levels with small fixtures taped to the dashboard, for example. Some DPs like to have several small lights mounted at various angles to achieve the appearance of passing traffic and streetlights by bringing the lights up and down on dimmers or panning them across the actors.

With fast film, the lighting need not consume a lot of power. A night scene could be very minimally lit using a couple of 12-V fixtures (Kino-Flos, stick-ups, Dedolights, or other 12-V fixtures) running off of the car battery or a deep-cycle marine battery. In a pinch, I once liberated a headlight from the grip truck; bounced, diffused, and wrapped in black wrap, it looked fantastic.

CHAPTER 10

Specialty Lighting

Big Guns

From its very beginning, motion pictures have used big lights. At first, it was purely out of necessity—using carbon arc lights allowed the early motion pictures to be moved indoors. As technology progressed, film stocks became increasingly sensitive. Meanwhile, the technical difficulty of light level has been replaced with an aesthetic necessity for virtual realism in the photography. To light up a big room as if it were filled with sunlight, you have to use the biggest lights there are, and the DP still sometimes has to stretch to get to the desired f-stop. The truth is, sometimes you just need a whole boatload of light. To make sunlight play naturally, it needs to reach into the set and still be overexposed a couple stops. In addition, the DP knows the lenses look a lot better at an f-4 than at an f-2.8. Even though, these days, a DP could shoot everything with 500ASA film stock, he or she won't if it can be helped (especially if the shot is to be part of an optical effect). On top of that, the scene might need to ramp into slow motion, a narrow shutter angle is needed for a visual effect, or a heavy tobacco filter on the lens whittles down the f-stop. In these situations, you need to get out the big guns.

I was told once that, years ago at one of the studios, someone actually built a 50,000-W tungsten lamp. It was water cooled. Only one was ever made and it was only used once. I have to assume it didn't work out all that well. People are always trying to design bigger, brighter, more efficient lights. The problem is always heat. In the *Professional Lighting Handbook* (2nd ed., Boston: Focal Press, 1991), Verne and Silvia Carlson describe an early prototype 18k HMI fitted with cooling air-jets and foam aluminum heat sinks. If air circulation wasn't just right, the lamp had "been known to warp reflectors, crack lenses, and vaporize the interiors of the fixture, as well as melt electrode tips." The efforts of these developers combined with new space-age materials and refinements in the designs brought several very powerful lights to market in recent years. Here again, the most recent information may be available on the Internet (see Appendix H).

Set Lighting

Softsun

Softsun fixtures come in sizes from moderate to enormous (3.3k, 10k, 15k, 25k, 50k, and 100k). They are daylight balanced (5400 K), flicker free, and can be dimmed from their power supply from 100% to just 5% via a handheld digital remote control (or any DMX control signal). Most models are rectangular in shape, to accommodate the linear ESL lamp (enhanced spectrum long arc). Thus, the Softsun lamp and reflector form a large-aperture direct light source (Figure 10.1). The rectangular units have a wide spread horizontally (most models 100° or more) but a focusable vertical spread (the 50k unit has an 11° spread in spot position and 35° spread in flood). While these units normally are oriented horizontally, they can be deployed in any orientation.

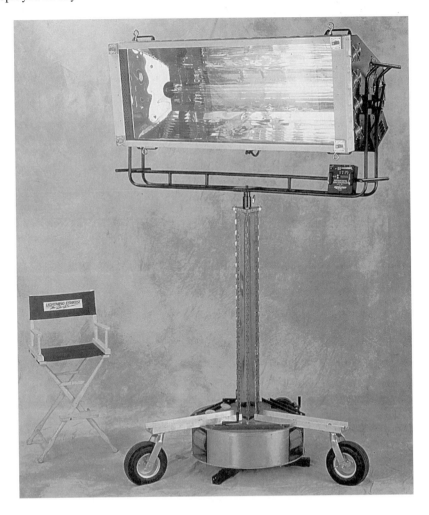

Figure 10.1 50k Softsun. (Courtesy of Lightning Strikes!, Los Angeles, CA.)

Figure 10.2 3.3k Softsuns rigged to a car. (Courtesy of Lightning Strikes!, Los Angeles, CA.)

The larger Softsun units have proven themselves invaluable for day exteriors to help create a consistent sun source, especially when the real sun ducks in and out of clouds or sinks behind the horizon. In these changing conditions, the dimming feature is especially helpful for maintaining balanced light levels. Because of its greater power and spread, the light can be backed up to cover more area with a single source. Compared to an 18k HMI at full flood, the 50k is approximately a two-thirds stop brighter (at full flood) to two stops brighter (at full spot). Due to the light's wide horizontal spread it can replace two or three 12k or 18k Fresnels. DPs find this advantageous, because it allows them to deploy a single source, eliminating the problem of multiple shadows, and effect a natural look. See Appendix B for photometrics.

The 3.3k unit has proven especially good for lighting car interiors (Figure 10.2). Softsun lamps pose no explosion hazard, and the lamps are shock mounted and rugged enough to survive a high-speed chase. The size and shape of the 3.3k lends itself to lighting through car windows (26 in. long, 12 in. high, 9 in. deep). It weighs 24 lb.

The ESL lamps keep consistent color temperature as they age, and therefore they also match lamp to lamp. They also remain consistent (within 200 K) throughout their dimmable range. The spectral power distribution is regular with no spikes, which shows a truer match to daylight than other daylight sources. The CRI is 96 or better.

The 50k and 100k units are very large (the 50k is 72 in. long, 29 in. high, 22 in. deep) and heavy (the 50k head weighs 210 lb, the 100k weighs 300 lb). The bail is equipped with three 1 1/8-in. junior pins: center and outboard sides. The light is most stable placed on two side-by-side super cranks, although a single Cinevator can handle the 50k. Very often, the necessary flexibility is gained by placing the fixture in a Condor so it can be easily moved around, on the arm. Especially on uneven terrain moving the light on two stands is difficult.

All the larger Softsun units have Cam-Lok tails. The 50k flicker-free ballast requires a three-phase power 208/240 V AC at 220 A per leg (three phase wires plus ground), 50/60 Hz. The non-flicker-free ballast is a single-phase 208/240 V AC (two phase wires plus ground) at 250 A per leg, 50/60 Hz. So be prepared with 4/0 cable to power this light. The 100 kW runs off a 480-V three-phase (380/415 in Europe) generator. Many generators this size are switchable to 480 V. This also allows the 100-kW unit to still use 4/0 cable feeds.

All the Softsun heads require cooling fans. A normal/silent switch puts the fans on a quieter setting during sound takes.

12k and 18k PAR HMIs

With spot lenses, these are the brightest fixtures there are. At this writing, these fixtures are in their infancy—or perhaps adolescence—they are a little surly. A few problems still need to be ironed out. Nonetheless, several manufacturers now offer 12k and even 18k SE PAR fixtures. An LTM 12k PAR with a superwide lens puts out more than 100 FC at 100 ft. With a spot lens, it puts out a scorching 492 FC at 200 ft. With a medium lens at 20 ft, it is brighter than the sun on a clear day. Clearly, these fixtures are ideal for re-creating sunlight. Figure 10.3 shows 12k PARs on a feature set. Among tall downtown buildings in Los Angeles, the DP and gaffer maintained a consistent backlight all day long by lining up nine 12k PARs on a rooftop 400 ft from the set.

While their awesome power fills a niche no other light can, it also makes them essentially ungelable when using medium or spot lenses. This makes color correction a problem. Gels work by absorbing selected parts of the color spectrum by converting that spectral energy into heat. The result, in this case, is that even 4 × 4 frames

Figure 10.3 12k PAR fixtures line the roof of a downtown building giving an edge light to actors 400 ft and nine stories below. At that distance, the eight fixtures did not cast multiple shadows but acted as a single source. (Courtesy of gaffer Mike Bauman.)

placed away from the light burn up almost immediately. Heat shield (an expensive clear, UV-absorbing gel used to save gels from heat) puts up a fight only for a minute or so before burning through. The only solution seems to be for the light manufacturers to design sets of specially suited high-temp glass filters in an array of necessary colors.

At this writing, bulb failure is also a concern. They seem to fail (explosively) somewhat more frequently than we are used to with other HMI types. Manufacturers recommend removing 6k, 12k, and 18k lamps before moving the light. These bulbs are heavy and supported only at one end. They can easily be cracked by a bump in the road or by being set down hard. This, and the fact that they are excruciatingly hot to work around, should make electricians especially cautious. Changing lenses is like working in a foundry—use gloves and pliers or channel locks. Get thick leather gloves that cover your forearms if you are going to be doing it a lot, but if possible, turn the light off. Mole's 12/18k PAR does not use lenses. Instead it has a flood/spot knob that moves the reflector to intensify or widen the beam.

In cold weather, the abrupt change of temperature when shut down can cause lenses to crack. You can avoid this by lengthening the time during which they cool down. Do this by adding scrims to the light a minute or two before shutting off the light. The hot scrims help warm the lens when the light is shut off.

20k and 24k Tungsten Lights

For almost a century the biggest single source tungsten light was the 10k. The advent of 20k and 24k lamps (in 1998) paved the way for a variety of 20k and 24k fixtures, including Fresnel fixtures, sky pans, and beam projectors (so far). The large tungsten lamps were first designed in Japan and introduced in the United States as 220-V lamps, a strange voltage to have chosen, as it does not match any U.S. or Japanese electrical system. The bulbs are now available in various voltages: 208 V, 220 V, 230 V, and 240 V. It is very important to specify the bulb you need and match it to the voltage of the system you are using. A 208-V bulb will burn out if 240 V is applied to it (a very expensive mistake). Conversely, a 240-V bulb running on 208 V will have poor output and an overly warm color temperature. The 230-V lamps are used in European electrical systems.

Carbon Arc Lights

From the very earliest days of motion pictures, carbon arc lights have been lighting movies (Figure 10.4). In their heyday, there were quite a variety of arc fixtures, from Fresnels of various sizes, to broads, ellipsoidal spotlights, and follow spots (see Table A.8). Pick out any movie in the Classics section of your video store and you will be watching a film lit with arcs. The silhouette of a Brute arc is a Hollywood icon. By the 1970s, arc lights were being replaced by another type of high luminance daylight technology, the HMI. Discharge sources had clear advantages over arcs. Each arc light requires a full-time operator. The carbons must be constantly trimmed and changed every 20–30 minutes. The lights must be shut off whenever possible to save the carbons and prevent excess heating. The phrase, "Lights, camera, action," comes from the days when the lights were turned on

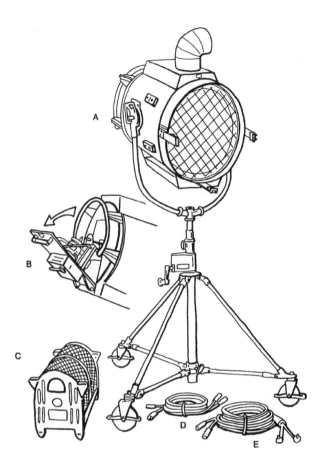

Figure 10.4 Components of a studio arc light. (A) Head with chimney attached, (B) access to the carbons and internal mechanism is gained by folding out the back of the unit, (C) power grid, (D) head cable, (E) grid cable with lug connectors. (Equipment courtesy of Mole-Richardson Co., Los Angeles, CA.)

immediately before each take. Arcs are noisy and make smoke. With today's general shift to a more thrifty and speedy mode of production, arcs are rarely used. They sit in rows on the top shelves of the studios' lamp docks, dusty hulks, relics of a time gone by.

Still, arcs are by no means extinct. Every year, at least a few films and commercials haul out Brutes. In fact, they seem to have even made a small comeback in the last couple years. Why? Ask any gaffer or DP who worked with them. The quality and color of an arc is beautiful; no other source truly replicates it. Many gaffers consider them the nicest of all sources.

Operation

An arc light operates by maintaining an arc flame between the positive and negative carbon electrodes. As the arc flame burns away the ends of the carbons, a motor feeds the carbons so that the arc gap remains constant. The arc flame emanates

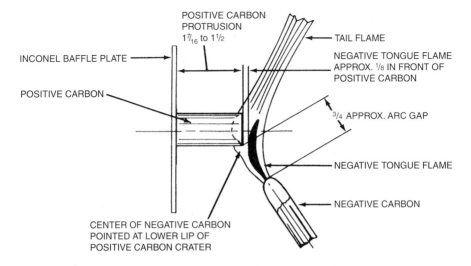

Figure 10.5   Ideal carbon arc flame. (Courtesy of Mole-Richardson Co., Los Angeles, CA.)

from the pointed tip of the negative carbon, licking upward toward the cratered end of the positive carbon. As a result, the positive carbon burns away twice as fast as the negative. On average, a positive carbon will last about 30 minutes, depending on the length and type of the carbon. The positive carbon is constantly rotated by a motor so that its crater burns away symmetrically.

With a perfectly trimmed arc light, the feed motor maintains exact alignment of the positive and negative carbons as they burn away (Figure 10.5). The tip of the negative electrode should be pointed directly at the lower lip of the crater on the positive. The gap between them should be $^3/_4$ in. The positive carbon should protrude from the baffle plate about $1^7/_{16}$ to $1^1/_2$ in.

A rheostat controls the speed at which the positive carbon is fed and rotated. The arc light operator checks the alignment of the carbons during the operation by peering through one of the darkly tinted peepholes in the side of the housing. By checking the alignment and gap of the carbons from time to time, the operator can determine if the positive carbon is burning faster or slower than the feed rate. If the gap is getting bigger, the operator must increase the feed rate; if the gap is growing smaller, the operator must decrease the feed rate.

The alignment of each electrode is adjusted manually by turning one of two knobs on the back of the fixture. Turning the knob clockwise screws the electrode in; counterclockwise pulls it back. If the carbons burn themselves out of alignment, first realign them with the manual knobs, then adjust the feed rate to keep the carbons aligned. Do not attempt to use the feed rate to bring the carbons back into alignment.

Installing the Electrodes

On the Litewate Brute, manufactured by Mole-Richardson Co., the entire carbon feed assembly is mounted to the back panel of the light. This panel hinges down and out to give access to the interior mechanics (Figures 10.6 and 10.7). In the event that the mechanism breaks down, the back panel can be replaced without exchanging

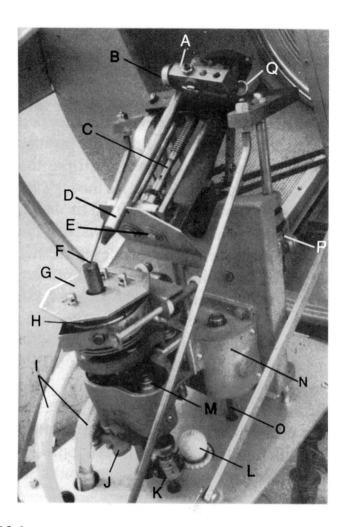

Figure 10.6 The carbon feed mechanism of a Litewate Brute arc hinged out of the back of the light. (A) Negative carbon holder, (B) carbon roller, (C) negative drive rod, (D) negative carbon, (E) negative baffle plate, (F) positive carbon, (G) positive baffle plate, (H) positive brushes, (I) power leads, (J) carbon release lever, (K) manual hand-crank shaft for positive carbon, (L) work light, (M) feed gear, (N) gear box, (O) manual hand-crank shaft for negative carbon, (P) feed motor, (Q) dimpled release lever. (Photo by Rob Lewbel. Equipment courtesy of Mole-Richardson Co., Los Angeles, CA.)

the entire light. On older models, access to the inner workings is gained through a door on the side of the light.

The lamp operator keeps a supply of carbons in a metal can hanging from the light stand on a chain. Before installing new electrodes, the power switch (Figure 10.7D) must be off. Determine whether the light is cool. If it is hot, use pliers to operate the internal levers. Lamp operators make it a practice to use pliers even when the lamp is cool in order to form safe habits.

Figure 10.7 The back panel of a Litewate Brute Arc. (A) Spring-loaded door latch, (B) handle, (C) polarity indicator light, (D) power switch, (E) recessed power cable receptacles, (F) striker lever, (G) flood/spot crank, (H) negative manual hand crank, (I) feed-rate rheostat, (J) positive manual hand crank, (K) butt end of positive carbon. (Photo by Rob Lewbel. Equipment courtesy of Mole-Richardson Co., Los Angeles, CA.)

For the following discussion letters in parentheses refer to Figure 10.6. The carbon holders are likely to be in the position where the last set of carbons were removed; that is, cranked in toward each other. Drop the negative carbon carriage (A) to the bottom position by pressing the dimpled release lever (Q). The lever disengages the carbon holder from the drive rod (C) and allows it to slide freely.

On the Litewate Brute, a spring-loaded lever on the negative carbon holder allows you to hold back the roller clamp (B) to slide the butt end of the carbon in to the V-block against the stop. On the Brute, the negative carbon is held by a thumbscrew.

The positive carbon is held in place by the brushes (H). Rotate the *camming lever* (carbon release lever, J) clockwise to spread the brushes and allow installation of the positive carbon. Before inserting the positive electrode, depress the *striker lever* to bring the negative electrode up into striking position. Slide the positive carbon in through the back panel, crater end first, until it *gently* touches the negative carbon. It should protrude from the baffle plate by 1 1/2 in. The butt end of the positive carbon will stick out of the back of the housing. Align the carbons so that the tip of the negative carbon touches the center of the positive carbon. Release the striking lever. Clamp the positive carbon in place with the carbon release lever. Close the back of the housing or the access door. Note: Align the carbons so that the negative carbon touches the center of the crater of the positive carbon, not the lower lip. If the negative carbon hits the lower lip during striking, it may shatter the edge of the crater, causing uneven burning for several minutes.

Carbons and Filtration

There are two types of carbons: white-flame carbons and yellow-flame carbons. Both carbons produce a light that is very high in UV frequencies and both must be filtered with gels to reduce the UV emissions to a usable level.

Unfiltered white-flame arcs have a color temperature of approximately 6200 K. A Y-1 gel filter corrects the color to 5700 K. Using both a Y-1 and an MT2 gel on a white-flame arc corrects the color temperature to between 3200 and 3400 K.

Yellow-flame arcs naturally produce a light at approximately 4100 K. A YF or YF-101 filter corrects the color temperature to approximately 3200 K. Yellow-flame carbons have a greater tendency to flicker than white-flame carbons, and arc light operators often prefer to use a white-flame carbon and color correction gel instead.

The following lists the different types of arc correction gels available, what they are used for, and various manufacturers' names for them:

Y-1 Straw-colored gel used with white-flame carbons to reduce UV and convert color to daylight (GAM 1560, Y-1 L.C.T. Yellow; Lee 212, L.C.T. Yellow [Y-1]; Mole Y-1; Rosco 3107, Tough Y-1).

WF Green Preferred in Europe for same use as Y-1 (Rosco 3110, Tough WF Green; Lee 213, White Flame Green).

MT2 Used with Y-1 to convert white-flame arcs to 3200 K. Also used as an amber conversion for HMI and CID lights (Rosco 3102, Tough MT2; Lee 232, Super Correction WF Green to Tungsten; GAM 1570, MT2).

1/2 MT2 Used with Y-1 to make a partial conversion to tungsten. Light looks slightly yellow to daylight film and slightly blue to tungsten film (Rosco 3115, Tough 1/2 MT2; Gam 1575, 1/2 MT2).

1/4 MT2 Used with Y-1 to warm the daylight-balanced arc slightly (Rosco 3116, Tough 1/4 MT2).

MTY Combination Y-1 and MT2. Reduces UV and converts white-flame arcs to 3200 K (Rosco 3106, Tough MTY; GAM 1565, MTY).

MT 54 Straw-colored gel used to warm the color of white-flame arc lights and HMIs (Rosco 3134, Tough MT 54).

YF-101   Green gel used with yellow-flame carbons to reduce UV and correct to
   3200 K (Lee 230, Super Correction L.C.T. Yellow; Mole YF-101).
UV Filter   Almost clear gel used to remove UV from arc and HMI sources (Rosco
   3114, Tough UV Filter; Lee 226, UV; GAM 1510, UV Shield).

Powering an Arc Light

Arc lights run exclusively on DC power either from a rectified generator or
the DC powerhouse on the studio lot. When using a 120-V DC power source, the
arc light plugs into the grid, which supplies the light with its operating voltage of
about 73 V from a 120-V DC source. When only AC power is available, a rectifier
must be used instead of the grid. Most rectifiers operate off of three-phase AC power
and provide 73 V DC to the light.

The polarity of the cables is critical to the operation of the light. Connecting
the unit with reversed polarity causes the light to sputter and hiss during striking,
and if left on for more than a few seconds, it will burn out the core of the negative
carbon, and the tip of the positive carbon is likely to split or crack. Be sure that
positive is connected to positive and negative is connected to negative. If you are
unsure about which is which and they are not identified with color codes, check the
connectors with a DC voltmeter before striking the light. A red warning light in the
back panel of the fixture glows if the polarity is reversed, but the light is not always
reliable (Figure 10.7C).

It is good practice to fire up the light to check for proper operation as soon
as you have power. If there is any kind of problem, you can fix it without holding
up the entire production.

If the grid voltage is too high or too low, it will adversely affect the performance of the light. If the negative electrode becomes burned to a slender point, it
is a signal that the voltage is too high and the carbons are burning too fast. If the
negative carbon burns to a blunt end, the voltage is too low. In either case, the arc
flame becomes unstable and can start to flicker.

Striking an Arc Light

For the following discussion letters in parentheses refer to Figure 10.7. When
the carbons are properly aligned, trimming an arc light is as simple as turning the
power switch on (D, this energizes the electrodes and engages the feed motor),
gently turning the striker lever (F) until the carbons momentarily touch, causing an
arc, then immediately releasing the striker lever. When the negative carbon contacts
the positive carbon, the arc flame immediately ignites. Once the light is fired, check
the arc flame through the peephole. Advance the positive carbon using the hand
crank (J) so that the tip of the negative points directly at the lower lip of the crater
on the positive—about three half turns of the knob. Do not hold the striker lever
down for too long, because this can damage the carbons and the generator.

Striking Partially Used Carbons

Every time you turn off an arc light, immediately check and realign the carbons
so that they are ready for immediate restrike. When the gaffer asks for the lights
again, it is too late to start realigning the carbons.

Realignment is simple. With the power switch off, back off the positive carbon with the hand crank. Press the striker lever to bring the negative carbon into striking position, then crank the positive carbon forward until the negative carbon touches it in the middle of the crater. Release the striker lever. Now, you are ready to go as soon as the gaffer asks for light.

If you have to restrike without realigning the carbons, there is a good chance you will chip the edge of the crater, which can make the flame unstable. To fix a cracked positive carbon, turn up the rheostat (I) and even out the edge of the positive by burning it away. Once it is even again, return the rheostat to normal speed.

Daily Maintenance and Lubrication

For consistent, quiet operation, arc lights need to be lubricated three times daily: once at the start of the day, once after lunch, and once at the end of the day. The lubrication holes are shown in Figure 10.8; however, it is better to remove the gear housing cover and lubricate these parts more carefully if time permits and the light is cool. Be careful not to get lubricant on the clutch, because this will cause the clutch to slip and make manual adjustment of the carbons difficult. Lubricate gears and all joints or places where there is metal-to-metal friction.

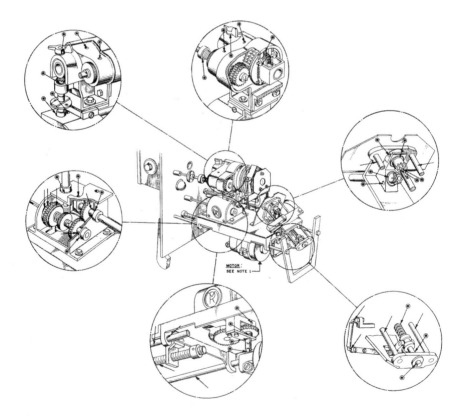

Figure 10.8 Carbon arc light lubrication holes. (Courtesy of Mole-Richardson Co., Los Angeles, CA.)

Arc lights are lubricated with a solution of finely powdered graphite and kerosene. The kerosene acts as a carrying agent to work the graphite into the gears and other moving parts. Heavy lubricants such as WD-40 and oil should not be used, because the high temperature of the light evaporates the liquid, leaving only a gummy residue that impedes the operation of the light. Once the oil has worked its way in, the residue can be cleaned out only by taking apart every mechanical part of the gear and clutch assembly. If a graphite/kerosene solution is unavailable, diesel fuel also provides lubrication without gumming up the gears.

During use, fragments of carbon and smoke dirty the inside of the lens. To clean the inside of the lens and the housing, access is gained by swinging open the floor of the housing. The floor is hinged and held in place by a pin at the bottom front of the light. Additional trays on the bottom of each side of the light hinge open for quick cleaning. During daily maintenance, the lens should be cleaned with household glass cleaner and the inside of the light blown out with compressed air. All debris and carbon chips should be emptied from the lamp trough.

Moonlight Rigs

Lighting Balloons

By placing HMI or tungsten lamps inside sealed diffusion balls, filling them with helium, and floating them over the action areas, you can create soft 360° light without the need for a high platform (Figure 10.9). Lighting balloons are particularly well suited for illuminating large delicate interior locations, such as an old cathedral or historic building, where rigging lights could damage the location. Lighting balloons are also often used simply for time efficiency, because they can eliminate rigging time and are relatively easy to adjust and move.

Balloons are often enlisted to create soft-light ambiance on exterior night scenes. For this application, balloons may afford the DP some advantages over rigging large lights in a Condor, depending on the look desired. Balloons provide a more even light, with softer shadows, and spreads 360° with a gradual fall-off. For night exteriors, the softer look helps disguise the presence of artificial lights. This is especially valuable in wilderness or rural settings, where the only motivated ambient source is moonlight. A soft source is also useful in urban scenes to lessen specular glints off of parked cars. Balloons also have practical advantages. To create an equivalent soft source from a Condor requires quite a bit of rigging. Most balloons can be set up in an hour or less and moved from one position to another relatively quickly. It is a fairly simple matter to hide the cable and tag lines, compared to hiding a Condor. They can be controlled (tungsten versions can be dimmed) from the ground. Balloon lights can afford a more efficient use of the electrician's and rigger's time.

Balloons are available from various suppliers and individuals. Check out the manufacturers' websites (see Appendix H, under Aerial Brilliance, Lights Up, Airstar, Leelium, or LTM).

Specifications for balloon lights are listed in Table A.15. The 4.8k HMI (12.5-ft diameter) balloon set at a height of 46 ft provides 20 FC directly below the balloon, which tapers off to 9.8 FC at a 50-ft radius and 2.8 FC at 115 ft from the center

Figure 10.9 Here, lighting balloons provide ambiance under the thick canopy of a Hawaiian jungle. They are much faster to move around in the dense undergrowth than 18ks on stands. The gaffer also used these 6k balloons as key light by bunching two or three and employing ¹/₂ soft-frost diffusion. As an added bonus, the balloons could be floated to soften direct sunlight when the grips would have had a hard time flying a diffusion frame. (Balloons are by Aerial Brilliance. Photo by gaffer Mike Bauman.)

(Figure 10.10). The 16k HMI (16.5-ft diameter) balloon set at 82.5 ft provides 20 FC directly below, 11 FC at a 50-ft radius, and 2.8 FC at a 200-ft radius from center.

Tube balloons, which are sausage-shaped, have a lower profile, so they afford the camera a wider shot when the balloons are used on interiors with lower ceilings such as indoor swimming pools, auditoriums, or churches. Vertical dimensions range from 5 to 8¹/₂-ft, depending on wattage (see Table A.15). Different suppliers have different dimensions. Tube balloons tend to cast the most light out the sides of their long axis, making them ideal for lighting a church aisle, for example. A long aisle might be lit with two or three tube balloons in a line.

Different manufacturers use different materials and design strategies, and some are more successful than others. Some balloons deliver more foot candles per watt than others by virtue of the envelope material they use. The placement of the globes inside the balloon also affects brightness. Those with the globes hung in the middle of the balloon are generally more efficient than those that light upward from the bottom of the balloon.

The availability of user-friendly accessories also differs from one supplier to another. To give just one example, Lights Up accessories include their Yarmulke

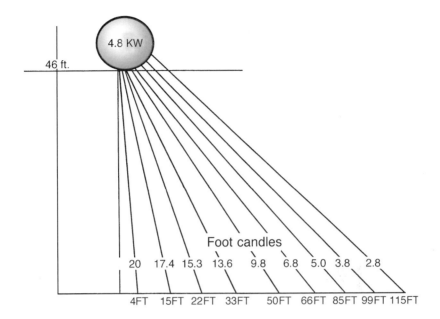

Figure 10.10 Sample photometric data for 4.8k HMI lighting balloon. (Courtesy of Lights Up Industries, Los Angeles, CA. Check the website for current information.)

polysilk top cover, which cuts top spill. Black-out skirts (designed with snaps and Velcro for quick adjustable application) contain side spill and prevent the walls from being lit on interior sets). Lights Up balloons use black tag lines, which attach with a snap ring or quick link. The black lines are fairly easy to hide and do not have reflective highlights (unlike monofilament lines). Most Lights Up units are available with detachable head cables, so the balloon can be moved easily when working around architectural obstacles. Some balloons are flicker free or adaptable to flicker-free ballasts (from your own supplier). Some suppliers can provide head cable extensions as necessary.

Most balloon companies send out their equipment with a technician. Experience has shown that sending balloons up and taking them down is a tricky enough operation to warrant having one person single-mindedly dedicated to supervising operations and caring for the balloon.

On the larger balloons, the balloon is attached by its head cable to its road case, which houses the ballasts (HMI units) and winch. Three tag lines are also attached to set the position and height of the balloon. These are tied off to weights, sandbags, or other sturdy tag points. Rigging and stabilization equipment are often required to set the balloon in a difficult spot and prevent the balloon from bobbing and twisting excessively in wind. Lights Up deploys a "wind net" (a netting that wraps over the top of the balloon to help distribute forces evenly around the envelope of the balloon, stabilize it, and prevent unnecessary stresses).

Balloons cannot generally be used in winds greater than 25 mph. They cannot be used if there is lightning in the area. They must be kept well clear of power lines and sharp objects. Also keep them away from sprinkler heads. Balloons can be rained on, although the smaller balloons may not stay afloat if they get too heavy with water. The larger balloons have more lift and can withstand rain and downdrafts better than the smaller balloons. At higher elevations, balloons lose lift and may need to be supported with rigging.

Balloons can be rigged any number of ways, the main concern being not to puncture or overstress the envelope. A balloon can be rested against a ceiling, provided the ceiling is stable and free of sharp edges. Cabling can be draped off to one side or, if necessary, the balloon turned 90° on its side to accommodate running the cables out the side, which helps maximize head room and avoid using tag lines. Balloons can be supported on cable lines run between trees in a forest. They can be flown from a Condor arm for stability. In long-term, semi-permanent sets on a sound stage, balloons can be filled with air instead of helium and hung upside down from the perms on sound stages. This approach limits their flexibility. Without helium, they become quite heavy. While air can be used, other gasses such as nitrogen are not advisable because they discolor the envelope and do not have as much lift. Helium is an inert gas—not combustible. In fact, it is a cool gas, which helps ventilate the enclosed lamps.

Soft Box

Some DPs prefer an even larger, soft source for night moonlight ambiance. For this, they might design a 12 × 12-ft. soft box constructed of box truss and speed rail, lit with an array of 2500 PARs or 12ks suspended from a crane arm. The rig shown in Figure 10.11 is actually a soft box for keeping a consistent *daytime* ambiance on a downtown street with constantly changing sunlight.

Fisher Lights

Fisher Productions, Inc. (which makes specialized suspended soft banks for car photography) makes a special rig, named appropriately, the *Moonlight*. It is an 8 × 17-ft soft bank lit with 10 2500-W DCI lamps (an 18k tungsten version is also available). Flicker-free DCI electronic ballasts allow for about 1½ stops of dimming and color temperature adjustment from about 4500 to 6000 K with no gel added. Slide-in filters allow even greater color correction. The bank is suspended from an 80-ft telescoping arm. Stabilizing cables run from the light bank to the arm, so it can be panned and tilted. All lamp adjustments are made remotely from the ground. Power requirements are 208Y/120 three-phase AC (75 A per leg) Cam-Lok (with adapters supplied for other connectors).

Because a large source can create soft shadows only if it is relatively close to the subject, rigs of this type are best positioned fairly close overhead. Distant backgrounds can be more easily lit with standard hard sources.

Truck-Mounted Tower Lights (Musco)

The Musco Light Company began as a mobile sports lighting service but found a place in the motion picture industry for lighting very large expanses. A Musco consists

Figure 10.11 Sixteen 6k Goya fixtures pointed straight down into a huge 20 × 20-ft soft box made of box truss. The box was built for a major exterior location on a feature film, where it would provide daytime ambience and extend precious daylight. The bottom of the box is covered with two layers of diffusion material and is skirted with duvetyn. It is rigged to a large crane. (Courtesy of Kevin Brown.)

of a truck-mounted boom arm with a bank of 6–15 high-efficiency 6k open-face HMI fixtures. Because of its high-efficiency reflector, each 6k unit puts out as much light as a standard 12k HMI Fresnel. The smallest Musco truck has a maximum boom height of 80 ft, and the largest goes to 100 ft (120 ft with a jib arm). The trucks are completely self-contained and self-sufficient, with their own sound-baffled generators and operators (Figure 10.12).

The lights can be controlled by the gaffer or DP with a handheld remote-control unit or by the Musco operator with levers at the base of the boom. Each light can be panned 359°, tilted 220°, flooded, and spotted remotely. The entire boom arm rotates 180° on its base.

The fixtures have a standard daylight color temperature of 5600 K. Some are available with flicker-free electronic ballasts. A 15-head array can flood a 300-sq ft area up to half a mile away from the truck at a level of 20 FC. At maximum spot, a 50-sq ft area that is 100 ft from the light can be illuminated to 13,000 FC.

When gel or diffusion is needed, it is placed on a large frame that surrounds the entire bank of lights on three sides. The frames can be gelled ahead of time by Musco's field operators, or they can be gelled by set grips on the day before use. It takes exactly three rolls of 48-in. gel to cover the whole frame of the 15-light array.

Figure 10.12 A Musco truck. (Courtesy of Musco Mobile Lighting, Ltd., Oskaloosa, IA.)

Effects Lights

Xenon Lights

Xenon globes have a very short arc length and an extremely bright arc, which makes them easy to collimate into a highly focused beam with very little scatter (Figure 10.13).

The beam is perfectly circular and very narrow. The beam diameter can be controlled with an electronic flood/spot switch on the head and ballast. The intense shaft of daylight-balanced (5600 K) light is sometimes used to simulate sunlight or a searchlight. Xenon fixtures are used in concerts and light shows to create spectacular air lighting effects. Their vibration-resistant design also makes them suitable for use in helicopter and armored tank searchlights.

Xenotech, among other manufacturers, developed a line of high-output xenon lights designed primarily for concert, theatrical, and motion picture use. They are made in various sizes. The smallest is a powerful 75-W flashlight that can be powered by

Figure 10.13   Xenon lights have a very small arc gap, allowing the beam to be focused into an intense, very narrow shaft. (Courtesy of Xenotech, Inc., Sun Valley, CA.)

a clip-on battery or by 110 V mains. In full spot, the flashlight can deliver 600 FC at a distance of 100 ft. The smaller xenon fixtures (150 W, 500 W, 750 W, and 1000 W) run on single-phase 120 V. The power supplies for larger units (2000 W, 4000 W, 7000 W, and 10,000 W) may take either 208–230-V single-phase or 208–230-V three-phase, depending on the type. The power supplies provide the start-up charge and regulate power to the head. On/off and flood/spot functions can be controlled from the ballast and the head. Xenon lights operate on a pulse DC (equivalent to square-wave current), which allows flicker-free filming at any frame rate up to 10,000 fps.

The lights can be ordered with a normal yoke or a remote-control articulating base and color changer and douser accessories. When operated by a computer-controlled remote, a line of xenon lights can be preprogrammed to perform moving beam effects in unison, or each unit can be controlled separately for different purposes.

Xenon lamps have long lives, greater than 2000 hours. There is no color shift over the life of the globe, and the color temperature is independent of voltage and current fluctuations. Xenon lamps require very careful temperature regulation, and they must use forced air cooling, which makes them somewhat noisy. Forced air cooling should continue for at least 5 minutes after the light has been turned off. Xenons cannot be aimed downward. A mirror accessory must be used to redirect the beam when steep downward angles are required.

During the life of the globe (Figure 10.14), evaporated tungsten is deposited on the upper inner wall of the envelope and slowly reduces light output. The globe should be turned over after half its rated life. These unavoidable deposits are what define the end of a globe's usefulness. Frequent ignition charges accelerate the wear of the electrodes and hasten the darkening of the envelope. Xenon light operators should therefore try to avoid unnecessary shut-downs and start-ups. If the light is temporarily not needed, pan it into the sky rather than shut it off.

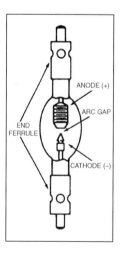

Figure 10.14 A xenon globe.

A xenon bulb is always under substantial internal pressure, and the pressure increases when hot. A xenon globe does not break, it explodes. It must always be handled with the utmost care and should never be handled until completely cooled. Bulb manufacturers recommend the use of protective eyewear (or, better, a full-face mask), cotton gloves, and even protective bodywear when handling the globes. For safety reasons, globes should not be operated more than 25% past their rated lifetime. Xenon globes must be installed with proper polarity (Figure 10.14). If operated with improper polarity, the bulb can be rendered useless in a short amount of time.

Beam Projectors

The beam projector (BP, as they are known in the theater) has been around since before movies were invented. While they are commonly used in theater lighting, until their recent revival, they hadn't seen too much action on the silver screen. In 2000, Mole-Richardson redesigned the BP in large sizes for use in motion picture work, and they proved a valuable tool (Figure 10.15). The lamp in a BP is set in front of a large parabolic glass mirror, which fills the back of the unit. Fins or channels in concentric circles around the bulb cut side spill. The resulting beam is a straight, almost parallel column of light, similar to that of a xenon unit but not as sharp. Unlike a xenon lamp, however, tungsten BPs can be put on dimmer. A flood/spot knob widens or concentrates the beam slightly (5–15°) by sliding the lamp base relative to the mirror. The fixtures come in several sizes: an 18-in. fixture, either 2k tungsten or 1.2k HMI; a 24-in. fixture, either 5k tungsten or 2.5/4k HMI; and a huge 36-in. fixture, either 10k or 20k tungsten or 12k HMI.

Beam projectors are all about showing shafts of light in atmosphere. Diffusion fog, special effects smoke, or dust in the air give the shafts shape. The field of a BP is slightly uneven. If you point the light at the wall you can almost make out the magnified image of the lamp filament projected on the wall by the mirror reflector.

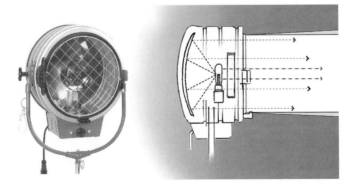

Figure 10.15 A 2.5k HMI beam projector. The large parabolic mirror directs the light into a shaft of parallel rays. (Courtesy of Mole-Richardson, Co., Los Angeles, CA.)

Automated Lights

Lighting showmanship has always been a tradition in rock-and-roll lighting and dance clubs. State-of-the-art automated luminaires are capable of creating breathtaking effects in the hands of a creative designer and a skilled console operator. Dozens of lights can be programmed—choreographed—to make sweeping pans and flourishes, weaving beams of light into patterns in the air. The lights have dozens of features. The operation of lighting systems such as Vari-lite, Intellabeam, Cyberlight, and Roboscan is complex, typically requiring the skills of a specialist. However, without getting into too much detail, we can get a general idea of what is possible by looking at one fixture as an example.

The Cyberlight, designed by Lightwave Research, employs a 1200 SE HMI source (5600 K) (Figure 10.16). Light travels through a complex tunnel of mechanisms, including motorized zoom, variable iris, variable frost (hard or soft edge), optical dimming and blackout, a three-tier color system (infinitely variable dichroic color mixing system, eight-position color wheel, color correction), bidirectional variable-speed rotating gobo wheel (four gobos), fixed gobo wheel (eight gobos), and variable-speed strobe shutter. The fixture is 44 in. long and weighs 91 lb. The light can also produce a number of optical effects, such as a multi-image prism, split color, near photo-quality image projection, wave glass, and a mosaic color effect. The light comes out the end of the fixture and hits a moving mirror, which is panned and tilted by a high-resolution, microstepping motor capable of panning the beam smoothly 170° and tilting 110°. All features are remotely controlled using a special LCD lighting controller or a USITT DMX-512 console. The control cable is standard XLR.

Figure 10.16 Cyberlight. (Courtesy of High End Systems, Austin, TX.)

Each feature of an automated light takes up one dimmer channel on the control console. Each light may use 10–25 channels (some lights require even more). A sophisticated computer-based control console is required to program coordinated movement of hundreds of channels. Programming automated lights requires the skills of a specialist, a board operator with automated lighting experience.

Black Lights

Ultraviolet (UV) light, black light, occupies a place in the electromagnetic spectrum just below violet, the shortest visible wavelength of light. It is invisible radiant energy. The UV spectrum is subdivided as follows:

UV-A 350–380 nm black light.
UV-B 300–340 nm used for suntanning.
UV-C 200–280 nm harmful, burns can result.

Right around 365 nm, in the middle of the UV-A spectrum, you get maximum transmission for exciting luminescent pigments and materials. When acted on by UV rays, fluorescent and phosphorescent materials are excited to a retroreflective state and emit visible light and vibrant color. Because black light works on some materials and not others, you can create interesting images, such as a disembodied pair of white gloves juggling three glowing orange balls.

Black Light Fixtures

Black-light blue fluorescent lamps (BLB: 4 ft, 40 W typically) have little punch; however, when used in close they can be quite effective. In a 4-bank, 8-bank, or 10-bank Kino Flo fixture with its bright reflector and high-output ballast, fluorescent black lights offer an even, soft light from a large source.

Mercury-vapor or metal-halide floodlights ranging from 250 to 400 W are also available from theatrical rental houses. These lamps use a deep-dyed, pot-poured, rolled, or blown glass filter. To create radiant energy at about 365 nm, one needs a light with high-UV output (mercury vapor or metal halide) and a carefully designed UV filter that blocks the visible light (400–700 nm) and the UV-B and UV-C wavelengths.

For lamps larger than 400 W, a UV dichroic coating is necessary to take the extreme heat. Such filters can be used on fixtures up to 18k HMI and xenon lights. Xenotech and Phoebus both carry dichroic UV lenses for their xenon lights. Automated Entertainment, in Burbank, developed UV filters for 12k and 18k HMIs and 200-W, 1200-W, 2500-W, and 4k SE PARs. Automated also has its own UV and "glow-in-the-dark" pigments and dyes.

Wildfire Inc. is another innovator in this area. It developed a line of UV lights, including a 400-W Fresnel, 400-W floodlight, 400-W ellipsoidal spotlight, and 250-W wide spotlight in a 20°, 50°, or 90° beam diameter. The units operate with ballasts and head feeders like HMIs. Wildfire also offers a wide variety of luminescent materials and paints, including nontoxic dyes, hair spray, lipstick, fabrics, plastics, adhesive tapes, confetti, PVC flexible tubing, and more.

DN Labs is also active in this market, with a line of small lights and specially formulated, highly efficient luminescent rods and sheets that can be machined and won't break.

Photographing with Black Light

To determine the exposure with black light, take spot meter readings of the luminescent materials to be filmed under the UV lights. To glow vibrantly on film, they should be overexposed by one stop. The effect is less vibrant at exposure and slightly dull one stop under exposure. A UV filter must be used on the camera lens because the lens cannot focus UV light the same way it can focus the visible spectrum. Without the UV filter, UV produces a hazy softening in the image.

UV light can be combined with conventional light and still create a luminescent effect. The balance depends on how much the effect is to be featured. One could light the scene normally and add UV lights on luminescent materials to give them an extra vibrancy, or a scene could be lit to a lower level with conventional lights so that the luminescent materials stand out. With nothing but black light lighting a scene, a woman wearing a luminescent wig and dress, for example, will appear to have no hands or face, only the clothes and hair show up.

Fiber Optics

A fiber-optic cable is a flexible or semiflexible glass cable that conducts light energy produced by an illuminator light box. A number of fiber-optic systems are available, with different features and applications: for miniatures, to light car interiors, and for table-top product shots, where a conventional bulb would melt the product or cause an electrical hazard (lighting up inside soaps or fluids), or underwater. The light emitted from the end of the fiber-optic cable comes out as a beam and can be fitted with a lens and barn doors, a miniature light bar, or used bare. Because of the makeup of the cable, the light can become green in lengths longer than 8 ft, and a magenta correction gel may need to be used.

DN Labs makes a 1200-W HMI illuminator (either electronic or magnetic) that illuminates 11 $1\frac{1}{2}$-in. diameter fiber-optic cables very brightly. DN Labs also makes a 250-W (3000-K) illuminator, and a 75-W, 12/24-V AC/DC illuminator, which is ideal for moving car work. These illuminate a single fiber-optic cable. Clearflux™ fiber-optic cable comes in various sizes and types: outside diameter $\frac{1}{4}$- in., $\frac{3}{8}$-in., $\frac{1}{2}$-in., and $\frac{3}{4}$-in. core, either side lit (entire length glows) or end lit (which transmits light to the end).

Innovision Optics makes a fiber-optic system that uses either 150- or 250-W tungsten or a 150-W metal-halide illuminator that has a choice of dichroic colored glass filters built into it. Flexible and semiflexible optic cables come in various types and sizes. One type glows along its entire length, like a flexible neon rope. It can be heated and bent into semipermanent shapes and letters. Core sizes are $\frac{3}{16}$ in., $\frac{1}{4}$ in., $\frac{3}{8}$ in., and $\frac{1}{2}$ in., in up to 70-ft unspliced lengths. To increase intensity, you can attach an illuminator at both ends.

Neon

When the art department provides neon lights, it is often necessary to dim the neon to make it look good on film. Bobinette or black hose stockings work if the neon is out of focus in the background, but when the neon is seen clearly, it is useful to dim them electronically. Variac or triac dimmers can generally be used for short periods, but when the neon is to be left on, the art department should order special neon dimmers. Other dimmers can overheat and burn out the neon transformer. The way to know if a dimmer is overheating a transformer is to use an ammeter on the power line either going into or coming out of the dimmer. If the dimmer setting is a bad match for the transformer, the amperage flow will jump way above the rated amperage of the transformer. A transformer rated at 2 or 3 A can start drawing 15 or 20 A and burn up.

Neon transformers are sized to the particular tube they are lighting. The voltage and milliamp output of the transformer depends on a number of factors, including the type of gas used and the length of the tube. If you run into trouble with the neon going out when dimmed, using a larger transformer helps. The milliamp output of the transformer drives the neon tubes. A transformer with a higher milliamp output keeps the tube lit when dimmed.

Follow Spots

Follow spots, with their powerful long throw, are a staple of music concerts, skating events, circus events, and theatrical performances (Figure 10.17). Follow spots are designed to follow a performer on a distant stage, necessitating the following controls: an *iris* lever, which controls the size of the circular pool of light; a *douser* lever for "blacking out"; *shutters*, which "strip out" the top and bottom of a circular pool, creating more of a rectangle; and a *color changer*, which introduces any of several colored gels. The *trombone handle* is used to set the size and intensity

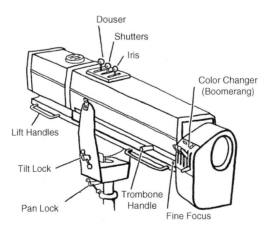

Figure 10.17 The Strong Super Trouper follow spot. (Equipment courtesy of Strong International, Inc., Omaha, NE.)

of the beam. A *fine focus* knob is used to sharpen or soften the edges of the beam. The setting of this knob varies with the distance to the subject and the trombone setting used. Follow spots are mounted on gimbals, which allow the operator to pan and tilt the light smoothly to follow action on the stage.

The size and light source type vary with application. Small 1k quartz-bulb follow spots, such as the Strong Trouperette, are common for short throws of 30–60 ft (100 FC), such as in a night club or school auditorium. Slightly larger 575-W HMI and 700-W xenon units have throws of 50–160 ft (100 FC). Large follow spots, such as the Strong Super Trouper with a 1k or 2k xenon globe, are used for lighting performers from the back of very large auditoriums and arenas. The Super Trouper has a throw of 130–340 ft (100 FC). The Gladiator and other similar follow spots, using 2500- and 3000-W xenon globes, have throws of up to 460 ft (100 FC).

Operating the Follow Spot

Operating a follow spot smoothly and properly is something of a specialty. There are a few important points to remember. Unless otherwise specified, the trombone and iris should be arranged to light the performer from head to foot. Always keep the performer's face lit, if necessary lose other parts of the body. Panning and tilting must be smooth and in perfect harmony with the movements of the performer, neither leading them nor getting left behind, and keeping small movements fluid and subtle so as not to be distracting. When you receive direction to *iris out* from head and shoulders to full body, tilt the light down as you iris out so that the light stays centered on the body. If you are to come out of black on a performer, get the light aimed before opening the douser. If necessary, you can surreptitiously get accurate aim by closing the iris down to a pinpoint, then quickly open the douser, aim the light, douse it, and open the iris up again. Very often follow spots are used to *ballyhoo*, the classic sweep of light over the stage and the audience in big random figure eights. You can expect to be asked to ballyhoo at some point. When a group of performers are to be covered with a single light, the beam has to be widened out so much that the top and bottom of the beam start to create unwanted spill problems. In this case, you may be asked to *strip it out*; use the shutter to cut the top and bottom of the beam, again making the beam cover the performers from head to foot.

In film work, it is convenient to be able to adjust the intensity of the beam. This can be accomplished in a couple ways. The simplest way is to use the trombone. Trombone forward to intensify the light, and trombone back to dim it. The gaffer meters the light on stage and gives you one or more working intensity settings; mark the settings on the barrel and make sure the trombone does not slide out of adjustment. Once the trombone is set for intensity, the iris is used to size the beam. A second way to dim a spot is to put neutral density gel in one or two gel slots.

The *boomerang* (color changer) typically has six gel frames, which can be introduced into the beam using one of six levers on the end of the barrel. By common convention, the changer levers are numbered from 1 to 6 from front to back. Most changers are designed so that you can roll through the colors; as each new lever is applied, the previous lever automatically releases. You can release all the levers and go to white light by pressing a button underneath the changer levers.

When the spot is not in use on stage, it may be panned off into the ceiling of the arena or into the sky, or it may be doused. Xenon lights should not be turned off unnecessarily, as this drastically decreases the life of the very expensive xenon bulbs. The douser can be closed for several minutes without causing damage to the light. Do not use the iris or shutter to do this, however, as they will be damaged. Like any xenon light, xenon follow spots use a power supply that converts current to DC. Xenon bulbs are flicker free at any frame rate and have a daylight color temperature. The bulbs are extremely sensitive to temperature and must be cooled with fans when running. After shutdown, the bulb must be allowed to cool with fans running for at least 5 minutes. *Never shut down the power before the light has been allowed to cool.*

Follow spots are designed to be used with colored gels. Despite their candle power, they should not burn through gel; the optics are arranged so that the beam is least hot as it passes through the gel stage of the barrel. In addition, large follow spots use cooling fans to cool the gel in use. If the gel burns through quickly in one place, it is a sign that the bulb or reflector may be out of alignment. Adjustment knobs on the back of the larger lights are used to align the bulb. If the gel fades quickly, you may want to check that the gel fan is working (on the underside of the boomerang) and that the air intake is not clogged.

Lightning Effects

Creating a convincing flash of lightning can be difficult. It requires a very bright, very brief flash, several stops brighter than the exposure used for the set lighting. To be convincing, it should flicker slightly and vary from flash to flash. For a small area, shutters are sometimes used in front of a fairly large fixture; however, this is a marginally effective technique when used in a large area.

For many years, the brightest, most convincing lightning effect was accomplished with a scissor arc. A scissor arc consists of a bundle of carbon rods wrapped in wire and attached to a scissor device that brings the carbons into contact with the opposite electrode. When the two are brought together, all hell breaks loose, and an extremely bright sputtering flash lights up everything within a block. The scissor arc is positioned a distance from the action and is placed up high on a scaffold. Should you ever be on a set where a scissor arc is used, stand clear of the fixture, and watch out for fragments of hot carbon falling from the fixture. A hot piece of carbon can melt right through asphalt.

Lightning Strikes!

More recently, Lightning Strikes! developed a line of programmable lightning fixtures that can drench the set in light for up to 3 seconds (Figure 10.18). The lights are available in a wide range of sizes: 25k, 40k, 70k, 250k, 500k, and 2 mW (2 million W). Several heads can be connected to a central control unit and fired simultaneously

Figure 10.18 A 250,000-W Lightning Strikes! unit. (Courtesy of Lightning Strikes!, Los Angeles, CA.)

or separately. The color temperature is 5600 K, and the unit is dimmable to about 20% output with no change in color temperature. The units can be very precisely controlled and flash sequences can be programmed, so identical flashes can be repeated in take after take. The units can be ordered fully sealed in waterproof housings for use with rain towers. The 70k head's peak output yields 350 FC at 100 ft with a 45°-beam spread. The smaller lightning units are ideal for interior sets or narrow exterior shots (25 kW or 40 kW for small sets, 70 kW for moderately large sets and night exteriors).

The Lightning Strikes! controllers and lighting units offer an open field of effects possibilities. Experimenting with different combinations and timing will help you create an optimal effect for your application. For example, I find a lightning effect is enhanced by firing two units separately, moments apart, from slightly different directions, and reducing brightness on the second flash, as if the secondary lightning were more distant.

The 4-kW unit can be fitted with a QuickColor system, a specially adapted Wybron color changer and programmable control unit. The color changer provides additional heat protection for the gel scroll. A choice of 10 colors can be selected by DMX control. A special handheld control unit comes with the system that provides flash and color control. It can be programmed with up to three color sequences.

The larger units (250 kW and up) are powerful enough to drench even large expansive sets. They can compete with daylight, so they are ideal for lighting daytime exterior storm scenes.

Control Units

A variety of different control units may be used. The *undulating controller* comes standard with each light and is used for manual or automatic random lightning flashes.

The *precision fader* is a programmable controller with which one can create, repeat, and loop up and down fades. It is great for creating an explosion effect; for example, with a big initial flash and slow decay, spiked with lesser secondary explosions. Each sequence can last up to 4 seconds, and the unit can hold up to four sequences. The unit comes with four preprogrammed sequences, but you can create custom sequences using a simple joystick to edit the sequence. Each sequence can change level up to 24 times a second. Machine gun fire flashes can also be created with an on, off, on, off pattern.

The *quad controller* controls up to four lights separately or in unison with eight memory banks that record firing sequences for playback. The quad controller can also be hooked up to a MIDI sequencer running on a laptop computer and triggered from SMPTE time code. The flash sequence is preprogrammed into the MIDI sequencer. During filming, the MIDI sequencer synchronizes to the time code (from a video or audio playback unit), triggering the flashes at exact (repeatable) points in time.

The lights can also be run from a standard DMX dimmer console by using an interface box called the *DMX to LS ISO converter*. Brightness level and "mode" are controlled on two adjacent channels and constant, slow undulation; medium undulation or fast undulation are controlled by the "mode" pot. By your assignment of the DMX addresses, multiple lights can either be synchronized or operated separately.

Lightning Strikes! units can also be triggered by an optical or acoustic sensor hidden in the set. A flash camera or a loud noise (gunshot) can be used to trigger the lightning strikes. The duration of strike can be extended from 1 to 36 frames with a choice of intensity level for each frame. Because the Lightning Strikes! flash lasts a minimum of $1/24$th of a second it will be caught on film (whereas a normal strobe flash is about $1/10,000$ second, which is caught on film only if the shutter of the motion picture camera happens to be open at that instant). A custom 20k handheld unit is available to simulate a paparazzi flash.

The *16-light Sequencer* can chase up to 16 lights at a time. Frames on and off can be preset and repeated. The Sequencer can be synchronized to the camera shutter for multiple passes or blue screen work.

Power Requirements

Table 10.1 lists specifications for the Lightning Strikes! units as well as power requirements. All units operate on 208–250-V service (single phase, or two legs of a three-phase service), except the 25k unit, which is 120 V AC, and the 2 mW unit, which runs off its own special trailer-mounted Thundervoltz power pack.

The 70k unit draws about 300 A when fired. Because the time is so short, it can safely be run on 100-A house current. (It is treated like an electric motor starting load.) Although this is a fairly substantial intermittent load, the peak power is within

Table 10.1 Lightning Strikes! Units

Fixture	Number of Units	25,000W	40,000W	70,000W	250,000W	500,000W	2 Mega-Watts
Weight		24 lbs	30 lbs	34 lbs	55 lbs	63 lbs	275 lbs
Head dimensions		25 × 12 × 9 in.	29 × 12 × 9 in.	32 × 12 × 9 in.	42 × 17 × 11 in.	42 × 19 × 15 in.	76 × 29 × 22 in.
Mount				1-1/8 in. Jr. Pin	1-1/8 in. Jr. Pin		
Voltage		120 only	208–250 V AC 50/60 Hz	208–250 V AC 50/60 Hz	208–250 V AC 50/60 Hz	208–250 V AC 50/60 Hz	Battery Pack Operation only
Current (momentary)		210 A	175 A	300 A	1050 A	2100 A	
Power Requirements							
Mains or house	1	40 A minimum	40 A minimum	63 A minimum, 100 A optimum	200 A minimum, 300 A optimum	400 A minimum	
	2	80 A	80 A	125 A	400 A	800 A	
	3	120 A	120 A	200 A	600 A	1200 A	
Generator	1	24 kW 200 A (at 120 V)	25 kW 200 A (at 120 V)	40 kW 350 A (at 120 V)	180 kW 1500 A (at 120 V)	360 kW 3000 A (at 120 V)	
	2	42 kW 350 A (at 120 V)	60 kW 500 A (at 120 V)	90 kW 750 A (at 120 V)	360 kW 3000 A (at 120 V)	720 kW 6000 A (at 120 V)	
	3	60 kW 500 A (at 120 V)	90 kW 750 A (at 120 V)	144 kW 1200 A (at 120 V)	540 kW 4500 A (at 120 V)	1.080 megawatts 9000 A (at 120 V)	
Battery pack			Thundervoltz 40,000 W	Thundervoltz 70,000 W	Thundervoltz 250,000 W	Thundervoltz 500,000 W	Thundervoltz 2,000,000 W
Input required			8 A, 100–250 V AC	10 A, 100–250 V AC	20 A, 100–250 V AC	30 A, 100–250 V AC	80 A, 100–250 V AC
Dimensions			29 × 29 × 26 in.	29 × 29 × 26 in.	2 units, each 26 × 24 × 26 in.	2 units, each 31 × 32 × 34 in.	Trailer-mounted 15 × 6 × 2 ft
Weight			425 lbs	425 lbs	1000 lbs	1300 lbs	5000 lbs

5% of nominal RMS power, meaning that there is no momentary drain much greater than the nominal power, as there is when striking HMI units, for example.

Thundervoltz Battery Packs

Alternately, all units (except the 25k) can be run off Thundervoltz battery packs. These are specially designed oversized battery-powered packs with an inverter and charger to provide AC specifically for Lightning Strikes! units. The packs deliver power enough to flash the units indefinitely, so long as the AC charger is connected to a power source. The packs can also be run with no AC power for up to 12 hours or 125 flash sequences using an optional 12-V, 12-A battery. The 450-lb Thundervoltz runs two 40k units or a single 70k unit. The 1300-lb double Thundervoltz runs two 250-kW units or a single 500-kW unit. The battery packs are mounted on heavy-duty pneumatic tires so they can be pushed around more easily.

Generators

In general, the generator can be sized as little as almost half the kilowatt output of the fixture. For example, a 70-kW Lightning Strikes! unit can be run off a 40-kw generator (350 A at 120 V AC). Generator companies recommend that, when two 70,000-W heads are used, the plant should have at least a 750-A capacity; when three 70,000-W heads are used, the plant should have at least a 1200-A capacity. A sudden heavy load like that of Lightning Strikes! affects all the lights on a generator. They may blink each time the strike hits. To guard against surge current affecting the set lighting, most gaffers order an additional generator to handle the Lightning Strikes! units. If you have to run both on the same generator, use the smaller units (70k or less), keep the bursts short, and have no more than half the amperage capacity of the generator devoted to lighting units.

Lighting Matte Photography

It seems almost every film and TV show we work on, at some point requires at least a couple composite shots using a green or blue screen. For a composite, the foreground action and the background action are filmed separately, then combined to make it appear as if the two coexisted in the same space and time. Take for example a shot of a man dangling from a 40th-story ledge with antlike taxicabs visible far below. This is two shots: (1) a view from the 40th floor looking down at the taxicabs in the street (with no ledge in the foreground) and (2) a shot looking down at a man dangling from a ledge with a matte screen behind him. (The shot looking down at the taxicabs could even be a miniature model.) The composite is made by scanning the two shots at very high resolution into a computer and compositing them digitally. For a television show, the composite is made digitally after the film is transferred to tape. For the two shots to be wed effectively, there are a number of considerations for lighting.

Pure Screen Color and Density

The details of how the background is removed and replaced with the background plate are beyond the scope of this discussion, but it suffices to say that the compositor is able to get the best results with the purest color screen, especially in separating fine detail like blowing hair or transparent elements like smoke. If the screen is contaminated with other color, shadows, or differences in saturation, it is much more difficult for the compositor to retain fine edge detail, and the image may need to be cleaned up by rotoscoping frame by frame. Rotoscoping is a time-consuming, expensive solution. Most often it would have been far easier and cheaper to fix on set.

Special effects professionals developed a number of ingenious ways to produce the purest possible matte. They start by controlling the color of the screen and the lights and refining them to a very specific single color, usually a specific green but maybe a blue or red. Composite Components, one of the central innovators in compositing, developed the Digital Green™ screen and Digital Green™ paints. The color of the screen was reverse engineered by looking at the spectral sensitivity curves of particular Eastman Kodak film stocks to find a narrow portion of the color spectrum where the film captures the purest color (best localized to one color layer of the emulsion). They then designed fluorescent tubes that radiate only in the same spike of spectral energy. These tubes are extremely bright in their selected part of the spectrum (around 436-nm blue, 545-nm green). Flo Co. manufactures and distributes these tubes in Digital Green™, Digital Blue™, and Digital Red™ along with their own fixtures. Kino Flo also supplies special green and blue fluorescent tubes for lighting green and blue screens. Kino Flo's effects tubes are off-the-shelf tubes originally manufactured for another purpose, yet they produce a very pure color output (green 560 nm or blue 420 nm) and fully saturate the matte color.

The matte screen must also be lit evenly. The compositor relies on uniformity in density to produce good separations. One should shoot for a variation across the visible section of the matte screen of not more than a stop. At one time, this was done quite effectively by lighting a transmission screen from the rear with panels of fluorescent tubes. With bigger and bigger matte screens being required, this system became impractical. Front-lighting a solid green or blue screen using fluorescent fixtures yields very good results and has become the norm. Because fluorescent banks produce such soft light and the green or blue tubes are so surprisingly bright, fluorescent fixtures are more than adequate to front-light even a very large matte screen. A row of evenly spaced four-bank, 4-ft fixtures along the bottom and top of a 20-ft high matte screen typically produce an adequate brightness. With larger screens, you can bump up to 8-bank or 10-bank fixtures. Using dimmable ballasts allows you to easily adjust the screen brightness as needed. Egg crate louvers, diffusion, door extensions, and black wrap can be handy to help even out the light from top to bottom.

Lighting the Foreground

The foreground lighting must make the subject appear to be in the same environment as appears in the background plate. Contrast and color temperature should be matched as closely as possible. Attention to the direction and feel of the key light and the kind of ambient light shown in the plate shot are important when lighting the foreground shot.

Backlight, edge light, or side light are important with matte shots. Keep in mind that, when the background is dropped out, the foreground subject may as well be standing in black limbo. If the background plate is of a bright environment, some of that light should appear to be hitting the subject in the form of edge and backlight. Backlights also help wash out any green light wrapping onto the actor from the screen.

Some forethought is required in hanging the backlights. The lights must be arranged in such a way that the fluorescent lights front-lighting the matte screen and the backlights do not interfere with one another (Figure 10.19). They often want to occupy the same place or cast shadows on one another.

The foreground lighting has to be kept completely off the matte screen, and the matte screen has to be kept completely off any reflective or glossy parts of the foreground subject. Reflections of the matte screen appear as holes in the matte. Contamination on the matte screen makes it hard for the compositor to pull a good matte. To keep front light off the matte screen, *allow plenty of space between the screen and the foreground action, 15 to 25 ft.* It is a common mistake to underestimate both the size of the screen and space in the soundstage needed for matte screen shots. These shots also require more floor space for flags in front of the front lights to cut white light off the background.

Reflections of the matte screen in props, set dressing, and wardrobe can be helped by masking off the matte screen where it is not needed. Dulling spray can be used on shiny objects. If a garbage matte can be used, white cards and flags can be set around the edges of shiny objects to block the reflection. The grip equipment can be removed from the shot later by the compositor, so long as it is separated from the subject by the green background. Angle them so the card or flag is reflected in the shiny surface from the camera's viewpoint instead of the screen. Note: Shots of curved chromelike objects may have to be dealt with using another compositing technique, because depending on the shot and the action, it may be impossible to properly contend with reflections.

Matte photography poses many even more-complex lighting challenges. For example, when an actor is to be seen from head to foot walking around in a virtual set, the matte screen behind the actor must seamlessly meet the floor under his feet. This can be accomplished by laying out a mirror-plex floor, which reflects the green screen to camera (Figure 10.19). This can be a very effective technique. Precautions must be taken to allow the screen and the mirrored floor to meet seamlessly. Also the back lights will want to kick onto the actor's legs off the floor, requiring lots of subtle grippage and time. The compositors have to rotoscope where the actor's feet touch their own reflection in the mirror. For them, making this small concession to have an otherwise clean matte is far preferable to the alternative: lighting the virtual set, the actors, and the screen with the same (white) light, which creates even more challenges for the DP and the compositor.

MARK DOERING POWELL
APRIL 2002

Lighting Automobiles

Directors of photography sometimes specialize in one type of work; photographing automobiles for commercials is one such niche, sometimes referred to as *sheet-metal photography*. Lighting a car requires special consideration, because the metal is glossy and highly reflective. When lighting any shiny object, you are not so much projecting light onto the subject as creating an environment around it that, when reflected, defines its shape, separates it, and creates highlights and shadow. By manipulating the shape of the reflected highlights and shadows, you can actually alter the apparent shape of the subject. Car lighting specialists use this technique to de-emphasize less appealing contours of their subject with the same delicate care that feature DPs often take in lighting the face of a star.

Fisher lights are large rear-lit soft banks specifically designed for this type of work (Fisher Productions, Inc.). They are made in 10 × 40-ft and 17 × 52-ft sizes. The bank is suspended from overhead support and can be panned, tilted, and angled remotely. The banks are lit with rows of 1k tungsten lamps, which are individually controlled by a dimmer, 40 kW (10 × 40 ft) or 96 kW (17 × 52 ft). Dimmers are standard 208Y/120 three-phase AC with Cam-Lok tails (adapters when necessary). When flicker-free, daylight-balanced light is needed, the 10 × 40-ft bank can be fitted with a 50-kW DCI system (20 2500-W DCI lamps, powered by dimmable electronic ballasts). By manipulating brightness and color across the whole area of the bank, effects such as twilight sky can be created. Fisher supplies its own technicians with the special rig.

Chimera Photographic Equipment also makes large soft banks, called *F-2 banks* (5 × 10, 10 × 20, 10 × 30, 15 × 30, or 15 × 40 ft). Lights can be rigged to the center suspension bar or to a grid above.

Figure 10.19 Using the thinnest possible Mirrored Plexi™ sheets on a small platform under the actor, the camera sees a seamless matte color background all the way to the actor's feet. At the bottom, the screen is rolled onto a pipe to hold it flat to the ground (ties would be seen by camera). The fluorescent fixtures lighting the screen from below and above are placed a distance away from the screen (7 ft in this case); for even coverage, it works well if this distance is about half the height of the matte screen (14 ft). The lights are spaced no more than 3 or 4 ft apart and must extend beyond the edge of the screen to light the screen evenly all the way to the edge. Each fluorescent is capped on both ends with black wrap to prevent spill onto the actor.

Note that all the lights must be flagged, teased, or wrapped in black wrap to prevent spill from the foreground onto the background screen and vice versa, as are the lights lighting the actor (not shown here). The backlights cannot be placed where they will block the upper fluorescent lights. If there were more space behind the matte screen, the backlights could also be hung there, which also helps prevent spill back onto the screen. Note that the backlights kick off the mirror floor onto the actor's legs. This can be helped with judicious use of bottom barn doors and black wrap or flags. The teaser is adjustable up and down and so it can be placed to keep all the backlights from flaring the camera lens. (Illustration by Mark Doering-Powell.)

Underwater Lighting

The developments in underwater lighting and camera housings in the 1990s turned a corner for this specialty of filmmaking. Increasingly sophisticated developments made lighting underwater safer and more efficient. Simultaneously, new equipment greatly expanded what is possible underwater and improved the quality of underwater cinematography. Underwater lights have been put to work in swimming pools, in large water tank sets, in lakes, and in the open ocean. Underwater lights are often enlisted to light up swimming pools or fountains, even when the camera is not submerged. A light placed at the bottom makes the entire pool glow and can be applied to throw moving highlights on surrounding people, buildings, and so on. The lights work great in rain scenes, flood scenes, and storm scenes aboard ship, in which gallons and gallons of water may pour across the deck. These can be treacherous sets to shoot, because with wind and water, things can easily get knocked down. Deploying underwater units in water-laden areas of the set eliminates any risk of electrical hazard should a light be knocked into the water or broken.

Scuba Training and Certification

Scuba stands for self-contained underwater breathing apparatus. To work on underwater sets, a lighting technician must be scuba certified; that is, must have at least Open Water Diver certification, preferably an Advanced Diver certification. To be a diver, you must be very comfortable in and under water, be in good physical shape, and be able to swim at least moderately well. The open water diver training teaches a student the basics of diving. It involves some relatively simple book learning, quizzes and tests, several pool dives, and several open water dives (in a lake or ocean). You can get certified in as little as a couple weeks if your schedule permits. Open Water Diver certification allows the diver to plan and make "no stop" dives without an instructor (no decompression) and get tank refills. This certification restricts a diver in a couple ways: you can make only daytime dives; you cannot swim into caves, wrecks, or other restrictive areas; and you cannot go below 60-ft depth. An Advanced Diver certification is required to do any of these things.

I would not recommend that an electrician go directly from a beginner scuba class to working in underwater sets. Scuba diving involves skills that need some time and experience to fully get a handle on. A beginner diver who is not giving his full attention to diving can easily forget a simple thing that could have serious consequences. Beginning divers are still learning important skills, like equalizing the pressure in their ears and achieving neutral buoyancy in the water. Forgetting to equalize or accidentally increasing buoyancy when you meant to decrease it could lead to serious injury. Ear injuries in particular are far too common among novice divers. An electrician interested in doing underwater work should get certified well before a work opportunity comes up. A number of Scuba training organizations offer standardized courses (PADI and NAUI are the main two). In my experience, the single most-important decision that affects the quality of training is the individual instructor (not the school or the course). You hear a lot of salesmanship when you start talking to dive instructors and dive shops. Get referrals from other divers. Find out whom they got their training from. Look for experience over price. After certification make an effort to dive regularly with more experienced divers and build up hours. Take a weeklong trip to a tropical dive resort. Invest in some advanced training. Make some wreck dives, deepwater dives, and night dives with an experienced instructor, and learn the hazards and safety procedures associated with different environments.

Diving is a blast. It is a lifelong recreational sport as well as a source of potential employment.

The Old Drop-a-Bulb-in-the-Pool Method

In the days of Esther Williams, it was standard procedure to light water ballet sequences by submerging bare 10k incandescent bulbs in the pool. The power was DC. The feeder cable was soldered to the terminals of the globe, and the connection was potted with a big glob of epoxy or latex rubber to make it watertight. (In the early days, they used tar.) As daring as it may sound, this technique and a similar scheme using a small PAR bulb were the predominant methods of underwater lighting until the 1980s.

Note that *tungsten halogen* bulbs cannot be used underwater in this way; they must be surrounded by air. Water cooling prevents the globe from reaching 250°C, which is required to activate the halogen cycle. Without the halogen cycle, the globe blackens with tungsten deposits in a matter of hours.

Naturally, there are a number of safety and efficiency concerns with this arrangement. For starters, if the bulb burns out, you have to pull up the whole cable to solder on a new globe, which creates a lot of downtime. Second, having a large amperage running though every cable increases the danger posed in the event that a hot wire contacts the water. Third, the bulbs must be submerged before they are turned on, because the temperature differential between the hot globe and the cool water can cause the glass of a bulb or PAR lens to crack or explode. Finally, if the bulb breaks under water, the result is a hot wire in contact with water.

In the late 1960s, Birns Oceanographic lights, underwater lights manufactured for the oil industry, began to be used in underwater cinematography. These were standard double-ended tungsten bulbs mounted in front of a reflector in a casing with a heavy cover glass. They could be used to depths of 3000 ft. The lights had to be submerged before they were turned on to prevent the cold water from shock-cooling the glass and cracking it. The lights were an improvement over what was available before, but they were heavy and very inefficient.

Modern Underwater Fixtures

For an underwater lighting system to be safe, it must (1) be a completely sealed system, watertight from cable to bulb; (2) provide a sensing device and shutdown mechanism in case an electrical fault occurs; and (3) overcome the problem of thermal stress on the glass that is in contact with water.

James Cameron's epic adventure film, *The Abyss*, revolutionized underwater lighting technology. Forty percent of the live action footage was filmed underwater in a huge tank, 209 ft in diameter and 55 ft deep. The project offered two young inventors the opportunity to realize a project they had had in mind for some time. Pete Romano, an underwater cameraman, and Richard Mula, a gaffer and engineer, developed the 1200-W HMI SeaPAR®, an efficient underwater PAR light, to meet the needs of this extremely demanding project (Figures 10.20 and 10.21). The SeaPARs work equally well out of water, in the rain, or submerged to depths of more than 250 ft. Subsequently, a whole line of lights sprung from this initial system, which are now available from HydroFlex® and Pace.

The system is watertight. Ballasts and main distribution cables remain above the surface. The head cables run down into the water. The lights use watertight plugs that can be plugged and unplugged underwater with the power off. The connectors have locking sleeves to prevent kick-outs. A hot female lead can be left unplugged in water because the female plug naturally holds air within the deep contact pockets so that electricity does not come into contact with water. All cables and connectors are watertight. The connection point on the head is made so that, even if the head cable gets cut, water cannot enter the head.

To provide a fault-sensitive shutdown mechanism, the system operates on AC current with a grounding lead. All metal parts are grounded. The HMI ballasts are fitted with two Class A ground-fault circuit interrupter (GFCI) devices, which sense the presence of leakage current. If there is more than a 5-mA differential between the hot leg (outgoing current) and the neutral leg (return current), indicating that fault current is leaking through to ground, a relay cuts power to the ballast. This is less current than required to harm an individual, even if the person is in contact with the fault source.

The second GFCI serves as a redundant backup. In addition, a fourth lead is used: A ground-return lead connected to a relay circuit constantly monitors the integrity of the grounding lead and shuts down the power if the ground is removed or lost. Finally, the outside glass covers on these fixtures are made of special thermoshock-resistant glass that can withstand sudden extreme temperature changes.

The Underwater Lighting Arsenal

An entire line of underwater HMI, tungsten, fluorescent, and xenon light fixtures are available commercially. HydroFlex® offers various HMI PARs including 4k SE, 2.5k SE, 1200-W SE HydroPARs®, and the 1200-W SeaPAR (a PAR 64-type HMI). An 8k HMI broad/cyc fixture, called the *HydroRama*, employs twin, axially opposing 4k SE globes set in a reflector. This is a very bright broad fixture, good for lighting large areas, large sets, or green screens. HydroFlex also offers tungsten PARs in 5k SE, 2k SE, 1k (PAR 64), and 650-W (Par 36) sizes as well as a small MR16 fixture. The HydroRama fixture is adaptable to take twin 5k SE bulbs making it a 10k tungsten-balanced broad/cyc light. HydroFlex has several self-contained flashlight fixtures, which can be used either by actors on camera or as a small off-camera fill light. Among them are the 21-W MHL Splashlight (daylight balanced) and the 100-W tungsten Hartenberger (dimmable to three settings). HydroFlex adapted many of the familiar Kino fixtures for underwater use. The lights include the HydroFlo® 9-in. kit, 6-ft, 4-ft, 2-ft, 15-in., and 9-in. individual tubes; 4-ft, four-bank

(A)

(B)

Figure 10.20 (A) SeaPAR lights in use underwater. A 1200-W SeaPAR HMI lights a rusted wreckage for the cameraman, (B) a diver holds two battery-powered incandescent PAR-46 lights. The underwater weight of the lamps with batteries is about 2 lb each. (Courtesy of Hydro Image Inc., Los Angeles, CA.)

(A)

(B)

Figure 10.21 (A) A green-screen shot for a Pepsi commercial on the floor of a water tank. Note the two 1200 PARs and the 2500 PAR shining onto a 4 × 4 bounce board. (B) Jennifer Brown music video. Lattice floating on the surface of the water breaks up the light from above into dramatic shafts. (Courtesy of Hydro Image Inc., Los Angeles, CA.)

and 4-ft, eight-bank, and 15-in., two-bank (Mick Light) soft boxes, and 4-ft, four-bank, and 4-ft, eight-bank panel lights for lighting green screens.

Pace offers its WetSet™ line of underwater lights including 8k (twin 4k HMI lamps) and 5k (twin 2.5k HMI lamps) cyc lights, and HMI PAR lights in sizes as follows: 4k SE, 2.5k SE, 1.2k PAR, 1.2k SE, and 200-W SEB. Tungsten PARs include 2k SE, 1k SE, and 1k PAR. Pace developed a system of interchangeable parts: a single lamp base that can accept one of four different bulbs (2.5 HMI, 4k HMI, 2k tungsten, or 5k tungsten), which fit in any of three reflectors or housings (PAR, soft light, or cyc). The result is that with one fixture, four bulbs, and three reflectors, the assembled fixture can have any of 12 configurations; (Well almost; actually, the cyc lights require a pair of lamps and lamp bases.)

Pace also offers a 1k cyc light and tungsten flashlights of 400 W and 250 W and a xenon (daylight-balanced) torch. Pace offers fluorescent panels with Kino-Flo lamps. Pace carries a number of underwater props such as a desk light and a computer monitor. Both Pace and HydroFlex offer underwater practical bulbs and fixtures.

Features of Underwater Fixtures

On the SeaPAR, a retaining ring buckles to the front of the fixture. The retaining ring holds scrims, gels, and diffusion and simultaneously prevents any light leakage to the sides. The retaining ring allows water to circulate around the gel for heat dissipation. Barn doors and snoots can be mounted to the front of the retaining ring.

Two lock knobs are on the bail, on either side of the light. One is the tilt lock. The other, the rotation lock, is used to orient the elliptical beam. The fixtures can be used in any orientation.

It is a property of physics that spreader lenses have very little effect if they are on the outside of the fixture, surrounded by water. Most underwater PARs house their spreader lens inside the watertight cover glass. Spreader lenses can be exchanged (out of water) by simply unbuckling the cover on the front of the fixture.

The 4k HMI HydroPAR and 5k tungsten HydroPAR do not use spreader lenses but spot, medium, or wide reflectors (which can be exchanged in or out of water without disturbing the sealed globe envelope). The 2.5k HMI and 2k tungsten HydroPAR use changeable Fresnel lenses, which are inside the buckled fixture and must be changed on dry land. The larger fixtures cannot be used out of water, or only for timed periods. Table A.12 in Appendix A lists additional specifications for each fixture.

Lighting Underwater

Underwater DPs use underwater lights and grip gear in all the ways you normally do on a dry sound stage. You bounce light off griffolyn, use griffolyn flags to control the light (duvetyn turns brown in water), use color and diffusion on the lights, and so on. It is worth taking note of some important differences in the way light behaves, however.

Water acts as a color filter. Within 10 ft of the surface, 70–80% of the red end of the spectrum is absorbed, leaving only blue light. Water acts as a continuous filter, absorbing the longer wavelengths (red, yellow, and orange). The brilliant colors of sea life and face tones of actors appear dull in the blue light that filters down from the surface. Only when you shine a light on them do the magnificent colors come to life. Fill light is therefore used to help bring back good color to subjects at depths greater than about 16 ft, even when existing exposure is sufficient.

An underwater scene lit only from underwater looks dead and flat. Except for the bubbles, you can't even tell that you are underwater. To bring the water to life, you need light coming through the surface, creating dancing striations of light. For a night scene, you might use a heavy backlight from above the surface and a small amount of soft underwater bounce (a 1200-W HMI into a 4-by white griffolyn, for example). Light reflection off the surface of the water affects the amount of light penetrating through the surface. Better penetration occurs at steeper angles and with calmer water. Penetration can be substantially reduced in heavy seas.

Water is usually somewhat cloudy and acts as a diffusion, much like fog, scattering the light. It reduces light transmission and softens the light as it bounces off the particles in the water. However, the beam angle of the light in clear water is the same as in air. The reflection of light off particles in the water causes a phenomenon known as *backscatter*, which is like using your high beams when driving in snow or fog; the light traveling through the foreground obscures the subject. The problem is worst when the light is attached to the camera. You can minimize backscatter by using less frontal light and more side light and by favoring multiple medium-sized units over one very bright one. A narrow-beam light with a stronger beam creates less backscatter than a wide one, and snoots and barn doors are also very helpful. It is important to keep the cloudiness consistent. In a pool, a filtering system must be used, and the floor of the pool must be vacuumed to start with a clean pool. Once all the divers are in the water, you can add substances to make it murkier if necessary. When filming *The Abyss*, fuller's earth, diatomite (a swimming pool filter agent), small amounts of milk, and blue dye were added to the water to make it very blue and hazy. To avoid stirring up particles resting on the bottom, underwater crews often do not use fins. Instead, they wear weights and walk around on the bottom of the pool.

Fill light may also be called for when shooting a subject from below. Light can be bounced off the bottom of a white pool, or a griffolyn may be laid on the bottom surface, a white board might be used, or a light can be shone directly at the subject. When the subject is moving, it works well to have the fill light handheld by a diver at a 45–90° off-lens axis, moving with the subject. The lamp operator can maintain an even fill level by keeping a consistent distance between the light and the subject.

Exposure readings are taken using an underwater reflected light meter, because this type of reading automatically accounts for light loss in the water. The Sekonic L-164, for example, has a 30° angle of acceptance. You aim the meter in the direction you wish to shoot and set the aperture accordingly. The Ikelight digital is also self-contained and can take reflected readings (10° angle of acceptance) or incident readings. Both meters can be used to depths of 200 ft. The water is brighter above the diver and falls off into darkness below the diver, so meter readings should be taken in the appropriate direction. Underwater cases are available for various standard light meters, including the Spectra IV, Minolta Auto IV, Minolta 1° Spot, and Minolta Color Temperature meter.

Electricity and Water

The danger of water is that it is a conductor. Salt water (which is essentially what the body is made of) is a better conductor than fresh water. Neither is a very good conductor, but enough of one to pose a threat to life under certain circumstances.

Insulated cables can be run underwater (type W cables are approved for use underwater). However, carefully check the condition of the cables. Discard any cable with cuts or abrasions in the insulation. Cable insulation becomes permeable to moisture over long periods of time. Therefore, a safety system that continuously checks for leakage current should be installed when cables are run in wet ground or water for more than a day or so.

GFCI Protection

Remember that, to get a shock, a diver must become part of a closed circuit. Water is ground, and in water a diver becomes part of the ground. The greatest danger is to reach out of the water and touch a hot wire or a metal housing with a fault in it, directing electricity exclusively straight through the body: in through the arm, through the lungs and heart, and out through the lower half of the body. This scenario could very easily kill a person. That is why it is so critical that the casing of a light and all accessible metal parts be at ground potential and, if there is a ground fault, that the circuit is automatically interrupted by a Class A GFCI (also called *GFI*) before an accident can occur. There are different types of GFCI devices. A Class A GFCI is designed to protect people from shock current. These devices are required to be prominently marked as such. If you find a GFCI without Class A marked on it, it is not an appropriate type of protection for safety. Other types of GFCIs are less sensitive, designed to protect equipment and distribution. A Class A GFCI cuts power to a circuit if it senses more than 6 mA leakage current.[1] This is below a level that would cause a serious shock. (It takes about 9 mA to make a painful shock for men, 6.0 mA for women, although you can feel a shock as low as 1.8 mA for men and 1.2 mA for women with 60-Hz AC current.) GFCIs are available up to 100 A, single and three-phase, 120-V and 208/240 V. A normal GFCI does not work properly outside its specified voltage range. Specially designed GFCIs are available for use behind dimmers and can handle variable voltages (see the next subsection).

---

[1]UL 943 defines a Class A GFCI. It specifies that the following equation be used to determine the combination of current and time at which a GFCI will break the circuit:

$$t = (20/i)^{1.43}$$

through the range of 6 mA to 264 mA. This gives a current/time curve that triggers the GFCI in a few seconds at 6 mA and in 25 ms at 264 mA.

Shock-Block GFCI Equipment

Shock-Block, manufactured by K-Tec Corporation, makes several Class A GFCI devices for the motion picture industry:

Shock-Block 100 Variable voltage from 0 to 120 V AC, 100-A (12 kW) protection.

Shock-Block 250 208-V AC or 240-V AC applications (200–240 V AC), 100-A (25-kW) protection.

Shock-Block 300 Three-phase, 208/240-V AC applications, 100-A (40-kW) protection.

These are in-line, plug-in devices housed for use in rain and wet environments. To help the lighting technician identify a faulty load, when multiple lights may be in use, the Shock-Block has a chain of five LED lights that monitor the level of leakage at any given moment. Each load may contain some small (safe) amount of leakage current. The LEDs tell you when you are getting close to tripping the GFCI. By monitoring the LEDs while equipment is plugged and unplugged, an electrician can discover which load is causing the GFCI to trip. The unit also monitors ground presence and power phasing. If either of these is not correct, the unit does not reset and identifies the problem on its display.

Shock-Block also makes a number of (non-Class A) equipment protection devices to offer GFCI protection upstream, from the 100-A Shock-Blocks back to the generator. These devices are three phase and have higher amperage capacity (125, 250, or 400 A per phase). Using a coordinated system of devices in which the trip time and trip current are lower on the GFCIs near the load and higher on the GFCIs toward the source, the system assures that the downstream elements trip before the upstream elements. This arrangement assures that, if a hard short occurs at the load, the GFCI immediately upstream of the short trips and removes the fault current before any larger circuit protection upstream trips, thus preempting a larger power outage. The effect is to isolate and keep the problem circuit from bringing the whole system down. The SB-3400 (the 400-A version) is equipped with a sensitive meter, which gives a continuous read-out of any fault current present. This reading helps lighting technicians know the change in fault current when each load is added or removed, simplifying the task of isolating problem equipment and providing predictive information to avoid trips.

As a matter of safety, all electrical equipment, including submersibles, submarines, pumps, cables, and lights, should be routinely checked for leakage current before being put in the water.

Electricity in Water

A bare wire underwater sets up an electrical field around it as it seeks all paths to complete a circuit (to ground or the neutral wire). The primary route is the path of least resistance. If the neutral or grounding wire is close by, as in the case of a sheared cable, the field is very strong between the two wires and spreads around the fault, weakening with distance. The size of the field depends on the amperage available and the impedance imposed by the size of the wires. This is the reason why it is better to use lots of lower-amperage cables rather than a few very high-amperage ones. For example, if a 10-A circuit power cord in fresh water gets cut by a boat propeller, water sets up a field with a diameter of about 5.6 ft (minimum safe distance). A cable carrying 100 A, on the other hand, sets up a field 49 ft in diameter.

Another reason many low-amperage cables are preferable to a few high-amperage ones is that GFCIs on 20-A circuits are very dependable. The higher is the amperage, the greater the noise in the system and the less dependable the GFCIs become. You often get a lot of nuisance trips.

A diver can feel it when he or she is coming close to an electrical field. If you ever put your tongue on a 9-V battery, you know the taste that comes into your mouth and you can feel a tingle in the fillings in your teeth. Closer to the field, you begin to feel the tingle of electricity in your body. A diver inside a strong field may experience the effects of electrical shock: trouble breathing, muscle freeze, cardiac fibrillation, and cardiac arrest.

In Chapter 12, the effects of AC and DC on the body are discussed. DC current poses a less lethal threat because it requires more amperage to cause muscle freeze and interfere with other important muscles, such as the heart and lungs. Although HMIs are always AC (even AC/DC ballasts run AC to the head), their increased light output means that they replace an incandescent light of much higher amperage, so they pose no greater threat than the alternative. However, because AC circuits are grounded, the safety features previously discussed diminish any potential threat to a safe level.

High-Speed Photography and Camera-Synchronous Strobe Lighting

Both Clairmont Camera and Unilux, Inc., offer high-speed strobe lighting systems that synchronize the flash of the lighting units with the shutter of the camera. Each frame of film is given a very bright, very short flash of light. When a camera operates at 24 fps, the exposure time is normally $1/48$ second. With the Unilux strobe unit, the flash is $1/100,000$ second. The effect is to remove all motion blur from an image. Strobe units are often used for shooting slow-motion close-ups of pouring liquids, such as in beer and soft drink commercials. Each drop of beer is sharp because in each frame the moving drops are frozen in a microsecond of flash. The lights can be synchronized with the camera shutter at frame rates from 1 fps up to 650 fps.

Unilux strobes have been used in music videos to capture dance in an ultrasharp, jerky style. By using a special-effects generator box, the lights can create a strobe effect by not exposing every frame. This appears on film as a series of flashes with performers jumping suddenly from one position to another. Using a sequencer circuit, the lights can also be made to chase so that in each frame light comes from a different head.

Unilux H3000 System

Unilux has been designing and improving strobe systems since the late 1960s. The first such system was so large that it required a special studio. With each model, the lights have become smaller, lighter, and simpler to operate. Today's strobes are as portable and as easy to operate as 1200-W HMIs.

Figure 10.22 The Unilux H3000 system pictured here has five heads, two control units, and the shipping case. (Courtesy of Unilux, Inc., Hackensack, NJ.)

The H3000 system consists of three heads and a control console to which the three lights are connected. Figure 10.22 shows a system using two control units and five heads.

Control consoles can be daisy-chained together to control as many lights as needed. The H3000 system takes single-phase, 50- or 60-Hz, 220-V power at about 10 A per head. An older Unilux system uses three-phase 208/120-V power and draws about 5 A per head.

Unilux heads use a special spiral-shaped quartz xenon bulb, which resembles something out of Dr. Frankenstein's lab. They have a daylight color temperature of 6000 K, and they operate relatively cool. The heads can be oriented in any position.

The strobe system synchronizes to the speed of the camera using a sync cable connected to the camera's speed control accessory receptacle. The strobe speed follows the camera shutter speed to give one flash each time the shutter is open and one flash each time it is closed, which is when the camera operator can see through the lens.

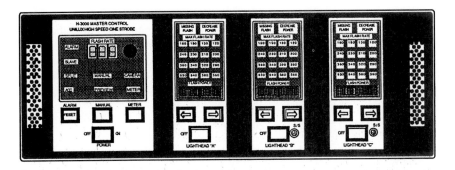

Figure 10.23 The front of the Unilux H3000 control unit. (Courtesy of Unilux, Inc., Hackensack, NJ.)

Operation

Figure 10.23 shows the front panel of the control console. When you turn the power switch on, the lights go into preview mode. They flicker at 60 flashes per second at a relatively low light level. This speed is just fast enough that the strobing is not annoying while setting the lights. Once the lights are roughly positioned, you are ready to take some light readings. Before you can take readings, however, select the maximum flash rate for each light. The maximum flash rate settings are, in frames per second, as follows: 120, 130, 150, 160, 200, 210, 230, 240, 290, 320, 340, 360, 560, 580, 640, and 650 fps. The maximum flash rate should be set at or above the fastest film frame rate to be used in the shot. If filming at less than 120 fps, set the flash rate to 120 fps. The brightness that the lights can attain is inversely proportional to the speed of the flashes you set. When you set the flash rate, you also set the intensity of the flash. When the camera rolls, the flashes are uniform in intensity at any speed up to the maximum speed you set. Electronics within the control console monitor the operation of the equipment and signal errors such·as camera speeds above the maximum flash rate setting or missing flashes.

Note that high-speed cameras sometimes give off a spike pulse when they are coming up to speed. This will trigger an alarm on the console. Press the alarm reset button. If the alarm is not triggered again, you can safely assume there is no problem once the camera is at speed.

Let's say that we will be filming at 200 fps. We set the maximum flash rate to 200 for each of the light heads. Now, we are ready to take light readings. A word of warning: If the main power switch is turned off, the settings will be lost, so it is helpful to circle the setting numbers on the console with a white grease pencil.

Strobe light must be measured with a flash meter. A flash meter is able to sense and capture an exposure measurement from a quick flash of light. Unilux provides Minolta flash meters with its lights. To take a reading, press the meter button on the control console. The lights will come up to the intensities you set. Note that the lights continue to flash at 60 flashes per second in meter mode. When you're done taking readings, press the meter button again to return to preview mode. The control console automatically returns the lights to preview mode after 3 minutes.

When you are ready to start filming, the lights automatically come up to the preset intensity when you turn the camera on. The flash rate is slaved to the camera speed and increases and decreases speed in tandem with the camera motor. The frame rate at any given moment is shown on the control console. The control console also displays the source of the flash rate signal: camera, meter mode, preview, accessory port (such as the special effects generator), or slave input (used when the console is slaved to another console).

Controlling the Light

A focusing snoot can be used to concentrate the beam into a spot of adjustable size. Unilux lights don't generally come with barn doors, but Mole Studio junior barn doors and 10 1/8-in. scrims fit the ears.

Mixing Sources

In many instances, cinematographers find that the strobe by itself is overly sharp. To make the image look more natural, you can mix strobe with tungsten or flickerless HMI sources. A good mix is to set the strobe two stops brighter than the supplemental sources.

To calculate the exposure when mixing Unilux with supplemental sources, measure the two sources separately, then add the two readings. Remember that twice as much light equals one stop more, so if the Unilux reading and the supplemental readings are the same, effectively doubling the light, the exposure is one stop more than the individual readings. If Unilux is one stop brighter, the supplemental lighting is half as bright; and you would add a half-stop to the Unilux reading. If Unilux is two stops brighter, the supplemental light is one quarter as bright; you would add a quarter stop to the Unilux reading.

When Unilux lights are used alone, changing the frame rate does not change the exposure. Because the heads flash the same amount of light on each frame, the exposure time does not change with the frame rate as it does with normal lights. When mixing Unilux with supplemental light, if you double the frame rate, the exposure time of the supplemental light is cut in half. You would need to double the intensity of the supplemental light to keep the same proportion of light from the two sources. In other words, the f-stop you read from the tungsten sources must take the frame rate (shutter speed) into account before it is compared with the Unilux reading for setting light levels.

Sync Delay Box

The sync delay box is a separate circuit box that comes with every system. With all cameras except Arriflex, the camera sync cable is connected to the sync delay box, and the box is connected to the "others" camera input on the back of the control console (Figure 10.24). The sync delay box serves three potentially helpful functions: shutter sync, cutoff speed, and polarity.

Shutter Sync

With each camera used, the shutter sync should be checked by removing the lens and observing the shutter opening with the Unilux lights running. If the shutter

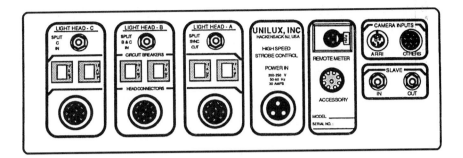

Figure 10.24 The back of the Unilux H3000 control unit. (Courtesy of Unilux, Inc., Hackensack, NJ.)

is not completely open each time the light flashes, the sync delay circuit should be used. Turn the circuit on, and set the angle of shutter delay from 1° to 359°.

Cutoff Speed

When set to automatic, the cutoff speed circuit does not let the flash rate go below 60 fps. This is to avoid annoying strobe speeds as the camera slows down at the end of each take (used when filming at frame rates above 60 fps). The switch can also be set to cut off at 10 fps or 1 fps.

Polarity

With some Panavision cameras, the polarity of the sync pulse is inverted. The polarity switch flips the polarity so that the control console gets a usable signal. If the shutter won't sync up, try changing the polarity.

Split Sync

The split sync configuration allows you to get two stops more light when operating at frame rates above 60 fps with any camera that has a rotating shutter. As noted earlier, each head normally flashes twice for each shutter rotation, once for an exposure (shutter open) and once for the camera operator (shutter closed). The split-sync configuration eliminates the second flash, which cuts the flash rate in half, provides extra power to the heads, and quadruples the light output.

To provide light for the viewfinder, the viewfinder flash is diverted to one or two separate heads. The viewfinder lights do not affect the exposure because they are off when the shutter is open. When the system is in meter mode, the viewfinder light is off so that it does not affect the exposure readings.

Special Effects Generator

The special effects generator makes strobe and chase effects possible. These are used quite often for music videos. Strobe effects have also been used on such features as *Throw Momma from the Train* and *Jacob's Ladder* to create the flashing light of a train passing in a tunnel.

The special effects generator has eight channels. Each channel can control an individual light or an entire console of three lights. Each channel can be set to skip one to nine frames between flashes.

A sequencer circuit makes the channels chase, firing each head separately in sequence. Simply select the number of channels, from one to eight.

Notes

Be aware that the strobes can trigger a seizure in people who have photosensitive epilepsy. Make sure that everyone on the set is aware that strobes will be used. People with this very rare reaction generally know to stay away from strobes and avoid them.

CHAPTER **11**

Electricity

The Fundamentals of Electricity and Electrical Equations

First, a quick and dirty explanation of how electricity works. Electricity is the flow of electrons through a conductor. Electrons are forced into motion though a conductor when a power source is applied. As you know, a DC battery provides two terminals to power an electrical device, such as a light; one terminal has a positive charge (+), the other has a negative charge (−). The amount of difference between their states represents the potential to do work. It is therefore referred to as the *potential* or *potential difference*. The greater the potential difference, the greater the force with which electrons are made to flow. When a light fixture is connected to the battery terminals, the wires and lamp provide a path for electrons to flow from the negative terminal to the positive terminal of the battery. The chemical reaction taking place within the battery maintains the potential difference, which forces electrons to flow *continuously* through the circuit.

The flow of electricity and the electrical properties of components in a circuit are quantified by four basic units of electrical measure:

Unit	Description	Variable (used in equations)	Abbreviation (used to identify values)
Amperes	Current	I	A (amps)
Volts	Electromotive force, potential difference	E	V (volts)
Watts	Power output	P or W	W (watts)
Ohms	Resistance	R	Ω (Ohm

Amperes (Current)

The flow of electrons is called *current*. In an electrical circuit, the volume of electricity per second (rate of flow) of electricity is measured in *amperes*, *amps* for short (one coulomb per second equals one ampere). Amp is abbreviated A (as in a

1k pulls 8.3 A). In practical terms, amps represent the amount of current being drawn by the load (lights) connected to the power source. The amperage of a circuit is important to electricians, mainly because cable, connectors, and other distribution equipment must be large enough to carry the amperage required by the load. If cables are too small, they heat up, which causes a number of problems, including the potential to start a fire. Every element in an electrical distribution system, from the generator to the lamps, has to be sized to handle the amperage (current).

By convention, the letter I is used to represent current when it is an unknown quantity in electrical equations. If you are not used to using electrical equations, the difference between I and A may be confusing, after all they are both amperage, right? A is an abbreviation for ampere, used to identify a stated value (for example, we are pulling 80 A on this feeder cable). I is a variable used to stand in for an unknown or unspecified value of current in electrical equations (for example, $I = \frac{9600 \text{ W}}{120 \text{ V}}$, so $I = 80$ A).

Volts (Electromotive Force)

The *potential difference* (the difference in the amount of charge between the positive terminal and the negative terminal of the power source) determines how much force the electricity has. This is called *electromotive force* or *voltage*. It is measured in volts (V). A flashlight operates on 1.5 V, a car battery at 12 V, and a wall socket at 120 V. Voltage is the force with which current is pushed through a resistance. When we measure voltage with a voltmeter, we read the difference in voltage potential between the hot wire and the neutral wire (or any two points in a circuit).

E is the variable used to represent voltage (*E*lectromotive force) in equations.

Watts (Power)

Wattage can be thought of as total power *output*; in the case of lighting fixtures, wattage is the amount of total output (light and heat). A high-wattage bulb is brighter than a lower-wattage one. The total amount of electrical power being delivered at any one moment is measured in watts, abbreviated W (a baby is a 1000-W light, or a 1-kW bulb, or simply a 1k). (k stands for kilo meaning thousand. 1 kilowatt is 1000 watts.) The wattage is the product of the amperage (amount of current) and the voltage (electromotive force). Wattage is the measure of the amount of work being done in any one instant. It is the same idea as horsepower; in fact, 746 W = 1 hp.

Again, the letter P is conventionally used as a variable to represent wattage (power) in equations. However, W is also used.

For the purpose of billing, the power company's meter counts the electricity consumed in kilowatt-hours (kWh). The wattage used at any given time is reflected in the speed at which the disk in the meter turns. Kilowatt-hours measure the total amount of electrical power consumed over a given amount of time: the rate at which power is consumed in a given moment, measured in kilowatts, multiplied by the hours that power is consumed at that rate.

The Power Equation

Watts are mathematically related to volts and amps as follows:

$$P = IE \quad \text{or} \quad \text{Watts} = \text{Volts} \times \text{Amps}$$

An easy way to remember the power equation is to think of West Virginia ($W = VA$), or *PIE*.

From this we can see that both voltage and current (amperage) contribute to the total output (wattage). Consider two 60-W bulbs, a household bulb and a car headlight. The household bulb runs on 120 V and pulls a current of 0.5 A. The car headlight uses a 12-V battery but pulls electricity at a rate of 5 A. The total power consumed and the total amount of light emitted are the same for the 60-W household bulb and the 60-W car headlight:

$$\text{Household bulb: } 120 \text{ V} \times 0.5 \text{ A} = 60 \text{ W}$$
$$\text{Car headlight: } 12 \text{ V} \times 5 \text{ A} = 60 \text{ W}$$

To make the same point another way, in Great Britain and Western Europe, the standard voltage is 240 V. Consider what this means for a 10k lamp.

$$\text{United States: } 120 \text{ V} \times 83.3 \text{ A} = 10,000 \text{ W}$$
$$\text{United Kingdom: } 240 \text{ V} \times 41.67 \text{ A} = 10,000 \text{ W}$$

Note the amperage of the 240-V lamp is half of that of the 120-V lamp. The two lamps are the same brightness regardless of voltage. So a 10k is a 10k the whole world over, but in the United Kingdom, a 10k can use a much smaller cable.

Take a look at Table 11.1. The table lists the amperage of a variety of wattage lights for various voltage systems. Note the various permutations of the relationships between voltage, amperage, and wattage. Note that a 100-W lamp operating at 12 V pulls the same amperage as a 2000-W lamp operating on a 240-V system.

The power equation can be stated three different ways:

$$P = IE \quad \text{or} \quad \text{Watts} = \text{Volts} \times \text{Amps}$$

$$E = \frac{P}{I} \quad \text{or} \quad \text{Volts} = \frac{\text{Watts}}{\text{Amps}}$$

$$I = \frac{P}{E} \quad \text{or} \quad \text{Amps} = \frac{\text{Watts}}{\text{Volts}}$$

Calculating the Amperage of Lights

Actual Amps and Paper Amps   We frequently use the power equation to calculate the current (amperage) pulled by a given load ($I = P/E$). Remember, the amount of *current* needed determines all the major parameters of our work when installing a distribution system: the size cables, the size of the power plant, the balance of load between phases, and the amount of line loss.

Table 11.1   Amperage of Lights with Various Voltage Systems

Lamp Wattage	System Voltage					
	240 V	230 V	208 V	120 V	30 V	12 V
100 W	0.4 A	0.4 A	0.5 A	0.8 A	3.3 A	8.3 A
200 W	0.8 A	0.9 A	1.0 A	1.7 A	6.7 A	16.7 A
300 W	1.3 A	1.3 A	1.4 A	2.5 A	10.0 A	25.0 A
400 W	1.7 A	1.7 A	1.9 A	3.3 A	13.3 A	33.3 A
500 W	2.1 A	2.2 A	2.4 A	4.2 A	16.7 A	41.7 A
650 W	2.7 A	2.8 A	3.1 A	5.4 A	21.7 A	54.2 A
750 W	3.1 A	3.3 A	3.6 A	6.3 A	25.0 A	62.5 A
1000 W	4.2 A	4.3 A	4.8v	8.3 A	33.3 A	83.3 A
1500 W	6.3 A	6.5 A	7.2 A	12.5 A		
2000 W	8.3 A	8.7 A	9.6 A	16.7 A		
3000 W	12.5 A	13.0 A	14.4 A	25.0 A		
4000 W	16.7 A	17.4 A	19.2 A	33.3 A		
5000 W	20.8 A	21.7 A	24.0 A	41.7 A		
6000 W	25.0 A	26.1 A	28.8 A	50.0 A		
8000 W	33.3 A	34.8 A	38.5 A	66.7 A		
9000 W	37.5 A	39.1 A	43.3 A	75.0 A		
10,000 W	41.7 A	43.5 A	48.1 A	83.3 A		
12,000 W	50.0 A	52.2 A	57.7 A	100.0 A		
20,000 W	83.3 A	87.0 A	96.2 A			

To calculate the amperage pulled by a given light fixture, divide the lamp's wattage by the line voltage. For example, for a 1000-W light operating at 120 V, we make the following calculation:

$$I = \frac{P}{E} \quad \text{or} \quad \text{Amps} = \frac{\text{Watts}}{\text{Volts}}$$

$$\frac{1000 \text{ W}}{120 \text{ V}} = 8.3 \text{ A}$$

Table 11.1 gives the current for all the most common wattages.

Paper Amps   A quick method for calculating amperage is to divide the wattage by 100, an easy calculation to do in your head. Dividing by 100 overestimates the amperage, which introduces a safety margin of several amps per light. This is known as the *paper method* of calculating amperage.

Table 11.2 Paper Method Example

Wattage	Paper Amps	Real Amps
300	3	2.5
500	5	4.2
1000	10	8.3
2000	20	16.7
4000	40	33.3
5000	50	41.7
10,000	100	83.3
Total	228	190 (rounded to the nearest amp)

To calculate the total current being pulled through a cable, simply add up the amps pulled by each light. In Table 11.2, note how much easier it is to add the paper column than the real column.

Paper quantities are 1.2 times the real amperage. There are several reasons it is useful to maintain this safety margin. First of all, cables cannot be run at their full rated capacity continuously (the NEC defines *continuous use* as more than 3 hours). For continuous use, the cables must be derated to 80%. We often need to run lights for unspecified periods of time, so using paper amps derates the cable (to about 83%) automatically. Derating using paper amps also helps reduce line loss (loss of voltage with long runs of cable). There are other ways in which using paper amps provide a useful safety margin. For example, when a generator is loaded to near full capacity, an HMI ignition (which momentarily pulls a high current) can overload the power plant, resulting in the generator shutting down or tripping the main breaker.

Resistance and Ohm's Law

So far we have a mental picture of a lamp operating at the standard 120 V, drawing current (amps) to generate a particular wattage output. However, this is an incomplete picture of the forces acting on a circuit. What prevents an ambitious 60-W light bulb from drawing more current and becoming a 600-W light bulb? The force we are missing is resistance. Understanding resistance and how it relates to power and current gives a much clearer picture of the forces at work in a circuit.

Resistance is the opposition to the flow of current created by the load (the fixtures plugged into the circuit) and by the resistance of the wires themselves. Resistance is measured in ohms, abbreviated as the Greek letter omega (Ω). Example: A 2-kW light has a resistance of 7.20 Ω (on a 120-V system). *R* is used to denote resistance when it is an unknown value in electrical equations ($R = 7.20 \ \Omega$).

The resistance of a particular conductor or lamp filament can be considered constant,[1] determined by its physical properties and construction. The resistance of the filament limits the amperage that can be pushed through it by a particular voltage and, therefore, determines its ultimate output in watts.

Ohm's Law

Ohm's law can be stated three ways:

$$I = \frac{E}{R} \quad \text{or} \quad \text{Amps} = \frac{\text{Volts}}{\text{Resistance}}$$

$$R = \frac{E}{I} \quad \text{or} \quad \text{Resistance} = \frac{\text{Volts}}{\text{Amps}}$$

$$E = I \times R \quad \text{or} \quad \text{Volts} = \text{Amps} \times \text{Resistance}$$

Figure 11.1 shows the formulas wheel that gives all the possible relationships between voltage, wattage, amperage, and resistance. Figure 11.2 shows an easy way to remember these relationships.

Resistance of a Light

Ohm's law stated as $R = E/I$ can be used to calculate the resistance of a load (a light fixture). The resistance of a particular load can be calculated by dividing its rated voltage by the amperage. For example, a 5k bulb (rated 5000 W at 120 V) pulls 41.67 A. The resistance of the lamp can be calculated as follows:

$$\frac{120 \text{ V}}{41.67 \text{ A}} = 2.88 \ \Omega$$

Resistance of Cable

The resistance of a particular length of cable is equal to the voltage drop in the cable divided by the amperage running through it. If there is a 4-V drop in a length of cable carrying a 40-A load, the resistance of that length of cable is

$$R = \frac{E}{I} \quad \text{or} \quad \text{Ohms} = \frac{\text{Volts}}{\text{Amps}}$$

$$\frac{4 \text{ V}}{40 \text{ A}} = 0.1 \ \Omega$$

---

[1]The resistance of a piece of wire is constant at a given temperature. Any metal has less resistance at a lower temperature; as temperature increases, so does resistance. With tungsten, this effect is very pronounced—when cold it has very little resistance but when heated it has very high resistance. As a result, tungsten lights have high in-rush current with a cold start. Once at operating temperature, however, resistance is constant. In contrast, the resistance of copper changes very little with temperature.

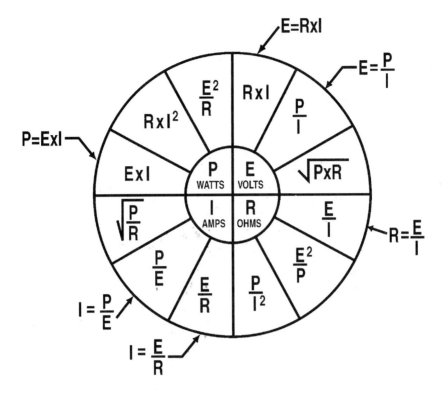

Figure 11.1 The formulas wheel gives every permutation of the relationships between voltage, amperage, wattage, and resistance.

Using Ohm's Law

$I = E/R$ calculates the amperage drawn by a particular load, knowing the line voltage and the load's resistance. To see how this equation works, let's use it to illustrate the dramatic effect of line loss.

All conductors, such as cable, have resistance. In a long length of cable, the resistance causes a perceptible drop in voltage from source to load because resistance turns some power into heat in the cables. This is known as *line loss*. Looking at $I = E/R$, we can see that, if voltage decreases (due to line loss), the amperage also decreases. We can calculate that, if the voltage is reduced to 108 V, a 2000-W bulb (normally 16.6 A, 7.36 Ω) draws less current than it should. Using Ohm's law we can calculate the actual current:

$$I = \frac{E}{R} \quad \text{or} \quad \frac{108 \text{ V}}{7.36 \text{ Ω}} = 14.7 \text{ A}$$

The actual current is only 14.7 A, instead of 16.6 A. Now, using the power

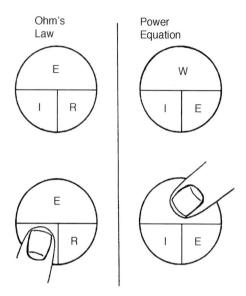

Figure 11.2 A simple way to remember the most common equations in Figure 11.1 is to use "magic circles." On either of the circles shown, cover the symbol you want to find with your finger. The relationship that remains is the formula. For example, to determine amperage (*I*) from a known resistance (*R*) and voltage (*E*), put your finger on the *I* and read *E* divided by *R*. To determine wattage (*W*) from amperage and voltage, put your finger over the *W* and read *I* times *E*.

equation, we can calculate the actual power output of the 2000-W lamp:

$$W = I \times E \quad \text{or} \quad 108 \text{ V} \times 14.7 \text{ A} = 1584 \text{ W}$$

The output is sliced down to 1584 W.

The problem is compounded by the fact that a light operates at full efficiency only at its rated voltage. Operating at 108 V (90% of its rated power), the 2k in fact produces only about 68% of its normal light output. That's one wimpy 2k—a 32% loss of output caused by a 10% loss of voltage. Light output decreases geometrically with line loss.

Parallel and Series Circuits

Several lamps can be connected in a single circuit in one of two ways: in parallel or in series (Figure 11.3). Lighting equipment is almost always connected in parallel; however, series circuits also become important to us in a number of ways.

In a *parallel* circuit (Figure 11.4), each load is connected across the full potential difference (voltage) of the power source. The *voltage* is therefore the same across every load on the circuit ($E_T = E_1 = E_2 = E_3$, etc.). Each of the loads provides a separate path for current to flow. The amount of current in each path depends on

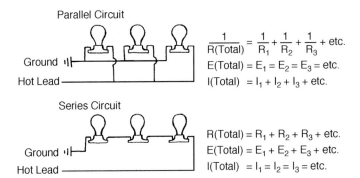

Parallel Circuit

$$\frac{1}{R(\text{Total})} = \frac{1}{R_1} + \frac{1}{R_2} + \frac{1}{R_3} + \text{etc.}$$
$$E(\text{Total}) = E_1 = E_2 = E_3 = \text{etc.}$$
$$I(\text{Total}) = I_1 + I_2 + I_3 + \text{etc.}$$

Series Circuit

$$R(\text{Total}) = R_1 + R_2 + R_3 + \text{etc.}$$
$$E(\text{Total}) = E_1 + E_2 + E_3 + \text{etc.}$$
$$I(\text{Total}) = I_1 = I_2 = I_3 = \text{etc.}$$

Figure 11.3 In a parallel circuit, voltage is constant everywhere in the circuit and the sum of the amperages of the fixtures equals the total amperage of the circuit. In a series circuit, amperage is constant everywhere in the circuit and the sum of the voltages of each fixture equals the voltage of the circuit.

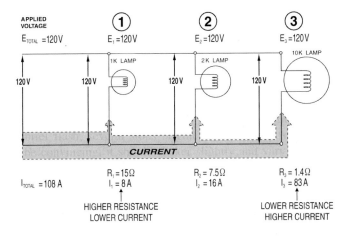

Figure 11.4 In a parallel circuit, the same voltage is applied to each load in the circuit. The current divides among paths in inverse proportion to the resistance present in that path.

the resistance in that path. The sum of the amperages of the separate loads is equal to the total amperage of the whole circuit ($I_T = I_1 + I_2 + I_3$, etc.).

In a *series* circuit, the components are connected end to end (Figure 11.5). The current has only one path to complete the circuit and has to pass through every component to complete the circuit back to the power source. (I use the general term *component* here. In our case, a component most likely is a load such as a light, but it might also be a battery or an electronic device such as a resistor.) The *amperage* is therefore the same throughout the circuit, found by calculating total current (I_T).

In a series circuit, the voltage divides among the components. The sum of the voltages across each component ($V_1 + V_2 + V_3$, etc.) equals the total voltage of the

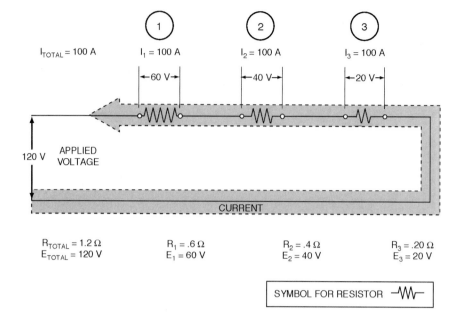

Figure 11.5 In a series circuit, the total current flows through every part of the circuit. The total voltage is divided among components in proportion to their resistance.

circuit (V_T). The voltage across each component depends on the resistance of that component.

In a series circuit, the total resistance of the circuit (R_T) equals the sum of the resistances of the separate components ($R_1 + R_2 + R_3$, etc.).

It is important to remember that, in a series circuit, the total current of the circuit runs through every component. You cannot calculate the current of a single component knowing the wattage and voltage of that component as you can with a parallel circuit, unless the loads are all identical. The current running through each component depends on what other components are connected in the series circuit. Therefore, to calculate the current for any component you must calculate the total current (I_T). To find the total current, add the resistances of all the components. Now, divide the circuit voltage (E_T) by the total resistance, R_T (using Ohm's law to find I_T):

$$\frac{E_T}{R_T} = I_T$$

If all the components in a series circuit have *exactly the same resistance*, then you can simply calculate the current of any individual component (e.g., $I_1 = P_1/E_1$) and the result will be the same as calculating I_T.

As you can see, in a series circuit, if there is a break in the circuit at any point (if one of the filaments blows, for example), the entire circuit is interrupted and none of the lights receive power.

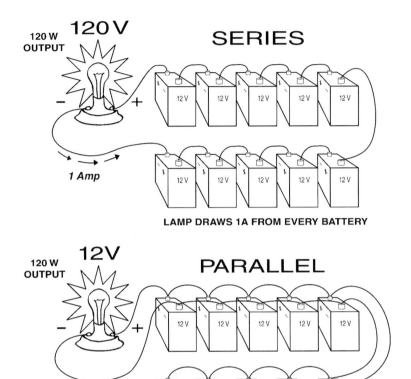

Figure 11.6 In the series circuit (top), the voltage across all 10 batteries adds up to the total voltage of 120 V. If the light bulb is a theoretical 120-W, 120-V bulb, the total current (1 A) travels though every part of the circuit. In a parallel circuit (bottom), the voltage is the same (12 V) at every point in the circuit no matter how many batteries are used. The theoretical 120-W, 12-V light bulb pulls 10 A, which divides among the 10 batteries (1 A each). Both light bulbs have the same light output.

To help show how voltage and current behave differently in a series circuit than in a parallel circuit, let's look at a simple example of series connected components: a battery pack. A 120-V battery pack consists of 10 12-V batteries connected in series: negative to positive, end to end (Figure 11.6). When connected in series, the total voltage of the pack is equal to the sum of the voltages of the individual batteries. If just two batteries were connected in series, the voltage would be 24 V (12 V + 12 V = 24 V). If five 12-V batteries were connected in series, the total voltage would be 60 V (12 V + 12 V + 12 V + 12 V + 12 V = 60 V). To get 120 V, therefore, you need 10 12-V batteries in series.

If the 10 series-connected batteries were connected to a 120-V lamp, you would complete a *series circuit*. As you know, the total current flows through every component (each of the batteries, and the 120-V lamp), because the series circuit provides only one path through the entire chain of batteries and the lamp. The current is therefore the same measured across any component in the circuit. In contrast, if any number of batteries were connected in parallel, the voltage would always remain 12 V. Increasing the number of batteries in parallel would increase the *current* available, or to put it another way, the current drawn by the lamp would divide among the batteries.

To put it simply: voltage is *the same* across each component of a parallel circuit; current is *the same* across each component of a series circuit. Current *divides* among the multiple paths provided by a parallel circuit (in inverse proportion to the resistance in each path); voltage *divides* among multiple components connected in series (in proportion to the resistance across each component).

How Not to Use Electrical Equations—Beavis the Electrician

It is a little-known fact that, before Beavis hit it big with the show Beavis and Butt-head, he was an electrician. He asked someone, "Dude, like, what do you really need to know to be one of the those lighting dudes?" and the person answered, "Never overamp the cable."

"How do I do that?" asked Beavis.

"Just remember: Watts divided by Volts always equals Amps."

Armed with this information Beavis joined the union and got a job.

The first day on the job, the gaffer gave Beavis a baby and a 1k variac dimmer and asked him to do a lighting cue. As Beavis sat there waiting to do his cue, he looked at the dimmer and thought, if I dial the dimmer from 100% to 50%, that's half as much voltage. So if Watts divided by Volts always equals Amps, then when the voltage goes to half, the amperage must double. To make sure he was right about this he wrote the equation on his hand:

$$\frac{1000 \text{ Watts}}{120 \text{ Volts}} = 8.3 \text{ Amps}$$

So,

$$\frac{1000 \text{ Watts}}{60 \text{ Volts}} = 16.7 \text{ Amps}$$

Beavis jumped up from his seat and yelled, "Cut, Cut, Cut!" When the gaffer demanded to know what was up, Beavis explained, "Like dude, if I dim this down I'll overamp this little 1k variac, huh, huh." That was the end of Beavis's first job. On his way out the door, the best boy explained. "You see, Beavis, when a light is dimmed down, it gets dimmer."

"Yeah, I know. So?"

"Think of wattage as *output*. If the light is dim, it is not giving full output. It is not putting out 1000 watts any more."

"But it says 1000 W. It's stamped right on the bulb," complained Beavis.

"To know the amperage when the light is dimmed you have to use resistance and Ohm's law." And the best boy scribbled the following equation on Beavis's forehead.

$$I = \frac{E}{R}$$

For a 1000-watt lamp, $R = 14$ Ohms; so,

$$I = \frac{60 \text{ V}}{14 \text{ }\Omega} \quad \text{or} \quad 4.3 \text{ A}$$

"At 60 volts the 1k draws 4.3 amps—and since Watts = Volts × Amps, 60 V × 4.3 A = 258 W."

"So," concluded the best boy, "a 1k at 50% is actually putting out only 258 watts."

"So the variac wasn't going to blow up? Okay, thanks," said Beavis. "Hey, but that was pretty funny when the director got a gun and chased me all over the set, huh? Ha, Ha-ha, ha."

A few months went by and Beavis watched what the other electricians did and didn't ever call cut. He kept his job. One day, the gaffer gave Beavis a bunch of cute little tiny 12-V, 100-W bulbs and said, "Hook these up and hide them in the set." Beavis didn't have a 12-V power supply, so he decided to use the variac dimmer and dial it down to 12 V. He counted the little 100-W lamps. There were 10 of them. That's 10 100-W lamps, Beavis calculated, or 1000 W. Perfect, he thought, I'll use a 1k dimmer and hook them up with #12 wire.

Beavis wired the little bulbs to plugs, and ran a #12 stinger to the lamps. He carefully adjusted the voltage from the variac to 12 V using his voltmeter, then plugged in a couple of the lamps to see if they worked. They worked just fine for about a minute then shut off. Beavis checked all his connections and finally figured out the little fuse on the variac had blown. He cursed the rental house for their shoddy equipment. Using a trick he'd learned from one of the old timers on set, he replaced the fuse with a slug of copper to keep it from blowing. Then he started plugging in the cute little lamps again, just as the gaffer came back to check on his progress.

All of a sudden the dimmer started smoking, the insulation melted off the wires and the set caught on fire. The gaffer screamed and yelled, the AD had a heart attack, and the director chased Beavis around with a gun again.

As studio security escorted Beavis off the lot, Beavis kept asking, "What happened?" The best boy explained, "Remember Watts ÷ Volts = Amps. Each of those cute little 100-watt lamps pulls 8.3 amps!" He worked out the math on a piece of charred paper:

$$\frac{100 \text{ Watts}}{120 \text{ Volts}} = 8.3 \text{ Amps}$$

Beavis remembered his experience with the dimming cue his first day and said, "But before, when I turned the voltage down, you said amperage went *down*. Now you're saying, at 12 V, the amperage is *higher*?"

"Current and wattage decrease when you are using the variac to *dim* the lights," explained the best boy. "But, when you use it as a transformer, the lights operate at full intensity. The total wattage really is 1000 W. And the total circuit voltage is only 12 V, not 120 V. If you'd have turned on all 10 of those little lamps …

$$\frac{1000 \text{ Watts}}{12 \text{ Volts}} = 83 \text{ Amps}$$

You would have been pulling 83 amps. That's like hooking up a 10k to a 1k variac."

That was the end of Beavis's time as an electrician. After that, he paired up with Butthead and the rest is history.

Ironically, there was a way for Beavis to have connected the lights without any problem, if he had put them in series. Remember, current is the same every place in a series circuit, and it is equal to the total wattage divided by total voltage:

$$\frac{1000 \text{ W}}{120 \text{ V}} = 8.3 \text{ A}$$

The voltage in a series circuit divides among the components of the circuit in proportion to the resistance of each component. In this case, all the bulbs have the same resistance, so voltage would have divided evenly, 12 V per light.

The moral of this story is to be sure you have properly identified which quantities are fixed and which depend on other variables. Understand what is going on in the circuit (drawing it helps) before choosing the equation to apply.

Circuits, Circuit Protection, and Cable

The essential parts of a safe electrical circuit are illustrated in Figure 11.7: the power source, the load, the conductor cables, a control device (such as a switch or dimmer), and circuit protection (a fuse or circuit breaker). A circuit should not be considered complete without a control device and circuit protection. The control

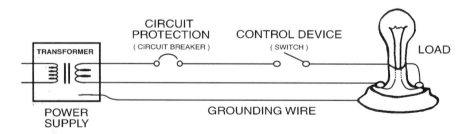

Figure 11.7 The components of a safe circuit.

device is used to open and close the circuit. (A *closed* circuit forms a complete circle through the load and other devices back to the power source. In an *open* circuit, the circle is interrupted by an open switch or lost connection.) Plugging or unplugging a cable is not a good way to close and open a circuit, except in an emergency. Similarly, using a circuit breaker as a switch is bad practice. It wears out the breaker.

Short Circuit and Overcurrent Protection

In a *short* circuit, the conductor inadvertently shortcuts the path from source to load, allowing current to flow directly across the power source from the outgoing wire to the return wire. *Overcurrent* results from having too large a load on a circuit.

From Ohm's law ($R = E/I$), you can see that the higher the amperage flowing through a fixture, the lower the resistance in the circuit; conversely, the lower the resistance of a fixture, the more amperage is allowed to flow. What happens if there is no resistance? If you create a dead short by touching the two wires together, the uninhibited current flow rapidly increases to the maximum available from the power source, which may be thousands of amps. The amperage in the circuit becomes extremely high, far beyond the amperage capacity of the cables. The wires heat up, burn, and melt (quite possibly setting the building on fire) or, if the amperage is high enough, vaporizes the cables in a matter of seconds. Overcurrent protection is needed for this reason.

An overcurrent device (a fuse or circuit breaker) cuts off power to the circuit if the current exceeds a specified limit. The amperage capacity of cables used downstream of the overcurrent device is matched to the amperage capacity of the overcurrent device. Thus, circuit protection is designed to prevent the possibility of thermal meltdown from an overloaded or shorted circuit.

Circuit Breakers and Fuses

The most common type of circuit protection today is the circuit breaker. In our industry, we like to use *magnetic* breakers. A magnetic circuit breaker interrupts the circuit if there is an overcurrent or short circuit. *Thermal-magnetic* breakers are common in homes. These are sensitive to temperature as well, which is an important safety feature when the wires are buried inside walls. In set lighting, thermal-magnetic breakers tend to cause nuisance tripping.

An alternative, less expensive than a circuit breaker, is a fuse. Most large fuses (100 A or more) are of the cartridge fuse type, which may be renewable (the end caps screw off and the broken strips are replaced) or nonrenewable. Nonrenewable fuses tend to heat up less and are favored in situations where there is little chance of an overcurrent. Fuses may or may not have a time delay type. A time-delay fuse is designed to allow for start-up loads, which may exceed the nominal current rating of a piece of equipment. This is the case with motors and with HMIs. Circuit breakers are designed to provide a time delay automatically.

Ground-Fault Circuit Interrupter

A ground-fault circuit interrupter (GFCI) is an additional protective device (incorporated into either a specially designed circuit breaker or a 120-V outlet) that detects fault currents much smaller than would trip a normal circuit breaker or fuse. GFCIs are also called *ground-fault interrupters* (GFIs), *residual-current devices* (RCDs) in England, and *earth-leakage detectors* (ELDs) in Australia.

A Class-A GFCI is designed to protect people against shock current in the event of a fault. In household wiring, GFCIs are required in bathroom outlets, outlets near sinks, outdoor circuits, and on any electrical equipment operated in proximity to a swimming pool, hot tub, or the like. Similarly, when filming in a bathroom or near a pool, a GFCI should be incorporated into the circuits powering the lights near the water. The danger of wet environments is that water underfoot greatly increases the conductivity of one's body to ground. Should leakage current occur, the GFCI will trip so fast that the shock current is less than that required to cause any serious injury.

A GFCI works by continuously comparing the current of the phase lead to that of the neutral lead. Normally, the current flowing to a load on the phase lead is identical to the current returning on the neutral lead. However, if there is a defect in the wiring or the fixture, some current will leak to ground, causing a differential between the two leads. If there is a differential of 0.005 A or more, the GFCI disconnects the circuit in $^1/_{40}$ second.

GFI-equipped distribution equipment was covered in the section on Underwater Lighting, Chapter 10. Some rental houses can provide special Edison outlet boxes with GFCI circuit breakers or outlets for use near water. Shock-block and others provide larger capacity GFCI equipment (100 A and higher).

The Current-Carrying Capacity of Cable

An amperage capacity, or *ampacity*, is assigned to each type of cable in the National Electrical Code based on the wire gauge, the maximum operating temperature of the insulation, and the conditions under which it will be used.

Wire Gauge

Wire sizes are numbered using the American wire gauge (AWG) sizes shown in Figure 11.8. For wire sizes from 18 AWG to 1 AWG, the smaller the number, the bigger the wire. Cables larger than 1 AWG are numbered 0, 00, 000, and 0000 (pronounced "one-ought," "two-ought," "three-ought," and "four-ought"). These sizes are usually written 1/0, 2/0, 3/0, and 4/0.

Cables bigger than 4/0 are referred to by their cross-sectional area, measured in circular mils (cmil) and are rarely used as portable power cable in film production.

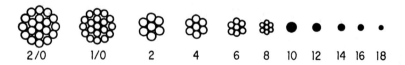

Figure 11.8 Actual diameters of common sizes of copper wires without insulation. (From H. Richter and W. Schwan, *Practical Electrical Wiring*, 15th ed. New York: McGraw-Hill, 1990. Reproduced with permission of McGraw-Hill.)

Multiconductor cable is labeled with the gauge and the number of conductors, denoted as follows: 12/3, where 12 is the gauge of the cable, and 3 is the number of conductors.

Cable (Europe)

Conductor size in the United Kingdom and continental Europe is given in square millimeters. The conductor size, type of insulation, operating temperature, and number of conductors (cores) is marked on the cable. Cable reference codes are usually marked CENELC. A typical code would be HO7RN-F1, which would indicate the cable rated for 750 V (7), heat and oil resistant (HO), rubber insulated on the conductors (R), with neoprene outer insulation (N), and the (F) indicates flame retardant. The number following the (F) indicates the number of cores.

In the United Kingdom, cables are often marked with their British standard code number, which does not immediately give information, but references lookup tables.

Maximum Operating Temperature

Testing laboratories test each type of cable insulation and assign it a maximum temperature rating. The more current runs through the cable, the warmer it becomes. The rating reflects the temperature that the wire can safely reach without damaging the insulation. When insulation becomes overheated, it may become brittle, crack apart, or melt. The temperature rating provides a margin of safety between the maximum operating temperature of the cable and its breakdown point.

Tables C.1 and C.2 list the ampacity of various sizes and temperature ratings of cable. Note that the ampacity of a cable rated at 60°C or 75°C is substantially lower than that of cable rated at 90°C. Be sure you assign the proper amperage to the cable you use.

If a cable rated at 90°C is connected to a fuse rated at only 75°C, the cable must be derated to the temperature of the fuse. This is necessary because the higher rated cables may transfer heat and overheat the fuse. To use the cable at its full capacity, a larger jumper cable must be used to connect between the fused panel and the first junction point to prevent heat transfer. The jumper cable must be sized to carry the needed amperage at the lower temperature rating.

Other Factors That Affect Ampacity

Ampacity is not printed on cable because outside factors influence the operating temperature of the cable and may lower its effective maximum amperage: the ambient temperature around a cable, the number of cables and the distance between them, whether the cables are in a raceway or conduit or standing in free air, and whether the circuit is run continuously or intermittently (periodically allowed to cool). The NEC specifies how much a cable must be derated in each of these circumstances (NEC article 400, Table 400-5B). Keep this in mind when cabling. When cable runs are in well-ventilated areas, the room temperature is normal or cool, and the loads are used intermittently, no derating is necessary. When cables are tightly bundled or stacked one on another, placed in narrow raceways, strung out across hot asphalt and left baking in the desert sun or otherwise subject to hotter than normal ambient temperatures, the insulation may be overheated if the cable is loaded to full ampacity. Keep this in mind when selecting cable gauge under such circumstances.

Ampacity of Overcurrent Devices

Because electrical conductors heat up over time, when circuits are to be loaded continuously for more than 3 hours NEC 220.10(b) requires that the overcurrent devices (such as circuit breakers) be derated to 80% of their maximum rated ampacity, unless the circuit breaker is a special type, designed to operate at 100% continuously. Many modern distro boxes use continuous rated breakers (see Table 12.3). For example, a circuit protected by a 100-A breaker may not be loaded beyond 80 A continuously for more than 3 hours. If the circuit is loaded continuously beyond 80%, a cool-down period is required, lasting at least half as long as the "on" time. When a feeder supplies a circuit having a combination of continuous and noncontinuous loads, the rating of the overcurrent device may not be less than the noncontinuous load plus 125% of the continuous load. (A *continuous load* is defined by the code as a load that is expected to continue for 3 hours or more.)

Ampacity and Operating Temperature of Connectors

Like cable, connectors have a maximum amperage rating. Obviously, you must not run more power through a cable than the connector is rated for, regardless of the rating of the cable. Connectors tend to be the weakest part of the system. Bates and Edison connectors overheat and melt if they are overamped or (more commonly) if there is poor electrical contact between connectors. If left too long, the connector melts, is destroyed, and not uncommonly starts a fire in the process. The amperage ratings of connectors are discussed in Chapter 12.

Like cable the connectors have a maximum rated operating temperature. Los Angeles city regulations further require that the ampacity rating of the cable may not be based on a temperature rating that is higher than that of the connectors. If the connectors are rated for 75°C the cable must be rated according to the 75°C column on the ampacity tables, even if the cable is rated for a higher temperature.

Types of Feeder Cable

Type W Cable

Type W cable is a portable, extrahard-usage power cable, manufactured to meet the requirements of NEC Article 400 (portable cords and cables) and is acceptable for temporary wiring according to Articles 520 (Theaters and Similar Locations) and 530 (Motion Picture and Television Studios and Similar Locations). It is flexible and abrasion resistant and usually double insulated. It may be oil, solvent, and sunlight resistant and flame tested. Carol Super Vutron cable is also flexible down to –50°C.

Entertainment Industry and Stage-Lighting Cable EISL
(Types SC, SCE, and SCT)

EISL cable, commonly called *entertainment cable*, is a portable, extrahard-usage cable with the same insulation characteristics as type W cable but is 20%

smaller and lighter than type W, due to the improved materials used in the insulating jacket. You often see 105°C cable used, but it is not listed in the ampacity tables because the temperature rating must also match the temperature rating of the circuit protection, which is usually no more than 90°C. Use the 90°C column of the ampacity table for 105°C cable.

Welding Cable

For many years, welding cable was commonly used for feeder because it was more flexible and lighter than other types of cable available at the time. However, welding cable has never been approved for this purpose. The misapplication of welding cable became an issue during the 1984 Olympic Games in Los Angeles, after which there was a general conversion to type W and entertainment cable on the West Coast. Although some small rental houses may still rent it, the NEC prohibits the use of welding cable in motion picture distribution systems, except as a grounding wire.

Decoding Feeder Cable Labels

Electricians learn to identify wire gauge by appearance. Occasionally, however, you have to check the gauge by reading it off the insulation. For example, 2/0 type W cable is almost as large as type SC 4/0 cable.

Single-conductor feeder cables are imprinted something like this:

Royal Entertainment Industry & Stage-Lighting Cable 2/0 AWG 90°C 600V (UL) NEC 520 & 530 Outdoor

- Royal is the manufacturer.
- Entertainment. . . . Cable is the type of cable.
- 2/0 AWG is the size of the cable according to the American wire gauge standard.
- 90°C is the maximum operating temperature of the insulation.
- 600V is the maximum voltage of the cable.
- UL indicates that the cable is listed with Underwriters Laboratories.
- NEC 520 & 530 indicate that the cable meets the requirements of National Electrical Code Articles 520 and 530, which apply to the entertainment industry.
- Outdoor indicates that the cable is approved for outdoor use.

Decoding Multiconductor Cable Labels

Multiconductor cable, used for stingers and power cords, is marked as follows:

12/3 Type SJOW-A 90°C P-123-MSHA—Type SJO 90°C

- 12/3 indicates the gauge (12) and the number of conductors in the cable (3).
- Type SJOW-A is a code for the type of insulation (S cord with a light oil- and water-resistant jacket).
- 90°C is the maximum operating temperature of the cable.

Table 11.3 Insulation Designations

S	Portable cord designed to withstand wear and tear, consisting of two or more stranded conductors with a serving of cotton between the copper and the insulation to prevent the fine strands from sticking to the insulation. Fillers are twisted together with the conductors to make a round assembly held together by a fabric overbraid. The outer jacket is of rubberlike thermosetting material.
SJ	Junior service. The same as S, but with a thinner jacket. Junior service cord may not be used in areas governed by NEC Section 520-53(h), 520-62(b) (live audience situations). It may be used in other situations, so long as it is not subject to abuse (continually stepped on or rolled over).
SV	Junior service. The same as S, but with an even thinner jacket.
SO	S cord with an oil-resistant neoprene jacket. Designated for extrahard use.
SOW	S cord with an oil- and water-resistant jacket.
SPT	Standard two-conductor "zip cord" or household lamp card. Cord with thermoplastic insulation. Warning: In long lengths, 18 AWG or 16 AWG zip cord burns up before it trips the circuit breaker. Even with a dead short, 100' of #18 zip has so much resistance that 20 A start a fire without tripping the breaker.

- P-123-MSHA indicates that the cable is approved by the Mine Safety and Health Administration (MSHA).
- Type SJO 90°C is an alternative designation given to this particular cable. Note: SJO is not rated for extrahard usage; SO cable is rated for extrahard usage.

Table 11.3 gives the meaning of some common insulation designations.

Types of Distribution Circuits

There are three basic types of distribution circuits:

- Direct current (DC).
- Single-phase alternating current (AC).
- Three-phase alternating current.

In the United States, Canada, and Mexico, the three systems are three-wire DC (240/120 V), three-wire single-phase 60-Hz AC (240/120 V), and four-wire three-phase 60-Hz AC (208Y/120 or 240Δ/120). In the United Kingdom, Australia, and Western Europe, higher voltage 50-Hz systems are used (415/240 V or 400/230 V AC.) We discuss each of these.

Direct Current and Alternating Current

To start with, the most basic distinction between these circuits is the difference between AC and DC current. A *direct current* power source (a battery or DC generator) has a positive terminal and a negative terminal. Electrons flow from the negative terminal through the circuit to the positive terminal. The *polarity* (direction of flow) never changes, and the voltage remains at a constant value.

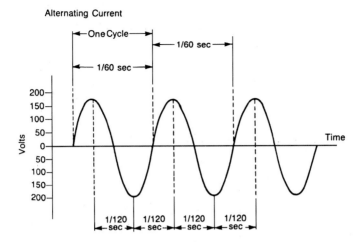

Figure 11.9 A 60-Hz alternating current makes one full cycle in one second and hits peak voltage every second. Note that the effective, or RMS, voltage is 120 V.

Alternating current, which is supplied by the power company through transformers or by an AC generator, has one, two, or three, or "hot" leads, known as the *phase leads*, and a neutral lead, sometimes called the *return* lead. The polarity of the circuit alternates continuously from positive to negative and back to positive again. Electrons flow first in one direction, then polarity is reversed and they flow in the other direction. The polarity changes 120 times per second in the United States (60 cycles per second), or 60 hertz (Hz) (Figure 11.9). On AC circuits, the hot legs are more properly called the *phase* leads. The return wire is called the *common, neutral*, or *return*.[2]

Europe and other parts of the world use a 50-Hz, 240-V system or another system. Appendix I gives the kind of power used in cities throughout the world.

During each cycle, the voltage of a 60-Hz 120-V system goes from 0 to *peak voltage*, +170 V, back to 0, reverses polarity, goes down to –170 V, and back to 0 again. It does this 60 times every second. Because the cycles occur rapidly, there is no time for the filament of a bulb to dim during the short time when the voltage passes 0, which is the reason the bulb provides a constant glow. The *effective*, or RMS (root mean square), voltage of a circuit is 120 V:

$$\frac{\sqrt{2}}{2} \times \text{Peak Voltage} \quad \text{or} \quad 0.707 \times 170 = 120 \text{ V}$$

[2]The term *grounded lead* is officially the correct term for the neutral. As *neutral* is the more familiar term to most electricians, I use it throughout this text. Officially, however, this is considered incorrect usage; the common wire is not actually "neutral" unless the phase wires are equally loaded. I do not use the term *grounded lead* because it is too easily confused with *grounding wires*. They serve two completely different functions in a power system. See the section on Grounding later in this chapter.

A voltmeter reading gives you the effective voltage. A lamp connected to the circuit operates at the effective voltage of 120 V.

Alternating Current and Direct Current on the Set

Both AC and DC power are used on sound stages and on location. Many of the large Hollywood studios, including Warner Brothers, Paramount, Universal, Sony, Twentieth Century Fox, Walt Disney Studios, CBS Studio Center, and Culver Studios, still use DC house power in some or all of their stages. Most new studio facilities use AC, and AC is used for most location filming as well.

Either AC or DC can be used to power tungsten lights. A 120-V DC circuit lights the bulb to the same brilliancy as a 120-V AC circuit. DC current cannot be used with AC HMIs, variac dimmers, or other equipment that has an AC transformer. Plate dimmers or electronic DC dimmers must be used to dim DC circuits. Carbon arc lights run on DC. To convert AC power to DC, a *rectifier* must be used. To convert DC to AC, an *inverter* must be used.

Safety Considerations

DC is often used when filming near water on a backlot because it is considered to be safer. You are less likely to get a shock from a DC system. With an AC system, you can complete a circuit by touching a hot wire and standing on the ground, but with a DC circuit, you can complete the circuit only by touching the positive and the negative wires simultaneously. The ground beneath your feet does not complete the circuit unless the DC system is grounded, and few are.

The shock from a DC circuit and the shock from an AC circuit are different (see the section on Electrical Shock and Muscle Freeze later in this chapter). However, this safety benefit does not apply to portable generators, which convert AC to DC using rectifiers. Rectified AC current is pulsating and reacts with the body the same as AC. True DC power plants are only found on older studio facilities.

Switches and Breakers

There are some important differences between AC and DC switches and circuit breakers. A property of DC current is that, when there is a narrow gap between contacts, the current arcs and begins to burn the contacts (the carbon arc light operates on this principle). Every time a switch is opened or closed, a short gap exists for an instant. If the current is allowed to arc each time the switch is opened or closed, it will burn away the contacts of the switch very quickly. To prevent the arc, DC switches and circuit breakers are spring-loaded so that the contacts snap together quickly.

The most common household switches, AC-only switches, do not require this feature and operate quietly, without a snap. Do not use AC-only switches or breakers with DC circuits. The letters AC appear after the rating on the switch.

AC-DC switches can be used with either AC or DC power. If AC does not appear on the rating of the switch, it is an AC-DC type. If an AC-DC switch is to be used to control an incandescent light, it must have a "T" (tungsten) rating

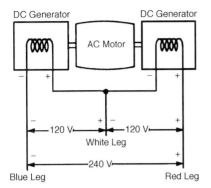

Figure 11.10 The three-wire 120/240-V DC generator configuration for DC sound stages. An AC motor drives two DC generators connected in series. The blue leg is usually the negative leg, and the red leg is the positive. The voltage potential between them is 240 V. The white leg gives a voltage potential of 120 V when connected to a circuit with either hot leg.

(a slightly beefier switch is needed to handle the high initial inrush current drawn by a cold tungsten filament).

Direct Current: Three-Wire Edison System

Most DC stages are actually powered by two generators connected in series to provide a three-wire system with two hot legs (red and blue) and one common leg (white) (Figure 11.10).

Connecting the load between either one of the hot legs and the common leg gives 120 V. Connecting the load between the negative blue leg and the positive red leg gives 240 V.

At one time, true DC generators were used on location to power arc lights. True DC generators have all but passed into history. Some AC generators can provide a rectifier circuit to create rectified two-wire DC. In other words, they use electronics to approximate DC. This *pulse DC*, as it is sometimes called, can be used to power arc lights and other DC equipment, but it does not provide the safety aspects of true DC around water. Pulse DC causes the same types of harmful reactions in the body as AC.

Polarity

Polarity is the direction of flow of electricity in a circuit. In DC circuits, electricity flows from the negative terminal of the power source, through the circuit, to the positive terminal. Polarity is important when powering carbon arc lights. This equipment does not operate properly if the polarity is reversed. *In a three-wire DC circuit, the blue leg is always negative and the red leg is always positive* (see Figure 11.10). If you were connecting a carbon arc light to the blue leg, you would connect the positive lead to the white wire. If you were connecting it to the red leg, you would connect the negative lead to the white wire. The white wire is negative with respect to the red leg and positive with respect to the blue leg.

You can check the polarity of a DC circuit by using a DC voltmeter or a magnetic compass, which will point in the direction of flow when held next to a current-carrying wire.

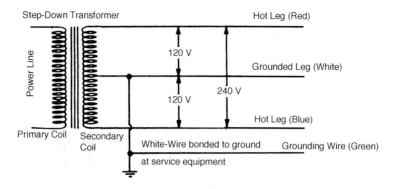

Figure 11.11 The three-wire 120/240-V AC configuration common in all types of buildings. The coils represent the primary and secondary coils of the transformer that steps down the voltage from the power lines. The neutral (white) wire taps into the midpoint of the secondary coil and is a grounded wire. The voltage potential is 240 V between red and blue and 120 V between white and red or between white and blue.

Alternating Current: Single-Phase Three-Wire System

While most incandescent lights run on 120 V, larger HMIs and 20ks run on 208 V or 240 V. A single-phase three-wire AC system, which provides both 120- and 240-V power from three wires, is commonly used in film distribution systems as well as in most homes and commercial buildings (Figure 11.11).

Like the three-wire DC system, this system consists of two 120-V phase legs and a neutral. By connecting the load between one phase leg and the neutral, you get 120 V. By connecting the load between the two phase legs, you get 240 V. The neutral wire is always white. The two phase legs are two other colors (blue, red, or black) but never white or green. A voltage reading between a phase wire and the neutral is referred to as a *phase-to-neutral* reading. A voltage reading between two phase wires is referred to as a *phase-to-phase* reading.

You might wonder whether using the neutral wire to serve two circuits doubles the load on the neutral wire. Would the neutral wire have to be twice as thick as in a single circuit to carry twice the amperage? No, the current flowing through one phase lead always flows in the direction opposite that of the current in the other phase lead. When the loads are the same on both legs, the current in the neutral wire is effectively zero. When the load on one phase is greater than that on the second, the neutral wire carries the difference in amperage of the two hot legs.

For example, assume that the red leg and the blue leg are carrying 50 A each. The loads are even, so the two loads traveling through the neutral wire cancel each other out. If we remove 10 A from the red leg and put it on the blue leg, making the red leg 40 A and the blue leg 60 A, the neutral wire carries the difference (20 A).

Note that this type of circuit actually has four wires including the ground, but it is properly referred to as a *three-wire circuit plus ground*. This gets a bit confusing because we refer to our cable as *four-wire banded* (single phase) or *five-wire banded* (three phase). The phase wires and the neutral are "current-carrying wires," the fourth (or fifth) wire is a green-coded grounding wire used for grounding non–current-carrying parts of the lights and electrical hardware (see the section on Grounding later in this chapter).

Note also that electrical systems are referred to as either *120/240* or *120/208 three-phase*. It is not proper to refer to the U.S. system as *110/220 V*. This is misleading and can cause confusion.

Cautions

There are a couple of disastrous mistakes to avoid when cabling. You must be careful not to connect the wires incorrectly. If you do, the lights on one circuit receive 240 V, which blows out 120-V lamps as soon as you try to turn them on. When a plugging box is intentionally wired to serve a 240-V light, it must be clearly marked. If in any doubt, check the voltage with a voltmeter before plugging in any lights.

Second, be sure that the neutral wire is never inadvertently disconnected once the lights are on. If the neutral wire is taken out of the circuit, the voltage applied to the circuit becomes 240 V and the two sides of the circuit become connected in series (Figure 11.12).

Theoretically, if the amperage load on both legs were exactly the same, the voltage on each side would still be 120 V (240 divided by 2). However, chances are that one leg pulls more amperage than the other. The difference in resistance creates an imbalance in the voltage. The voltage on one side of the series circuit drops, while the other side shoots up and starts to blow out bulbs on that side of the circuit in a matter of seconds.

Consider a simple example of a three-wire system with a 5k fixture on the red leg and a 2k fixture on the blue leg (Figure 11.13).

With the neutral connected, each light receives 120 V. The 5k pulls 41.67 A and has a resistance of 2.88 Ω. The 2k pulls 16.67 A and has a resistance of 7.2 Ω.

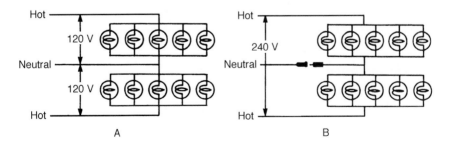

Figure 11.12 (A) A typical three-wire 120/240-V system with five lamps connected to each leg. The red and blue legs are separate circuits sharing the grounded lead. (B) When the white wire is pulled, the red and blue legs become connected in series with 240 V total voltage. If both sets of lamps have exactly the same resistance, the voltage is divided evenly in two, at 120 V each. However, if one leg has more resistance, it receives more voltage and the other leg receives less. (They always add up to 240 V.)

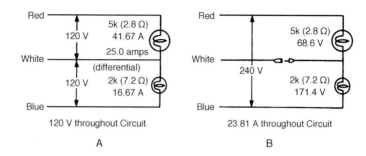

Figure 11.13 (A) A three-wire system with a 5k on one leg and a 2k on the other. (B) With the white wire pulled, the two legs are connected in series with 240 V applied to the circuit. The 2k is blown by the 171-V power.

If the neutral wire were disconnected, the two lights would become connected in series in a 240-V circuit. Unlike a parallel circuit, the amperage in a series circuit is the same in every part of the circuit, and the total resistance of the circuit equals the sum of the resistances of all the lights.

We can calculate the amperage for the circuit as follows:

$$I(\text{total amperage}) = \frac{E(\text{total voltage of circuit})}{R(\text{sum of the resistances})}$$

$$I = \frac{240 \text{ V}}{2.88 \ \Omega + 7.2 \ \Omega} = 23.81 \text{ A}$$

Knowing the amperage of the whole circuit (23.81 A), we can now calculate the voltage ($E = I \times R$) being applied to each light:

Voltage of the 5k: 23.81 A $\times$ 2.88 Ω = 68.6 V
Voltage of the 2k: 23.81 A $\times$ 7.2 Ω = 171.4 V

From this, we can see that the fixture with the greater resistance, the 2k, receives a higher voltage, which blows the lamp. Note that the sum of the voltages of the lights is equal to the voltage of the whole circuit (68.6 V + 171.4 V = 240 V).

Three-Phase, Four-Wire Systems

Most commercial buildings, including sound stages, have three-phase power. Almost all location generators also put out three-phase power. You will sometimes see the word phase abbreviated with the Greek letter phi (ϕ).

A three-phase, four-wire system consists of three 120 V phase leads (referred to as phase A, B, and C, coded black, blue, and red) and a neutral lead (white). Each of the three phases operates at 60 cycles per second. Each phase, however, operates a third of a cycle out of phase with the next. If you think of one cycle as a 360° circle, each phase begins the cycle 120° after the last. Figure 11.14 compares the generator windings and sine wave of a single phase generator with that of a three-phase generator.

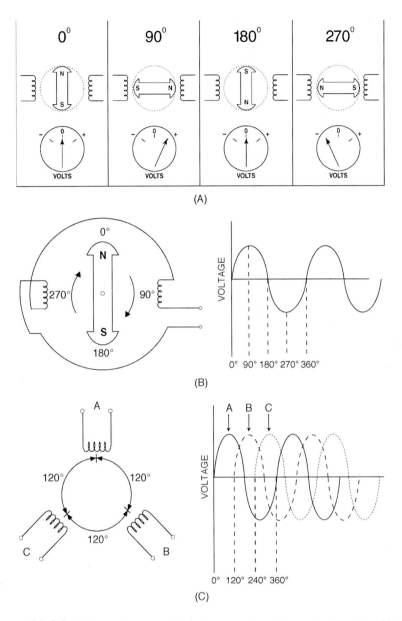

(A)

(B)

(C)

Figure 11.14 When a wire moves through a magnetic field, a current is induced in the wire (a voltage potential is produced that pushes the current when connected to a complete circuit). (A) A simplified diagram shows how this is used to produce electricity in an alternator (an AC generator). As the rotor (magnetic field) rotates past the armature windings, voltage increases to a maximum; current moves first in one direction (at 90°), then in the opposite direction (at 270°). As the rotor passes 0° and 180°, the voltage passes 0 and the current changes direction. (B) The result is a continuous sinusoidal waveform as the armature rotates. (C) A three-phase alternator has three sets of armature windings (A, B, and C), each spaced 120° from the last. This produces three separate sine waves, 120° out of phase, commonly referred to as the *three phases*. For simplicity and clarity, all the windings for each phase are represented here by a single winding and the rotor is not shown.

As with the single-phase system, if all three phases are evenly loaded, the neutral wire carries no current (assuming purely resistive loads). When the phase legs are not evenly loaded, the neutral carries the difference of the phases. The difference was easy to calculate with a single-phase system, but with a three-phase system it has to be calculated using vectors and geometry (because of the 120° phase difference between the legs). This leads to a rather complicated calculation. If the currents on the three phase legs are radically different from one another you can find I_N (the current on the neutral) as follows: plug the phase currents I_A, I_B, and I_C into the following (somewhat verbose) equation:

$$I_N^2 = \left[I_A - \frac{1}{2}(I_B - I_C) \right]^2 + \frac{3}{4}(I_B - I_C)^2$$

Note that this equation calculates I_N^2. You have to hit the square root key on your calculator to get I_N.

If you are like me, you wouldn't touch this equation with a ten-foot pole so here is a simpler rule of thumb. If two of the three phase leads are evenly loaded (at 100 A, for example) and the third phase is loaded to, say, 60 A, the neutral carries the difference between the current on the two even phases and current of the third phase lead (100 A − 60 A = 40 A).

208Y/120V System

The circuit shown in Figure 11.15 is a wye-connected three-phase system. It is called a *wye* or *star* because of its shape. When a load is connected to any one of the phase wires and the neutral wire, the voltage is 120 V. When a load is placed between any two phase wires, the voltage is 208 V because the two phases are 120° apart.

Note that a three-phase, four-wire system actually uses five wires. The fifth is a green-coded grounding wire used for grounding non–current-carrying parts of the lights and electrical hardware (not shown in Figure 11.15; see the section on Grounding later in this chapter). In our business we typically call this a *five-wire run*. A "real-world" electrician would call this a *four-wire, plus ground*.

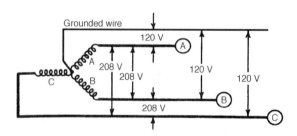

Figure 11.15 A 208Y/120-V three-phase system. The three coils shown represent the secondary coils of the transformers that step down the voltage from the power line. A 208/120-V system can supply 120-V single-phase circuits and 208-V three-phase circuits at the same time. (From H. Richter and W. Schwan, *Practical Electrical Wiring*, 15th ed. New York: McGraw-Hill, 1990. Reproduced with permission of McGraw-Hill.)

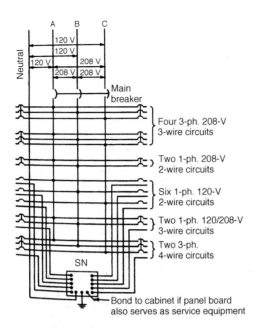

Figure 11.16 Five types of circuits can be derived from a 208Y/120 (four-wire, three-phase) system. (From H. Richter and W. Schwan, *Practical Electrical Wiring*, 15th ed. New York: McGraw-Hill, 1990. Reproduced with permission of McGraw-Hill.)

There are five types of circuits that can be derived from a wye-connected, four-wire plus ground, three-phase system (Figure 11.16):

120-V, two-wire circuit plus ground, single-phase Three separate circuits can be made by tapping any one of the phase leads and the neutral lead. When loading the three phases, it is important to keep them evenly balanced.

208-V, two-wire circuit plus ground, single-phase This circuit is made by tapping any two of the three phase leads. The larger HMI ballasts run on 208, 230, or 240 V. When running three-phase (208Y/120) power, select 208-V input power on the ballast. Again, as much as possible, keep the load evenly balanced among the phases by tapping A and B, B and C, and C and A evenly.

120/208-V, three-wire circuit plus ground, single-phase By tapping two of the three phase leads and the neutral lead, you have the option of providing 120- or 208-V power. Doing this, you can use distribution boxes made for three-wire systems. Be sure to label each box (red/blue, blue/black, or black/red) so you remember what is plugged into what. Keep the load evenly balanced by tapping evenly: A and B, B and C, and C and A.

208-V, three-wire circuit plus ground, three-phase This type of circuit uses all three phase leads and no neutral. Some xenon ballasts are wired this way. A service panel wired this way is usually a designated branch circuit for machinery, such as a large air-conditioning unit or three-phase motor. Such circuits are not suitable for tie-ins. It is unsafe and forbidden by the NEC to use a ground wire tapped from another circuit to get 120-V single-phase circuits from the legs of a three-wire, three-phase system.

208Y/120, four-wire circuit plus ground, three-phase   Branch circuits with this configuration provide all the possibilities just mentioned.

Delta-Connected Four-Wire, Three-Phase System

You sometimes come across a four-wire, three-phase delta-connected system. Its name comes from the circuit's resemblance to the Greek letter delta (Δ). The voltage across each of the secondary coils of the transformer is 240 V (Figure 11.17).

To supply 120/240-V service, one coil is tapped in the center. The tap is grounded and becomes the neutral lead for a three-wire, single-phase 120/240-V circuit. Single-phase 120-V power can be gained by connecting to A and N or B and N. The tapped coil is usually larger than the other two, so it can handle the extra load.

Connecting to C and N produces 208-V, single-phase power (Figure 11.18). This is called the *high leg* or *stinger leg*, and it has caught many an electrician by surprise. If you are used to a wye configuration, you would expect any of the three phase leads to give 120 V when connected with the neutral. The high leg on a delta-connected system gives 208 V because it has the added voltage of an extra half-coil. Because the extra half coil is 120° out of phase, it adds 88 V to the 120 V of the full coil (88 + 120 = 208 V). Obviously, the high leg would burn out any 120-V light connected to it.

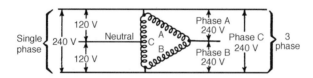

Figure 11.17   A 240-V, three-phase, delta-connected system delivers single-phase 240/120-V current and three-phase 240-V current. (From H. Richter and W. Schwan, *Practical Electrical Wiring*, 15th ed. New York: McGraw-Hill, 1990. Reproduced with permission of McGraw-Hill.)

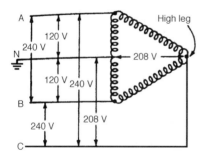

Figure 11.18   In a delta-connected system, the voltage from the neutral to the high leg is 208-V power, not 120-V power as you would expect from a wye-connected system. (From H. Richter and W. Schwan, *Practical Electrical Wiring*, 15th ed. New York: McGraw-Hill, 1990. Reproduced with permission of McGraw-Hill.)

Other Systems Used in Industrial Applications

When shooting on location it is sometimes convenient to tap into unused existing service. Location panel tie-ins require a permit and may be performed only by a trained and qualified person. Empty warehouses sometimes have a number of service panels and subpanels that could provide a small amount of supplemental power. You may find a 208Y/120V or 240Δ/120 system you can use. Other systems are also quite common in this type of environment; however, they may or may not be of any use.

Large fluorescent lighting installations operate more efficiently on 277-V power, so most industrial buildings use a 480Y/277-V system. The system is on a separate transformer from the 120-V service. The cables are usually coded brown, orange, and yellow. This system has no direct applications for film lighting and would require a step-down transformer to be a usable power source. (Mole-Richardson offers step-down transformers of this type.)

There are a couple of variations on the delta-connected system. Three-wire systems may carry either 240 V or 480 V across each coil. In an alternative delta configuration, one corner of the delta is sometimes grounded. A step-down transformer would have to be installed (again requiring a permit and properly qualified electrician) and a neutral wire derived to use this system as a power source.

Electrical Systems in Other Parts of the World

Various voltage configurations are used in other parts of the world. The United Kingdom and Australia generally use a three-phase, star-connected 415/240-V 50-Hz AC system. The European "harmonized standard" is star-connected 400/230-V 50-Hz AC. Some European countries still use 220-V service (three-phase, delta-connected 127/220). Appendix I gives a complete listing for nations around the world.

The star-connected system used in the United Kingdom and Australia is shown in Figure 11.19. Note that it is exactly like the 208Y/120-V system used in the United States but at twice the voltage. The 400Y/230-V standard is again the same configuration of coils stepped to a slightly lower voltage at the transformer. While, on the North American continent, we require both voltages available from the 208Y/120-V system, this is not necessary in Europe, where virtually all lighting equipment runs at one voltage (230–240 V). This makes distribution that much simpler, as no lights are connected phase to phase; they connect to one phase wire and neutral, with the exception of three-phase equipment, which connects to all three phases.

The U.K. system of color coding for fixed wiring (permanent building wires) is as follows:

Earth (protective conductor)	*Green/Yellow*
Single phase (live)	Red (or yellow or blue)
Neutral	Black
Phase R	Red
Phase Y	Yellow
Phase B	Blue

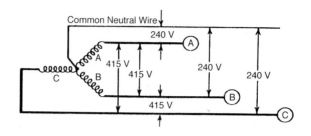

Figure 11.19 The U.K. electrical standard 415Y/240-V AC.

The UK system of color coding for flexible cables is

Earth (protective conductor)	*Green/Yellow Stripe*
Neutral	Blue
Phase wires	Brown or black

In four- and five-core cables, if conductors of the same color are used for the three phases or for different functions, then coded sleeves are added to the cores (e.g., L1, L2, L3).

Grounding

There are two kinds of grounding: (1) system grounding, the grounding of one of the current-carrying wires of the installation to earth; and (2) equipment grounding, grounding the non–current-carrying parts, such as lamp housings and ballast casings.

System Grounding

As noted in the preceding discussion, the white, or neutral, wire is always a current-carrying *grounded* lead. The white wire is grounded to the service equipment (the main power box in the building), which in turn is grounded to the transformer delivering the electricity from the power line. The service equipment is grounded to earth by some means (e.g., a metal pipe of an underground water system, a ground rod, sunken building steel, or a made electrode, which is a large electrode placed in the ground during construction). In the case of portable generators, the frame of the generator serves in place of the earth. Generator grounding is discussed in detail in Chapter 13, Power Sources.

Equipment Grounding

Grounded neutral wires are not to be confused with *grounding* wires. The U-shaped prong on an Edison plug is for the grounding wire. Grounding wires are not meant to carry current under normal circumstances. They carry current only when

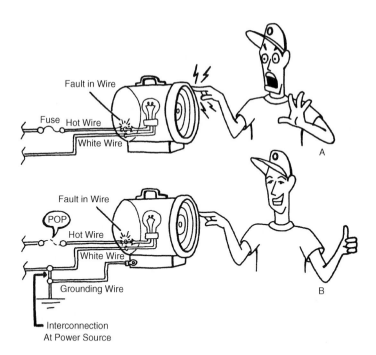

Figure 11.20 (A) A fault in a metal fixture makes the entire housing hot. Anyone who touches the hot fixture may complete a circuit to ground and get a shock. (B) A grounding wire carries the fault current safely to ground. Bonding the grounding wire and the white wire at the service entrance creates a dead short between the hot wire and neutral. If enough current flows through the grounding wire, the fuse or circuit breaker pops in response. However, if the fault makes only loose contact (high resistance), it creates a lot of heat but may not pop the fuse.

there is a fault (such as inside a piece of equipment) and the metal housing becomes electrified. If no grounding wire were connected (Figure 11.20A), anyone who touched the fixture would complete the circuit to ground through his or her body and would receive a shock. With a grounding wire connected to the housing (Figure 11.20B), electricity seeks the path of least resistance, and the bulk of the electricity completes the path to ground through; the grounding wire instead of through a human body. The faulty fixture remains safe to touch.

Another way to think of equipment grounding is the intentional connection of all exposed metal ports of the system together; this way all exposed metal ports at the same potential. A person touching any two metal surfaces will not experience a difference in potential—they won't be shocked.

The grounding wire is bonded to the service box, as is the neutral wire of the circuit. When a fault occurs, current coming back on the grounding wire makes a dead short with the bonded neutral. If enough current flows through the grounding wire, it will blow the fuse or trip the circuit breaker protecting the circuit. However, if the fault makes only loose contact (high resistance), it will create a lot of heat but may not pop the fuse.

Proper equipment grounding is essential to safety. It is one of the things that the fire marshal and electrical inspector look for on the set.

The grounding wire can be smaller than the current-carrying wires; however, it must not be so small that the resistance in the wire prevents it from tripping the breaker in case of a fault. The NEC provides a table indicating the minimum sizes for grounding wires (see Table B.3).

Line Loss

The National Electrical Code (NEC) states voltage drop should not exceed 3% on the main feeder cables or 5% total, where 3% of 120 V is 3.6 V and 5% is 6 V. The U.K regulations have similar provisions. The IEE regulations state that the voltage drop should not exceed 4% of the nominal voltage; that is, 9.2 V in a 230-V system or 9.6 V in a 240-V system.

As a rule of thumb, electricians assume that most feeder cable loses about 4 V per 100 ft when running at the full ampacity of the cable. You can anticipate a significant line loss any time there is a fairly long run of cable and the cable is loaded near its maximum ampacity rating. As a rule, the values in Table 11.4 give an approximation of what to expect.

The three major variables that affect the amount of line loss are length, wire thickness, and amperage load. Remember these three principles:

1. The resistance of a conductor increases directly with its length. The longer the run, the greater the line loss.
2. The resistance of a conductor decreases in proportion to its cross-sectional area. The larger the conductor, the less the line loss.
3. Voltage drop varies directly with the load. The larger the amperage load, the larger the line loss.

Table 11.4   Rule of Thumb Voltage Drop per 100 Feet for Various Cables at (Near) Full Capacity

Cable Size	Paper Load	Actual Load	Voltage Drop per 100-Ft Length
4/0	400 A	333 A	4 V
2/0	300 A	250 A	5 V
#2	200 A	160 A	6 V
#4	100 A	83 A	4 V
#6	50 A	42 A	4 V
#12	20 A	16 A	5 V

Note: These figures have been rounded up and down as necessary to make numbers that are easy to remember. Table C.4 gives exact voltage drop per 100 ft for various cables under various loads.

To overcome line loss, the generator operator might try to increase the voltage at the generator so that the voltage at the set is correct (115–120 V). Small adjustments in voltage can be made this way (up to 5%), but any larger adjustment destabilizes the frequency control of the generator. In addition, when increasing the voltage at the generator to overcome line loss, keep two things in mind. First, if equipment is being powered at the upstream end of the cable run (such as the producer's trailer at base camp), the upstream equipment will be over voltage (the producer's computer is toast). Second, voltage drop is proportional to amperage load. When the amperage load is reduced significantly, voltage must be turned down at the generator to prevent any remaining lights from being over voltage. If a lot of big lights are suddenly turned off, the voltage jumps up and the remaining load is over voltage (the sound cart is toast). I use these examples for dramatic emphasis. Clearly neither base camp nor sound should be powered on the same system as lighting.

In any case, to avoid these problems, it is necessary to minimize line loss by increasing the wire gauge.

Effects of Line Loss and Low Voltage

Line loss that results in low voltage at the set causes a number of serious problems for the operation of lights. As already discussed, light output falls off geometrically as the voltage decreases. The dramatic loss of output was shown in our earlier example.

Additionally, as the light intensity decreases, so does the Kelvin color temperature of the emitted light. As the intensity decreases, the color goes from white to yellow to orange.

A final reason why it is important to keep line loss within reasonable tolerances is that a loss of voltage also translates into a loss of power. From the equation $W = I^2R$, we see that the power loss in a given cable increases as the square of the amperage. If you double the ampere load on the cable, the voltage drop also doubles, but the power loss increases fourfold. The power source has to work harder, burning more fuel, or more kilovolt-amperes, because it uses power in heating the cables in addition to running the lights. The performance of the generator (its maximum effective load) is reduced.

Other Causes of Line Loss

Resistance, heat, and line loss also occur when a connection is weak or loose, when a cable is frayed, when a connector is only partially inserted, and when a connector or conductor is loaded beyond its capacity. Stacking cables closely together or within one multiconductor cable (Socapex) or making severe bends in the cable creates a hot spot in the cable and connector, which also increases resistance and line loss and further degrades the insulation.

Circular coils in a single-conductor, current-carrying cable create impedance, resulting in line loss and increased heating. Good set practices, such as checking for good contact between connectors, locking connectors tightly, taping connectors where necessary, avoiding circular coils, and replacing overheating parts, help rid you of the annoyance of inexplicable line loss and melted connectors.

Line Loss Calculations

Figure 11.21 shows equations we can use to make various kinds of voltage drop calculations. We can calculate the

- *Thickness* of cable needed to limit the voltage drop to a selected percentage.
- *Distance* a particular cable can carry a known amperage.
- Exact *voltage drop* for a particular cable at a stated amperage.
- Maximum *current* we can send through a given length of cable and not exceed a chosen voltage drop.

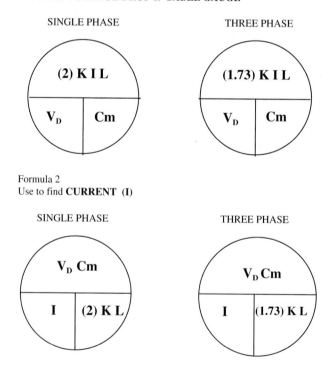

V_D = Voltage Drop
I = Current
Cm = Area of cable (see Table 11.3 to convert to AWG wire gage)
L = Length in feet (one way distance)
R = Resistance
K = 10.8 for copper at 25° C.

Formula 1
Use to find **VOLTAGE DROP** or **CABLE GAUGE**

SINGLE PHASE · THREE PHASE

(2) K I L · (1.73) K I L

V_D · Cm · V_D · Cm

Formula 2
Use to find **CURRENT (I)**

SINGLE PHASE · THREE PHASE

V_D Cm · V_D Cm

I · (2) K L · I · (1.73) K L

Figure 11.21 Voltage drop equations.

Formula 3
Use to find **CABLE LENGTH**

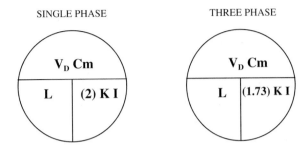

SINGLE PHASE   THREE PHASE

Formula 4
Use to find **RESISTANCE OF CABLE**

SINGLE AND THREE PHASE

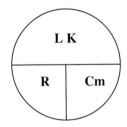

Figure 11.21 Continued.

To use these equations, we first have to define the variables we are using:

L L is the *length* of the wire in feet. This is the *one-way distance* from source to load. (Note that, in the equations, this number is multiplied by 2 to get the two-way distance the current has to flow to complete the circuit.)

V_D V_D is the voltage drop from source to load.

I I is the current carried by the cable.

1.73   When making calculations for 3-phase circuits we substitute 1.73 for 2 in the equations.

K K is the specific resistance of the material of which a conductor is composed. For copper cable, $K = 10.8$ at 25°C. Usually K and 2 are combined in the equations: $2K = 21.6$. For three-phase circuits, $1.73K = 18.34$.

Cm Cm is the cross-sectional area of a wire measured in circular mils (cmil):

$$1 \text{ mil} = 1/1000 \text{ in.}$$

$$\text{cmil} = (\text{diameter in mils})^2$$

Table 11.5 Cross-Sectional Area and Ampacity of Cables

AWG (wire gauge)	Cross-Sectional Area (cmil)	Actual Maximum Ampacity (90° cable)*
4 × 4/0	846,400	1620 A
3 × 4/0	634,800	1215 A
2 × 4/0	423,200	810 A
4/0	211,600	405 A
2/0	133,100	300 A
#2	66,360	190 A
#4	41,740	140 A
#6	26,240	105 A
#12	6530	20 A

*Noncontinuous loads, single-core cable, well ventilated.

These tend to be pretty big numbers. For example, 4/0 cable has a cross-sectional area of 211,600 cmil. Table 11.6 correlates cmil to wire gauge numbers for common gauges. Table C.2 (Appendix C) lists complete cable data.

Finding the Voltage Drop

The voltage drop equation (Figure 11.21, Formula 1) is used to find the voltage drop when the length, gauge, and current are known:

$$V_D = \frac{(2)KIL}{Cm}$$

$2K$ is 21.6
$1.73K$ is 18.34

so for single phase,

$$V_D = \frac{(21.6)IL}{Cm}$$

and for three phase,

$$V_D = \frac{(18.34)IL}{Cm}$$

For example, what would be the voltage drop if a 1k is plugged into 200 ft of stingers (#12 AWG)? We know a 1k draws 8.3 A and Table 11.5 tells us #12 cable has a cross-sectional area of 6530 cmil, so

$$V_D = \frac{(21.6)(8.3 \text{ A})(200 \text{ ft})}{6530 \text{ cmil}} = 5.5 \text{ V}$$

If our stinger were plugged in to a 120-V source we would be on the hairy edge of acceptable voltage after 200 ft. What would happen if we put on a 2k instead?

$$V_D = \frac{(21.6)(16.67 \text{ A})(200 \text{ ft})}{6530 \text{ cmil}} = 11 \text{ V}$$

We would end up with 109 V after 200 ft. Clearly, this is unacceptable. We need to use a larger cable if we have to run it out 200 ft. If we ran a 100-A Bates (#2 AWG) to the light, our V_D would decrease. Table 11.5 tells us Cm for #2 cable is 66,360 cmil, so

$$V_D = \frac{(21.6)(16.67 \text{ A})(200 \text{ ft})}{66,360 \text{ cmil}} = 1.08 \text{ V}$$

Finding the Cable Gauge

We can use the same equation (Figure 11.21, Formula 1) to find the thickness of cable necessary to keep within a given V_D for a given length and current:

	Single Phase	Three Phase
$Cm = \dfrac{2KIL}{V_D}$	$Cm = \dfrac{(21.6)IL}{V_D}$	$Cm = \dfrac{(18.34)IL}{V_D}$

For example, we are running four 10ks per leg on a 4/0 run 400 ft from the can. If we allow no more than a 5-V drop, how many pieces of 4/0 do we need per leg?

$$Cm = \frac{(21.6)IL}{V_D} = \frac{(21.6)(4)(83.33 \text{ A})(400 \text{ ft})}{5 \text{ V}} = 575,769.6 \text{ cmil}$$

Each piece of 4/0 is 211,600 cm. To find the number of pieces we need, we divide 575,769 cmil by 211,600 cmil and round up (or just check Table 11.5):

$$\frac{575,769 \text{ cmil}}{211,600 \text{ cmil}} = 2.7 \text{ pieces of 4/0 per leg}$$

To go 400 ft, we need three pieces of 4/0 per leg.

Finding the Current

To calculate the maximum amount of current you can pull through a given length and gauge of cable and remain within a specified voltage drop, use the equation in Figure 11.21, Formula 2:

	Single Phase	Three Phase
$I = \dfrac{V_D Cm}{(2)KL}$	$I = \dfrac{V_D Cm}{(21.6)L}$	$I = \dfrac{V_D Cm}{(18.34)L}$

For example, how many amps can we draw per leg on a piece of 5-wire banded (#2 AWG), 250 ft long, if we allow no more than 6-V drop. The circuit is three phase:

$$I = \frac{V_D Cm}{(18.34)L}$$

$$I = \frac{(6 \text{ V})(66{,}360 \text{ cmil})}{(18.34)(250 \text{ ft})} = 86.8 \text{ A per leg}$$

We can put only 86.8 A per leg. That's just enough for a 10k (83.3 A) on each leg.

Finding the Length

Finally, we can calculate the maximum length a given cable may be expected to carry a given amperage and remain within a specified voltage drop using the equation in Figure 11.21, Formula 3:

	Single Phase	Three Phase
$L = \dfrac{V_D Cm}{(2)KI}$	$L = \dfrac{V_D Cm}{(21.6)I}$	$L = \dfrac{V_D Cm}{(18.34)KI}$

For example, a piece of #4 cable (head cable for 10ks) is rated for a maximum amperage of 140 A. What is the longest length we can go with a 10k load and a 3.6-V drop?

$$L = \frac{V_D Cm}{(21.6)I}$$

$$L = \frac{(3.6 \text{ V})(41{,}740 \text{ cmil})}{(21.6)(83.3 \text{ A})} = 83.5 \text{ ft}$$

Use a 50-ft extension and a 25-ft head feeder and you maxed out your voltage drop.

The final equation (Figure 11.21, Formula 4) allows you to calculate the actual resistance of a cable or the area of a cable given its resistance in ohms.

The figures we've been coming up with may seem very surprising. We routinely load cables to near their maximum ampacity and run them out a couple hundred feet. However, the result is (1) less output from the lights; (2) warm color temperature; (3) hot cables and connectors, which leads to trouble over time; and (4) loss of capacity from the power source. To avoid these problems, when long lengths of cable are needed, increase the cable size a size or two and run the same load. Instead of running 200 ft of stingers, use a 100-A Bates. Instead of running a city block with banded, put in a 4/0 run. When long lengths of cable are involved you can no longer think in terms of using a cable's full capacity.

Using U.K. Voltage Drop Tables

In the United Kingdom, the method of determining voltage drop is as follows. The IEE and cable manufacturers produce tables that give the voltage drop in millivolts per ampere per meter. Different figures are given to take account of single- and

Table 11.6   U.K. Voltage Drop for Various Cables

Typical Current Rating	Conductor Size	Type	Millivolt Drop per Meter per Amp	Number of Current Carrying Wires in Insulation
16 A	2.5 mm^2	Copper	19	2
45 A	6.0 mm^2	Copper	7.7	2
125 A	25 mm^2	Copper	1.7	2
180 A	120 mm^2	Copper	0.46	2
400 A	185 mm^2	Copper	0.27	1 (short runs)
400 A	240 mm^2	Aluminum	0.45	1 (long runs)

three-phase systems, together with allowances for "impedance" loss. The tables give the total voltage drop in all the circuit conductors for each meter of cable route. The values given assume the maximum operating temperature of the cables. In most practical cases, the voltage drop is less, because the cables probably are not at full capacity and the conductor temperatures are not at maximum rating; therefore the resistance is lower than that given in Table 11.6.

For example, two 120-mm^2 feeder cables, rated for 85°C, used as a phase and neutral are taken 200 meters from a generator to a distribution point. The voltage drop for this cable is given as 0.46 mV/A/m. If we assume the cables are loaded to 180 A, the voltage drop is

$$0.46 \times 180 \times 200 = 16{,}560 \text{ mV} = 16.56 \text{ V}$$

British regulations require that the voltage drop should be no greater than 4% in most cases, which amounts to 9.6 V on a 240-V system. As can be seen, the preceding value is not acceptable; therefore, either a larger conductor size or parallel feeders have to be used.

Power Problems from Electronic Loads

Much of today's lighting technology relies on electronics such as DC rectifiers, silicone-controlled rectifiers (SCRs), capacitors, and high-frequency switching power supplies (IGBTs). These kinds of load can have undesirable effects on the current waveform, revealing themselves in the form of overheating or failing equipment, efficiency losses, circuit breaker trips, excessive current on the neutral wire, interference and instability with generators, noisy or overheating transformers and service equipment, and even loosened electrical connections. In the following sections, we discuss the power factor and current harmonics and look at their effects. Your awareness of these effects will help you to build systems that avoid or mitigate problems and show you how to test for problems.

Like a landslide, technology continues moving, toward more and more dependence on electronic devices that have such effects. Office buildings full of fluorescent lights and computer equipment experience the same problems because the power supply of every PC, printer, copy machine, and electronic ballast in the building creates harmonics that build on one another. These problems will continue to escalate until they reach a point where technology and regulation are forced to address the situation and provide new tools for dealing with it. Much discussion and research is underway already. In the meantime, here's what to look for. We start with the milder problem of power factor, then look at the bigger problem of harmonics.

Power Factor

When we calculate cable loads and generator loads we use the equation

$$\frac{\text{Watts}}{\text{Volts}} = \text{Amps}$$

However, with some AC equipment, this statement is not true, *it underestimates the actual current.* When a piece of equipment has inductive properties (magnetic ballasts) or capacitive properties (electronic ballasts and electronic dimmers), the *power factor* must be considered to make proper load calculations.

Inductive Reactance

An incandescent light or heating element has no inductive or capacitive properties. It merely creates resistance in a circuit. A purely resistive circuit is said to have a power factor of 1.0 (also called a *unity* power factor or *100%* power factor) and the equation watts/volts = amps is correct. When an AC load involves coils, such as those in a transformer, motor, or magnetic ballast, it creates resistance *and inductance.* As the current increases and decreases (120 times per second) in a coil carrying AC current, a magnetic field expands outward from the wire's center then collapses back inward again. As the current increases, the circuit stores energy in the magnetic field; then as the current decreases, the circuit gets the energy back. No actual work is accomplished, energy just keeps circulating back and forth between the coil and the power source. When the lines of flux of the magnetic field grow and collapse they self-induce a voltage in the coil; this is called the *counterelectromotive force* (counter EMF). The counter EMF has the opposite polarity of the applied voltage. As a result, the applied voltage must overcome the induced voltage before current can flow through the circuit. This opposition to the flow of current is called *inductive reactance.*

The effect of reactance is clear when you look at the waveforms of voltage and current (Figure 11.22). The increase and decrease of current normally corresponds with the increase and decrease of voltage, 60 times a second (Figure 11.22A). Inductive reactance causes current to *lag* behind the voltage (Figure 11.22B). The degree to which the two waveforms are put *out of phase* depends on the relative amount of resistance and inductance offered by the coil. The more they are out of phase, the lower (poorer) the power factor.

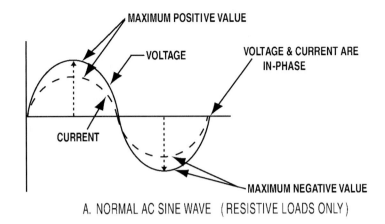

A. NORMAL AC SINE WAVE (RESISTIVE LOADS ONLY)

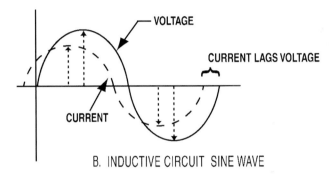

B. INDUCTIVE CIRCUIT SINE WAVE

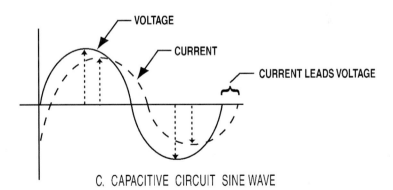

C. CAPACITIVE CIRCUIT SINE WAVE

Figure 11.22 The effect of resistance, inductance, and capacitance on the voltage/current phase relationship.

Capacitive Reactance

Similarly, if the circuit has a capacitive component (electronic ballasts), *capacitive reactance* produces a power factor of less than 100%. Capacitive reactance acts on the waveform in a way opposite to inductive reactance. It causes current to *lead* voltage (Figure 11.22C). As mentioned in Chapter 4, some HMI ballasts have power factor correction circuits, which help restore the efficiency of a ballast. In fact, because a capacitor has the effect on the current waveform opposite to an inductor, capacitors are used to help correct the effects of inductive reactance. Conversely, inductors help counter capacitive reactance, which aids in returning a waveform that is out of phase to normal.

What Is the Power Factor?

The power factor (pf) is the ratio of *true power* to *apparent power*:

$$\frac{\text{True Power (W)}}{\text{Apparent Power (VA)}} = \text{Power Factor}$$

If you measure the current and the voltage, then multiply the two together, you get what's called the *apparent power* (expressed in volt-amperes).[3] This is the amount of power traveling back and forth in the cables.

For single-phase circuits, volt-amperes = volts × amps:

$$E_{RMS} \times I_{RMS} = \text{VA (apparent power in volt-amperes)}$$

For three-phase circuits, volt-amperes = 1.732 × volts × amps (1.732 is the square root of 3).

True power is the actual amount of energy being converted into real work by the load. You can read true power using a *wattmeter* (see the section on Meters for Measuring Electricity later in this chapter).

$$E_{RMS} \times I_{RMS} \times pf = \text{True Power (Watts)}$$

As one electrician put it, if apparent power is a glass of beer, power factor is the foam that prevents you from filling it up all the way. The size of the feeder cables and the rating of the power source must be sufficient to supply the *apparent power* (beer plus foam), even though only the beer (true power) counts as far as how much actual drinking is possible. Load calculations must therefore include the power factor.

Power Factor Calculations

The power factor of a ballast or motor is sometimes, but not always, written on the equipment. To calculate the actual amperage needed to power equipment when the power factor is known, use the following equation:

$$\frac{\text{True Power}}{E \times pf} = I$$

where true power is the rated wattage of the equipment, E is the voltage, pf is the power factor, and I the current.

---

[3]These measurements must be made with a true RMS meter, not a common multimeter.

To illustrate, suppose we are powering four 6k HMIs. If we made the mistake of discounting the power factor, we would incorrectly calculate the amperage as follows:

$$\frac{4 \times 6000 \text{ W}}{120 \text{ V}} = 200 \text{ A}$$

If the units have a power factor of 0.80, the actual amperage required is

$$\frac{4 \times 6000 \text{ W}}{120 \text{ V} \times 0.80} = 250 \text{ A}$$

From this we see the importance of taking the power factor into account. The amperage is significantly higher than thought, 50 A higher.

Excessive Current on the Neutral Wire

With incandescent lights, if we draw equal current from the phase leads, there will be no return current on the neutral; the current cancels out between legs. In some situations, this allows the neutral wire of the feeder cables to be smaller than the phase wires.

When an inductive or capacitive load causes current and voltage to be out of phase, the phase currents no longer cancel when they return on the neutral. When using magnetic ballasts, it is normal to have as much as 20–25% of the total amperage return on the neutral when the legs are evenly loaded. For this reason, when using many magnetic ballasts, it is wise to provide a neutral that is at least as large as the phase wires.

Electronic dimmers and electronic ballasts inject additional chaos into the waveform. In addition to pulling the voltage and current out of phase, the electronics create harmonic currents that can stack on top of one another, creating very high currents returning to the power source on the neutral wire. When using large numbers of electronic dimmers and electronic ballasts (which have no power factor correction), about 80% of the current does not cancel out between legs. The neutral wire of the feeder cable must be substantial enough to carry the *sum of the currents of the phase legs times 80%*.

It is common practice to double or triple the neutral wire when powering large numbers of electronic dimmers or electronic ballasts. By the same token, you can overload the neutral wiring of the transformer or generator if it is not sized to handle return current, especially with 208Y/120 circuits. When return current could be a problem, it is wise to oversize the generator.

Meters for Measuring Electricity

Set electricians should carry some kind of voltage tester with them at all times (Figure 11.23). An inexpensive voltmeter (Figure 11.23C) is quite adequate because, with constant use, meters run the risk of being damaged. Meters and testers come in many shapes and sizes. A simple voltage tester (Figure 11.23H), when connected across a circuit, indicates with an LED display whether a circuit is 110 or 220 V.

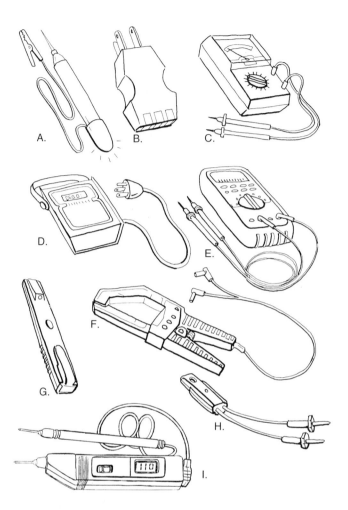

Figure 11.23 Meters for measuring electricity. (A) Continuity tester, (B) circuit tester, (C) voltmeter, (D) line frequency tester, (E) digital multimeter, (F) amp probe attachment for a multimeter, (G) voltage sensor, and (H) voltage tester. (I) A common digital multimeter can read continuity, voltage AC and DC, and resistance.

Most electricians invest in a small digital multimeter (Figure 11.23I), such as the Beckman DM73 or an equivalent, that measures AC and DC voltage, detects continuity, and measures resistance. These are usually "average-responding" or "RMS-calibrated" meters. This type of meter assumes the waveform being measured is close to a pure sine wave and works fine for most lighting loads; however, they read 30–70% low when harmonic distortion is present. A *true RMS* voltage meter and amperage meter are necessary to make accurate readings when using nonlinear loads such as electronic dimmers and ballasts. A true RMS meter's analytical circuits can measure and calculate the actual heat caused by a current regardless of the wave shape.

More expensive digital multipurpose meters, such as those manufactured by Fluke (Figure 13.23E), incorporate hertz and amp features in addition to voltage, resistance, and continuity. This type of meter may also be true RMS. These features come in handy when troubleshooting or ringing out a new rig.

Circuit Testers

A circuit tester (Figure 11.23B) is used to test Edison outlets. It tells (1) if the circuit is hot, (2) if the polarity is correct, and (3) if the grounding wire is present.

A voltage sensor (Figure 11.23G) is a handy device that senses the magnetic field of electricity. Although it gives no quantitative reading of amperage, the sensor is useful for checking if a wire is hot. Put the sensor near the wire, and press the button. If it beeps or lights up, then the wire *may be* hot. I say *may be* because I have gotten positive readings from wires that were connected to nothing at both ends. These testers are prone to giving false positive readings.

Measuring Voltage

Here are some general precautions when you are setting up to take readings:

- Voltage readings require that you touch the two meter probes to two live exposed terminals in the circuit. When probing exposed terminals, be extremely careful as you position the probes not to hold a probe between two terminals and not to put your fingers on or close to the terminals. Voltage can arc between terminals, which can cause a kind of electrical explosion.
- Be sure your hands, shoes, and work areas are dry.
- Set the meter on a stable surface or hook it over a stable vertical surface. If one of the probes is attached to the meter, place your body so you will not have to strain, twist, or get off balance to see the readout.
- Avoid taking readings in extremely humid or damp conditions.
- Be sure the meter leads are in good condition with no exposed wire and that they are connected to the proper meter jack.

Select the type of service being read (AC or DC) and select the voltage range (if applicable). If metering unknown values, start with the highest range, then change to a more accurate setting once you know the correct range. Touch the probes to the terminals of the circuit to be measured or insert the probe into an Edison outlet. When accuracy is critical, average several readings and eliminate stray readings. Hold the probes to the terminal long enough for the meter to settle at a constant reading. Digital meters often show ghost voltages before they are connected to the circuit because the test leads act like antennas picking up electromagnetic interference. Ghost voltages typically change rapidly from one number to another. Let the reading settle.

The nicer digital multimeters have two displays that simultaneously display voltage. A large digital readout gives you the number of volts. This display is updated four times a second. A smaller bar graph under the number gives an almost instantaneous readout of voltage (30 times a second). The bar graph is helpful in spotting momentary voltage drops.

When measuring a DC circuit, if the needle deflects to the left off the bottom of the scale (analog) or if the meter shows a minus sign (digital), the polarity is reversed. Check that your probes are properly connected; reverse them to get a measurement.

Measuring Frequency (Hertz Rate)

A frequency meter is used to measure the frequency of an AC circuit in cycles per second (Hz). There are several types of frequency meters. The most popular frequency meters simply plug into an Edison outlet (Figure 11.23D). In addition, some clamp-on ammeters have a hertz-reading function.

Another type of frequency meter, the Cinecheck meter, does not take the reading from the power lines at all but from the light emitted by an HMI fixture (magnetic ballast only). Simply hold the meter up to the light and read the frequency.

Measuring Amperage

An "amp probe," or clamp-on ammeter (Figure 11.23F), is used to determine the amperage traveling through a single conductor. Amp probes are generally AC only; however, some more sophisticated meters can measure DC amperage as well. The amp probe has two curved fingers that close around an insulated single conductor cable. The probe measures the strength of the magnetic field created around the cable by the current running through it. The strength of the field is proportional to the amperage running through the wire. The amp probe gives a reading in amperes.

When reading nonlinear loads (electronic dimmers and ballasts), use an AC-only true RMS ammeter. The AC/DC types do not give accurate readings when harmonics are present.

When using the clamp-on pick-up with a Fluke multimeter, the meter reads amps on a millivolt scale. One millivolt equals one amp.

Testing Continuity and Testing for Shorts

Unlike all the other testing equipment discussed in this section, a continuity tester (Figures 11.23A and I) is only used when power is *not* connected to the circuit. The tester is used to check for a break in the line. If the line is continuous, the tester will beep or light up.

A continuity tester is handy to check if a bulb or fuse has blown or if there is a broken wire somewhere in a cable. If the filament of the bulb is intact, the tester will show continuity across the terminals of the bulb.

If you are checking continuity on a piece of cable, it is often easier to do it from one end, rather than having to touch one probe to each end. If the cable has bare wire ends you can do this by simply twisting the wires together on one end, and then reading continuity (up and back) from the other end (Figure 11.24A). If the

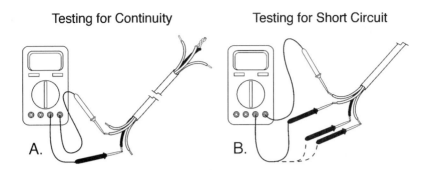

Figure 11.24 An easy way to check continuity in a cable is to twist the wires together at one end and read continuity at the other end, as shown. If you get a beep, both wires are good. (Use a jumper wire or make a testing plug to short out the conductors when the cable has connectors attached.)

You can also use the continuity meter to check for shorts between wires by touching a meter probe to one wire, then checking each of the other wires. If you get a beep, there is a short between those two wires. You can use these techniques to check for shorts and breaks in the line throughout a distribution system. Just be sure the system is not connected to a power source and the lights are switched off.

cable has connectors on the ends, make a testing aid—a male connector with a jumper wire connecting all the contacts. Now, it is a simple process to plug the connector onto the female end of the cable and read continuity between each of the male contacts at the other end. (Note: You might want to label your device with a warning like: Testing Aid. WARNING DEAD SHORT.)

If you suspect there may be a short in a piece of cable or equipment, you can use a continuity tester to check for continuity between wires (Figure 11.24B). If you find continuity, there is a short. Check each combination of wires (neutral and phase, neutral and ground, phase and ground). You can check a whole cable run this way. If you find a short, just be sure you haven't overlooked a path for continuity before you jump to conclusions (remove the bulb before testing for shorts on a light fixture).

Wattmeter or Power Meter

A wattmeter or power meter is a clamp-on device like an ammeter, with probes like a voltmeter. It reads true power (watts) in a circuit. This meter can account for the phase difference between current and voltage when there is inductive or capacitive reactance in the circuit. Some power meters require you to turn off power to the circuit when connecting and disconnecting the meter, then turn on power to take readings. A wattmeter also reads amperage and voltage separately, which together give you the apparent power (see the section on the Power Factor). You can determine the efficiency of power use by dividing true power by apparent power (which gives you the power factor), and multiply by 100 to get efficiency as a percentage.

Electrical Shocks and Muscle Freeze

In the event that an electrician comes into contact with a hot wire and completes a circuit, the biggest danger is that his muscles will be frozen by the current and he will not be able to pull away from it. If this happens, the most important thing is to *turn off the electricity* and get him away from the current as quickly as possible. The length of time a person is shocked determines the severity of injury and the likelihood of cardiac arrest and death. *Do not touch someone who is being electrocuted.* Unless you can move faster than 186,000 miles per second (the speed of light), you will become part of the circuit. *Turn off the power first.* If you cannot turn off the power quickly, pushing the victim with a wooden plank or an apple box is a safe way to disengage him from the circuit. A running, jumping body block can work as long as you are in the air when you hit the victim and do not complete a circuit to ground.

Once the victim is away from the circuit, check for pulse and breathing. Begin CPR immediately if there is no pulse. Call for professional medical assistance. It is very important that a person who has received a shock go to the hospital, have his blood checked, and be looked over by a doctor. With DC, the typical signs of electrocution are burns—blackened fingernails or toenails. There may be no exterior signs of injury after a shock, yet even without any outward signs, electrocution can cause serious injury to internal muscles and organs. It has happened that a person walked away from a shock accident, only to have a heart attack 2 days later when the injured muscle seized up. A doctor can check the electrolytes in the patient's blood and prescribe muscle relaxants and other therapy if he sees a potential risk. The electrician who has been shocked may not even want to go to the hospital. He may feel embarrassed and want to play down the accident. He may feel fine and not want to be taken out of work. Keep in mind, he is probably not thinking very straight. Always report any kind of injury. It could seem like nothing at the time, yet turn out to be something serious. If you report it to the medic, you have started a paper trail, which will be necessary later to establish that the injury was work related.

In addition to the duration of contact, the severity of damage from a shock is determined by the number of vital organs traversed, especially the heart. The most lethal path electricity can take is into one arm and out of the other. As electricity travels across the chest and through the heart and lungs, it can very easily cause ventricular fibrillation or stop the heart entirely. For this reason, when making a tie-in or dealing with hot, exposed wires, many electricians handle the wire with one hand and put the other hand in their pocket or behind their back.

It is a common misconception that voltage is what kills a shock victim. In truth, high voltage can be dangerous because it has a tendency to arc, but the amperage is what damages the muscles and heart.

The amperage of a shock is a combination of the current in the circuit and the resistance present (Table 11.7). The resistance of dry skin, for example, is about 100,000 Ω. This resistance is enough for brief contact with a 100-V circuit to allow about 1 milliampere (mA), or 0.001 A, to flow through the body, which is enough

Table 11.7 Effect of Resistance on Amperage of Shock

Condition	Resistance	Milliamps
Dry skin @ 100 V	100,000	1
Wet skin @ 100 V	1000	100
Through an open cut @ 100 V	500	200
Dry skin @ 10,000 V	100,000	100

Table 11.8 Effect of Ampacity on Shock Victims

Current	Effect on Body
1 mA or less	No sensation (not felt).
More than 5 mA	Painful shock.
More than 10 mA	Muscle contractions, could "freeze" some people to the electrical circuit.
More than 15 mA	Muscle contractions, can cause most people to become frozen to the electrical circuit.
More than 30 mA	Breathing difficult, could cause unconsciousness.
50–100 mA	Ventricular fibrillation of the heart possible.
100–200 mA	Ventricular fibrillation of the heart certain. Death is possible.
Over 200 mA	Severe burns and muscular contractions, the heart is more apt to stop beating than to fibrillate. Death is likely.
1 ampere or more	Permanent damage to body tissues, cardiac arrest, severe burns, and probable death.

to bite but not enough to cause damage (Table 11.8). In contrast, the resistance of wet skin is about 1000 Ω, which allows about 100 mA to flow through the body. This is enough to cause ventricular fibrillation, impede breathing, and cause unconsciousness and possibly death. Wearing thick rubber electrician's gloves is recommended any time you are exposed to live lugs and cables.

AC current can be more deadly than DC current for several reasons. Although both types of current have the effects listed in Table 11.9, AC can freeze a body to a conductor with one-fifth the current of DC. Alternating current can more easily cause fibrillation and cardiac arrest because the 60-Hz polarity cycle is a harmonic of the rhythm of the heart and AC current has a peak voltage of 170 V, while DC is a constant 120 V. However, this is not to say that DC power cannot hurt or kill a person.

Every electrician must have a healthy respect for electricity if he or she aims to have a long and successful career. People are killed every year by accidental electrocution—the majority by faulty equipment that has been poorly maintained, but some by their own ignorance or foolishness. Pressure from the powers that be, long hours, and physical exhaustion can cloud good judgment and clear thinking.

Be aware of your physical and mental state. As a professional, your judgment of a situation has weight; don't discount it. No matter how frantic things get, when it comes to dealing with exposed live conductors, remember to slow down, think about what you are doing, and don't let anyone distract you. No situation in filmmaking is worth the risk to your life and health.

Electrical, Building, and Fire Codes

A number of bodies impose regulations on the operations of the electrical crew: the National Electrical Code, local city codes (Department of Building and Safety), studio safety regulations, OSHA, and the local fire department.

The National Electrical Code

The National Electrical Code is a book of regulations and requirements developed in the interest of protecting life and property. The code is sponsored and published by the National Fire Protection Association (NFPA). The code itself is purely advisory as far as the NFPA is concerned. However, individual states can adopt the code as law. When it adopts the code, the state, or any city or municipality in it, may add to the rules of the code, but none may relax its requirements.

You can buy a copy of the current code at any technical bookstore; be warned, however, that the code is written in NEC-speak. It can be frustratingly confusing to read if you do not understand the unexplained context behind each directive. This section attempts to explain the rules of the code that are important to film lighting technicians. I do not address every rule.

The code covers every conceivable use of electricity, from basic wiring methods and materials to pipe organs and "hydromassage bathtubs." The two sections of the code that deal directly with film and television production are Article 520, "Theaters and Similar Locations," and Article 530, "Motion Picture and Television Studios and Similar Locations." However, many other sections of the code also apply, most importantly grounding (Article 250), cable types (Article 400), and overcurrent protection (Article 240).

Article 520 covers live theaters, concert halls, movie theaters, and motion picture and television studios that incorporate assembly areas such as those used for game shows, situation comedies, variety shows, or concerts. This article covers only those areas of an auditorium occupied by or within 10 ft of a live audience. Article 530 covers all the areas of stages that have no audience. Codebooks 1996 and later include a separate section, Article 6 (formerly Article 525), to cover carnivals, circuses, fairs, and similar events.

Outdoor Use

The code provides definitions for various types of equipment used in motion picture and television production (530.2). Our equipment is defined by the code as portable equipment. Article 530.6 allows that portable lighting and distribution equipment "shall be permitted for temporary use outdoors provided the equipment is supervised by qualified personnel while energized, and barriered from the general public."

Cords and Cables

For areas covered by Article 520 (audience areas), cords must be designated for "extra hard usage." The following types are permitted: S, SO, SEO, SOO, ST, STO, STOO, G, EISL, and W (NEC 400.4, note 5, and Table 400.4). No junior service (e.g., SJO) cable may be used, except in breakout assemblies, such as from a Socapex dimmer line (1996 NEC 520.68 Exception No. 4).

In areas covered by Article 530, cords may not be fastened by uninsulated staples or nails. For circuits protected by a 20-A breaker or smaller, splices and taps may be made in the cord as long as "approved devices," such as wire nuts, are used (NEC 530.12).

Switches

Each lighting fixture or other electrical device must have an externally operable on/off switch within 6 ft of the fixture. This is in addition to any remote switches that may be connected (NEC 530.13). Keep this in mind when building or adapting your own lights. A switch is necessary for safety.

UL Listing

Underwriters Laboratories and similar agencies test electrical parts such as plugs, sockets, switches, and wire as well as lights, appliances, and other electrical equipment. If a product is approved, it is said to be *listed* and marked UL. Common plugs and sockets that are unlisted are usually of poor quality and should be avoided. The specialized equipment used in filmmaking may be unlisted simply because the manufacturer must pay to put the product up for testing.

All electrical equipment and hardware used on a set must be either listed or specially approved by the local authority that has jurisdiction. Los Angeles has the luxury of having its own testing laboratory to get city approval for unlisted products.

Guarding Live Parts

It can be stated generally that all live parts must be enclosed or guarded to prevent people and conductive material from making accidental contact. This is true for all types of equipment, connectors, cables, bull switches, panelboards, splicing boxes, dimmers, rheostats, lights, and so on (NEC 530.15). The NEC defines *guarded* as "covered, shielded, fenced, enclosed, or otherwise protected by means of suitable covers, castings, barriers, rails, screens, mats or platforms to remove the likelihood of approach or accidental contact by persons or objects to a point of danger" (NEC 100). The intent of this rule is to protect unsuspecting laypeople.

Overcurrent Protection

Fuses and breakers interrupt only the hot legs. The neutral grounded lead should not be interrupted by circuit protection.

Location Automatic overcurrent protection (circuit breakers or fuses) must be provided within 25 ft of every reduction of wire size (NEC 240.21 Exception No. 3). For example, when splitting from 2/0 cable to 100-A whips, there must be breakers in the junction box or along the wires within 25 ft of the split. To meet this requirement, soft-Y connectors (e.g., 100-A Bates to two 60-A Bates) are supposed to have in-line fuses.

The 400% Rule: Oversizing DC Circuit Protection Circuit protection may be up to 400% of the amperage rating of the cable (NEC 530.18). For example, this allows you to make a 4/0 run from a 1600-A DC service panel and run up to the cable's rated capacity (400 A/leg), without the need for further circuit protection. You can run a 5k directly off a deuce board (which has a 200-A fuse; NEC 530.18c). Note: This allows you to oversize the circuit protection. It does not allow you to load the cables for more than their rating.

"Plugging Boxes" and Distro Boxes

Plugging boxes (e.g., four-hole boxes) are not permitted to be used for AC power. Any wire smaller than no. 8 AWG connected to a paddle or stage box must have appropriate fuses in the connector.

An AC power distribution box (AC plugging box, scatter box) is an AC distribution center containing grounded, polarized receptacles and may contain over-current protection.

Feeder Cables

You may not load cables beyond their rated capacity. Amperage capacity tables appear in Articles 310 and 400 of the code; these tables are reprinted in Appendix C. All neutral and ground cables must be identified by color coding, either by the color of the single conductor connector or by being wrapped with 6 in. of colored tape or sheath. White and neutral gray are reserved for grounded neutral leads only. Green is for grounding leads (sometimes green with yellow stripes). In addition, if more than one electrical system is used in the same area, the hot wires must also be color coded at each end (e.g., a 480-V air conditioner in use at the same time as a 120-V system). Yellow is not a great color to use around sodium lights because it looks the same as white.

Connectors

Branch Circuit Connectors The code defines a *branch circuit* as the conductors between the last overcurrent protection device and the load. In other words, a branch circuit is the portion of the circuit between the last set of breakers or fuses and the lights. The code requires that multipole connectors used in AC branch circuits be polarized and the grounding wire make contact first and disconnect last. A standard U-ground plug or Bates connector is an example of such a connector. Also required is that the amperage rating of plugs and receptacles not be less than that of the overcurrent protection. Plugs and receptacles, such as Edison twist-lock and Bates, can be used interchangeably for either AC or DC as long as they are listed for AC/DC use and marked to identify the system to which they are connected (Article 530.21[b]).

Feeder Connectors   Connecting *single-pole cables* to a hot system must be done in the following order: (1) ground (where used), (2) neutral, and (3) hot conductors. Disconnect from a hot system in the reverse order.

The code lists three permissible ways to ensure that ground is made first and broken last:

1. The connection makes it impossible to connect or disconnect wires when the source is hot.
2. A mechanical device makes it possible to connect the wires in only the proper order. The same device ensures that disconnection is made in the reverse order. Abbott panels are an example of a connector that works this way.
3. A caution notice adjacent to the line connectors indicates the order in which the connection should be made.

Starting in 1996 the code required that single-pole connectors be listed (UL) or approved by local authority. It also requires that, when used with AC, the male and female connectors lock together with a mechanical locking device (Article 530.22).

Single-conductor cables must be attached to the connectors with *solder, crimping*, or a *setscrew*. Grounding connections are not allowed to depend solely on a solder contact because, if a fault exists, the heated solder will melt. Solder connections are allowed with other legs because, if the connection breaks, the worst that can happen will be loss of power. However, if the grounding connection breaks, electrocution and fire are possible.

Grounding

NEC Article 250 covers grounding in depth. The important points for set lighting applications follow.

All equipment supplied with AC must be grounded back to the source of power (the can or generator) by means of a continuously connected equipment-grounding conductor. When using house power, use the grounding bus of the particular can from which the power is being drawn; you may not ground to a different can.

The grounding wire may be smaller than the current-carrying wires in accordance with Table 250.122 of the code, which is reprinted in Table C.3 of this book.

Alternating Current Generators   When using an AC generator, the non–current-carrying metal parts of the lighting equipment and grounding receptacles shall be bonded to the generator frame (via the grounding wires), and the neutral must be bonded to the generator frame (NEC Article 250.34[c]). If the generator is mounted on a vehicle, the frame of the generator must be bonded to the frame of the vehicle. (Vehicle-mounted generators are bonded together on installation; this is not something the electrician has to do.)

Direct Current Equipment   DC equipment operating at not more than 150 V does not have to be grounded, although grounding is not prohibited.

A DC HMI ballast provides AC to the head. Therefore, the head must be grounded to the ballast so that, if there is a fault in the head, it will trip the breaker in the ballast. A DC ballast need not be grounded to the power source. When using several DC ballasts within 10 ft of one another, the grounds should be connected together.

Connections for grounding must use an approved ground fitting or ground rod clamp. Tie-in clips or spring clamps are not permitted.

Fire and Building Codes

Fire codes provide that there must be fire lanes leading to exits. There must be a space of 4 ft between the walls of the sound stage and sets or equipment. These fire lanes must be kept completely clear of equipment. Outside doors surrounding the area of filming must be unlocked and unobstructed.

Fire codes are different in every city, and they change regularly. It is up to the best boy electric to keep up to date on the code having jurisdiction over the city in which filming is taking place. The best boy electric checks in with the fire marshal on the first day of filming to establish rapport, inform the fire marshal of his plan, and to see if any plans raise problems or require special action.

OSHA and the Industry-Wide Labor-Management Safety Committee

The Industry-Wide Labor-Management Safety Committee is sponsored by the Contract Services Department of the Association of Motion Picture and Television Producers. It is an advisory body made up of studio safety professionals, labor union business managers, and producers to publish safety bulletins in response to accidents and common safety complaints. There are safety bulletins on a full range of topics, from firearms to helicopters to sky diving. The ones that apply to set lighting directly are Bulletin #22, "Guidelines for the Use of Elevating Work Platforms . . . ," and Bulletin #23, "Guidelines for Working with Lighting Systems and Other Electrical Equipment." Most rules are based on electrical code or commonsense safety, and the concepts they address are expressed throughout this book.

Your union and the Producers Association can provide any safety bulletins. In situations where a producer asks a crew member to do something unsafe, refer them to bulletins as well as OSHA regulations. Remind the producer of the personal liability he or she is creating. Disregarding manufacturers' safety requirements or OSHA rules may void a producer's insurance. If OSHA finds grievous safety problems they can shut down the production until the safety concerns are dealt with. Similarly, most studio lots have their own safety departments with total jurisdiction over the productions filming on their property. They will take anonymous tips.

CHAPTER 12

Distribution Equipment, Rigging, and Dimmers

The components of a distribution system are as follows:

Power source   The power may come from one or more of a number of sources: (1) a mobile generator; (2) designated studio circuits, which are powered by a municipal transformer or turbine generators; (3) a tie-in to the service panel on location; (4) a location power drop; (5) a battery or battery pack; or (6) available wall circuits. Power sources are covered in Chapter 13.

Main disconnect   The main disconnect, a bull switch with current-limiting fuses or circuit breakers, provides a main switch to shut down all power at the end of the day or in an emergency. It also provides main circuit protection for the power source. In the case of a generator, the main breaker switch or fuse is part of the generator.

Main feeder cable   This cable, usually 4/0 or 2/0 copper cable, carries power from the power source to the set. The four most common types of feeder cable connectors are lug, Mole-pin, Cam-Lok, and Abbott connectors.

Splicing box   A spider box, or junction box, functions as a cable splicing point to connect one length of cable to the next. It also provides a means of splicing a trunk line off the main line.

Main distribution boxes   Feeder cables terminate into distribution boxes, which provide a point to subdivide current into a number of smaller-gauge subfeeder cables. Any time you reduce cable size, the NEC requires that there be proper overcurrent protection within 25 ft of the change (NEC Article 240-21). Distribution boxes provide circuit protection and multiple outlets (usually 100 A each) for subfeeders and lights. A portable remote switchboard provides one or more main switches, usually 200 A per leg.

Dimmers   Dimmer packs are powered from the main feeder and used to control some or all of the lights.

Subfeeders Smaller-gauge feeder cable delivers power from the distribution box to outlet boxes or to subsequent distribution boxes. Banded 2 AWG cable is typical. (Banded cable is simply four or five single-conductor cables held together in a bundle by bands of tape at regular intervals.)

Lamp and extension connectors and cables Extension cables usually having 100-A or 60-A Bates connectors or some other type of connector run from the distribution boxes to the larger lights (2,500–10,000W).

Edison outlet boxes Gang boxes, quad boxes, or lunch boxes provide 20-A outlets for plugging in the smaller lights. Typically location equipment uses Edison outlets. On-stage, you sometimes run into lamps and outlet boxes fitted with 20-A twist-lock or 20-A Bates outlets. Outlet boxes plug into 100- or 60-A distribution boxes or extension cables.

DC Three-Wire System

The original electrical system of Hollywood movie making is still used today. It is a simple and adaptable system for DC power. When Hollywood started using AC equipment for the first time in the 1970s, it simply continued to use the old DC distribution system. Eventually, DC connectors were phased out of use with AC (because of the need to provide a ground wire with AC and similar concerns). Other components of the original DC system were modified and are now used with AC systems. Through all this, the original DC system has not changed much and is basically the same today as it was in 1950.

DC Cans

On DC sound stages, the powerhouse runs power to permanently installed service panels known as the *cans*, which is a fused (or sometimes unfused) safety switch. A sound stage might have two or three 2400-A circuits distributed among six or eight cans around the floor and in the perms of the sound stage. Individual cans are typically fused at 400 or 800 amps per leg. Some stages have numbered circuits that can be controlled from a central point on the stage. Each can contains copper bus bars onto which lug cable are bolted. Bus bars have a maximum ampacity of 1000 A per square inch of cross-sectional area. In other words, a $\frac{1}{4}$ in. bar, 4 in. wide can carry 1000 A ($\frac{1}{4} \times 4 = 1$).

Sister Lugs

Lugs are heavy-duty copper or bronze-cast clamps that screw onto the copper bus bars of the service cans and spider boxes (Figure 12.1). Lugs are used also for arc light feeder cables and other large equipment.

A 4/0 or 2/0 lug cable is used for primary feeders, running from the bus bar to the spider box and from spider box to spider box. When connecting lugs to the power supply busses, use a crescent wrench or speed wrench (ratcheted) to ensure a tight connection. Always place the lug nuts on the right side of the bus bar. We do

Table 12.1 Ampacity of Spider Boxes

Cable Slots per Bar	Continuous			Intermittent		
	Amps per Cable	*Amps per Bar*	*Amps per Cable*	*Amps per Bar*	*Minutes On*	*Minutes Off*
4	300	600	325	650	20	6
6	280	840	325	975	20	10
8	270	1080	325	1300	20	14

Note: The amperage data in Table 12.1 apply to spider boxes that are not listed if they have the same number of lugs per bar. This table gives Mole-Richardson's recommended maximum loading.

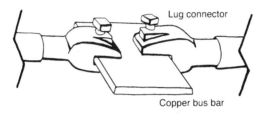

Figure 12.1 Lugs attach to a bus bar or spider box.

this because the nuts chew up the bars. If you chew up both sides of the bus bar, the flat part of the lug no longer mates with the bus bar.

By coincidence, the gap of the jaw of the lug is the same size as the square head of the lug bolts, so in a pinch, you can use one lug to tighten the bolt of another lug.

Spider Boxes

A spider box is an intermediate cable splicing block used to join lengths of lug cable or divide power in several directions. (A four-bar AC spider box will be shown in Figure 12.8. The DC version would be a two-bar or three-bar.) A three-bar spider box houses three copper bars $\frac{1}{4}$ in. thick held in a transparent Plexiglas insulated frame. Spider boxes provide a bar for each wire of the distribution cable, usually color-coded blue, white, and red for a three-wire DC system. Each bar can accommodate between four and eight lugs. Mole-Richardson's design has holes in the Plexiglas frame to provide access to the lug bolts, which are tightened to the bars using a T-handle $\frac{3}{16}$-in. Allen wrench.

Westlinghouse spiders are made of opaque gray nonconductive materials. The ampacity per cable and per bar of a spider box is determined by the number of lugs per bar. See the amperage data in Table 12.1.

Remote Switchboards

Once the main feeder cables in the perms have reached the vicinity above the set, they are usually connected to a switchboard. The switchboards provide circuit protection at a workable amperage, 200 A/leg. In most cases, the circuit protection

Figure 12.2 A deuce board with two high-amperage, remote-control, fused switches in a stackable casing. The deuce board shown is designed for a three-wire 800-A AC or DC input and two three-wire 400-A outputs (200 A per leg). (Courtesy of Mole-Richardson Co., Hollywood, CA.)

for DC cans is located in the powerhouse, not on the sound stage, and is set at 400, 800, or 1200 A per leg.

Switchboards control power to various areas of a large set or to several separate sets within one stage. Switchboards (commonly called *location boards* or *deuce boards*) work with any three-wire system, AC or DC. An ace board has a single switch (two 200-A circuits, 400 A total). A deuce board divides power between two switches (four 200-A circuits, 800 A input total) (Figure 12.2). A four-way board divides power among four switches (eight 200-A circuits, 1600 A input total). The input feeder lugs connect to bus bars on the switchboard. Sets of output bus bars are provided on the front of the unit. The contactors can be controlled by toggle switches on the switchboard or from a remote toggle switch box. They can even be controlled by a practical switch wired into the set. A master switch is provided on the remote switch and on the switchboard itself to switch all contactors at once. Typically, the remote switch cables run down to stage level for ease of use. Modern AC deuce boards are DMX controlled and have Bates outlets. Old switch-controlled deuce boards can be wired to a DMX relay box that translates a DMX signal and controls the relay contacts in the deuce boards. This feature gives on/off control of the switchboards to the dimmer board operator.

Switchboards are designed to be stacked. An eyelet is provided on the top of each unit for hoisting it onto catwalks.

A   Lug to female pin adapter

B   Lug to male pin adapter

C   MoleLock three-fer

D   Male to male suicide adapter

E   Female to female suicide adapter

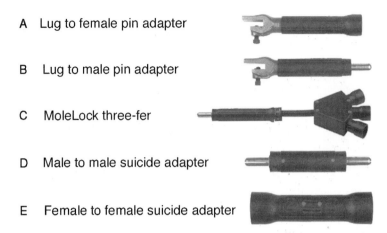

Figure 12.3   Mole pin adapters.

Mole Pin Connectors

Today's mole pin connectors are single-conductor, .515-in. diameter, slip-pin connectors. Today, most studios and rental houses have replaced the original Mole pin connection (used on DC systems) with locking connectors (such as MoleLock or Cam-loc), which can be used with either DC or AC systems. Mole pins are used on subfeeder cables and on the head cables of some larger lights. A lug-to-Mole pin adapter, or jumper (Figure 12.3A), connects mole-pin feeders to the spider box or deuce board.

Mole pin connectors are used for 2/0 cable (and rated at 200 A) and on banded #2 AWG cable (and rated at 150 A). On banded cable, the legs are color-coded with rubber sheaths at the base of the connectors. Mole pins can fit cable sizes from 2/0 to as small as 10 AWG.

The pins of a mole pin connector have a thin slit cut down the center, which allows the pin to flex and put friction on the inside of the female receptacle. With use, the pins can become bent together, so that the pin no longer creates the friction that makes a good connection. If this happens, wedge the blades of a wire snipper or knife into the gap to pry the two halves apart. Similarly, the female connector can get spread and loose, especially those of three-fers. Weed out and replace ill-fitting connectors.

Equipment has been manufactured for the motion picture industry without any standards, and some manufacturers in the past intentionally made their equipment so it would not be interchangeable with other manufacturers. You will find pin and sleeve connectors of various sizes that do not fit appropriately. Mole's original pin diameter was .501 in. Today's pin and sleeve connectors are all .515 in. in diameter.

Three-Fers

Three-fers are used to branch three feeder cables off of one (Figure 12.3B). A standard three-fer interconnects one male pin with three female receptacles.

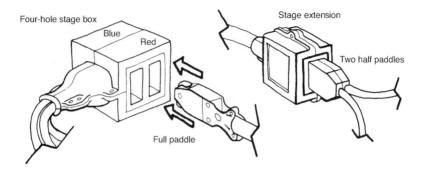

Figure 12.4 Plugging boxes and paddle connectors.

One three-fer is used on each leg. They are color coded. Three-fers are rated as per the size of the single pin (Mole-pin 200 amps; Cam-loc 400 amps).

Suicide Pins

A suicide pin is a male-to-male Mole pin adapter (Figure 12.3D). It gets its name from the fact that, when the adapter is plugged in, it exposes a hot pin. Obviously, you should never leave a bare suicide pin plugged into a live wire. Suicide pins are used to reverse the direction of the connectors on the grounding wire or to make a feeder loop (see the section on Rigging later in this chapter).

DC Paddle-and-Stage Box System

Stage boxes (four- and six-hole boxes) are DC plugging boxes that accommodate male paddle connectors (Figure 12.4). This system predates the use of AC in film production. This equipment is not permitted on AC systems and may only be used on DC sound stages and back-lots. Plugging boxes are hardwired to a 25- or 50-ft cable with lug ends. These connect directly to the remote boards and are run along the catwalks to a point above their final drop point. They are either tied to the rail or dropped to the floor or to the green beds (lower catwalks around the sets) and tied off.

Stage boxes with short tails and Mole pin connectors are also commonly used (these are connected back to the deuce boards with banded #2 AWG Mole pin cable).

Stage boxes are referred to by the number of holes they have: one-hole, two-hole, four-hole, or six-hole box. Lights with stage, or paddle, connectors plug directly into the stage box.

A normal full stage plug (1 in. thick) can carry a maximum of 85 A. A half stage plug ($^1/_2$ in. thick) can carry 20 A and fit two to a hole in a stage box (Table 12.2). A gang box plugs into the stage box with a paddle connector (Figure 12.5).

Stage boxes come in both two-wire (single-circuit) and three-wire (two circuit) versions. The color-coded sheath at the base of the Mole pins or lugs identifies the legs. When you connect a three-wire box normally (blue to blue, red to red, and white to white), you get two 120-V circuits (Figure 12.6A). Three-wire boxes are painted red on one side and blue on the other to show the leg into which the paddle is plugged.

Table 12.2 Ampacity of Stage Boxes

Stage Box	Circuit Type	Amps per Hole	Amps per Side	Amps, Total
One-hole	Two-wire	50	—	50
Two-hole	Two-wire	45	—	90
Four-hole	Two-wire	85	—	170
Four-hole	Three-wire	85	110	220
Six-hole	Two-wire	85	170	265
Six-hole	Three-wire	85	170	340

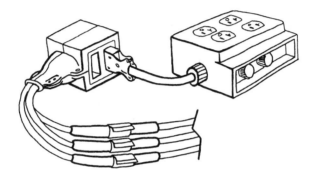

Figure 12.5 A fused gang box plugged into a stage box.

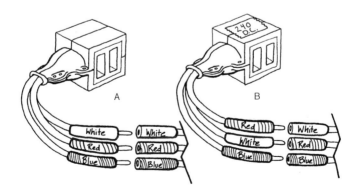

Figure 12.6 (A) A four-hole stage box connected normally provides four 120-V outlets: two on the red leg and two on the blue leg. (B) A four-hole box connected red to white and white to red provides 240-V power on the blue side and 120-V power on the red side.

Connecting a Stage Box for 240/120-V Power

To get 240-V current from a stage box, connect the feeder to the box as follows: red to white, white to red, and blue to blue (Figure 12.6B). This connects the two hot legs to the blue side of the stage box, making it 240 V. The red side still runs 120 V on the red leg. Whenever you "240" a stage box, be sure to mark it boldly with a big piece of tape.

Stage Extensions

A stage extension has a stage plug on one end and a one-hole or two-hole box on the other. It is used as an extension for the bigger lights that have paddle connectors or for Edison gang boxes.

Precautions with the Stage Box System

- The holes of stage boxes are large enough to put your fingers into, which presents a hazard. Tape over holes that are not in use, especially when children or animals are present.
- Be very careful not to misplug a three-wire system to the stage box and run 240 V accidentally. Always label 240-V circuits.
- There is little to prevent moisture from getting into the connections when water is present. When shooting around moisture (e.g., on dewy grass, near a sprinkler system, in the rain, in a bathroom, near a pool), raise the pin and stage box connections on apple boxes. Wrap the connections in Visqueen or plastic garbage bags.
- When plugging in cables and lights using DC current, make sure that the fixtures are turned off. Making a hot stab (plugging in a light when it is turned on) with DC is a dangerous business because the contacts arc and start to weld before they can become fully connected. Gases can build up and cause an explosion. If you have to make a hot stab, insert the connector with one well-aimed, straight, firm motion, so it goes in all the way at once. Avoid hot stabs whenever possible.

Plate Dimmers

Plate dimmers are large, variable-resistance dimmers that can be used with either AC or DC circuits running incandescent lights (Figure 12.7). Because better dimmers are available for AC circuits, plate dimmers see most of their action dimming DC on the older studio sound stages. Unlike other types of dimmers, a plate dimmer can provide blackout dimming only when a minimum wattage is pulled through it; if the fixture connected to it is too small, the dimmer will not dim all the way down to blackness. To provide sufficient wattage, it may be necessary to run a *ghost load*, an additional light that does not light the set but provides the added wattage to make the dimmer operate.

Plate dimmers come in various sizes: 1k (775 W minimum), 2k (1655 W minimum), 3k (2705 W minimum), and 5k (500 W minimum, a huge 88-lb unit). Each is equipped with an on/off switch. DC sound stages use large consoles housing 12 or so plate dimmers. The console typically has a number of 1k circuits, some 2k circuits, and a couple 5k circuits.

Figure 12.7 A 2k plate dimmer. (Courtesy of Mole-Richardson Co., Los Angeles, CA.)

AC Systems

Main Feeder Run

Three types of locking connectors are widely used on AC for 4/0 and 2/0 main feeder cables: sister lugs, Cam-Lok, and MoleLock (up to 2/0 only). The table below shows how each is rated:

	4/0 cable	*2/0 cable*	*#2 cable (banded)*
Cam-Lok	400 amps	300 amps	200 amps
Sister Lugs	400 amps	300 amps	200 amps
MoleLock	N/A	200 amps	150 amps

Cam-Lok and MoleLock Connectors

Cam-Lok is widely used for main feeder (4/0 and 2/0 cable) as well as subfeeder (banded cable #2 AWG) and for some large lights. Cam-Lok is also the most common input connector for dimmer packs. Male and female Cam-Lok connectors are mated by lining up the arrows, inserting the male connector then twisting the male 180°, which engages a locking pin into a cam mechanism that pulls the connectors tightly together. No tools are necessary. The cam ensures full contact yet is relatively easy to connect and disconnect. To ensure a good connection, the connectors must be twisted until tight, not simply inserted.

MoleLocks are locking connectors that evolved from the old Mole pin system. The slip pins are basically unchanged but they are housed in a hard plastic color-coded sleeve that twist-locks to the mating sleeve once the pin is fully inserted.

Cam-Lok and MoleLock connectors are shielded so that bare metal cannot be left exposed, and the connection is protected from water. The sleeves are color-coded red, blue, black, white, or green, appropriately.

Cam-Lok connectors should not be connected or disconnected "hot" (when powering a load). This is true for all connectors but especially with Cam-Loks, because if the pin within the Cam-Lok connector gets pitted and warped from arcing, it can eventually seize up and the connectors will be permanently stuck together.

Both Cam-Lok and MoleLock connectors are made as adapters (lug to cam, lug to pin), three-fers, and suicide pins. A Cam-Lok T allows two Cam-Lok connectors to be plugged into one. A "soft two-fer" or "soft three-fer" is simply two or three female connectors wired to one male connector with a short piece of wire (see Figure 12.3).

Reversed Ground System

With pin and cam connectors, the male and female are oriented with "pins to power," meaning that the male pins point toward the power plant and the female end goes toward the lights. This is true of all cable, except the ground. In our industry, a reverse ground system has been (almost universally) adopted. Most equipment (banded cable and distro boxes with panel-mounted connectors) is set up with the ground reversed. The male connector on the grounding wire points downstream, toward the load. The idea is to make it impossible to plug a hot wire into the grounding wire by mistake.

Grounding Stars and Grounding Clusters

A grounding three-fer, or grounding star used with a reverse ground system, interconnects three male pins with one female receptacle. A grounding cluster or "squid" is a softwired set of connectors that serves the same purpose.

Spider Boxes

For lug cable, four-bar spiders provide *bus bars* for three wires plus a green-coded grounding bar for single-phase AC systems (Figure 12.8). Five-bar spiders provide four bars (blue, black, red, and white) plus a green grounding bar for three-phase systems. *Warning: Never use a green bus bar as a current-carrying bus; it is a grounding bar only.* The green bus bar is connected directly to the external metal straps and handles, which create a serious short and shock hazard if the bus bar is connected to a hot lead.

Spiders come in different configurations. Small (two holes per bar), larger (four holes per bar), and the super spider (four holes per bar plus two neutral buses for double neutral applications, like dimmers). The maximum amperage rating of the bus bars is specific to the particular model of spider box. Check the manufacturer's label for (1) the total current carrying capacity of the spider and (2) the rating

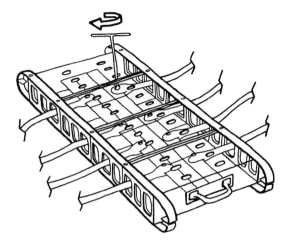

Figure 12.8 A four-bar spider box allows up to six lugs per bar. Lug nuts are tightened with a T-handle Allen wrench through the holes in the Plexiglas frame.

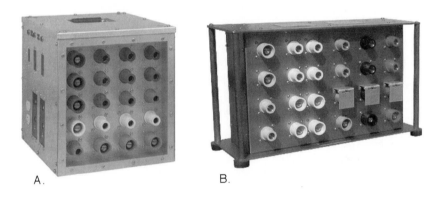

A.   B.

Figure 12.9 (A) This distribution hub can branch out into three additional (Cam-Lok) runs, with all cable runs coming from one side, which can be toward the wall and out of the way. That leaves open access to the six 100-A Bates outlets. (Courtesy Mole-Richardson Co., Los Angeles, CA.) (B) This 2400-A Cam-Lok spider has a two rows of 4/0 inputs (note the second set of male connectors are capped when not in use). The spider can branch to as many as six rows of outputs. The neutral is doubled in accordance with 130% requirements for electronic ballasts and dimmers. (Courtesy of Dadco, Sun Valley, CA.)

per cable. Mole-Richardson also offers spider boxes with a single disconnect breaker (1200 or 2400 A). This would usually be used when no other main disconnect is convenient.

Unlike lug cable, *Cam-Lok and MoleLock* cable can be joined directly together. A spider box is necessary only when you want to break off runs in different directions; for example, when several dimmer packs or distro boxes need to be plugged into one large main run. The Cam-Lok spider shown in Figure 12.9 provides two rows of inputs and six rows of outputs. This box accommodates a double 4/0 run input (2400 A max). Spiders are also available for a single 4/0 run (1200 A max) and seven output rows. Similar boxes are available for MoleLock. Both are also available with double neutral connectors.

Regardless of how many connectors are available on a spider, the total amperage is rated based on the bus bars inside. Check the manufacturer's rating of the buss bars.

When a spider box is used to splice smaller subfeeders to the main run, circuit protection is required within 25 ft of the reduction of cable size (NEC Article 240.21). If no other circuit protection exists that close, protection can be provided by breakers or switch boxes, which offer a main three-phase switch at 200 A per leg.

AC-Power Distribution Boxes

Regardless of the type of connectors used, the main feeder run terminates into some sort of distribution box. The distro box provides circuit protection for subsequent smaller circuits, which power the lights. A wide variety of AC distribution boxes are manufactured to make any transition you might need. Configurations typically include a combination of output connectors and usually also include a courtesy 20-A duplex outlet. The most common configurations follow. Almost all boxes are available in either single-phase (four-wire) or three-phase (five-wire) versions.

Input Connector	Output Connectors
Lug to	Bus bar (spider)
	2/0 MoleLock feeder with 200-A breakers (drop-down box)
	2/0 Cam-Lok feeder with 200-A breakers (drop-down box)
	100-A Bates (usually six circuits with 100-A breakers)
	208-V 100-A Bates (usually two–four circuits with 100-A breakers)
Cam-Lok to	Direct feedthrough in combination with the following:
	100-A Bates (usually six circuits with 100-A breakers)
	208-V 100-A Bates (usually two–four circuits with 100-A breakers)
	Socapex (usually four Socapex with 24 20-A breakers)
	20-A duplex outlets
MoleLock to	Direct feedthrough in combination with the following:
	100-A Bates (usually six circuits with 100-A breakers)
	208-V 100-A Bates (usually two–four circuits with 100-A breakers)

Figure 12.10 shows some typical distribution boxes. Table 12.3 lists specifications of a sample of commonly used distro boxes.

Some questions to consider when ordering boxes:

Single phase or three phase?
Input connector type?

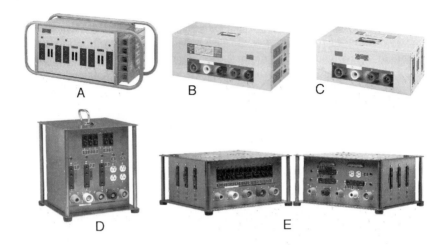

Figure 12.10 (A) 1200-A, three-phase lug box, 12 100-A outputs; (B) 600-A, three-phase MoleLock through box: six 100-A outputs and 20-A duplex courtesy outlet; (C) 400-A single-phase version of the MoleLock box; (D) Dadco cat box, reduces cable spaghetti in catwalks by having all cable flow in one direction; (E) 1200-A Duzz-all Distro, outputs are six 100-A, three 100-A 240-V, and one 20-A duplex courtesy outlet. (A, B, and C courtesy of Mole-Richardson, Los Angeles, CA; D and E courtesy of Dadco, Sun Valley, CA.)

AC/DC or AC only?
Do you need 240-V 100-A outlets for 12ks and 20ks?
Do you want some boxes that feed through?

Features I find very useful are indicator lights (help with troubleshooting) and courtesy outlets (in a dark stage it's good to have a small work light at each box). On catwalks it is often preferable to use boxes that feed in and out along only one axis (Figure 12.10D). This keeps the cable runs a lot neater than boxes that feed out in four directions. Some boxes can be stood on end, taking up less horizontal space. Some boxes are arranged in such a way that you cannot connect hard three-fers directly to the box because they run into each other or the ground. Use three-fers with tails to connect to these boxes.

Bates Three-Pin Connectors

Bates connectors come in several sizes: 20 A, 30 A, 60 A, 100 A in the 120-V variety. Bates connectors are also available for 240-V equipment in 40 A and 100 A (Figure 12.11). These are three-pin connectors: hot wire, neutral, and ground (except the 240-V connectors, which have a ground and two hot wires, no neutral). The 100-A and 60-A extensions (100 ft, 50 ft, or 25 ft) run from the distro boxes to the lights and gang boxes. The 100-A Bates connectors are used on lights of more than 7.2k: 10ks, 9k maxibrutes, 8k soft lights. The 60-A Bates are used on lights 2k–7.2k: 5ks, 9-lite FAYS (5850 W), 4ks, 2500s, 4k soft lights, 5k skypans, and the like.

Table 12.3 Distribution Boxes

Input Connector	Total Amps	Model	Description	Phase	Output Connectors	Features
Mole-Richardson						
CamLok	900-A AC	4801	120/208-V	Three	6 100-A 120-V, 3 100-A 208-V, 1 20-A duplex	Circuit breakers, circuit lights
	600-A AC	4671 4681	Face-mounted input, pigtail input	Three	6 100-A 120-V, 1 20-A duplex	Circuit breakers, circuit lights
	300-A AC	4621 4631	Face-mounted input, feedthrough	Three	6 100-A, 120-V, 1 20-A duplex	Circuit breakers, circuit lights
	400-A AC	4881	120-V, feed-through	Single	4 100-A, 120-V, 1 20-A duplex	Circuit breakers, circuit lights
	200-A AC	4661	240-V, feed-through	Single	2 100-A, 240-V, 1 20-A duplex	Circuit breakers, circuit lights
Remote switchboards	800-A	3801	AC or DC deuce board	Single AC/DC	4 200-A fuses	2 remote switches, dimmable, casters, stackable
	1600-A		AC or DC four-way board	Single AC/DC	8 200-A fuses	4 remote switches, dimmable, casters, stackable
Spider boxes (lugs)	800-A AC	3951	208/120-V	Three	6 100-A, 120-V, 2 100-A, 208-V, 1 20-A duplex	Circuit breakers, circuit lights
	600-A AC	4891	208/120-V	Three	4 100-A, 208-V, 2 100-A, 120-V	Circuit breakers, circuit lights
	400-A AC	4901	120-V	Single	4 100-A, 120-V, 1 20-A duplex	Circuit breakers, circuit lights

Table 12.3 Distribution Boxes (continued)

Input Connector	Total Amps	Model	Description	Phase	Output Connectors	Features
Mole pin	400-A AC	4851	Pin-through banded box	Single	4 100-A, 120-V, 1 20-A duplex	Circuit breakers, circuit lights
	300-A AC	4911	120/240-V Pin-through banded box	Single	2 100-A, 120-V, 1 100-A, 240-V	Circuit breakers, circuit lights
	200-A AC	4861	240-V, feed-through	Single	2 100-A, 240-V, 1 20-A duplex	Circuit breakers, circuit lights
100-A Bates	100-A AC	3961 4961	Lunchbox 5-duplex out, feedthrough version	Single	5 20-A duplex	Circuit breakers, circuit lights
	100-A AC	3941 4841	Lunchbox 5 20-A Bates out, feedthrough version	Single	5 20-A Bates	Circuit breakers, circuit lights
	100-A AC	3991	60-A Bates	Single	2 60-A Bates, 1 20-A duplex	Circuit breakers, circuit lights
	100-A AC	3971	30-A Bates/duplex	Single	2 30-A Bates, 2 20-A duplex	
	100-A AC	4651	30-A Bates	Single	3 30-A Bates	
	100-A AC	4641	60-A Bates, 240-V	Single	2 60-A Bates 240-V	
	100-A AC	5001432	100-A gang	Single	4 20-A Edison	Circuit breakers
60-A Bates	60-A AC	5001545	60-A gang, 3 circuit	Single	3 20-A duplex	Circuit breakers
	60-A AC	5001467	60-A gang, 2 circuit	Single	2 20-A duplex	
Matthews						
Cam-Lok (or with pin adapters)	1200-A	387639	Feedthrough, "spider", bull switch	Three	2 sets of Cam-Loks	Circuit lights, 400-A fuses
	600-A	387627	"TDB 60,000-W AC," 120-V	Three	6 100-A Bates	Continuous-rated circuit breakers, circuit lights

Table 12.3 Distribution Boxes (continued)

Input Connector	Total Amps	Model	Description	Phase	Output Connectors	Features
	600-A	387638	Bull switch, 200-A fuses	Three	1 set of Cam-Loks	Circuit lights, 200-A fuses
	600-A	387637	Feedthrough, 120-V	Three	6 100-A Bates	Continuous-rated circuit breakers, circuit lights
	400-A	387601	"TDB 40,000-W AC," 400-A box, 120-V	Single	2 100-A Bates, 4 60-A Bates	Continuous-rated circuit breakers, circuit lights
	400-A	387636	Feedthrough, 120/220-V	Single	2 100-A 120-V, 2 100-A 220-V	Continuous-rated circuit breakers, circuit lights
100-A Bates	100-A	387643	100-A through box	Single	5 20-A duplex	Circuit breakers, circuit lights
	100-A	387630	"Hollywood box"	Single	5 20-A Edison	5 fuses
60-A Bates	60-A	387623	Hollywood box, 20-A Bates	Single	3 20-A Bates	3 fuses
	60-A	387606	"Hollywood box"	Single	3 20-A duplex	3 fuses
	40-A	387602	"Hollywood box"	Single	2 20-A duplex	2 fuses
Dadco Spiders						
2 rows cam	2400	DAD 2400 SC	Cam-thru Spider	Three	6 rows cam	Double neutral
4 rows cam	2400	DAD 2400 SC	Cam-thru Spider	Three	4 rows cam	Double neutral
2 rows cam	1200	DAD 1200 SC	Cam-thru Spider	Three	6 rows cam	Double neutral
1 row cam	1200	DAD 1200 SC	Cam-thru Spider	Three	7 rows cam	Double neutral
Dadco Distro						
1 row cam	1200	DAD 1200 FT	3-phase Duzz-all Distro	Three	1 row cam-thru 3 100-A Bates 240-V 6 100-A Bates 120-V 1 20-A Duplex 120-V	

Table 12.3 Distribution Boxes (continued)

Input Connector	Total Amps	Model	Description	Phase	Output Connectors	Features
1 row cam	900	DAD 900 FT3	3-phase Distro box	Three	1 row cam-thru 2 100-A Bates 240-V 4 100-A Bates 120-V 4 20-A Duplex 120-V	
1 row cam	600	DAD 600 FT3	3-phase Distro box	Three	1 row cam-thru 6 100-A Bates 120-V 4 20-A Duplex 120-V	
1 row cam	600	DAD 600 FT	1-phase Distro	Single	1 row cam-thru 6 100-A Bates 120-V 4 20-A Duplex 120-V	
1 row cam	400	DAD 400 FT	1-phase Distro	Single	1 row cam-thru 4 100-A Bates 120-V 4 20-A Duplex 120-V	
Dadco Catwalk Distro						
	900	DAD 900 CAT	Catwalk Distro	Three	1 row cam-thru 2 100-A Bates 240-V 4 100-A Bates 120-V 4 20-A Duplex 120-V	
	600	DAD 600 CAT	Catwalk Distro	Three	6 100-A Bates 120-V 4 20-A Duplex 120-V	
Dadco Socapex and 240-V L6 Twist Distro						
1 row cam	1200	DAD 6SP FT3	Socapex Distro	Three	1 row cam-thru 6 6-circuit 20-A Soco 2 20-A Duplex 120-V	Individual breakers for each circuit
1 row cam	1200	DAD S14 FT3	U-ground, Socapex Distro	Three	1 row cam-thru 4 6-circuit 20-A Soco 14 20-A Duplex 120-V	

Table 12.3 Distribution Boxes (continued)

Input Connector	Total Amps	Model	Description	Phase	Output Connectors	Features
1 row cam	1200	DAD S9U FT3	Combo Distro	Three	1 row cam-thru 6 20-A 240-V L6 Twist-lock 1 6-circuit socapex 240-V 10 20-A Duplex 120-V	
1 row cam	1200	DAD 18U FT3	Edison u-ground distro	Three	1 row cam-thru 18 20-A Duplex 120-V or 24 20-A Duplex 120-V	
1 row cam	1200	DAD S62 FT3	Moving Light distro	Three	1 row cam-thru 12 20-A 240-V L6 Twist-lock 2 6-circuit socapex 240-V 2 20-A Duplex 120-V	
1 row cam	1200	DAD L62 FT3	Moving Light Distro	Three	1 row cam-thru 12 20-A 240-V L6 twist-lock 2 20-A Duplex 120-V	
Dadco Lunch Boxes						
100-A Bates	100	DAD 100 FT	Lunch Box	—	100-A Bates feed-thru 5 20-A Duplex 120-V	Light-weight lunch box. Available with pipe clamp adapter
100-A, 240-V Bates	100	DAD 240 FT	Twist lock Distro	—	100-A, 240-V Bates feed-thru 4 30-A Twist Lock	For use with 240-V 4k HMI ballasts
100-A Bates	100	DAD 620 PBS	Six Pack	—	100-A Bates feed-thru 6 20-A Single U-ground 120-V 1 6-circuit socapex 120-V	
100-A Bates	100	DAD 620 PBG	Bakers dozen	—	100-A Bates feed-thru 6 20-A Single U-ground 120-V	

Note: This list is meant to give a representative sample of the configurations commonly available. By no means does this table represent a complete list of manufacturers or types.

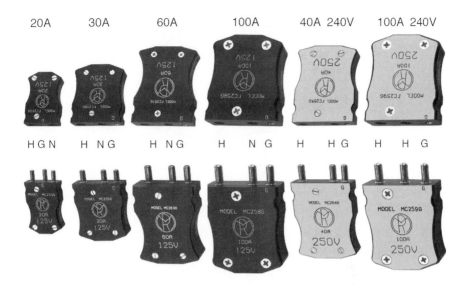

20A	30A	60A	100A	40A 240V	100A 240V

Figure 12.11 Pin configurations for Bates connectors of various sizes. The 100-A 240-V connector is similar to the 100-A connector but the neutral pin is a hot pin and positioned closer to the center of the plug. The 240-V connectors are yellow. (Courtesy of Mole-Richardson Co., Los Angeles, CA.)

A 100-A to 60-A adapter/splitter must be used to connect these lights to the 100-A outlet on the distro box. The 30-A Bates are used in theater and not in film work. The 20-A Bates plugs are found only on theatrical lamps (ellipsoidals and PAR cans) and in television studios, in which all the lighting equipment is used in-house only. Such facilities are typically installed with permanent numbered circuits around the walls of the stage, in the floor, and mounted to overhead pipes. This permanent feeder system is hardwired to a patch panel and dimmer board. The 20-A Bates extensions are used instead of Edison stingers. If you are using a large number of Bates-fitted lamps, distro boxes with 20-A Bates outlets can be ordered, but ordinarily in motion picture work, Edison outlets are used for lamps 2k or less. Lamps with 20 Bates plugs require an adapter "pigtail" adapter (Edison male/Bates female).

Bates connector pins are sized and positioned asymmetrically so they make ground first, break ground last, and they are polarized—they cannot be plugged in incorrectly. Bates connectors melt if they become overheated; keep them strictly within their designated amperage limits. Where one Bates cable plugs into another, tape the connection so they don't pull apart (Figure 12.12).

Bates is not the name of a manufacturer. It used to be the name of a theatrical lighting company on Bates Street in LA—the Bates Rental Company. Because all their equipment was identified with "Bates" written on the plugs, the connectors came to be known as Bates connectors. Manufacturers include Mole-Richardson, Paladin, Union Connector Co., ADI, and Group 5 Engineering, but they continue to be referred to as *Bates*. They are also sometimes called *Union connectors*: Union Connector Co. makes several designs, including some with mechanical hooks that

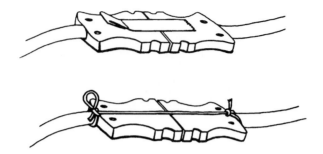

Figure 12.12 Bates connectors often need to be held together by tape or sash card.

Figure 12.13 Edison boxes. (A) The classic 100-A lunch box with five duplex outlets, (B) a 60-A gang box with three 20-A duplex outlets, (C) a 100-A gang box with five single 20-A Edison outlets. (Courtesy of Mole-Richardson Co., Los Angeles, CA.)

lock one connector to another. Bates connectors are also commonly called *3-pin connectors*, which is not to be confused with single-conductor, Mole pin connectors, also referred to simply as *pin connectors* or *pin and sleeve connectors*.

Like other connectors in our industry Bates connectors are not made to any standard. Two listed plugs from different manufacturers might fit tight mechanically but not make a good electrical connection. To check for a good fit, insert the single hot pin into the female and check for snugness. Inspect the pin and sleeve. Look for discoloration due to overheating, burnt, pitted, or deteriorating pins due to arcing and signs of overheating inside the plug due to a weak connection to the cable. In the past some connectors used on cable and on dimmer packs were made with solid female sleeves. For these especially the male plugs must be the proper size.

Edison Boxes

Lunch Boxes and Gang Boxes with Breakers

Edison outlet boxes are fitted with either a 100-A or a 60-A male Bates (Figure 12.13). A *lunch box* is a 100-A box that provides five 20-A duplex circuits (10 Edison outlets) with 20-A circuit breakers and indicator lights on each circuit. Alternately, boxes may be fitted with 20-A Bates or 20-A twist-lock outlets instead of duplex. Most also provide a 100-A female outlet, so you can feed through to subsequent boxes.

The duplex outlets on most Edison boxes are a heavy-duty type commonly known as *hospital grade outlets*. They are designed for constant use, plugging and unplugging equipment. A normal household outlet would wear out. Hospital grade outlets have a small green dot on the face of the outlet. Hospital grade receptacles come in all colors, white, brown, blue, and red, but it is only the green dot that signifies it is hospital grade.

Some electricians like to use the green dot to signify which outlet a 2k should be plugged in to. However, this is not a good system because some boxes have the dot on top, others on the bottom, and some have no dot at all (see Chapter 9, 2k Plugging Policy).

The advantages of breakers are that a tripped breaker is easy to find and breakers can be used to switch a circuit on and off (making it a lot easier to switch off a light that is hung out of reach). The disadvantages are that circuit breakers are more expensive and more delicate than fuses and can be tripped only a finite number of times before they need to be replaced, which drives up the maintenance costs for the rental house.

Fused Gang Boxes

A fused gang provides two to five fused duplex outlets. Each circuit has a separate 20-A fuse. Spring holders for spare fuses are mounted next to the fuses. These fuses blow from time to time. It is worthwhile to keep a couple of spares with you, so you can replace a bad one immediately and return the circuit to service.

Socapex Connectors and Cable

Socapex cable, "Soco" for short, carries six separate 15- to 20-A circuits together in one multiconductor cable. It is commonly used to carry dimmer circuits up to the lights. At that point, a Soco *break-out adapter* separates the six circuits, providing either Edison outlets or 20-A Bates outlets for the lights. Dimmer packs with 2.4-kW dimmer circuits are often configured with panel-mounted Socapex connectors for direct connection to Socapex cable. Packs that provide single circuit outputs (usually 20-A Bates) can be fed into Soco cable by attaching a Soco *break-in adapter*.

Some six-circuit light fixtures, such as coops and space lights, use Soco input connectors, which allows you individual control over each lamp in the fixture. Also non-dim AC Socapex distro boxes can be used to plug Soco lines directly into hard power. These boxes provide manual on/off control of the individual circuits and some provide DMX-controlled remote switches, which you can patch to the dimmer console (Figure 12.14).

Rating Socapex Cable

Socapex typically uses #12 wires (rated for 20-A per circuit). Some Socapex cable currently in the field is #14 guage (rated at 15-A per circuit). The connectors were not originally designed for this high a load. If you load up the cable with six

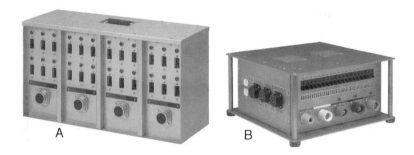

Figure 12.14 (A) 600-A MolePlex distribution box, Cam-Lok inputs. Four Socapex outputs with six individual 20-A breakers per outlet, six 20-A duplex. (Courtesy of Mole-Richardson Co., Los Angeles, CA.) (B) Dadco Socapex Distro Box: Cam-Lok inputs, Cam-Lok flowthrough, six six-circuit Socapex outputs with six individual 20-A breakers per Soco, two 20-A courtesy outlets. (Courtesy of Dadco, Sun Valley, CA.)

2ks, the Socapex connectors heat up excessively. If these lights are left on for extended periods of time, especially in long runs, the results can be catastrophic. Some historical perspective might be helpful here. Socapex originated in theater and concert lighting and was first used in England on a 240-V system (carrying half as much current). It was designed to make long runs from the dimmer room out to the lighting bars in theaters and concert halls. To cut down on connection points, Soco cable comes in unusually long lengths, rental houses carry lengths up to 200 ft. While it is a great convenience to have six bundled circuits in one long cable, it is also a recipe for high resistance and heat. Inside each connector, 12 current-carrying connection points are held very close together. If current is too high, heat builds excessively at the connection points. To ensure reliability, many rigging gaffers rate the cable at no more than 12.5 A (1500 W) per circuit if the lights are to be left on for extended periods (more than 3 hours) or the runs are long. Avoid piling connectors on top of one another where they can conduct heat between metal parts.

Socapex Pin Configuration and Troubleshooting

A Socapex connector has 19 pins (Figure 12.15). The outer circle of pins are the line and neutral wires of the six circuits. The inner circle are grounds for each circuit. The center pin, 19, is not used or may be used as an additional ground.

If the cable used is 18 or 19 conductor cable, each circuit gets an individual ground wire. If used with 14 conductor cable, all the ground pins are bused together.

The male Soco connector has a key at the top to orient the connectors and a threaded collar that twists and pulls the connectors together, then click-locks with the female. A keeper inside the connector keeps the key properly oriented. If it breaks, the whole connector can spin and you can end up with the wrong dimmer number coming up. The key should always be located between pins 6 and 7 (as shown in Figure 12.15). When checking over cable before installing the cable, be sure the strain relief is tight. If the outer insulation has pulled out of the strain relief and you can see the inner wires, do not use the cable. When the strain relief is loose,

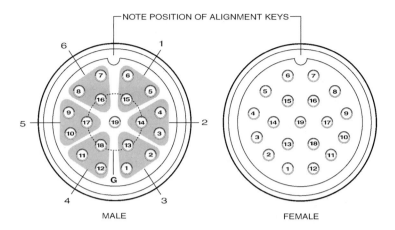

Figure 12.15 Each of the six circuits in a Socapex cable has its own hot, neutral, and ground wires (shown here in gray). The position of the keyway and condition of the pins are essential to proper function.

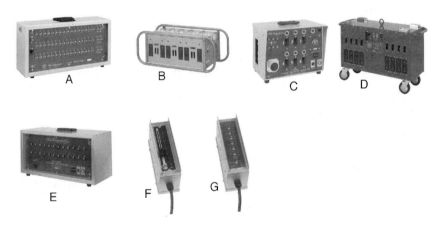

Figure 12.16 DMX-controlled distribution boxes and accessories. (A) DMX switchbox, (B) DMX 600-A distribution box, (C) DMX Socapex lunch box, (D) DMX 800-A deuce board, (E) relay box, (F) DMX remote slider, (G) six-channel DMX remote switch. (Courtesy of Mole-Richardson Co., Los Angeles, CA.)

the bare pins (male end) or receptacles (female end) start to pull out of the insulating housing into the connector. The wires can get pulled and twisted when the connector is handled—bad things can result.

Remote Switch Control

Manufacturers offer various ways of providing remote on/off control of individual circuits from specially equipped distribution boxes. A variety of them are shown in Figure 12.16. Mole makes a three-phase DMX-controlled remote boxes with six 100-A Bates outputs (Figure 12.16B). Each 100-A circuit can be switched via a DMX signal. In the days of DC distribution, this type of control was provided by remote switches connected to deuce boards or DC cans with remote-controlled contactors. Mole's modern AC/DC deuce board (Figure 12.16D) evolved for use with three-wire AC or DC using Cam-Lok inputs and providing eight 100-A Bates outlets, each with 100-A breaker protection. The modern deuce boards still have two contactors (switches) per box, controlling four outlets per switch. Control is via a DMX control signal run to a dimmer board or DMX switch box. A DMX switch box (Figure 12.16A) generates DMX to provide on/off control of DMX-controllable distro boxes, or relay boxes; an alternative to dimmer board control.

You can control old-style deuce boards with DMX by employing a DMX relay box (Figure 12.16E). The 24-channel relay box can control up to eight old-style two-unit type 3801 deuce boards.

You can avoid running long runs of DMX cable by using a wireless DMX transmitter and receivers. Multiple receivers can be used throughout a large set to provide DMX control for dimmers, remote boxes, color scrollers, shutters, smoke machines, wind machines, and any other DMX-controlled device.

Test Meter Inputs on Distro Boxes

Mole incorporates a set of banana plug outlets for testing the circuits with a multimeter (Figure 12.17A). This brilliantly simple idea eliminates the crazy process of scrounging for bare copper to which you can touch the test meter probes. As this is something we do routinely when checking voltage or troubleshooting a problem, it would make our job a lot easier if all distro boxes were supplied with a way to safely connect a test meter. The banana plugs are protected by a small fuse.

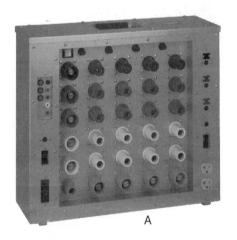

A

B

Figure 12.17 Electrician-friendly distro features. (A) A Cam-Lok spider with built-in banana plugs for easy metering. (Courtesy Mole-Richardson Co., Los Angeles, CA.) (B) A 100-A, 240-V lunch box with four 30-A twist-lock outlets. This gets rid of the mess of three-fers and cam connectors at the distro boxes and makes it possible to run a lightweight extension to your 240-V HMIs (up to four 4k fixtures). (Courtesy of Dadco, Sun Valley, CA.)

240-V Lunch Box for HMI Ballasts

Dadco makes a box the size of a gang box for feeding four 2500 or 4k 240-V ballasts (Figure 12.17B). This eliminates a big mess of three-fers and adapters and allows four 4ks to run off a single 100-A whip (240 V). Our industry does not yet have a commonly used 240-V connector smaller than 100 A, so the box employs a 30-A 240-V twist-lock connector. Each circuit is protected by a double-pole 25-A breaker (240 V × 25 A = 6000 W max per circuit). The ballasts require an adapter to a male 30-A twist-lock. (Mole makes a 40-A 240-V Bates-type connector that works the same way with a 240-V 40-A Bates outlet box).

Adapters

There are as many kinds of adapters as there are different combinations of connectors: lugs to MoleLock, lugs to Cam-Lok, full stage to 60-A Bates, 20-A Bates to Edison, 20-A twist-lock to 20-A Bates, and so on. Adapters often come in the form of a pigtail, or soft-wired adapter, which is nothing more than a foot or so of cable with a different connector on each end. When ordering equipment, the best boy must take care to order the adapter needed to connect each piece of equipment. When referring to an adapter, designate the male end first (e.g., a Bates to Edison adapter has a male Bates and gives you a female Edison).

100-A to two 100-A splitters   The idea of this splitter is to give you more outlets for 60-A splitters, 100-A gangs, and lights. Note: Under no circumstances should this splitter be used to pull more than 100 A total.

100-A to two 60-A splitters   Order as many of these as you have lights and Edison boxes with 60-A tails. Note: Some adapters are fitted with in-line 60-A fuses. Be sure to stock spares and be on the lookout for burnouts.

240-V 100-A bates snakebites (MoleLock or Cam-Lok to Bates adapters)   If you get caught without a 240-V Bates outlet for a 20k or 12/18K, this solves the problem. Note: The circuit breaker on the dimmer or ballast serves as branch circuit protection.

Three-wire 100-A bates snakebites (three-wire MoleLock or Cam-Lok to two 100-A Bates)   In the absence of a distro box, a snakebite patches directly into three-fers. Note: Although very handy, there is no circuit protection here (a violation of NEC).

Edison to 20-A Bates pigtails   You may need adapters with any theatrical lights you order.

100-A Bates to MoleLock or Cam-Lok adapters   Be sure to ask the type of connector for any large lights you order. If the light has pins of cam, you may need to adapt to 100-A Bates.

Socapex break-in and break-out adapters   A break-in adapter has six numbered male connectors (usually either 20-A Bates or Edison), leading to one female Socapex connector. They are used to channel power from separate circuits into a Socapex line. A break-out adapter is used at the load end of the Socapex cable to go from male Socapex to six numbered female connectors (20-A either Bates or Edison).

Jumpers   Lug to Cam-Lok jumpers are typically used to lug dimmer packs into a spider box. The 10-ft lug jumpers are handy to connect deuce boards to a nearby spider box. Banded jumpers (MoleLock or Cam-Lok) are handy to wire a distro box into a spider box.

Figure 12.18 shows a number of PBU (parallel blade U-ground) and twist-lock plug types, some of which you will rarely run into.

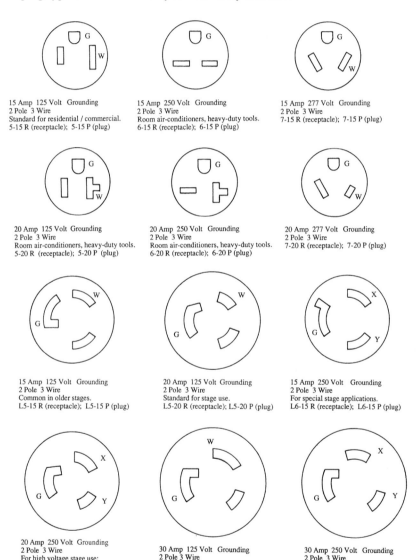

Figure 12.18   Edison and Twist-loc connectors. (Reprinted with permission from the *Backstage Handbook* by Paul Carter. New York: Broadway Press, 1988.)

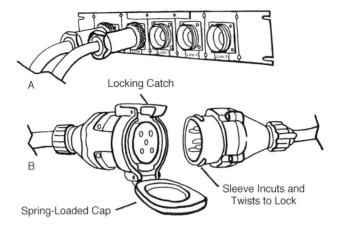

Figure 12.19 (A) An Abbott sequentially locking panel, (B) Meltric connectors.

Meltric and Abbott System

The Meltric and Abbott system (Figure 12.19) is used on a limited number of stages around Hollywood. The system uses 400- or 200-A Abbott connectors on the feeder cable and Meltric 225-, 100-, and 60-A connectors for the subfeeders. The entire system is equipped with five wires for three-phase AC power, but it can be used for single-phase AC if not all of the wires are used. Wheeled distribution boxes provide step-down points with circuit protection. There are several kinds of distribution boxes: the main disconnect, the feeder splicing block, the feedthrough feeder distribution box, and the subfeeder distribution boxes. Meltric 100-A banded cable extensions are used for subfeeder. Meltric 100-A to 100-A "octopus" three-fers and Meltric 100-A to 60-A "squid" three-fers divide the three-phase power into single-phase 120-V circuits. Fused 90- and 50-A gang boxes provide Edison or twist-lock outlets for the smaller fixtures.

Meltric Connectors

Meltric connectors feature a positive mechanical lock, spring-loaded connector caps, and a five-wire polarized "make first, break last" pin configuration that prevents wires from being plugged incorrectly. The connectors are spring-loaded so they spring apart when released and must be pushed together with force to connect them. Because of their rugged design and many features, the connectors are larger and heavier than other distribution connectors.

Abbott Connectors and Sequentially Locking Panels

The sequential safety-lock panel is designed to make it impossible to connect and disconnect the feeder cables in the wrong order. A locking mechanism prevents any connectors from being connected before the ground. Once the ground is connected, the neutral must be connected next, and only then can the hot wires be connected.

Other brands of connectors have similar sequentially locking panels. Posi-loc is a system for Cam-Lok connectors, and VEAM B-lok is a similar panel for VEAM single-conductor connectors. Sequentially locking panels are not required by code, and while some feel that they make the distribution system idiotproof, the use of panels on every female connection is generally an unnecessary encumbrance.

European Distribution Systems

There are many similarities between the U.K. and American systems of distribution, although the amperage requirements are much less in Europe, due to the higher voltages used. The U.K. system of distribution is based on BS5550, which was introduced in 1981 and is periodically revised. It has been very successful in streamlining the number of connectors and cable systems in use, together with the types of switchgear and distribution units. The primary distribution units consist of the following (see Figure 12.20):

Intake switch unit (ISU)   Power intake from the mains or generator, 400 A.
Control centre (CC)   Intermediate distribution, 400 A/125 A/63 A.
Final distribution unit (FDU)   125 A/32 A/16 A.

The main power distribution cables are single core, typically, 400 A, 250 A, or 150 A and commonly use BAC connectors. BAC, Spade, and Tec connectors or bare wires are used to connect to the power supply. It is essential to identify each of these cables clearly to show whether it is a phase, neutral, or earth conductor. Obviously, any misplugging can cause a huge fault or a very dangerous situation. Several modern distribution systems have sensing circuits to prevent misplugging. The system (shown in Figures 12.21–12.23) is used by Michael Samuelson Lighting Ltd of Pinewood Studios. It incorporates four system status lights on the top of each distribution unit. A green light indicates the box is properly grounded. A red light warns of reversed polarity, and a blue light and buzzer indicate ground leakage. The buzzer lets an electrician know that there is a ground leak as soon as a lighting unit is plugged in, even when the flashing blue light is out of sight. The buzzer can be turned off with a key (held by the gaffer), in which case a yellow light comes on to indicate when the buzzer is disabled.

The main feeder cables terminate into a control centre distribution box. In a three-phase system, this box feeds multiple three-phase 125-A subfeeders that run to either a splitter unit (which separates the phases into three 125-A single-phase runs) or a distribution unit (which offers a variety of single-phase outlets).

Generally, multicore connectors and cables are used for circuits 125-A and less. BS4343 connectors are commonly used. Figure 12.21 shows the four single-phase connector sizes. Typically, these would be color coded blue for single phase.

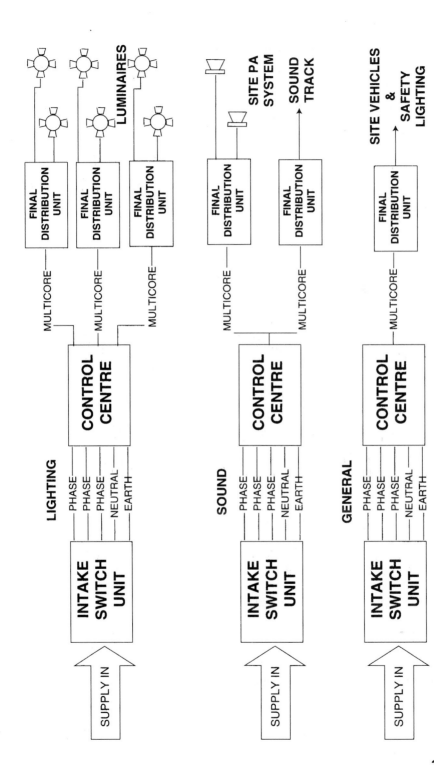

Figure 12.20 U.K. distribution systems overview.

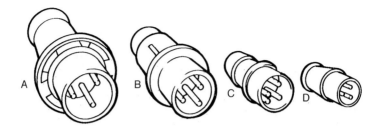

Figure 12.21 BS 4343 single-phase plugs: (A) 125 A, (B) 63 A, (C) 32 A, (D) 16 A. (From *David Samuelson's Hands-on Manual for Cinematographers*. Oxford: Focal Press, 1994. Reprinted with permission of Focal Press.)

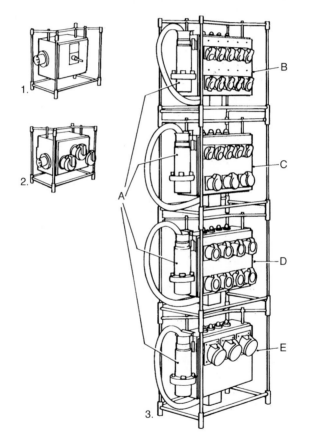

Figure 21.22 MSL electric distribution system: (1) 125 isolation switch unit, (2) 125 three-phase splitter unit, (3) stacked 125 distribution units: (A) 125-A single-phase (with inlet plugs on short cables), (B) 10 × 16-A outlets, (C) 5 × 32-A outlets, (D) 8 × 32-A outlets. (From *David Samuelson's Hands-on Manual for Cinematographers*. Oxford: Focal Press, 1994. Reprinted with permission of Focal Press.)

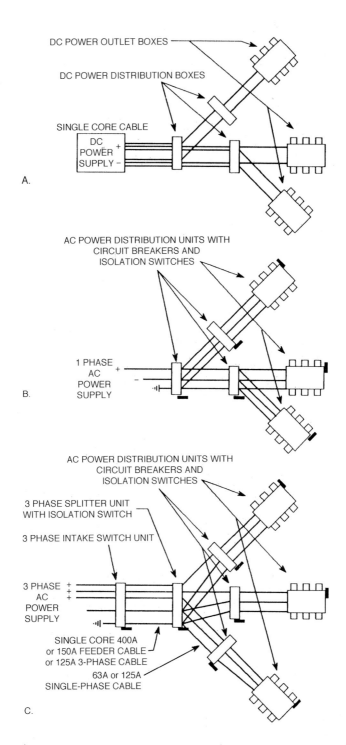

Figure 21.23 Power distribution schematics. (A) DC system, (B) single-phase AC system, (C) three-phase system. (From *David Samuelson's Hands-on Manual for Cinematographers*. Oxford: Focal Press, 1994. Reprinted with permission of Focal Press.)

Three families of connectors are color coded: red for three-phase connectors, blue for single-phase ones, and yellow for low-voltage connectors.

Several different input and output power arrangements of the units cater to the variety of connectors used and for three-phase and single-phase operation. Figure 12.22 shows some examples. The six boxes shown here form a system: 125-A intake switch unit (1), 125-A three-phase to three 125-A single-phase splitter unit (2), and junction boxes that distribute power to all the various outlet sizes (3). The system also incorporates splitter units to divide 125-A to 63-A outlets and 63-A to 32-A outlets. There are outlet boxes with 63- or 32-A inputs and multiple 16-A outputs, and Y-splitters and jumper leads to adapt to domestic type plugs. The 16-A connectors are typically used on lights up to about 3500 W. The 32-A connectors can be used on luminaries up to about 7000 W. The 63-A connectors are typical for lights up to 12k.

Distribution units are fitted with the necessary power intake switchgear and subdistribution fuses or MBCs contained within one unit, which makes rigging so much safer by reducing the amount of interconnections on site. Each outlet has its own mechanical circuit breaker and neon indicator. Most modern distribution units are fitted with RCDs (GFCIs) to prevent nuisance tripping.

Figure 12.23 shows the step-down structure generally used with DC circuits, single-phase AC circuits, and three-phase AC circuits.

Many other types of connectors used for various purposes and by various vendors. Electrical regulations specify that all connectors must be approved to either a British standard or an International standard and should be used only with the correct pin connections and relevant color codes. Under the British Health and Safety regulations, all items used on the temporary installation must be tested for electrical safety prior to being delivered to site and have to be marked that the test was satisfactory. It is essential that, when any temporary installation is complete, wherever it is, it is fully checked to ensure that all connections and equipment have been installed correctly prior to the application of power to the system.

Rigging

A rigging crew prerigs the cabling and hangs lights prior to the arrival of the shooting crew. The rigging crew is supervised by the *rigging gaffer*, who plans the cabling for the sets. Responsibilities include

- *Placement* of distribution boxes, outlets boxes, and dimmer circuits for ease of use.
- *Control* of lighting via dimmers, remote switches or manually.
- *Routing* of cable (an efficient use of cable combined with routing that keeps cable out from under foot and invisible to camera).
- Providing sufficient *amperage capacity*.
- *Minimizing line loss*.
- *Estimating and requesting personnel* for all the work, including rigging, wiring practical fixtures, and setting up the dimmer board.

- *Ordering all the cable and lighting equipment* for the rigs.
- *Ordering special equipment*, including generators, condors, genie lifts, scissor lifts, "mule" winches, fork lifts, all terrain vehicles (ATVs), and so forth needed to accomplish the work.
- *Safety*: Assuring the rigging is free of electrical hazards, neatly squared away, and eliminating or postwarning for physical hazards that the crew could trip over, get hooked on, bonk their heads on, get poked in the eye with, get burned by, run into in the dark, fall from, and the like.
- *Testing* the power system from beginning to end, including the lights.
- *Prelighting*: Placing, focusing, gelling, diffusing, and flagging the lights, roughing it in for the shooting crew.
- *Labeling* everything and providing a light plot for gaffer and first unit crew, and a dimmer hook-up sheet for the dimmer board operator. Electricians unfamiliar with the rig need to be able to quickly orient themselves to the layout.
- *Coordinating with other departments*, in particular the production designer, set dresser, construction coordinator, locations manager, transportation department, grip department, and of course, the production manager and production staff. This includes providing the locations manger with a schedule of the rigging crew's activities, so the manager can make arrangements for parking, bathrooms, and transportation for the rigging crew. Arranging with transportation to have stake-bed trucks or other vehicles available.

On small productions, the best boy may serve as the rigging gaffer and go out with a couple of extra electricians to prerig locations.

Distribution Strategy

Preparing the cabling and distribution for a set or location requires planning, forethought, and calculation. During filming, an electrician working the set should need only to glance around his immediate area to find power for a light, yet the cable must remain neat and invisible to the camera at all times. An electrician rarely requires a 50-ft stinger on a set that is properly cabled, nor should a stinger have to cross a room if the distribution is effectively laid out. You should never find yourself having to run four or five stingers out a door and around a corner; one properly placed 100-A box can eliminate a lot of work, mess, and task time. No matter how far away the gaffer wants a light, getting power should not create a crisis; cable should be standing by, ready to be run out to it.

Set Power—the "Ring of Fire"

Here are some rules of thumb for laying out set power on location and sound stages alike. Provide a "ring of fire"—surround the set with power on all sides. Rigging is not only a matter of having sufficient amperage available but having outlets placed so that one is always close at hand. No matter where the camera is placed, you should have a 100-A gang box ready to pull in behind camera. In each room where action is to take place, have 100-A whips (with gang boxes) coiled outside each door ready to come in when needed. In a room with only one door, provide 100-A whips on the opposite side of the room (through a window, through a rat hole in the set, over the top of the set wall, or dropped from the grid), ready to come in should the door have to close. Provide at least 100 A to each side of a room. In a large room, provide 100-A whips every 50 ft (hidden outside windows, in side rooms, through rat holes, or ready to drop from the grid). In a house with a staircase, you need power at the top of the stairs. Hide cables that cross doorways by routing the cable up and over the top of the door.

Substantial amounts of power are often required outside windows to power large units pointing into the room, as well as units lighting up an exterior (at night). When shooting on a stage, a *translight* or *scenic painting* often is hung outside windows to provide an exterior backdrop (a cityscape, suburban street, mountain woodland, or what have you). Translights are typically backlit with a row of sky pans. When shooting in a room with a lot of windows, you can expect the gaffer to want some large units outside. Have the necessary distribution box positioned accordingly. Provide 120-V *and* 208- or 240-V service.

The DP may want lights inside buildings across the street or streetlight effects on background buildings. There may be platforms for area lighting, such as Condors or scissor lifts, which will require power, perhaps a separate generator and cable run.

Planning the Rig

The first step in planning is to draw a plot. The gaffer and DP may have already drawn a basic light plot showing the sets and indicating where lights will be rigged. It is up to the rigging gaffer to then plan the specifics and fill in the blanks. On his own copy of the plot he adds the distribution boxes. This may include AC "hard" power, AC dimmer circuits, DC power, or all three. Devise a system of symbols to identify each type of distribution equipment in the rig. Use a standard lighting template to draw the lights.

Once location and type of distribution have been established you can draw in the cable runs. Colored pencils are handy to distinguish different types of runs. Add up the power demand. The total will be the amperage carried by the main feeder run. On a large studio stage there will be many main feeder runs from the service cans around the stage. For each area, power is drawn from the nearest can.

Note that stages are often wired with more than one can per circuit. On a feature stage, for example, there may be eight cans that serve four circuits—two cans per circuit. If the amperage of each circuit is 3200 A, you must run the loads so that the two cans that serve that circuit do not carry more than 3200 A between them. Each studio keeps a rigging bible, which charts the hook-up and capacity of the cans on each of the studio's stages. If you are unfamiliar with the stage, check the rigging bible.

You now know all the equipment that will be needed for the rig: feeder cable, switchboards, dimmers, distro boxes, subfeeder cable, extensions, and plugging boxes. The best boy can place the equipment order with the rental house or studio

Table 12.4 DC Cable Runs

Type of Run	No. of 4/0 Pieces	Amps per Leg	Total Amps	Configuration		
				Hot	Neutral	Hot
4-2-4 (million run)	10	1600	3200	4	2	4
3-2-3 (750 run)	8	1200	2400	3	2	3
2-1-2 (1/2 million run)	5	800	1600	2	1	2
1-1-1 (1/4 million run)	3	400	800	1	1	1
Two wire	2	400	400	1	1	0

lighting department. Order slightly more than your initial calculations in order to cover contingencies. Better to return some equipment later than to have to order more.

Paralleling DC Cable Runs

Let's begin by calculating the DC cable runs. The 4/0 cable has a maximum amperage rating of approximately 400 A. A normal three-wire circuit using 4/0 cable delivers 400 A per leg, 800 A total. If more amperage is required, the cable can be doubled (this is known as a half-million run), tripled (a 750 run), or quadrupled (a million run). This is called *paralleling* the cable. Table 12.4 shows the maximum amperage that can be drawn by various configurations, and Figure 12.24 shows the configuration of wires for each run.

The term *million run* comes from the days when the main feeder cables were larger than 4/0 (believe it or not!) and rated in circular mils. The cable size was 250,000 circular mils. Therefore, one run (250,000 cm) was referred to as a *quarter million run*. If two paralleled cables were used per leg (making 500,000 cm of copper per leg) it was called a *half million run*. Three cables per leg (750,000 cm) was called a *750 run* or *3/4 million run*, and four cables per leg made a *million run*. Today 4/0 cable has a cross-sectional area of only 211,600 cm, but we still refer to a four cable run as a million run (easier to say than 846,400 run).

When running fewer neutral wires than hot leg wires, it is crucial that you maintain a balanced load. The neutral wires will not be overloaded as long as the two hot legs remain evenly balanced. Remember that the neutral carries only the difference in amperage between the two hot legs. During operation, the best boy must never let the two legs become unevenly loaded by more than the amperage capacity of the neutral wires.

Paralleling AC Cable Runs

A 4/0 run of three-phase AC can deliver up to 1200 A, at 400 A per leg. A 4/0 run of single-phase three-wire AC delivers 800 A, at 400 A per leg. If more amperage is required, a parallel run (all wires) is made from the power source. When nonlinear loads are to be used, the NEC requires that the neutral be able to carry 130% of the load on the phase wires. In practice we simply double the neutral when powering dimmers or other nonlinear loads.

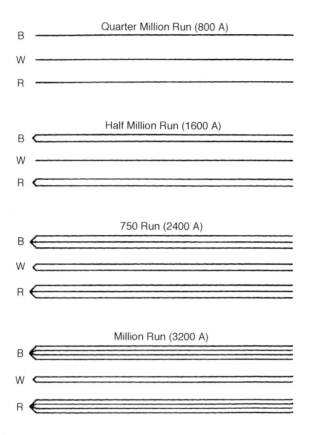

Figure 12.24 Parallel cable configurations for DC runs.

For example, if the demand is 1600 A and the AC service is single phase, we could meet this demand by paralleling two 4/0 runs of single-phase, three-wire AC. At 800 A each, the total is 1600 A. If the AC service is three-phase, we would parallel two 1200-A runs for a total of 2400 A (provided to power source has 2400-A capacity).

Figure 12.25 shows the effect on line loss of increasing the cable. You might think that doubling the cable also allows you to pull more amperage; however, increasing the amperage increases the line loss. The doubled cable gives you a longer run without problems from line loss, but you cannot then add amperage without the problem of line loss returning. Appendix C gives the line loss per 100-ft for various types of cable and load circuits.

Looping a Circuit

A trick used to increase the effective amperage of the cable or to cut line loss is to form a *cable loop*, complete circle of cable around a set, running cable around either side of the set and joining the legs at the back of the set at a spider box or with suicide pins. Joining the cables does not change the total maximum amperage but increases the maximum amperage you can have on either cable run. For example,

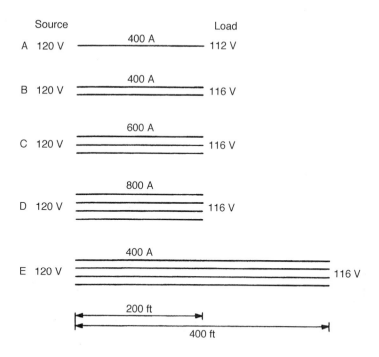

Figure 12.25 Double, triple, and quadruple cable effect on line loss.

if the cable were #2 AWG (rated at 150 A), the maximum amperage you could have without joining the cables would be 150 A per leg on each run (300 A per leg total). With the cables joined, you can run *up to* 300 A per leg anywhere in the circle depending where the loads are distributed (Figure 12.26). The actual amount of current on the cables depends on where in the loop the loads are applied. Given two paths back to the power source, most of the current will go via the shortest route (least resistance). If the load is mostly on one side of the set, most of the current will draw from the feeder on that side, and the benefit of looping the cable would be diminished. If the load is mostly in the center of the loop, the load will draw from both sides evenly and you can increase the load up to the ampacity of both cables combined. In effect, this is like paralleling cables.

For example, say you loop banded cable around a house. The loop has a total length of 300 ft. If the load is balanced around the loop, or if the bulk of the load is located about halfway around the loop (150 ft around the loop) then the cable will carry about 150 A in either direction per leg (300 A per leg total). In effect, you are paralleling the cables. However, if the entire 300 A load is moved to one side of the house located only 50 ft from the start of the loop, the current will divide *unevenly*. Only about 30 A will be carried back the long way (the 250 ft side of the loop); about 270 A will be carried by the 50 ft side of the loop. As you can see, this would over-amp the cable (we like to keep #2 cable around 150 A). *The current will be carried in two directions in inverse proportion to the distance in each direction.* In other

Table 12.5 Ampacity Increase and Total Ampacity on 300-Foot Looped Cable When the Entire Load Is Placed in One of Various Locations Around the Loop

Location of Entire Load Around 300-ft Loop	Distance Around/ Distance Remaining	Ampacity Increase (by looping cable)	Total Ampacity at This Location
50 ft	50 ft/250 ft = 0.2	0.2 × 150 A = 30 A	150 + 30 A = 180 A
100 ft	100 ft/200 ft = 0.5	0.5 × 150 A = 75 A	150 + 75 A = 225 A
150 ft	150 ft/150 ft = 1	1 × 150 A = 150 A	150 + 150 A = 300 A

Note: In practice the load is spread all around the loop. This example is a worst-case scenario to illustrate how the resistance of the length of the cable can limit the benefit of a cable loop.

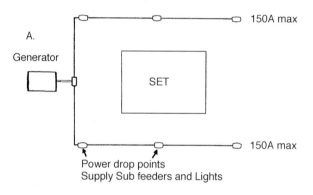

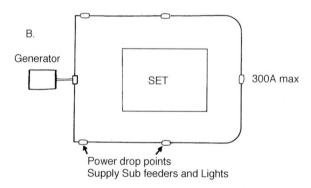

Figure 12.26 (A) Two runs of 2 AWG banded cable allow 150 A per leg on each run. (B) By connecting the cables at the ends, up to 300 A can be run anywhere in the loop. Note: Actual current depends on where in the loop lights are connected. Most current travels the shortest route. Be sure to measure loads with an amp probe.

words if the load is one-sixth of the way around the loop, then the current will be split five-sixths the short way, one-sixth the long way. The closer you are to an even load throughout the loop, the closer you are to optimum (paralleled cables). Table 12.5 shows the maximum amperage you could put on the 300-ft looped cable we have been talking about, without overloading the cable. This example assumes you are trying to put the load all in one place; a worst case scenario which probably would not happen in practice. Note that running a ghost load will not help "balance the load" around a cable loop.

In practice, you'd want to make sure your current is within tolerances by periodically checking the current on each side of the loop with an amp probe. Typically after each setup you are running different amounts of power all around the loop. Measure the current of each side at the point where they split, closest to the power supply.

Rigging the Set

During rigging, the distribution system remains disconnected from the power source and from the lights and electrical appliances. Only after the whole distribution system has been laid out and the system tested for shorts and discontinuity is the system connected to the power source and the main switch turned on. The crew checks the line voltage before any lights are plugged in to make sure that the power plant has been adjusted and is running properly and that cabling is properly connected.

Rules for Cabling

Avoid running feeder cable on the floor of the sound stage across traffic areas. The stage floor is a freeway of heavy equipment coming in and out: set pieces, Condors, forklifts, carts, and so on. Run cable from the can (or generator) straight up into the perms (or grid). This river of cable hanging down the wall of a sound stage is affectionately termed a *waterfall*. If a cable must cross the fire lane or other walkway, cover it with a cable crossover or tape rubber matting over it.

In the perms, the main feeder cable carpets the catwalks and runs to strategic locations above the set. From here the main feeder may feed a distribution box from which whips drop to the stage floor and the green beds, or it may split into smaller feeder runs and drop to feed distro boxes on the stage floor.

When laying cable, the crew typically starts at the power source and works toward the set, first laying out the feeder cable, then placing and connecting the switchboards, then running power to the greens and stage floor, and finally hanging the lights.

In rigging, neatness counts. Keep the cables as out of the way as possible and well organized. A fire marshal or electrical inspector gets the first clue that a set is unsafe from a quick look around at the general neatness of the work. If everything is nicely squared away, the inspector knows he or she is unlikely to find much at fault on further inspection; if the work is sloppy and possible hazards are visible, the inspector will keep looking for violations until he or she finds them. Any excess cable should be left at the load end of the cable, where it will be available if needed later. In green beds and catwalks, excess cable should be run out in a straight line, turned back on itself, and run to its end point (Figure 12.27).

Avoid sharp bends in cable. These cause hot points in the cable. Never leave a live cable in a circular coil because this can cause serious line loss and heat up and ruin the cable.

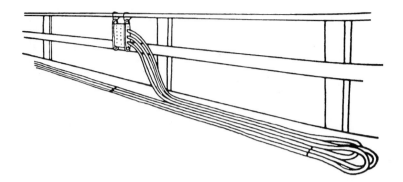

Figure 12.27 Cable turned back on itself.

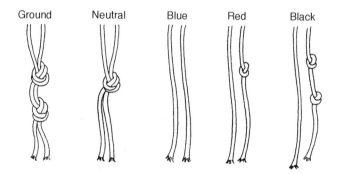

Ground   Neutral   Blue   Red   Black

Figure 12.28 On single conductor cable, use knots in the tie ropes to identify the wires. Figure eight knots are easy to untie after use. Use knots even when cables are color coded. Knots have the advantage of being readable in the dark.

Identifying Cable, Labeling Circuits

When laying out single conductor cable, it is extremely important to identify each cable properly. Each end of each cable can be identified with knots in the tie ropes (Figure 12.28) or with colored tape. Tie the appropriate knots at both ends of each cable before uncoiling it.

Many different runs of cable are often placed on a single catwalk. It is useful to be able to identify quickly the cables of a single run. To do this, lace the wires of each run together, as shown in Figure 12.29. Lacing the cables also helps keep the runs neat.

At each junction point between cables, the switch number, circuit number, or dimmer number should be labeled with 2-in. white tape on the spider box, deuce board, or distribution box. Switchboards should be labeled with the switch number and circuit number. It is also helpful to identify the intended function of the circuit, such as drop-in, high box, top lights, and so forth. A set lighting technician who is unfamiliar with the layout must be able to understand the circuitry by reading the labels on the cables and equipment.

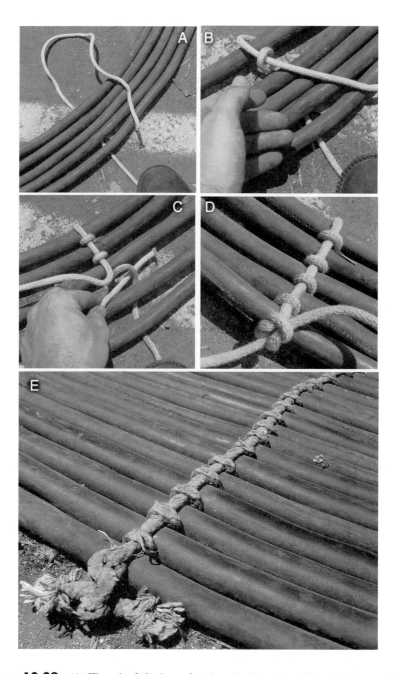

Figure 12.29 (A) Thread a 3-ft piece of sash under the cables, (B) pull a loop up from between the cables and thread the upper line through it. (C) With one foot anchoring the lower line, pull each loop tight and (D) tie it off with a square knot. (E) Laced cable lies flat and neat. Each run is united and cannot get tangled. The sash provides spacing between cables and aids in ventilation.

When AC and DC are being used on the same set, be sure to mark all outlet boxes either AC or DC. Write DC labels in black pen and AC labels in red pen so that the type of power is immediately obvious.

On spider boxes and distro boxes, identify the color of the hot legs with colored electrical tape or simply by writing red, blue, or black on a piece of tape. During filming, an electrician can immediately see what leg is being plugged into and tell the best boy if need be.

Each dimmer circuit serves a single light or a group of lights that always acts as a single unit. Each circuit has a number that corresponds to a dimmer address on the dimmer pack. Every cable between the dimmers and the lights is labeled with the circuit number. When rigging lots of dimmer circuits, affix white tape to both ends of all the cable before you run it. That way it is an easy matter to mark the cable as you run it, and you need not carry tape around with you. Tab spare cable also so that it can be easily labeled when added.

Make First, Break Last

When cabling is added to or removed from a system that is hot, the ground connection must be made first and broken last. This is called the *make first, break last rule*. Many electricians make it a habit to make connections in the proper order, regardless of whether the system is hot. The idea is that, if you get in the habit of doing it the right way every time, you never do it the wrong way when it matters.

Connect in this order: (1) ground, (2) neutral, (3) phase wires.

Disconnect in this order: (1) phase wires, (2) neutral, (3) ground.

Root Out Bad Contacts

Each time you attach two pieces of cable, check the pins and be sure each connector is making solid contact. Use a pin-splitter tool to bend apart smooshed pins. Nightmarish flicker problems are caused by bad, bent contacts in Bates cable or pin cable. Having to track down a bad cable because lights start flickering during filming is a horrible experience. The expression on the DP's face while watching banks of lights go dark one after another as the crew scrambles around behind the sets yelling, "Repatch" is enough to ruin a gaffer's whole day. Any questionable cable should be put aside and tagged boldly with tape.

Knots

Every electrician should know the following knots:

Bowline   When lifting equipment onto a catwalk, use a bowline (Figure 12.30A) to tie the rope to the equipment.

Highwayman's hitch or draw hitch   A highwayman's hitch is a self-tightening knot that also has the advantage of having a "quick-release" (Figure 12.31). This is a good one for raising and lowering equipment on a line.

Clove hitch   A cable tension relief is made using a clove hitch on the cable (Figure 12.30C). A clove hitch uses the weight of the cable to grip the cable tightly. The two loose ends of rope are looped around a support and tied with a square knot (Figure 12.30B). When tying off a cable drop from a catwalk or green

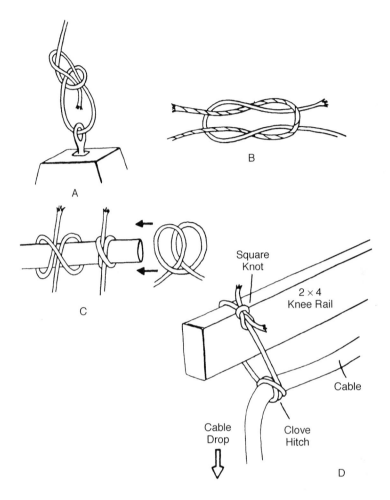

Figure 12.30 Useful knots: (A) The bowline is a very reliable knot that does not come loose when stressed. It is often used for tying ropes to equipment for lifting aloft. A real ace can tie this knot with one hand, a useful trick. (B) The square knot is used to tie one rope to another. (C) The clove hitch is used to hold tight to a deadweight, such as a vertical cable drop. (D) The clove hitch and square knot are used as tension relief on a cable drop.

bed, tie the cable to the knee rail or standing post (Figure 12.30D). Do not tie off to wood smaller than a 2 × 4.

High safety knot   A high safety knot (Figure 12.32) is used to tie off a line that has tension on it, such as that from a dead weight or block and tackle. The *saddle* cinches the line so that it will not slip while you tie the two half hitches to secure it.

Trucker's hitch   The trucker's hitch (Figure 12.33) is used to tighten a rope, as when tying something down or securing a rope around equipment to hold it during travel. A better trucker's hitch is shown in Figure 12.34.

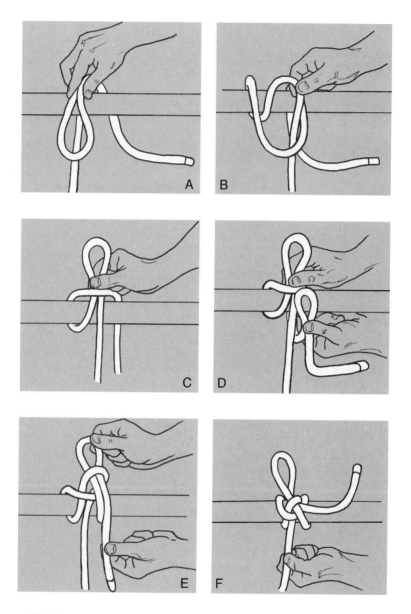

Figure 12.31 A highwayman's hitch is great for raising and lowering objects; it will not come loose when you put tension on the standing line, but it is also fast to untie—just pull on the loose end. Be sure to tighten the knot (F) by pulling on the standing line before hoisting gear.

Rigging Lights

When lights are mounted to pipe, all cable should run to one end of the pipe and from there up to a tie-off point. The bundle of cable is sashed to the pipe at regular intervals. Leave two loops of slack at each head so it can be panned and tilted.

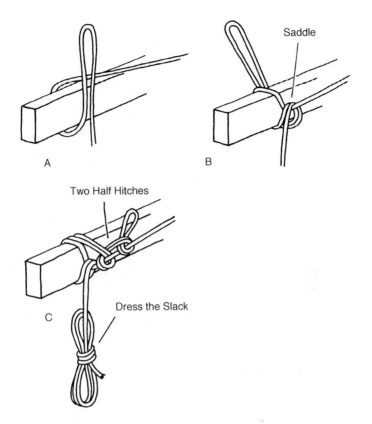

Figure 12.32 The high safety knot is used to tie off a taut line.

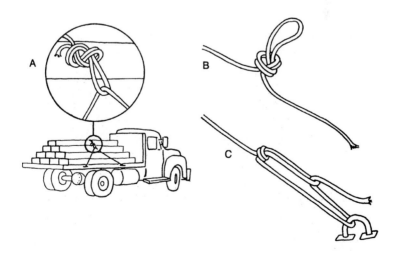

Figure 12.33 The trucker's hitch is used to tighten a rope around equipment to secure it in place. (A) A trucker's hitch using two ropes, (B and C) a trucker's hitch using a single rope.

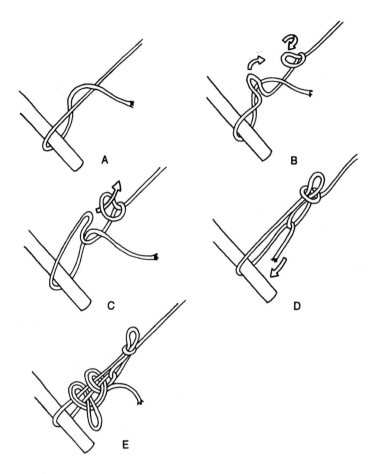

Figure 12.34 This hitch allows you to tighten the rope as you would a trucker's hitch; however, it is more easily adjustable and the knot can be removed quickly by simply removing the half hitches and tugging on the loose end. Unlike the standard trucker's hitch, no knots are left in the rope.

In some situations lights must be suspended (Figure 12.35) by rope using a block and tackle to hoist them into position. A one-to-one block and tackle can be used for smaller lights. For larger and heavier lights, a two-to-one or three-to-one block and tackle is necessary (Figure 12.36).

Testing

Once the entire distribution system is in place, it must be thoroughly wrung out; that is, each circuit from beginning to end must be tested for short circuits, continuity, correct voltage (120, 208, or 240), and line loss. In the process of testing, you may find blown fuses, tripped circuit breakers, blown bulbs, bad connections, burnt-out cable, and the like. By the time you are finished, you have a pristine rig ready for the shooting crew.

Figure 12.35 A row of eight-banger soft lights shining down through the ceiling of the set, rigged to the rafters with blocks and tackle. This rig creates soft top light for a three-level set built for *Star Trek: Deep Space Nine* on Stage 17 at Paramount Studios. Note that the blocks and tackle are tied off to the handrail with high safety knots. In addition, each light is tied off with guy wires and secured with chain. (Rig by Frank Valdez. Photo by author.)

Before connecting the lights to the distribution systems, and before connecting the feeders to the power source, *check all lines for short circuits.* You can do this quite simply by taking a 120-V test bulb plugged into a hot outlet and touching the two contacts to two of the feeder wires at a time. If the test bulb lights, there is a short between those wires. Check each wire in combination with each of the other wires. Note: a continuity tester is not appropriate because lights in the distro boxes provide continuity between hot and neutral wires.

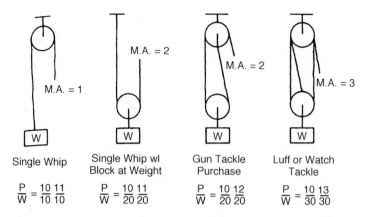

Figure 12.36 Block and tackle mechanical advantage configurations. The moving part of the block and pulley is called the *sheave*. Heavy lights, like the eight-bangers shown in Figure 12.35, are rigged with the luff tackle, which gives a three-to-one mechanical advantage. Smaller lights could have a single whip with no mechanical advantage. (Reprinted with permission from *Backstage Handbook* by Paul Carter. New York: Broadway Press, 1988.)

Next, turn the power on, and *check the voltage* at each outlet box. Be sure that none of the boxes accidentally has the wrong voltage (120 or 240).

At this point, you can plug in all the lights and begin to turn them on. *Check that each light is working.*

With all the lights on, use a precise voltmeter to *check for line loss.* First check the voltage at the power source, then check it at the end of each run. Be sure that you are checking at the farthest point from the power source on each run. If the line voltage is abnormally low, check for bad connections and bad cable on that run. Remember resistance increases as the load increases, so a voltage test tells you nothing about the line loss unless *all* the lights are burning.

If magnetic HMI ballasts are to be used, *check the line frequency.* It should be constant at 60 Hz.

Electronic Dimmer Systems

An electronic dimmer system consists of a control console (which controls and displays the dimmer status of the dimmers) and the dimmer packs (the actual dimmers), as shown in Figure 12.37.

How an SCR Dimmer Works

An electronic dimmer is a *silicon-controlled rectifier* (SCR). Rather than increasing or decreasing voltage (the amplitude of the AC sine wave), as with a variable transformer, an SCR dimmer increases and decreases power by chopping up the sine wave (Figure 12.38).

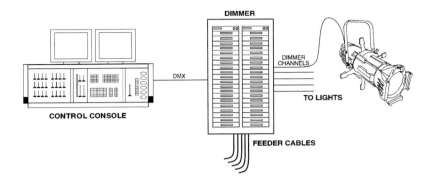

Figure 12.37 Dimmer system overview.

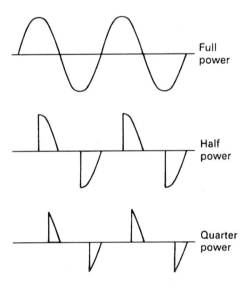

Figure 12.38 The AC wave form of a SCR dimmer circuit. At half power, the sine wave is actually clipped off halfway through its cycle.

At 100% power, the sine wave looks normal. At 50% power, the dimmer switches off the circuit during the rise in the sine wave, then switches on at the peak of the wave. The level to which the dimmer is set determines the point in the sine wave at which the dimmer activates. The dimmer deactivates each time the wave passes through zero. *Note: Because the sine wave is chopped up, SCR dimmers cannot be used on line with fluorescents, HMI fixtures, or electric motors (such as motorized stands and fans). Using electronic dimmers with such loads can cause damage to both the dimmer and the load.*

With the power source turning off and on with each half cycle (120 times per second), one might worry that the lights would flicker, especially when the shutter speed is set at non–flicker-free speeds. Most of the time this does not happen, because the glow of filament in the lamp does not have time to decay appreciably between half cycles. However, when using very small lamps at very low dimmer settings and filming off-speed, you *can have flicker register on film*, just as you would with HMIs using magnetic ballasts. A friend of mine was filming a large sign fitted with hundreds of tiny 100-W bulbs. The sign was patched into the SCR dimmer system and was set at 35%. For normal filming (24 fps), this was fine; however, when the camera was set to 48 fps and the shutter angle set to 90° (giving an effective shutter speed of $\frac{1}{96}$ th of a second, which is not a flicker-free speed), the lights flickered on film. The main ingredient to this disaster was the small size of the lamp filaments. The smaller is the filament, the more quickly it responds to changes in voltage. Lamps with larger filaments do not cause this problem. In this case, if variac dimmers had been used instead of SCR dimmers, if the dimmer setting were higher, or if the camera had run at 40 or 60 fps (which are flicker-free speeds), the lights would not have flickered on film.

Control Signals

The console communicates with the dimmers using a small signal cable. Older consoles use an analog system with individual 10-V DC control signal circuits running to each dimmer, requiring a multiwire cable (one wire per dimmer plus a common). The dimmer matches its power output proportionally to the voltage of the control signal from 0 to 10 V. Modern systems communicate using a multiplexed analog signal (AMX 192) or digital protocol (DMX 512). Dimmer levels are encoded by the control console and connected using an AMX four-wire or DMX five-wire control cable. A controller card in the dimmer pack decodes the multiplexed or digital signal. An AMX 192 signal can control as many as 192 channels with a single control cable. A DMX 512 protocol can control up to 512 channels. The control cable from the console is daisy-chained from one dimmer pack to the next, looping the signal through as many packs as needed.

Control Consoles

Control consoles have three levels of sophistication: manual boards, memory boards, and computer boards. The *manual board* has a set of sliding faders that directly correspond to the channel numbers. A typical two-preset board has a duplicate row of faders used to preset the fader positions for the next lighting cue. The two sets of faders are typically referred to as scenes X and Y. A cross-fade fader is provided to make a smooth transition from dimmer settings for scene X to those of scene Y. Most modern boards provide a single-handle or split-handle proportional dipless cross-fade, which cross-fades smoothly between presets without an intensity dip during the fade. Each set of fader levels is called a *scene preset*. In the days when manual boards were in common use, the board operator had to write down all the fader settings as the lighting designer created them during the prelight or tech rehearsals. During the performance, the board operator was constantly busy setting faders for the next lighting cue on the inactive scene preset. When prompted, he or she executed the cross-fade to the new scene, then began to reset all the faders for the next cue. Because cues sometimes needed to follow each other in rapid succession, boards with three, four, or more scene presets (hundreds of faders) were common.

Fortunately, the memory board was invented. A *memory board* is an enhanced manual board that memorizes and replays channel settings, freeing some or all the faders to be reset to a new state. In this way, a limited number of presets can be set up, memorized, and replayed without having to reset fader levels.

Other common features are separate nondim (switch) circuits, timed cross-fades, a grand master blackout switch, and on some boards, chase effects circuits. Momentary switches, which allow the board operator to flash the lights with a touch of his fingers, are a common feature on rock-and-roll boards.

Most dimmer boards provide *submaster faders*, which allow you to group faders and control each group with a separate submaster fader. When a submaster is created, the board records the levels of all the dimmers and assigns those levels a given submaster fader. When the board operator brings the submaster fader up to full, all the dimmers come up to their assigned levels. A board may have anywhere from four to several dozen submasters, and each submaster can be "piled on" to the others. In other words, if the board operator creates a submaster for the key lights, another submaster for the gobo pattern lights, and a third submaster for backlights, each group of lights can be added to the others. When a dimmer is assigned different levels in two or more active submasters, the dimmer takes the level of the higher submaster setting.

Sophisticated *computer boards* provide automatic, timed, cross-fade memory so that the cues cross-fade automatically at the preprogrammed speed. All the board operator has to do during the performance is hit the cue button when prompted; the board automatically executes the cross-fade. A cross-fade may be programmed to happen instantaneously, to dim smoothly over a couple of seconds, or even to fade almost imperceptibly over a matter of minutes. Computer boards can handle hundreds of complex timed level manipulations and even overlap multiple cues with ease.

Definitions

As you can already tell, when you start talking nuts and bolts about dimmer systems, you quickly run into a whole new language. It is important to understand the standardized meanings of terms like *patch, circuit, channel, preset,* and *cue.* These terms are very often misused or used interchangeably. Understanding the following list of definitions also helps clarify the way this equipment works in general. Most of what follows is taken almost directly out of the Strand CD80 operators manual.

Circuit Everything downstream of the dimmer, from the dimmer's output (Bates connector) to the lighting fixtures themselves.
Dimmer The device controlling power to a circuit and lighting fixtures. Two lights on one dimmer circuit cannot be controlled separately.

Channel Device controlling a dimmer or group of dimmers. In a simple system, there is a slider for each channel. On most current control systems, channels are numbers, accessed by a numeric keypad. Multiple dimmers may be controlled by a single channel to which they are *patched*.

Patch Historically, the process of physically connecting circuits to dimmers. Now usually refers to electronic assignment of dimmers to channels. *Patch* does not refer to the assignment of channels to cues or submasters.

Preset A predefined set of intensities for a set of channels, stored in memory for later replay.

Memory The storage location for preset information.

Cue The process of recalling a preset from its memory location and putting the result on stage.

Submaster A controller (usually a linear slider) that allows manual control of groups, effects, cues, or channels.

Fade A gradual change in stage levels from one set of intensities ("look") to another.

Up-fade The portion of a fade that involves only channels that are increasing in level.

Down-fade The portion of a fade that involves only channels that are decreasing in level.

Cross-fade A fade that contains both an up-fade and down-fade. This also may refer to any fade where the levels of one cue are replaced by the levels of another cue.

Bump An instantaneous change in stage levels from one set of intensities ("look") to another.

Strand CD 80 Pack

The Strand CD 80 digital pack is among the most commonly used portable dimmer packs in motion picture work. What follows are some crib notes on operation and trouble-shooting.

CD 80 packs are configured in one of the following ways (see Table G.3, Appendix G, for additional specifications):

24	1.2-kW dimmers, 15-A circuits.
12	2.4-kW dimmers, 20-A circuits.
24	2.4-kW dimmers, 20-A circuits.
6	6-kW dimmers, 50-A circuits.
6	12-kW dimmers, 100-A circuits.

For larger dimming jobs, a rolling rack combines multiple packs into a single compact rolling welded aluminum cabinet.

48	2.4-kW dimmers, 20-A circuits.
24	6-kW dimmers, 50-A circuits.
24	12-kW dimmers, 100-A circuits.

Input power feeder connectors are typically Cam-Lok. Output connectors are Bates (20-A, 60-A, or 100-A, according to circuit size). Some 1.2k and 2.5k dimmer packs are fitted with Socapex outputs. A single Socapex cable carries six separate 20-A circuits. When lights are individually controlled on 20-A circuits, Socapex cable makes cabling much less cumbersome. It comes in long lengths: 200, 150, 100, 50, and 25 ft. At the lamp end of the cable, a breakout adapter connects to the Socapex cable, providing six numbered 20-A Bates receptacles.

Installation and Setup

CD80 packs must receive adequate ventilation and be kept within reasonable temperature and humidity levels with no condensation. The packs are not designed to be used outdoors. As many as eight packs may be stacked vertically. Do not place more than two units side by side unless there is at least 24 in. between packs. Otherwise, the exhaust heat from one pack is blown directly into the intake vent of the next pack. Keep vents clear from obstruction, dirt, fibers, paint particles, and so forth.

Ideally, the rack is mounted in a special air-conditioned, soundproof cabinet, which eliminates the problems of both cooling and noise.

The brains of the CD80 pack is the *digital pack controller*, commonly known as the *card*. The digital controller is made of a faceplate mounted on a control card. The control card slides into slots in the front panel of the dimmer pack. Two thumb-screws secure it in place. In case of failure, the entire card can be replaced in the field. The digital pack controller can be removed and installed without disconnecting any wiring. With the input power turned off, loosen the thumbscrews and pull on the thumbscrews to slide the controller out of the pack.

To install the controller (again power off at source), line the controller up with guides on each side of the slot and slide the module in carefully until it touches the connector in the pack. Firmly set the controller by pressing on both ends of the module. Tighten in place with thumbscrews.

The faceplate contains the connectors, buttons, and indicator lights that affect everything the dimmer pack does (Figure 12.39):

Input and output connectors for AMX control cable (four-pin XLR).

Input and output connectors for DMX/SMX control cables (five-pin XLR).

Input connectors for 12 or 24 discrete analog control signals.

Input connectors for fiber optic cable (obsolete).

RS232 connector for connection with computer (obsolete).

Three power indicator lights (green) that show each input power phase present (ϕA, ϕB, ϕC). Use these to check the input power lines.

Three protocol indicator lights (yellow), which show the protocol currently being decoded (AMX, DMX, or analog).

Six mode-select dip switches, used to set various important parameters of operation. Table 12.6 outlines the function of each of these six dip switches. Be especially sure switches 2 and 6 are set properly or the dimmer pack may not work properly. If you change dip switch settings during operation, press the reset button to enter changes.

Overtemperature indicator light (red)—the dimmer pack shuts down automatically and this light comes on if the heat sink temperature exceeds 85°C. This would happen if the vents were blocked, if ventilation were inadequate, or if the fan motor failed.

Table 12.6 Dimmer Controller Card Dip Switch Settings

Position 1	<u>Off</u>: No effect
	On: No effect
Position 2	<u>Off</u>: Three phase
	On: Single phase
Position 3	When using analog and multiplexed protocol simultaneously, this switch determines if the output signal to the dimmer is the *sum* of the two signals (up to 100%) or the *higher* of the two signals (pile-on).
	<u>Off</u>: Highest takes precedence (pile-on)
	On: Dimmer level is analog + protocol
Position 4	Off: 0–15-V DC input level for analog input
	<u>On</u>: 0–10-V DC input level for analog input
Position 5	<u>Off</u>: In the event of loss of control signal, the dimmers retain current levels for 30 minutes
	On: In the event of loss of control signal, the dimmers black out
Position 6	Off: Uses every *other* control signal, starting with the thumbwheel number (use with 6-kW and 12-kW dimmers when using Strand lighting systems AMX 192 where 6-kW/12-kW dimmer assignment is made in the control console)
	<u>On</u>: Uses the first 12 control signals starting with the thumbwheel number

Notes: I underlined the setting that you typically want. Press the reset button to enter changes during operation. The control board reads these settings only during start-up. Changing them while in operation does nothing in most cases, until you press reset.

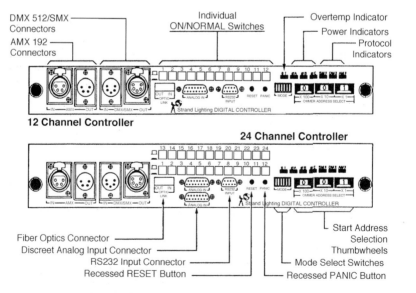

Figure 12.39 CD80 dimmer pack controller card faceplate.

Three numbered thumbwheels used to assign the first dimmer number for the pack. For example, when several 12-channel packs are daisy-chained together, the first pack would be assigned channels 1–12 by setting its thumbwheel to 1. The second pack's thumbwheel would be set to 13 (assigned channels 13–24).

Recessed "panic" button. When pressed, this button turns all dimmers on. Push it again to return dimmers to normal operation. Use a bent paper clip or other small probe to get to the recessed button.

Recessed reset button. When pressed, this button tells the card's processor to restart.

12 or 24 two-position pushbuttons. When set to the in position, each button turns on the associated dimmer to full and overrides the control signal or operates the dimmer in the absence of a control signal. When the button is in the out position, the dimmer operates normally and the backlit button shows the approximate level of the associated dimmer.

Three small (0.250-A fast-blow) phase fuses are located on the controller card. If a phase B or C fuse blows, the controller does not work the dimmers connected to that phase. If the phase A fuse blows, the controller is completely disabled. Replacing the fuses requires no special tools or procedures. With input power turned off, remove the controller card from the pack, replace the faulty fuse, and carefully reinsert the controller module.

The *dimmer law* refers to the response of the dimmer to the control signal over the range of fader settings. A direct one-to-one relationship between the control signal and dimmer output gives a fairly abrupt rise in light level as the fader is increased, whereas a modified square law gives smoother control over the lower end of the dimming curve. Dimmer law selection is made using the jumper on the control board, as shown in Figure 12.40.

To match the law with an analog control signal, disable the jumper. To use the modified square law, install the jumper as shown.

In addition to the mode-select switch in position 2 (setting for single or three phase), 1.2-kW, 2.4-kW, and 6-kW packs have an interior single/three-phase selection plug on the power terminal block. The factory default setting is three phase. To check the setting, remove the top cover of the pack and check the position of the phase selection plug shown in Figure 12.41. Close the pack and connect the input leads. Check the green power indicator lights to confirm that proper phases are powered.

Set the thumbwheels to the first dimmer number to which this dimmer pack is to respond. The digital controller will start looking at dimmer signals starting at the signal number set on the thumbwheel.

For example, if three 12-channel packs are to be controlled by a 36-channel console, you would set the pack 1 thumbwheel to 1, the pack 2 thumbwheel to 13, and the pack 3 thumbwheel to 25. This assigns channels 1–12 to the first pack, channels 13–24 to the second pack, and channels 25–36 to the third pack.

Each pack is independent of the others. You can set two packs to the same set of signal numbers if you require more than one physical dimmer for each dimmer number.

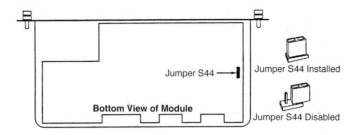

Figure 12.40 Dimmer law curve jumper location on controller card.

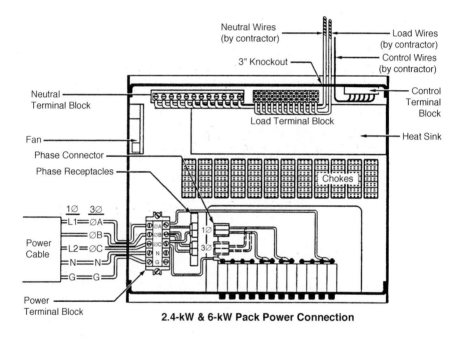

Figure 12.41 The CD80 internal phase selection plug (1.2-kW, 2.4-kW, and 6-kW packs only) factory default setting is three phase.

The start numbers need not be a multiple of 6 or 12. You can start one dimmer pack at 1 (dimmers 1–12) and the second pack at 9 (dimmers 9–20). This will give you two dimmers each on dimmers 9 to 12.

Troubleshooting

Problems Affecting the Entire Pack

No phase LED lit.

- No power to the dimmer pack. Check distribution and cable connectors.
- Controller may not be seated correctly. Remove and reinstall the controller.

- Fuse F1 (phase A) may be open (blown). Replace with a .0250A fast blow fuse if required (discussed previously).
- If the fuses are okay and you can turn the dimmers on with their individual pushbuttons, the controller module is defective. Replace it with a spare and return it to the owner or Stand Lighting for repair.

Phase B or C LED not lit. Fuse F2 or F3 is probably open. Replace the fuse (discussed previously).

All phase LEDs lit but no protocol indication.
- Control console is unplugged or control cable is disconnected.
- Incoming control wiring may be miswired or one or more conductors broken.
- Replace control cable or check its continuity and wiring.

No control of dimmers (dimmers are always OFF).
- If the OverTemp light is on, the pack has shut down from overheating. Make sure that the air intake and exhaust are not blocked and wait for the thermostat to reset.
- The thumbwheel settings may be set to an incorrect address. Double-check your settings.

No control of dimmers (dimmers are always on). The "panic" button may be on or the individual dimmer pushbuttons may be on.

Line Noise

The chopped waveform of an electronic dimmer can cause electromagnetic interference, current harmonics commonly called *line noise*. As described in Chapter 8, this can cause residual current to be carried on the neutral wire. In some situations and with some equipment, the neutral wire of the feeder cable may need to be doubled and even tripled when powering large numbers of dimmers. Symptoms of this problem are visible flicker in the lights and unusually large return current on the neutral wire. Also keep in mind that beefing up the neutral only transfers the problem to the power source. Make sure the power source is capable of handling excess current on the neutral.

Problems Confined to One Phase

Problems that are confined to one phase are usually related to controller problems or to the dimmer pack being incorrectly set up for the type of power in use.

Consecutively numbered dimmers will not go on.
- One phase of the power feeding the pack is off or not connected.
- The controller module may be incorrectly inserted. Remove it and carefully reinsert it into the dimmer pack.
- One or more output control circuits (in the controller) have failed. Swap the controller card with a known good spare. If the problem goes away, return the defective controller for repair.

One or more dimmers on the same phase do not come up to full or do not track correctly.
- The mode-select switch in position 2 may be incorrectly set. Make sure the pack is set up for the type of power being used.

- The phase fuse may be open.
- One or more output control circuits (or the controller) may be defective. Replace the controller with a spare and return the defective card for repair.

Problem with Individual Dimmers
Check the following:

Dimmer circuit breaker on.

Load wiring and lamp operating properly (not burnt out). Check the load wiring and lamp by turning on the pushbutton switch for that dimmer circuit. If nothing comes on, the problem is in the wiring or the lamp itself.

If you still have a problem, it is either a defective controller, defective discrete analog control wiring, or a defective SSR, circuit breaker, or choke. Each of these parts is designed to be easily replaced in the field.

Check the controller module by replacing it with a known good spare. Make sure the mode-select switches are set the same way on the replacement controller. If the problem goes away with the new controller, return the defective controller for repair.

Check for defective SSR, choke, or circuit breaker by checking the voltage at the circuit breaker output, choke output, and SSR output with the dimmer on (see Figure 12.41). The component with an input but no output is defective (most commonly the SSR). Replace the defective component.

If the dimmer works from the console (protocol input), but not from the discrete analog input, there is a problem in the discrete analog circuitry, external to the pack.

If the dimmers flicker when at 50%, the control card is defective. Replace it.

CHAPTER **13**

Power Sources

Generators

Putt-Putts (Portable Honda Generators)

For small amounts of remote power, a portable Honda-style "putt-putt" generator is a very handy unit to carry on any show. In rough terrain, it enables lighting in places a heavy diesel plant cannot reach. At night a putt-putt can save running hundreds of feet of cable to power one 2500 PAR to light the deep background. A Honda can power work lights during wrap, allowing the main plant to be shut down and the cable wrapped. One Hollywood insert company (which shoots mostly MOS establishing shots and pickups for movies and television shows) lights all its night exteriors quite nicely with little more than three putt-putts and a dozen PAR 64s.

A typical 45-A (5500-W) Honda generator that you get from a film equipment supplier will have been retrofitted with precision speed control and appropriate output connectors—60-A Bates, twist-lock, or Edison. (There is also a 6500-W model, which is significantly noisier.) Fuel capacity is generally 4.5–5 gallons, which will last 6–8 hours. The arrangement of the electrical circuits is also commonly modified for our use. From the factory, the alternator has two windings, wired in series, which provide two 20-A 120-V circuits and one 45-A 240-V circuit. In this configuration, you cannot pull more than 20-A per side, and it works best if you keep the two circuits evenly loaded. In this configuration, for example, you could not run a 5k or 4k PAR HMI (unless you used a European 240-V lamp or ballast). To use all 45 A available, on one 120-V circuit, a special retrofit must be made to the alternator. When Crawford or Young retrofits a generator, it splits the windings so that you can switch between parallel windings (one 45-A 120-V circuit) or series (two 20-A 120-V, one 45-A 240-V circuit). When using the 60-A Bates outlet, be sure that the unit is switched to 120-V mode. You will also encounter generators that are hardwired with the coils in parallel, with no 240-V outlets, that you can run to full capacity on one 45-A circuit.

Troubleshooting

With such a small engine, the governor can be touchy and easily upset by variations in the load or fuel flow. The resulting variations in the hertz rate can cause HMI "flicker." It is a wise precaution to monitor the hertz rate with an in-line meter, and many gaffers use flicker-free ballasts when powering HMIs from a putt-putt to allow greater tolerance for variation in hertz rate. The governor tends to be less stable with light loads. You get more consistent performance if you load the unit to near full capacity and do not change the load during the shot (with flicker devices or sudden light cues).

Hiccups in the power line are commonly caused by inconstant fuel flow. The generator must be on level ground. The fuel tank is mounted only slightly above the carburetor; if the putt-putt is on a slope, with the fuel tank on the low side, fuel can get too low to flow properly, which disrupts the power. When powering lights on a moving vehicle or vessel, rocking or jerking can interrupt fuel flow, which causes hiccups in the power line. This can be helped by keeping the tank topped off, but the best solution is to use a unit retrofitted with a fuel pump.

A common area of breakdown on the Honda is the circuits that recharge the battery. If they fail, the battery goes flat; as it does, the governor has difficulty maintaining consistent RPM. First the hertz rate becomes unstable, starts oscillating, and then slowly drifts lower and lower. If this happens, you can fix the problem temporarily (and get the shot) by jumping the battery with a car battery.

Another common trouble with these units is difficulty in starting due to the motor flooding. To avoid flooding the carburetor during transport, the fuel valve must be shut off. The carburetor has a very low head and floods and dribbles fuel all over the place if the valve is left open.

The performance of a small engine is greatly affected by air density. At high elevations (above 3000 ft), power output decreases 3% per 1000 ft. In the mountains, the mixture must be leaned out or the fuel/air mixture will be too rich, causing the engine to run rough and possibly foul the spark plugs.

Young Generators, Inc., extensively retrofit its Hondas to remedy the weaknesses mentioned. A fuel pump reduces fuel flow problems. The circuitry is completely reworked, with a split solenoid (50-A 120-V, or 120/240-V AC), beefier regulator, better battery charging system, and numerous other refinements. A fuel solenoid automatically shuts off fuel on shutdown to eliminate dribbling and flooding. The generator is mounted on four large pneumatic tires and encased in a protective metal roll-cage. It weighs about 440 lb.

Full-Size Generators

Movie generators are baffled to minimize noise for sound recording. They are very precisely electronically governed at 60 + 0.2 Hz to be reliable when used with HMI lights and are equipped with a hertz readout and hertz adjustment on the main control panel. Similarly, voltage is precisely maintained electronically and can be adjusted. Dual plants of 750-A to 1200-A are commonly mounted on the tractor of the production van (see Figure 2.2). Trailer-mounted "tow plants" are also common,

Figure 13.1 Trailer-mounted 1000-A generator. The vents on the top open automatically when the engine is turned on. The side doors provide access to the engine. On the back of the unit, the bottom doors cover the bus bars and power distribution outlets and above that is the digital control panel. (Equipment courtesy of Young Generators, Inc., Arroyo Grande, CA.)

ranging from small 200-A up to 2400-A. The smaller sizes (200 A, 350 A, 450 A, and 500 A) commonly use gasoline engines. Larger plants (500 A, 750 A, 900 A, 1000 A, 1200 A, 1500 A, 1800 A, 2400 A, 2500 A, or 3000 A) require diesel engines. (Rating generator capacity in amps is actually an anomalous and confusing invention of our business. In all other applications, generators are rated in kilowatts. A 60-kW generator is said to have a 500-A capacity at 120 V; a 144-kW generator has a 1200-A capacity, and so on.) A 1000-A AC/DC generator, like the one shown in Figure 13.1, is the typical workhorse for motion picture work.

Most generators used today are relatively simple to operate, fully automated, and self-diagnostic. The Young generator shown in Figure 13.1 is typical. It has a selection switch (either on the control panel or inside one of the rear doors) that allows you to choose between single-phase 240/120, three-phase 208Y/120, or two-wire DC with up to 200-A single-phase AC delivered concurrently. Some models also offer the option of 480Y/277 three-phase power. Circuit breakers or electronic overcurrent protection protect the generator from short circuits. Most generators on the West Coast provide copper bus bars for the connection of lug feeder cable. Generators are also commonly fitted with Cam-Lok or Mole-pin receptacles or both (Figure 13.2). The Young generator shown has dual voltage regulators, dual electronic governor controllers, and dual fuel pumps to provide redundancy in case a

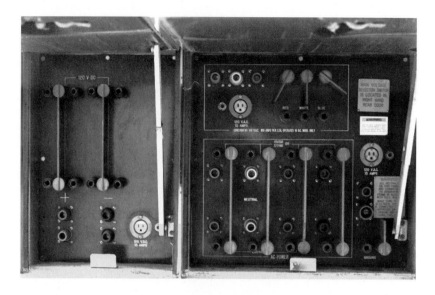

Figure 13.2 The distribution panel provides bus bars and Mole-pin and Cam-Lok connectors for each wire. On the left are the DC bus bars. On the bottom right are the AC bus bars, which can service three-phase 120/208-V power (or three-phase 277/480-V power by turning a selector switch inside the generator) or single-phase 120/240-V power using the three left bus bars. Above right are 120/240-V bus bars for AC when run concurrently with DC. There is also a 15-A Edison outlet for a courtesy light. At the far right bottom is the grounding bus. (Equipment courtesy of Young Generators, Inc., Arroyo Grande, CA.)

part fails. Young generators automatically shut down when they are about to run out of fuel. (This is not true of all generators. You can have significant downtime when a diesel motor has run out of fuel, because you have to bleed the fuel lines to get the air out.)

Smaller trailer-mounted generators typically have a fuel capacity of 80–150 gallons. A 500-A diesel generator under full load burns fuel at a rate of about 3.8 gallons per hour. The larger plants typically hold 200 gallons. A 750-A plant burns between 3 and 8 gallons per hour, depending on the load. A 1200-A plant burns 15 gallons per hour at full load, 8 at half load. A 500-A gasoline generator consumes about 6 gallons per hour at any load.

Generator Placement

The sound department has a vested interest in where the generator is placed. Despite baffles that deaden engine noise, generators can be a nuisance for the sound department. Place the generator around the corner of a building or behind a big vehicle, far from the set. Point the noisiest parts (the exhaust ports) away from the set. Electricians must sometimes run very long lengths of feeder cable to get the generator far enough from the set; once placed it can be a lot of trouble to move it, so it is worth getting it well placed initially.

The quieter the location, the harder it is to hide the generator. For example, one crew was shooting in the desert, where it is very quiet and very hard to find large structures to hide things. The crew had already run every piece of cable it had, and the generator was sitting miles away but was still ruining the sound takes. Finally, out of desperation, the best boy had a hole dug 14 ft deep and backed the generator into the hole. There is a theory among best boys that a sound mixer who can't see it won't hear it. Unfortunately, in this case, the sound mixer could still hear the interred generator. This just goes to show that you can't always please the sound mixer, no matter how hard you try, but you have to exhaust every possibility before you can give up. Another tactic I tried on a remote Western shoot was to build a thick haystack around the plant on three sides (allowing plenty of clearance so as not to create a fire hazard).

The generator operator or transportation personnel must make sure the plant is secured and stationary. The emergency brake must be engaged, if equipped, or chocks placed under the wheels to prevent movement (fire code regulations). It is a common misconception that the generator must be perfectly level to operate. Although a good policy when possible, this is not generally true. The main consideration is for the fuel in the fuel tank, but if the fuel intake is properly installed (in the *center, curbside*, at the *bottom* of the tank), being out of level does not adversely affect fuel intake. If conditions dictate that you must run the generator out of level, make sure the fuel filler and vents are high and the fuel pickup point is low.

Finally, the fire marshal will have several concerns related to generators. The generator must not be parked under anything that is likely to catch on fire, such as dry foliage. (Remember exhaust ports point up.) It must not block fire hydrants or exits. A multipurpose fire extinguisher (20-BC) or equivalent must be available. If the generator requires refueling, it must be shut down before refueling begins, and a "static line" attached between the fueler and the genie. There must be no smoking near the generator.

Generator Operation
Walk-Around Inspection
Before starting the generator each day, the operator makes a walk-around inspection of the plant that includes the following:

1. Open manual air vents if necessary. Most large generators' vents open automatically when the engine is started (they use oil pressure to hold them open). This is a great convenience, but you could forget to open them when they must be opened manually. The engine overheats very quickly without proper cooling. In rain or snow, the top air intake must be closed to prevent water getting in the air supply. The secondary air intake door must be opened instead. A valve, usually found near the back doors, may have to be closed to cut off oil pressure from the top door.
2. Check the oil at the beginning of every day. Add oil when needed. Inspect the engine compartment for leaky hoses or oil-soaked insulation.
3. Check the water level once or twice a week, and add water if necessary.

4. Remove the fuel cap and check the fuel level. The tank should be topped off each night to prevent water condensation inside the fuel tank overnight. (With gasoline engines, do not switch a flashlight on at the mouth of an open fuel tank. The spark in the switch can ignite the gas fumes.)
5. Check the Racor fuel filter for water and crud, which may have collected on the bottom of the clear bowl. Drain if necessary (draining the Racor filter is discussed in the section on Basic Troubleshooting).
6. Check fan and alternator belts.

Startup and Shutdown

Before starting the generator, run the distribution cables. Be sure no lights or other loads are connected to the distribution system. Connect the feeder cables to the generator. Place the generator's master power switch in the off position.

1. Check that the generator is set for single-phase AC 240/120, three-phase AC 208Y/120, or DC operation as desired. Some generators use a large selection switch (located inside, back, right) to switch large contactors from one configuration to another. Be aggressive when turning this switch. A solid connection is needed. Make sure the switch is fully locked in position. If the switch fails to make full contact or is left between settings, the results can be catastrophic.
2. Flip the stop/run switch to run (Figure 13.3), press the ignition switch or turn the ignition key. Leave the idle/run switch in idle while the generator is not

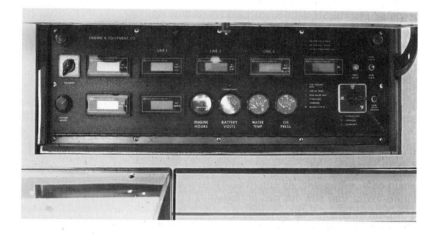

Figure 13.3 The digital control panel. Top row, from left to right, are the voltmeter selector switch, which selects which leg the voltmeter reads; AC voltmeter; three ammeters, one for each leg; and frequency meter. The lights below the frequency meter show engine diagnostics; the lights above the frequency meter indicate which type of power is being used. To the right of the frequency meter are the hertz adjustment knob and the panel-lights switch. Bottom row, from left to right, has the voltage adjustment knob, DC voltage meter, DC ammeter, four engine instruments, and ignition /power switch. (Equipment courtesy of Young Generators, Inc., Arroyo Grande, CA.)

feeding the distribution system. Most generators have automatic starters and start easily. Allow the generator to warm up in idle for a few minutes before switching it to run. Look up as soon as the engine starts; watch that the cooling doors are open and watch the exhaust color (more on exhaust shortly).

3. When the best boy is ready to turn on the power, alert the gaffer and electricians that "the lines are going *hot*." You do not want to shock someone down the line who may still be connecting the lugs to a spider box.
4. When you are ready for power, flip the idle/run switch to run, and turn the main power switch or breaker on.
5. Check the voltage output meter and set the voltage using the adjustment knob. Be sure to recheck voltage after changing from single phase to three phase or vice versa. The voltage will need adjustment. You can use this knob to offset voltage drop in the cables. The voltage reading should be taken from the farthest outlet from the generator.
6. Check the hertz reading. It should be hovering right around 60 ± 0.2 Hz, and it should be stable, never jumping more than 0.1 Hz at a time. If a small adjustment is necessary, adjust the frequency with the adjustment knob or screw.
7. If you are in a public area, cover the live panel with rubber matting and mark it "Danger Live Wires."
8. During operation, periodically monitor the ammeters. It is best to keep the load evenly distributed between legs, no more than 50 A between legs as a rule of thumb.
9. Periodically check the engine instruments: oil pressure, battery charge, water temperature, and fuel pressure (if installed). These gauges can warn you of impending problems, such as a fuel filter clogging or a battery losing its charge—problems that could shut down the generator (and the production). More on this in the section on Troubleshooting.

In shutting down the generator,

1. Turn off all the lights and other loads.
2. Turn off the generator's main breaker or power switch.
3. Switch the generator to idle and allow several minutes for cool down.
4. After 3–5 minutes turn the ignition switch off.
5. Close manual air vents if necessary.

Grounding Generators

The discussion of system grounding earlier in this book described how an electrical system is connected to earth at the power source. Typically the neutral tap of the step down transformer supplying the system is grounded to earth. This establishes the neutral wire at ground potential and anchors the system to the large mass of the earth. In the case of a building this connection is made by sinking large conductors underground when the foundation is built.

As portable generators have been used more and more in film production, over the years the issue of grounding the generator to earth has been in contention. NEC article 250.6 states that the frame of the generator (including the frame of the vehicle) can serve as the grounding electrode for the system supplied by the generator so long as the generator is *isolated* from earth (by virtue of having rubber tires or other means). Generally a portable generator does not need to be grounded to earth; in fact the City of Los Angeles and various Industry Safety Bulletins recommend not attempting to ground the generator to earth for several reasons.

1. Making a proper ground to earth is an involved procedure. The grounding electrode must be either an 8-ft copper or steel stake driven fully into the ground (NEC Section 250.6[c]) or a building's grounding electrode. Driving an 8-ft stake into the ground would be impractical if not impossible in most situations.
2. Driving a rod into the ground without a site survey is potentially dangerous. You could hit buried gas lines, electrical cable, telecommunications cable, or water lines. Imagine hundreds of productions at work in Los Angeles driving 8-ft stakes into the ground willy nilly all over town on a daily basis.
3. Grounding connections must be made with an approved connections device. The connection to the electrode must be made with an approved bolted clamp (spring clamps are not allowed). You can't use a water pipe or lawn sprinkler system pipe for ground. The pipe may not be metal underground, and it is not an approved ground in any case. The connection must then be metered with approved testing devices and inspected by the authority having jurisdiction (A.H.J.)—the electrical inspector.

When a generator is fully insulated from the ground, it operates as a closed system. All the lighting fixtures are grounded to the generator. If there is a ground short, the generator's circuit breakers will trip to protect the circuit.

For these safety features to work, the generator must be set up such that the neutral wire is bonded to the generator frame and the generator frame is bonded to the truck frame. On some older AC/DC generators, the neutral was lifted (not bonded to the frame). In the event of a ground short, the current coming through the ground wire could not make a dead short and trip the main breaker, leaving the entire frame of the generator truck hot. You can double-check that the neutral is bonded to the frame using a wiggy (a type of voltage tester) or a test lamp, and connecting the test leads to the neutral and to the ground on the truck's frame. (Note: an electronic voltage meter will give erroneous readings in this application.)

When Generators Must be Grounded

When two electrical systems, supplied from different sources are being used in close proximity to one another, the grounds of the two systems should be bonded to one another. When equipment is being supplied from multiple portable generators, or when a generator is being used in addition to building service, the grounds of the two systems must be bonded.

For example, when a generator is being used in addition to a tie-in to building power, the generator should be grounded with a stake, *and* the ground must also be bonded to the ground of the building. This puts both circuits at the same voltage potential. By neutralizing any difference in potential, you eliminate the chance of getting a shock from touching a light powered by the genie while touching the building ground—a metal handrail, radiator, or plumbing pipe. However, if the generator is only powering equipment on the outside of the building and equipment powered by the two sources are never used in proximity to each other, the generator need not be bonded to the building ground.

Selecting a Generator

The size of generator selected for a job should be based on the power requirements of that job. While one naturally might want a larger generator "just in case," overkill can be bad for the plant. A generator should not be run continuously at less than 20% of its maximum load. Over time, running under very light loads causes all sorts of problems, including glazing the cylinders, which can destroy the engine. Nothing is better for a rough-running engine than to be run at full capacity for a couple hours. You see a lot of soot and smoke in the exhaust at first, until the engine cleans itself out. Generator rental companies use *load banks* (big resistance banks) for this very purpose as part of a regular maintenance schedule.

Flexibility in load capacity is one advantage of having two tractor-mounted plants. In addition to having backup in case one plant fails, you have the ability to run a lot of power or very little as necessary. Tractors provide increased fuel capacity, up to 300 gallons, enough to keep a plant running for as long as 3 or 4 days.

The advantage of a tow plant is that it is generally quieter than a tractor-mounted plant; the large flat fuel tank effectively blocks sound so it does not reverberate out from under the plant as it does with a tractor-mounted plant. When filming a period Western in a peaceful, remote stretch of New Mexico, you can hear a car 3 miles away, let alone a 200-hp diesel engine 500 ft up the mesa. You need a quiet plant or you'll be running cable up hill and down dale.

Young Generator, Inc., has custom- built cargo vans with 250-A, 500-A, and even 750-A capacity generators installed inconspicuously inside. The van makes relocating the generator fast and easy and allows it to be hidden in the shot if necessary.

Either a gasoline engine or a diesel engine drives the alternator. There are pros and cons to each. The advantages of a gasoline engine are that it runs very quietly, has low NOx emission (nitrogen oxide), and is not as heavy as a diesel engine. A basic carburetor can digest inferior fuels without serious effects on the engine's operation better than a fuel injection system used by diesel engines. The disadvantages of gasoline engines are that gas engines have limited power output, up to 60 kW (500 A); they have higher fuel consumption (gas engines have static fuel consumption under any load, even under no load); and they use flammable gasoline, which is not permitted in harbors and other fire-critical areas.

The primary advantages of a diesel engine are high reliability, low maintenance, and high fuel efficiency. It has more power and can turn larger alternators. Also, diesel fuel is "combustible" rather than "flammable," so it is safer. On the downside, diesel engines are hard cold starters, more sensitive to fuel contamination, and more critical of lubricants and coolants. As a result of the higher combustion pressures, diesel engines must be made of heavy materials. A 1200-A tow plant can weigh upward of 10,000 lb. High combustion pressure also means more noise (you can always tell the distinctive diesel knock), higher emissions (NOx and particulate matter (PM)—soot), but much lower hydrocarbon and ROG emissions.

Electrical Configurations

A generator alternator has three sets of coils, each 120° offset from the last, creating three-phase AC current. To provide 120-V DC or single-phase AC (or both), additional circuitry is required. To allow flexibility, alternator coils are tapped at various strategic places. Each phase (marked L1, L2, and L3) is tapped in four places. The tap points are marked 1–12. From this, many configurations are possible (Figures 13.4 and 13.5).

Basic Troubleshooting

A fully equipped, modern generator automatically shuts down if it senses a mechanical problem, such as low oil pressure, low coolant pressure, high water temperature, overspeeding, or overcranking. Any of these problems is easily diagnosed

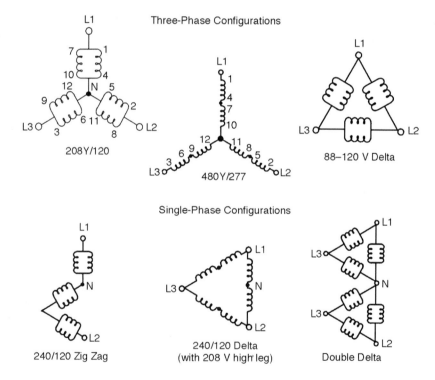

Figure 13.4   Alternator coils are tapped in 12 places to allow versatility in possible electrical configurations. A multipole, heavy-duty, rotary switch configures the coils. 208Y/120 three-phase is the standard configuration. A 88–120-V delta three-phase is used to create AC and DC concurrently (see Figure 13.5). The zigzag configuration uses all three coils to create 240/120 single phase. (The gap between N and L2 is the "open leg" of a delta, giving 120 V.) Note that, in each configuration, all six coils are tapped evenly, regardless of the ultimate output. (Courtesy of Young Generators, Inc., Arroyo Grande, CA.)

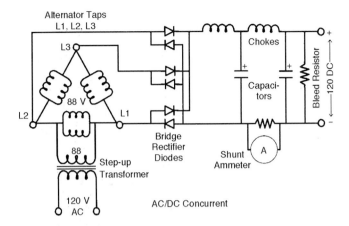

Figure 13.5 AC and DC derived concurrently from an 88-V delta three-phase AC configuration. A step-up transformer creates 120-V AC by tapping between L1 and L2 (a second transformer between L2 and L3 would be used to create 120/240 AC). The three 88-V AC legs are converted to 120-V DC using rectifier diodes, chokes, and capacitors. (Courtesy of Young Generators, Inc., Arroyo Grande, CA.)

by inspecting the engine warning lights and instruments, followed by poking around inside the generator housing and looking for the problem. If a generator shuts down, check the indicator lights before turning the start switch off.

If you have a familiarity with engines, you may be able to make a reasonable guess at the cause of the shutdown. Overheating could be caused by a rupture in the cooling system (low coolant pressure and high temperature) or a blocked or burnt-out thermostat (high water temp). Most likely is a plugged radiator (pollen, insulation fluff, etc.) or broken fan belt.

Low oil pressure indicates a ruptured oil line, leaking oil, or low oil.

A "charge" light indicates the battery has not been charging, pointing to a problem with the alternator, a broken belt, a break in the wiring between the alternator and the battery (some generators have a fuse or circuit breaker in this line), or a bad battery. An important note here is that the electronic governor that controls the engine speed relies on battery power to operate. Unlike a car motor, which requires little battery power to run, the electronic governor requires much more battery power. A failed charging system typically shows itself in a slow loss of AC hertz rate and an inability to pick up a load (it bogs down when big lights are turned on).

Troubleshooting—Mechanical

Fuel System

The fuel system is vital to the proper running of a diesel engine and the biggest area of potential problems. Bubbles of air in the fuel lines can make it impossible to maintain consistent hertz rate. Contaminants in the fuel can clog fuel lines over time.

Fuel is drawn into the pickup at the bottom of the fuel tank. If you have problems after the plant has been moved and there is a lot of crud coming into the fuel filter, it may be because the fuel intake is raised off the bottom of the tank and crud on the bottom of the tank has been stirred up. Or the tank may now be on a slight incline, causing water at the bottom of the tank to reach the intake. The water and crud on the bottom of the tank gradually build up until the mixture reaches the (raised) fuel intake, at which time the engine does not run because it is drinking pure water and crud.

Fuel is pumped through the Racor filter, which separates out water and contaminants. The clear bowl on the bottom of the filter shows any water or crud that has accumulated. It can be drained out using the valve on the bottom of the bowl. In wet, humid climates (northwest and eastern United States), the filter fill up much faster than in dry climates.

To drain water, hold a container under the drain, open the valve at the bottom of the filter bowl, and activate the electric fuel pump to force the water from the bottom of the filter assembly. If your generator has no fuel pump upstream of the filter, you may have to loosen the T-handle and remove the top cover before draining fuel from the valve. Refill the filter with clean fuel before closing the cover.

Fuel is pumped to the primary and secondary fuel filter canisters, which are usually close to the main fuel pump. This pump raises fuel pressure to 20–50 psi and pumps fuel to the fuel injector. A fuel pressure gauge is sometimes installed at this point in the system. The fuel pressure gauge is helpful to forewarn the operator if a clog is developing somewhere in the fuel system. Make note of the normal fuel pressure. A downward trend in fuel pressure usually indicates a clogging fuel filter. If pressure is unstable and the gauge is all over the map, it indicates that the system is sucking air.

Bleeding the Lines   If a diesel engine is allowed to run out of fuel, the fuel lines get air in them, and must be bled before the generator will restart. Use the following procedure to *bleed the lines*:

1. Fill the fuel tank.
2. Activate the electric fuel pump. On some plants this is accomplished by pressing the engine on/off button. Others have a switch installed next to the pump inside the engine housing. If the fuel pump stops clicking, repeat this step.
3. Bleed the Racor filter. Unscrew the top of the filter and let the fuel pump fill the filter to the top. Then screw the top back down.
4. Operate the small hand pump on the side of the injector pump for 60 seconds.
5. Start the generator.
6. If it doesn't start, open injector 1 with a 19-mm or $^{11}/_{16}$-in. wrench until fuel spurts out.
7. Repeat steps 5 and 6 with injectors 2, 3, and 4.

Bad Fuel   If you get *bad fuel in the system*, you must clean out the entire system. Start by adding a dewatering additive or biocide to the fuel (see the next paragraph). Switch to the backup fuel system (if equipped). Next clean the fuel filters and fill them with clean fuel. There are *four* fuel filters: one in the electric fuel pump, the Racor filter, and two canister filters near the injectors.

Fuel Care and Additives   Condensation on the insides of the fuel tank causes *water in the fuel*. Avoid this by filling the tank before leaving it overnight. Daily use of a dewatering additive is a great insurance policy, as such agents remove their weight in water, eliminating the most common cause of generator failure, dirty fuel. Additives such as Fuel Power combine a water dispersant and antigumming agent; they clean the injectors and reduce smoke.

There are two types of diesel fuel. In warm states such as California, you see only one type, diesel 2; however, diesel 2 turns to a gel and becomes gooey and waxy at about 15–32°F. In *cold climates*, diesel 1, which is thinner, becomes necessary. Diesel 2 is normally preferable because it contains more BTUs (more energy). Use local fuel when in cold climates. "Pour point depressants" such as Polar Power prevent diesel fuel from waxing up at freezing temperatures. Use it before the fuel has a chance to gel. If you get caught in the sudden freeze with diesel 2 in the tank, use the Melt Down additive to unclog gooey fuel lines. (Kerosene is sometimes used but is illegal because of EPA requirements.) Warming the fuel tank with a heater also helps.

Troubleshooting—Electrical Problems

The two control systems of the electrical component of a generator are the voltage regulator and the electronic governor. The *voltage regulator* increases or decreases the magnetic field strength inside the alternator to control output voltage. It then compares output voltage to a preset (adjustable) target value and automatically adjusts field strength to match it.

The *electronic governor* controls engine RPM, which is directly proportional to hertz rate, so delicate control of the throttle (gas engine) or fuel injector (diesel) is required. The governor receives a signal from a sensor, which tells it how fast the engine is turning. (The sensor is a magnetic pickup that actually counts teeth on the flywheel as it turns.) The governor compares this speed to the desired speed (which results in 60 Hz) and increases or decreases the gas accordingly.

Snags in either the voltage regulator system or the governor system can cause electrical problems; however, more often than not, problems that show up in fluctuations in voltage or hertz rate are caused by other factors.

Visible Flicker in the Lights   *Visible flicker* is rarely caused by faulty frequency regulation, as is often erroneously assumed. Do not confuse "HMI flicker" (a pulsing visible only on film) with visible flicker. Most often visible flicker is caused by poor connections in the distribution cables. I tracked down many a flicker and found a bad Bates connector or pin connector was at fault. Especially if flicker is limited to particular lights or a single leg of power, the problem is unlikely to be with the generator.

Lights Flicker on All Phases—Voltage Periodically Jumps and Dips

Peaks and dips in voltage are sometimes caused by a buildup of corrosion on the voltage adjustment knob on the control panel. This would be seen as visible flicker on all phase wires. Several swift twists back and forth (load disconnected) usually clean it out and should get rid of the problem. This knob is one of the weakest links in the system. Subjected to the elements, the rheostat can get a buildup of dirt and corrosion. Faulty contact in the rheostat can make it very hard for the voltage regulator to work effectively.

As a second possibility, *flicker and voltage fluctuations occurring on all three phases* are often caused by a bad neutral connection. Feel the cable connections for hot spots. This will lead you to the problem cable or connector.

A final possibility is fluctuations coming from the voltage regulator itself. This usually occurs as a "bouncing" instability, about two pulses per second. Very occasionally, you have to switch to the backup voltage regulator, which can be selected with a switch inside the generator housing. Be sure to shut down the generator before changing from 1 to 2. *Never switch between regulators with the engine running.*

Generator Does Not Produce Any Power   If the generator produces no power, the voltage regulator power input or field output may have become disconnected or the regulator may have failed.

Voltage Goes through the Roof   *High voltage* indicates that the voltage regulator's sensing input is disconnected. If the sensing input is disconnected, the voltage regulator senses that the voltage is too low (it senses zero voltage). It increases the voltage in the field output more and more to try to compensate, and the generator output voltage goes through the roof.

Unpredictable, Irregular Changes in Frequency   These may be caused by air bubbles rising up through the Racor fuel filter. Air bubbles may be caused by low fuel in the tank or a pinhole leak in a fuel line. A restriction in the fuel line has a similar effect.

Unstable Frequency   If you find *unstable frequency*, the governor lever may be "hunting," overshooting then undershooting. Check that there is no play in the throttle/governor linkage and that the linkage moves freely without stickiness. Clean it and spray it with lubricant if necessary. In the case of a carburated engine, this may be caused by a sticky throttle due to (1) high venturi pressure hampering the throttle valve (wiping some oil on the bearings often frees up a stiff butterfly and allows the governor to control the hertz rate properly) or (2) carburetor ice. Placing a load on the generator lowers the vacuum and usually eliminates the problem; otherwise, shut down the generator and allow the ice to melt.

If you have *unstable frequency and the governor lever oscillates and does not stabilize*, the governor control may need calibration. An adjustment is made with the "I", "A," and gain controls on the little electronic governor box.

Engine Overspeeds   The "I" pot on the governor controller adjusts overshoot. The engine *overspeeds* briefly when load level changes if it is set too high. Alternately, hertz may be set too high or be faulty, or governor is faulty.

Slow Frequency Drift   If you notice a *slow frequency drift* (typically downward), the battery may be going flat (failed engine alternator) or you may have moisture in electronic governor controller (dry it with a hair dryer or work light) or a bad electronic governor controller.

Wet Cell Battery Packs and Inverters

In situations in which no other power source is practical, such as when shooting in a moving car, a boat, a remote cave, or some equally inaccessible place, battery packs or inverters can provide the needed power.

Inverter Systems

When shooting on a boat, bus, or car you can run up to 1800 W (Kino-flo, tungsten, or HMI lights) off the Kino-flo inverter (Figure 13.6). The system employs a 194-A/hour, sealed, nonspillable, lead-acid battery, battery charger, and 1800-W inverter. The entire system is small enough to fit in the trunk of a car. The inverter supplies 120-V AC with a true sine wave. It provides AC feedthrough to power the system off "shore power" while prelighting, then switches instantaneously to battery power when disconnected. No restrike is necessary. The inverter works with 10–16-V DC input and weighs 40 lb. The charger can recharge the battery to 75% power in about 2 hours and weighs 21 lbs. The battery with casters weighs 188 lb.

Battery Packs (120-V DC)

By connecting 10 12-V wet cell (lead-acid) batteries in series, a DC voltage of 120 V can be obtained. Commercially available battery packs are specially made with nonspill caps on the cells, typically housing five 12-V cells to a case. Each case

Figure 13.6 This inverter system has a charger, 1800-W inverter, and 184-AH battery pack. The inverter creates 120-V AC 60 Hz (or 230 V on European model) from 12-V DC input (the battery). Each battery pack can power four four-bank, 4-ft fixtures for up to 56 minutes from a full charge. (Courtesy of Kino Flo, Inc., Sun Valley, CA.)

weighs about 130 lb. Batteries are made in various capacities, ranging up to 100 ampere-hour (AH) and more; however, a 45-AH rating is typical. As an example, when fully charged and operated continuously at 80°F, the Molepower battery pack, manufactured by Mole-Richardson, provides power as follows:

4000 W for 20 minutes.
3000 W for 40 minutes.
2000 W for 1 hour.
1000 W for 2 hours and 40 minutes.

As you can see, a battery's capacity is affected by its rate of discharge: The lower the rate, the greater the total power output. At lower temperatures, wet cell batteries have reduced capacity; the times noted should be reduced by 7% for each 10°F below 80°F. Additionally, if the battery is not run continuously, its total running time is greater than the times noted. Finally, the performance of wet cells decreases with age. In a given battery pack, there will likely be a mix of newer and older cells, making it hard to predict the battery's performance precisely.

The voltage of a lead-acid battery decreases as it discharges, very slowly at first and more rapidly as it nears the end of its charge. The state of charge can be found by checking the specific gravity of the electrolyte with a hydrometer. The water level should be checked and topped off with distilled water when necessary.

It takes 6–8 hours to charge a wet cell battery pack properly. A trickle charger is often used (input: 120-V AC, 15 A, 60 Hz; output: 120-V DC, 12 A). A battery pack can be shock-charged in about 15 minutes, but this is very dangerous—it can cause permanent damage to the batteries, does not fully charge the electrolyte, and is not recommended.

Great care must be taken not to tip a lead-acid battery. Spilled sulfuric acid causes serious damage to the equipment and people with which it comes into contact. If a battery spills, the area must be thoroughly doused in water to dilute the sulfuric acid.

There is also a more expensive, lightweight, maintenance-free, lead-acid battery that is fully sealed, in which the electrolyte is in the form of jelly or absorbent felt. The battery can be operated in any orientation except completely upside down with no danger of spill. Fully sealed lead-acid batteries typically have a lower AH capacity than other types: 20–30 AH is typical.

Power on Location

When shooting in a location where a generator is impractical, you can use one of the following alternatives to provide power: (1) have the power company make a line drop and install a kilowatt-hour meter at the location or (2) tie into the building's service at a panelboard.

Line Drops

A line drop is sometimes less expensive than renting a generator. If shooting takes place in one location over several weeks and the building cannot supply sufficient power, you can have the power company make a line drop from the power lines and install a kilowatt-hour meter at the location. A licensed electrician can then install a panelboard with main breakers for the system from which the film's distribution system can draw power. The line drop has advantages over a tie-in because it is a designated circuit with sufficient amperage; it has advantages over a generator because it is silent and does not burn fuel.

Tie-ins

A tie-in taps power directly from a building's service box, drawing power from the building's permanent feeder cables. In many locations, such as homes, hotels, and warehouses, a tie-in to house power may save a tremendous amount of cabling and expense.

Tying in can be very dangerous. You can be killed by inadvertently contacting hot wires. Furthermore, a mistake can cause serious damage to the facility and the film equipment. If you are going to do tie-ins, learn the procedure from an experienced electrician. Do not attempt it yourself until you know the routine thoroughly. Tying in can be relatively simple in some locations and difficult in others. If the tie-in is difficult, do not hesitate to have the production company call a licensed electrician to make the tie-in.

The information that follows is not sufficient for a novice to attempt the procedure. It is included merely to help lighting technicians identify types of house circuits, know the procedures that are legal and safe, and understand the safety role of the person assisting the electrician who performs the tie-in.

Obtaining a Permit

In Los Angeles, when there is some likelihood that a tie-in will be needed at a location, the location manager files an application for an electrical inspection for that location. In California, temporary electrical work does not require a licensed contractor. The code requires that the tie-in must be made by a "qualified person." At this writing, the term *qualified person* is not defined by the NEC and is subject to the interpretation of the jurisdiction that has authority. City inspectors can be expected to visit the location to confirm that the tie-in is properly made. An inspector who finds deficiencies with the work can shut down a production until the problems are remedied. It is therefore very important that tie-ins be made by the book. Any questions about a given situation should be directed to the local building and safety department. Rules differ in other cities. Check with the agency that has jurisdiction in the area in which filming is to take place.

Power Demand

Depending on the demands of the situation, a tie-in can work in one of two ways: by adding to the load of an existing service or by replacing the load of an existing service. If the power demand is not very large, for example, when running a few supplemental lights that are hard to reach with generator power, a tie-in may be made that relies on the surplus amperage available on house circuits. An amp probe is used to measure the existing current flow to determine the surplus that may be used and to monitor the loads once the tie-in is made.

On the other hand, if the power demand is large or if insufficient surplus amperage is available from the existing service, then the only way to use house circuits is to shut off or disconnect the circuits to supply the needed amperage to the film's distribution system. In a factory warehouse, for example, there might be some large machinery that won't be operating during filming and that has 100-A or 200-A breakers in the panelboard. The electrician can remove these breakers, disconnect the wires to the machinery, and install breakers with wires running to the film's distribution system.

Investigating the Existing Service

Two important factors determine if a tie-in is practicable in a given location: (1) whether the service has the surplus amperage needed and (2) whether and how the distribution cables can be connected to the panel.

Warning: When investigating service panels, remember that everything is hot. You will receive a serious shock if you allow any part of your body or any metal object you are holding to touch the hot buses or come between two hot buses, which may catalyze an arc. Stand on an insulating material. Wear insulating rubber electrician's gloves whenever working inside a hot panelboard.

Types of Service

Every panelboard has a small metal placard that gives the amperage, voltage, and number of phases of the panel. This information should be confirmed by inspecting the panel carefully and measuring the voltage across the legs with a voltmeter (see Chapter 11).

The amperage rating of the service varies with the size of the installation. A small older house, for example, might be equipped with two 60-A fuses (three wire, single phase). A commercial building is likely to have three-phase service panels of 600 A or more. In addition, this type of installation often has three-wire, single-phase subfeeders of sufficient amperage to be of use.

Commercial buildings may also have high amperage, three-wire, three-phase circuits designated for large air conditioning units or other big machinery. These circuits are inappropriate for tie-ins because they are designated specifically for the machinery they feed, and they provide no grounded neutral lead.

Existing Amperage Load

The next step is to determine how much power the installation is already servicing. Use an amp probe to measure the current running through each hot leg and through the neutral. The surplus amperage available is the amount running through each leg subtracted from the amperage rating on the fuses.

For example, suppose you are working with 200-A fuses on a single-phase circuit. The red leg measures 75 A, the blue measures 125 A, and the neutral measures 50 A. (The neutral carries the difference between the two hot legs.) This leaves 125 A available on the red leg and 75 A available on the blue leg. Subtracting a safety margin of 20 A per leg, you have 160 A available for the lights as long as the building's load does not change.

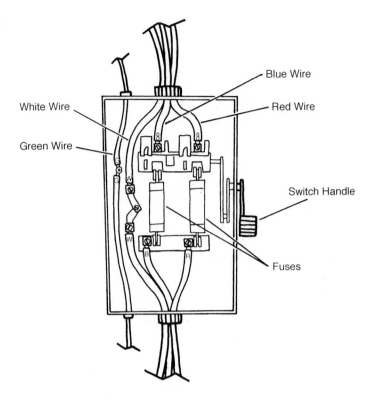

White Wire

Green Wire

Blue Wire

Red Wire

Switch Handle

Fuses

Figure 13.7 A single-phase three-wire bull switch.

If you will rely on the tie-in for most of the power, it is wise, before shooting at a location, to take several measurements at different times and determine the peak demand. Take measurements when the building is fully occupied. Watch for variables, such as air conditioning, that cycle on and off.

Before Tying In

The power should be turned off at a main switch (Figure 13.7) while the tie-in is performed. If there is a main switch that can be shut off, shut it off. More often than not, power cannot be cut off, and the tie-in must be made to a hot circuit.

An assistant should always be present while the electrician makes the tie-in. The assistant is there to help the electrician should he get into trouble. If there is a main switch for turning off the power in an emergency, the assistant should stand with her hand on the switch. (Should an accident occur, the priority becomes saving the electrician from electrocution, and the switch should be used and the consequences dealt with later.) If there is no switch, the assistant should hold a 2 × 4 or an apple box to use to knock the electrician away from the panelboard should he make contact and become frozen to the terminals. The assistant should have a flashlight handy in case the lights go out. She can also help guard against distractions.

Make it a policy not to let anyone talk unnecessarily while the electrician is making a tie-in.

The electrician performing the tie-in must be insulated from the ground. He should stand on an apple box or a piece of rubber matting.

Making the Connections

The electrician first suspends the tie-in cables from a structural support above the box with sash cord, so that the ends of the cable dangle. This takes the weight off the connections. The tie-in cables are not connected to the rest of the distribution system when making the tie-in. A bull switch should be connected immediately downstream of the tie-in, and it should be switched off.

If it is possible to make the tie-in with one hand, it is good practice for the electrician to put the other hand in his pocket or behind his back to prevent the possibility of completing a circuit through the heart.

The tie-in is made downstream of the main breaker or fuses. It should never be made upstream (on the service side) of the main breakers. If a short circuit is accidentally created upstream of the main breaker, the breaker in the transformer on the pole will be tripped and could shut off electricity for a whole city block.

There are two approved ways of connecting wires to a panelboard. The first is to connect wires to circuit breakers. The second is to insert wires into existing wire holes in lugs on the panelboard.

There is a third way to connect wires to a panelboard: Clamp onto the lugs in the panelboard with power clamps. However, at this writing, it is in question whether the use of power clamps for tie-ins is allowable. Power clamps do not qualify under NEC Articles 110.14 and 110.14(a) as suitable electrical connectors or suitable grounding connectors under NEC Article 250.113. Authorities vary in their policies regarding the use of power clamps.

Connecting to Circuit Breakers

If there are identifiable circuits not needed during filming, the easiest way to tie in is to remove one or more of the installation's circuit breakers and replace them with two larger breakers of equivalent total amperage (Figure 13.8).

If the panelboard has 100- or 200-A breakers in it already, they can be disconnected from the house load and connected instead to jumper cables that lead to suitable connectors (Mole-pins, Cam-Loks, lugs, or what have you). This approach guarantees that the distribution system does not overload the panelboard.

To remove a circuit breaker, first switch the breaker off. Then unplug the breaker from the bus bar by rocking it back away from the bus and sliding it out of its channel. When tightening down the terminals of the circuit breaker, use a torque screwdriver or wrench and observe the tightening torque marked on the circuit breakers. The NEC requires proper torquing, which is critical to the proper functioning of the breakers.

Manufacturers have various designs for circuit breakers and panelboards. If you plan to replace several breakers with one or two larger ones, check the make and model of the breakers used at the site. If the panelboard has a placard reading

Figure 13.8 A tie-in to 100-A breakers. The tie-in cables are the black cables that are run out the bottom of the panel box. The bus on the left is the neutral. The smaller bus on the right is the ground.

"Caution—series rated system," circuit protection depends on the breakers of branch circuits and the upstream breakers operating together. When tying into such a system, you must provide a current-limiting fused switch box downstream of the tie-in to protect the circuit properly.

Connecting to Lugs

Do not attempt this type of tie-in on an energized system. The power must be switched off at a main switch before any lugs may be loosened. Connecting wires directly to the panelboard lugs requires that you loosen the lugs. If any lug is loosened when the panel is energized, the wire would arc violently and very likely burn up. You could 220 the building, the same as pulling the neutral on a three-wire circuit.

When tying in directly to the panel lugs, you must provide a fused switch box with current-limiting fuses within 25 ft of the tie-in point. Be sure that the fuses are the current-limiting type.

The lugs on the panelboard are normally occupied by the wires feeding the house. If the hole in the lug is oval, it is a multiwire lug and approved for more than one wire. If the hole in the lug is round, it is a single-conductor lug and not approved for two wires; nonetheless, it is sometimes possible to get a second wire into a single-conductor lug, depending on the sizes of the wires and the lugs.

After Tying In

To comply with the NEC, once the tie-in is complete, the open panelboard must be guarded from accidental contact. Rubber matting attached to the face of the panelboard provides proper protection. You can secure the matting with the screws and screw holes of the panelboard cover. The panelboard can be further guarded by locking the door to the room. Place a sign that says, "Danger Live Cables" or "Danger High Voltage" across the face of the panelboard. Place additional signs across the doorway to the room to prevent people from getting near the open panelboard.

When the system is ready to be energized, notify the gaffer and electricians. Everyone must be warned before current starts running through the cables. Once the connection is made and the bull switch is on, make a point of telling the gaffer and other electricians, "We're hot."

Using Available Power

Sometimes you simply don't have the option of using your own distribution system. You are forced to use the existing circuitry at the location. When you use available power, the best boy electric should first find the breaker box and check the amperage of the circuits. They are usually 15 A or 20 A. Count the number of separate circuits. Number the circuits and label the outlets with the circuit numbers. If hair-curling irons or blow dryers are going to be plugged in, determine which circuit they are on. Run stingers from different sections of the house to have as many circuits as possible available.

The electrical code specifies that in new houses there must be two designated 20-A circuits around the counter of the kitchen. These circuits are handy because they are not wired to any other outlets. Other designated circuits are those for the laundry and the water heater, which may be 208 V or 240 V. Wall outlets, including the fused 20-A bathroom outlet, usually share circuit breakers with other outlets and overhead fixtures.

CHAPTER **14**

The Work World

This chapter gives a brief overview of labor standards that are considered fair and acceptable in the film industry and, in doing so, explains how both union and nonunion productions conduct business. For union employees, the conditions of employment are spelled out in great detail in the union labor agreement. If a production company is a union signatory, the union represents the crew members, instituting standard minimum wage and overtime requirements, providing rules regarding turnaround, meals, number of crew members hired, and so on. The variables involved in nonunion deals are discussed later in this chapter. The union contract provides a yardstick by which nonunion labor arrangements can be measured; it is, therefore, a good starting point for this discussion.

The Unions

The largest and most powerful technician's union in the motion picture industry is the International Alliance of Theatrical and Stage Employees (IATSE, or IA). The National Association of Broadcast Employees and Technicians (NABET) once also represented film and television technicians, but NABET film technicians have been absorbed into the IA in New York and Los Angeles. NABET now represents mostly broadcasting technicians. Table 14.1 lists some union locals for the United States and Canada. All the major film studios and many independent producers are union signatories and have a standard 3-year agreement with the IA. IA organizers work to organize nonunion shows and union business agents enforce contracts with signatories.

Hollywood: Local 728

In most areas, set lighting technicians are included in the stagehands' or studio mechanics' local, along with grips, shop craftsmen, re-recording mixers, sound department personnel, video engineers, property personnel, and projectionists. Hollywood Local 728 is unique in that it is strictly a set lighting local.

Table 14.1 Union Locals in the United States and Canada

State	City or Region	Type	Local
Arizona	Phoenix/Tucson	SM	IATSE Local 485
California	Los Angeles	MPSELT	IATSE Local 728
	San Jose	M	IATSE Local 134
	San Francisco	S	IATSE Local 16
	San Francisco		NABET Local 134
Colorado	Denver/Boulder	S	IATSE Local 7
	Colorado Springs	M	IATSE 62
District of Columbia	Washington, DC	SM	IATSE Local 22
Florida	Miami/Orlando	SM	IATSE Local 477
Georgia	Atlanta	SM	IATSE Local 479
Hawaii	Honolulu	M	IATSE Local 665
Illinois	Chicago	SM	IATSE Local 476
Massachusetts	Boston (all New England)	SM	IATSE Local 481
Michigan	Detroit	SM	IATSE Local 38
Minnesota	Minneapolis (statewide)	SM	IATSE Local 490
Missouri	Saint Louis	S	IATSE Local 6
Nevada	Las Vegas	M	IATSE Local 720
New Mexico	Santa Fe	SM	IATSE Local 480
New York	New York	SM	IATSE Local 52
North Carolina	See South Carolina		
Ohio	Cleveland (statewide)	SM	IATSE Local 209
Oregon	Portland (Pacific NW)	SM	IATSE Local 488
Pennsylvania	Pittsburgh (greater Pittsburgh)	SM	IATSE Local 489
South Carolina	Wilmington (Carolinas)	SM	IATSE Local 491
Texas	Houston (statewide)	SM	IATSE Local 484
Canada	Burnaby, British Columbia	MPSPT	IATSE Local 891
	Toronto, Ontario	MPSPT	IATSE Local 873
			NABET Local 700

Abbreviations: SM = studio mechanics; S = stagehands; MPSELT = motion picture studio electrical lighting technicians; MPSPT = motion picture studio production technicians; M = mixed.

In Los Angeles, a worker's name must be listed on the *Industry Experience Roster* to work under the basic labor agreement. The roster is provided to producers by the contract services department of the Association of Motion Picture and Television Producers (AMPTP). The roster lists union members from which producers can select their crew. To get on the experience roster you must have worked 30 days on a union show. This sounds like a Catch 22; however, there are two scenarios in which a nonunion worker can earn this 30 days and get on the experience roster.

1. If a worker is hired on a nonunion show whose employees vote to seek union representation and the show is organized by the union and the producers sign an agreement, that worker typically can count all the days (retroactively to the beginning of the employment) as union days.
2. During the busiest times of the year, the union runs out of people, and the Local hall goes into *permit status*. At that time nonunion workers can be hired on permit.

Once a worker has accumulated 30 permit days within a 1-year period, the worker applies to contract services, fills out CSATF (Contract Services Administration Trust Fund) paperwork, takes a color blindness test, and if eligible, his or her name is added to the experience roster. Once on the roster, the individual is eligible to work in Los Angeles and must join the union and pay the dues before taking other union work. Each local office keeps a list of member availability. Union members are required to call in and report any work they take, including work on nonunion shows.

There is no written entrance test for Local 728, as there is for Local 52 in New York and some other locals. Rules for entrance vary from city to city.

Basic Agreement

The following is an abbreviated summary of the current conditions provided in an IA *Basic Agreement* on the West Coast. They are included here as an example of the types of concerns workers have on any production. The rules may vary from one union local to another, and as signatories renew their contracts, negotiations may change the current agreements, but the issues remain the same.

Daily employee   Gaffer, best boy, and rigging gaffer, set electricians, 8 hours guaranteed. Wage shown in Table 14.2 under Schedule A.

Weekly employee   Gaffer, best boy, and rigging gaffer. 5 consecutive days and at least 54 hours, with at least 9 hours of pay per day. Wage shown in Table 14.2 under Schedule B.

Studio   Shooting on premises.

Studio zone   Within 30 miles of central location. Reimbursed for mileage or travel time, or ride furnished to set. 10 hour turnaround.

Nearby location   More than 30 miles away. Ride furnished. Go on the clock when you meet the van.

Distant location   Overnight necessary. 8 hour turnaround; golden time after 14 hours elapsed; 6-day workweek. Production pays for accommodations, meals, and all other out-of-pocket expenses. The production supplies transportation from the hotel to the set every day, and crew members go on the clock when they are picked up at the hotel, rather than when they arrive at the set; they go off the clock when they are dropped off again.

Table 14.2 Sample Union Wage Table, Studio Minimum Rates

Classification	Schedule A, Daily Employees $1^1/_2$ after 8 hours/day or 40 hours/week; minimum call 8 hours	Schedule B, Weekly Employees Weekly Guarantee: 54 cumulative hours; 5 consecutive days; minimum call 9 hours	
	Per Hour	Per Hour	Per Week
Chief Lighting Technician (gaffer)	$24.69	$24.355	$1485.68
Assistant Chief Lighting Technician	$22.33	$21.908	$1336.38
Chief Rigging Electric	$23.15	$21.908	$1336.38
Running Repair (special operator)	$22.82		
Lighting Technician	$21.32		
Entry Level Employee	$18.65		

Note: Sample wage scale August 1, 1992–July 31, 1993, for Local 728 in Los Angeles.

Turnaround   Generally 9-hour minimum, except where noted (distant location, studio zone).

Forced call   Less than required turnaround. Hours worked on forced call are added to the previous day's hours for the purpose of calculating overtime pay.

Base wage   Shown in Table 14.2. After 8 hours: Time and a half. After 12 hours: Golden time. Double-time normally; sixth day, triple-time; seventh day, quadruple-time.

Meals   After every 6 hours work; 30–60 minutes.

12-minute grace period   A 12-minute grace period allows the production to continue to shoot for 12 minutes beyond the 6-hour limit with no penalty.

30-minute grace period   A 30-minute extension allows the production to finish a camera take that is in progress. No lighting or camera changes may be made. The extension is meant to be used when there is some sort of urgent extenuating circumstance, such as the need to get an expensive actor off the clock.

Other agreements   Special agreements for specific types of productions that were frequently formerly nonunion (e.g., NBC Agreement, HBO Agreement, etc.). Rules vary. Generally rate schedule is lower, as much as 24% lower for lighting technicians. Double-time pay starts after 14 hours, instead of 12 hours. Contractual holidays and vacation days not worked are unpaid, whereas under the Basic Agreement a percentage is paid, and there is no "drive to" pay.

A complete copy of each union contact is distributed to the union membership and reissued every time a contract is renegotiated. If you have no contract handy when a question arises, you can call your local. The call steward or business agent can clarify any questions you have.

Lamp Specification Tables

Table A.1 Fresnel Fixtures

	Amps	Volts	Bulb	Lens	Scrim	Chimera Ring Size	Weight (lbs)	Beam Angle Candle Power Flood	Spot
Altman									
300L	2.5	120	FKW	3"	5"	5"	5 lb	55° 4200	13° 15,000
650L	5.4	120	FRK	4.5"	6⅝"	6½"	8 lb	59° 9000	11° 55,000
1000L	8.3	120	EGT	5"	7¾"	7⅝"	11 lb	60° 20,200	10° 125,000
Studio 1k	8.3	120	EGT	7"	9"	9⅝"	14 lb	60° 18,000	9° 175,000
2000L	16.7	120	CYX	7"	9"	9⅝"	19 lb	58° 42,000	10° 325,000
Studio 2k	16.7	120	CYX	10"	13"	13½"	26 lb	55° 32,000	8° 330,000
5000L	41.7	120	DPY	10"	13"	13½"	26 lb	55° 82,500	14° 375,000
Studio 5k	41.7	120	DPY	12"	15½"	—	55 lb	87° 56,000	18° 464,000
Arri									
300 W	2.5	120	FKW	3.2"	5"	5"	6.5 lb	60° 4590	16° 16,200
650 W	5.4	120	FRK	4.3"	6⅝"	6½"	7.1 lb	52° 10,800	14.5° 46,800
1000 W	8.3	120	EGT	5.1"	7¾"	7⅝"	11.2 lb	57° 19,800	11° 116,000
Studio 1k	8.3	120	EGT	6.9"	9"	9⅝"	15.2 lb	62° 18,000	11° 162,000
2000 W	16.7	120	CYX	6.9"	9"	9⅝"	17.5 lb	60° 42,500	15° 182,500
Studio 2k	16.7	120	CYX	10"	13"	13½"	27 lb	62° 36,250	10° 252,000
5000 W	41.7	120	DPY	10"	13"	13½"	34 lb	62° 70,000	13° 370,000
Studio 5k	41.7	120	DPY	11.8"	15½"	—	36 lb	67° 70,000	13° 435,150
Studio 10k/12k*	83.3 100	120 120	DTY Koto 12k	16.7"	19½"	—	48 lb	51° 205,000	14° 950,000
Cinemills									
10/12k	100 A	120	DTY or 12 k	20"	—	—	—	—	—
20k	100 A	240	20 kW	24"	29"	29"	98 lb	455,000	3,020,000

* Uses Koto 12k tungsten lamp and maximized reflector/lens system for output rivaling a 20k.

Table A.1 Fresnel Fixtures (continued)

	Watts	Volts	Bulb	Weight (lbs)	Power Supply	Beam Angle Candle Power Flood	Spot
DedoTech							
DLH	100	12	FCR	2 lb	DT-4 (four 12-V outlets) or DT-5 (five 12-V outlets)**	2800 40°	66,000 3.4°
	50	12	BRL			—	—
	20	12	Special			—	—
DLHM	100	12	FCR	6 lb	Internal 120-V AC transformer	—	—
DLH-150	150	24	FCS	3 lb	DT-150 (three 24-V outlets)	— —	77,300 6°
COOLH	250	24	ELC	4 lb	COOLT-2 (two 24-V outlets)	— —	94,066 13°
DLH436	400	36	EVD	7.5 lb	DT-36 (one 36-V) with 24-step dimmer	7380 56°	120,600 5.5°
DLH650	650	117	DL 650	7.5 lb	None	7200 56°	96,300 8°

**All power supplies have selectable input voltage: 110-, 120-, 220-, 230-, or 240-V AC and three-position brightness switch that selects output level.

All Dedo Fixtures up to 150 W use 3" scrims and take a 3" Chimera adaptor ring

Dedocool power supplies have fan motors. Keep fans running after lights are turned off.

Table A.1 Fresnel Fixtures (continued)

	Amps	Volts	Bulb	Lens	Scrim	Weight (lbs)
Desisti						
Leonardo k	8.3	120	EGT	6"	7½"	—
Piccolo 2k	16.7	120	CYX	6"	7¼"	—
Leonardo 2k	16.7	120	CYX	10"	12"	—
Piccolo 5k	41.6	120	DPY	10"	12"	—
Leonardo 5k	41.6	120	DPY	12"	15½"	—
Leonardo 5k	41.6	120	DPY	14"	15½"	—
Piccolo 10k	83.3	120	DTY	14"	15½"	—
Leonardo 10k	83.3	120	DTY	24"	29¾"	—
Super Leo 20k	83.3	220	20k	24"	29¾"	—
Lee Colortran						
1k Fresnel	8.3	120	EGT	6"		11 lb
2k Fresnel	16.7	120	CYX	8"		19.5 lb

Table A.1 Fresnel Fixtures (continued)

	Watts	Amps	Volts	Bulb	Lens	Scrim	Chimera Ring Size	Weight (lbs)	Beam Angle / Candle Power Flood	Beam Angle / Candle Power Spot
Mole-Richardson										
Tiny Mole 200 W	200	1.7	120	FEV	2"	5"	3"	2.5 lb	37° / 3300	11° / 7700
Mini Mole 200 W	200	1.7	120	FEV	3"	4⁷/₁₆"	5¹/₄"	3 lb	50° / 2500	7° / 19,500
Midget 200 W	200	1.7	120	FEV	4¹⁵/₃₆"	5¹/₈"	5¹/₄"	5 lb	46° / 3000	7° / 29,500
InBetweenie 200 W	200 / 100	1.7	120	FVL FVM	2"	3"	—	1.5 lb	43° / 2300	15° / 5300
Betweenie 300 W	300	2.5	120	FKW	3"	5¹/₈"	5¹/₄"	5 lb	48° / 4500	9° / 24,800
Tweenie	650	5.4	120	DYS	4¹/₂"	5¹/₈"	5¹/₄"	5 lb	—	—
Tweeie II	650	5.4	120	FRK	4¹/₂"	5¹/₈"	5¹/₄"	5 lb	59° / 7800	8° / 66,600
Baby Baby	1000	8.3	120	EGT	5"	7³/₁₆"	7¹/₄"	7 lb	59° / 14,000	11° / 98,000
Baby	1000	8.3	120	EGT	6"	6⁵/₈"	6⁵/₈"	7.25 lb	47° / 18,000	8° / 172,000
Baby Junior	2000	16.7	120	CYX	6"	9"	9"	10.25 lb	46° / 40,500	11° / 148,500

Table A.1 Fresnel Fixtures (continued)

	Watts	Amps	Volts	Bulb	Lens	Scrim	Chimera Ring Size	Weight (lbs)	Beam Angle Candle Power Flood	Spot
Junior Solarspot	2000	16.7	120	CYX	9⅞"	10⅛"	10⅛"	22.5 lb	48° / 52,000	10° / 400,000
8" Junior	2000	16.7	120	CYX	8"	9"	9"	13.75 lb	48° / 50,000	10° / 400,000
Baby Senior	5000	41.6	120	DPY	9⅞"	13½"	13½"	26 lb	49° / 99,000	10° / 589,500
Senior Solarspot	5000	41.6	120	DPY	14"	15½"	15½"	56 lb	50° / 63,000	9° / 598,500
Baby Tenner	10k	83.3	120	DTY	14"	18½"	18½"	52.5 lb	54° / 156,500	9° / 1,287,000
Tenner Solarspot	10k	83.3	120	DTY	20"	21"	21"	129.5 lb	34° / 414,000	10° / 2,287,000
Big Eye	10k	83.3	120	DTY	24¾"	29"	29"	131 lb	55° / 189,000	9° / 1,917,000
20k "Big Mo"	20k	83.3	220	KP200	24¾"	29"	29"	98.5 lb	54° / 430,000	12° / 2,800,000

Table A.1 Fresnel Fixtures (continued)

	Amps	Volts	Bulb	Lens	Scrim	Chimera Ring Size	Weight (lbs)	Beam Angle Candle Power Flood	Spot
LTM Peppers									
Pepper	0.8	120	ESR	2"	3"	3"	2 lb	48°	14°
100/200	1.7	120	FEV					2300	5500
Pepper 200	1.7	120	FEV	3 1/8"	4 1/4"	4 1/4"		48°	8°
								3900	10,500
Pepper 300	2.5	120	FKW	3 1/8"	4 1/4"	4 1/4"	3 lb	60°	14°
							3 oz	4600	27,500
Pepper 420	3.5	120	EKB	3 1/8"	4 1/4"	4 1/4"	3 lb	54°	9°
							3 oz	6100	44,400
Pepper 650	5.5	120	FRK	4 3/8"	5"	5"	6 lb	67°	9°
							3 oz	11,000	52,800
Pepper 500/	4.2	120	EGN	5"	6 5/8"	7 1/4"	10 lb	48°	7°
1,000	8.3	120	EGT					16,500	142,000
20,000-W	83.3	220	KP200	24"	29"	29"	105 lb	53°	11°
Pepper								430,000	2,770,000

	Amps	Volts	Bulb	Lens	Scrim	Chimera Ring Size	Weight (lbs)
Sachtler							
Director 300H	2.5	120	FKW	3"	5 1/4"	5 1/4"	5.5 lb
Director 500C	4.2	120	FRG	3"	5 1/4"	5 1/4"	5.5 lb
Director 650H	5.4	120	FRK	5"	7 3/4"	7 3/4"	9.67 lb
Director 1000C	8.3	120	EGT	5"	7 3/4"	7 3/4"	9.75 lb
Director 1000H	8.3	120	EGT	6"	9"	9"	11.25 lb
Director 2000C	16.7	120	*	6"	9"	9"	11.5 lb
Director 2000H	16.7	120	*	8"	12"	12"	23 lb
Director 2000H	16.7	120	*	10"	13 1/2"	13 1/2"	29 lb
Director 5000H	41.7	120	DPY	10"	13 1/2"	13 1/2"	34 lb
Director 5000H	41.7	120	DPY	12"	13 1/2"	13 1/2"	34 lb
Director 10k	83.3	120					

Table A.1 Fresnel Fixtures (continued)

	Amps	Volts	Bulb	Lens	Scrim	Chimera Ring Size	Weight (lbs)	Beam Angle Candle Power Flood		Spot	
Strand/Quartz Color											
3" Mizar	1.7	120	FEV	3"	4³⁄₈"	4¹⁄₄"	4 lb	43°	3900	14°	14,000
3" Mizar 300/500	2.5 / 4.2	120 / 120	FKW / FRK	3"	4³⁄₈"	4¹⁄₄"	4.4 lb	46°	7920	13°	33,980
5" Bambino 1k	8.4	120	EGT	5"	7¹⁄₄"	7¹⁄₄"	13.2 lb	60°	12,000	9°	72,000
6" Polaris 1k	8.3	120	EGT	6"	9" or 7⁷⁄₈"	7⁵⁄₈"	13.2 lb	59°	—	10°	58,400
6" Bambino 2k	16.7	120	CYX	6"	9"	7⁵⁄₈"	13.4 lb	59°	24,000	10°	184,000
10" Castor 2k	16.7	120	CYX	10"	12⁵⁄₈" or 13¹⁄₂"	12³⁄₄"	29.7 lb	51°	36,000	9°	297,000
10" Bambino 5k	41.6	120	DPY	10"	12⁵⁄₈" or 13¹⁄₂"	13¹⁄₂"	33 lb	55°	162,500	14°	675,000
12" Pollux 5k	41.6	120	DPY	12"	16"	15³⁄₄"	37 lb	55°	108,000	12.5°	594,000
14" Vega 10k	83.3	120	DTY	14"	16"	15³⁄₄"	57 lb	51°	180,000	9°	936,000
20" Draco 20k	83.3	220	KP200	20"	29"	29"	151 lb	46°	439,400	23°	2,366,000

Table A.2 Soft Light Fixtures

Fixture	Amps	Volts	Bulbs		Face Dimensions	Weight (lbs)	Beam Angle	Candle Power
Arri								
Arrisoft 1000	8.3	120	1	FCM	$9\frac{1}{2} \times 7\frac{7}{10}$"	13 lb	74°	9200
Arrisoft 2000	16.7	120	2	FCM	$8\frac{2}{10} \times 17\frac{1}{10}$"	19 lb	73°	16,700
Desisti								
Botticelli 2k	16.7	120	2	FCM	21×1"	11.5 lb	70°	
Botticelli 4k	33.3	120	4	FCM	32×21"	34.6 lb	80°	
Lowel								
Softlight 2	16.7	120	2	FCM	28×24"	8 lb	66°	
LTM								
400 Soft	3.3	120	1	FDA	$4\frac{3}{4} \times 6\frac{7}{8}$"	3 lb	67°	1000
1000 Soft	8.4	120	1	FCM	$11\frac{1}{2} \times 17$"	6.5 lb	70°	5000
2000 Soft	16.8	120	2	FCM	$20\frac{1}{2} \times 17$"	12 lb	70°	10,080
4000 Soft	48	120	4	FCM	42×42"	48 lb	70°	18,000
Mole-Richardson								
Mini-Softlite	5.4	120	1	FAD	$6\frac{1}{4} \times 6\frac{1}{4}$"	5.75 lb	65°	2400
750 Baby Soft	6.3	120	1	EJG	8×8"	5 lb	70°	3000
1k Super Soft	8.3	120	1	FCM	18×18"	21.5 lb	70°	5000
2k Zip Baby Soft	16.7	120	2	FCM	$8 \times 17\frac{1}{2}$"	9.25 lb	72°	10,080
2k Super Soft	16.7	120	2	FCM	24×24"	31.5 lb	70°	10,080
4k Baby Soft	33.3	120	4	FCM	18×18"	27 lb	70°	18,000
4k Super Soft	33.3	120	4	FCM	36×30"	63 lb	74°	24,320
8k Super Soft	66.7	120	8	FCM	36×30"	99 lb	69°	48,000
Strand								
Arturo 1000/1500	8.4	120	1	FFT	—	24 lb	—	—
	12.5	120	1	FDB	—	24 lb	—	—
Arturo 2000	16.7	120	2	FFT	—	35 lb	—	—
Arturo 4000/6000	33.3	120	4	FFT	—	45 lb	68°	—
	50	120	4	FDB	—	45 lb	68°	—

Table A.3 Open-Face Fixtures

	Watts	Volts	Bulb	Scrim	Chimera Ring Size	Weight (lbs)
Arri						
Arrilite 600	600	120	DYS	5"	$5\frac{1}{8}$"	3.6 lb
	250	30	DYG			
Arrilite 650	650	120	FAD	$7\frac{1}{4}$"	$7\frac{1}{4}$" *	5.2 lb
Arrilite 1000	1000	120	DXW	$7\frac{1}{4}$"	$7\frac{1}{4}$" *	5.2 lb
Arrilite 2000	2000	120	FEY	10"	10"	8.1 lb
Desisti						
Minilite 1000	1000	120	FHM	—	—	5 lb
Lee Colortran						
Mini-Pro Broad	650	120	FAD	—	—	—
Mini-Broad	650	120	FAD	—	—	29 oz
Broad	1000	120	FHM	—	—	—
Mini-Lite Nook	1000	120	FHM	—	—	—
Set Light Nook	1000	120	FHM	—	—	—

Table A.3 Open-Face Fixtures (continued)

	Watts	Volts	Bulb	Scrim	Chimera Ring Size	Weight (lbs)
Lowel						
Pro-Light	125	120	FSH	Special	Special*	2 lb
	250	120	GCA			
	200	30-V DC	GCB			
	100	12/14-V DC	GCC			
V-light	500	120	GDA	Special	Special*	1.5 lb
Toto-Light	300	120	EHZ	Special	Special*	2.25 lb
	500	120	FCZ			
	750	120	EMD			
Omni-Light	420	120	EKB	Special	Special*	2.6 lb
	600	120	DYS			
DP Light	500	120	EHC	Special	Special*	3.9 lb
	1000	120	FEL			
LTM						
Pepper 650 Flood	650	120	FRK	6"	6"	4 lb
Mole-Richardson						
Teenie Weenie	600	120	EKD	5$^1/_8$"	5$^1/_4$"	1.75 lb
Teenie Mole	650	120	FAD	6$^1/_4$"	6" *	3.5 lb
Mickey-Mole	1000	120	DXW	7$^3/_{16}$"	7$^1/_4$" *	4 lb
Mighty	2000	120	FEY	10"	10"	6.5 lb
1k Broad	1000	120	FHM	8$^1/_2$ × 12"	—	4.25 lb
2k Super Broad	2000	120	FFW	10$^1/_4$ × 12"	—	4 lb
650 Nooklite	650	120	FAD	—	—	1.25 lb
1k Nooklite	1000	120	FCM	—	—	2 lb
2k Nooklite	2000	120	FEY	—	—	2.5 lb
1k Molette	1000	120	FCV	—	—	0.75 lb
2k Molette	2000	120	BWG	—	—	2.5 lb
Sachtler						
Reporter 20	20, 70	12-V DC				
Reporter 50	30, 50	12-V DC				
Reporter 100	100	12-V DC				
Reporter 250	250	30-V DC				
Reporter 300	150, 300	110				
Reporter 650	650	110				
Reporter 1000	1000	110				
Strand Quartz Color						
Pulsar 600	600	120	DYS	—	Special*	3.6 lb
Ianabeam 650 "Redhead"	650	120	FAD	7$^1/_4$"	Special*	2.9 lb
Ianabeam 1000 "Redhead"	1000	120	DXW	7$^1/_4$"	Special*	2.9 lb
Ianabeam 2000 "Blonde"	2000	120	FEY	10"	10$^5/_8$"	8.5 lb

* Fixture takes a dedicated, nonstandard Chimera ring. See Chimera tables, Appendix G.2.

Table A.4 PAR Fixtures

	Watts	Bulb	Weight (lbs)	Scrim	Lamps
ETC					
Source Four PAR	575	HPL575	7.5 lb	7½"	
Mole-Richardson					
MolePAR	1000	PAR 64	4.75 lb	10⅛"	
PAR Can	1000	PAR 64	4.5 lb	10"	
Lee Colortran					
Cine-Queen	1000	PAR 64	—	9"	
PAR Arrays					
Arri	7000	PAR 64	170 lb		
Ruby 7	7000	PAR 64	170 lb		7 × 1000
Mole-Richardson					
MoleFAY	650	PAR 36	2.25 lb		1 × 650
2-Light	1300	PAR 36	9 lb		2 × 650
4-Light	2600	PAR 36	10.5 lb		4 × 650
6-Light	3600	PAR 36	17 lb		6 × 650
9-Light	5400	PAR 36	29.5 lb		9 × 650
12-Light	7800	PAR 36	26.5 lb		12 × 650
5-Light	3250	PAR 36	10 lb		5 × 650
3-Light Obie	1950	PAR 36	4.5 lb		3 × 650
6-Light	6000	PAR 64	54 lb		6 × 1000
9-Light	9000	PAR 64	72 lb		9 × 1000
"Moleeno" 12k	12,000	PAR 64	92.5 lb		12 × 1000
"Moleeno" 24k	24,000	PAR 64	173 lb		24 × 1000
"Moleeno" 36k	36,000	PAR 64	198 lb		36 × 1000
MoleCool	600	DYS	3.25 lb		1 × 600
	250	DYG			
2-Light	1200	DYS	9 lb		2 × 600
9-Light	5400	DYS	29¼ lb		9 × 600
Ultra Light Mfg.					
24-Light Dino	24k	PAR 64	—		24 × 1000
30-Light Dino	30k	PAR 64	—		30 × 1000
Ultra Dino	36k	PAR 64	190 lb		36 × 1000

Notes:

1. Color temperature, beam angle, and intensity depend on the globe used. See bulb data Appendix E.

2. Source Four PAR uses interchangeable, rotatable lenses (Clear, VNSP, NSP, MFL, and WFL). Lumen output is equivalent to 1k PARs with smoother, rounder beam. Optional MCM reflector removes 90% of heat from beam.

3. MolePAR accesories include intensifier and dicroic daylight conversion filter.

4. Weights listed include PAR lamps.

5. The Ruby 7 takes standard 29" scrims and barn doors.

Table A.5 HMI Fresnels

Model	Globe	Lens	Scrim	Chimera Ring Size	Head Weight (lbs)	Beam Angle Candle Power Flood	Spot
Altman							
575 SE	575 SE	5"	7¾"	7⅝"	16 lb	35,000	250,000
1200 SE	1200 SE	7"	9"	9⅝"	17 lb	52,000	700,000
2500 SE	2500 SE	10"	13"	13½"	38 lb	120,000	1,060,000
4000 SE	4000 SE	12"	15½"	—	65 lb	123,000	1,853,000
Arri							
Compact 125	125 SE	3.1"	5"	—	3.7 lb	59° 9000	8° 75,000
Compact 200	200 SE	4.3"	6⅝"	—	5.5 lb	55° 9000	8.3° 75,600
200 W	200 PAR	4.3"	5¼"	—	5.5 lb	52° 6147	7° 47,060
200 MSR	200 MSR PAR	4.3"	6⅝"	6½"	8 lb	—	—
575 W	L1.71900.0 / 575 PAR	6.9"	8½"	8½"	18 lb	44° 22,000	8° 197,300
Compact 575 W	575 SE	5.1"	7¾"	7⅝"	12 lb	60° 30,000	6° 250,000
1200 W	1200	11.8"	13"	12¾"	35 lb	54° 57,600	7° 726,200
Compact 1200 W	1200 SE	6.9"	9"	9⅝"	20 lb	58° 125,000	6° 800,000
2500 W	2500	13.8"	16"	15½"	66 lb	56° 157,300	7° 1,299,100
Compact 2500 W	2500 SE	10"	13"	13½"	31 lb	60° 159,000	7° 1,500,000
4000 W	4000	19.7"	21"	21"	95 lb	56° 199,000	8° 2,697,700
Compact 4000 W	4000 SE	11.8"	15½"	16⅛"	49 lb	60° 175,000	7° 2,125,000

Model numbers (Arri): 501205, 502200, L1.73000.0, — (200 MSR), L1.71900.0 (575 W), 505205, L1.72050.0, 512205, L1.72180.0, 525205, L1.72340.0, 540205

Table A.5 HMI Fresnels (continued)

| | | | | | | Head | Beam Angle Candle Power | |
Model	Globe	Lens	Scrim	Chinera Ring Size		Weight (lbs)	Flood	Spot
6000 W L1.72460.0	6000	19.7"	21"	21"		96 lb	54° / 399,700	7° / 4,749,800
Daylight 6000 560200	6000	19.7"	21"	21"		85 lb	56° / 250,000	6° / 4,377,500
Daylight 12000 562200	12000	19.7"	21"	21"		137 lb	54° / 625,000	7° / 8,440,500
Daylight 12/18k 563205	12,000 / 18,000	24.6"	29"	29"		154 lb	60° / 725,000	7° / 10,000,000
Cinimills								
12k Silver Bullet —	12k	24"	29"	29"		135 lb	425,000	7,875,000
12/18k Super Silver Bullet —	18k	24"	29"	29"		150 lb		
DedoTech								
DLH 400D	400 MSR	—	—	—		8.75	50°	5°
Desisti								
Rembrandt 200 2490	200 MSR/SE	4.8"	—	—		5.29	47°	6°
Piccolo 575 2500	575 SE	6"	7¼"	7³⁄₈"		15.21	46°	5°
Rembrandt 575 2400	575	6"	7¼"	7³⁄₈"		—	—	—
Piccolo 1200 2510	1200/SE	6"	7¼"	7³⁄₈"		18.74	54°	9°
Rembrandt 1200 SE 2610	1200/SE	10"	12"	12³⁄₈"		27.78	—	15°
Rembrandt 1200 2410	1200	10"	12"	12³⁄₈"		—	—	—
Piccolo 2500 2520	2500/SE	10"	12"	12³⁄₈"		33	55°	6°
Rembrandt 2500 2420	2500	12"	15½"	15³⁄₄"		—	—	—
Rembrandt 4000 2430	4000	14"	15½"	15½"		—	—	—
Piccolo 6000 —	6000 SE	14"	15½"	15½"		—	—	—
Rembrandt 6000 2440	6000	14"	15¾"	15³⁄₄"		—	—	—
Rembrandt 12k 2450	12k	20"	24¼"	24½"		117 lb	—	—
Rembrandt 18k 2560	18k	24"	—	—		148 lb	—	—

Table A.5 HMI Fresnels (continued)

	Model	Globe	Lens	Scrim	Chimera Ring Size	Head Weight (lbs)	Beam Angle Candle Power Flood	Beam Angle Candle Power Spot
Mole-Richardson								
575-W Solarspot	6331	575 SE	6"	6⅝"	6⅝"	11.25 lb	46° 16,200	6° 216,000
1200-W Solarspot	6321	1200-W SE	8"	9"	9"	20.25 lb	38° 63,000	6° 706,500
2500-W Solarspot	6341	2500-W SE	9.88"	13½"	12"	28 lb	60° 160,000	6° 1,639,800
6000-W Solarspot	6431	6000-W SE	14"	18½"	18½"	31 lb	60° 270,000	5° 4,050,000
12k Solar-Arc Solarspot	6301	12k	24.75"	29"	29"	150.5 lb	57° 405,000	7° 7,560,000
18k Solar-Arc Solarspot	6351	18k	24.75"	29"	29"	125 lb	58° 684,000	8° 9,540,000
LTM								
Bonxia 200 SE	—	200 SE MSR	3.13"	4¼"	4¼"	3.3 lb	30° 10,176	8° 47,040
Luxarc 200	Mk II	200	5"	6⅝"	6⅝"	6 lb	50° 7600	5° 124,000
Luxarc 575	Mk III	575	7"	9"	9"	12 lb	32° 50,600	6° 455,400
Luxarc 1200	Mk III	1200	10"	12"	12"	22 lb	46° 65,800	5° 1,315,600
Luxarc 2500	Mk III	2500	12"	15½"	15¾"	50 lb	51° 111,600	5° 1,264,500
Luxarc 4000	Mk III	4000	14"	18⅜"	18½"	58 lb	55° 222,400	10° 2,075,200
Luxarc 6000	Mk II	6000	20"	21½"	21"	105 lb	54° 417,600	6° 5,256,000

Table A.5 HMI Fresnels (continued)

	Model	Globe	Lens	Scrim	Chimera Ring Size	Head Weight (lbs)	Beam Angle Candle Power Flood	Spot
Super Lite 12k	—	12k	24"	29"	29"	125 lb	65° 450,000	6° 7,430,000
Luxarc 18K	—	18k	24"	29"	29"	130 lb	59° 730,000	7° 9,330,000
Super 12/18k	—	12k or 18k	24"	29"	29"	143 lb	59° 730,000	7° 9,330,000
Sachler								
Director 125D	—	123-W/SE	3"	5 1/4"	5 1/4"	4.4 lb	—	—
Director 270D	—	250-W/SE	5"	7 5/8"	7 5/8"	10.75 lb	—	—
Director 575D	—	575 MSR	6"	8 1/2"	8 1/2"	14 lb	—	—
Director 1200D	—	1200 MSR	8"	12"	12"	—	—	—
Director 2500D	—	2500 MSR	10"	13 1/2"	13 1/2"	—	—	—
Director 4000C	—	4000 MSR	10"	13 1/2"	13 1/2"	—	—	—
Director 4000D	—	4000 MSR	12"	13 1/2"	13 1/2"	—	—	—
Strand Color Quartz								
575 Sirio	2060	575	6"	9"	9"	24 lb	55°	5°
1200 Sirio	2070	1200	10"	12 3/4"	12 3/4"	44 lb	57°	5.5°
2500 Sirio	2080	2500	12"	16"	15 3/4"	58.5 lb	63.5°	6°
Supernova 25/12	24147	2500 SE or 1200 SE	10"	13 1/2"	13 1/2"	36 lb	60°	7°
Supernova 40/25	24155	4000 SE or 2500 SE	12"	16"	15 3/4"	43 lb	70°	9°
4000 Sirio	2090	4000	14"	16"	15 3/4"	72 lb	53°	8.5°
6000 Sirio	3000	6000	14"	16"	15 3/4"	68 lb	56°	5.5°
12 kW Sirio	3890	12 kW	20"	29"	29"	187 lb	55°	6°
Sunray								
Sunray 12/18k		12 kW or 18 kW	24"	29"	29"	138 lb	—	—

Table A.6 HMI PAR Fixtures

	Model	Globe	Scrim	Chimera Ring Size	Head Weight (lbs)	Lens	Beam Angle	Candela
Arri								
Arrisun 5 PAR	L1.77175.0	BB575 PAR	—		11 lb	Very Narrow Spot	14° × 8°	450,000
						Narrow Spot	14° × 10°	400,000
						Medium Flood	26° × 12°	150,000
						Wide Flood	50° × 45°	25,000
Arrisun 1200-W PAR	L1.77500.0	BB1200 PAR	—	10"	19 lb	Very Narrow Spot	14° × 7°	1,800,000
						Narrow Spot	11° × 8°	1,300,800
						Medium Flood	22° × 10°	600,000
						Wide Flood	54° × 19°	169,600
Arrisun 12 plus	512305	1200 SE	13"	13½"	25 lb	Super Spot	3.5°	5,625,000
						Spot	6.5°	2,500,000
						Medium	12° × 20.5°	192,000
						Super Wide	21° × 47°	110,000
						Frosted Fresnel	39°	53,250
Arrisun 40/25 2500-W Bulb	540300	2500 SE	15½"	1⅛"	43 lb	Super Spot	5°	8,750,000
						Spot	8.5°	3,375,000
						Medium	11° × 20°	1,800,000
						Wide	11° × 44°	450,000
						Super Wide	48°	200,000
						Frosted Fresnel	18°	202,500
Arrisun 40/25 4000-W Bulb	540300	4000 SE	15½"	16½"	43 lb	Super Spot	4.5°	10,500,000
						Spot	10°	4,500,000
						Medium	12° × 21°	2,150,000
						Wide	19° × 45°	600,000
						Super Wide	50°	250,000
						Frosted Fresnel	22°	270,000

Table A.6 HMI PAR Fixtures (continued)

	Model	Globe	Scrim	Chimera Ring Size	Head Weight (lbs)	Lens	Beam Angle	Candela
Arrisun 60	560300	6000 SE	19½"	—	59 lb	Super Spot	7°	14,900,000
						Spot	10°	7,175,000
						Medium	11° × 20°	3,375,000
						Wide	20° × 38°	1,225,000
						Super Wide	42°	675,000
						Frosted Fresnel	37°	337,500
Arrisun 120	562300	12,000 SE	21"	21"	101 lb	Super Spot	6°	20,000,000
						Spot	10°	11,250,000
						Medium	10° × 30°	4,000,000
						Wide	20° × 45°	1,750,000
						Super Wide	45°	950,000
						Frosted Fresnel	41°	682,000
Cinimills								
200-W Wallylight[1]	—	200-W PAR	7¼"	7⅛"	11.5 lb	—	—	—
200-W SE[2]	—	200-W SE	7¼"	7⅛"	6 lb	—	—	—
575-W SE	—	575 SE	7¼"	7⅛"	12.5 lb	—	—	3,375,000
1200-W PAR	—	1200 PAR	10"	9"	16 lb	—	—	—
1200-W SE	—	1200 SE	10"	10⅛"	16 lb	—	—	4,600,000
2500-W SE	—	2500 SE	13½"	13½"	24.5 lb	—	—	6,575,000
4000-W SE	—	4000 SE	13½"	13½"	24.5 lb	—	—	11,000,000
6000-W SE	—	6000 SE	13½"	16⅛"	—	—	—	—
Desisti								
Remington 200	—	200-W MSR	—	—	—	—	—	—
Caravaggio 575	2310	575-W PAR	—	7⅜"	—	—	—	—
Caravaggio 1200	2320	1200-W PAR	—	—	19 lb	—	—	—
Remington 2.5/4k	—	2500-W SE	—	—	—	—	—	—
	—	4000-W SE	—	—	—	—	—	—
Remington Piccolo 6k	—	6000-W SE	—	—	—	—	—	—

Table A.6 HMI PAR Fixtures (continued)

Model		Globe	Scrim	Chimera Ring Size	Head Weight (lbs)	Lens	Beam Angle	Candela
DN Labs								
575 Durapar PAR	—	575 PAR	7½"	7⅞"	10 lb	—	—	—
575 Durapar SE	—	575 SE	10"	—	15 lb	—	—	—
1200 Durapar PAR	—	1200 PAR	10"	10⅛"	13 lb	—	—	—
1200 Durapar SE	—	1200 SE MSR	12"	12"	21 lb	—	—	—
2500 Durapar SE[1]	—	2500 SE MSR	12"	12"	21 lb	—	—	—
10kW Durapar (4-light cluster)	—	4 × 2500 SE	—		82 lb	—	—	—
40kW Durapar (16-light cluster)	—	16 × 2500 SE	—		338 lb	—	—	—
4000W Durapar	—	4000 SE	16"	15¾"	33 lb	—	—	—
6000 SE Durapar	—	6000 SE	16"	15¾"	48 lb	—	—	—
6000 DE Durapar	—	6000-W DE	22 × 25"	—	65 lb	21 × 24" square	—	—
12-kW Durapar	—	12-kW DE	22 × 25"	—	80 lb	21 × 24" square	—	—
K 5600								
Joker Bug 200[1]	U0200B	MSR/SE 200 W	5"	5"	4.4 lb	—	—	—
Joker Bug 400	U0400B	MSR/SE 400 W	6⅝"	6⅝"	5.2 lb	—	—	—
Joker Bug 800	U0800B	BA 0800 SE	7¾"	7¾"	6 lb	—	—	—
Joker 1200	U1200	1200-W SE	9"	9"	12 lb	—	—	—
LTM								
CinePAR 200 S/E		200S/E MSR	6⅝"	6"	2.4 lb	VNSP	6°	509,000
						NSP	19° × 12°	74,900
						MF	36° × 26°	24,000
						WF	62°	9,600
CinePAR 200		200-W PAR	6⅝"	6"	4 lb	NSP	—	—
						M	—	—
						WF		
						SWF		

Table A.6 HMI PAR Fixtures (continued)

Model	Globe	Scrim	Chimera Ring Size	Head Weight (lbs)	Lens	Beam Angle	Candela
CinePAR 575 S/E	575 S/E	6⅝"	6⅝"	7 lb	NSP	6°	1,350,000
					MF	28° × 14°	183,400
					SWF	62°	22,500
					FF	42°	24,800
CinePAR 575	575 PAR	7¼"	7¼"	8 lb	VNSP	13° × 7°	337,500
					M	17° × 10°	281,300
					WF	20° × 8°	135,000
					SWF	67°	16,900
CinePAR 1200 S/E	1200 SE	9"	9"	16 lb	VNSP	4°	4,601,600
					MF	25° × 12°	490,800
					WF	54° × 21°	131,300
					SWF	53°	72,100
CinePAR 1200	1200 PAR	9"	9"	13 lb	VNSP	12° × 6°	2,000,000
					NSP	12° × 8°	1,375,000
					MF	23° × 9°	805,100
					WF	54° × 22°	198,800
					SWF	64°	89,400
CinePAR 2500 S/E	2500/SE	13"	12¾"	32 lb	VNSP	6°	5,832,000
					NSP	8°	2,592,000
					MF	27° × 11°	856,000
					WF	60° × 25°	222,400
					SWF	54°	124,800
CinePAR 4000 S/E	4000/SE	15½"	15¾"	40 lb	VNSP	5°	10,530,000
					M	23° × 10°	1,260,000
					WF	38° × 15°	540,000
					SWF	20°	261,000
					FF	33°	180,000

Table A.6 HMI PAR Fixtures (continued)

	Model	Globe	Scrim	Chimera Ring Size	Head Weight (lbs)	Lens	Beam Angle	Candela
CinePAR 6000 S/E		6000 S/E	19½"	—	48.5 lb	S M WF SWF FF	7° 13° × 31° 18° × 37° 36° 34°	13,500,000 — — 380,000
CinePAR 6/12kw S/E		6k S/E or 12,000 S/E	—	—	74 lb	S M WF SWF FF	6° 13° × 28° 18° × 30° 40° 28°	19,000,000 36,000,000 1,790,000 1,090,000 660,000
Mole-Richardson								
200 MolePAR	6201	200 PAR	6¼"	6"	7.5 lb	VNSP, NSP, M, WF	—	—
575 MolePAR	6211	575 PAR	7³/₁₆"	7¼"	10 lb	VNSP, NSP, M, WF	—	—
1200 MolePAR[3]	6221	1200 PAR	10⅛"	10"	13 lb	VNSP, NSP, M, WF	—	—
1200 MolePAR[3]	6371	1200 SE	10⅛"	10"	15 lb	VNSP, NSP, M, WF	—	—
2500 MolePAR	6381	2500 SE	12"	12"	27 lb	VNSP, NSP, M, WF	—	—
4000-W MolePAR	6391	4000-W SE	13½"	13½"	28.5 lb	VNSP, NSP, M, WF	—	—
6000-W MolePAR[3]	6401	6000-W SE	15½"	—	39 lb	VNSP, NSP, M, WF	—	—
12k MolePAR	6601	12k SE	21"	21"	67 lb	VNSP NSP WF EWF	11° 14° 38° 45°	10,310,000 3,660,000 1,890,000 1,180,000
Sachtler								
Production 575D		575 MSR	6"	9"	14 lb	—	—	—
Production 1200D		1200 MSR	8"	9½"	—	—	—	—
Sunray								
575 PAR[4]		575 PAR	7¼" 12"	7⅜"	3 lb	VNSP, NSP, MF, WF, SWF	—	—
575 SE PAR		575/SE	7¼" 12"	7⅜"	11 lb	VNSP, NSP, MF, WF, SWF	—	—

Table A.6 HMI PAR Fixtures (continued)

Model	Globe	Scrim	Chimera Ring Size	Head Weight (lbs)	Lens	Beam Angle	Candela
1200 PAR[2]	1200 PAR	10" 15½"	10⅛"	10 lb	VNSP, NSP, MF, WF, SWF	—	—
1200 SE PAR	1200/SE	10" 15½	10⅛"	15 lb	VNSP, NSP, M, WF		—
2500-W SE[3]	2500/SE	10" 15½"	10⅛"	20 lb	VNSP, NSP, M, WF	—	—
4000-W SE[3]	4000 SE	15½" 21"	15½"	30 lb	SP, M, WF, SWF	—	—
Strand Quartz Color							
Quasar 12	4532	10³⁄₁₆"	10⅝"	19.8 lb	SP, M, WF, SWF	2°–21°	—
Super Quasar 25/12	24800	2500 SE or 1200 SE	10³⁄₁₆"	10⅝"	34 lb	SP, M, WF, SWF	3°–46°	—
Super Quasar 40/25	24900	4000 SE or 2500 SE	12⅝"	12¾"	44 lb	SP, M, WF, SWF	4°–44°	—

Notes:

1. 200-W WallylightHead and ballast are one self-contained unit.

2. Accesories include an *intensifier*, a polished aluminum bowl-shaped snoot attachment that can increase light output by about 34%.

3. Accesories for Durapar SE fixtures include a *diffusion module*, which converts the head into a very bright soft light.

4. Optional 200W Slimverter converts 30-V DC from battery pack to 120-V AC and can be used with fluorescents, electronic dimmers, incandescents (200-W or less) as well as the Joker Bug 200.

Table A.7   HMI Sun Gun Fixtures

	Globe	Lens	Scrim	Chimera Ring Size	Head Weight (lbs)	Power Supply
Arri						
125 Pocket PAR	125 W SE	3"	—	6"	2 lb	24–30-V DC electronic ballast or 120-V AC electronic ballast
Desisti						
Tiziano	200-W SE	Open Face	—	6"	3.95 lb	24–30-V DC electronic ballast 120-V AC mains adaptor
Remington 200		SE PAR	—	—	—	24–30-V DC electronic ballast 120-V AC mains adaptor
DN Labs						
200 PAR	200 PAR	—	—	5¼"	2.5 lb	—
K 5600						
Joker 200	200 SE		5"		4.4 lb	30-V DC
Joker 400	400 SE		6⅝"	6⅝"	5.2 lb	30-V DC
LTM						
Sungun 200S/E	200-W SE	None	5⅞"	6"	2.6 lb	DC ballast: 30-V electronic AC ballast: 100–260-V auto
Blue Torch 270	250-W SE	None	5⅞"	6"	5 lb	DC ballast: 24–30-V AC ballast: 110-V
Bonzai 200 S/E	200-W SE	3⅛"	4½"	4¼"	3.3 lb	DC ballast: 20–30 V AC ballast: 120–250 V
Sachtler						
Reporter 125D	123-W SE	—	5¼"	5¼"	1.5 lb	—
Reporter 270D	250-W SE	—	7⅝"	7⅝"	3.3 lb	—
Production 575D	575-W SE	—	8½"	8½"	8.4 lb	—
Production 1200D	1200-W SE	—	12"	12"	18.5 lb	—

Notes: The Arri Pocket PAR can be used with a number of accessories. Including glass CTO filters, hand grip, Chimera, pattern projector attachment with multiple lens choices, Flex light (flexible light tube attachment for miniatures and temperature-sensitive subjects), and Light Pipe (white tube attachment turns the light into a soft tube light).
The K5600 Joker lights also feature accessories including china lantern, soft tube light.

Table A.8 Other HMI Fixtures

Description	Manufacturer	Name	Globe	Dimentions	Weight (lbs)	Candela ($FC \times D^2$)
Chicken coop	Cinemills	4000 W/2500 W	2500-W DE	$49 \times 39"$	55 lb	—
			4000-W DE			
Soft lights	Desisti	Raffaello 575	575	$12^5/_8 \times 15"$	20.5 lb	—
	Desisti	Raffaello 1200	1200	$12^5/_8 \times 19"$	24.5 lb	—
	Desisti	Raffaello 2500	2500	$17 \times 24^3/_4"$	50.2 lb	—
	LTM	Softarc 575	575	$14 \times 20^1/_4"$	18 lb	10,500
	LTM	Softarc 1200	1200	$19 \times 30"$	31 lb	19,500
	DN Labs	Durapar 200T	—	—	—	—
Scoop	DN Labs	Spectra-Flux 1200	SE 1200	21" round	21 lb	—
Bare bulb in Pyrex tube used for Chinese lantern	K 5600	Bug Light	SE 200 W	Pyrex tube	3.5 lb	—
Open-face fixtures	Arri	X2	200W SE	—	4.4 lb	4950
	Arri	X5	575W SE	—	11 lb	11,250
	Arri	X12	1200 SE	—	22 lb	25,000
	Arri	X40/25	2500 or 4k SE	—	39.7 lb	75,000
	Arri	X60	6k SE	—	66.1 lb	112,500
	Desisti	Goya 1200	SE 1200W	—	—	67,700
		Shadowlight				
	Desisti	Goya 2500/4000	SE 2500	$20 \times 22"$	37 lb	116,000
		Shadowlight	SE 4000			

Table A.9 Mole-Richardson Studio Arc Fixtures

	Grid Input Watts	Amps	Volts	Carbon Dimentions (in.)	in/hr.	Head Lens	Scrim	Weight (lbs)
150	18k	150	120 dc	Pos .63 × 25 Neg 11/16 × 9	9 4-1/2	—	—	181 lb
Baby Brute	27k	225	120 dc	Pos .63 × 22 Neg 17/32 × 6¾	20 10	14"	18-½"	126 lb
Lightweight Brute	27k	225	120 dc	Pos .63 × 22 Neg 17/32 × 6¼	20 10	24-¾"	29"	152 lb
Brute	27k	225	120 dc	Pos .63 × 22 Neg 17/32 × 9	20 10	—	—	225 lb
Titan	42k	350	120 dc	Pos .63 × 25 Neg 11/16 × 9	20 10	—	—	250 lb

Table A.10 Fluorescent Fixtures

Fixture	Lamps	Lamp Length	Bulb Type	Dimensions of Face (in.)	Weight (lbs)	Ballast
Lowel						
Light Array	6	4 ft	T-12	30 × 54	18 lb	Detatchable, flicker-free
Mole-Richardson						
Eight-tube, 18 in.	8	18 in.	T-12	16.4 × 19	25.25 lb	Built-in, conventional
Four-tube, 4 ft	4	4 ft	T-12	21.75 × 55.25	42.74 lb	Built-in, conventional
Leonetti Sunray						
Four-tube, 4 ft	4	4 ft	T-12	8 × 48	23 lb	Flicker-free
Eight-tube, 4 ft	8	4 ft	T-12	16 × 48	36 lb	Flicker-free

Table A.10 Fluorescent Fixtures (continued)

Fixture	Lamps	Lamp Length	Bulb Type	Dimensions of Face (in.)	Weight (lbs)	Ballast
LTM						
Mini Moonlight	2	18 in.	Osram FT 36 DL/835 (3200K) Philips PL-L 36W/95 (5100K)	2 × 18	—	Built-in, flicker-free
Moonlight Single	6	18 in.	Osram FT 36 DL/835 (3200K) Philips PL-L 36W/95 (5100K)	18 × 18	25 lb	Built-in, flicker-free
Moonlight Double	12	18 in.	Osram FT 36 DL/835 (3200K) Philips PL-L 36W/95 (5100K)	36 × 18	50 lb	Built-in, flicker-free
Moonlight Triple	18	18 in.	Osram FT 36 DL/835 (3200K) Philips PL-L 36W/95 (5100K)	54 × 18	75 lb	Built-in, flicker-free
Moonlight Quadruple	24	18 in.	Osram FT 36 DL/835 (3200K) Philips PL-L 36W/95 (5100K)	36 × 36	100 lb	Built-in, flicker-free
Moonlight Sextuple	36	18 in.	Osram FT 36 DL/835 (3200K) Philips PL-L 36W/95 (5100K)	36 × 54	150 lb	Built-in, flicker-free

Table A.11 Kino-Flo Fixtures

Name	Length	No. of Tubes	Weight (lbs)	Mount	Ballast	Volts	Amps	Lamp	Output @ 6 ft (FC)
Portable Fixture Systems									
Four Bank	4 ft	4	10.5 lb	3/8 pin	Std Slt, Dim	117-V AC	5	F40/T12	80
	2 ft	4	6.5 lb	3/8 pin	Std Slt, Dim	117-V AC	3.5	F20/T12	45
	15 in.	4	5 lb	3/8 pin	Std Slt, Dim	117-V AC	2.5	F14/T12	25

Table A.11 Kino-Flo Fixtures (continued)

Name	Length	No. of Tubes	Ballast	Mount	Weight (lbs)	Amps	Volts	Lamp	Output @ 6 ft (FC)
Two Bank	4 ft	2	Std. Slt. Dim	3/8 pin	7 lb	2.6	117-V AC	F40/T12	53
	2 ft	2	Std. Slt. Dim	3/8 pin	4 lb	1.8	117-V AC	F20/T12	23
	15 in.	2	Std. Slt. Dim	3/8 pin	3 lb	1.4	117-V AC	F14/T12	14
Single	4 ft	1	Std. Slt. Dim	3/8 pin	4 lb	1.3	117-V AC	F40/T12	25
	2 ft	1	Std. Slt. Dim	3/8 pin	2 lb	0.9	117-V AC	F20/T12	10
	15 in.	1	Std. Slt. Dim	3/8 pin	1.5 lb	0.7	117-V AC	F14/T12	6
Flathead	4 ft	8	2 Slt	3/8 pin	26 lb	10	117-V AC	F40/T12	155
Diva-Lite 400	21 in.	4	Built-in[1]	3/8 pin	14 lb	0.92	117-V AC[2]	F55/T5	75
Diva-Lite 200	21 in.	2	Built-in[1]	3/8 pin	8.5 lb	0.6	117-V AC[2]	F55/T5	45
Wall-O-Lite	4 ft	10	Built-in[1,3]	Jr. pin	47 lb	12	117-V AC	F40/T12	180
Blanket Light	6 ft	16	Mega 4-Bank Frame		90 lb[4]	25.6	117-V AC	F72/T12	306
Mega Double	8 ft	2	Mega Double	3/8 pin	15 lb	3.7	117-V AC	F96/T12	64
	6 ft	2	Mega Double	3/8 pin	9 lb	3.1	117-V AC	F72/T12	50
Mega Single	8 ft	1	Mega. Slimline	3/8 pin	9 lb	2.2	117-V AC	F96/T12	25
	6 ft 10 in.	1	Mega. Slimline	3/8 pin	5 lb	1	117-V AC	F72/T12	10
12-V DC Systems									
12-V Single	4 ft	1	12-V DC Single	—	—	4.5	2-V DC[5]	F40/T12	
	2 ft	1	12-V DC Single	—	—	2.6	2-V DC[5]	F20/T12	
	15 in.	1	12-V DC Single	—	—	2.3	2-V DC[5]	F14/T12	
Mini-flo	9 in	1	Mini-flo 12-V DC	—	15 oz	0.8	2-V DC[5]	F6/T5	
Micro-flo	6 in.	—	Micro-flo 12-V DC	—	8 oz	—	2-V DC[5]		
	4 in.	—	Micro-flo 12-V DC	—	—	—	2-V DC[5]		
Studio Fixtures									
Image 80	4 ft	8	Built-in[3]	Jr. pin	37 lb	10	117-V AC	F40/T12	155
Image 40	4 ft	4	Built-in[3]	Jr. pin	22 lb	5	117-V AC	F40/T12	80
Image 20	2 ft	4	Built-in[3]	Jr. pin	14 lb	1.8	117-V AC	F20/T12	42

Notes:

1. Has dimming ballast.
2. Also available with universal ballast (100–265-V AC 50/60 Hz).
3. DMX control also available for this fixture.
4. Blanket light (30 lb) plus frame (60 lb).
5. Comes with 12-V DC transformer for use with 120-V AC or 220-V AC service.

Table A.12 Ellipsoidal Reflector Spotlight Specifications

Fixture	Field Angle	Multiplier	Candle Power (cd)	Lamp	K	Watts	Weight (lbs)	Gel Frame (in.)
Altman			*Flat Field Data*					
Shakespeare 50	50°	.93	27,500	FLK (HX600)	3200	575	18 lb	6-1/4"
Shakespeare 40	40°	.73	43,500	"	"	"	18 lb	6-1/4"
Shakespeare 30	30°	.54	104,000	"	"	"	18 lb	6-1/4"
Shakespeare 20	20°	.35	119,000	"	"	"	18 lb	6-1/4"
Shakespeare 10	10°	.17	265,000	"	"	"	30 lb	6-1/4"
Shakespeare 1535Z	15°–35°	.26–.63	233k–58k	"	"	"	30 lb	7-1/2"
Shakespeare 3055Z	30°–55°	.54–1.04	74k–23.5k	"	"	"	30 lb	7-1/2"
ETC			*Flat Field Data*					
Source Four 450	50°	.93	34,866	HPL 575	3250	575	16 lb	6-1/4"
Source Four 436	36°	.65	84,929	"	"	"	16.3 lb	6-1/4"
Source Four 426	26°	.46	138,079	"	"	"	16 lb	6-1/4"
Source Four 419	19°	.31	167,435	"	"	"	16 lb	6-1/4"
Source Four 410	10.3°	.178	800,300	"	"	"	16.3 lb	12"
Source Four 405	6.8°	.119	996,000	"	"	"	17.5 lb	14"
Altman			*Peak Field Data*					
Micro-Elipse	—		12,000	MR-16 EYC/EYJ	3050	75	5 lb	3-3/8"
3.5Q 3.5 × 5	48°	.89	15,200	EHD	3000	500	9 lb	4-1/8"
3.5 × 6	38°	.69	16,000	"	"	"	9 lb	4-1/8"
3.5 × 8	28°	.50	17,200	"	"	"	9 lb	4-1/8"
3.5 × 10	23°	.41	20,000	"	"	"	9 lb	4-1/8"
3.5 × 12	18°	.32	88k–55k	"	"	"	9 lb	4-1/8"
4.5-1530 Baby zoom	15°–30°	.26–.54	80k–40k	EHF	3200	750	15 lb	6-1/4"
4.5-2550 Baby zoom	25°–50°	.44–.93	50k–26k	"	"	"	15 lb	6-1/4"
4.5-3060 Baby zoom	30°–60°	.55–1.15	51,200	"	"	"	15 lb	6-1/4"
360Q 4.5 × 6.5	56°	1.06	88,000	EHF	3200	750	13.5 lb	7-1/2"
6 × 9	35°	.63	152,000	"	"	"	14 lb	7-1/2"
6 × 12	25°	.44	184,000	"	"	"	15 lb	7-1/2"
6 × 16	21°	.37	216,000	"	"	"	15 lb	7-1/2"
6 × 22	11°	.19		"	"	"	15 lb	7-1/2"

Table A.12 Ellipsoidal Reflector Spotlight Specification (continued)

Fixture	Field Angle	Multiplier	Candle Power (cd)	Lamp	K	Watts	Weight (lbs)	Gel Frame (in.)
Altman			*Peak Field Data*					
1KL6-12	12°	.21	342,400	FEL	3200	1k	24 lb	7-1/2"
1KL6-20	20°	.35	257,600	"	"	"	25 lb	7-1/2"
1KL6-30	30°	.54	195,200	"	"	"	24 lb	7-1/2"
1KL6-40	40°	.73	148,800	"	"	"	25 lb	7-1/2"
1KL6-50	50°	.93	97,600	"	"	"	24 lb	7-1/2"
1KL8-10	10°	.17	490,000	"	"	"	26 lb	10"
1KJL10-5	5°	.09	1,008,000	"	"	"	32 lb	12"
1KL6-2040Z	20°–40°	.35–.73	275k–85k	"	"	"	28 lb	7-1/2"
1KL8-1424Z	14°–24°	.25–.43	489k–262k	"	"	"	34 lb	10"
Colorttran			*Peak Field Data*					
5/50 Series 650-012	50°	.93	28,700	FEL	3200	1k		
5/50 Series 650-022	40°	.73	48,000	"	"	"		
5/50 Series 650-032	30°	.54	118,000	"	"	"		
5/50 Series 650-042	20°	.35	171,000	"	"	"		
5/50 Series 650-052	15°	.26	298,000	"	"	"		
5/50 Series 650-072	10°	.17	563,000	"	"	"		
5/50 Series 650-082	5°	.09	938,000	"	"	"		
Colortran			*Peak Field Data*					
Mini-zoom 213-302	40°–65°	1.27–.73	32k–8.9k	FMR	3000	600		
Mini-zoom 213-312	25°–50°	.44–.93	49k–18.3k	"	"	"		
Mini-zoom 213-322	15°–30°	.26–.54	61k–44.5k	"	"	"		
Mini Ellipse 213-152	50°	.93	9000	EVR	3000	500		
Mini Ellipse 213-152	40°	.73	16,500	"	"	"		
Mini Ellipse 213-152	30°	.54	24,000	"	"	"		
Ellipsoid 213-052	40°	.73	48,000	FEL	3200	1k		
Ellipsoid 213-062	30°	.54	118,000	"	"	"		
Ellipsoid 213-072	20°	.35	171,000	"	"	"		
Ellipsoid 213-092	12°	.21	298,000	"	"	"		
Ellipsoid 213-102	10°	.17	563,000	"	"	"		

Table A.12 Ellipsoidal Reflector Spotlight Specification (continued)

Fixture	Field Angle	Multiplier	Candle Power (cd)	Lamp	K	Watts	Weight (lbs)	Gel Frame (in.)
Ellipsoid 213-112	5°	.09	938,000	"	"	"	7.3 lb	6"
Ellipse Zoom 213-162	15°–35°	.26–0.63	206k–82k	"	"	"	10.5 lb	6"
Strand			**Peak Field Data**					
Quartet PC	7.5°–55.5°	.13–1.05	64,000	FRK	3200	650	10.6 lb	6"
Quartet 25	25°	.44	36,000	"	"	"	17 lb	7.5"
Quartet 22/44	22°–44°	.39–.81	408,000	"	"	"	13.2 lb	7.5"
Leko 15	15°	.26	190,800	FEL	3200	1k	13.2 lb	7.5"
Leko 20	20°	.35	185,000	"	"	1k	13.2 lb	7.5"
Leko 30	30°	.54	449,850	"	"	1k	13.2 lb	7.5"
Leko 40	40°	.73	118,825	"	"	1k	22 lb	10"
Leko 50	50°	.93	63,000	FEL	"	1k	26 lb	11-3/4"
8" Leko	12°	.21	582,400	"	"	1k	15 lb	6-1/4"
10" Leko	9°	.15	880,000	"	"	1k	27 lb	7-1/2"
4-1/2" Variable Focus	25°–50°	.44–.93	24,698	EVR	"	500	28 lb	7-1/2"
6" Variable Focus	15°–40°	.26–.73	92,800	FEL	"	1k	26.5 lb	7-1/2"
Cantata 11/26	11°–26°	.19–.46	265,000	FEL	"	1k	24 lb	7-1/2"
Cantata 18/32	18°–32°	.32–.57	165,000	"	"	"	28 lb	7-1/2"
Cantata 26/44	26°–44°	.46–.81	108,800	"	"	"	28 lb	7-1/2"
Optique 8/17	8°–17°	.17–.30	395,000	T-29	"	1200	37.5 lb	7-1/2 "
Optique 15/42	15°–42°	.26–.77	119,790	"	"	"	37.5 lb	7-1/2"
Alto 8/16 (2k)	8°–16°	.14–.28	595,200	CP92	"	2k	35 lb	9.6"
Alto 14/32 (2k)	14°–32°	.25–.57	357,192	"	"	"	45.2 lb	9.6"
Alto 20/38 (2k)	20°–38°	.35–.69	207,500	"	"	"	43.56 lb	9.6"
Toccata 10/26	10°–26°	.17–.46	605,756	CP92	"	2k		9.6"
Toccata 15/38	15°–38°	.26–.69	348,480	"	"	"		9.6"

Notes:

1. Lamp intensities for ETC Source Four and Altman Shakespeare fixtures are *cosine flat field* candle power. All others are *peak* candle power. Comparing the two is misleading because peak readings tend to exaggerate performance.

2. Altman 360Q lamps are manufactured with either a bi-pin base, or a mini-can base. The bi-pin bulb type is listed here.

3. Each fixture can take a variety of bulbs. The highest wattage bulb is shown here. See Table E.3 for bulb substitutions.

4. To determine beam width, multiply *multiplier* by distance.

5. To determine footcandle level, divide candle-power by distance squared, or use Table A.14.

Table A.13 Underwater Fixtures

Fixture	Bulb	Volts	Depth	Weight (lbs) in Air	Weight (lbs) in Water	Beam Control	Notes, Accessories
HydroFlex HMI							
HydroPAR 4k SE	4k SE MSR	220-V AC	100 ft	32 lb	11 lb	Removable reflectors: spot, medium, flood	Underwater use only
HydroPAR 2.5k SE	2500-W SE	120-V AC	150 ft	30 lb	4 lb	Exchangeable Fresnel lenses: VNSP—Very Narrow Spot MFL—Medium Flood WFL—Wide Flood UWFL—Ultrawide Flood	Timed intervals above water or continuous underwater use
HydroPAR 1200W	BB1200 PAR 64 Mark II	120-V AC	120 ft	29 lb	2 lb	Exchangeable Fresnel lenses: VNSP MFL WFL UWFL	Timed intervals above water or continuous underwater use
HydroRama 8k HMI	2 × MSR 4000HR	220-V AC	100 ft	58 lb	42 lb	Reflector adjustable through 180°	Underwater use only
Splashlight	21-W MHL		100 ft	8.5 lb	2 lb	Spot or flood reflectors	45 min battery life. Kit includes 3 batteries and a charger. 5500 K color temp.
Tungsten Incandescent							
HydroRama 10k Tungsten	2 × DPY (5k) or 2 × CP/85 (5k)	120-V 220-V AC/DC	100 ft	48 lb	32 lb	Reflector adjustable through 180°	Underwater use only. Low mode plate (to sit on bottom of pool) or yoke Jr. spud.
HydroPAR 5000 W SE	DPY or CP/85	120-V 220-V	100 ft	22 lb	6 lb	Removable reflectors: spot, medium, flood	Underwater use only
HydroPAR 2000 W SE	CYX	120-V AC/DC	120 ft	24 lb	4 lb	Exchangeable Fresnel lenses: VNSP MFL WFL UWFL	

Table A.13 Underwater Fixtures (continued)

Fixture	Bulb	Volts	Depth	Weight (lbs) in Air	Weight (lbs) in Water	Beam Control	Notes, Accessories
HydroPAR 1000 W	PAR 64	120-V AC/DC	150 ft	14 lb	4 lb	Change-out PAR 64 lamp VNSP NSP MFL NSP (dichroic) MFL (dichroic)	Can be mounted to yoke, handgrip, $5/8$" spud, or panel mounted
HydroPAR 650 W	PAR 36	120-V AC/DC	120 ft	5 lb	1 lb	Change-out PAR 36 lamp MFL SP MFL (dichroic) SP (dichroic)	
HydroPAR MR-16	12–300-W MR-16	12–120-V AC/DC	100 ft	1.5 lb	1 lb	A variety of bulbs available, spot to flood	2.75" long, 1.5" wide
HydroPAR 12-V Practical	50-W, 100-W, 150-W	12-V	100 ft	3.3 oz	2.3 oz		4 power output settings
Hartenberger UW Flashlight	100-W halogen			6 lb	2 lb		
Pace WetSet™ HMI							
8k/5k PaceCyc	Two 4k SE SE	220	150 ft				
5k PaceCyc	Two 2.5k SE	220-V AC	150 ft				
4k PaceSE	4k SE	220-V AC				Wide Lens	
2.5k PaceSE							
1.2k SE							
1.2k PacePAR	Osram/Sylvania 1200-W PAR 64	120-V AC	150 ft			Medium, wide, and very wide lenses	Includes scrims, gel holder, and barn doors

Table A.13 Underwater Fixtures (continued)

Fixture	Bulb	Volts	Depth	Weight (lbs) in Air	Weight (lbs) in Water	Beam Control	Notes, Accessories
200-W SEB		Lithium / Battery pack				Med and wide lenses	Scrims, battery kit
Xenon Searchlight		Lithium / Battery pack				Pencil beam flag	
Tungsten Incandescent							
10k PaceCyc	Two 5k tungsten	220-V AC	150 ft				
5k PaceSE	5k tungsten	220-V AC	150 ft				
2k SE	CYX 2k	120-V AC/DC	150 ft			12" wide lens	Scrims, gel holder
1k PacePAR	PAR 64	120-V AC/DC	150 ft			Diffusion lens	Gel holder and scrims
650 PacePAR	PAR 36	120-V AC/DC	150 ft			Diffusion lens or change out bulb	
1k Cyc	500 W	120-V AC/DC	15 ft	1k Cyc		Diffusion lens or change out bulb	
	1000 W						
	1500 W						
250-W Flashlight							
400-W Flashlight							

Note: All HydroFlex lights come equipped with a $\frac{5}{8}$" baby spud (except where noted), underwater mateable connectors and integrated ground-fault sensors (GFCI). On the PAR fixtures, barn doors and snoots can be used by removing the lamp head retaining ring and inserting the accessory. Scrims, filters and gels can also be used.

Table A.14 Xenotech Brightlight Xenon Fixtures

			Beam Diameter and Foot-Candles at 100 ft		Head Weight
Unit	*Reflector Size*	*Power Supply*	*Full Spot*	*Full Flood*	*(lbs)*
571	9 in.	120-V AC at 15 A	24 in., 1000 FC	87 in., 250 FC	36 lb
1000	13 in.	120-V AC at 15 A	35 in., 1000 FC	72 in., 250 FC	48 lb
2000	13 in.	208/240-V AC at 20-A Single Phase	35-in., 1875 FC	72 in., 444 FC	52 lb
4000	20 in.	208/240-V AC at 40A Single Phase	42 in., 3750 FC	130 in., 1000 FC	134 lb
7000	20 in.	208/240-V AC at 30-A Three Phase	42 in., 7500 FC	185 in., 2433 FC	130 lb
10,000	30 in.	208/240-V AC at 40-A Three Phase	53 in., 20,000 FC	145 in., 5000 FC	120 lb

Notes:

All units are 5600 K and unaffected by lamp age or input voltage.

All units are available with right angle mirrors for applications where the beam is to be pointed downward. The 1k and 2k mirror weighs 11 lb, the 4k and 7k mirror weighs 25 lb.

The smaller power supplies use either Edison or Bates connectors, the larger units (4k and up) use Cam-Loc only.

Table A.15 Balloon Light Fixtures

Unit	Volts	Amps	Bulb Configuration	Shape	Size	Power Supply	Operating & Max Height	Shipping Weight (lbs)	Notes
Lights Up HMI									
700-W HMI	120 V			Sphere	5 ft diam	Flicker free			Forced air, stand mounted
2.4k HMI	240 V	21 A	2 × 1200 W	Sphere	8 ft diam	S/P Flicker free			
4.8k HMI	240 V	42 A	4 × 1200 W	Sphere	12.5 ft diam	S/P Flicker free	20–50 ft, 90 ft max	240 lb	Typically lights up to 200-ft diameter circle
4.8k HMI	240 V	42 A	4 × 1200 W	Tube	18.5 × 8.5 ft	S/P Flicker free			
16k HMI	208 V, three phase	86 A	4 × 4000 W	Sphere	16.5 ft diam	Magnetic, FF adaptable	30–80 ft, 100 ft max	725 lb	Typically lights up to 400-ft diameter circle
Lights Up Tungsten									
2k Tungsten	120 V	20 A		Sphere	6.5 ft diam				Forced air, stand mounted
2.6k Tungsten	120 V			Sphere	6.5 ft diam				
4k Tungsten	240 V	20 A	4 × 1000 W	Sphere	6.5 ft diam		15–30 ft, 45 ft max	20 lb	Typically lights up to 125-ft diameter circle
4k Tungsten	240 V	20 A	4 × 1000 W	Tube	9 × 5 ft				
8k Tungsten	240 V	2 20 A	8 × 1000 W	Sphere	12.5 ft diam		20–45 ft, 90 ft max	90 lb	Typically lights up to 175-ft diameter circle
8k Tungsten	240 V	2 20 A	8 × 1000 W	Tube	13.5 × 6.5 ft				
16k Tungsten	240 V	4 20 A		Sphere	16.5 ft diam				
Fisher/Leelium									
5k HMI				Tube			16 ft		Typically lights up to 66 × 100-ft area
8k Tungsten				Tube			16 ft		Typically lights up to 66 × 100-ft area

Table A.16 Beam Projectors

	Watts	ANSI	Scrim	Weight	CD spot	CD flood
Tungsten						
18" Molebeam Projector	2000 W	CYX	21"	47 lb	3,400,000	360,000
24" Molebeam Projector	5000 W	DPY	29"	79 kb	2,500,000	720,000
24" Molebeam Projector	10k	DTY	29"	79 lb		
36" Molebeam Projector	20kW	KP 200	—	125 lb	8,500,000	2,250,000
HMI						
18" Molebeam Projector	1200 W	1200SE	21"	48 lb	3,600,000	450,000
24" Molebeam Projector	2500 W	2500SE	29"	81 lb	10,800,000	1,260,000
24" Molebeam Projector	4k	4000SE	29"	81 lb	14,800,000	1,260,000
36" Molebeam Projector	12k HMI	12kw SE	—	136 lb	43,120,000	4,290,000

Note: Beam angle is virtually parallel. All units can be adjusted from −5 degrees at full spot, +15 degrees at full flood.

APPENDIX **B**

Photometric Calculations

The tables in Appendix A offer photometric data about most of the lights listed, specifically beam angle and candle power. Beam angle data allows you to calculate the beam diameter of a light at any distance you choose. Knowing the candle power allows you to calculate foot-candle intensity at any distance. The tables in this section provide an easy way of making these calculations.

Converting to Foot-Candles

Use Table B.1 to figure out about how many foot-candles you need to achieve a desired f-stop. The ISO of the film may be that recommended by Kodak or Fuji or it may be adjusted to account for exposure differences due to filters, frame rates, and intentional over- or underexposure.

Table B.1 F-Stop vs. Foot-Candles for Various Film Speeds

ISO	f/1.0	f/1.4	f/2	f/2.8	f/4	f/5.6	f/8	f/11	f/16	f/22
10	120	250	500	1000	2000	4000	8000	16,000	32,000	64,000
12	100	200	400	800	1600	3200	6400	12,800	25,000	50,000
16	80	160	320	640	1250	2500	5000	10,000	20,000	40,000
20	64	125	250	500	1000	2000	4000	8000	16,000	32,000
25	50	100	200	400	800	1600	3200	6400	12,800	25,000
32	40	80	160	320	640	1250	2500	5000	10,000	20,000
40	32	64	125	250	500	1000	2000	4000	8000	16,000
50	25	50	100	200	400	800	1600	3200	6400	12,800
64	20	40	80	160	320	640	1250	2500	5000	10,000
80	16	32	64	125	250	500	1000	2000	4000	8000
100	12	25	50	100	200	400	800	1600	3200	6400
125	10	20	40	80	160	320	640	1250	2500	5000
160	8	16	32	64	125	250	500	1000	2000	4000
200	6.4	13	25	50	100	200	400	800	1600	3200
250	5	10	20	40	80	160	320	640	1250	2500
320	4	8	16	32	64	125	250	500	1000	2000
400	3.2	6.4	13	25	50	100	200	400	800	1600
500	2.5	5	10	20	40	80	160	320	640	1280
640	2	4	8	16	32	64	120	240	500	1000
800	1.6	3.2	6.4	12	24	50	100	200	400	800
1000	1.2	2.5	5	10	20	40	80	160	320	640

Notes: Incident light in foot-candles. Frame Rate 24 fps. Exposure Time: $1/50$ second (180° shutter opening).

Calculating Field Diameter

If you want to know how much area a beam of light covers at a particular distance, you can look it up in Table B.2. Use the tables in Appendix A to find the beam angle, then use Table B.2 to find the beam size at a given distance.

For ellipsoidal fixtures, manufacturers often list a "multiplier" to use to find field diameter. Table A.12 (Appendix A) lists specifications for various commonly used ellipsoidals. Included in this table (and in any manufacturer's catalogue) is the multiplier used to calculate field diameter at a given throw. For example the Source Four 36° fixture has a multiplier of 0.65. If the throw is 20 ft, we can calculate the field diameter:

$$\text{Distance} \times \text{Multiplier} = \text{Field Diameter}$$

$$20 \text{ ft} \times 0.65 = 13 \text{ ft}$$

Calculating Intensity

To get a rough idea on how much light you get from a given fixture at a given distance, you can look up the candle-power (cd) of almost any light fixture in Appendix A. Plug this number into Table B.3 to find the approximate reading in foot-candles. Then use Table B.1 to find the corresponding f-stop. Note that the values given in Appendix A are based on manufacturers' photometric data and optimal performance. Your situation on the set is never optimal. Many everyday factors conspire to reduce the performance of a fixture: the age of a bulb, dirt on the lens and reflector, lower than optimal voltage, smoke or dirt in the air, and so forth. Needless to say, your results may vary.

We can calculate the intensity of a light at any distance using the inverse square law. To find the amount of light, divide the source candle power given in candela (cd) by the distance squared:

$$\frac{\text{Source cd}}{D^2 \text{ (feet)}} = \text{fc}, \quad \text{or} \quad \frac{\text{Source (cd)}}{D \text{ (meters)}} = \text{lux}$$

Or, you can use Table B.3 to ascertain the light level of any fixture at any distance.

For example, a Source Four 36° fixture has a source intensity of 84,929 cd. The intensity at 20 ft is therefore

$$\frac{84,929}{(20)^2} = 212 \text{ FC}$$

You can use this equation to calculate the source intensity (cd) of a given fixture by measuring the FC level at a given distance or to calculate the distance necessary to achieve a particular FC level from a given fixture:

$$\text{cd} = \text{FC} \times D^2, \text{ where } D = \frac{\text{Fixture Intensity (cd)}}{\text{Light Level (FC)}}$$

Table B.2 Beam Diameter (in feet) at Various Distances

Beam Angle Degree	Multiplier	Distance in Feet												
		5	10	15	20	25	30	40	50	75	100	150	200	250
2	0.03	0.2	0.3	0.5	0.7	0.9	1.0	1.4	1.7	2.6	3.5	5.2	7.0	8.7
4	0.07	0.3	0.7	1.0	1.4	1.7	2.1	2.8	3.5	5.2	7.0	10.5	14.0	17.5
6	0.10	0.5	1.0	1.6	2.1	2.6	3.1	4.2	5.2	7.9	10.5	15.7	21.0	26.2
8	0.14	0.7	1.4	2.1	2.8	3.5	4.2	5.6	7.0	10.5	14.0	21.0	28.0	35.0
10	0.17	0.9	1.7	2.6	3.5	4.4	5.2	7.0	8.7	13.1	17.5	26.2	35.0	43.7
12	0.21	1.1	2.1	3.2	4.2	5.3	6.3	8.4	10.5	15.8	21.0	31.5	42.0	52.6
14	0.25	1.2	2.5	3.7	4.9	6.1	7.4	9.8	12.3	18.4	24.6	36.8	49.1	61.4
16	0.28	1.4	2.8	4.2	5.6	7.0	8.4	11.2	14.1	21.1	28.1	42.2	56.2	70.3
18	0.32	1.6	3.2	4.8	6.3	7.9	9.5	12.7	15.8	23.8	31.7	47.5	63.4	79.2
20	0.35	1.8	3.5	5.3	7.1	8.8	10.6	14.1	17.6	26.4	35.3	52.9	70.5	88.2
22	0.39	1.9	3.9	5.8	7.8	9.7	11.7	15.6	19.4	29.2	38.9	58.3	77.8	97.2
24	0.43	2.1	4.3	6.4	8.5	10.6	12.8	17.0	21.3	31.9	42.5	63.8	85.0	106.3
26	0.46	2.3	4.6	6.9	9.2	11.5	13.9	18.5	23.1	34.6	46.2	69.3	92.3	115.4
28	0.50	2.5	5.0	7.5	10.0	12.5	15.0	19.9	24.9	37.4	49.9	74.8	99.7	124.7
30	0.54	2.7	5.4	8.0	10.7	13.4	16.1	21.4	26.8	40.2	53.6	80.4	107.2	134.0
32	0.57	2.9	5.7	8.6	11.5	14.3	17.2	22.9	28.7	43.0	57.3	86.0	114.7	143.4
34	0.61	3.1	6.1	9.2	12.2	15.3	18.3	24.5	30.6	45.9	61.1	91.7	122.3	152.9
36	0.65	3.2	6.5	9.7	13.0	16.2	19.5	26.0	32.5	48.7	65.0	97.5	130.0	162.5
38	0.69	3.4	6.9	10.3	13.8	17.2	20.7	27.5	34.4	51.6	68.9	103.3	137.7	172.2
40	0.73	3.6	7.3	10.9	14.6	18.2	21.8	29.1	36.4	54.6	72.8	109.2	145.6	182.0
42	0.77	3.8	7.7	11.5	15.4	19.2	23.0	30.7	38.4	57.6	76.8	115.2	153.5	191.9
44	0.81	4.0	8.1	12.1	16.2	20.2	24.2	32.3	40.4	60.6	80.8	121.2	161.6	202.0
46	0.85	4.2	8.5	12.7	17.0	21.2	25.5	34.0	42.4	63.7	84.9	127.3	169.8	212.2
48	0.89	4.5	8.9	13.4	17.8	22.3	26.7	35.6	44.5	66.8	89.0	133.6	178.1	222.6
50	0.93	4.7	9.3	14.0	18.7	23.3	28.0	37.3	46.6	69.9	93.3	139.9	186.5	233.2
52	0.98	4.9	9.8	14.6	19.5	24.4	29.3	39.0	48.8	73.2	97.5	146.3	195.1	243.9
54	1.02	5.1	10.2	15.3	20.4	25.5	30.6	40.8	51.0	76.4	101.9	152.9	203.8	254.8
56	1.06	5.3	10.6	16.0	21.3	26.6	31.9	42.5	53.2	79.8	106.3	159.5	212.7	265.9
58	1.11	5.5	11.1	16.6	22.2	27.7	33.3	44.3	55.4	83.1	110.9	166.3	221.7	277.2
60	1.15	5.8	11.5	17.3	23.1	28.9	34.6	46.2	57.7	86.6	115.5	173.2	230.9	288.7
62	1.20	6.0	12.0	18.0	24.0	30.0	36.1	48.1	60.1	90.1	120.2	180.3	240.3	300.4

Table B.2 Beam Diameter (in feet) at Various Distances (continued)

Beam Angle Degree	Multiplier	Distance in Feet												
		5	10	15	20	25	30	40	50	75	100	150	200	250
64	1.25	6.2	12.5	18.7	25.0	31.2	37.5	50.0	62.5	93.7	125.0	187.5	249.9	312.4
66	1.30	6.5	13.0	19.5	26.0	32.5	39.0	52.0	64.9	97.4	129.9	194.8	259.8	324.7
68	1.35	6.7	13.5	20.2	27.0	33.7	40.5	54.0	67.5	101.2	134.9	202.4	269.8	337.3
70	1.40	7.0	14.0	21.0	28.0	35.0	42.0	56.0	70.0	105.0	140.0	210.1	280.1	350.1
72	1.45	7.3	14.5	21.8	29.1	36.3	43.6	58.1	72.7	109.0	145.3	218.0	290.6	363.3
74	1.51	7.5	15.1	22.6	30.1	37.7	45.2	60.3	75.4	113.0	150.7	226.1	301.4	376.8
76	1.56	7.8	15.6	23.4	31.3	39.1	46.9	62.5	78.1	117.2	156.3	234.4	312.5	390.6
78	1.62	8.1	16.2	24.3	32.4	40.5	48.6	64.8	81.0	121.5	162.0	242.9	323.9	404.9
80	1.68	8.4	16.8	25.2	33.6	42.0	50.3	67.1	83.9	125.9	167.8	251.7	335.6	419.5
82	1.74	8.7	17.4	26.1	34.8	43.5	52.2	69.5	86.9	130.4	173.9	260.8	347.7	434.6
84	1.80	9.0	18.0	27.0	36.0	45.0	54.0	72.0	90.0	135.1	180.1	270.1	360.2	450.2

Note: Simply multiply distance times multiplier to get diameter at any distance.

Table B.3 Brightness in Foot-Candles of Fixtures at Various Distances (Each shaded area represents a range of 1/3 of an f-stop)

Fixture	Modifiers	Candella	Output	F-Stop (250 ASA 1/50 sec) @20 ft	F-Stop (250 ASA 1/50 sec) @80 ft	2	3	5	10	15	20	25	30	40	50
200-W Joker-Bug		938		f-.7		235	104	38	9	4	2	2	1	1	0
Kino-Flo Diva-Lite 200	w/ Chimera	1,250	1,300			313	139	50	13	6	3	2	1	1	1
			1,500												
Kino-Flo 2-ft 4-bank	w/o Louvre	1,600	1,800	f-1		400	178	64	16	7	4	3	2	1	1
100-W Pepper	Flood	1,875	2,300	f-1		469	208	75	19	8	5	3	2	1	1
Kino-flo 2-ft 2-bank	w/o Louvre		2,100												
100-W Dedo	Flood		2,147												
Kino-Flo 4-ft 2-bank	w/o Louvre	2,500	2,700	f-1 1/3		625	278	100	25	11	6	4	3	2	1
Kino-Flo Diva-Lite 400			3,000												
750 Zip		3,200		f-1 2/3		800	356	128	32	14	8	5	4	2	1
400-W Joker Bug	SW w/Chimera		3,200												
150-W Dedo	Flood. 3400 K		3,483												
Kino-Flo 4-ft 4-bank	w/o Louvre		3,500												
200W Pepper	Flood	3,750	3,900	f-1.4		938	417	150	38	17	9	6	4	2	2
1k Soft	Spot	5,000	5,500	f-1.4 1/3		1,250	556	200	50	22	13	8	6	3	2
100-W Pepper	Flood		4,600												
300-W Pepper	w/o Louvre		6,000												
Kino-Flo Flathead 80	Flood														
420-W Pepper	Flood	6,400	6,100	f-1.4 2/3		1,600	711	256	64	28	16	10	7	4	3
200-W HMI fresnel	Flood	7,500				1,875	833	300	75	33	19	12	8	5	3

Table B.3 Brightness in Foot-Candles of Fixtures at Various Distances (Each shaded area represents a range of 1/3 of an f-stop) (continued)

Fixture	Modifiers	Candella	Output	F-Stop (250 ASA 1/50 sec) @20 ft	F-Stop (250 ASA 1/50 sec) @80 ft	____Distance in Feet____									
						3	5	10	15	20	25	30	40	50	60
650-W Fresnel	Flood	**7,500**		f-2		833	300	75	33	19	12	8	5	3	2
Kino-Flo Wal-o-lite	w/o Louvre		7,500												
400-W Dedo 436	Flood		7,614												
650-W Dedo 650	Flood		8,100												
200-W Joker-Bug	SW		9,000												
2k Soft		**10,000**		f-2 1/3		1,111	400	100	44	25	16	11	6	4	3
200-W Pepper	Spot		10,500												
650-W Pepper	Flood		11,000												
200-W Joker-Bug	FF		11,700												
400-W Dedo 400D	Flood		11,907												
Kino-Flo Blanket Light		**12,500**	13,700	f-2 2/3		1,389	500	125	56	31	20	14	8	5	3
400-W Joker Bug	FF		14,400												
4k Soft	Flood	**15,000**		f-2.8		1,667	600	150	67	38	24	17	9	6	4
1k Baby Fresnel	Flood														
1k Mickey Mole															
400-W Joker Bug	SWF		18,800												
575-W HMI Fresnel	Flood	**20,000**		f-2.8 1/3		2,222	800	200	89	50	32	22	13	8	6
300-W Pepper	Spot	**25,000**	27,500	f-2.8 2/3			1,000	250	111	63	40	28	16	10	7
3.3k SoftSun	Flood		27,500												
200-W Joker-Bug	W		30,200												
2k Mighty Mole	Flood	**30,000**		f-4	f-1		1,200	300	133	75	48	33	19	12	8
800-W Joker-Bug	FF		38,800												
8k Soft	Spot	**40,000**		f-4 1/3			1,600	400	178	100	64	44	25	16	11
420-W pepper	WF														
400-W Joker Bug	Flood		44,400												
2k Blonde or Arrilight	WF		44,400												
1k PAR 64	WF														

Table B.3 Brightness in Foot-Candles of Fixtures at Various Distances (Each shaded area represents a range of 1/3 of an f-stop) (continued)

Fixture	Modifiers	Candella	Output	F-Stop (250 ASA 1/50 sec) @20 ft	F-Stop (250 ASA 1/50 sec) @80 ft	3	5	10	15	20	25	30	40	50	60	70	80
										Distance in Feet							
2k 8" Junior Fresnel	Flood	**50,000**		f-4 2/3			2,000	500	222	125	80	56	31	20	14		
100-W Dedo	Spot		50,220														
650-W Pepper	Spot		52,800														
3.3k SoftSun	Spot		55,000														
		60,000		f-5.6	f-1.4		2,400	600	267	150	96	67	38	24	17		
										Distance in Feet							
1200-W HMI Fresnel	Flood	**60,000**		f-5.6	f-1.4		2,400	600	267	150	96	67	38	24	17	12	9
150-W Dedo	Spot, 3400 K		62,700														
5k Baby Senior Fresnel	Flood	**80,000**		f-5.6 1/3			3,200	800	356	200	128	89	50	32	22	16	13
200-W Joker-Bug	M		96,800														
1200-W HMI PAR	SWF	**100,000**		f-5.6 2/3			4,000	1,000	444	250	160	111	63	40	28	20	16
650-W Dedo 650	Spot		115,843														
10k Baby Tenner	Flood	**120,000**		f-8	f-2		4,800	1,200	533	300	192	133	75	48	33	24	19
400-W Dedo 436	Spot		120,366														
1k Mickey Mole	Spot		152,000														
400-W Joker Bug	M																
2500-W HMI Fresnel	Flood																
2500-W HMI Par	SWF																
1k PAR 64	MF																

Table B.3 Brightness in Foot-Candles of Fixtures at Various Distances (Each shaded area represents a range of 1/3 of an f-stop) (continued)

Fixture	Modifiers	Candella	Output	F-Stop (250 ASA 1/50 sec) @20 ft	F-Stop (250 ASA 1/50 sec) @80 ft	5	10	15	20	25	30	40	50	60	70	80
											Distance in Feet					
4k HMI Fresnel	Flood	**160,000**		f-8 1/3		6,400	1,600	711	400	256	178	100	64	44	33	25
1200-W HMI PAR	WF		181,000													
800-W Joker-Bug	SWF Frosted															
4k HMI SE Par	Fres															
2k Mighty Mole	spot															
2500-W HMI SE Par	WF	**200,000**		f-8 2/3		8,000	2,000	889	500	320	222	125	80	56	41	31
400-W Dedo 400D	Spot		201,852													
		240,000		f-11	f-2.8	9,600	2,400	1,067	600	384	267	150	96	67	49	38
4k HMI SE Par	SWF		315,000													
800-W Joker-Bug	MF															
6k HMI Fresnel	Flood	**320,000**		f-11 1/3		12,800	3,200	1,422	800	512	356	200	128	89	65	50
	Frosted															
6k SE HMI Par	Fres		380,000													
1k PAR 64	NSP															
6k Par LTM	FF															
		400,000		f-11 2/3		16,000	4,000	1,778	1,000	640	444	250	160	111	82	63
20k Fresnel	Flood	**480,000**		f-16	f-4	19,200	4,800	2,133	1,200	768	533	300	192	133	98	75

Table B.3 Brightness in Foot-Candles of Fixtures at Various Distances (Each shaded area represents a range of 1/3 of an f-stop) (continued)

Fixture	Modifiers	Candella	Output	F-Stop (250 ASA 1/50 sec) @20 ft	F-Stop (250 ASA 1/50 sec) @80 ft	Distance in Feet									
						10	15	20	25	30	40	50	60	80	100
12k HMI Fresnel	Flood	**480,000**		f-16	f-4	4,800	2,133	1,200	768	533	300	192	133	75	48
200-W Joker-Bug	S		591,800												
4k HMI SE Par	WF														
1k PAR 64	VNSP														
18k HMI Fresnel	Flood	**640,000**		f-16 1/3		6,400	2,844	1,600	1,024	711	400	256	178	100	64
12k Par LTM	FF		660,000												
6k Par LTM	SWF		730,000												
1200-W HMI Par	MF	**800,000**		f-16 2/3		8,000	3,556	2,000	1,280	889	500	320	222	125	80
2500-W HMI SE Par	MF														
4k HMI SE Par	MF	**960,000**		f-22	f-5.6	9,600	4,267	2,400	1,536	1,067	600	384	267	150	96
50k SoftSun	Flood		1,050,000												
12k Par LTM	SWF		1,090,000												
6k Par LTM	W		1,260,000												
1200-W HMI PAR	NSP	**1,280,000**		f-22 1/3		12,800	5,689	3,200	2,048	1,422	800	512	356	200	128
400-W Joker Bug	NSP		1,544,000												
1200-W HMI Par	W	**1,600,000**		f-22 2/3		16,000	7,111	4,000	2,560	1,778	1,000	640	444	250	160
12k Par ETM	W		1,790,000												
1200-W HMI par	VNSP	**1,920,000**		f-32	f-8	19,200	8,533	4,800	3,072	2,133	1,200	768	533	300	192
50k SoftSun	Spot		2,375,000												
800-W Joker-Bug	NSP		2,094,000												
6k Par LTM	M		2,480,000												
2500-W HMI SE par	NSP	**2,560,000**		f-32 1/3		25,600	11,378	6,400	4,096	2,844	1,600	1,024	711	400	256
		3,200,000		f-32 2/3		32,000	14,222	8,000	5,120	3,556	2,000	1,280	889	500	320
12k Par LTM	M	**3,840,000**		f-44		38,400	17,067	9,600	6,144	4,267	2,400	1,536	1,067	600	384

Table B.3 Brightness in Foot-Candles of Fixtures at Various Distances (Each shaded area represents a range of 1/3 of an f-stop) (continued)

Fixture	Modifiers	Candella	Output	F-Stop (250 ASA 1/50 sec) @20 ft	F-Stop (250 ASA 1/50 sec) @80 ft	Distance in Feet									
						15	20	25	30	40	50	60	80	100	150
2500-W HMI SE Par	VNSP	3,840,000		f-44	f-11	17,067	9,600	6,144	4,267	2,400	1,536	1,067	600	384	171
		5,120,000		f-44 1/3		22,756	12,800	8,192	5,689	3,200	2,048	1,422	800	512	228
12k HMI Fresnel	Spot	6,400,000		f-44 2/3		28,444	16,000	10,240	7,111	4,000	2,560	1,778	1,000	640	284
		7,680,000		f-64	f-16	34,133	19,200	12,288	8,533	4,800	3,072	2,133	1,200	768	341
4k HMI SE PAR	VNSP	10,240,000		f-64 1/3		45,511	25,600	16,384	11,378	6,400	4,096	2,844	1,600	1,024	455
6k HMI SE Par LTM	S	12,800,000	17,120,000	f-64 2/3		56,889	32,000	20,480	14,222	8,000	5,120	3,556	2,000	1,280	569
12k Par LTM	S	15,360,000	19,680,000	f-88	f-22	68,267	38,400	24,576	17,067	9,600	6,144	4,267	2,400	1,536	683
		20,480,000		f-88 1/3		91,022	51,200	32,768	22,756	12,800	8,192	5,689	3,200	2,048	910

Direct sun, 11 am, clear day, January, in Los Angeles = 8400 fc

APPENDIX **C**

Electrical Tables: Line Loss, Ampacity, and Resistance

Table C.1 Ampacity of Cables: Type W and Entertainment Industry Stage Cable (EISC) Types SC, SCE, and SCT[a] (NEC Table 400-5(8))

Size of Cable	No. of Current-Carrying Wires in Cable		
	1	*2*[b]	*3*[c]
Cable rated at 90°C and 105°C			
4/0	405	361	316
3/0	350	313	274
2/0	300	271	237
1/0	260	234	205
2 AWG	190	174	152
4 AWG	140	130	114
6 AWG	105	99	87
8 AWG	80	74	65
Cable rated at 75°C			
4/0	360	317	277
3/0	310	275	241
2/0	265	238	208
1/0	230	207	181
2 AWG	170	152	133
4 AWG	125	115	101
6 AWG	95	88	77
8 AWG	70	65	57
Cable rated at 60°C			
4/0	300	265	232
3/0	260	230	201
2/0	225	199	174
1/0	195	173	151
2 AWG	140	128	112
4 AWG	105	96	84
6 AWG	80	72	63
8 AWG	60	55	48

Source: Reprinted with permission from NFPA 70–1993, The National Electrical Code®, Copyright © 1992, National Fire Protection Association, Quincy, MA 02269. This reprinted material is not the complete and official position of the National Fire Protection Association on the referenced subject, which is represented only by the standard in its entirety.

[a]These amperage capacities are based on an ambient temperature of 30°C (86°F). They are allowable only where the individual conductors are not installed in raceways and are not in physical contact with one another, except in lengths not to exceed 24 in. where passing through the wall of an enclosure.

[b]See footnote b in Table C.2.

[c]See footnote c in Table C.2.

Table C.2 Amperage Capacities for Flexible Cords, Stingers, and Zip Cord[a]
(NEC Table 400-5 (A))

	No. of Current-Carrying Wires		
AWG Size	2[b]	3[c]	Asbestos[d]
18	10	7	6
16	13	10	8
14	18	15	17
12	25	20	23
10	30	25	28
8	40	35	—
6	55	45	—
4	70	60	—
2	95	80	—

Source: Reprinted with permission from NFPA 70-1993. The National Electrical Code®, Copyright © 1992, National Fire Protection Association, Quincy, MA 02269. This reprinted material is not the complete and official position of the National Fire Protection Association on the referenced subject, which is represented only by the standard in its entirety.

[a]These amperage capacities apply to the following types of cord: thermoset types C, E, EO, PD, S SJ, SJO, SJOO, SO, SOO, SP-1, SP-2, SP-3, SRD, SV, SVO, and SVOO and thermoplastic types ET, ETT, ETLB, SE, SEO, SJE, SJEO, SJT, SJTO, SJTOO, SPE-1, SPE-2, SPE-3, SPT-1, SPT-2, SPT3, ST, STO, STOO, SRDE, SRDT, SVE, SVEO, SVT, SVTO, and SVTOO.

[b]The amperage capacities in this column apply to multiconductor cable in which two of the wires are current-carrying (such as a hot wire and a neutral wire, or two hot wires of a 240-V single-phase circuit). The neutral wire of a balanced 240/120-V single-phase circuit is not considered a current-carrying wire for the purpose of this table, with one exception: If the major portion of the load consists of electronic ballasts, electronic dimmers, or similar equipment, there are harmonic currents present in the neutral conductor and it shall be considered to be a current-carrying conductor. The green grounding wire is never considered to be a current-carrying wire.

[c]The amperage capacities in this column apply to multiconductor cable in which three of the wires are current-carrying wires (such as a three-wire three-phase-circuit, a balanced four-wire three-phase circuit, or a single-phase three-wire circuit derived from the neutral and two-phased legs of a wye-connected three-phase system). The neutral wire of a balanced four-wire three-phase circuit is considered a current-carrying wire only when there are harmonic currents present. A cord or cable with four or more current-carrying wires must be derated in accordance with NEC Section 400-5. Cords and cables in which four to six of the conductors are carrying current must be derated to 80% of the ampacities given in this table.

[d]This column gives the amperage capacities of asbestos cords (types AFC, AFPD, and AFPO), which are often used inside fixtures.

Table C.3 Minimum Size of Grounding Wires (NEC Table 250-95)

	Gauge of Grounding Conductor Aluminum and Copper-Clad	
Rating of Overcurrent Protection of Circuit (A)	Copper Wire No.	Aluminum Wire No.
15	14 AWG	12 AWG
20	12 AWG	10 AWG
30	10 AWG	8 AWG
40	10 AWG	8 AWG
60	10 AWG	8 AWG
100	8 AWG	6 AWG
200	6 AWG	4 AWG
300	4 AWG	2 AWG
400	3 AWG	1 AWG
500	2 AWG	1/0
600	1 AWG	2/0
800	1/0	3/0
1000	2/0	4/0
1200	3/0	250 kcmil
1600	4/0	350 kcmil

Source: Reprinted with permission from NFPA 70-1993, The National Electrical Code®, Copyright © 1992, National Fire Protection Association, Quincy, MA 02269. This reprinted material is not the complete and official position of the National Fire Protection Association on the referenced subject, which is represented in its entirety only by the standard.

Table C.4 Voltage Drop in Volts per 100 Feet for Various Cables

Amps per Leg	Three Phase			Single-Phase Circuits from 3-phase Feeders		Single Phase and DC Circuits			
	4/0 Feeder	2/0 Feeder	#2 Banded	#2 Banded and "100-A"	#6 "60-A"	4/0 Feeder	2/0 Feeder	#2 Banded and "100-A"	#6 "60-A"
25	0.2	0.4	0.7	1.1	2.7	0.3	0.4	0.8	2.1
50	0.4	0.7	1.4	2.1	5.3	0.5	0.8	1.6	4.1
75	0.7	1.1	2.1	3.2	8.0	0.8	1.2	2.4	6.2
100	0.9	1.4	2.8	4.2	10.7	1.0	1.6	3.2	8.2
125	1.1	1.8	3.5	5.3		1.3	2.0	4.1	
150	1.3	2.1	4.2	6.3		1.5	2.4	4.9	
175	1.5	2.5	4.9	7.4		1.8	2.8	5.7	
200	1.8	2.8	5.6	8.4		2.0	3.2	6.5	
225	2.0	3.2				2.3	3.6		
250	2.2	3.5				2.5	4.1		
275	2.4	3.9				2.8	4.5		
300	2.6	4.2				3.1	4.9		
325	2.9					3.3			
350	3.1					3.6			
375	3.3					3.8			
400	3.5					4.1			

Table C.5 Resistance of Copper Wire

Size	Approx OD inches	Cross-Sectional Area (cmils)	Lb per M/100 ft	Ohms per M/100 ft	ft/Ohm
4/0	0.528	211600	65.3	0.00509	19646
2/0	0.418	133100	41.1	0.00811	12330
2 AWG	0.292	66360	20.5	0.0162	6173
4 AWG	0.232	41740	12.9	0.0259	3861
6 AWG	0.184	26240	8.0	0.0410	2439
8 AWG	0.1285	16510	5.1	0.0640	1529
10 AWG	0.1019	10380	3.1	0.1018	981.9
12 AWG	0.0808	6530	20.0	0.1619	617.0
14 AWG	0.0641	4110	1.2	0.2575	389.0
16 AWG	0.0508	2580	.8	0.4094	244.0
18 AWG	0.0403	1620	.5	0.6510	154.0

Note: Weights listed are of the copper itself, not the total weight or an insulated cable. Resistance at 25°C.

Flicker-Free Frame Rates

Table D.1 HMI Flicker-Free Frame Rates at Any Shutter Angle: 60-Hz Power

Frames/Second	Optimal Shutter Angle
120.000	180
60.000	180
40.000	120
30.000	180
24.000	144
20.000	180
17.143	
15.000	
13.333	
12.000	180
10.909	
10.000	
9.231	
8.000	198
7.058	
6.000	
5.000	
4.000	
3.000	
2.000	
1.000	

Table D.3 Flicker-Free Frame Rates at Any Shutter Angle: 50-Hz Power

Frames/Second	Optimal Shutter Angle
100.000	180
50.000	180
33.333	
25.000	180
20.000	144
16.666	
14.285	
12.500	
11.111	
10.000	
9.090	
8.333	
7.692	
7.142	
6.666	
5.000	
4.000	
3.125	
2.500	
2.000	
1.000	

Table D.2 Additional Flicker-Free Frame Rates at Specific Shutter Angles: 60-Hz Power

Frames/Second	Shutter Angle
57.6	172.8
50	144
48	144
45	135
36	108
35	105
32	92 or 96
28	168
26	156
25	150
22	198 or 132
18	162
16	192 or 144

Table D.4 Additional Flicker-Free Frame Rates at Specific Shutter Angles: 50-Hz Power

Frames/Second	Shutter Angle
48	172.8
40	144
36	129.6
32	115.2
30	108
28	108.8
26	187.2 or 93.6
24	172.8
22	158.4
18	194.4 or 129.6
16	172.8 or 115.2
12	172.8 or 129.6
8	172.8 or 144

Bulb Tables

Table E.1 Photo Floods, Mushroom Floods, MR-16s: Medium Screw Base Bulbs

Type	Bulb and Base Type	Volts	Watts	K Color	Life (hr)
Standard and Pear-shaped (PS) Photofloods					
PH-211	A-21 Medium	120	75	3200	100 hr
PH-212	A-21 Medium	120	150	3050	100 hr
PH-213	A-21 Medium	120	250	3400	3 hr
BBA (No 1)	A-21 Medium	120	250	3400	3 hr
BCA (B-1)	A-21 Medium	120	250	4800	3 hr
ECA	A-23 Medium	120	250	3200	20 hr
BAH	A-21 Medium	120	300	3200	20 hr
EBV (No 2)	PS-25 Medium	120	500	3400	6 hr
EBW (B-2)	PS-25 Medium	120	500	4800	6 hr
ECT	PS25/5 Medium	120	500	3200	60 hr
Mushroom Bulbs					
DAN (R-20)	R-20 Meduim	118	200	3400	4
BEP (R-30)	R-30 Medium	118	300	3400	4
EBR (R-30)	R-30 Medium	118	375	3400	4
DXH (PH/RFL-2)	R-40 Medium	118	375	3200	15
BFA (R-34)	R-40 Medium	118	375	3400	4
DXC (PH/RFL-2)	R-40 Medium	118	500	3400	6
EAL	R-40 Medium	120	500	3300	15
FAE	R-40 Medium	118	550	3400	10
MR-16 Bulbs Medium Screw Base					
FSA (NSP) or JDR120V75W NSP	MR-16, Medium	120	75	3000	—
FSB (MFL) or JDR120V75W MFL	MR-16, Medium	120	75	3000	—
FSD (WFL) or JDR120V75W WFL	MR-16, Medium	120	75	3000	—
FSC (NSP) or JDR120V100W NSP	MR-16, Medium	120	100	3000	—
FSE (MFL) or JDR120V75W MFL	MR-16, Medium	120	100	3000	—
FSF (WFL) or JDR120V75W WFL	MR-16, Medium	120	100	3000	—

The bulb type designation indicates type and size (in eighths of inches). For example, R-40 indicates it is a Reflector lamp with a 5-in. diameter (40/8 = 5). An R-30 bulb is 3-6/8 in. diameter, an MR-16 is 2 in. diameter, and so on.

The mushroom floods listed here are all 3000 K or more. Mushroom floods also come in a wide variety of wattages that have lower color temperature, flood, and spot. R-40s, for example, come in 75 W, 150 W, and 300 W.

The MR-16s listed are 120 V medium screw base. MR-16 and MR-11 bulbs also come in a wide variety of other configurations. The 6V and 12V versions with a small 2-pin base are the most common type.

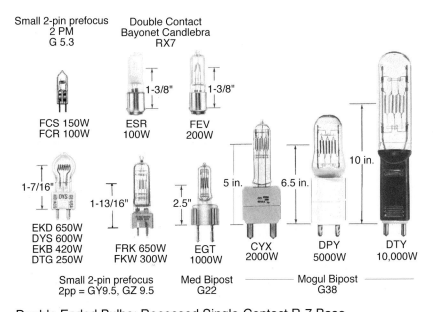

Small 2-pin prefocus
2 PM
G 5.3

Double Contact
Bayonet Candlebra
RX7

1-3/8"

1-3/8"

FCS 150W
FCR 100W

ESR
100W

FEV
200W

10 in.

1-7/16"

EKD 650W
DYS 600W
EKB 420W
DTG 250W

1-13/16"

2.5"

5 in.

6.5 in.

FRK 650W
FKW 300W

EGT
1000W

CYX
2000W

DPY
5000W

DTY
10,000W

Small 2-pin prefocus
2pp = GY9.5, GZ 9.5

Med Bipost
G22

Mogul Bipost
G38

Double-Ended Bulbs: Recessed Single-Contact R-7 Base

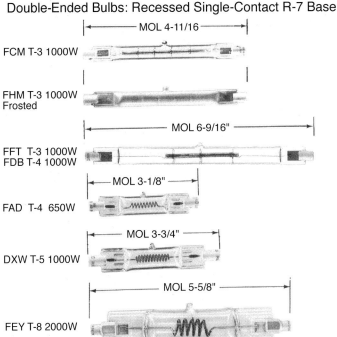

MOL 4-11/16"

FCM T-3 1000W

FHM T-3 1000W
Frosted

MOL 6-9/16"

FFT T-3 1000W
FDB T-4 1000W

MOL 3-1/8"

FAD T-4 650W

MOL 3-3/4"

DXW T-5 1000W

MOL 5-5/8"

FEY T-8 2000W

Figure E.1 Tungsten halogen lamps.

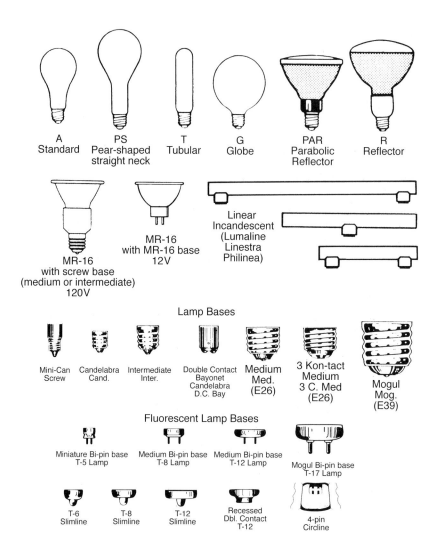

Figure E.2 Various types of practical bulbs and lamp bases.

Table E.2 Fluorescent Lamps

Watts	Bulb	Diameter	Length	Description	Kelvin	Base
KF55 (Daylight) Lamps						
6	T5	5/8"	9"	F6T5/KF55	5500K	Mini Bipin
14	T12	1-1/2"	15"	FI4T12/KF55 SFC	"	Med. Bipin
20	T12	1-1/2"	24"	F20T12/KF55 SFC	"	"
30	T12	1-1/2"	36"	F30T12/KF55 SFC	"	"
40	T12	1-1/2"	48"	F40T12/KF5S SFC	"	"
55	T12	1-1/2"	72"	F72T12/KF55/SL SFC	"	Single Pin
85	T12	1-1/2"	72"	F72T12/KF55/HO SFC	"	Med. Bipin
75	T12	1-1/2"	96"	F96T12/KF55/SL SFC	"	Single Pin
110	T12	1-1/2"	96"	F96T12/KF55/HO SFC	"	Med. Bipin
KF32 (Tungsten) Lamps						
6	T5	5/8"	9"	F6T5/KF32	3200K	Mini Bipin
14	T12	1-1/2"	15"	F14T12/KF32 SFC	"	Med. Bipin
20	T12	1-1/2"	24"	F20T12/KF32 SFC	"	"
30	T12	1-1/2"	36"	F30T12/KF32 SFC	"	"
40	T12	1-1/2"	48"	F40T12/KF32 SFC	"	"
55	T12	1-1/2"	72"	F72T12/KF32/SL SFC	"	Single Pin
85	T12	1-1/2"	72"	F72T12/KF32/HO SFC	"	Med. Bipin
75	T12	1-1/2"	96"	F96T12/KF32/SL SFC	"	Single Pin
110	T12	1-1/2"	96"	F96T12/KF32/HO SFC	"	Med. Bipin

Other Fluorescent Bulbs

Make and Name	Color Temp (K)	Color Rendering Index	Minus-Green Correction Required
Duro Test Optima 32	3200	82	0–1/4
Duro Test Vita-Lite	5500	91	1/8–1/4
GE Chroma 50	5000	90	1/2
GE IF 27	3000	—	—
GTE Sylvania Design 50	5000	91	1/2
Warm White (WW)	3000	52	Full
Deluxe Warm White (WWX)	3000	77	Full
Cool White (CW)	4500	62	Full

Colored Fluorescent Bulbs

Bulb	Description
Super Blue	420 nm blue spike for blue screen opticals
Green	560 nm green spike for green screen opticals
Black Light	UV A stimulates luminescent materials
Red	Party colors
Pink	Party colors
Yellow	Party colors

Table E.3 Tungsten Bulb Specifications and Substitutions

Bi-Pin Single-Ended Tungsten Halogen Bulbs

Watts	ANSI Code	Color Temp (K)	LCL	Finish	Volts	Bulb Life (hr)	Amps
	100 W and 200 W Fresnels: Peppers, Midget, Tiny Mole, Mini Mole, etc. Base: Double-contact bayonet candelabra RX7. Bulbs: B-12, G-16½, T-4 and T-8. Burn within 30 of vertical, base down.
250	ESS	2950	1³/₈"	C	120	2000	2.1
200	**FEV**	**3200**	**1³/₈"**	**C**	**120**	**50**	**1.7**
200	BDJ	3200	1³/₈"	C	120	20	1.7
200	CCM	3075	1³/₈"	C	115–125	25	1.7
150	CGP	3075	1³/₈"	C	115–120	25	1.3
150	ETF	3000	1³/₈"	F	120	2000	1.3
150	ESP	2900	1³/₈"	C	120	1000	1.3
150	ETC	3000	1³/₈"	C	120	2000	1.3
100	**ESR**	**2850**	**1³/₈"**	**C**	**120**	**750**	**0.5**
100	100Q/CL/DC	3000	1³/₈"	C	120	1000	0.8
100	CEB	2975	1³/₈"	C	115–125	50	0.8
75	CBX	2925	1³/₈"	C	115–125	50	0.6
50	CAX	2875	1³/₈"	C	115–125	50	0.4
	100 W and 150 W Dedo. Base: Small 2-pin : 2 PM = G 5.3 Bulb: T-3½, T-4. Burn base down to horizontal
150	**FCS**	**3400**	**1.181"**	**C**	**24**	**100**	**6.25**
100	**FCR**	**3300**	**1.181"**	**C**	**12**	**50**	**8.3**
50	BRL	3300	1.181"	C	12	50	4.2
	300 W, 650 W Fresnels: Tweenie II, Betweenie, 300 W Pepper, etc. Base: Small 2-pin prefocus: 2 PP = GY 9.5. GZ 9.5. Bulb: T-6. Burn with coil horizontal.
650	**FRK**	**3200**	**1¹³/₁₆"**	**C**	**120**	**200**	**5.4**
500	FRB	3200	1¹³/₁₆"	C	120	200	4.2
300	**FKW**	**3200**	**1¹³/₁₆"**	**C**	**120**	**200**	**2.5**
	Small 1k Fresnels (special high seal temp bulb made for specially designed high-temp heads—Sachtler, Desisti). Base: Small 2-pin prefocus GY9.5. Bulb: Phillips
1000	Blue Pinch	3200	1¹³/₁₆"	C	120	250	8.3
	Old Style Tweenie, 420 Pepper, Teenie Weenie Open Face. Base: 2-pin prefocus: 2 PP = GY 9.5. GZ 9.5. T-6 or T-7 bulb. Burn with coil horizontal.
650	**EKD-Q650/3CL2PP**	**3400**	**1⁷/₁₆"**	**C**	**120**	**25**	**5.4**
600	**DYS/DYV/BHC**	**3200**	**1⁷/₁₆"**	**C**	**120**	**75**	**50**
420	**EKB-Q420/4CL/2PP**	**3200**	**1⁷/₁₆"**	**C**	**120**	**75**	**2.5**
250	**DYG-Q250/4CL/2PP**	**3400**	**1⁷/₁₆"**	**C**	**30**	**15**	**5.3**
100	EYL	3300	1⁷/₁₆"	C	12	50	63

Table E.3 Tungsten Bulb Specifications and Substitutions (continued)

Watts	ANSI Code	Color Temp (K)	LCL	Finish	Volts	Bulb Life (hr)	Amps
1k Fresnels							
Base: Medium bipost., G22. Bulb: T-6, T-7, T-20, or T-24. Burn within 45 of vertical base-down.							
1000	**EGT-Q1000T7/4CL**	**3200**	**2½"**	**C**	**120**	**250**	**8.3**
1000	EGT	3200	2½"	C	120	250	8.3
1000	EBB-1M24/13	3350	2½"	C	120	12	8.3
750	EGR-Q750T7/4CL	3200	2½"	C	120	200	6.3
750	EGR	3200	2½"	C	120	200	6.3
750	DVH-750T24/16	3200	2½"	C	120	50	6.3
500	EGN	3200	2½"	C	120	100	4.2
500	DVG-500T20/63	3200	2½"	C	120	50	4.2
Small 2k Fresnels (special high seal temp bulb made for specially designed high-temp heads—Sachtler, Desisti).							
Base: Medium Bi-post, G22. Bulb: T-8 Phillips							
2000	Blue Pinch	3200	2½"	C	120	500	16.7
2k Fresnels							
Base: Mogul bipost., G38. Bulb: T-7, T-8, T-9 1/2, and T-48. Burn within 45 of vertical base down.							
2000	**CYX-Q2000T10/4**	**3200**	**5"**	**C**	**120**	**250**	**16.7**
1500	CXZ-Q1500T10/4CL	3200	5"	C	120	300	12.5
1000	CYV-Q1000T7/4CL/BP	3200	5"	C	120	200	5.3
5k Fresnel							
Base: Mogul bipost., G38. Bulb: T-17 and T-20. Burn base-down to horizontal.							
5000	**DPY-Q5000T20/4CL**	**3200**	**6½"**	**C**	**120**	**500**	**41.6**
5000	DPY	3200	6½"	C	120	500	41.6
10k and 12k Tungsten Fresnel							
Base: Mogul bipost, G38. Bulb: T-24. Burn within 45 of vertical base-down.							
10,000	**DTY**	**3200**	**10"**	**C**	**120**	**300**	**83.3**
12,000	**Koto 12k**	**3200**	**10"**	**C**	**120**	**—**	**100**
20k Fresnel							
Base: Mogul bipost., G38. Bulb: T32. Burn within 45 of vertical, base-down.							
20,000	KP200 208V	3200	13.937"	C	208	300	83.3
20,000	KP200 220V	3200	13.937"	C	220	300	83.3
20,000	**KP200 240V**	**3200**	**13.937"**	**C**	**240**	**300**	**83.3**
1k Molipso							
Base: medium prefocus, P28. Bulb: T-5 or T-6. Burn any position.							
1000	**EGJ-Q1000/4CL/P**	**3200**	**3½"**	**C**	**120**	**500**	**8.3**
1000	EGM-Q1000/CL/P	3000	3½"	C	120	2000	8.3
1000	EGJ	3200	3½"	C	120	400	8.3
750	EGF-Q750/4CL/P	3200	3½"	C	120	500	8.3
750	EGG-Q750/CL/P	3000	3½"	C	120	2000	6.3
750	EGF	3200	3½"	C	120	250	6.3
750	EGG	3000	3½"	C	120	2000	6.3

Table E.3 Tungsten Bulb Specifications and Substitutions (continued)

Watts	ANSI Code	Color Temp (K)	LCL	Finish	Volts	Bulb Life (hr)	Amps
2k Molipso							
Base: mogul bipost, G38. T-8 bulb. Burn any position.							
2000	**BWA-Q2000/4CL/**	**3200**	**5"**	**C**	**120**	**750**	**16.7**
2000	BWA	3200	5"	C	120	500	16.7
1k Molette, Ellipsoidal Spotlights							
Base: medium 2-pin. G9.5. T-4 or T-6 bulbs. Burn any position.							
1000	**FFL-Q1000/4CL**	**3200**	**2³⁄₈"**	**C**	**120**	**500**	**8.3**
1000	**FCV-Q1000/4**	**3200**	**2³⁄₈"**	**F**	**120**	**500**	**8.3**
1000	FEL	3200	2³⁄₈"	C	120	300	8.3
1000	FCV	3200	2³⁄₈"	F	120	300	8.3
750	EHF-Q750/4CL	3200	2³⁄₈"	C	122	300	6.3
750	EHF	3200	2³⁄₈"	C	120	300	6.3
750	EHG	3000	2³⁄₈"	C	120	2000	6.3
500	FHC/EHB	3200	2³⁄₈"	C	120	200	4.2
500	EHC/EHB-Q500/5CL	3150	2³⁄₈"	C	120	300	4.2
500	**EHD-Q500CL/TP**	**3000**	**2³⁄₈"**	**C**	**120**	**2000**	**4.2**
500	EHD	3000	2³⁄₈"	C	120	2000	4.2
2k Molette							
Base: mogul screw. T-8 bulb. Burn any position.							
2000	BWF-Q2000/4CL	3200	5¹⁄₄"	C	120	750	16.7
2000	BWF	3200	5¹⁄₄"	C	120	400	16.7
2000	**BWG**	**3200**	**5¹⁄₄"**	**F**	**120**	**400**	**16.7**

Double-Ended Tungsten Bulbs

Watts	ANSI Code	Color Temp (K)	MOL	Finish	Volts	Bulb Life (hr)	Amps
400 W and 650 W Soft Lights and Open Face Lights							
Base: Recessed Single-Contact R7S. 3¹⁄₈" double-ended T-4 bulb. Burn any position.							
650	**FAD**	**3200**	**3¹⁄₈"**	**C**	**120**	**100**	**5.4**
650	FBX	3200	3¹⁄₈"	F	120	100	5.4
650	DWY	3400	3¹⁄₈"	C	120	25	5.4
420	FFM	3200	3¹⁄₈"	C	120	75	3.5
400	**FDA (400T4Q/4CL)**	**3200**	**3¹⁄₈"**	**C**	**120**	**250**	**3.3**
400	EHR (400T4Q/CL)	2900	3¹⁄₈"	C	120	2000	3.3
300	EHP (300T4Q/CL)	2900	3¹⁄₈"	C	120	2000	2.5
1k Open Face, Mickey, 1k Arrilite							
Base: Recessed Single-Contact R7s. 3³⁄₄" double-ended T-3 bulb. Burn any position.							
1000	**DXW**	**3200**	**3³⁄₄"**	**C**	**120**	**150**	**8.3**
1000	FBY	3200	3³⁄₄"	F	120	150	8.3
1000	BRH	3350	3³⁄₄"	C	120	75	8.3
1000	DXN	3400	3³⁄₄"	C	120	75	5.0
600	FCB	3250	3³⁄₄"	C	120	75	5.0
500	FGD	3200	3³⁄₄"	C	120	100	4.2

Table E.3 Tungsten Bulb Specifications and Substitutions (continued)

Watts	ANSI Code	Color Temp (K)	LCL	Finish	Volts	Bulb Life (hr)	Amps
1k Nook, 1k, 2k, 4k, and 8k Soft lights							
Base: Recessed single-contact R7Ss. $4^{11}/_{16}$" double-ended T-3 bulb. Burn horizontal ± 4°.							
1000	**FCM-Q1000T3/4CL**	**3200**	**$4^{11}/_{16}$"**	**C**	**120**	**500**	**8.3**
1000	FCM-Q1000T3/4	3200	$4^{11}/_{16}$"	F	120	500	8.3
1000	FCM	3200	$4^{11}/_{16}$"	C	120	300	8.3
1000	**FHM**	**3200**	**$4^{11}/_{16}$"**	**F**	**120**	**300**	**8.3**
750	EJG-Q750T3/4CL	3200	$4^{11}/_{16}$"	C	120	400	8.3
750	EMD-Q750T3/4	3200	$4^{11}/_{16}$"	F	120	400	6.3
750	**EJG**	**3200**	**$4^{11}/_{16}$"**	**C**	**120**	**400**	**6.3**
500	FDF-Q500T3/4CL	3200	$4^{11}/_{16}$"	C	120	400	4.2
500	FDN-Q500T3/4	3200	$4^{11}/_{16}$"	F	120	400	4.2
500	EDF	3200	$4^{11}/_{16}$"	C	120	400	4.2
500	EDN	3200	$4^{11}/_{16}$"	F	120	400	4.2
500	Q500T3/CL	3000	$4^{11}/_{16}$"	C	120	2000	4.2
500	Q500T3	3000	$4^{11}/_{16}$"	F	120	2000	4.2
500	FCL	3000	$4^{11}/_{16}$"	C	120	2600	4.2
500	FCZ	3000	$4^{11}/_{16}$"	F	120	2600	4.2
300	EHM-Q300T2 1/2/CL	2980	$4^{11}/_{16}$"	C	120	2000	2.5
300	EHZ-Q300T2 1/2	2950	$4^{11}/_{16}$"	F	120	2000	2.5
2k Nook							
Base: Recessed single-contact R7s. $5^5/_8$" double-ended T-6 or T-8 bulb. Burn any position.							
2000	**FEY-Q2000T8/4CL**	**3200**	**$5^5/_8$"**	**C**	**120**	**500**	**16.7**
2000	FEY (2MT8Q/4CL)	3200	$5^5/_8$"	C	120	400	16.7
1000	FER/EHS-Q1000T4/6CL	3200	$5^5/_8$"	C	120	500	8.3
1000	FER (1000T6Q/4CL)	3200	$5^5/_8$"	C	120	500	8.3
1000	DWT-Q1000T6/CL	3000	$5^5/_8$"	C	120	2550	8.3
1000	DWT (1000T6Q/CL)	3000	$5^5/_8$"	C	120	2000	8.3
Cyc Strips							
Base: Recessed single-contact R7s. $6^9/_{16}$" double-ended T-3 or T-4 bulb. Burn horizontal ±4°.							
1500	**FDB-Q1500T4/4CL**	**3200**	**$6^9/_{16}$"**	**C**	**120**	**400**	**12.5**
1500	FGT-Q1500T4/4	3200	$6^9/_{16}$"	F	120	400	12.5
1000	**FFT-Q1000T3/1CL**	**3200**	**$6^9/_{16}$"**	**C**	**120**	**400**	**8.3**
1000	FGV-Q1000T3/1	3200	$6^9/_{16}$"	C	120	400	8.3

LCL = Light Center Length, the distance from the center of the bulb's filament to the bottom of its base. If the wrong LCL is used, the filament will not be centered on the reflector and fixture performance will be greatly reduced.

MOL = Maximum Overall Length, the distance from the top of the lamp to the tip of the pins on the base or from end to end for double-ended lamps. For double-ended lamps, MOL is necessary to match lamp to fixture size.

Interchangeability = Bulbs within each grouping in this table are interchangeable—they have the same base (type and dimensions) and the same LCL (or MOL in the case of double-ended lamps).

The most commonly used lamps for motion picture work are highlighted in bold print.

C = Clear finish

F = Frosted finish

Table E.4 PAR 64 Bulbs, 120-V, EMEP Base (Extended Mogul End Prong)

Beam	500 W		1000 W		1200 W
	2800 K (2000 hrs)	3000 K (4000 hrs)	3200 K (800 hrs)	5200 K (200 hrs)	3200 K
Very narrow spot	—	—	FFN (VNSP) Q1000PAR64/1	—	GFC (VNSP)
Narrow spot	500PAR64NSP	1000PAR64QNSP	FFP (NSP) Q1000PAR64/2	FGM (NSP) Q1000PAR64/3D	GFB (NSP)
Medium flood	500PAR64MFL	1000PAR64QMFL	FFR (MFL) Q1000PAR64/5	FGN (MFL) Q1000PAR64/7D	GFA (MFL)
Wide flood	500PAR64WFL	1000PAR64QWFL	FFS (WFL) Q1000PAR64/6	—	GFE (WFL)
Extrawide flood	—	—	GFF (XWFL)	—	GFD (XWFL)

Table E.5 PAR 64 Lamp Performance Data for PAR 64 and Aircraft Landing Lights

ANSI Code	Volts	Watts	Base	Color Temp	Ave. Life (hr)	Beam	Beam Angle (degrees)	Candle Power
FFN	120	1000	EMEP	3200	800	VNSP	12 × 6	400,000
FFP	120	1000	EMEP	3200	800	NSP	14 × 7	330,000
FFR	120	1000	EMEP	3200	800	MFL	28 × 12	125,000
FFS	120	1000	EMEP	3200	800	WFL	48 × 24	40,000
GFF	120	1000	EMEP	3200	800	XWFL	—	—
GFC	120	1200	EMEP	3200	400	VNSP	10 × 8	540,000
GFB	120	1200	EMEP	3200	400	NSP	10 × 8	450,000
GFA	120	1200	EMEP	3200	400	MFL	24 × 13	160,000
GFE	120	1200	EMEP	3200	400	WFL	58 × 25	45,000
GFD	120	1200	EMEP	3200	400	XWFL	—	—

ACL (Aircraft Landing Light) Bulbs in PAR 64 size

4559	28	600	Screw Terminal	—	25	VNSP	12 × 11	600,000
Q4559	28	600	Screw Terminal	—	100	VNSP	12 × 8	600,000
Q4559X	28	600	Screw Terminal	—	100	VNSP	11 × 7 1/2	600,000

Table E.6 PAR 36 Bulbs, 650 W, 120 V, Ferrule Base

Beam	5000 K (35 hr)	3400 K (30 hr)	3200 K (100 hr)
Spot	—	FBJ Q650PAR36/3	—
Medium	FAY Q650PAR36/3D	DXK Q650PAR36/2	FCX Q650PAR36/7
Wide	—	—	FCW Q650PAR36/6

Gels and Diffusions

Table F.1 Kelvin Scale/MIRED Scale Conversion Table

Kelvin	0	100	200	300	400	500	600	700	800	900
2000	500	476	455	435	417	400	385	370	357	345
3000	333	323	313	303	294	286	278	270	263	256
4000	250	244	238	233	227	222	217	213	208	204
5000	200	196	192	189	185	182	179	175	172	169
6000	167	164	161	159	156	154	152	149	147	145
7000	143	141	139	137	135	133	132	130	128	127
8000	125	123	122	120	119	118	116	115	114	112
9000	111	110	109	108	106	105	104	103	102	101

Example: To find the MIRED value for a 6500 Kelvin source, look across from 6000, and down from 500. The MIRED value is 154.

Table F.2 Kelvin Conversion: Lee Color-Correction Conversion

Light Source Lee Color (K)	CTO (Orange)				CTB (Blue)			
	Lee 223 Eighth	Lee 206 Quarter	Lee 205 Half	Lee 204 Full	Lee 218 Eighth	Lee 203 Quarter	Lee 205 Half	Lee 201 Full
2000	1901	1773	1642	1517	2075	2151	2370	2755
2300	1786	1672	1555	1443	1938	2004	2193	2519
2600	2433	2227	2024	1838	2725	2857	3257	4032
2900	2695	2445	2203	1984	3058	3226	3745	4808
3200	2959	2660	2375	2123	3401	3610	4274	5714
3500	3205	2857	2532	2247	3731	3984	4808	6711
3800	3460	3058	2688	2370	4082	4386	5405	7937
4400	3953	3436	2976	2591	4785	5208	6711	11111
5000	4425	3788	3236	2786	5495	6061	8197	15873
5600	4878	4115	3472	2959	6211	6944	9901	23810
6200	5348	4444	3704	3125	6993	7937	12048	41667
6800	5780	4739	3906	3268	7752	8929	14493	100000
7400	6211	5025	4098	3401	8547	10000	17544	
8000	6623	5291	4274	3521	9346	11111	21277	
9000	7299	5714	4545	3704	10753	13158	30303	
Kelvin MIRED	26	64	109	159	−18	−35	−78	−137

Table F.3 Kelvin Conversion: Rosco Color-Correction Conversion

Light Source Color (K)	CTO (Orange) R-3410 Eighth	R-3409 Quarter	R-3408 Half	R-3411 ¾	R-3401 Sun 85	R-3407 Full	CTB (Blue) R-3216 Eighth	R-3208 Quarter	R-3206 Third	R-3204 Half	R-3203 ¾	R-3202 Full	R-3220 2×CTB
2000	1923	1845	1721	1585	1585	1499	2049	2128	2217	2315	2500	2710	4115
2300	1805	1736	1626	1504	1504	1427	1916	1984	2062	2146	2304	2481	3610
2600	2469	2342	2146	1938	1938	1812	2681	2817	2976	3155	3509	3937	7813
2900	2740	2584	2347	2101	2101	1953	3003	3175	3378	3610	4082	4673	11364
3200	3012	2825	2545	2257	2257	2088	3333	3546	3802	4098	4717	5525	18182
3500	3268	3049	2725	2398	2398	2208	3650	3906	4219	4587	5376	6452	34483
3800	3534	3279	2907	2538	2538	2326	3984	4292	4673	5128	6135	7576	166667
4400	4049	3717	3247	2793	2793	2538	4651	5076	5618	6289	7874	10417	
5000	4545	4132	3559	3021	3021	2725	5319	5882	6623	7576	10000	14493	
5600	5025	4525	3846	3226	3226	2890	5988	6711	7692	9009	12658	20833	
6200	5525	4926	4132	3425	3425	3049	6711	7634	8929	10753	16393	33333	
6800	5988	5291	4386	3597	3597	3185	7407	8547	10204	12658	21277	62500	
7400	6452	5650	4630	3759	3759	3311	8130	9524	11628	14925	28571		
8000	6897	5988	4854	3906	3906	3425	8850	10526	13158	17544	40000		
9000	7634	6536	5208	4132	4132	3597	10101	12346	16129	23256	90909		
Kelvin MIRED	20	42	81	131	131	167	-12	-30	-49	-68	-100	-131	-257

Table F.4 Kelvin Conversion: GAM Color-Correction Conversion

Light Source Color (K)	CTO (Orange)						CTB (Blue)					
	1555 Eighth	1552 Quarter	1549 Half	1546 ¾ CTO	1543 Full	1540 Extra CTO	1535 Eighth	1532 Quarter	1529 Half	1526 ¾ Blue	1523 Full	1520 Extra CTB
2000	1916	1852	1721	1585	1520	1294	2037	2110	2315	2577	2703	2817
2300	1799	1742	1626	1504	1445	1239	1905	1969	2146	2370	2475	2571
2600	2457	2353	2146	1938	1842	1520	2660	2786	3155	3663	3922	4167
2900	2725	2597	2347	2101	1988	1618	2976	3135	3610	4292	4651	5000
3200	2994	2841	2545	2257	2128	1709	3300	3497	4098	5000	5495	5988
3500	3247	3067	2725	2398	2252	1789	3610	3846	4587	5747	6410	7092
3800	3509	3300	2907	2538	2375	1866	3937	4219	5128	6623	7519	8475
4400	4016	3745	3247	2793	2597	2000	4587	4975	6289	8696	10309	12195
5000	4505	4167	3559	3021	2793	2114	5236	5747	7576	11364	14286	18182
5600	4975	4566	3846	3226	2967	2212	5882	6536	9009	14925	20408	29412
6200	5464	4975	4132	3425	3135	2304	6579	7407	10753	20408	32258	62500
6800	5917	5348	4386	3597	3279	2381	7246	8264	12658	28571	58824	500000
7400	6369	5714	4630	3759	3413	2451	7937	9174	14925	43478	200000	
8000	6803	6061	4854	3906	3534	2513	8621	10101	17544	76923		
9000	7519	6623	5208	4132	3717	2604	9804	11765	23256			
Kelvin MIRED	22	40	81	131	158	273	−9	−26	−68	−112	−130	−145

Table F.5 Daylight Color Correction (CTO Gels)

Name	Rosco Cinegel	MIRED Shift	Lee	MIRED Shift	GAM	MIRED Shift	K Shift	Light Reduction (Stops)
Extra CTO	—	—	—	—	1540	+273	20,000 K to 3200 K	1
Full CTO	3407	+167	204*	+159	1543	+163	5500 K to 2200 K	
Full Straw	3441		441				6500 K to 3200 K	2/3
Sun 85	3401	+131	—	—	—	—	5500 K to 2900 K	2/3
85 Acrylic	3761						5500 K to 3200 K	
3/4 CTO	3411	+130	285	—	1546	+130	5500 K to 3200 K	2/3
1/2 CTO	3408	+81	205*	+109	1549	+81	5500 K to 3800 K	1/2
1/2 Straw	3442		441					
1/2 CTO Acrylic	3751							
1/4 CTO	3409	+42	206*	+64	1552	+40	5500 K to 4500 K	1/3
1/4 Straw	3443		441					
1/8 CTO	3410	+20	223*	+26	1555	+22	5500 K to 4900 K	1/4
1/8 Straw	3444		441					

*Also available in 60-in. rolls.

Table F.6 Neutral Density and ND/Daylight Correction Gels

Gel	Rosco Cinegel	MIRED Shift	Lee	MIRED Shift	GAM	K Shift	Light Reduction (Stops)
0.15 ND	3415	0	298	0	1514	0	½
0.3 ND Acrylic	3402	0	209*	0	1515	0	1
	3762						
0.6 ND Acrylic	3403	0	210*	0	1516	0	2
	3763						
0.9 ND Acrylic	3404	0	211*	0	1517	0	3
	3764						
1.2 ND	—	—	299	0	1518	0	4
CTO 0.3 ND	3405	+131	207	+159	1556	5500 K to 3200 K	1
CTO 0.6 ND	3406	+131	208	+159	1557	5500 K to 3200 K	2
CTO 0.9 ND	—	—	—	—	1558	5500 K to 3200 K	3

*Also available in 60-in. rolls.

Cinemills Corporation makes gels that share the same product numbers as Lee.

Table F.7 Tungsten Color Correction (CTB Gels)

Name	Rosco Cinegel	MIRED Shift	Lee	MIRED Shift	GAM	K Shift	Light Reduction (Stops)
Double Blue	3220	−257	200	—	—	2800 K to 10,000 K	4
Extra CTB	—	−150	—	−137	1520	3200 K to 6200 K	1¾
Full CTB	3202	−131	201	—	1523	3200 K to 5700 K	1⅓
¾ CTB	3203	—	281	—	1526		1¼
½ CTB	3204	−68	205	−78	1529	3200 K to 4300 K	1
⅓ CTB	3206	−49	—	—	—	3200 K to 3800 K	⅔
¼ CTB	3208	−30	203	−35	1532	3200 K to 3600 K	⅔
⅛ CTB	3216	−12	218	−18	1535	3200 K to 3400 K	⅓

Cinemills Corporation makes gels that share the same product numbers as Lee.

Table F.8 Blue/Orange Correction: Colormeter LB Index (MIREDs)

Colormeter LB Reading (MIREDs)	Kodak Wratten Filter		Light Loss Due to Filter	Approximate Equivalent Gel	Kelvin Shift	
	Amber	Blue			From	To
−257	—	—	4	Double CTB	3200	10,000
−133	—	80A	2	Full CTB	3200	5500
−112	—	80B	1²/₃	—	3400	5500
−100	—	80C + 82A	—	³/₄ CTB	3200	4700
−90	—	82C + 82C	1¹/₃	—	2490	3200
−81	—	80C	1	¹/₂ CTB	3800	5500
−77	—	82C + 82B	1¹/₃	—	2570	3200
−66	—	82C + 82A	1	—	2650	3200
−56	—	80D	¹/₃	—	4200	5500
−55	—	82C + 82	1	¹/₃ CTB	2720	3200
−45	—	82C	²/₃	—	2800	3200
−32	—	82B	²/₃	¹/₄ CTB	2900	3200
−21	—	82A	¹/₃	¹/₈ CTB	3000	3200
−10	—	82	¹/₃	—	3100	3200
+9	81	—	¹/₃	—	3300	3200
+18	81A	—	¹/₃	—	3400	3200
+27	81B	—	¹/₃	¹/₈ CTO	3500	3200
+35	81C	—	¹/₃	—	3600	3200
+42	81D	—	²/₃	¹/₄ CTO	3700	3200
+52	81EF	—	²/₃	—	3850	3200
+81	85C	—	¹/₃	¹/₂ CTO	5500	3800
+112	85	—	²/₃	—	5500	3400
+133	85B	—	²/₃	³/₄ CTO or Sun 85	5500	3200
+167	85B + 81C	—	²/₃	Full CTO	5600	2900

Table F.9 Green/Magenta Correction: Colormeter CC Index

| Colormeter II | Colormeter III | | Gel Source With | Rosco | Lee | GAM | Compensation | Conversion |
Color Compensation	CC Filter Magenta	CC Filter Green	Gel Name	Cinegel No.	Gel No.	Gel No.	in f-Stops	
+18	40M	—	—	—	—	—	2/3	Removes Green
+13	30M	—	Full Minus Green	3308	247	1580	2/3	"
+8	20M	—	—	—	—	—	1/3	"
+6	15M	—	Half Minus Green	3313	248	1582	1/3	"
+4	10M	—	—	—	—	—	1/3	"
+3	7.5M	—	1/4 Minus Green	3314	249	1583	1/3	"
+2	5M	—	—	—	—	—	1/3	"
+1	3.5M	—	1/8 Minus Green	3318	279	1584	1/4	"
−1	—	3.5G	1/8 Plus Green	3317	278	—	1/4	Adds Green
−2	—	7.5G	1/4 Plus Green	3316	246	—	1/3	"
−4	—	10G	—	—	—	—	1/3	"
−5	—	15G	1/2 Plus Green	3315	245	1587	1/3	"
−7	—	20G	—	—	—	—	1/3	"
−10	—	30G	Full Plus Green	3304	244	1585	2/3	"
−13	—	40G	—	—	—	—	2/3	"
—	30M	—	Fluoro-Filter	3310	—	1590	1 2/3	Converts cool whites to 3200 K
—	—	30G	Plus-green 50	3306	—	—	1 1/4	Converts 3200 K source to match cool whites
—	—	30G	Fluorescent 5700	—	241	—	1 2/3	Converts 3200 K source to 5700 K (cool white fluorescents)
—	—	30G	Fluorescent 4300	—	242	—	1 1/2	Converts 3200 K source to 4300 K (white fluorescents)
—	—	30G	Fluorescent 3600	—	243	—	1 1/4	Converts 3200 K source to 3600 K (warm white fluorescents)

Minolta Colormeter II and earlier read out + or − color compensation index number (first column). Newer models read out in CC filter numbers (second and third columns).

Table F.10   Theatrical Gel Colors

Gamcolor Gels		
The Great American Market		

105	Antique Rose (Minusgreen)	440	Very Light Straw	950	Purple	
		450	Saffron	960	Medium Lavender	
106	¹/₂ Antique Rose (¹/₂ Minusgreen)	460	Mellow Yellow	970	Special Lavender	
		470	Pale Gold	980	Surprise Pink	
107	¹/₄ Antique Rose (¹/₄ Minusgreen)	480	Medium Lemon	995	Orchid	
		510	No Color Straw			
		520	New Straw	**Lee Gels**		
108	¹/₈ Antique Rose (¹/₈ Minusgreen)	535	Lime (¹/₂ Plusgreen)	*Cosmetic Range*		
		540	Pale Green (Plusgreen)	184	Cosmetic Peach	
110	Dark Rose	570	Light Green Yellow	185	Cosmetic Burgundy	
120	Bright Pink	650	Grass Green	186	Cosmetic Silver Rose	
130	Rose	655	Rich Green	187	Cosmetic Rouge	
140	Dark Magenta	660	Medium Green	188	Cosmetic Highlight	
150	Pink Punch	680	Kelly Green	189	Cosmetic Silver Moss	
155	Light Pink	685	Pistachio	190	Cosmetic Emerald	
160	Chorus Pink	690	Bluegrass	191	Cosmetic Aqua Blue	
170	Dark Flesh Pink	710	Blue Green			
180	Cherry	720	Light Steel Green	**Theatrical Colors**		
190	Cold Pink	725	Princess Blue	002	Rose Pink	
195	Nymph Pink	730	Azure Blue	003	Lavender Tint	
220	Pink Magenta	740	Off Blue	004	Medium Bastard Amber (HT)	
235	Pink Red	750	Nile Blue	007	Pale Yellow (HT)	
245	Light Red	760	Aqua Blue	008	Dark Salmon (HT)	
250	Medium Red XT	770	Christel Blue	009	Pale Amber Gold (HT)	
260	Rosy Amber	780	Shark Blue	010	Medium Yellow (HT)	
270	Red Orange	790	Electric Blue	013	Straw Tint (HT)	
280	Fire Red	810	Moon Blue	015	Deep Straw (HT)	
290	Fire Orange	820	Full Light Blue	019	Fire (HT)	
305	French Rose	830	North Sky Blue	020	Medium Amber (HT)	
315	Autumn Glory	835	Aztec Blue	021	Gold Amber (HT)	
320	Peach	840	Steel Blue	022	Dark Amber (HT)	
323	Indian Summer	842	Whisper Blue (¹/₂ CTB)	024	Scarlet (HT)	
325	Bastard Amber	845	Cobalt	026	Bright Red (HT)	
330	Sepia	847	City Blue (Extra CTB)	027	Medium Red (HT)	
335	Coral (Extra CTO)	848	Bonus Blue	035	Light Pink (HT)	
340	Light Bastard Amber	850	Primary Blue	036	Medium Pink (HT)	
343	Honey (Full CTO)	860	Sky Blue	046	Dark Magenta (HT)	
345	Deep Amber	870	Whinter White (¹/₈ CTB)	048	Rose Pink	
350	Dark Amber	880	Daylight Blue	052	Light Lavender (HT)	
360	Amber Blush (¹/₂ CTO)	882	Southern Sky (Full CTB)	053	Paler Lavender (HT)	
363	Sand	885	Blue Ice (¹/₄ CTB)	058	Lavender (HT)	
364	Pale Honey (¹/₄ CTO)	888	Blue Bell (³/₄ CTB)	061	Mist Blue (HT)	
365	Warm Straw	890	Dark Sky Blue	063	Pale Blue (HT)	
370	Spice (CTO/N.6)	905	Dark Blue	068	Sky Blue	
375	Flame	910	Alice Blue	079	Just Blue (HT)	
380	Golden Tan (CTO/N.3)	920	Pale Lavender	085	Deeper Blue (HT)	
385	Light Amber	930	Real Congo Blue	089	Moss Green (HT)	
390	Walnut (CTO/N.9)	940	Light Purple	090	Dark Yellow Green (HT)	
420	Medium Amber	945	Royal Purple			
		948	African Violet			

HT = High-temperature polycarbonate base.

Table F.10 Theatrical Gel Colors (continued)

101	Yellow	172	Lagoon Blue (HT)	21	Golden Amber
102	Light Amber	174	Dark Steel Blue	321	Soft Golden Amber
103	Straw	176	Loving Amber	22	Deep Amber
104	Deep Amber	179	Chroma Orange	23	Orange
105	Orange	180	Dark Lavender	24	Scarlet
106	Primary Red	181	Congo Blue (HT)	25	Orange Red
107	Light Rose	182	Light Red	26	Light Red
109	Light Salmon	183	Moonlight Blue	27	Medium Red
110	Middle Rose	192	Flesh Pink	30	Light Salmon Pink
111	Dark Pink	193	Rosy Amber	31	Salmon Pink
113	Magenta	194	Surprise Pink	32	Medium Salmon Pink
115	Peacock Blue (HT)	195	Zenith Blue (HT)	332	Cherry Rose
116	Medium Green Blue	196	True Blue	33	No Color Pink
	(HT)	197	Alice Blue (HT)	333	Blush Pink
117	Steel Blue	332	Follies Pink	34	Flesh Pink
118	Light Blue (HT)	332	Special Rose Pink	35	Light Pink
119	Dark Blue (HT)	343	Special Medium Lavender	36	Medium Pink
120	Deep Blue (HT)	344	Violet	37	Pale Rose Pink
121	Lee Green (HT)	353	Lighter Blue	337	True Pink
122	Fern Green (HT)	354	Special Steel Blue	38	Light Rose
124	Dark Green (HT)	363	Special Medium Blue	39	Skelton Exotic Sangria
126	Mauve		(HT)	339	Broadway Pink
127	Smoky Pink			40	Light Salmon
128	Bright Pink	**Roscolux Gel**		41	Salmon
129	Heavy Frost	*(in sheets and 24 in. rolls)*		42	Deep Salmon
130	Clear	00	Clear	342	Rose Pink
132	Medium Blue (HT)	01	Light Bastard Amber	43	Deep Pink
134	Golden Amber	02	Bastard Amber	44	Middle Rose
135	Deep Golden Amber	03	Dark Bastard Amber	344	Follies Pink
136	Pale Lavender	04	Medium Bastard Amber	45	Rose
137	Special Lavender	304	Pale Apricot	46	Magenta
138	Pale Green	05	Rose Tint	47	Light Rose Purple
139	Primary Green (HT)	305	Rose Gold	48	Rose Purple
141	Bright Blue (HT)	06	No Color Straw	49	Medium Purple
142	Pale Violet	07	Pale Yellow	349	Fisher Fuchia
143	Pale Navy Blue	08	Pale Gold	50	Mauve
144	No Color Blue	09	Pale Amber Gold	51	Surprise Pink
147	Apricot	10	Medium Yellow	52	Light Lavender
148	Bright Rose	310	Daffodil	53	Pale Lavender
151	Golt Tint	11	Light Straw	54	Special Lavender
152	Pale Gold	12	Straw	55	Lilac
153	Pale Salmon	312	Canary	355	Pale Violet
154	Pale Rose	13	Straw Tint	56	Middle Lavender
156	Chocolate	14	Medium Straw	57	Lavender
157	Pink	15	Deep Straw	357	Royal Lavender
158	Deep Orange	16	Light Amber	58	Deep Lavender
159	No Color Straw	316	Gallo Gold	358	Rose Indigo
161	Slate Blue	17	Light Flame	59	Indigo
162	Bastard Amber	317	Apricot	359	Medium Violet
164	Flame Red	18	Flame	60	No Color Blue
165	Daylight Blue	318	Mayan Sun	360	Clearwater
166	Pale Red	19	Fire	61	Mist Blue
170	Deep Lavender	20	Medium Amber	62	Booster Blue

Table F.10 Theatrical Gel Colors (continued)

63	Pale Blue	389	Chroma Green	624	Pink
363	Aquamarine	90	Dark Yellow Green	625	Pale Rose Pink
64	Light Steel Blue	91	Primary Green	626	Flesh Pink
364	Blue Bell	92	Turquoise	627	Rose Pink
65	Daylight Blue	93	Blue Green	631	Middle Rose
365	Cool Blue	94	Kelly Green	632	Salmon
66	Cool Blue	95	Medium Blue Green	638	Light Rose Purple
67	Light Sky Blue	395	Teal Green	639	Lilac
68	Sky Blue	96	Lime	641	Lavender
69	Brilliant Blue	97	Light Grey	642	Surprise Pink
70	Nile Blue	397	Pale Grey	644	Deep Lilac
71	Sea Blue	98	Medium Grey	645	Indigo
72	Azure Blue	99	Chocolate	647	Pale Blue
73	Peacock Blue			648	No Color Blue
74	Night Blue	**Rosco Cinecolor Gel**		649	Booster Blue
76	Light Green Blue	*(in 48 in. rolls)*		651	Light Steel Blue
376	Bermuda Blue	602	Bastard Amber	652	Azure Blue
77	Green Blue	603	Warm Rose	654	Daylight Blue
78	Trudy Blue	604	No Color Straw	657	Primary Blue
378	Alice Blue	605	Pale Gold	658	Medium Green Blue
79	Bright Blue	608	Warm Straw	659	Green Blue
80	Primary Blue	609	Straw	661	Medium Blue
81	Urban Blue	610	Light Flame	669	Pale Yellow Green
82	Surprise Blue	611	Rose Amber	671	Light Green
83	Medium Blue	612	Golden Amber	672	Moss Green
383	Sapphire Blue	613	Light Amber	673	Turquoise
84	Zephyr Blue	614	Flame	674	Primary Green
85	Deep Blue	615	Deep Straw	675	Light Blue Green
385	Royal Blue	617	Peach	676	Blue Green
86	Pea Green	618	Orange	677	Medium Blue Green
87	Pale Yellow Green	620	Deep Salmon	680	Light Grey
88	Light Green	621	Light Red	681	Medium Grey
388	Gaslight Green	622	Pink Tint	682	Chocolate
89	Moss Green	623	Light Pink		

Table F.11 Diffusion Materials

Types of Diffusion	Product No.	Light Reduction	Notes
Lee			
Full Tough Spun	214	2^1/$_2$	Slight softening of field and beam edge.
Half Tough Spun	215	1^1/$_2$	Slight softening of field and beam edge.
Quarter Tough Spun	229	^{3}/$_4$	Slight softening of field and beam edge.
Full Tough Spun	261	2	Flame retardant. Slight softening of field and beam edge.
^{3}/$_4$ Tough Spun	262	1^2/$_3$	Flame retardant.
^{1}/$_2$ Tough Spun	263	1^1/$_3$	Flame retardant.
^{1}/$_8$ Tough Spun	264	1	Flame retardant.
^{1}/$_4$ Tough Spun	265	^{3}/$_4$	Flame retardant.
216 White Diffusion	216	1^1/$_2$	Very popular moderate/heavy diffusion. Available in 60" width.
^{1}/$_2$ 216	250	^{3}/$_4$	Moderate beam spread and softening.
^{1}/$_4$ 216	251	^{1}/$_3$	Moderate beam spread and softening.
^{1}/$_8$ 216	252	^{1}/$_8$	Moderate beam spread and softening.
Blue Diffusion	217	1^1/$_2$	Increases color temperature very slightly.
Daylight Blue Frost	224	2^1/$_4$	CTB frost.
Neutral Density Frost	225	2	ND 0.6 frost.
Brushed Silk	228	^{3}/$_4$	Diffuses light in one direction only.
Hampshire Frost	253	^{1}/$_4$	Very light frost.
New Hampshire Frost	254	—	High-temperature polycarbonate base
Hollywood Frost	255	—	—
Half Hampshire	256	—	—
Quarter Hampshire	257	—	—
Heavy Frost	129	1^1/$_3$	Flame retardant.
White Frost	220	1^1/$_3$	Flame retardant.
Blue Frost	221	1^1/$_3$	Flame retardant. Increases color temperature very slightly.
Grid Cloth	430	—	Heavy white fabric 52-in.width.
Light Grid Cloth	432	—	Lighter white fabric in 52-in. width.
Rosco			
Tough Spun	3006	2^1/$_2$	Slight softening of field and beam edge.
Light Tough Spun	3007	1^2/$_3$	Slight softening of field and beam edge.
^{1}/$_4$ Tough Spun	3022	1	Slight softening of field and beam edge.
Tough Frost	3008	2	Slight to moderate softening, moderate beam spread but with discernible beam center.
Light Tough Frost	3009	1^1/$_2$	Slight to moderate softening, moderate beam spread but with discernible beam center.
Opal Tough Frost	3010	1	Popular light diffusion with slight to moderate softening, moderate beam spread but with discernible beam center.
Light Opal	3020	^{1}/$_2$	Slight to moderate softening, moderate beam spread but with discernible beam center.
Tough White Diffusion	3026	3^1/$_2$	Like Lee 216. Dense diffusion with wide beam spread creating even field of shadowless light.
^{1}/$_2$ White Diffusion	3027	2^1/$_2$	Like Lee 250. Moderately dense diffusion with wide beam spread.
^{1}/$_4$ White Diffusion	3028	1^1/$_2$	Like Lee 251. Moderate diffusion with wide beam spread.

Table F.11 Diffusion Materials (continued)

Types of Diffusion	Product No.	Light Reduction	Notes
Tough Rolux	3000	$2^1/_2$	Moderately dense diffusion with wide beam spread.
Light Tough Rolux	3001	—	Moderate diffusion with wide beam spread.
Grid Cloth	3030	5	Comes in 54-in. rolls. Very dense diffusion with very wide beam spread, which creates soft shadowless light. Ideal for large area diffusion. Not tolerant of high heat.
Light Grid Cloth	3032	$3^1/_2$	Smaller weave than grid cloth. Considerable softening. Comes in 54-in. rolls.
$^1/_4$ Grid Cloth	3034	$2^1/_2$	Considerable softening. Comes in 54-in. rolls.
Silent Frost	3029	3	Diffusion made of a rubbery plastic that does not crinkle and rattle in the wind.
Hilite	3014	1	Quiet like silent frost. Comes in 54-in. rolls.
Soft Frost	3002	2	Quite like silent frost, denser than Hilite.
Wide Soft Frost	3023	2	In 72 in. width.
$^1/_2$ Soft Frost	3004	$^1/_2$	Quiet, light diffuser.
Tough Silk	3011	$1^1/_2$	Considerable softening in one direction only.
Light Tough Silk	3015	1	Considerable softening in one direction only.
Tough Booster Silk	3012	—	Raises color temperature from 3200 K to 3500 K with silk softening characteristics.
Tough Booster Frost	3013	—	Raises color temperature from 3200 K to 3800 K with frost softening characteristics.
Full Blue Frost	3017	—	Raises color temperature from 3200 K to daylight with frost softening characteristics.
GAM—The Great American Market			
Medium GAM Frost	10	—	Soft light, warm center, diffuse edge.
Light GAM Frost	15	—	Soft light, warm center, diffuse edge.
Full GAM Spun	32	$2^1/_2$	Textural, warm center defined edge.
Medium GAM Spun	35	$1^2/_3$	Textural, warm center defined edge.
Light GAM Spun	38	1	Textural, warm center defined edge.
Gamvel	45	3	Soft light with diffuse shadow line.
216 GAM White	55	—	Shadowless, white light. Heavy diffusion with no center or edge visible.
Medium GAM Silk	65	—	Spreads light predominantly in one direction.
Light GAM Silk	68	—	Spreads light predominantly in one direction.
Gam Fusion	10-10	$^1/_4$	Almost clear with no color shift.
Gam Fusion	10-20	$^1/_4$	Very light diffusion with no color shift.
Gam Fusion	10-30	$^1/_2$	Light diffusion with no color shift.
Gam Fusion	10-40	$^1/_2$	Medium-light diffusion with no color shift.
Gam Fusion	10-50	1	Medium diffusion with no color shift.
Gam Fusion	10-60	2	Medium-heavy diffusion with no color shift.
Gam Fusion	10-70	5	Heavy diffusion with no color shift.
Gam Fusion	10-75	5	Heavy diffusion with no color shift.
Gam Fusion	10-80	6	Very heavy diffusion with no color shift.
Gam Fusion	10-90	6	Fully diffuse with no color shift.

Light reduction values given here are manufacturers' approximate figures. The actual transmission will depend on the beam angle of the light and the distance from the diffusion.

Lighting Accessories

Ring sizes for all fixtures are listed in Appendix A. Table G.1 shows which banks correspond to which ring sizes. Table G.2 lists ordering numbers for lights requiring dedicated speed rings not given in Appendix A.

Table G.1 Chimera Light Bank Specifications

Chimera Type	Ring Sizes	Size	Dimensions (in.)	Depth (in.)
Video Pro	3–9"	Extra Small	16 × 22	12
		Small	24 × 32	18
		Medium	36 × 48	24
Quartz Bank	9–21"	Small	24 × 32	22
		Medium	36 × 48	29
		Large	54 × 72	38
Daylight Junior Bank	$6^5/_8$–21"	Extra Small	16 × 22	21
		Small	24 × 32	30
		Medium	36 × 48	36
Daylight Bank	9–21"	Small	24 × 32	33
		Medium	36 × 48	40
		Large	54 × 72	48
Daylight Senior Bank	$24^1/_2$–29"	Large	54 × 72	50

Table G.2 Chimera Bank Ring Sizes and Ordering Numbers

Light Fixture	Video Pro	Daylight Junior Bank	Quartz Bank	Daylight Bank	Ring Frame Size (in.)
Lowel					
DP Light	9500AL				8
Tota-light	9510AL				8.5
Omni Light	9530AL				7.3
Pro-light	2945				5.9
V-light	2955				5.9
Quad DP Light			9011	9013	15.5
Triple Tota-light			9031	9033	13.5
Mole-Richardson					
Baby 407	2970				$6^5/8$
Tennie-Mole 650	2990AL				8.5
Mickey 1k	9540	9542			8.5
Quad Mickey			9071	9073	15.5
Mighty 2k			9731	9733	13.5
Arri					
Arrilite 650, 800, and 1000 W	2900				
Quad Arrilite			9051	9053	15.5
Strand Quartz Color					
Quad Ianebeam 650/1000			9061	9063	15.5
Reporter 200	9710				6.2
Sachtler					
Reporter 100H, 250H, 125D	9570				6.2
Reporter 270D, 650H	9580				7.5
Production 575	9590				7.5
Reporter 200, RL 250-300 DLF	9710				6.2

Table G.3 Dimmers

Dimmer	Model No.	Type	Ouput Voltage	Amps per Chnl.	Total Amps	Input Power	Input Connector	Output Connector
Mole-Richardson								
1200-W Molestat	5241	Auto-transformer	0–140-V AC	10 A	10 A	120-V AC	Edison	Edison
1800-W Molestat	5231	Auto-transformer	0–140-V AC	15 A	15 A	120-V AC	Edison	Edison
2.4-kW DC Molelectronic	5321	Electronic	118-V DC	20 A	20 A	120-V DC	20-A Bates	20-A Bates
6-kW DC Molelectronic	5331	Electronic	118-V DC	50 A	50 A	120-V DC	60-A Bates	60-A Bates
12-kW DC Molelectronic	5351	Electronic	118-V DC	100 A	100 A	120-V DC	100-A Bates	100-A Bates
72-kW DC 6-pack	53570	Electronic	118-V DC	100 A	600 A 300 A per leg	120/240-V DC	Bus bars	100-A Bates
12-kW AC Molelectronic	42590	Electronic	118-V AC	100 A	100 A	120-V AC	100-A Bates	100-A Bates
20-kW AC Molelectronic	42450	Electronic	206/238-V AC	100 A @ 240 V	100 A per leg	208/240-V AC	100-A 250-V Bates	100-A 250-V Bates
144-kW AC 12-Pack	8881	Electronic	116-V AC	100 A	1200 A, 400 A per leg	208/240-V AC	Bus bars, 4-wire + ground	100-A Bates
1000-W Plate Dimmer	504	Resistance	120-V AC or DC	8.3 A	8.3 A	120-V AC or DC	Full stage plug	Edison
2000-W Plate Dimmer	503	Resistance	120-V AC or DC	16.6 A	16.6 A	120-V AC or DC	Full stage plug	Edison
3000-W Plate Dimmer	5091	Resistance	120-V AC or DC	25 A	25 A	120-V AC or DC	Mole pin	Full stage plug
5000-W Plate Dimmer	2301	Resistance	120-V AC or DC	41.6 A	41.6 A	120-V AC or DC	Full stage plug	Full stage plug
22,000-W Plate Console	367	Resistance	120-V AC or DC	2 41.6 A / 4 16.6 A / 4 8.3 A	183.3 A	120-V AC or DC	2 Full stage plugs	10 Full stage plugs
2–5 k								
4–2 k								
4–1 k								
LTM								
1-Channel Pepper Pot		Triac	120-V AC	8.3 A	8.3 A	120-V AC	Edison	Edison
3-Channel Pepper Pot		Triac	120-V AC	3–8.3 A	25 A	120-V AC	As ordered	3 Edison
6-Channel Pepper Pot		Triac	120-V AC	6–10 A	60 A	120-V AC	As ordered	6 Edison

Table G.3 Dimmers (continued)

Dimmer	Model No.	Type	Output Voltage	Amps per Chnl.	Total Amps	Input Power	Input Connector	Output Connector
20-kW Dimmer	IA-925 WA	Electronic	120 or 240 V	100 A @ 240 V	100 A @ 240 V	120-V AC or 240 V	240-V 100-A Bates	240-V 100-A Bates
Strand								
20k Single	73118	Electronic	208-V AC	83.3 A @ 240 V	83.3-A per leg	120/208-V AC	240-V 100-A Bates	240-V 100-A Bates
12k Single Analogue Multiplex	73115 73116	Electronic	120-V AC	100 A	100 A	120-V AC	100-A Bates	100-A Bates
6k Single Analogue Multiplex	73113 73114	Electronic	120-V AC	50 A	60 A	120-V AC	60-A Bates	60-A Bates
2.4k Single Analogue Multiplex	73111 73112	Electronic	120-V AC	20 A	20 A	120-V AC	20-A Bates	20-A Bates
CD80 Pack 24 1.2 kW	—	Electronic	120-V AC	24 10 A	240 A, 80 A × 3 240 A, 120 A × 2	Three-phase Single-phase	Cam Lok	20-A Bates
CD80 Pack 12 2.4 kW	—	Electronic	120-V AC	12 20 A	240 A, 80 A × 3 240 A, 120 A × 2	Three-phase Single Phase	Cam Lok	20-A Bates
CD80 Pack 24 2.4 kW	—	Electronic	120-V AC	24 20 A	480 A, 160 A × 3 480 A, 240 A × 2	Three-phase Single-phase	Cam Lok	20-A Bates
CD80 Pack 6 6 kW	—	Electronic	120-V AC	6 50 A	300 A, 100 A × 3 300 A, 150 A × 2	Three-phase Single-phase	Cam Lok	60-A Bates
CD80 Pack 6 12 kW	—	Electronic	120-V AC	6 100 A	600 A, 200 A × 3	Three-phase only	Cam Lok	100-A Bates
CD80 Rolling Rack 48 2.4 kW	—	Electronic	120-V AC	48 20 A	960 A, 160 A × 6 960 A, 320 A × 3	Three-phase Three-phase	2 sets Cam-Lok or 1 set Posi-Lok or 1 set Abbott	20-A Bates or Socapex
CD80 Rolling Rack 24 6 kW	—	Electronic	120-V AC	48 20 A	1200 A, 200 A × 6 1200 A, 400 A × 3	Three-phase Three-phase	2 sets Cam-Lok or 1 set Posi-Lok or 1 set Abbott	60-A Bates
CD80 Rolling Rack 24 12 kW	—	Electronic	120-V AC	48 20 A	2400 A, 200 A × 12 2400 A, 400 A × 6 2400 A, 400 A × 6	Three-phase Three-phase Three-phase	4 sets Cam-Lok or 2 sets Posi-Lok or 2 sets Abbott	100-A Bates

Table G.3 Dimmers (continued)

Dimmer	Model No.	Type	Ouput Voltage	Amps per Chnl.	Total Amps	Input Power	Input Connector	Output Connector
Standard Variacs								
1k Variac		Auto-transformer	0–140-V AC	8.3 A	8.3 A	120-V AC	Edison	Edison
2k Variac		Auto-transformer	0–140-V AC	16.6 A	16.6 A	120-V AC	Edison	Edison
5k Variac		Auto-transformer	0–140-V AC	41.5 A	41.5 A	120-V AC	60-A Bates	60-A Bates
Household Dimmers								
150-W Socket Dimmer		Small Triac	120-V AC	1.25 A	1.24 A	120-V AC	Med screw-base socket	Med screw-base socket
600-W Household		Small Triac	120-V AC	5.0 A	5.0 A	120-V AC	Edison	Edison
1000-W Household		Small Triac	120-V AC	8.3 A	8.3 A	120-V AC	Edison	Edison
Magic Gadgets								
Low Volt DC Dimmer		Transistor	0–24-V DC	10 A	10 A @ 12 or 24-V DC	24-V DC	Screw terminals	Screw terminals
2k In-line Dimmer (w/flicker box input)		Triac	120-V AC	16.6 A	16.6 A	120-V AC	Edison	Edison
5k In-line Dimmer (w/flicker box input)		Dual SCR	120-V AC	41.6 A	41.6 A	120-V AC	60-A Bates	60-A Bates
10k In-line Dimmer (w/flicker box input)		Duel SCR	120-V AC	83.3 A	83.3 A	120-V AC	100-A Bates	100-A Bates
20k In-line Dimmer (w/flicker box input)		Duel SCR	220/240-V AC	83.3 A @ 240 V	83.3 A per leg	220 or 240-V AC	100-A, 240-V Bates	100-A, 240-V Bates

All units are also available for foreign voltage.

Table G.4 Flicker Boxes

Device	Channels	Amps per Chnl.	Input Volts	Controls	Functions
Magic Gadgets—William A. McIntire Enterprises					
Shadowmaker	3-channel	16.6 A	120-V AC	3 high limit pots 3 low limit pots 1 speed pot 4 function switches Manual on/off buttons	Manual dimmers, Full on (test), All blink 5 chase sequences 2 lightning flashes 3 TV screen effects 2 candlelight, 2 firelight
Shadowmaker Programmable	3-channel	16.6 A	120-V AC	As above	User programmable from Mac or PC
Flicker 2k	1-channel	16.6	120-V AC	1 speed pot	Manual dimmer or
Dimmers 5k		41.6	120-V AC	1 high limit pot	Flickers at random to levels
10k		83.3	120-V AC	1 low limit pot	between high and low settings.
20k		83.3	240-V AC	1 dim/off/flicker	
Flicker Dimmer Progammable	1-channel	As above	As above	As above	User progammable from Mac or PC
Flicker 2D 2k	1-channel	16.6 A	120-V AC	1 high limit pot	4 TV/film, 6 firelight
5k		41.6 A	120-V AC	1 low limit pot	2 lightning, 2 pulsating
10k		83.3 A	120-V AC	1 speed pot	1 blink, Full on (test) or
20k		83.3 A	240-V AC	4 function switches Manual on/off buttons	Manual dimmer
Flicker 3D	3-channel	Drives any number of 20-A, 50-A, and 100-A Magic Gadgets dimmers (Table G.3)	120-V AC	1 speed pot 4 function switches Manual on/off buttons	Full on (test) Blink 5 chase sequences 2 lightning flashes 3 TV screen effects 2 candlelight 2 firelight
Flicker DC	1-channel	10 A	0–24-V DC	Same as 2D above	Same as 2D above
21D Sequencer	21-channel	Drives any number of 20-, 50-, & 100-A Magic Gadgets dimmers (Table G.3)	120-V AC	1 speed pot 5 function switches Manual on/off buttons	Full on (test) Blink 5 chase sequences 2 lightning flashes 3 TV screen effects 2 candlelight 2 firelight

Table G.4 Flicker Boxes (continued)

Device	Channels	Amps per Chnl	Input Volts	Controls	Functions
Flicker Torch	1-channel	Battery-powered three 9-V	27-V DC	on/off dimmer	Small flickering bulb for use in prop torch or lantern.
Lightning Stepper	3 inputs 9 outputs	Drives photo strobe packs	120-V AC	None	None
Great American Market					
Flickermaster	1-channel	8.3 A	120-V AC 9-V battery	1 speed pot 1 dimmer pot 1 4-position selector (off, test, 0–100, 10–100)	Random flicker, Manual dimmer
SPE-5 Flickermaster	1-channel	16.6 A	120-V AC	1 speed pot 1 threshold pot 1 dimmer pot 1 4-position selector (off, test, 0–100, V-100) Flicker/Strobe Switch	Strobe Random flicker Manual dimmer
SPE-X3 Flickermaster	3-channel	16.6 A	120-V AC	3 channel on/off 3 dimmer pots 3 delay pots 1 master speed pot 1 master dimmer Selector knob A/B toggle Memory set button 1 reverse/forward 1 chase/dark chase	Off, test, chase, random flicker, independent flicker, strobe, and 16 memory positions (recalls previous delay, dimmer, and speed settings), manual dimmers. Retains memory settings between uses.

Internet Resources and Equipment Manufacturers

Abbott and Co., 1611 Cascada Dr., Marion, OH 43302. Electrical connectors.

Aerial Brilliance, Helium balloon lights.

Contact Industrial Wholesale Electric Co., 1500 S. Griffith Ave., Los Angeles, CA 90021. Airstar, Lenix helium balloon lights. http://www.airstar-light.com

Altman Stage Lighting Company, Inc., 57 Alexander St., Yonkers, NY 10701. Tungsten and HMI fixtures, ellipsoidal and theatrical fixtures. http://www.altmanltg.com

American Grip Inc., 8468 Kewen, Sun Valley, CA 91352. Studio and grip equipment. http://www. americangrip.com

Arri, 500 Route 303, Blauvelt, NY 10913, 600 N. Victory Blvd., Burbank, CA 91502. Tungsten and HMI lights. http://www.arri.com

Automated Entertainment, P.O. Box 7309, Burbank, CA 91510-7309. Range of dichroic filters, black-lights, fully stocked theatrical rental house. http://www. automatedhd.com

Backstage Studio Equipment, 8052 Lankershim Blvd., North Hollywood, CA 91605. Studio equipment. http://www.backstageweb.com

Benjamin Electric Co., 1615 Staunton Ave., Los Angeles, CA 90021. Distribution boxes, deuce boards, studio distribution equipment. http://www.benjaminelectric.com

Cam-Lok, 6142 Highway 19, Zacahary, LA 70791. Electrical connectors. http://www.camlok.com

Carol Cable Co., Inc., 249 Roosevelt Ave., Pawtucket, RI 02862. Cable.

Chimera Photographic Lighting, 1812 Valtec La., Boulder, CO 80301. Soft boxes. http://www. chimeralighting.com

Cinemills Corp., 2021 Lincoln St., Burbank, CA 91504. HMI bulbs and lights, gel. http://www. cinemills.com

Clairmont Camera, 4343 Lankershim Blvd., North Hollywood, CA 91602. Synchronous strobe system, camera rental. http://www.clairmont.com

Colortran Inc., 1015 Chestnut St., Burbank, CA 91506-9983. Ellipsoidal and theatrical fixtures. http://www.nsicorp.com/proddir1.htm

Dadco LLC, Portable Power Distribution Systems, Sun Valley, CA. http://www.dadco-llc.com

Dedotec USA Inc., 216 Little Falls Rd., Cedar Grove, NJ. Tungsten lights. http://www.dedolight.com

Desisti, Desmar Corp., 1109 Grand Ave., North Bergen, NJ 07047. Tungsten and HMI lights. http://www.desisti.it

Di-Lite (Koto Luminous Corp.), Fujita Estate Building, 5th Floor, 4–8 Ueno 1-Chrome, Taito-ku, Tokyo, Japan 110. HMI bulbs.

DN Labs, 1430 Willamette St., Suite 18, Eugene, OR 97401. HMI lights. http://www.dnlabs.com

Electronic Theatre Controls (ETC), 3030 Laura Ln., Middleton, WI 53562. Dimmer systems, ellipsoidal and par fixtures. http://www.etcconnect.com/default.asp

ExCel Wire and Cable Co., 108 Elm Ave., Tiffin, OH 44883. Cable.

Filmtools, 1930 W. Olive Ave., Burbank, CA 91506. http://www.filmtools.com

Fisher Lights, 5528 Vineland Ave., North Hollywood, CA 91601. Large soft boxes for car photography, soft light crane light. http://www.fisherlight.com

John Fluke Mfg. Co., Inc., P.O. Box 777, Everett, WA 98206. Electrical meters. http://www.flukenetworks.com

General Electric, Nela Park, E. Cleveland, OH 44112. Tungsten and HMI bulbs. http://www.gelighting.com

Genie USA, 18340 N.E. 76th St., P.O. Box 69, Redmond, WA 98073-0069. Man lift. http://www.genielift.com/index.html

Giddings Pace, Inc., 10741 Sherman Way, Suite #1, Sun Valley, CA 91352. Underwater HMI lights. http://www.pacetech.com

Great American Market, 826 N. Cole Ave., Hollywood, CA 90038. Stick-up lights, flicker boxes, GAM gels, color changers. http://www.gamonline.com

Group 5 Engineering (Advanced Devices), 11620 Exposition Blvd., Los Angeles, CA 90064. Bates connectors. http://www.stagepin.com/index.htm

High End Systems, 2217 West Braker Lane, Austin, TX 78758. Automated lights. http://www.highend.com

Hydro Image, Inc., 4121 Redwood Ave., Los Angeles, CA 90066. Sea Par underwater lights and cameras.

HydroFlex, Inc., 5335 McConnell Ave., Los Angeles, CA 90066. Underwater lights. http://www.hydroflex.com

ILC Technology Inc., 399 Java Dr., Sunnyvale, CA 94089. HMI bulbs.

Innovision Optics, 1719 21st St., Santa Monica, CA 90404. Fiber Optics lighting systems. http://www.innovision-optics.co

K 5600, 10434 Burbank Blvd., North Hollywood, CA 91601. HMI Joker fixtures and 200 W Bug light and 200 W inverter. http://www.k5600.com

K-tec Corporations, 7224 Winterwood Ln., Dallas, TX 75248. Shock block. http://www.ktec.org

Kino Flo, Inc., 10848 Cantara St., Sun Valley, CA 91352. Fluorescent lights. http://www.kinoflo.com

Lee Colortran, Inc., 1015 Chestnut St., Burbank, CA 91506, 40B Commerce Way, Totowa, NJ 07512. Lighting fixtures, Lee filters, color changers, studio distribution equipment.

Leelium Balloons Ltd., 12A Belvue Business Centre, Northolt, London UB5 5QQ England. Helium balloons. http://www.leeliumballoons.com

Leonetti (Sunray), 10601 Glenoaks Blvd., Pacoima, CA 91331. HMI and fluorescent fixtures. http://www.leonetticompany.com

Lightmaker, 28145 Crocker Ave., Valencia, CA 91355. AC/DC and AC lightweight flicker-free ballasts.

Lightning Strikes, 6601 Santa Monica Blvd., Hollywood, CA 90038. Lightning effects lights. www.lightningstrikes.com

Lowel-Light Manufacturing, Inc., 140 58th St., Brooklyn, NY 11220. Tungsten fixtures. http://www.lowel.com

L.P. Associates, 6650 Lexington Ave., Hollywood, CA 90038. DCI lights and globes.

LTM Corp. of America, 11646 Pendleton St., Sun Valley, CA 91352-2501. Tungsten and HMI fixtures. http://www.ltmlighting.com/products.html

Magic Gadgets/William A. McIntire Enterprises, P.O. Box 4244, Portland, OR 97208. Dimmers, flicker effects boxes, various gadgets. http://www.magicgadgets.com

Matthews Studio Equipment, Inc., 2405 Empire Ave., Burbank, CA 91504. Studio equipment. http://www.matthewsgrip.com

Meltric Corp., 4640 Ironwood Dr., Franklin, WI 53132. Electrical connectors. http://www.meltric.com

Minolta, 11150 Hope St., Cypress, CA 90630. Light meters. http://www.minoltausa.com

Mole-Richardson Co., 937 N. Sycamore Ave., Hollywood, CA 90038-2384. Tungsten and HMI fixtures, studio equipment, distribution equipment, carbon arc lights. http://www.mole.com

Musco Mobile Lighting, Ltd., 100 1st Ave. West, P.O. Box 808, Oskaloosa, IA 52577. Mobile lighting trucks. http://www.musco.com

Norms, 5219 Craner Ave., North Hollywood, CA 91601. Studio equipment.

Osram Corp., 110 Bracken Rd., Montgomery, NY 12549-9700, 7658 Haskell Ave., Van Nuys, CA 91406. HMI bulbs.

Peterson Systems International, P.O. Box 1557, Duarte, CA 91009. Cable crossovers. http://www.petersonsystems.com

Phillips Lighting Co., P.O. Box 6800, Somerset, NJ 08875-6800. Bulbs. http://www.lighting.philips.com

Phoebus Manufacturing, 2800 Third Street, San Francisco, CA 94107. Xenon follow spots and search-lights, electronic shutters, xenon projector and other specialty items. http://www.phoebus.com

Power Gems Corporation, 7034 Sophia Ave., Van Nuys, CA 91406. Electronic HMI ballasts. http://www.powergems.net

Rosco Laboratories, Inc., 1120 North Citrus, Hollywood, CA 90038. Gels. http://www.rosco.com

Royal Electric, Inc., 3233 Hunting Park Ave., Philadelphia, PA 19132. Cable. http://www.royalelectric.com

Sachtler, 55 N. Main St., Freeport, NY 11520. Tungsten and HMI fixtures. http://www.sachtler.com

Shotmaker, 10909 Vanowen St., North Hollywood, CA 91605. Custom tow vehicles. http://www.shotmaker.com

Snorkelift, P.O. Box 4065, St. Joseph, MO 64504-4065. Telescoping boom platforms.

SpectraCine, Inc., 820 N. Hollywood Way, Burbank, CA 91505. Light meters. http://www.spectracine.com

Strand Lighting, Inc., 6603 Darin Way, Cypress, CA 90630. Tungsten and HMI fixtures, ellipsoidal and theatrical fixtures, dimmer packs. http://www.strandlight.com

Strong International, Inc., 4350 McKinley St., Omaha, NE 68112. Xenon, HMI, and tungsten follow spots. http://www.strong-cinema.com

Studio Lighting, Inc., 13831 Herrick Ave., Sylmar, CA 91342. Space lights.

Sylvania, 100 Endicott Street, Danvers, MA 01923. Tungsten and HMI bulbs. http://www.sylvania.com

Teatronics, P.O. Box 508, Santa Margarita, CA 93453. Dimmers. http://www. teatronics.com

Ultra Light Manufacturing Co., 1816 Industrial Rd., Las Vegas, NV 89102. Tungsten lights and grip equipment. http://www.ultralightmfgco.com

Unilux, Inc., 59 N. 5th Street, Saddle Brook, NJ 07663. Strobe lighting system. http://www.unilux.com

Union Connector, 300 Babylon Tpk., Roosevelt, NY 11575. Distribution boxes, electrical connectors. http://www.esta.org/homepages/unionconnector/

Ushio America, Inc., 5440 Cerritos Ave., Cypress, CA 90630. Tungsten bulbs. http://www.ushio.com

VEAM (a division of Litton Systems, Inc.), 100 New Wood Rd., Watertown, CT 06795. Electrical connectors. http://www.littonveam.com

Wildfire Inc., 5200 West 83rd St., Los Angeles, CA 90045. Ultraviolet light technology. Black light fresnel and theatrical fixtures, paints and accessories. http:// www.wildfirefx.com

Wolfram, 30 Janis Way, Scotts Valley, CA 95066. HMI bulbs.

Xenotech, Inc., 7348 Bellaire Ave., North Hollywood, CA 91605. Xenon lights. http://www.xenotechusa.com

Woody Light, Inc., Keith Morgan, Granada Hills, CA. http://www.woodylight.com

Young Generators, Inc., 2442-A Willow Road, Arroyo Grande, CA 93420. Generators. http://www.gepower.com

Internet Directories

http://www.stagelighting.com/index.html
http://www.1000bulbs.com/
http://www.usfilmproduction.com/CA/Regions/Los_Angeles/LACompanies/ lighting_equip.htm
http://www.nsicorp.com/
http://www.mts.net/~william5/links2.htm
http://www.armadillo.uk.com/home.htm
http://www.lighting-inc.com/searchman.html
Gaffer's/Electrician's reference Library www.lightingtech.net

Power and Television Systems Throughout the World

Country	Language	Television Standard	Line Voltage	Line Frequency
Afghanistan	Pashtu/Persian	PAL	220/380	50
Algeria	Arabic/French	PAL	220/380	50
Angola	French/Portuguese	PAL	220/380	50
Antigua and Barbuda	English	NTSC	230	60
Argentina	Spanish/Castellano	PAL	220/380	50
Australia	English	PAL	240/415	50
Austria	German	PAL	220/380	50
Bahamas	English	NTSC	120/240	60
Bahrain	Arabic/English	PAL	230/400	50/60
Bangladesh	Bengali	PAL	230/400	50
Barbados	English	NTSC	115/200/230	50
Belgium	Dutch/French	PAL	220/380	50
Benin	French	PAL	220	50
Bermuda	English	NTSC	115/230	60
Bolivia	Spanish	NTSC	220/380	50
Botswana	English/Sitswana	PAL	220/380	50
Brazil	Portuguese	PAL	127/220	60
Brunei	Malay/English	PAL	230	50
Bulgaria	Bulgarian	SECAM	220/380	50
Burma	Burmese	NTSC	220/240	50
Burundi	French	Mono	220	50
Cameroon	English/French	PAL	220/380	50
Canada	English/French	NTSC	120/240	60
Canary Islands	Spanish	PAL	127/220	50
Central African Rep.	French/Sango	Mono	220/380	50
Chile	Spanish Castellano	NTSC	220/380	50
China	Chinese, regional	PAL	220/380	50
Colombia	Spanish	NTSC	110/220	60
Congo	French	SECAM	220/380	50
Costa Rica	Spanish	NTSC	120/240	60
Cuba	Spanish	NTSC	115/120	60
Curacao and Aruba	Dutch	NTSC	127/220	50
Cyprus	Greek/Turkish/English	PAL	240/415	50
Czechoslovakia	English/Czechoslovak	SECAM	220/380	50
Denmark	Danish	PAL	220/380	50
Djibouti	French/Arabic	SECAM	220	50
Dominican Rep.	Spanish	NTSC	110/220	60
Ecuador	Spanish	NTSC	110/120/127	60
Egypt	Arabic/English	SECAM	220/380	50
El Salvador	Spanish/English	NTSC	115/230	60
Ethiopia	Amharic/English	Mono	220/380	50

Country	Language	Television Standard	Line Voltage	Line Frequency
Fiji	—	—	220/415	50
Finland	Finnish	PAL	220/380	50
France	French	SECAM	220/380	50
Gabon	French/Fang	SECAM	230	50
Gambia	English	Mono	230	50
Germany	German	PAL/SECAM	220/380	50
Ghana	English/Acan	PAL	220/400	50
Gibraltar	English	PAL	240/415	50
Greece	Greek	SECAM	220/380	50
Greenland	—	—	220/380	50
Grenada	English	NTSC	230	50
Guadeloupe	French	SECAM	220	50/60
Guatemala	Spanish	NTSC	120/240	60
Guinea Rep.	French	SECAM	220/380	50
Haiti	French/Creole	SECAM	115/220/230	60
Honduras	Spanish	NTSC	110/220	60
Hong Kong	Cantonese/English	PAL	200/346	50
Hungary	Hungarian	SECAM	220/380	50
Iceland	Icelandic	PAL	220/380	50
India	Hindi/Urdu	PAL	230/400	50
Indonesia	Indonesian	PAL	127/220	50
Iran	Farsi/Kurdish/Arabic	PAL/SECAM	220/380	50
Iraq	Arabic/Kurdish	SECAM	220/380	50
Ireland	English	PAL	220/380	50
Israel	Hebrew/Yiddish/Arabic	PAL	230/400	50
Italy	Italian	PAL	220/380	50
Ivory Coast	French	SECAM	220	50
Jamaica	English/Spanish	NTSC	110/220	50
Japan	Japanese	NTSC	100/200/210	50/60
Jordan	Arabic/English	PAL	220	50
Kampuchea	—	—	120/208	50
Kenya	English/Swahili	PAL	240/415	50
Korea (N)	Korean	SECAM/NTSC	220	60
Korea (S)	Korean	NTSC	100/200	60
Kuwait	Arabic/English	PAL	240/415	50
Laos	Lao	PAL	220/380	50
Lebanon	Arabic/French	SECAM	110/190	50
Lesotho	English	Mono	220	50
Liberia	English	PAL	120/240	60
Libya	Arabic/Italian/English	PAL	127/220	50
Luxembourg	French	PAL/SECAM	220/380	50
Macau	Portuguese/Cantonese/ English	PAL	110/220	50
Madagascar	Malagsy/French	PAL	127/220	50
Madeira	Portuguese	PAL	220	50
Malaysia	Malay	PAL	240/415	50
Mali	French	Mono	127/220	50
Malta	English	PAL	240/415	50
Mauretania	Hassaniya Arabic/French	SECAM	230	50
Mauritius	English/Creole	SECAM	230	50
Mexico	Spanish	NTSC	120/127/220	60
Mongolia	Mongol	SECAM	127/220	50
Morocco	Arabic/French	SECAM	115/127/220	50
Mozambique	Portuguese	PAL	220/380	50
Nepal	Nepali	PAL	230/380	50
Netherlands	Dutch	PAL	220/380	50
New Zealand	English	PAL	230/400	50

Country	Language	Television Standard	Line Voltage	Line Frequency
Nicaragua	Spanish	NTSC	120/240	60
Niger	French	Mono	220/380	50
Nigeria	English	PAL	230/415	50
Norway	Norwegian	PAL	230	50
Oman	Arabic/English	PAL	220/440	50
Pakistan	Urdu/English/Punjabi	PAL	230/400	50
Panama	Spanish/English	NTSC	120/240	60
Papua New Guinea	English	PAL	240	50
Paraguay	Spanish	PAL	220	50
Peru	Spanish	NTSC	110/220	60
Philippines	Filipino	NTSC	120/220/240	60
Poland	Polish	SECAM	220/380	50
Portugal	Portuguese	PAL	220/380	50
Puerto Rico	Spanish	NTSC	120/240	60
Qatar	Arabic/Farsi	PAL	240	50
Reunion	French	SECAM	220	50
Romania	Romanian	SECAM	220/380	50
Russia	Russian	SECAM	127/220	50
Saudi Arabia	Arabic	SECAM	127/220	50
Senegal	French	SECAM	110/220	50
Seychelles	English/French	Mono	230	50
Sierra Leone	English	PAL	220/440	50
Singapore	Mandarin/English	PAL	230	50
Somalia	Arabic/Italian/English	Mono	220/440	50
South Africa	English/Afrikaans	PAL	220/380	50
Spain	Spanish	PAL	220/380	50
Sri Lanka	English/Sinhala/Tamil	PAL	230/400	50
St Vincent	English	NTSC	230	50
Sudan	Arabic	PAL	240/415	50
Suriname	Dutch/English	NTSC	115/230	50/60
Swaziland	English	PAL	230/380	50
Sweden	Swedish	PAL	220/380	50
Switzerland	French/German/Italian	PAL	220/380	50
Syria	Arabic/Kurdish	SECAM	115/220	50
Taiwan	Mandarin	NTSC	110/220	60
Tanzania	Swahili/English	PAL	230/400	50
Thailand	English/Thai	PAL	220/380	50
Togo	French	SECAM	220/380	50
Trinidad and Tobago	English	NTSC	115/230	60
Tunisia	Arabic/French	SECAM	220/380	50
Turkey	Turkish	PAL	220/380	50
Uganda	English	PAL	240/415	50
United Arab Emirates	Arabic/Farsi	PAL	220/240	50
United Kingdom	English	PAL	240/415	50
Upper Volta	—	—	220/380	50
Uruguay	Spanish	PAL	220	50
USA	English	NTSC	120/208/240	60
Venezuela	Spanish	NTSC	120/208/240	60
Vietnam	Vietnamese	SECAM	220/380	60
Virgin Islands	English	NTSC	110/220	60
Yemen Arab Rep.	Arabic	PAL	220	50
Yemen Dem. Rep.	Arabic	NTSC	250	50
Yugoslavia	Croatian	PAL	220	50
Zaire	French/English	SECAM	220/380	50
Zambia	English	PAL	230	50
Zimbabwe	English	PAL	220/380	50

Lighting Equipment Order Checklist

HMI Fresnels

To include barn doors, five-piece scrim set, gel frame, scrim box, magnetic ballast, two 50-ft head cables, ballast feeder cable

____ 18k Fresnel
____ 12k Fresnel
____ 6k Fresnel
____ 4k Fresnel
____ 2500 Fresnel
____ 1200 Fresnel
____ 575 Fresnel
____ 200 Fresnel
____ Electronic ballasts
____ 12k Clear glass lens

HMI PARs

To include barn doors, three-piece scrim set, gel frame, scrim box, four- or five-piece lens set, magnetic ballast, two 50-ft head cables, ballast feeder

____ 6k PAR
____ 4k PAR
____ 2500-W PAR
____ 1200-W PAR
____ 575-W PAR
____ 400-W Joker
____ 200-W PAR
____ Electronic ballasts

Sun Guns

____ Sun Gun
____ 30-V Nicad Belt-Battery
____ AC Power Supply

HMI Soft Lights

To include egg crate, magnetic ballast, two 50-ft head cables, ballast feeder

____ 6000 Soft
____ 2500 Soft
____ 1200 Soft
____ 575 Soft
____ Electronic ballasts

Tungsten Fresnels

To include five-piece scrim set, gel frame, scrim box or bag, four-leaf barn doors, power feeder

____ 20k Fresnel w/ramp-up dimmer
____ 10k Studio Fresnel
____ 10k Big Eye Fresnel
____ 10k Baby Tenner
____ 5k Studio Fresnel
____ 5k Baby Senior
____ 2k 8" Junior Fresnel
____ 2k Baby Junior Fresnel
____ 2k Studio Junior Fresnel
____ 1k Studio Fresnel (407)
____ 1k Baby Baby Fresnel
____ 650-W Fresnel
____ 420 Pepper
____ 300 Pepper
____ 200 Pepper
____ 200-W Midget/Tiny/Mini
____ 100-W Pepper

Dedos

____ 150-W Dedo Kit
____ 100-W Dedo Kit
____ 250-W Dedo Cool Kit

Fresnel Accessories

____ Snoots
____ Focal Spots
____ Shutters
____ Chimera Banks
____ Chimera Speed Rings

Tungsten Soft Lights

To include egg crate, power feeder

____ 8k Soft Light
____ 4k Softlight
____ 4k Zip Soft
____ 2k Super Soft
____ 2k Zip Soft
____ 1k Zip Soft
____ 750 Zip Soft
____ 400 Soft

Tungsten Open Face
To include five-piece scrim set, gel frame, scrim box or bag, four-leaf barn doors

____ 2k Mighty Mole
____ 2k Blonde
____ 1k Mickey Mole
____ 1k Red Head
____ 650 Open Face
____ 2k Nook
____ 1k Nook
____ 650-W Nook
____ 1k Molette
____ 2k Molette
____ Pinza (Med Screw Base)

Kits

____ R-40 Kit
____ Lowel Tape-up Kit
____ Stick-up Kit

Tungsten PARs

____ 1k Mole PAR (with three-piece scrim set, barn doors)
____ 1k PAR Cans (with gel frame, bail block)
____ Six-light PAR (6 PAR 64s)
____ Maxi-brute (9 PAR 64s)
____ Dino (24 PAR 64s)
____ Ultra Dino (36 PAR 64s)
____ VNSP PAR 64
____ NSP PAR 64
____ MFL PAR 64
____ WFL PAR 64
____ Nine-light FAY
____ Six-light FAY
____ Four-light FAY
____ Two-light FAY
____ One-light FAY
____ PAR 36 Dichroic
____ PAR 36 Tungsten MFL
____ PAR 36 Tungsten WFL

Tungsten Area Lights

____ Sky Pan (10k, 5k, or 2k)
____ Chicken Coop 6k
____ Space Light 6k
____ 2k Scoop Light
____ 1k Scoop Light

Ellipsoidal Spotlights

____ 2k Molipso
____ 1k Molipso
____ 50° 1k 4.5 × 6 equivalent
____ 36° 1k 6 × 9 equivalent
____ 26° 1k 6 × 12 equivalent

____ 19° 1k 6 × 16 equivalent
____ 10° 1k 6 × 22 equivalent
____ 5° 1k 10 × 23 equivalent
____ Edison Pigtails
____ Bail Blocks

Other Theatrical Lights

____ Cyc Strip
____ Follow Spot
____ Beam Projector
____ Scene Machine

Fluorescents

____ Wall-o-light (10 bank)
____ 4-ft Four bank
____ 4-ft Double Bank
____ 4-ft Single
____ 2-ft Four bank
____ 2-ft Double bank
____ 2-ft Single
____ 15-in. Four bank
____ 15-in. Double bank
____ 15-in. Single
____ 8-ft tubes with Slimline Ballast
____ 6-ft tubes with Slimline Ballast
____ 12-V Single 15-in. Kit
____ 12-V Mini Flo 9-in. Kit
____ 12-V Micro Flo 6-in. Kit
____ 12-V Micro Flo 4-in. Kit

Xenons

____ 10k Xenon
____ 7k Xenon
____ 4k Xenon
____ 2k Xenon
____ 1k Xenon
____ 750-W Xenon
____ 500-W Xenon
____ 150-W Xenon
____ 75-W Xenon Flashlight

Stands

____ Cinevator, Crank-o-vator
____ Super Crank
____ Crank-o-vator
____ Low Crank Stand
____ Mombo Combo 4-riser Stand
____ Steel Three-Riser Junior Stand
____ Steel Two-Riser Junior Stand
____ Aluminum Three-Riser Junior
____ Aluminum Two-Riser Junior
____ Junior Rolling Stand Three-riser
____ Junior Rolling Stand Two-riser
____ Low Boy Junior Stand

____ Steel Three-Riser Baby Stand
____ Steel Two-Riser Baby Stand
____ Baby Rolling Stand Three-riser
____ Baby Rolling Stand Two-riser
____ Low Baby Stand
____ Preemie Stand
____ Blade Stand
____ Low Blade Stand
____ Runway Base
____ Turtle Stand
____ T-bone
____ Wheel Set (three piece)

Carts
____ Cable Cart
____ Doorway Dolly
____ Head Cart
____ Milk-Crate cart
____ Work Box

Dimmers
____ Control Console
____ CD80 (6 × 100 A)
____ CD80 (6 × 60 A)
____ CD80 (24 × 20 A)
____ CD80 (24 × 15 A)
____ 20k Stand Alone Dimmer
____ 12k Stand Alone Dimmer
____ 6k Stand Alone Dimmer
____ 5k Variac
____ 2k Variac
____ 1k Variac
____ 5k Plate Dimmer
____ 3k Plate Dimmer
____ 2k Plate Dimmer
____ 1k Plate Dimmer
____ 1k Hand dimmer
____ 650-W Hand Dimmer

Distribution
____ Three-Bar Spider Box
____ Four-Bar Spider Box
____ Five-Bar Spider Box
____ 600-A Bull Switch Three-Phase
____ 400-A Bull Switch Single Phase
____ 200-A Bull Switch Single Phase
____ 900-A Distro Box
____ 600-A Distro Box
____ 400-A Banded Box
____ Lug to Female Adapters
____ Lug to Male Adapters
____ Three-fers (pin)
____ Ground Squid (pin)
____ Female Suicide Pin Adapter

____ Male Suicide Pin Adapter
____ Cam-Loc T-splitter
____ Lug to Cam-Loc Jumper
____ Two-wire Pin to 100-A 240-V Bates Adapter
____ Two-wire Pin to 100-A Bates Adapter
____ Three-wire Pin to Two 100-A Bates Adapter
____ 100-A to Two 100-A Bates Adapter
____ 100-A to Two 60-A Bates Adapter
____ 60-A to Two 60-A Bates Adapter
____ 100-A Lunch Box (five duplex Edison outlets with circuit beakers)
____ 100-A Gang Box (five 20-A fused Edison)
____ 60-A Gang Box
____ In-line Hertz Meter
____ Flicker Box
____ Cable Crossovers
____ Tie-in Clamps

Cable
____ 4/0 100-ft
____ 4/0 50-ft
____ 4/0 25-ft
____ 4/0 Jumper
____ 2/0 100-ft
____ 2/0 50-ft
____ 2/0 25-ft
____ 2/0 Jumper
____ 50-ft #2 Grounding Cable
____ 50-ft #2 Banded (three-wire plus ground)
____ 50-ft #2 Banded (four-wire plus ground, three-phase)
____ Banded Jumper 10-ft
____ 100-A 100-ft Bates Extension
____ 100-A 50-ft Bates Extension
____ 100-A 25-ft Bates Extension
____ 60-A 100-ft Bates Extension
____ 60-A 50-ft Bates Extension
____ 60-A 25-ft Bates Extension
____ 50-ft Stinger
____ 25-ft Stinger
____ Socapex 150-ft (six 20-A dimmer circuits)
____ Socapex 100-ft
____ Socapex 50-ft
____ Socapex Break-out
____ Socapex Break-in

Generator
____ 46-A EX 5500 Honda
____ 350-A
____ 450-A
____ 750-A
____ 1000-A
____ 1200-A
____ 1400-A

Expendables Checklist

Gel and Diffusion

Orange

____ roll Extra CTO
____ roll full CTO
____ roll Sun 85
____ roll ³/₄ CTO
____ roll half CTO
____ roll quarter CTO
____ roll eighth CTO
____ roll full Straw
____ roll half Straw
____ roll quarter Straw
____ roll eighth Straw

Blue

____ roll Extra CTB
____ roll full CTB
____ roll ³/₄ CTB
____ roll half CTB
____ roll quarter CTB
____ roll eighth CTB

Magenta

____ roll full minus-green
____ roll half minus-green
____ roll quarter minus-green
____ roll eighth minus-green

Green

____ roll full plus-green
____ roll half plus-green
____ roll quarter plus-green
____ roll eighth plus-green

Neutral Density and ND CTO

____ ND 0.3
____ ND 0.6
____ ND 0.9
____ ND 1.2
____ 85 ND 0.3
____ 85 ND 0.6
____ 85 ND 0.9

Diffusion

____ roll 216
____ roll 250
____ roll 251

____ roll opal
____ roll grid cloth
____ roll light grid
____ 1000H Velum

Other Gels

____ Other color correction (e.g., CID, SCI, Y1, Fluorofilter)
____ Heat shield
____ Cosmetic colors
____ Party colors
____ Party gel sheets

Bulbs

3200 K

____ PH 211 75 W (100 hrs)
____ PH 212 150 W (100 hrs)
____ ECA 500 W (60 hrs)
____ MR-16 75 W narrow spot
____ MR-16 100 W narrow spot
____ ECA 250 W (20 hrs)

3400 K

____ PH 213 (250 W) (3 hrs)
____ No. 1 BBA 250 W (3 hrs)
____ No. 2 EBV 500 W (6 hrs)

4800 K

____ 60 W (blue)
____ 100 W (blue)
____ No 1 BCA 250 W (3 hrs)
____ EBW 500 W (6 hrs)

Other Bulbs

____ 75-W R-40 flood
____ 150-W R-40 flood
____ 300-W R-40 flood
____ EAL 500-W R-40 flood (3200 K)
____ 25-W Softwhite household
____ 40-W Softwhite household
____ 60-W Softwhite household
____ 75-W Softwhite household
____ 100-W Softwhite household
____ 12" 35-W 1613 Linestra (Osram)
____ 20" 60-W 1614 Linestra (Osram)
____ 40" 150-W 1106 Linestra (Osram)

____ Socket 661 Linestra (Osram)
____ 60-W or 100-W blue
____ 60-W or 100-W red
____ 60-W or 100-W green
____ 60-W or 100-W clear
____ 40-W candella base makeup table bulbs

Fluorescents
____ 4-ft Optima 32
____ 4-ft Vita-lite
____ 8-ft Optima 32
____ 8-ft Vita-lite

Tape
____ 2" gaffers tape (gray)
____ 2" gaffers tape (black)
____ 2" gaffers tape (white)
____ Black 2" paper tape
____ Photo black 2" paper tape (matte black)
____ White 1" camera tape
____ Electrical tape (Bk, Bl, Rd, Gr, Wt)
____ $^1/_2$" snot tape
____ $^3/_4$" snot tape

Hardware
____ Bags clothespins
____ Trick line (black) #4
____ Mason line (white) #4
____ Hanks sash cord #6
____ Hank sash cord #8
____ Hank sash cord #10
____ Box large garbage bags
____ 12" rolls blackwrap
____ 24" rolls blackwrap
____ 36" rolls blackwrap
____ Bottle pure isopropyl alcohol
____ Clean lint-free rags
____ Roll bailing wire
____ Box cotter pins
____ Box Sharpie markers
____ Box pens

____ Rubber matting (by the ft)
____ Roll Visqueen
____ Refracil (by the yard)
____ Crutch tips $1^1/_4$"
____ Crutch tips $^3/_4$"
____ Bungy cords (36", 24", 18", 12")
____ S-hooks

Electrical
____ Box 20 A cartridge fuses
____ Box 60 A fuses
____ AA batteries
____ 6 V meter batteries
____ A 76 meter batteries
____ 9 V batteries
____ Spare Mag light bulbs
____ Cube taps (w/ground)
____ Ground lifters
____ Roll zip cord (18/2) 250' black
____ Roll zip cord (18/2) 250' white
____ Roll red/black #12 wire (twisted pair)
____ Roll red/black #14 wire (twisted pair)
____ Porcelain sockets (med. screw base)
____ In-line taps female Edison
____ Add-a-tap male Edison
____ Add-a-tap female Edison
____ Plug-in switch (Edison in/out)
____ Hubble female Edison
____ Hubble male Edison
____ Box wire nuts
____ In-line dimmers 1000 W
____ In-line dimmers 600 W
____ Socket dimmers (screw base)
____ Medium screw base extension
____ 6" swivel screw base extension
____ 9" swivel screw base extension
____ Pig nose adapters (screw base to Edison)
____ Mogul to medium screw base adapters
____ Medium to candella screw base adapter
____ Candella to medium base adapter

Glossary*

A Ampere.

Abbott A manufacturer of single-conductor connectors used on feeder cable.

Abby Singer The second to last shot of the day. The shot before the *martini*.

above-the-line costs Production costs of the producer, director, writer, and principal actors.

AC (1) Alternating current. (2) Camera assistant.

ace A 1k Fresnel light.

AD *See* assistant director.

adapter A device used to convert from one type of connector to another.

ammeter A meter for measuring amperage.

ampacity Amperage capacity of cable, connectors, etc.

amperage (I) A unit of current. One ampere will flow through a resistance of 1 ohm under a pressure of 1volt.

ampere-hour A quantity of electricity equal to the number of amperes times the number of hours of charge that a battery can deliver.

AMPTP Association of Motion Picture and Television Producers.

anode A negative electrode.

ANSI American National Standards Institute. Three-letter ANSI codes are used to identify light bulbs (e.g., EGT is a 1k bulb).

apple box A reinforced plywood box used on the set for many purposes, including to raise an actor who is too short or to raise furniture. Apple boxes come in four sizes: full, half, quarter, and pancake.

arc light Any light that makes light by forming an arc, including arc discharge lights such as HMIs. On the set, *arc light* is normally understood to mean a carbon arc light.

ASA (1) American Standards Association (now the ANSI). (2) The exposure index (EI) rating of a film emulsion, also referred to as ISO.

aspect ratio The ratio of the width to the height of the film frame. The standard aspect ratios are 1.33:1 (television), 1.66:1 (high-definition television and European theatrical film standard), 1.85:1 (American theatrical film standard), and 2.36:1 (Anamorphic 35 mm).

assistant director (AD) The person who runs the set. The AD is responsible for coordinating the actions of the many departments so that everyone is ready when the time comes to roll cameras.

AWG American Wire Gauge.

baby A 1k Fresnel lighting fixture manufactured by the Mole-Richardson Co.

baby stand A stand with a ⁵/₈-in. stud.

baby stud A ⁵/₈-in. mounting stud that mates with a ⁵/₈ in. receptacle.

backdrop A scenic painting or enlarged photograph transparency used outside set windows and doors when filming in a studio.

---

*Entries that have an asterisk are taken from *Practical Electrical Wiring* by Herbert P. Richter and W. Creighton Schwann. New York: McGraw-Hill, 1990.

bail   U-shaped part of a lighting fixture that attaches the fixture to the stand.

ballast   A device required to operate any discharge light, such as HMI, fluorescents, and xenon lights. The ballast provides the ignition charge and then acts as a choke, regulating the power to maintain the arc.

banded cable   Several single-conductor cables banded together at intervals, forming one bundle.

barn doors   Metal shields on a ring that mounts to the front of a lighting fixture. Barn doors are used to shape and control the beam of light.

base   (1) The basket on the underside of a fixture. (2) The base of a bulb is the porcelain part. (3) The lamp socket is also sometimes called the *base*.

Bates   A common name for three-pin connectors (20 A, 30 A, 60 A, 100 A, and 100 A/ 220 V).

batten   Usually refers to 1 × 3-in. lumber. May also refer to pipe on which lights, scenery, curtains, blacks, and borders can be hung.

battery belt   A battery pack, usually containing nickel-cadmium batteries, mounted in a leather belt that can be worn around the waist during mobile shooting.

bead board   Styrofoam used to make soft bounce light.

beam angle   The diameter of the beam angle is defined as the area of the light field that is 50% or more of the peak intensity of the beam.

beam projector   A theatrical lighting fixture that provides relatively strong, parallel rays of light.

beaver board   A nail-on plate mounted to a pancake.

below-the-line costs   The production costs of all members of the crew but not the producer, director, writer, and principal actors.

best boy   The assistant chief lighting technician, or second electrician. The best boy is the gaffer's chief assistant.

big eye   A 10k incandescent fixture with an extra large lens (Mole-Richardson).

black wrap   A thick, durable black foil used on hot lights to control spill and to shape the beam.

blackbody radiator   A theoretical incandescent source used in defining the concept of color temperature. The spectral power and color distribution of a blackbody source depend only on temperature.

blonde   An Ianero 2k open-face fixture.

boom operator   The sound person who operates the microphone boom and affixes microphones to the talent.

branch circuit   As defined by the NEC, circuits that are downstream of the last overcurrent protection.

branchaloris   A branch of a tree or bush held in front of a light to create a moving or stationary foliage pattern.

broad   A nonfocusing, wide-angle lighting fixture, typically using a double-ended bulb, installed in a rectangular fixture with a silver reflector.

Brute   A 250-A carbon arc light manufactured by Mole-Richardson, Co.

bull switch   A main switch used on the main feeder or on subfeeder lines.

bump   A feature on a dimmer console—an instantaneous change in stage levels from one set of intensities ("look") to another.

bus bar   Copper bars ($1/4$ in. thick) to which lug connectors are attached.

butterfly set   A frame used to support a net or silk over the top of the action. The silk reduces and softens direct sunlight.

C   Celsius (temperature scale).

C-47   A common, wooden spring-type clothespin.

C-74   A clothespin inverted to be used as a scrim puller.

C-clamp   A large C-shaped clamp with a baby stud or junior receptacle welded to it that is used to mount lights to beams.

C-stand   A multipurpose stand used for setting flags and nets. Short for *Century stand.*

cable crossover   A special rubber ramp used to protect cable from being damaged by being run over and to protect pedestrians from tripping over cable.

call sheet   A sheet distributed by the production department before the end of each day that indicates the scenes to be shot on the following day, the call time of all cast and crew members, special travel instructions, special equipment that will be used, and general notices to the cast and crew.

Cam-Lok   A type of single-conductor connector used for feeder cable.

can   A permanently installed panelboard bus bar in a sound stage.

Candela (cd)   A unit of light intensity derived from brightness and distance. cd = FC $\times$ feet^2 or, in Europe, cd = lux $\times$ meters^2.

carbon arc light   A very bright DC lighting fixture that creates light by igniting an arc flame between two carbon electrodes.

cathode   A positive electrode.

catwalk   A metal or wooden walkway above a sound stage.

CC   *See* color compensation.

CCT   Correlated color temperature.

celo cuke   A wire mesh painted with a random pattern and placed in front of a light to throw a subtle pattern.

chain vice grip   A mounting device that uses a bicycle chain and vice grip to create a tight clamp around pipes, poles, or tree limbs.

channel   Device controlling a dimmer or group of dimmers. In a simple system, there is a slider for each channel. On most current control systems, channels are numbers, accessed by numeric keypad. Multiple dimmers may be controlled by a single channel to which they are *patched.*

chaser lights   A linear string of lights similar to those on a theater marquee. The lamps are wired in three, four, or five circuits; equally spaced lights are connected to the same circuit, which can be sequentially energized, creating the effect of light chasing along the line of lights.

cheater   An Edison plug adaptor that allows three-prong grounded plugs to be plugged into a two-prong ungrounded outlet found in older buildings. Also called a *ground lifter, ground plug adaptor,* or *two-to-three adaptor.*

chiaroscuro   A strongly contrasting treatment of light and shade in drawing and painting. Translated from the Italian, the word means "half-revealed."

chicken coop   An overhead suspended light box that provides general downward ambient or fill light. Also called a *coop.*

chief lighting technician   *See* gaffer.

Chimera   A specially designed, lightweight, collapsible soft box manufactured by Chimera Photographic Lighting.

CID   *See* compact indium discharge.

cinevator stand   A heavy-duty stand used for the largest types of lights. The mechanism that raises and lowers the light is driven by an electric motor.

circuit   When talking about dimmer circuits refers to everything downstream of the dimmer, from the dimmer's output connector to the lighting fixtures themselves.

circuit breaker   An overcurrent protection switch. It trips and disconnects a circuit if the current drawn exceeds the rating of the circuit breaker.

clothesline cable   A cable hanging in the air at a level at which someone could trip on it or run into it. Cable should instead be routed so that it runs along the ground away from traffic areas.

Cmil   Cross-sectional area of cable in circular mil.

color chart   A chart of standard colors filmed at the head of a roll of film as a color reference for the lab.

color compensation (CC)   A reading gained from a color meter indicating the amount of green or magenta gel needed to neutralize off-color hues, usually present in fluorescent lights.

color temperature   A temperature expressed in degrees Kelvin (K) that defines the color makeup of light emitted by a source, such as the sun or a filament lamp, that has a continuous color spectrum.

combo stand   A junior stand with a 1 $1/8$-in. receptacle used to hold reflector boards and larger lights.

compact indium discharge (CID)   A 5500-K gas discharge globe often used in sun guns.

compact source iodine (CSI)   A type of gas discharge bulb similar to an HMI.

Condor   A vehicle with a telescoping boom arm used as a platform to position lights 30 to 120 ft in the air.

continuity   (1) Script continuity (the job of the script supervisor): the task of making sure that all the details of the scene remain consistent from take to take and from angle to angle. Shots may be filmed hours and even weeks apart, but they will be cut back to back in the final film. (2) Electrical continuity: the unbroken flow of electricity through various conductors.

continuity tester   A device that runs a small amount of voltage through a conductor and lights a small bulb or makes a sound if the conductor is continuous.

continuous load   An electrical load that is to be delivered continuously for more than 3 hours.

continuous spectrum   The color makeup of light from a source, such as an incandescent bulb or natural daylight, which includes all the wavelengths of light without spikes or holes anywhere across the spectrum of colors.

contrast ratio   The ratio of the intensity of the key light plus the fill light to the intensity of the fill light alone.

cookie   *See* cucaloris.

cool the lights   To turn the lights off.

crank-up stand   A heavy-duty stand that provides a crank to raise and lower heavy lights.

CRI   Color rendering index.

cribbing   Blocks of wood used to level dolly track.

Croney cone   A cone-shaped attachment fitted with diffusion that fits on the front of a light to soften and control the beam.

cross-fade   A fade that contains both an up-fade and down-fade. Also may refer to any fade where the levels of one cue are replaced by the levels of another cue.

crowder hanger   A fixture mount that fastens to the top of a set wall and provides two studs.

crystal-controlled   A crystal-based circuit that maintains a camera's frame rate very precisely. A wild camera has no crystal control.

CSI   *See* compact source iodine.

CTB gel   A blue gel that corrects a tungsten source to daylight.

CTO gel   An orange gel that corrects a daylight source to tungsten.

cube tap   A device that allows three Edison plugs to plug into one Edison socket.

cucaloris   A wooden cutout pattern placed in front of a light to create a pattern.

cue   The process of recalling a *preset* from its memory location (in a dimmer console) and putting the result on stage.

cue light   A flashing or rotating light positioned outside the set to warn people when the camera is rolling.

cup blocks   Wooden blocks with concave indents. Cup blocks are placed under the wheels of light stands to prevent them from rolling.

current   The rate of flow of electricity measured in amperes.

cutter   A long, thin flag used to make cuts in the light.

cyc strip   A strip of open-face fixtures used to light a cyclorama. The lights are often wired in two, three, or four separate circuits to provide individual control of different colors.

cyclorama   A seamless hanging or set piece, usually white, often curved where it meets the floor. It is used to create a limbo background, having no discernible horizon or texture.

day rate   The wage for a day's work.

daylight   Light commonly considered to have a color temperature of 5500 K to 6000 K. Daylight-balanced film renders colors naturally when lit with 5600-K light.

DC   *See* direct current.

dead-man pedal   A floor pedal that must be pressed by the operator's foot to operate or drive a Snorkelift. The dead-man pedal is a safety device to prevent runaways.

Dedolight   A small, special light fixture with a wide range of beam angle adjustment.

deferred pay   Payment for the crew's work made in lieu of salary when and if the production turns a profit.

delta-connected system   A system that provides four-wire, three-phase and three-wire, single-phase current with 120-V, 208-V, and 240-V current from four wires. The voltage between each leg must be carefully measured to determine which is the high leg (the leg that gives 208 V).

depth of field   The depth of the scene that will be in focus on the screen. Depth of field varies with the camera's aperture, focal length, and distance from the subject and the film format.

deuce   A 2k Fresnel light.

deuce board   A fused AC/DC distribution box having two high-amperage contactors that can be controlled from remote switches.

dichroic filter   A filtering lens used on some tungsten lights to convert tungsten to about 4800 K.

diffusion   Material used in front of lighting fixtures to soften the light they produce.

dike   A dichroic filter lens.

dikes   Wire cutters.

dimmer   The device controlling power to a circuit and lighting fixtures. Two lights on one dimmer circuit cannot be separately controlled.

direct current (DC)   Current that does not alternate polarity. Batteries and DC generators create DC.

director of photography (DP)   The person in charge of the lighting and camera departments. The DP has direct creative control of the image.

discontinuous spectrum   A light source with a discontinuous spectrum, such as a standard fluorescent bulb, that does not emit light evenly across the color spectrum, but instead has spikes at particular wavelengths and emits little or no light at others, resulting in poor color rendering.

distant location   A location that is far enough from the production's town of origin that the crew must stay overnight.

distribution box   An electrical box with circuit protection, used to stepdown cable size and connector size and provide a variety of sizes of outlets for subfeeders, stage extensions, and various sizes of lights.

dog collar   A short length of aircraft cable used to secure lights hung above the set. The collar is fitted with a loop at one end and a leash clip or carabiner at the other.

dolly grip   The grip in charge of laying dolly track and executing dolly moves and crane moves.

doorway dolly   A small, steerable, flatbed dolly with large inflated tires, frequently used to move cable and large lights.

dot   A very small, circular flag, net, or silk used to alter only a small portion of the beam of light.

douser   The mechanism on a follow spot used to make a quick blackout without the operator having to extinguish the light itself. On a carbon arc follow spot, the douser protects the lens while the arc is struck.

down-fade   The portion of a fade that involves only channels that are decreasing in level.

DP   *See* director of photography.

dress a light   To neaten up the light or cable.

duck bill   A vice grip with a baby stud on the handle and two 6-sq in. plates welded to the jaws. Used to mount foamcore and bead board on a C-stand.

dummy load   *See* ghost load.

duvetyn   Thick, black cloth used to block light.

E   Electromotive force, measured in volts.

ears   The metal brackets on the front of a light that hold the barn doors and scrims.

Edison plug and socket   A typical household plug and socket with two parallel blades and a U-shaped grounding pin. Also called a *U-ground parallel-blade plug*.

egg crate   An accessory for a soft light fixture that cuts stray light and narrows the beam angle.

electrician   Common name for a lighting technician.

18% gray   Medium gray used to determine exposure.

electromotive force   Voltage.

electronic ballast   A solid-state ballast. The term *electronic ballast* is synonymous with flicker-free square-wave ballast (HMI) or high frequency (fluorescent).

ellipsoidal reflector spotlight (ERS)   A spotlight of fixed or adjustable focal length that has framing shutters and a projection gobo slot and produces a long, narrow throw of light. Also called a *Leko*.

Elvis   A gold lamé stretched on a frame and used to bounce light.

emulsion   The photochemical substance on a piece of film that captures the image.

equipment grounding   The grounding of non–current-carrying parts of equipment via a green grounding wire.

expendables   Supplies, such as tape, that are used up during the course of a production.

eye light   A light used to create a twinkle of light in the eye of the subject.

F   Fahrenheit (temperature scale).

f-stop   A scale used to set the aperture of the camera.

fade   A gradual change in stage levels from one set of intensities ("look") to another.

fall-off   The diminishing intensity of light from one position to another.

FAR cyc   A lighting fixture that lights a cyclorama.

FAY   An incandescent PAR light with dichroic coating that creates daylight-colored light.

FC   *See* foot-candle.

feeder cable   Large single-conductor cable used to run power from the power source to the set.

field   The area that is at least 10% of the maximum candle power of a beam of light.

field angle   The angle from the light fixture to the opposite edges of the field.

filament   The tungsten coil inside a bulb that glows when voltage is applied to it, creating light.

fill light   Soft light used to reduce the darkness of the shadow areas.

finger   A very small rectangular flag, net, or silk used to make minute cuts of the beam of light.

first team   The director and actors.

fixture   A luminaire, light, lamp, instrument, head, or lantern.

flag   Black duvetyn cloth stretched over a metal frame and used to shape and cut light.

flag box   A wooden box in which flags, nets, and silks are stored.

FLB filter   A filter used on the camera to remove the green hue of fluorescents.

flex arm   A small jointed arm used to hold fingers and dots.

flicker box   An electrical circuit box used to simulate the flickering of a flame or television screen. A flicker box randomly increases and decreases the intensity of the lighting fixtures.

flicker-free   An HMI or fluorescent ballast that provides a square-wave or high-frequency signal that eliminates light-level pulsation when filmed at any shutter speed.

flood   The spread of the beam from a fixture that is broad and relatively weak.

foamcore   A white, glossy card material reinforced with 1/4-in. Styrofoam and used to bounce light.

focal length   The distance from a lens at which an image comes into focus (the focal point). For camera lenses, it is usually expressed in millimeters. A long lens has a very narrow angle of view and a short depth of field. A short lens has a wide angle of view and greater depth of field.

focal spot   An accessory that mounts on a Fresnel fixture, essentially changing the fixture into an ellipsoidal spotlight.

follow spot   A high-power, narrow-beam spotlight suitable for very long throws. It is designed to follow performers on stage.

foot-candle (FC)   An international unit of illumination. One foot-candle equals the intensity of light falling on a sphere placed 1 ft away from a point source of light of one candela. One footcandle equals one lumen per sq ft. *See also* lux.

foot-lambert   An international unit of brightness. One foot-lambert equals the uniform brightness of a perfectly diffusing surface emitting or reflecting light at a rate of one lumen per sq ft.

forced call   When less than the minimum turnaround time is given between wrap on one day and call on the following day.

format   The film or video medium and the aspect ratio of the image.

4-by cart   A cart for moving and storing 4 × 4-ft frames, flags, nets, bounce boards, and so on.

4-by floppy   A 4 × 4-ft flag with an additional flap that folds out to make a 4 × 8-ft flag.

fps   Frames per second.

frequency   The number of cycles per second of alternating current, measured in hertz.

Fresnel   (1) A type of lens that has the same optical effect as a plano-convex lens but has reduced weight and heat retention. (2) The light fixture that uses a Fresnel lens.

furniture clamp   An adjustable clamp used for mounting lights.

furniture pad   A packing blanket used to protect floors, deaden sound, soften a fall, and so on.

fuse   An overcurrent device that uses an alloy ribbon with a low melting point. The circuit is broken when the current exceeds the rating of the fuse.

gaffer   The head of the lighting crew. The gaffer works directly under the director of photography.

gaffer's tape   Heavy, fabric-based tape that rips cleanly in the direction of the weave. It is used for securing cables and lights on the set.

gamma   A graph line that describes a film emulsion's reaction to tonal gradation and its innate contrast. Also called *D log E curve* or *characteristic curve*.

gang box   An outlet box that provides Edison outlets and plugs into a larger connector, such as a 60-A Bates or a 100-A stage box.

gator grip   A baby stud on a spring-loaded clamp with rubber jaws, used for mounting lightweight fixtures to doors, poles, furniture, and so on.

gel   Polyester-based colored gelatin used to color a beam of light.

generator   The power plant used to create power on location. Motion picture generators are sound-baffled and provide bus bars or other common feeder connectors.

genny   *See* generator.

GFCI, GFI   *See* ground fault interrupter.

ghost load   A load not used to light the set and placed on a circuit to balance the various legs of power or to bring the load on a resistance-type dimmer up to its minimum operating wattage. Also called *dummy load* and *phantom load*.

globe   A bulb.

gobo arm   The arm of a C-stand.

gobo head   The metal knuckle that attaches the gobo arm to a C-stand.

golden time   Premium overtime pay after 12 hours of work (14 hours when on a distant location). Golden time is normally double the regular hourly rate.

gray scale   A chart showing gradations of gray from white to black.

greens   The wooden catwalk suspended above the set in a sound stage.

grid   (1) A transformer unit used with a carbon arc light. (2) The structure of metal pipes suspended above the stage floor for hanging lighting fixtures.

grid clamp   A clamp that attaches to grid pipe.

grid cloth   A white nylon diffusion fabric with a gridlike weave.

griffolyn   Nylon-reinforced plastic tarp material. Griffolyns are typically black on one side and white on the other; they are used as a bounce for fill. Also called *griff*.

grip   A crew member responsible for the nonelectrical aspects of lighting and rigging and for the camera dolly and other camera platforms.

grip clip   A metal spring clamp.

grip helper   A metal arm that mounts to a junior stand. A gobo head angles down and out from the stand to which a 4-by frame can be attached in front of the fixture.

grip truck   The lighting truck that houses the lights and grip equipment during location shooting.

ground fault interrupter (GFI)   A special type of circuit protection. There are a number of different types of GFIs. One type compares the outgoing current of a circuit to the returning current. If it detects a difference in the two (indicating a ground fault), it trips a switch to disconnect the circuit.

ground lifter   *See* cheater.

ground row   Cyclorama lights placed along the ground at the base of the cyc. A mask normally hides the lights from view.

grounded wire   The grounded, white, current-carrying wire of an AC circuit. Do not confuse this term with the green *grounding wire*.

grounding star   A mole-pin connector to which a number of grounding leads can be attached.

grounding wire   The green, non-current-carrying equipment grounding wire of an AC circuit.

halogen cycle   The cycle by which halogen in a bulb returns tungsten deposits to the filament, preventing blackening on the inner wall of the bulb.

head   A light fixture.

head cable   The cable running from the ballast of a lighting fixture to the head.

hi boy   An extra tall stand.

HID   High-intensity discharge. A type of street lamp.

high leg   The 208-V leg of a delta-connected three-phase system.

high roller   An extra tall rolling stand, often used to fly an overhead frame.

high-key   A bright lighting style with low contrast and bright highlights.

HMI   *See* mercury medium-arc iodide.

honey wagon   The trailer that houses the lavatories used when shooting on location.

hot spot   (1) The beam center. (2) A shiny spot or glare reflection that is distracting to the eye.

house lights   The permanent lighting in the audience area of a theater or sound stage.

housing   The metal casing that surrounds the bulb and reflector of a lighting fixture.

Hz   Hertz (cycles per second).

I   Current, measured in amperes.

IA, IATSE   International Alliance of Theatrical and Stage Employees.

IBEW   International Brotherhood of Electrical Workers.

Impedance (Z)   A measure, in ohms, of the opposition to current flow in an AC circuit. Impedance includes resistance, capacitive reactance, and inductive reactance.*

incandescent   Any type of electric light that creates light by making a metallic filament (usually tungsten for film lights) glow by applying current to it.

incident light meter   A light meter that reads the light falling onto the face of the meter.

inductance   A measure, in henrys, of the opposition to current change in an AC circuit (causing current to lag behind voltage). Inductance is exhibited by turns of wire with or without an iron core.

infrared (IR)   Wavelengths above the highest visible wavelength of light, felt as heat.

inky   A 100-W or 200-W Fresnel fixture manufactured by Mole-Richardson Co.

instrument   In the theater, a lighting fixture.

intermittent duty   Operation for alternate intervals of load, no load, and rest.

IR   *See* infrared.

iris   The mechanism on a follow spot that adjusts the diameter of the beam.

ISO   *See* ASA.

J-box   A junction box. The term usually refers to an Socapex HMI head cable junction box used to connect an extension head cable to the existing head cable.

jockey boxes   Metal storage containers on the underside of a truck. Jockey boxes usually store sandbags, cable, and so on.

juicer   A set lighting technician.

junior   A 2k Fresnel fixture.

junior stand   A stand with a 1 1/8-in. junior receptacle.

junior stud   A 1 1/8-in. stud.

K   Kelvin (temperature scale).

k   One thousand.

Kelvin   A unit of measurement of temperature (0 K = −273°C). In set lighting, the term refers to the color temperature (color makeup) of light and not to its physical temperature.

key light   The main source lighting the subject.

kick-out   The accidental unplugging of a light.

kicker   A side backlight.

kit rental   An additional fee a technician charges for the use of his or her own tools, equipment, and hardware. Also called *box rental.*

knuckle   The part of a C-stand gobo head that grips the flag.

ladder   A metal ladderlike structure, suspended from above or mounted to a wall, that provides a position from which to hang lights. Ladders are often used in theaters to position a stack of lights in the wings.

lantern   A lighting fixture (British theater).

layout board   Cardboard sheets, 4 × 8 ft, commonly used to protect floors.

Leko   Leko is a trademark of Strand's ellipsoidal reflector spotlight.

light-balancing (LB) scale   Scale used on Minolta color meters.

Lightmaker   A manufacturer of flicker-free AC and AC/DC ballasts.

Linnabach projector   A simple small-point-source lamp mounted inside a black box that projects cutout shapes or transparencies onto a cyclorama. The images are slightly diffuse shadows.

louvers   Thin, parallel strips with a black finish arranged in a grid pattern that is placed in front of a soft light source. Louvers reduce spill light and direct the light in one direction.

low boy   A very short stand.

low-key   A dark, shadowy lighting style.

lug   An extremely heavy-duty brass connector that bolts feeder cables to bus bars, deuce boards, and spiders. Also called *sister lugs.*

lumen   A unit of light (flux).

luminaire   A light fixture.

lux   An international unit of light intensity used primarily in Europe. One lux equals one lumen per square meter. One foot-candle equals 10.764 lux. lux = $cd/meters^2$.

MacBeth   A blue glass conversion filter used on some open-face lights. Converts tungsten sources to daylight.

mafer clamp   An all-purpose grip clamp (cam screw tightening) that can receive a number of different mounting attachments, such as a baby stud or a flex arm.

magic hour   The hour of light after sunset, during which the western sky creates a warm-colored soft light.

make first, break last   A rule of thumb when connecting single-conductor cables. The grounding connection must be made first, before any of the other wires. When disconnecting the cables, the grounding wire connection should be broken last.

martini   The last shot of the day.

matth pole   A pole that braces against two opposite walls to provide a structure from which to hang a lightweight fixture.

meal penalty   The fee paid by the production company (on union films) when shooting continues beyond six hours without breaking for a meal.

meat ax   An arm mounted to the pipe of a catwalk or to the basket of a boom platform that provides a way to place a flag in front of a fixture.

Meltric   A five-pin, heavy-duty connector used in some power distribution systems.

memory   On a dimmer console, the storage location for preset information

mercury medium-arc iodide (HMI)   A type of gas discharge bulb with a color temperature of 5600 K and high efficiency of more than 90 lumens per watt.

Mickey   A 1k open-face fixture manufactured by Mole-Richardson.

Midget   A 200-W wide-beam Fresnel fixture manufactured by Mole-Richardson.

Mini   (1) A 100-W or 200-W Fresnel fixture manufactured by Mole-Richardson, or a miniature soft light manufactured by LTM. (2) Minnie: Girlfriend of Mickey manufactured by Walt Disney.

minusgreen gel   A magenta gel used to take the green out of fluorescent light.

MIRED   One million times the reciprocal of the Kelvin rating of a given light source. The MIRED scale is used to determine the color shift of a given gel when used with any source. Short for *microreciprocal degree*.

Mole-pin   A 0.5 in. slip pin used as a distribution system connector.

MOS   A scene filmed without recording sound.

mountain leg   The leg of a three-leg stand that extends to allow the stand to remain upright on uneven ground.

MT-2   A color-correction gel used on carbon arc lights with a Y-1 gel to correct the color temperature of a white-flame arc to 3200 K.

multiline spectrum   The spectral energy distribution graph of an HMI light. Instead of a continuous line across the color spectrum, the color makeup is created by numerous single spikes.

Musco Light   A very powerful mobile lighting truck.

NABET   National Association of Broadcast Employees and Technicians.

nanometer (nm)   A unit of length used to measure the wavelengths of the colors of light. One nanometer equals one-billionth of a meter.

ND   *See* neutral-density.

NEC   National Electrical Code.

net   A black honeycomb netting material sewn onto a rod frame that is used to reduce the intensity of part or all of a light's beam.

neutral-density (ND)   A gel or filter that reduces light transmission without altering the color of the light.

NFPA   National Fire Protection Association.

nook light   A small, lightweight open-face fixture that typically uses a double-ended bulb and a V-shaped reflector.

offset   A piece of grip hardware used to hang a light out to the side of a stand.

ohm (Ω)   A unit of electrical resistance equal to the resistance through which 1 V will force 1 A.

opal   A popular, thin diffusion.

open-face light   A fixture that has no lens, only a bulb mounted in front of a reflector.

OSHA   Occupational Safety and Health Administration.

overcurrent device   A circuit breaker or fuse.

overhead set   A large frame with one of several types of material stretched across it, including a solid, single net, double net, silk, or griffolyn.

O-zone   The open spaces between the perms, in the rafters of a sound stage. Only rigging grips are typically allowed to work in the O-zone using safety lines.

PA   *See* production assistant.

paddle   The male plug that is plugged into a stage box.

pancake   A $3/4$-in. piece of plywood matching the dimensions of the large side of an apple box.

paper method   A method of calculating the amperage of 120 V fixtures by dividing the wattage by 100.

PAR can   A rugged fixture used often in rock-and-roll concerts. A PAR can is simply a PAR globe mounted in a cylindrical can that provides a slot for colored gel.

parabolic reflector   A reflector shaped like a parabola, giving it a focal point from which all light rays will be reflected outward in a parallel beam.

parallel circuit   The connection of two or more fixtures across the same conductors of a circuit such that current flow through each is independent of the others.*

parallels   A small, easy-to-assemble scaffold platform.

party gel   Colored gels, also called *effects gel* or *theatrical gel*

patch   Historically, the process of physically connecting circuits to dimmers. Now usually refers to electronic assignment of dimmers to channels. *Patch* does not refer to the assignment of channels to cues or submasters.

Peppers   A line of small, lightweight tungsten lights manufactured by LTM in sizes of 100 W, 200 W, 300 W, 420 W, 500 W, 650 W, 1000 W, and 20k.

perms   Permanent catwalks near the high ceilings of sound stages.

phantom load   *See* ghost load.

phase   (1) An energized single conductor, usually ungrounded and never the neutral.* (2) The positioning of an AC cycle in time, relative to the phases of the other hot legs. Most electrical services are either single-phase or three-phase services.

photoflood   A bulb, typically with a standard medium screw base that has a color temperature of 3200–3400 K

piano board   Originally, a portable dimmer switchboard or road board. This term has come to be used for many types of portable dimmer switchboards.

pigeon plate   A baby nail-on plate.

pins   Any of several types of connectors. Mole-pins and *.515* pins are single-conductor slip pins used on feeder cable. Three-pin connectors, commonly called *Bates connectors*, are also sometimes called *pins*.

pipe clamp   A clamp used to hang a light from an overhead pipe.

plano-convex   A lens that is flat on one side and convex on the other. Light comes from the flat side and converges or diverges as it passes though the lens, in proportion to the lamp's distance to the lens.

plate dimmer   A resistance-type dimmer commonly used with DC circuits.

plugging box   A stage box. May also refer more generally to any outlet box.

plusgreen gel   A gel used to add green to lights to match their color to that of fluorescent bulbs.

pocket   Outlets for stage circuits, often located under a protective trapdoor; for example, floor pockets, wall pockets, and fly pockets.

polarity   The orientation of the positive and negative wires of a DC circuit or the hot and neutral wires of an AC circuit. A polarized plug cannot be plugged in with reversed polarity.

pole cats   Lighting support equipment consisting of extendible metal tubes that wedge between two walls or between floor and ceiling to which lights can be mounted.

power   The total amount of work, measured in watts. The term is also generally understood as electricity, or juice.

power factor   In AC, the ratio of the actual or effective power in watts to the apparent power in volt-amperes, expressed as a percentage. Inductive loads cause the current to lag behind the voltage, resulting in a power factor of less than 100%.*

practical lamp   A lamp, sconce, or fixture that is shown in the scene.

prefocus base   The type of lamp base.

prelight or prerig   To rig in advance. During production, the grip and electrical crew may form a second crew or bring in a second crew to work ahead, rigging the sets that are to be shot during the following days.

preset   Of a dimmer console, a predefined set of intensities for a set of channels, stored in memory for later replay.

primary colors For light, red, blue, and green. When the primary colors of light are projected onto a white surface, the area where all three colors intersect should theoretically make white light.

prime fixture A focusable, open-face fixture.

Priscilla A silver lamé stretched on a frame and used to bounce light.

producer The person who oversees the production of the film or television show from the very beginning (obtaining the script, raising money, finding the backing to produce the show) to the very end (selling the finished film in domestic and world markets, trying to maximize its sales and profitmaking potential). The producer is the ultimate authority on all money-related decisions and most others. Everyone on the production works for the producer.

production assistant (PA) An assistant in the production department who performs any number of menial and administrative tasks.

PSA Public service announcement.

quick-on plugs and sockets Low-amperage, parallel-blade, no-ground Edison plugs and sockets that are designed to be quick and convenient to wire.

R Resistance, measured in ohms. *See* resistance.

rag The cloth part of an overhead set.

rain tent A tent to cover lights and electrical equipment in case of precipitation.

reactance (X) A measure, in ohms, of the opposition to AC due to capacitance (X_C) or inductance (X_L).

receptacle A female connector or female mounting hardware.

rectifier An electrical unit that converts AC to DC.

redhead A 1k open-face fixture.

reflected light meter A light meter that reads the amount of light reflected by the scene into the meter. A standard reflected meter has a relatively wide angle of view and averages the areas of light and dark to give the reading. *See also* spot meter.

reflectors Silver-covered boards typically used to bounce light, usually sunlight. Also called *shiny boards*.

resistance (R) A measure, in ohms, of the opposition to current flow in a conductor, device, or load. In DC, volts ÷ amperes = ohms of resistance. For AC, see impedance.

rheostat A resistance dimmer.

rigging bible A set of diagrams showing the power layout of a studio's sound stages.

rigging gaffer The gaffer in charge of designing and installing the cabling and electrical distribution for a large set.

rim A backlight that makes a rim around the head and shoulders of the subject from the perspective of the camera.

Ritter fan A large effects fan used to blow snow and rain and to give the appearance of wind or speed.

safety A wire, chain, cable, or rope looped around the bail of a light to prevent it from falling should it come loose from its stud.

sandbag A sand-filled bag used to stabilize stands and equipment by adding deadweight or counterweight.

scale The minimum pay scale set forth by the labor union representing the crew or cast.

scene machine A lighting unit that projects an image on a screen, usually from the back. The image can be made to move by scrolling through the machine or to rotate by using adjustable-speed motors. Scene machines are often used to create moving clouds across the cyclorama in theatrical productions.

scissor arc A special carbon arc machine used to create a lightning effect.

scissor clip   A device that provides a means of hanging lights from a false ceiling, such as those found in many modern commercial buildings.

scissor lift   A self-propelled electric lift.

scoop   A lighting fixture that consists of a large 1k or 2k bulb mounted in a reflector. Scoops are used for general area light.

scosh   A very small amount, as in "Flood it out a scosh."

scrim   A circle of wire mesh, which slides into the ears on the front of a fixture and reduces the intensity of the light. A single dims the light about a half-stop. A double dims it about one stop. A half-single or double affects only half of the beam.

second team   The stand-ins used as models during lighting.

secondary colors   The colors formed by combining two primary colors. Also called *complementary colors.*

senior   A 5k incandescent Fresnel fixture manufactured by Mole-Richardson Co.

series circuit   Connection of two or more devices or loads in tandem so that the current flowing through one also flows through all the others.*

service   Electrical service. This term can refer to the types of circuits installed, for example, single-phase, three-wire service.

service entrance   The main panelboard into which the power lines running to a building terminate.

shock   The sensation or occurrence of an electrical circuit being completed through a person's body.

short   A film of 30 minutes or less. Directors and students often shoot a short as a resumé or promotional piece to demonstrate their abilities or to help them move into a new area.

short circuit   Unwanted current flow between conductors.

Shotmaker   A customized tow vehicle for shooting moving car scenes.

show card   Thick card stock, usually white on one side and black on the other, used to bounce light.

shutter   In a motion picture camera, a butterfly-type device that spins in front of the aperture plate.

shutters   Venetian blind–like metal slats that are mounted on a fixture in place of barn doors for use as a douser.

silicone spray   A dry lubricant used on dolly track.

silk   Silk fabric used to soften and cut the intensity of light. It is used in all sizes, from very small dots and fingers to very large 20 × 20-ft overheads.

Silver Bullet   A 12k or 18k HMI light manufactured by Cinemills Corp.

single-phase   A type of alternating current typically used in circuits that have two hot wires and one neutral.

sister lugs   *See* lug.

sky pan   A large, soft light fixture used for general fill, comprising a 2k, 5k, or 10k bulb and a large pan-shaped reflector.

snoot   A black metal cylinder or cone mounted on the ears of a fixture to narrow the beam.

Snorkelift   A telescoping-boom vehicle similar to the Condor.

snot tape   Sticky adhesive substance used to attach gel to a frame.

Socapex cable   Multiwire cable connector used (1) on HMI head feeder and (2) on multi-circuit cable for dimmer circuits.

soft box   A device used to create very soft, diffuse light.

soft light   A light fixture with a large, curved, white reflector surface that bounces light onto the scene. No direct light is used. The large aperture and reflected light creates light with soft shadows that is often used as fill light.

solid   A black "rag" stretched on a frame and used to cut light.

sound mixer   The person who operates the audio recording machine, usually a DAT or Nagra tape recorder.

space light   A large silked cylinder that hangs above the set to create soft ambient illumination.

spark   A nickname for set lighting technician.

SPD   Spectral power distribution (graph).

specular   An adjective used to describe hard light emitted by a point source.

spider box   A cable splicing box used to join lug feeder cables. The cable's lug connectors bolt to copper bus bar plates.

spot   A beam focused into a narrow, relatively strong beam of light.

spot meter   A type of reflected meter having a very narrow angle of acceptance (1° to 20°) used to determine the light value of a specific point on the set.

square wave   A type of AC created by an electronic ballast that renders HMI lights flicker free.

squeezer   A dimmer.

stage box   A distribution box with pockets that accept a male paddle connector. Stage boxes are normally referred to by the number of pockets they have: one-hole, two-hole, four-hole, or six-hole boxes.

stage extension   A high-amperage extension cable; it has a paddle on one end and a one-hole or two-hole box at the other.

staging area   The area on the sound stage or location selected as a temporary place to keep the lighting equipment and carts.

stick-up   An extremely small, lightweight fixture that can be taped to the wall.

stinger   An extension cord; officially, a hot extension cord.

stop   An f-stop or a t-stop.

strain relief   A rope tie used to reduce strain at the point at which a cable attaches to its connector.

streaks and tips   Cans of hair color that are often handy for darkening reflective surfaces.

strike   (1) To dismantle a set or to take down and put away a piece of equipment. (2) When referring to an HMI, to strike the light can mean to turn it on.

strobe light   A light that creates short, bright, regular flashes of light at an adjustable speed.

studio zone   In California, the area within 30 miles of a specific point in Hollywood. Labor rules are different inside and outside of this zone.

submaster   A controller (usually a linear slider) on a dimmer board that allows manual control of groups, effects, cues, or channels.

suicide pin   An adaptor with two male ends.

swing   A crew member who performs the tasks of both grip and electrician, as needed.

system grounding   The grounding of the service equipment and the current-carrying, neutral white wire to the transformer and to earth.

T-bone   A metal T-shaped base with a junior receptacle, used to place larger lights at ground level.

T-stop   The aperture setting of a zoom lens after compensation for light lost in the numerous optical elements of the lens.

taco cart   A special cart that carries grip equipment, such as C-stands, apple boxes, wedges, mounting hardware, and grip expendables.

tag line   A line dropped from aloft and used to hoist equipment into a catwalk, green beds, or Condor.

talent   On-camera people and animals, usually actors, not necessarily talented ones.

three-fer   A connector that provides three female connectors from one male connector.

three-phase   A type of alternating current that has three hot legs. The alternating voltage cycle of each leg is a third of a cycle apart.

three-riser   A stand that has three extensions.

throw   The distance at which a fixture can effectively light a subject.

tie-in   The connection of distribution cables to a facility's service panel box.

Titan   A 350-A carbon arc light manufactured by Mole-Richardson.

tracing paper   Thin, translucent paper used to white out windows.

transformer   A device with no moving parts and two or more insulated windings on a laminated steel core that is used to raise or lower AC voltage by inductive coupling. Volt-amperes into the primary coil and volt-amperes out of the secondary coil arc the same, less the small current necessary to magnetize the core.*

tree   A tall stand or tower that has horizontal pipes on which lights can be hung. Used a great deal in theater and concert lighting.

trombone   Fixture-mounting hardware that hooks over the top of the set, drops down the set wall, is adjustable, and provides a baby or junior stud or receptacle to which a light is mounted.

truss   A metal structure designed to support a horizontal load over an extended span. Trusses are used largely in concert lighting to support lighting fixtures aloft.

tungsten color temperature   A color temperature of 3200 K.

tungsten halogen lamp   A lamp designed to maintain an almost constant color temperature and a high lumen output throughout its life. The halogen cycle is a regenerative process that prevents the blackening of the inside of the bulb.

turnaround   The time between the time you go off the clock on one day and call time on the next.

turtle stand   A squat junior stand that enables a large light to be positioned at ground level.

tweco clamp   An electrical clamp consisting of two sawtooth jaws that clamp together by turning the threaded screw base.

Tweenie   A 650-W Fresnel light manufactured by Mole-Richardson Co.

twist-lock   A connector for which the plug inserts into the socket and then twists, locking the plug to the socket.

216   A popular, relatively heavy diffusion.

type W cable   Cable manufactured to meet the requirements of NEC Articles 520 and 530 regarding portable entertainment cable. It is abrasion, oil, solvent, and ozone resistant and flame tested.

U-ground   A standard Edison plug with a U-shaped grounding pin.

UL   Underwriter Laboratories.

ultraviolet (UV)   The wavelengths of light below the shortest visible wavelength. UV-A is black light. UV-B radiation can cause skin burns and eye damage as well as skin cancer if not filtered.

Unilux   A manufacturer of strobe lighting equipment that can be synchronized to a motion picture camera shutter.

up-fade   The portion of a fade that involves only channels that are increasing in level.

UV   *See* ultraviolet

V   *See* volt

VA   *See* volt-ampere.

variac   An autotransformer dimmer.

VEAM connector   VEAM Litton is a manufacturer of connectors, including multipin HMI head feeder connectors and single conductor feeder cable connectors.

velum   *See* tracing paper.

Visqueen   Plastic material used to protect equipment from precipitation.

volt (V)   A unit of electrical force. One volt is required to force 1 A of electricity though a resistance of 1Ω (ohm).

volt-ampere (VA)   Voltage times amperage. In DC, volts × amps = watts, but in AC, inductance and capacitance in the circuit may introduce reactance, causing a discrepancy between watts and volt-amperes.

voltage drop   The difference in voltage between two points in a circuit due to the intervening impedance or resistance.

voltmeter   A meter used to measure voltage potential between two points in a circuit.

W   *See* watt.

wall sled   A fixture-mounting device that hangs from the top of the set wall and rests against the wall.

wall spreader   Hardware that mounts to either end of a piece of lumber, creating a span from one wall to another from which lights can be hung.

watt (W)   A unit of electrical power, the product of voltage and amperage.

wedge   A triangular wooden block used to level dolly track.

welding cable   A flexible electrical cable once widely used for power distribution. Welding cable can no longer be used legally, except as a grounding wire.

western dolly   A large flatbed camera platform with large inflated tires that steer at one end. A western dolly can be useful for moving lights and cable.

wet cell battery   A car battery.

wiggy   A continuity or resistance-testing device.

woof   Stop.

wrap   The process of taking down lights and coiling cable that begins after the last shot of the day has been completed successfully.

wye-connected system   A common type of three-phase transformer arrangement. Voltage reads 208 V between any two of the hot legs and 120 V between a hot leg and the neutral white leg.

xenon lights   An extremely bright type of arc discharge light that has a color temperature of 5600 K. Because the arc is very small, the light can be channeled into a very narrow shaft of extremely bright light.

Y-1   A type of gel that converts a white carbon arc to normal daylight color balance.

Y-connected system   *See* wye-connected system.

yoke   *See* bail.

zip cord   Two-wire, 18-AWG electric lamp cord.

zip light   A small soft light.

zone system   Ansel Adams's system of 11 gradations of gray from pure black to pure white. The zones are numbered in Roman numerals from 0 to X. There is a one-stop difference from zone to zone.

Φ   Phase.

Ω   Resistance (ohms).

Bibliography

The following publications were consulted in the writing of this book. Each is an excellent reference for further reading in specific areas.

Carlson, Verne, and Sylvia E. Carlson. *Professional Lighting Handbook*. 2d. ed. Boston: Focal Press, 1991.

Carter, Paul. *Backstage Handbook: An illustrated Almanac of Technical Information*. New York: Broadway Press, 1988.

Detmers, F., ed. *American Cinematographer Manual*. Hollywood: American Society of Cinematographers Press, 1989.

Fitt, B, and Thornley, J. *Lighting by Design*. Boston: Focal Press, 1992.

Goodell, Gregory. *Independent Feature Film Production: A Complete Guide from Concept to Distribution*. New York: St. Martin's Press, 1982.

Local 728, International Alliance of Theatrical and Stage Employees. *Working Manual for Studio Electrical Technicians*. Hollywood: IATSE.

Maikiewicz, Kris. *Cinematography*. New York: Prentice Hall, 1973.

Matthews Studio Equipment Inc. *Matthews 1992 Product Catalog*. Burbank, CA, 1992.

Mole-Richardson Co. *Mole-Richardson Co. Catalog*. Hollywood, 1990.

Moody, James L. *Concert Lighting: Techniques, An and Business*. Boston: Focal Press, 1989.

National Fire Protection Association. *National Electrical Code*. Quincy, MA: NEPA, 1991.

Pilbrow, Richard. *Stage Lighting*. New York: Drama Book Publishers, 1970.

Richter, Herbert P., and Creighton W. Schwan. *Practical Electrical Wiring*. New York: McGraw-Hill, 1990.

Samuelson, David W. *Motion Picture Camera and Lighting Equipment: Choice and Technique*. 2d. ed. Boston: Focal Press, 1986.

Schaefer, John P. *An Ansel Adams Guide: Basic Techniques of Photography*. Boston: Little, Brown, 1992.

Strand Lighting, *CD80 Digital Pack, Users Manual*. Rancho Domingues, CA, Revision Date 9/28/92.

Sylvania GTE. *Lighting Handbook for Television, Theatre and Professional Photography*. 8th ed. Danvers, MA: Sylvania. 1989.

Van Valkenburgh, Nooger and Neville, Inc. Basic Electricity. Revised Edition, complete course. Indianapolis, IN: Prompt Publications an imprint of Sams Technical Publishing, 1992.

Additional References for Further Reading

Periodicals

American Cinematographer
ASC Holding Corporation
1782 N. Orange Drive
Hollywood, CA 90028

Lighting Dimensions
Lighting Dimensions Associates
135 Fifth Avenue
New York, NY 10010-7193

Books

Brown, Blain. *Motion Picture and Video Lighting*. Boston: Focal Press, 1992.

Glerum, Jay. *Stage Rigging Handbook*. Carbondale, IL: Southern Illinois University Press, 1989.

Hirshfield, Gerals. *Image Control*. Boston: Focal Press, 1993.

Lowell, Ross. *Matters of Light and Depth*. Philadelphia, PA: Broad Street Books, 1992.

McCandless, Stanley. *A Method of Lighting the Stage*, 4th ed. New York: Theater Arts Books, 1992.

Schaefer, Dennis, and Larry Salvato. *Masters of Light: Conversations with Contemporary Cinematographers*. Berkeley and Los Angeles, CA: University of California Press, 1984.

Uva, Michael. *The Grip Book*. Michael C. Uva, 1988.

Wilson, Anton. *Cinema Workshop*. Hollywood, CA: ASC Holding Co., 1983.

Index

Page references followed by "f" denote figures; those followed by "t" denote tables.